The Reinterpretation of the
AMERICAN REVOLUTION
1763–1789

The Reinterpretation of the

AMERICAN REVOLUTION
1763–1789

Edited with an Introduction by
JACK P. GREENE
The Johns Hopkins University

HARPER & ROW, PUBLISHERS
NEW YORK, EVANSTON, AND LONDON

CONTENTS

IV. TRANSFORMATION

V. BETWEEN FEAR AND HOPE

VI. THE TRIUMPH OF HOPE

VII. ACHIEVEMENTS AND PERSPECTIVES

PREFACE

———◦◦————◦◦◦————◦◦———

This anthology is intended to be neither comprehensive nor representative of the vast body of literature on the era of the American Revolution: it includes no statements of earlier interpretations and reflects my personal point of view at this time. What it is intended to do is collect in one volume many of the more significant shorter essays and portions of a few of the more important longer works published on the Revolution over the past two decades. Although there are some glaring contradictions among the individual selections, they capture, I think, something of the thrust of recent Revolutionary scholarship and, when taken together and read against the perspective provided by the introductory essay, provide a coherent, if obviously incomplete, statement of the nature and contemporary meaning of the Revolutionary experience.

JACK P. GREENE

Baltimore, Md.

[I]

INTRODUCTION

INTRODUCTION

———— ◄►◆► ►◄ ————

The Reappraisal of the American
Revolution in Recent Historical Literature

Both because of its crucial position in modern history as the
first of the great revolutions and because it gave birth to the
United States of America, the American Revolution has always
exercised a powerful appeal for historians. Its causes and consequences, its nature and meaning have never ceased to fascinate
—and to puzzle—them, and each generation of historians has
approached it anew, seeking to understand it in terms that would
be meaningful to them. The result has been a welter of interpretations of why the Revolution occurred and what exactly it
was. Those interpretations can be explained partly by changing
intellectual styles, social, economic, and political imperatives, and
psychological currents in the public world and partly by shifting
conceptions of human nature and historical change within the
community of historians. But they also stand as dramatic testimony to the one indisputable truth about the event itself: the
American Revolution, like every other historical phenomenon of
comparable magnitude, was so complex and contained so many
diverse and seemingly contradictory currents that it can support
a wide variety of interpretations and may never be comprehended
in full. Yet, the extensive and intensive reappraisal of the Revo-

---

This essay is adapted from a pamphlet of the same title published as
Publication Number 68 (Washington, D.C.: Service Center for Teachers,
1967). Portions of it are derived from "The Flight from Determinism:
A Review of Recent Literature on the Coming of the American Revolution,"
South Atlantic Quarterly, LXI (Spring, 1962), 235–259 (reprint: Bobbs-
Merrill Co.), and "Changing Interpretations of Early American Politics," in
*The Reinterpretation of Early American History: Essays in Honor of John
Edwin Pomfret*, ed. Ray A. Billington (San Marino, Calif.: 1966).

lution that has occurred since World War II may have brought us closer than ever before to such a comprehension.

EARLIER CONCEPTIONS

The Whig Conception

Through most of the nineteenth century it was customary to view the Revolution as a classic struggle for liberty. The most celebrated, detailed, influential, and authoritative exposition of this view came from George Bancroft, a fervid nationalist and devoted democrat who had grown to manhood in the years of intense national self-consciousness and democratic pride in American institutions that followed the War of 1812. His monumental *History of the United States*,[1] which brought the story of American development through the formation of the Constitution, was above all a patriotic ode to the foundation of American freedom. Sharing the conventional nineteenth-century Whig and democratic belief that the desire for freedom was the strongest drive in man, he limned a vivid portrait of the colonists' relentless striving for freedom, from the first landing at Jamestown in 1607 to the final victory at Yorktown in 1781, against a background of more or less continuous oppression from mother England. Although the Revolution was occasioned by the tyrannical assaults of George III upon American liberties in the 1760's and 1770's, it was merely the logical culmination of a century and a half of struggle against arbitrary English interference in American affairs.

For Bancroft, however, the final victory for freedom, the real triumph of American democracy and the successful conclusion of the Revolution, came not with the Treaty of Paris in 1783 but with the adoption of the Constitution in 1788. Immediately after the war, during what John Fiske, one of Bancroft's younger contemporaries, movingly described as *The Critical Period*,[2] petty local jealousies, uncertainty, and political impotence almost deprived Americans of the fruits of victory. Only with the embodiment of the libertarian and democratic principles of the Revolution in the Constitution and the establishment of a strong federal union were the achievements of 1776 and 1783 firmly secured.

That Americans had been blessed with an environment peculi-

---

[1] 10 vols., Boston, 1834–1874.
[2] Boston and New York, 1888.

arly well suited to the growth of freedom and, above all, with the special favor of God, Bancroft had little doubt, and in his conception of the Revolution as part of the "grand design of Providence" he found its deepest meaning. Americans were God's chosen people marked out for a special purpose, and their Revolution was the necessary prelude to the "political regeneration" of mankind, an important milestone on man's inevitable march toward a freer and more nearly perfect world.

Shared in large measure by such respected British contemporaries as W. E. H. Lecky[3] and George Otto Trevelyan,[4] Bancroft's simple Whiggish view of the Revolution as well as his intense patriotism did not set well with a new generation of American historians who, trained in the methods of scientific history during the closing decades of the nineteenth century, demanded a more objective reading of the American past. After 1890 two new tendencies in Revolutionary scholarship profoundly altered the traditional interpretation.

The Imperial Conception

The first of these tendencies was manifest in the work of a large group of historians who have since come to be referred to as the imperial school. Deeply offended by Bancroft's narrow nationalism and thoroughly caught up in the general movement toward Anglo-American accord that gained increasing vigor in the decades immediately preceding World War I, these historians insisted that the Revolution could be understood only when considered in terms of the empire as a whole, that the imperial, as well as the colonial, point of view had to be taken into account.

One of the most prominent of the imperial historians was Herbert Levi Osgood. Though he himself never produced a major work on the Revolution, he anticipated both the direction and many of the conclusions of the imperial historians in a notable essay published in 1898.[5] Calling for a "more just and scientific view of the Revolution," Osgood boldly suggested that the British government not only was not "guilty of intentional tyranny toward the colonies" but also had ample provocation for pursuing the measures that led to revolution after 1763. From the per-

---

[3] *A History of England in the Eighteenth Century* (8 vols., London and New York, 1878–1890).

[4] *The American Revolution* (4 vols., London and New York, 1899–1913).

[5] "The American Revolution," *Political Science Quarterly*, XIII (March, 1898), 41–59.

spective of imperial officials in London, he argued, the "vexatious delays" that resulted from the "narrow, prejudiced and unstatesmanlike" behavior of colonial lower houses of assembly during the Seven Years' War clearly justified the attempted reform of colonial administration at the end of the war. Like Bancroft, Osgood thought that the roots of the American Revolution were deeply embedded in the colonial past, but unlike Bancroft he expected to find them not in British oppression but in the "social and political tendencies . . . toward independence" within the colonies.

George Louis Beer, a tobacco merchant turned scholar and a protégé of Osgood, was the first to amplify and work out the implications of Osgood's suggestions in a study of *British Colonial Policy, 1754–1765*, which appeared in 1907.[6] As Beer carefully pointed out, he wrote strictly within the framework of imperial history, and his study made it clear that from the point of view of British administrators at Whitehall, American conduct during the Seven Years' War was marked not only by extreme provincialism, as Osgood had suggested, but also by patent disloyalty. Unmindful that the struggle extended beyond the narrow confines of the North American continent, Americans continued to trade with the French and Spanish in the West Indies throughout the war. Such behavior understandably persuaded imperial officials to try to tighten imperial ties and increase the administrative efficiency of the empire when the war was over. But this movement for centralization unfortunately—unfortunately because Beer tended to regard the Revolution as a tragic mistake, a "temporary separation of two kindred peoples"—came into direct and violent conflict with a movement for independence that dated from the very foundation of the colonies. Previously restrained only by the presence of the French and Spanish at the rear of the colonies, this movement could proceed without restraint after the removal of the French and Spanish menace in 1763. For Beer, then, as for Osgood and Bancroft, the ultimate cause of the Revolution was the incipient and long-developing desire for independence among the colonists.

The origin and nature of those desires were not spelled out in any detail until the 1920's when Charles McLean Andrews, the most influential and productive of all the imperial historians, turned after years of working on earlier colonial developments to speculate about the origins of the Revolution in a brilliant series

---

[6]New York, 1907.

of essays[7] and in his presidential address to the American Historical Association in 1925.[8] Like both Osgood and Beer, Andrews
was strongly influenced by a conception of historical change that
stressed the overwhelming influence of the physical environment,
the evolutionary character of historical development, and a view
of human nature that saw man as the agent of vast, impersonal
forces largely beyond his control. The supreme challenge to historians, he indicated in his presidential address, was to discover
those many "deeplying and almost invisible factors and forces
which influence and often determine human action." Revolutions,
he argued, were never sudden and never made by men; rather,
they were the products of complex long-range developments
which were the "masters, not the servants, of statesmen and
political agitators." A sound explanation of the American Revolution had therefore to be sought not in the behavior of individuals
or groups during the 1760's and 1770's but in the differing "states
of mind" produced by profoundly divergent conditions in the
colonies and Great Britain during the previous century and a
half. The American environment had given birth to "new wants,
new desires, and new points of view," to a completely "new order
of society," characterized by growth and change and contrasting
sharply with a way of life in Britain that seemed to Andrews to
have been "intellectually, socially, and institutionally in a state
of stable equilibrium." Andrews was convinced that a collision
between two such disparate and incompatible "yokefellows," the
one absolutely committed to keeping the colonies dependent and
the other demanding, through its ever maturing representative
assemblies, an ever increasing amount of self-government, was
inevitable.

The most notable contribution of these historians was a deeper
understanding of the imperial side of American development. No
one could read either the more substantial works of Osgood, Beer,
Andrews, and their contemporaries or important contributions
from the second generation of imperial historians—such as Leonard Woods Labaree's *Royal Government in America*,[9] which surveyed in detail the political relations between the imperial government and the colonies, and Lawrence A. Harper's *The English*

---

[7]*Colonial Background of the American Revolution: Four Essays in American Colonial History* (New Haven, 1924).

[8]"The American Revolution: An Interpretation," *American Historical
Review*, XXXI (January, 1926), 219–232.

[9]New Haven, 1930.

Navigation Laws,[10] which described at length the rationale and operation of the mercantile system—and still regard the British as tyrants. By the late 1920's, in fact, no serious student of early American history could doubt that the British had, or at least thought they had, good and substantial reasons for undertaking the measures they did, however the colonists might have interpreted them.

Perhaps because they were so thoroughly engrossed in exploring the nature of imperial administration during the seventeenth and early eighteenth centuries and in putting colonial developments into their proper imperial setting, none of the first generation of imperial historians ever produced a systematic or detailed treatment of the critical decades just before the Declaration of Independence. That task was not undertaken until the 1930's, when Lawrence Henry Gipson, Andrews' most prolific student, began to publish a massive study, *The British Empire Before the American Revolution*, which in the thirteen volumes thus far published has carried the story from 1748 to 1776. From these volumes as well as from two shorter studies[11] has emerged what may be assumed to be the final version of the imperial interpretation of the origins of the American Revolution. In its broader outlines it does not differ substantially from the more tentative formulations of Beer and Andrews. Like Andrews, Gipson places heavy emphasis upon the role of the American environment in causing the colonists to develop ideals and interests that diverged sharply from those of Englishmen. With Beer, he views the removal of the French menace as the decisive event in the coming of the Revolution. Already "politically mature, prosperous, dynamic, and self-reliant" by the 1750's, Americans gained physical security as well with the conquest of Canada; and when the British government justifiably sought to exert stricter controls over them in the 1760's and 1770's, nothing was left to deter them from throwing off the burdensome responsibilities of membership in the empire. By providing a solid substructure of detailed evidence to support these notions, Gipson is finally supplying what Osgood had called for in 1898: a comprehensive study, free from the patriotic distortions of the nineteenth-century nationalists, that is seeking to account rationally and historically

---

[10]New York, 1939.
[11]*The Coming of the Revolution, 1763–1775* (New York, 1954) and "The American Revolution as an Aftermath of the Great War for Empire, 1754–1763," *Political Science Quarterly*, LXV (March, 1950), 86–104.

for the conduct of the British government on the eve of the American Revolution.

The Progressive Conception

At the very time Osgood and Beer were calling for a more dispassionate analysis of the British side of the American Revolution, another group of historians was focusing its attention upon internal divisions within the colonies. Where Bancroft had found unanimity among the patriots, they found disagreement and conflict. Where the imperial historians emphasized the political and constitutional aspects of the controversy, they stressed the social and economic. To a very large extent, their interpretations were shaped by the rhetoric and assumptions of Progressive politics and social thought and by a conception of revolution that derived largely from the experience of the great European revolutions. Their sympathies, like those of all good Progressives, lay with the little man—the yeoman farmer, agricultural tenant, artisan, and town laborer. Not only the Revolutionary era, but all of American history seemed to have been dominated by a fundamental conflict between such groups, who stood for human rights and democracy, and the upper classes, who advocated property rights and the political predominance of special interest groups. The American Revolution was thus thought to have exhibited patterns of class conflict and internal political and social upheaval similar to those of the French Revolution; and it came to be seen largely and most importantly as part of a sweeping struggle for democracy on the part of disfranchised and unprivileged groups, who by their constant pressures were slowly bringing about that equality of condition that was characteristic of the age of Andrew Jackson but had subsequently been undermined and subverted by the machinations of selfish businessmen and manufacturers in the decades after the Civil War. Also, like all good Progressives, they automatically assumed that man was primarily an economic creature and that economic interest largely determined political behavior and developments. Believing that men could both see their interests clearly and perceive the best way to secure them, most of these historians were profoundly skeptical of ideas, which they regarded as either simple reflections of deeper social forces or mere abstractions designed to cloak "real" motives so sinister and selfish that they necessarily had to remain concealed. It was their mission, therefore, to break down the dominant political abstractions of the Revolution and, by "employing the ruthless methods of modern scholarship," to ferret out and expose the concrete interests and motives that lay behind them, to discover, as it were, the "real" American Revolution.

Two early works, Charles H. Lincoln, *The Revolutionary Movement in Pennsylvania, 1760–1776* (1901),[12] and Carl L. Becker, *History of Political Parties in the Province of New York, 1760–1776* (1909),[13] provided the foundations for the Progressive interpretation of the Revolution. Lincoln and Becker found that the Revolutionary controversy in both colonies was strongly conditioned by pre-existing conflicts within them. In Pennsylvania there were "two opposing forces, one radical," composed of Scotch-Irish Presbyterians and Germans in the west and non-Quaker lower- and middle-class Philadelphians in the east, and the other "conservative," consisting of the Quaker mercantile oligarchy in the east. In New York the radical unprivileged and unfranchised common freeholders, tenants, mechanics, and artisans were aligned against a tightly-knit landowning and commercial aristocracy. In both colonies the conflicts between these groups and the struggle of the radicals to push their way into the political arena and to achieve a wider area of economic and social freedom—the fight over "who should rule at home" and the radical demands for the "democratization of . . . politics and society"—and not the debate with Great Britain were most important in shaping political developments in the years between 1763 and 1776. The aristocratic elements in both colonies took the lead in opposing the Grenville program in 1764 and 1765, but they began to draw back as it became increasingly clear over the next decade, as Lincoln wrote, that "the arguments . . . used against English misrule" could be "turned against minority control and misgovernment" within the colonies. In the crucial years from 1773 to 1776 the extralegal committees, conventions, and congresses, not the conservative-dominated and legitimate colonial legislatures, were chiefly responsible for the achievement of independence, and in the process they also effected—more thoroughly in Pennsylvania than in New York—the "internal revolution" for which they had primarily been striving over the previous decade. The contest with Britain, then, was chiefly important not because it brought the colonies their independence but because it unleashed the "latent opposition of motives and interests between the privileged and the unprivileged" and provided the opportunity for the

---

[12]Philadelphia, 1901.
[13]Madison, Wis., 1909.

latter to score the first great victory for American democracy by driving some of the privileged to become loyalists and compelling others to give the forces of democracy a larger share in the direction of public affairs.

The striking similarity between developments in Pennsylvania and those in New York strongly suggested that what was true for those colonies was also true for the others, that the debate with Britain had everywhere been accompanied by an internal struggle for democracy between radicals and conservatives, unprivileged and privileged, democrats and aristocrats. Added weight was given to this suggestion in 1918 with the publication of Arthur Meier Schlesinger's *The Colonial Merchants and the American Revolution*.[14] In this volume Schlesinger argued at length that the merchants in all of the colonies exhibited a similar pattern of behavior between 1763 and 1776. Strongly opposed to the new commercial restrictions introduced in 1763 and 1764, they spearheaded the protest against the Stamp and the Townshend Acts. When, however, they began to lose control of the situation to "political agitators" and the "proletarian element," first during the riots over the Stamp Act and then during the enforcement of nonimportation from 1768 to 1770, they realized that they "were unavoidably releasing disruptive forces which, like Frankenstein, they were finding it impossible to control." Thereafter, they discouraged or at least sought to moderate the intensity of further opposition to British policy. Only when the Tea Act of 1773 raised the specter of parliamentary-granted monopolies did the merchants again encourage a firm stand, and the results thoroughly confirmed their earlier fears as the radicals seized the initiative, pushed the colonies down the road to independence and to a more democratic polity, and left the merchants with the unsatisfactory alternatives of either becoming loyalists or acquiescing in the political domination of their "natural" rivals.

In a brilliant article[15] which appeared just after the publication of his book, Schlesinger spelled out the implications, for an understanding of the coming of the Revolution, of his own and other recent works on the political, social, and economic divisions within the colonies. In the process, he erected a general framework of interpretation which for the next three decades determined the limits of much of the discussion of the Revolutionary controversy. The Revolution, he argued, could no longer be looked upon simply

---

[14]New York, 1918.
[15]"The American Revolution Reconsidered," *Political Science Quarterly*, XXXIV (March, 1919), 61–78.

as a "great forensic controversy over abstract governmental rights." At best, Schlesinger declared, the history of the constitutional defenses of the colonists was "an account of their retreat from one strategic position to another," and, in any case, the big merchants (and presumably the planters)—the men who "dominated colonial opinion"—were, like all "practical men of affairs, . . . contemptuous, if not fearful, of disputes upon questions of abstract right." Rather, the Revolution had to be seen in the context of the "clashing of economic interests and the interplay of mutual prejudices, opposing ideas and personal antagonisms." In general, Schlesinger emphasized, those interests and prejudices, those ideals and antagonisms, were determined by conflicting economic interests within the empire and by sectional and class considerations within the colonies. Hard economic interests—the fear among the merchants in the middle and northern colonies of the new commercial regulations and later of parliamentary-granted monopolies and the desire among the southern plantation aristocracy to repudiate their enormous debts—and not devotion to constitutional principles per se drove the colonial upper classes to oppose the new colonial policy. Inside the colonies, there were not "thirteen units of population thinking alike on most public questions," but instead, he argued, in applying the frontier hypothesis of Frederick Jackson Turner, two "major groupings" of population—the eastern seaboard, divided into the commercial North and the agricultural South, and the West—which were "differentiated by physiographical conditions, economic interests and political ideals." It was the union between the "interior democracies" and the "democratic mechanic class" in the cities, a union promoted by a new breed of professional revolutionaries epitomized by Samuel Adams, that shaped the course of internal politics between 1763 and 1776. "Fundamentally," Schlesinger concluded, "the American Revolution represented the refusal of a self-reliant people to permit their natural and normal energies to be confined against their will, whether by an irresponsible imperial government or by the ruling minorities in their midst."

That the deep-seated economic forces and sectional and class divisions in the pre-Revolutionary years emphasized by Lincoln, Becker, and Schlesinger were, in fact, fundamental to early American political life had been confirmed in 1913 by Charles A. Beard in *An Economic Interpretation of the Constitution*,[16] a study of the other end of the Revolutionary era and one of the

---

[16]New York, 1913.

half dozen most influential books ever written in American history. Assuming that "real economic forces . . . condition great movements in politics," Beard analyzed the economic interests of all members of the Constitutional Convention of 1787. A close examination of a group of previously unused Treasury records revealed that most members of the convention owned government securities. Along with other evidence this discovery led him to conclude that the Constitution "was not the product of an abstraction known as 'the whole people [as jurists were prone to argue],' but of a group of economic interests which must have expected beneficial results from its adoption." Specifically, Beard argued, the holders of personalty—personal property in money, manufactures, trade and shipping, and especially public securities, which promised to rise in value with the establishment of a stronger and more effective central government—as opposed to real property in land and slaves provided the "dynamic element in the movement for the new Constitution." Welded together by economic concerns that cut across state lines, a "small and active group of men" with strong personalty interests and expectations of large profits inaugurated the movement for the new Constitution, which was written in secrecy by a convention which was with few exceptions composed of men who were "immediately, directly, and personally interested in, and derived economic advantages from, the establishment of the new system." Despite strong opposition from small farming and debtor interests, the personalty interests were able to push the Constitution through the ratifying conventions because a large majority of adult males did not vote either because they were disfranchised or because they did not realize what was happening. The Constitution thus became "essentially an economic document" written by a group of self-interested men to forward their own personal economic interests and to secure the rights of property; it was, therefore, necessarily inimicable to the interests of the vast bulk of Americans, who had either no property or only small holdings. Implicit in Beard's conclusions was the idea that the Constitution, instead of being the logical culmination of the Revolution, as Bancroft and Fiske had argued, was actually a repudiation of it, a counterrevolutionary instrument conceived by conservatives to curb the democratic excesses of the war and Confederation periods.

Around the theme of a deeply rooted and pervasive conflict over democracy between rival groups of radicals and conservatives representing fundamentally antagonistic sectional and class interests, Becker and Lincoln, Schlesinger and Beard had together built what appeared to be a coherent explanation of the entire Revolutionary era. The pressures of 1774–1776 finally gave the radicals the opportunity they had been waiting for to wrest the lion's share of political power from the conservatives. Over the next decade they pushed through the Declaration of Independence and inaugurated a program of democratic reform that succeeded in the various states according to the strength of radical domination but was checked, if only temporarily, in 1787–1788 by the Constitution and the conservative resurgence it represented.

In 1926, J. Franklin Jameson added significantly to this interpretation with *The American Revolution Considered as a Social Movement*,[17] a survey of the democratic achievements of the radicals. Allan Nevins had described in detail some of these achievements two years earlier in *The American States During and After the Revolution*,[18] but it was Jameson who fitted them all together to support the thesis that the American Revolution, like the French Revolution, was truly revolutionary in character and profoundly altered many aspects of colonial society. "The stream of revolution," he wrote in a now famous sentence, "once started, could not be confined within narrow banks, but spread abroad upon the land." The extension of the suffrage, abolition of feudal holdovers such as quitrents, primogeniture, and entail, redistribution of loyalist estates to small holders, disestablishment of the Anglican church, abolition of slavery and the slave trade in many states, and changes in the relation of social classes to one another were all products of the democratic impulses set free by the Revolution. Taken together they represented a significant advance toward a "levelling democracy."

Still other studies published in the 1920's and 1930's amplified the Progressive interpretation of the coming of the Revolution in significant ways. Two analyses of the arguments of the colonial opposition between 1763 and 1776, Randolph G. Adams, *The Political Ideas of the American Revolution*, [19] and Carl L. Becker, *The Declaration of Independence*,[20] agreed, as Becker put it, that the colonists had "step by step, from 1764 to 1776, . . . modified their theory to suit their needs." Denying only Parliament's right to levy internal taxes at the time of the Stamp Act, they extended their argument to include all taxes for revenue after Parliament had humored them by levying external duties with the Town-

---

[17]Princeton, 1926.
[18]New York, 1924.
[19]Durham, N.C., 1922.
[20]New York, 1922.

shend Acts; and, after Parliament had threatened the internal constitutions of the colonies by legislation as well as taxation with the Coercive Acts of 1774, they denied that Parliament had any authority over the colonies whatever. Neither Becker nor Adams said as much, but their conclusions could be taken to indicate that the colonies had no firm devotion to the constitutional arguments they employed, that, in fact, it was the economic motive, the desire to escape any form of taxation, that lay behind their behavior.

From this position it was only a short step to the idea that the colonists had not taken seriously any of the ideas they spouted in the vast flood of literature that poured from colonial presses in the pre-Revolutionary debate. This was the clear inference of two other studies, John C. Miller's *Sam Adams: Pioneer in Propaganda* (1936),[21] and Philip Davidson's *Propaganda and the American Revolution* (1941),[22] both of which were written in the dark days of the Great Depression when the Progressive view of the American past had an especially powerful appeal and when in Fascist Italy and Nazi Germany the manipulation of large segments of the population by clever propaganda made it easy to see propaganda as a major element in American politics at virtually every stage in the nation's history. Both Miller and Davidson recognized that propaganda might be true or false, sincere or insincere, but they tended in general to treat it only as a mask for deeper motives. The net results of their studies was to throw still greater doubt upon the depth of the Americans' commitment to the ideas they advanced and, along with the works of Randolph Adams and Becker, to contribute to the conception of the Revolution as a movement begun by a group of wealthy conservatives for essentially economic motives and subsequently arrogated by a small band of radical conspirators using the debate with Britain to accomplish other, more important political, economic, and social ends within the colonies.

By the early 1940's the only parts of the Revolutionary era that had not been thoroughly studied from the Progressive point of view were the war and Confederation periods, the years between the Declaration of Independence and the adoption of the Constitution. Two general surveys, Charles and Mary Beard's *The Rise of American Civilization*,[23] a popular text, and Vernon Louis Parrington's *Main Currents in American Thought: The Colonial*

---

[21]Boston, 1936.
[22]Chapel Hill, N.C., 1941.
[23]2 vols., New York, 1927.

Mind,[24] the first of a dramatic three-volume account of the struggle between aristocratic and democratic forces in the American past as expressed in intellectual life, had traced the conflicts of the 1760's and 1770's through the 1780's and the debate over the Constitution. Other studies had described the conflict in two critical states: New York and Pennsylvania.[25] But it remained for Merrill Jensen to present the first really comprehensive study in *The Articles of Confederation*[26] and *The New Nation,*[27] the most important books written in the Progressive tradition on the Revolutionary era, with the single exception of Beard's great work on the Constitution.

Jensen's primary achievement was to demonstrate that the Confederation period was not one of complete "stagnation, ineptitude, bankruptcy, corruption, and disintegration," as Fiske and others had suggested. The Confederation government, Jensen showed, made significant accomplishments in the disposition of western lands, and within its framework states and individuals were able both to survive a postwar depression in the mid-1780's and to make a strong beginning toward solving the problems of developing a foreign trade, paying off wartime debts, and paving the way for smoother commercial intercourse among the states. The Fiske view derived, Jensen argued, from the "uncritical acceptance of the arguments of the victorious party in a long political battle" over the nature of the central government, which had been carried on from the outset of the Revolution by the adherents of "two consistently opposed bodies of opinion" deriving to some extent from differing material interests and representing fundamental economic, social, and political divisions in American society. The nationalists, composed largely of those members of the colonial aristocracy who became patriots and new men who gained economic power during the war, demanded a stronger central government that could preserve them from the "horrors of unchecked democracy" by suppressing internal rebellions, regulating trade, collecting taxes, and checking the "power of the states and the democracy that found expression within their

---

[24]New York, 1927.

[25]Most notably, E. Wilder Spaulding, *New York in the Critical Period, 1783–1789* (New York, 1932); J. Paul Selsam, *The Pennsylvania Constitution of 1775: A Study in Revolutionary Democracy* (Philadelphia, 1936); and Robert L. Brunhouse, *The Counter-Revolution in Pennsylvania, 1776–1790* (Harrisburg, 1942), all of which, it should be reiterated, dealt with New York and Pennsylvania.

[26]Madison, Wis., 1940.

[27]New York, 1950.

bounds." On the other side were the true federalists, consisting primarily of the prewar radicals described by earlier writers and inaccurately labeled antifederalists. This group was generally satisfied with the Articles, which by providing for decentralization and states' rights were the embodiment of the "agrarian democracy" for which they stood, the constitutional expression of the philosophy of the Declaration of Independence, and the "natural outcome of the revolutionary movement." Having won their real goal, local self-government, with the war, the radicals displayed little interest in maintaining the organization they had created to bring about the Revolution; as a result, they were caught off guard by the dedicated, well disciplined efforts of the nationalists to overturn the Articles and with them some of the major achievements of the Revolution, and the nationalists were able in 1787 to engineer a "conservative counter-revolution" and erect a "nationalistic government whose purpose in part was to thwart the will of 'the people' in whose name they acted."

With the works of Jensen the Progressive conception of the Revolutionary era achieved its fullest expression. It was a story of internal revolution and counterrevolution, the rise and fall of democratic radicalism. Everywhere in the years between 1765 and 1776 radical leaders "seized on British acts as heaven-sent opportunities to attack the local aristocracy . . . under the guise of a patriotic defense of American liberties" and united the masses "in what became as much a war against the colonial aristocracy as a war for independence." It was the course of social revolution within the colonies—which Jensen argued was often far more important in determining political behavior than the more remote dangers of British policy—and not the debate with Britain which thus came to receive primary emphasis. The Revolution was to be viewed as "essentially, though relatively, a democratic movement within the thirteen American colonies," and its significance lay in its "tendency to elevate the political and economic status of the majority of the people." With the Constitution the movement was temporarily reversed, but all was not lost, because the nationalists—the aristocratic enemies of democracy—had failed to reckon with the possibility "that the government they created might be captured by the radicals united on a national scale."

By calling attention to the importance of internal divisions, the Progressive historians added a new dimension to the study of the Revolution; more importantly, for over four decades they supplied most of the leading ideas and intellectual energy in Revolutionary scholarship. They had never won the complete endorsement of all of the specialists who wrote about the Revolution, and most of the standard narrative accounts continued to treat it as a struggle for liberty, albeit in much more moderate tones than Bancroft and with a heavy imperial and Progressive veneer.[28] Among the vast body of American historians, however, and especially among the writers of the most widely-used American history texts, the Progressive interpretation by the late 1930's had become the standard version of the Revolutionary experience.

NEW DIRECTIONS

Since World War II a new group of scholars has subjected the writings of the imperial and Progressive historians to a massive, critical reassessment. Reexamining and rethinking the evidence at almost every major point, they have proceeded along two distinct yet complementary and overlapping lines of investigation. One line has been concerned mainly with exploring the substantive issues both in the debate with Britain and in the politics of the new nation between 1776 and 1789 and in examining the nature of internal political divisions and assessing their relationship to the dominant issues. A second line of investigation has been through the history of ideas, especially through the underlying assumptions and traditions of social and political behavior, and has sought to explain the relationship between those ideas and the central developments of the Revolutionary era.

Each line of investigation rests upon a conception of human nature that contrasts sharply with older interpretations. For the new group of scholars man is no longer simply a pawn at the mercy of powerful incomprehensible forces entirely beyond his

---

[28]This statement refers especially to Claude H. Van Tyne, *The Causes of the War of Independence* (Boston and New York, 1922), and *The War for Independence* (Boston and New York, 1929); H. E. Egerton, *The Causes and Character of the American Revolution* (Oxford, 1923); and John C. Miller, *Origins of the American Revolution* (Boston, 1943), and *The Triumph of Freedom, 1775–1783* (Boston, 1948). The statement is even more applicable to the several important studies of constitutional and political thought published between 1920 and 1940: Charles Howard McIlwain, *The American Revolution: A Constitutional Interpretation* (New York, 1923); Robert Livingston Schuyler, *Parliament and the British Empire* (New York, 1929); Benjamin F. Wright, Jr., *American Interpretations of Natural Law* (Cambridge, 1931); Andrew C. McLaughlin, *Foundations of American Constitutionalism* (New York, 1932, and *A Constitutional History of the United States* (New York: 1935); Charles F. Mullett, *Fundamental Law and the American Revolution, 1760–1776* (New York, 1933, 1966); and Edmund Cody Burnett, *The Continental Congress* (New York, 1941).

control, as he was for both the nineteenth-century nationalists and the imperial historians. Nor is he a creature so strictly devoted to the pursuit of his own self-interest and so extraordinarily prescient as to be able to calculate ends and means, as he so often appeared in the writings of the Progressives. Instead, he is an extraordinarily limited and insecure being, tenaciously attached to what he conceives to be his own interests and, often more importantly, to those principles, values, institutions, and aspirations around which he has built his life, and he responds intensely and emotionally to every contingency that seems to threaten any portion of his existence—his ideals as well as his interests. Man's limitations necessarily mean that his perceptions of the threat will rarely be accurate (indeed, he will probably see threats that do not exist), that he will be perpetually subject to self-delusion so that even his understanding of his own behavior will be distorted, and that he will rarely be able to foresee the results of his actions, though he will often try to do so. In short, he is a creature who, as A. O. Lovejoy has put it, "is forever 'rationalizing' but . . . is scarcely ever rational," a being who is at once at the mercy of history—of the larger developments within his lifetime—and, within the limits imposed by his nature and the physical and cultural environment in which he lives, free to make choices and take actions—perhaps even great creative and selfless actions—which impinge upon and perhaps even alter in significant ways the course of history. To understand the historical process, then, the new group of scholars assumes, one must understand the nature of broad historical forces, the behavior of individuals and groups, and the interaction between historical forces and human behavior. To understand human behavior, moreover, one must understand man's explanations of his own actions because, no matter how grossly distorted those explanations may be, man does act upon them and they become, therefore, powerful causative forces.

The new investigations have focused upon seven major problems: 1) the nature of the relationship between Britain and the colonies prior to 1763; 2) the nature of social and political life within the colonies and its relationship to the coming of the Revolution; 3) the reasons for the estrangement of the colonies from Britain between 1763 and 1776; 4) the explanations for the behavior of the British government and its supporters in the colonies between 1763 and the loss of the colonies in 1783; 5) the revolutionary consequences of the Revolution; 6) the character of the movement for the Constitution of 1787 and its relationship to the Revolution; and 7) the nature and meaning of the Revolution to the men who lived through it.

Relationships Prior to 1763

In the evaluation of the causes of the Revolution, one of the central problems has been the character of the relationship between Great Britain and the colonies prior to 1763. Most earlier interpretations viewed that relationship as essentially an unhappy one for the colonists, who, it was suggested, deeply resented the navigation system and chafed under the political restrictions imposed upon them by the home government. This view, which was widely held in Britain and among British officials in the colonies during the eighteenth century, has been sharply challenged by several of the newer investigations. In *The Navigation Acts and the American Revolution*,[29] Oliver M. Dickerson examined the navigation system as it operated in the eighteenth century and concluded that it did not work serious hardships upon the colonies. This view was similar to the interpretations of earlier imperial historians, especially George L. Beer. But Beer and other imperial writers assumed that the widespread smuggling was symptomatic of American discontent with the navigation acts, and it was upon this point that Dickerson sharply disagreed. He denied that the colonists in the period before 1763 either regarded the system as a grievance or made any serious attempt to evade it except in the case of tea and sugar after the passage of the Molasses Act in 1733. In general, he found that the system was adequately enforced without major objections from the colonists, who appreciated the fact that its benefits far outweighed its objectionable features. These findings, Dickerson argued, indicated that the navigation acts were the "cement of empire," a positive force binding the colonies to the mother country.

This happy arrangement was upset in 1764, when the British undertook to substitute a policy of trade taxation for the older system of trade protection and encouragement. With the Sugar Act of that year British officials introduced stricter customs and commercial arrangements designed to produce more revenue. This new policy, Dickerson argued, destroyed the empire in little more than a decade. Taxes and incidental charges arising from measures adopted over the next twelve years drained over £600,000 from the colonies, and the effect of these regulations was com-

---

[29]Philadelphia, 1951.

pounded because the bulk of the taxes fell most heavily upon the more important commercial towns, which were at the forefront of the Revolutionary movement. But "England's most fateful decision," Dickerson declared in his most important new conclusion, was included as part of the Townshend revenue program: the establishment, in 1767 at Boston, of a separate Board of Customs for the continental colonies. Previously, American customs collection had been supervised from London, and administration, tempered by the desire of British merchants to keep American trade running smoothly, had been relatively mild. Receiving their salaries out of collections, the commissioners of the new board, however, literally began to wage war on colonial commerce. Between 1768 and 1772 they engaged in what Dickerson, accepting at face value contemporary colonial opinion, judged was little less than "customs racketeering," as they employed legal technicalities and unscrupulous methods to plunder large amounts from colonial merchants, including such future Revolutionary leaders as John Hancock and Henry Laurens. The more blatant abuses came to an end after 1770 as the commissioners and their supporters lost influence in Britain, but the damage had been done, and it was their wholesale attack on American liberty and property, not American opposition to the old navigation system or addiction to smuggling, that caused the intense colonial hostility to the new board.

At no time after 1763, Dickerson concluded, did Americans express dissatisfaction with either the philosophy or the operation of the old navigation acts. In fact, they opposed the new measures because they were not primarily trade regulations of the older type. Nevertheless, convinced that colonial resistance meant Americans were trying to throw off the navigation system, British officials took an increasingly stricter line and thus provided the only real foundation for the subsequent charge by later historians that colonials were unhappy with the navigation acts. Only insofar as colonial discontent was fostered by British efforts to enforce a system thought to be under attack, Dickerson declared, were the navigation acts in any sense an important issue in the controversy with Britain.

Other historians have disagreed with Dickerson about the colonial attitude toward the navigation system and the effects of the system on the colonial economy. In his detailed study of the operation of the customs service, *Trade & Empire: The British Customs Service in Colonial America, 1600–1775*,[30] Thomas C.

---

[30]Cambridge, Mass., 1967.

Barrow agreed with Dickerson that American discontent with the navigation system in the years immediately piror to the Revolution stemmed largely from the reforms adopted after 1763. But he argued convincingly that the early opposition of the colonists to the system, between 1660 and 1720, indicated that they found it and the philosophy behind it fundamentally objectionable and that their acquiesence between 1720 and 1760 depended not upon their acceptance of the system, as Dickerson contended, but upon its lax enforcement. Two other students, Lawrence A. Harper[31] and Curtis P. Nettels,[32] argued that the burdens placed on the colonies by the navigation acts far exceeded the benefits. Although both admitted that there was little overt dissatisfaction with the acts among the colonists prior to 1763, they argued, like Barrow, that the colonists' failure to protest against the acts was not because they were the cement of empire but because they were not strictly enforced. And while Harper and Nettels also admitted that colonial objections after 1763 were limited primarily to the new regulatory and revenue measures, they suggested that those objections implied, even if few colonists were conscious of the implication, a fundamental discontent with the intent and thrust of the navigation system. On the basis of more sophisticated and systematic analytical techniques, however, Robert Paul Thomas has recently indicated that Dickerson was closer to the truth than either Harper or Nettels. Finding that between 1763 and 1772 the annual per capita loss to the colonists averaged only about twenty-six cents per person or about one-half of one per cent of estimated per capita income, Thomas concluded that neither the navigation acts nor the new trade regulations adopted after 1763 imposed significant economic hardships upon the colonial economy.[33] Of course, Thomas' discoveries do not mean that powerful and articulate segments of the colonial population such as the New England merchants or the large Virginia planters might not have borne an unduly high proportion of the total loss and that for some such groups the navigation acts as they were enforced after 1763 might have constituted a serious grievance,

---

[31] "The Effects of the Navigation Acts on the Thirteen Colonies," in *The Era of the American Revolution: Studies Inscribed to Evarts Boutell Greene*, Richard B. Morris ed. (New York, 1939), 1–39, and "Mercantilism and the American Revolution," *Canadian Historical Review*, XXIII (March, 1942), 24–34.

[32] "British Mercantilism and the Economic Development of the Thirteen Colonies," *Journal of Economic History*, XII (Spring, 1952), 105–114.

[33] "A Quantitative Approach to the Study of the Effects of British Imperial Policy upon Colonial Welfare: Some Preliminary Findings," *ibid.*, XXV (December, 1965), 615–638.

as Harper and Nettels suggested. Obviously, additional research will be required before these arguments can be evaluated more fully, but one point seems to have been rather firmly established: the colonists were not unhappy with the navigation system as it operated in the decades just before 1763, although their acceptance of the system may have depended largely on the fact that it was only loosely administered.

That political relations for much the same reasons were equally satisfactory to the colonists prior to 1763 was my argument in *The Quest for Power: The Lower Houses of Assembly in the Southern Royal Colonies, 1689–1776.*[34] From the last decades of the seventeenth century, colonial officials in London had envisioned a highly centralized empire with a uniform political system in each of the colonies and with the imperial government exercising strict supervision over the subordinate governments. But they had never made any sustained or systematic attempt to achieve these goals during the first half of the eighteenth century. The result, if the experience of the four southern royal colonies was typical, was the development of a working arrangement that permitted colonial lower houses considerable latitude in shaping the constitutions of the colonies without requiring Crown officials to relinquish any of their ideals. Sporadic and largely ineffective opposition from London officials and royal governors did not prevent the lower houses from acquiring an impressive array of *de facto* powers and privileges and, in the process, transforming themselves from the dependent lawmaking bodies they originally were intended to be into miniature Houses of Commons and, in almost every colony, shifting the constitutional center of power from the executive to themselves. The growing divergence between imperial ideals and colonial reality mattered little so long as each side refrained from openly challenging the other. Severe friction in this area did not develop until after 1763 when Parliament and the Crown in its executive capacity challenged at several important points the authority of the lower houses and the constitutional structures they had been forging over the previous century and a half. Then, the sanctity of the rights and privileges of the lower houses became a major issue between the home government and the colonists as imperial officials insisted upon an adherence to the old imperial ideals while colonial legislators, in the course of trying first to draw a line between the authority of Parliament and the lower houses and then to delimit the

---

[34]Chapel Hill, N.C., 1963.

boundaries of royal power in the colonies, came to demand rigid guarantees of colonial rights and eventually imperial recognition of the autonomy of the lower houses in local affairs and the equality of the lower houses with Parliament. Like the navigation system, then, which was satisfactory to the colonists largely because it was laxly enforced, political and constitutional relations were not a source of serious tension prior to 1763 largely because imperial authorities had never made any sustained attempt to make colonial practice correspond to imperial ideals.

Carl Bridenbaugh reached a somewhat different conclusion about the impact of the Anglican attempt to secure a complete episcopal establishment in the colonies. His detailed exploration of that subject, *Mitre and Sceptre: Transatlantic Faiths, Ideas, Personalities, and Politics, 1689–1775*,[35] not only pointed out the importance of this concrete religious issue in the coming of the Revolution in the middle colonies and New England but also argued that the "aggressive" tactics of the Anglicans in those colonies and the long, and at times bitter, debate over the episcopacy question between 1689 and 1760 already had helped to alienate many American dissenters from the mother country long before 1763. Because the advocates of episcopacy were never able to persuade the custodians of the empire to take any concrete steps toward implementing their program, however, the threat of an American bishopric remained no more than a threat and, however alarming to the dissenting clergy and others actively engaged in opposing it, it does not seem to have created sufficient discontent among the colonists at large to have made them unhappy with their connection with Britain. Significantly, as Bridenbaugh indicated, the climax of the episcopacy dispute came during the crucial years between 1760 and 1765 when the vigorous efforts of Archbishop Thomas Secker to secure an American episcopate convinced many American dissenters that an Anglican plot was in the making, caused them to fear lest the Grenville legislation and an American bishropric might be part of the same general scheme to curtail American liberties, and contributed substantially to the explosive reaction to the Stamp Act in the northern colonies. If, however, the furor over the episcopacy question helped to increase the intensity of the northern reaction to other measures in 1764–1765, the issue also appears to have loomed much more seriously in association with those measures and to have been distinctly secondary to them.

---

[35]New York, 1962.

With the profusion of British patriotism that poured from the colonies throughout the Seven Years' War and their notable propensity for quarreling among themselves, the absence of serious friction between the mother country and her North American possessions, in the economic, political, or religious realm, in 1763 made the possibility of a united revolt by the colonies against Britain seem remote indeed. But the patriotism and the bickering, like the absence of friction, were, several writers have recently indicated, extremely deceptive. As Clinton Rossiter has argued in *Seedtime of the Republic*,[36] a lengthy discussion of the formal concepts of colonial political thought, by the middle of the eighteenth century colonial Americans had developed, out of their English intellectual heritage and a century and a half of practical experience, a common political faith. At the heart of that faith was a philosophy of "ethical, ordered liberty" that found expression in and served as the foundation for the arguments advanced by Americans during the Revolutionary crisis. That the development of these common political ideas was accompanied by the emergence of common attitudes, values, and traditions in all other areas of colonial thought was the thesis of Max Savelle in *Seeds of Liberty: The Genesis of the American Mind*,[37] a general survey of eighteenth-century colonial culture. By 1750, Savelle contended, the colonists were one people culturally, with a latent American loyalty and American nationalism. Savelle was careful to emphasize that during the closing years of the Seven Years' War this American loyalty was submerged under an orgy of British patriotic sentiment as Americans celebrated the great British victories in Canada, the West Indies, and Europe; the accession of a vigorous young king, George III, in 1760; and the great Peace of Paris in 1763, which made the British Empire the most extensive and powerful in the Western world since Rome. Never, Savelle admitted, had British nationalism been stronger in the colonies. Yet, he argued, the effusions of British patriotism, however sincere, served to conceal a powerful, if still largely dormant, spirit of American nationalism that was waiting to be nourished by the British challenge between 1763 and 1766.[38]

These conclusions have recently been confirmed by Richard L.

---

[36]New York, 1953.

[37]New York, 1948. Savelle expanded on this theme later in "Nationalism and Other Loyalties in the American Revolution," *American Historical Review*, LXVII (July, 1961), 901–923.

[38]For another discussion of this point see Paul A. Varg, "The Advent of Nationalism, 1758–1776," *American Quarterly*, XVI (Summer, 1964), 160–181.

Merritt in *Symbols of American Community, 1735–1775*.[39] Seeking some way to measure more precisely the American sense of community, he turned to colonial newspapers, the importance of which in stimulating opposition to Britain after 1763 had been emphasized earlier by Arthur M. Schlesinger.[40] By using content analysis and counting the explicit verbal symbols of identification —e.g., "American," "Europe," "Great Britain," "Virginia," "Massachusetts"—in a carefully selected sample of the newspapers, he discovered that the colonists had already "developed a fairly high degree of community awareness" well before 1763. By stimulating the colonists' pride in being Britons and by demanding an unusual amount of American attention to the home country and its military exploits, the Seven Years' War had, in fact, actually operated as a temporary brake upon the growth of that awareness. As soon as the war was over, however, the American sense of community increased perceptibly. The "takeoff" point, Merritt found, came during the early summer of 1763, well before any of the British measures that Americans found objectionable had gone into effect. The nature of his data did not enable him to explain *why* the colonists were becoming increasingly interested in one another, and to answer that question he fell back upon some of the integrative forces—the emergence during the middle decades of the eighteenth century of intercolonial trading patterns and communications networks, an interlocking elite, and closer interurban ties—previously emphasized by Michael Kraus[41] and Carl Bridenbaugh.[42] Whatever "caused" this development, however, it was, Merritt suggested, an important element in enabling the colonists to offer united resistance during the Stamp Act crisis, "which, in its turn, made a further contribution to the developing sense of American community." The debate with Britain, then, was, as Savelle had suggested, not the origin of American national sentiment but a powerful "impetus to a moving political force already underway." Each successive crisis reinforced "the colonists' growing sense of American separatism" until by 1775 they had crossed what Merritt called the "threshold" of functional and psychological political amalgamation which enabled them to form national political institutions and to fight a war against Britain. This growing sense of American community, then, helps to ex-

[39]New Haven, 1966.
[40]*Prelude to Independence: The Newspaper War on Britain, 1764–1776* (New York, 1958).
[41]*Intercolonial Aspects of American Culture on the Eve of the Revolution, with Special Reference to the Northern Towns* (New York, 1928).
[42]*Cities in Revolt: Urban Life in America. 1743–1776* (New York, 1955).

plain how thirteen diverse and often quarreling colonies could in just twelve short years sufficiently overcome their differences and unite against the mother country.

That the colonists' strong feelings of British patriotism in 1763 depended to a large extent upon a conception of the role of the colonies in the British Empire that itself reflected the expanding sense of community among the colonies was suggested by Richard Koebner in *Empire*,[43] a study in political semantics. This investigation of the history of the terms "empire," "imperial," and "imperialism" in the language of Western Europe from Rome to the Congress of Vienna contained a large section on British and colonial uses of the terms in the seventeenth and eighteenth centuries. It showed that the notion of the British Empire did not acquire a prominent place in British historical consciousness until after the Glorious Revolution and that even then it was an extremely restricted concept that referred only to Great Britain and Ireland and not to British possessions overseas. Only after 1740 did the colonies acquire a place in the empire, and then the impetus for that development came from the colonies, not the home islands. Aware of their increasing importance to Britain and exhilarated by their vision of future greatness, Americans began to conceive of the colonies as the "British Empire in America," and out of this concept emerged the idea of the empire as a world-wide political system held together by mutual allegiance and the harmony of interests among the constituent parts. This vision was, however, strictly an American creation, and in the decade preceding the Revolution it became clear that British officials had not yet come to regard the colonies as part of the empire, much less as the equal partners some Americans thought them to be. That British officials, with the notable exception of Massachusetts Governor Francis Bernard, did not understand that the American view of the empire included the colonies and could not, therefore, appreciate the implications of equality inherent in that concept helps to explain why they were constantly surprised at the extent of American demands, were unable to grasp the fundamental assumptions behind American constitutional arguments, and so thoroughly misconstrued the nature of American intentions. When they did begin in the 1760's to employ a broader concept of empire that took in the colonies, they used it as a device to bring about a more unified constitutional arrangement that would guar-

---

[43]Cambridge, England, 1961.

antee the subordination, not the equality, of the colonies. This profound divergence of thought between Great Britain and the colonies about the current and future role of the colonies in the British political community—a divergence that contributed substantially to the breakdown in communications that occurred between 1763 and 1776—helps make clear both why American leaders felt such an extraordinary sense of betrayal at the new measures adopted after 1763 and how the extreme British national feeling they expressed in the early 1760's could be dissipated so quickly over the next decade as it became increasingly clear that the imperial government did not share their conception of the place of the colonies in the empire.

What all of these newer studies seem to indicate, then, is that imperial-colonial relations were largely satisfactory to the colonies prior to 1763 only because potentially objectionable aspects of British economic and political policy were loosely enforced and that British national sentiment in the colonies remained high to an important extent because of the colonists' exaggerated view of their own importance within the imperial community. It is clear in retrospect that the shattering of that view and/or the strict enforcement of imperial policy was bound to stir resentment and opposition in the colonies. Had relations continued to follow the same pattern after 1763 that they did before, however, it is entirely possible that the colonists would have been as pleased with their British connection in 1776 and 1787 as they were in 1763. The Whig and imperial historians to the contrary notwithstanding, then, recent studies strongly suggest that the Revolution cannot be attributed either primarily or directly to colonial discontent with conditions as they operated before the 1760's.

Political, Social, and Economic Divisions
Within the Colonies

Still other scholars have directed their attention to the detailed study of political life within the individual colonies during the era of the Revolution, and their findings indicate that major modifications are required in the Progressive conception of both early American politics and the Revolution. Investigators of Maryland, New Jersey, Connecticut, Pennsylvania, Rhode Island, Georgia, and Virginia have analyzed the impact of the debate with Britain upon local politics and assessed the importance of the peculiar configuration of the economic, social, and political life of each colony in shaping its response to that debate.[44] Although these works reveal that the relative importance of the major substantive issues and the pattern of the Revolutionary movement varied considerably from colony to colony and that there were special, and occasionally extremely significant, local grievances against the imperial government in almost every colony, they also call attention to some important common features. Everywhere relations with Britain were relatively harmonious prior to 1763 and politics within the colonies were primarily elitist in nature. Public office—both appointive and elective—and political leadership were securely in the hands of upper-class groups, and, although there were occasional manifestations of social and economic discontent among the lower classes, that discontent never resulted in widespread demands for basic changes in the customary patterns of upper-class leadership. Political divisions, despite the earlier contentions of Lincoln and Becker, were not along class lines and not between rival ideological groups of radicals and conservatives. Rather, they revolved around the ambitions of rival factions among the elite. The debate with Britain was in many instances the occasion for one faction to gain political predominance at the expense of its rivals, but, significantly, the faction that stood for the strongest line of resistance to British policy usually emerged victorious. Within the colonies, then, the direction of local politics and the balance of political forces were influenced, and in some cases altered profoundly, by the debate after 1763 over Parliament's authority and the extent of the Crown's prerogative in the colonies. The constitutional debate was thus not only the primary political concern within most colonies from 1763 to 1776, these studies seem to indicate, but also the most powerful agency of political change.

---

[44]Charles A. Barker, *The Background of the Revolution in Maryland* (New Haven, 1940); Donald L. Kemmerer, *Path to Freedom: The Struggle for Self-Government in Colonial New Jersey, 1703–1776* (Princeton, 1940); Oscar Zeichner, *Connecticut's Years of Controversy, 1750–1776* (Chapel Hill, N.C., 1949); Theodore Thayer, *Pennsylvania Politics and the Growth of Democracy, 1740–1776* (Harrisburg, Pa. 1953); David Hawke, *In the Midst of a Revolution* (Philadelphia, 1961); Arthur L. Jensen, *The Maritime Commerce of Colonial Philadelphia* (Madison, Wis., 1963); David S. Lovejoy, *Rhode Island Politics and the American Revolution, 1760–1776* (Providence, 1958); Kenneth Coleman, *The American Revolution in Georgia, 1763–1789* (Athens, Ga., 1958); W. W. Abbot, *The Royal Governors of Georgia, 1754–1775* (Chapel Hill, N.C., 1959); and Thad W. Tate, "The Coming of the Revolution in Virginia: Britain's Challenge to Virginia's Ruling Class, 1763–1776," *William and Mary Quarterly*, 3rd series, XIX (July, 1962), 323–343.

An even more direct challenge to the Progressive conception of the Revolution came from Robert E. and B. Katherine Brown in two studies of the relationship between politics and social structure in Massachusetts and Virginia (*Middle-Class Democracy and the Revolution in Massachusetts, 1691–1780* and *Virginia, 1705–1786: Democracy or Aristocracy?*).[45] The Browns' discoveries that in both colonies the economic structure was highly fluid, property widely distributed, and lower-class economic and social discontent minimal indicated that neither colony was so rigidly stratified as to produce the kind of social conflicts which Progressive historians thought were the stuff of colonial politics. By showing as well that the franchise was considerably wider than had previously been supposed, the Browns also demonstrated that the predominance of the upper classes in politics did not depend upon a restricted franchise, that they had to have the support of men from all classes to gain elective office.

That both of these conclusions are probably also applicable to most other colonies is indicated by the findings of several other recent independent investigations of Connecticut, New York, New Jersey, Pennsylvania, and Rhode Island.[46] All of these studies argue that the franchise in these colonies was very wide and that the vast majority of free adult males could expect to acquire enough property during their lifetimes to meet suffrage requirements. Similarly, Jackson Turner Main in *The Social Structure of Revolutionary America*[47] demonstrated that, although there were great extremes in wealth and in standards and styles of living in American society during the late eighteenth century, it was everywhere relatively free from poverty and had, especially by European standards, a high rate of vertical mobility, great social and economic opportunity, and a remarkably supple class structure. This combination of economic abundance and social fluidity, Main concluded, tended "to minimize those conflicts which might have grown out of the class structure and the concentration of wealth" that was occurring in older settled areas on the eve of the Revolution.

---

[45]Ithaca, N.Y., 1955, and East Lansing, Mich., 1964, respectively.

[46]Charles S. Grant, *Democracy in the Connecticut Frontier Town of Kent* (New York, 1961); Milton M. Klein, "Democracy and Politics in Colonial New York," *New York History*, XL (July, 1959), 221–246; Richard P. McCormick, *The History of Voting in New Jersey: A Study of the Development of Election Machinery, 1664–1911* (New Brunswick, 1953); Thayer, *op. cit.*; and Lovejoy, *op. cit.*

[47]Princeton, 1965.

Other studies of the underlying assumptions and modes of behavior of early American politics by J. R. Pole[48] and Richard
Buel, Jr.,[49] have helped to resolve what, within the modern democratic conceptions employed by the Progressive historians and
such recent writers as Robert E. Brown, was such a massive and
incomprehensible paradox: why, in the words of Pole, "the great
mass of the common people might actually have given their consent to concepts of government" that by "systematically" excluding
them "from the more responsible positions of political power"
restricted "their own participation in ways completely at variance
with the principles of modern democracy." Revolutionary society,
these studies have found, was essentially what Walter Bagehot
called "a deferential society" that operated within an integrated
structure of ideas fundamentally elitist in nature. That structure
of ideas assumed, among other things, that government should
be entrusted to men of merit; that merit was very often, though
by no means always, associated with wealth and social position;
that men of merit were obliged to use their talents for the benefit
of the public; and that deference to them was the implicit duty
of the rest of society. All society was therefore divided between
the rulers and the ruled, and the rulers, including the representatives of the people, were not the tools of the people but their political superiors. "The mass of the people," Buel argued, thus
"elected representatives not to order them around like lackeys to
do the people's bidding, but to reap benefit from the distinguished
abilities of the few upon which the safety of society might in
large measure depend" and to utilize the "political *expertise* of the
realm in the people's behalf." To be sure, representative institutions provided the people with the means to check any unwarranted
abuses of power by their rulers, but the power the people possessed
was "not designed to facilitate the expression of their will in
politics but to defend them from oppression." Both Pole and Buel
concluded that, although these assumptions were undermined by
the Revolution and eventually gave way after 1790 to an expanded
conception of the people's role in the polity, they continued to be
the predominant elements underlying American political thought
over the whole period from 1763 to 1789.

Obviously, many more specialized studies of developments
within individual colonies will be required before the nature of

---

[48] "Historians and the Problem of Early American Democracy," *American Historical Review*, LXVII (April, 1962), 626–646.
[49] "Democracy and the American Revolution: A Frame of Reference," *William and Mary Quarterly*, 3rd ser., XXI (April, 1964), 165–190.

internal political divisions and their relationship to the coming of the Revolution will be understood fully. The investigations already published do, however, suggest four tentative conclusions that flatly contradict earlier arguments of the Progressive historians: the configuration of politics and the nature of social and economic divisions varied enormously from state to state; social and political opportunity was remarkably wide; class struggle and the demand for democracy on the part of unprivileged groups were not widespread and not a primary causative factor in the coming of the Revolution; and colonial political life operated within a structure of commonly-accepted values that assigned positions of leadership in the polity to members of the social and economic elite.

The Estrangement of the Colonies, 1763–1776

One of the results of the discoveries that tensions between Britain and the colonies prior to 1763 were relatively mild and that political rivalries within the colonies were, in most cases, distinctly secondary in importance to the constitutional debate with Britain between 1763 and 1776 has been that historians have increasingly come to focus more directly upon that debate in their search for an explanation for the coming of the Revolution. The guiding question in this search has been why the colonists became unhappy enough in the years after 1763 to revolt. To answer this question a number of historians have sought to identify and assess the importance of the several substantive issues between the colonies and Great Britain.

Thus Bernhard Knollenberg explored the nature and areas of American discontent during the early 1760's in *Origin of the American Revolution: 1759–1766*.[50] Although he agreed with other recent writers that Americans were generally happy with existing political and economic relationships with Britain through the middle decades of the eighteenth century, he contended that trouble began not in 1763 but in 1759, when British military successes made it unnecessary to placate the colonies further and permitted imperial authorities to inaugurate a stricter policy. Under the leadership of the Earls of Granville and Halifax, presidents respectively of the Privy Council and Board of Trade and longtime advocates of a tougher colonial policy. Crown officials undertook a series of new and provocative measures intended to weaken colonial self-government and, Knollenberg implied, check

---

[50]New York, 1960.

tendencies which British officials feared might be leading toward independence. Over the next four years a wider and more intensive use of such traditional checks as the royal instructions and legislative review seriously antagonized colonial leaders in almost every colony. Separately, none of these measures was very important, but their concentration within a short period, Knollenberg contended, produced a significant amount of discontent throughout the colonies. That discontent increased measurably beginning in the spring of 1762, when first the Bute and then the Grenville ministries undertook a variety of general reform measures designed to tighten up the colonial system. In 1763 came a series of steps that was particularly unpopular in New England, including the decision to use the royal navy to curb smuggling and to enforce the previously laxly administered Molasses Act of 1733 and various white pines acts. Also in 1763, imperial officials decided to station a large standing army in the colonies and to limit western expansion into the region beyond the Allegheny mountains. Security was the primary consideration behind both measures, but it was easy for Americans to interpret the former as an attempt to overawe them with force and the latter as a strategem to confine them to the seacoast—motives, Knollenberg found, which actually did play some small part in the decisions. The necessity of paying for the army led to the decision to tax the colonies and to Parliament's passage in 1764 of the Sugar Act, which provided for extensive reforms in colonial administration, and in 1765 of the Stamp Act, which touched off the colonial uprising in 1765–1766. According to Knollenberg, then, the cumulative effect of British policy over the previous six years, and not the Stamp Act alone, brought the colonies to the brink of rebellion during the Stamp Act crisis.

That the Stamp Act and the threat of parliamentary taxation which it contained were easily the most important sources of American dissatisfaction in the uprising of 1765–1766 has, however, been persuasively argued by Edmund S. Morgan and Helen M. Morgan in *The Stamp Act Crisis: Prologue to Revolution*,[51] one of the two or three most important books published on the era of the Revolution since World War II. On the basis of a new and thorough reexamination of what was probably already the most studied of the events preceding the Revolution, the Morgans reached several important new conclusions that fundamentally challenged older interpretations. They found, for example, that

---

[51]Chapel Hill, N.C., 1953.

the offer by George Grenville to entertain suggestions from the colonies for taxing themselves was less than sincere, that he had, in fact, already decided upon a stamp tax by the time he first suggested it to Parliament in 1764. Both the Massachusetts Assembly and colonial agents in London tried unsuccessfully to act on the offer, but the fact was that Grenville neither communicated it to the colonies through official channels nor formulated it in terms precise enough to permit definite action. The year's delay, the Morgans concluded, was merely to permit the ministry to work out details of the Stamp Act.[52] This discovery seriously undermined one of the central arguments of both the imperial and Progressive historians: that the colonists' failure to suggest alternatives to the Stamp Act indicated that they were opposed not to taxation without representation but to taxation in general. The argument was weakened still further by the Morgans' findings that Americans objected to all forms of parliamentary taxation for revenue in 1764–1765 and not simply to internal taxes, as both imperial and Progressive historians had implied. That the colonists had distinguished between internal and external taxes was widely believed in England, but the Morgans found no such distinction in contemporary American statements. Both American legislators and pamphlet writers categorically denied Parliament's authority to levy any taxes for revenue purposes—a principle to which they consistently adhered for the next decade.[53] In the light of this evidence it became clear the traditional charge that Americans were inconsistent and continually enlarged their claims as the situation changed was not valid.

The Morgans' study strongly suggested that American concern for and devotion to the constitutional arguments they employed were considerably greater than most scholars during the previous half century had assumed, and demonstrated the importance of political and constitutional considerations in the American case against the Sugar and Stamp Acts. As the subtitle suggested, the work argued for the decisiveness of the Stamp Act crisis in the unfolding Revolutionary drama. Not only did it raise the issue of the extent of Parliament's jurisdiction in the colonies by forcing American leaders and Parliament into a precise formulation of directly opposing views, but it also created an atmosphere of

---

[52]This argument is set forth in greater detail in Edmund S. Morgan, "The Postponement of the Stamp Act," *William and Mary Quarterly*, 3rd ser., VII (July, 1950), 353–392.

[53]For a more thorough elaboration of this point see Edmund S. Morgan, "Colonial Ideas of Parliamentary Power," *ibid.*, V (July, 1948), 311–341.

mutual suspicion that pervaded all subsequent developments and quite possibly precluded any peaceful settlement of the issue. Thereafter, Americans scrutinized every parliamentary action for possible threats to their constitutional rights, while British authorities became increasingly convinced that American opposition was simply a prelude to an eventual attempt to shake off the restraints of the navigation acts and perhaps even political dependence.

Other scholars analyzed in detail the American reaction to still other issues during the period from 1760 to 1776. The works of Dickerson, Barrow, Bridenbaugh, and myself, treating respectively the colonial reaction to the new trade restrictions, customs regulations, proposals for an American episcopate, and attacks on assembly rights, have already been discussed. Carl Ubbelohde's *The Vice-Admiralty Courts and the American Revolution*[54] and John Shy's *Toward Lexington: The Role of the British Army and the Coming of the American Revolution*,[55] have, as the titles indicate, explored the response to the vice-admiralty courts and the army. Although the vice-admiralty courts had been in existence since 1696, they never, Ubbelohde found, became the object of deep colonial hostility prior to 1763, largely because colonial merchants and others involved with them had been able to avoid them. When, however, imperial authorities sought after 1763 to make the courts a "cornerstone in the new imperial rule" by a series of new and stricter regulations, colonial opposition hardened noticeably. Still, the courts did not come under major attack until after Parliament had given them jurisdiction over the enforcement of first the Sugar and Stamp Acts and then the Townshend Revenue Act. Americans, drawing a fundamental distinction between the old trade regulations and the new revenue measures, argued that to try cases arising under the revenue laws in juryless vice-admiralty courts deprived them of their ancient right of trial by jury. In Britain such cases were tried before juries in the common law Court of Exchequer, and to alter that procedure in the colonies seemed to be to create an invidious distinction, as well as a basic inequality of rights, between Englishmen and Americans.[56] Yet, Ubbelohde concluded, however intrinsically objectionable Americans found the courts, their hostility to them ebbed and flowed with their dissatisfaction over questions of greater moment, and

---

[54]Chapel Hill, N. C., 1960.
[55]Princeton, 1965.
[56]This aspect of the issue is treated more fully in David S. Lovejoy, "Rights Imply Equality: The Case against Admiralty Jurisdiction in America, 1764–1776," *William and Mary Quarterly*, 3rd ser., XVI (October, 1959), 459–484.

it was really the association of the courts with the new revenue laws and other broad objectives of British policy after 1763 that made them seem so onerous to the colonists.

Shy reached a similar conclusion about the army. Kept in the colonies after the Seven Years' War largely to occupy and defend the non-English rim of the expanded North American empire and to help in the management of Indian affairs, the army was viewed with suspicion by some colonials who suspected that it might be intended as a coercive force. These suspicions, Shy found, were in part true: the possibility that an American garrison could help to put "some teeth in the imperial system" was actually a secondary consideration with British administrators. Not until the Stamp Act crisis did they come to conceive of the army as primarily "a police force." Yet, because the army was not used in that way during the crisis, there was relatively little overt colonial opposition to it. Only after September, 1768, when troops had been sent to Boston specifically to quell the disturbances over the Townshend Acts, did colonial leaders begin to suggest widely that the ostensible motive—the security of the colonies from external attack—for originally stationing the army in America was simply a pretext for forcing the colonists to obey the authority of Parliament and the directions of the ministry. Thereafter, polemicists repeatedly warned of the dangers of a standing army to the liberties and morals of the public, and the Boston Massacre, though it led to the removal of most of the troops from Boston and the eventual diminution of hostility to the army, only seemed to justify the warnings. Like the vice-admiralty courts, however, the army did not in the years before Lexington and Concord become "a major grievance in itself." Rather, Shy concluded, its primary importance lay in the fact that it "reinforced American attitudes on other issues."

The final crisis of the pre-Revolutionary years was analyzed in detail by Benjamin Woods Labaree in *The Boston Tea Party*.[57] The tea party, he argued, was the decisive event in the chain of events that led to the outbreak of war and the Declaration of Independence. It was the tea party, he pointed out, that produced a new spirit of unity among the colonies, after more than two years of disharmony following the abandonment of the nonimportation agreements against the Townshend duties in 1770, and finally determined British officials to take a firm stand against colonial opposition to parliamentary taxation by making an example of

---

[57]New York, 1964.

Boston. The punitive measures they adopted posed the new and disturbing question of whether the colonists had any rights at all with which to protect themselves from the naked power of Parliament, caused the rest of the colonies to unite behind Boston, drove patriot leaders to deny that Parliament had any authority whatever over the internal affairs of the colonies, and put both sides into an inflamed state that made war a virtual certainty. In an important modification of a long-accepted interpretation, Labaree also discovered that among American smugglers of Dutch tea the fear that the Tea Act of 1773 would enable the East India Company to undersell them and so gain a monopoly of the American market was less important in stirring resistance to East India Company tea than Progressive historians had suggested. Although he did not deny that the tea smugglers, who were largely confined to New York and Philadelphia, were concerned over the threat of monopoly, he found it a distinctly secondary issue among patriot leaders and the public at large. What concerned them far more was the possibility that the Tea Act was simply a clever ruse to inveigle them into paying the tea duty and admitting the long-contested right of Parliament to tax the colonies for revenue. By this discovery Labaree strongly seconded the argument of other recent writers: that constitutional rights, especially Parliament's attempts to tax the colonies for revenue, were the primary issues between Britain and the colonies in the fateful years from 1763 to 1776.

Although important issues, such as imperial prohibition of legal tender paper currency[58] and western expansion,[59] still require further study, these investigations have together made it possible to achieve a rather clear understanding of the importance and relative weight of the several substantive issues in the American case against the British government. Important segments of the colonists had occasionally been offended or alarmed by such things as the Anglican effort to secure an American episcopate or the sporadic attempts by imperial officials to curtail the power of the lower houses of assembly, but the colonists were generally

---

[58]A brief treatment of this issue is Jack P. Greene and Richard M. Jellison, "The Currency Act of 1764 in Imperial-Colonial Relations, 1764–1776," *William and Mary Quarterly*, 3rd ser., XVIII (October, 1961), 485–518.

[59]The conclusions of the classic study of British western policy—Clarence W. Alvord, *The Mississippi Valley in British Politics* (2 vols., Cleveland, 1917)—have been modified by the findings of several scholars, most notably Jack M. Sosin, *Whitehall and the Wilderness: The Middle West in British Colonial Policy, 1760–1775* (Lincoln, Neb., 1961), although neither Alvord nor Sosin explored in detail the extent and nature of colonial discontent with that policy.

satisfied with their connection with Britain before imperial officials adopted stricter measures after 1760 that fundamentally challenged American rights and property. Parliament's attempts to tax the colonies for revenue were far and away the most serious of these measures. Though the colonists found them profoundly disturbing in themselves and though their concentration over so short a period unquestionably contributed to the intensity of the colonial response to the challenge from Parliament, none of the other measures—the effort to tighten the navigation system, the attempt to undermine the authority of the lower houses, the employment of the army as a coercive force, the increased use of the vice-admiralty courts, or the threat to establish an American episcopate—loomed so importantly or stirred such widespread, determined, and pointed opposition. The remarkable consistency of their constitutional demands down to 1774 revealed both the intense commitment of the colonists to the constitutional principles on which they stood and their genuine concern about the constitutional question. Only after 1774, as I emphasized in *The Quest for Power,* did the American protest cease to be largely a series of defensive responses to immediate provocations by the imperial government and become an aggressive movement intent not just on securing exemption for the colonies from all parliamentary measures but also, in a striking escalation of their earlier demands, strict limitations upon the Crown's use of many of its traditional devices of royal control over the colonies. Throughout the entire debate, however, the primary issues in the minds of the colonists were, then, essentially of a political and constitutional nature involving matters of corporate rights, political power, individual liberty, security of property, and rule of law. Although, as Edmund S. Morgan has taken pains to emphasize (*The Birth of the Republic, 1763–89*),[60] all of these objects of concern were intimately coupled with "self-interest" and were conceived of as the necessary safeguards of the colonists' fundamental well-being —social and economic, as well as political—the opposition to Great Britain, these new studies would seem to indicate, was much less directly social and economic in character than earlier historians had suggested.

These conclusions have been considerably enriched and somewhat altered by several recent explorations of the assumptions, traditions, conventions, and habits of thought that underlay and conditioned the American response to the substantive issues in the

[60]Chicago, 1956.

quarrel with Britain. These studies of what is essentially the psychology of colonial resistance have been especially concerned with the role of the Americans' conception of human nature. At least since the early nineteenth century it has been conventional to attribute to the eighteenth century an optimistic conception of man and a belief in his ability, to paraphrase one of the most famous expositions of this view, to perfect the "good life on earth."[61] But this view, A. O. Lovejoy has insisted (*Reflections on Human Nature*),[62] is a "radical historical error." Some eighteenth-century writers did indeed subscribe to such a view of human nature, but, Lovejoy convincingly argued, the "most widely prevalent opinion about human nature" was that men were imperfect creatures who were usually actuated "by non-rational motives—by 'passions,' or arbitrary and unexamined prejudices, or vanity, or the quest for private economic advantage." Only because of their "craving for reputation, praise, and applause," which, eighteenth-century thinkers believed, was the "dominant and universal passion" in man, were men ever driven to behave in a manner "necessary for the good order of society and the progress of mankind." This unflattering view of human nature provided the foundation for an elaborate theory of politics which, in its essential elements, was traceable as far back as antiquity and which—as Z. S. Fink,[63] J. G. A. Pocock,[64] and, especially, Caroline Robbins,[65] among others, have shown—manifested itself in several forms in seventeenth- and eighteenth-century English thought and was especially congenial to those political groups on the fringes or completely out of political power. At the heart of this theory were the convictions that man in general could not withstand the temptations of power, that power was by its very nature a corrupting and aggressive force, and that liberty was its natural victim. The protection of liberty against the malignancy of power required that each of the various elements in the polity had to be balanced against one another in such a way as to pre-

---

[61]Carl L. Becker, *The Heavenly City of the Eighteenth-Century Philosophers* (New Haven, 1932).

[62]Baltimore, 1961.

[63]*The Classical Republicans: An Essay in the Recovery of a Pattern of Thought in Seventeenth Century England* (Evanston, 1945).

[64]"Machiavelli, Harrington, and English Political Ideologies in the Eighteenth Century," *William and Mary Quarterly*, 3rd ser., XXII (October, 1965), 547–583.

[65]*The Eighteenth-Century Commonwealthman: Studies in the Transmission, Development, and Circumstances of English Liberal Thought from the Restoration of Charles II until the War with the Thirteen Colonies* (Cambridge, Mass., 1959).

vent any of them from gaining ascendancy over the rest. A mixed constitution was the means by which this delicate balance was to be achieved, but power was so pervasive and so ruthless that nothing was safe from it.

That this theory of politics with its underlying view of human nature was widely diffused throughout the colonies had been indicated earlier by Gerald Stourzh in *Benjamin Franklin and American Foreign Policy*[66] and by Caroline Robbins and Richard Buel, Jr., in the works referred to previously, but it remained for Bernard Bailyn in *The Ideological Origins of the American Revolution*,[67] perhaps the most penetrating and original new study of any segment of the era of the Revolution, to show precisely how the theory shaped the American response to British measures after 1763. Within the context of the ideas associated with this theory of politics, Bailyn found, after an intensive examination of American polemical literature in the pre-Revolutionary years, the succession of restrictive and regulatory measures taken by the British government and royal officials in the colonies after 1763 appeared to be unmistakable "evidence of nothing less than a deliberate conspiracy launched surreptitiously by plotters against liberty both in England and in America." Far from being "mere rhetoric and propaganda," as Progressive writers had charged, such words as slavery, corruption, and conspiracy "meant something very real to both writers and their readers" and expressed "real fears, real anxieties, a sense of real danger." Above all else, Bailyn argued, it was this reading of British behavior and "not simply an accumulation of grievances" that "in the end propelled" the colonists into rebellion. The gross distortions in their interpretation of the actions of the British government, Bailyn implied, mattered much less than that Americans believed it. The inner reality behind the ostensible issues and concrete grievances, the "real" Revolution that had so successfully eluded the Progressive historians, Bailyn thus suggested, was not economic or even social in character but intellectual and psychological. It was not only hard economic interests or considerations of political power or constitutional principles, then, but also and, Bailyn strongly implied, more importantly, ideas that "lay behind the manifest events of the time" and provided the key to understanding the "contemporary meaning" of the Revolution. They revealed, Bailyn insisted, "not merely

---

[66]Chicago, 1954.
[67]Cambridge, Mass., 1967. This volume originally appeared as the Introduction to Volume I of *Pamphlets of the American Revolution* (Cambridge, Mass., 1965).

positions taken but the reasons why positions were taken" and the inner logic of American behavior.[68] Ideas thus played a dual role in the coming of the Revolution. They both provided a framework within which Americans could explain British and their own behavior and determined in significant and fundamental ways their responses to the developing situation.

The place of American conceptions of the past in this framework was the subject of H. Trevor Colbourn's monograph, *The Lamp of Experience: Whig History and the Intellectual Origins of the American Revolution*.[69] As Colbourn's subtitle suggested, it was the conception of history as set forth by seventeenth- and eighteenth-century Whig writers to which colonials were largely devoted. That conception saw the past as a continual struggle between liberty and virtue on one hand and arbitrary power and corruption on the other. Rome fell only after its citizens had sacrificed their temperance and virtue to luxury and vice. And, although the Glorious Revolution in England had promised to restore the ancient Saxon virtues and free constitution, which had been in abeyance ever since the Norman invasion, it had not been accompanied by a reformation in English character, with the result that the early eighteenth century presented a dreary scene of continuing moral degeneration and political irresponsibility—the harbingers, English Whig writers warned, of the total collapse of constitutional government and the eventual fall of Britain. This interpretation of Roman and British history, Colbourn argued, helped to lead American leaders irresistibly to the conclusion that the behavior of the British government toward the colonies after 1763 was a clear indication of its degeneration and that resistance was the only way to preserve not merely their liberty and property but their virtue as well and helped to turn a political and constitutional debate into a moral conflict.

The moral and emotional dimension of the American response to British policy, touched on by Bailyn and Colbourn, was further emphasized in two separate articles by Edmund S. Morgan[70] and Perry Miller.[71] Both writers called attention to an important as-

---

[68]Richard J. Hooker makes a similar point about Revolutionary toasts in "The American Revolution Seen Through a Wine Glass," *William and Mary Quarterly*, 3rd ser., XI (January, 1954), 52–77.

[69]Chapel Hill, N.C., 1965.

[70]"The Puritan Ethic and the American Revolution," *William and Mary Quarterly*, 3rd ser., XXIV (January, 1967), 3–43.

[71]"From the Covenant to the Revival," in *The Shaping of American Religion*, James Ward Smith and A. Leland Jamison, eds., (Princeton, 1961), 322–368.

pect of the Revolutionary experience that had largely eluded earlier historians: the extent to which the reactions of Americans to British measures had been accompanied and conditioned by an uneasy sense that it was not just British degeneracy but their own corruption that was responsible for their difficulties. Arguing that the American response to the Revolution "in all its phases" "was affected" by a group of inherited beliefs in industry, frugality, and simplicity which he called, for convenience, the Puritan ethic, Morgan showed how the widespread fear that British measures were a threat to those values both increased the intensity of the resistance movement and, ultimately, helped to persuade Americans that British persistence in such measures was a sure indication that "the British government had fallen into the hands of a luxurious and corrupt ruling class" and that the only way to preserve American virtue was to sever all connection with Britain. Equally important, however, Morgan suggested both that the colonists, "always uncomfortable in the presence of prosperity," were afraid that the rapid increase in colonial wealth during the eighteenth century had by encouraging idleness, extravagance, and luxury led to a precipitous decline in the old values and that these fears gave added impetus and meaning to the nonimportation and nonconsumption agreements employed by the colonists as weapons against British policy at various times between 1765 and 1776. Those agreements, Morgan pointed out, were seen not simply as a means of forcing the British government to repeal the measures in dispute but also of restoring American virtue. By removing the temptations to luxurious living represented by British imports and requiring "self-denial and industry" on the part of all colonials, those agreements, it was expected, would force the colonists to return to the old values and arrest the moral decay that was threatening the colonies with internal ruin. "Parliamentary taxation" was thus conceived of as "both a danger to be resisted and an act of providence to recall Americans from declension."

How these same fears of moral and spiritual decline affected and were revealed by the American reaction to the outbreak of fighting in 1775 was explained by Miller. Analyzing the religious ritual that became so manifestly a part of the Revolutionary process immediately after Lexington and Concord, Miller discovered a deep concern over the spiritual health of the colonists and a marked tendency to interpret the British government and the British army as the agencies of God's punishment for colonial sin. Receiving wide expression in public sermons in 1775–1776, as well as later in the war, this concern was behind the days of humiliation and prayer set aside by Congress and the local governments and was revealed through the application of the traditional Protestant philosophy of the jeremiad. That philosophy assumed both that "the sins of individuals brought calamity upon the commonwealth" and that humiliation before God, an acknowledgment of sin, and a sincere resolution "not only separately but in unison, to mend their ways, restore primitive piety, suppress vice, curtail luxury" were absolutely necessary before God would intervene to help them in removing their afflictions. The vindication of American rights and privileges and the success of American arms were thus, the clergy argued, "inextricably dependent upon a moral renovation." What was even more important, they realized in applying the philosophy of the social compact that was so integral to Protestant thought, moral renovation was equally dependent upon immediate and vigorous action against the agencies of their affliction. Resistance to British corruption, the clergy implied, was the means of reviving American virtue.

Although Miller did not explore either the sources or the nature of the social, religious, or psychological tensions that may have been behind the sense of guilt, of moral and spiritual decline, that gave this conventional, almost instinctual, procedure such compelling force in 1775–1776,[72] the implication was that the crisis in imperial relations over the previous decade had caused the Americans to go through a process of intensive self-examination, to become acutely aware of the vicious tendencies within themselves and their societies, and to come to the conclusion that it was not just the degeneracy of the British government and British society that they had to fear but their own imperfect natures and evil inclinations as well. Like Morgan, Miller thus inferred that the Revolution was an internal fight against American corruption as well as an external war against British tyranny. "The really effective work" of the clergy, he wrote, was therefore "not an optimistic appeal to the rising glory of America, but their imparting a sense of crisis by revivifying Old Testament condemnations of a degenerate people"; and what gave their message such power with the populace at large was its vivid portrayal of the "vengeance God denounced against the wicked [and of] . . . what dreary fortunes would overwhelm those who persisted in sloth." Yet, Miller pointed out, the words of the clergy carried an

---

[72]Some of the possible sources of these tensions are discussed briefly in Gordon S. Wood, "Rhetoric and Reality in the American Revolution," *William and Mary Quarterly*, 3rd ser., XXIII (January, 1966), 3–32.

implicit promise as well as an explicit threat. Social regeneration and the removal of British corruption, the successful assertion of "native piety against foreign impiety," would, many of the clergy came to infer, usher in a bright new day of "prosperity and temporal happiness beyond anything the world" had hitherto experienced.

Alan Heimert explored the religious aspects of the Revolution in far greater detail and over a much longer period in *Religion and the American Mind from the Great Awakening to the Revolution*.[73] An analysis of the intellectual divergence between "Liberal" (Arminian/Old Light) and Calvinist religious leaders that grew out of the Great Awakening and of their contrasting responses to the debate with Britain after 1763 convinced Heimert that the evangelical Calvinist followers of Jonathan Edwards were far more deserving of the title "spokesmen of rebellion" than the Liberals for whom it had usually been reserved. The elitist social ideology and the fear of mass popular uprisings manifested by the Liberals made them, Heimert argued, at best only timid revolutionaries, while the millenarian aspects of Calvinist thought— the hope for the establishment of a more affectionate union of Christians and the gradual restoration of the influences of the holy spirit in America—gave it a radical posture that made it far more congenial to the underlying thrust of the Revolution. Already in the habit of contrasting the corruption of the Old World with the promise of the New in the years before 1763, Calvinist clergymen were among the earliest and most persistent exponents of the theme that the degeneracy of Britain was responsible for and gave coherence to the various measures Americans found objectionable in the 1760's and 1770's; and for them resistance to Britain became the means not only to escape the seductive influences of British depravity and to secure the blessings of liberty for America, but also to revitalize "what for thirty and more years had been the social [and religious] goals of the evangelical scheme." By calling forth a vigorous exertion of will on behalf of liberty, by inspiring "sinners to oppose sin," the Revolution, the Calvinists hoped, would serve as the instrument for forging a spiritual union among the American people, "exorcising from America, not merely sinners, but the sinful spirit of selfishness itself," and thus initiating that moral revolution "within men" that would lead irresistibly to the creation of the "earthly Kingdom of the Calvinist Messiah" in America. Like Miller, Heimert thus

---

[73]Cambridge, Mass., 1966.

stressed that the spirit of 1775–1776 was "not universally one of moderation and calculated assessment of political privileges and rights." For the Calvinists, at least, the Revolution was "not so much the result of reasoned thought as an emotional outburst similar to a religious revival." Like both Miller and Morgan, Heimert pointed out the intensely introspective side to the Calvinist's response to the Revolution. Beneath his "zealous opposition to tyranny," Heimert declared, "lay an anxious awareness that, were something not done to change the course of history, the American character, his own included, might well not prove to be completely different from that of the British tyrant whom he opposed."

These studies of the psychology of American resistance have added several new dimensions to our understanding of the colonial reaction to British policy after 1763. First, they have shifted the focus from the ostensible to the underlying issues in the dispute by making fully explicit what, in the several investigations of substantive grievances, had been largely only implicit: that it was not only the *desire* to preserve their traditional rights and privileges against attacks by the imperial government but also the *fear* of what might happen to them once those bulwarks against arbitrary power had been removed that drove the colonists to revolt. Secondly, they have traced the origins of this fear directly to the colonists' conception of human nature with its strong sense of man's imperfections and especially of his inability to resist the corrupt influences of power. Thirdly, they have shown that that conception derived both, as Bailyn has argued, from a long philosophical tradition which came to the colonists largely through the writings of British dissenters and, as Morgan, Miller, and Heimert have suggested, from experiential roots. From their individual and collective experience the colonists understood how frail and potentially evil man was, and their deep-seated anxieties about the state of individual and social morality within the colonies helped to sharpen and shape their response to and was in turn heightened by the several manifestations of what they took to be corruption and the corrosive effects of power on the part of the imperial government. Finally, on the basis of these conclusions it becomes much clearer why the colonists had such an exaggerated reaction to what, in retrospect, appear to have been no more than a series of justifiable and not very sinister actions by the parent state and why they so grossly misunderstood the motives and behavior of the ministry and Parliament and insisted upon interpreting every measure they found objectionable as part of a malign conspiracy of power against colonial, and ultimately all British, liberty. From the perspective of these studies, then, the Revolution has become on the part of the Americans not merely a struggle to preserve the formal safeguards of liberty against flagrant violations by the British but, in a deeper sense, a moral crusade against British corruption, a crusade made all the more compelling by the American belief that only by a manly opposition to and, after 1776, a complete separation from, that corruption could they hope to restore American virtue and save themselves from becoming similarly corrupt.

The Roots of Tory and British Behavior

In their preoccupation with discovering and explaining the nature of American discontent between 1763 and 1776, most recent writers have neglected to give much attention to the Tory and British side of the Revolutionary controversy.[74] This is not to say that they have written "as partisans of the Revolutionaries" or that, like the men of the Revolution and the nineteenth-century patriotic historians, they have assumed either implicitly or explicitly that the patriots were right and their antagonists wrong. They have not, contrary to recent charges by Gordon S. Wood, attempted "to justify the Revolution."[75] Their findings and emphases do, however, raise two important questions. If, as they infer, the patriots stood for the maintenance of the *status quo* and represented the dominant drift of colonial opinion, what can be said of the Tories, the classic conservatives in the Revolutionary drama? If the British government was not trying to establish a tyranny in the colonies, as everyone now would agree, why did it continue to pursue policies that Americans found so objectionable? Both of these questions have been the subject of recent study.

That the Tories were indeed only a small minority of the total colonial population and that they were clearly out of step with the vast majority of their compatriots have been confirmed by the findings of two new works on loyalism. In *The King's Friends: The Composition and Motives of the American Loyalist Claim-*

---

[74]This neglect can be explained in large part as a reaction to the writings of the imperial historians, who, as Edmund S. Morgan suggested in 1957 ("The American Revolution: Revisions in Need of Revising," *William and Mary Quarterly*, 3rd ser., XIV [January, 1957], 3–15), had gone so far in presenting a sympathetic case for British officials that they had made it difficult to understand why the colonists revolted.

[75]"Rhetoric and Reality," *op. cit.* These charges are valid in the case of the works of Dickerson and Knollenberg.

ants,[76] Wallace Brown concluded on the basis of a systematic analysis of the social, economic, and geographical backgrounds of those loyalists who submitted claims for compensation to the British government that the total number of loyalists constituted no more than 7.6 to 18 per cent of the total white adult population. Earlier writers[77] had emphasized the upper-class character of loyalism, but Brown found that, although loyalism was "a distinctly urban and seaboard phenomenon"—except in New York and North Carolina where there were "major rural, inland pockets" of loyalists—with a clear "commercial, officeholding, and professional bias," its adherents came from all segments of society and represented a rough cross section of the colonial population. Only in Massachusetts, New York, and to a lesser degree Georgia were substantial numbers of the upper class represented, and even in those colonies the vast majority of the upper classes were clearly not loyalists. If, in terms of general social and economic background, the Tories were virtually indistinguishable from the Whigs, as Brown's investigation suggested, the question remains exactly how they were different.

This question has been taken up by William H. Nelson in *The American Tory,*[78] a penetrating study that focuses on the psychological character of the loyalists. The key to loyalism, Nelson argued, was weakness, weakness arising from the loyalists' inherent disparateness, lack of organization, unpopular political views, and marginal position in colonial society. Unlike their opponents, Tory leaders did not consult among themselves, never developed a community of feeling or a common sense of purpose, had no clear alternative to the Whig drift, and did not even know each other. Unable to cultivate public opinion, they held social and political ideas and values that could prevail in the colonies only with British assistance. Many, like Thomas Hutchinson, were passive and narrowly defensive with a sense of fatality, of inevitable misfortune and failure, that prevented them from taking the offensive. Others, like Joseph Galloway, found British measures as unacceptable as the patriots but waited until the opposition was too far advanced for them to seize the initiative. Similarly, rank and file Tories were concentrated among non-English and religious minorities and among people in peripheral areas, "regions already in decline, or not yet risen to importance" such

---

[76] Providence, 1966.

[77] Most notably, Claude H. Van Tyne, *The Loyalists in the American Revolution* (New York and London, 1902).

[78] Oxford, England, 1961.

as the western frontier and the maritime region of the middle
colonies, and represented a series of conscious minorities who
looked to Britain for support against an external enemy like the
Indians or the dominant majority. It was weakness, then, Nelson
argued, along with alienation from or suspicion of the prevailing
Whig majority, and not simple loyalty, that tied the Tories to
Britain and, he implied, was responsible for their choice after
the Declaration of Independence. Nelson's conclusions were seconded both by Brown, who suggested that most loyalists "had, or
thought they had, something material and spiritual to lose from
the break with Britain," and by Douglass Adair and John Schutz
in their introduction to *Peter Oliver's Origin & Progress of the
American Rebellion: A Tory View*,[79] where they explained that
Oliver's loyalism was in part attributable to his inability "to adapt
himself to the fast-changing events of American life after 1760."

If the work on American grievances did not imply that the
British politicians were in the wrong, it did suggest strongly that
they seriously misjudged the situation in the colonies at almost
every point between 1763 and 1783 and that, if the preservation
of the empire was one of their primary objectives, they blundered
badly. If, as imperial historians have argued, the measures of the
imperial government were wise, just, and well calculated to serve
the interests of the empire as a whole, imperial authorities failed
utterly to persuade the colonists of the fact. How this breakdown
in understanding could have occurred in a political community
so celebrated for its political genius has been partially explained
by Sir Lewis Namier in his exhaustive analyses of British politics
during the opening years of the reign of George III[80] and by other
scholars in a number of studies working out the implications of
his work.[81] A long line of earlier historians from Horace Walpole

---

[79]San Marino, Calif., 1961.

[80]*The Structure of Politics at the Accession of George III* (2 vols., London, 1929); *England in the Age of the American Revolution* (London,
1930); and *Crossroads of Power: Essays on Eighteenth Century England*
(London, 1962).

[81]The most important among these studies are Richard Pares, *King
George III and the Politicians* (Oxford, 1953), a general discussion of the
politics of the reign in the light of Namier's conclusions; John Brooke, *The
Chatham Administration, 1766–1768* (London, 1956), and Ian R. Christie,
The End of North's Ministry, 1780–1782 (London, 1958), two detailed
studies of the structure and course of British politics during important
segments of the Revolutionary years; Charles R. Ritcheson, *British Politics
and the American Revolution* (Norman, Okla., 1954), a narrative of the
impact of the American troubles upon British politics; and Eric Robson,
The American Revolution in its Political and Military Aspects, 1763–1783
(London, 1955), a collection of interpretive essays.

to Sir George Trevelyan had charged George III with attempting to destroy the influence of the Whig oligarchy and reestablish the supremacy of the Crown over Parliament. The King's American program, they had suggested, was part of the same pattern, and the English Whigs and the Americans were aligned against a common enemy in a common struggle against tyranny. Had the Whig party been in power, the argument ran, it would have pursued a more conciliatory course and prevented the Revolution.

Namier and his followers have sharply challenged this interpretation at every point. They have argued that there were no parties in the modern sense, only loosely organized factions and family groups; that what mattered most in politics was not ideology or the attachment to principle but the struggle for office, power, and advantage; that political issues revolved about local rather than national or imperial considerations; that the "political nation"—the people who took some active role in politics—was largely restricted to a narrow elite in the middle and upper echelons of British social structure; that all groups, as well as the King, accepted the traditional Whig principles that had evolved out of the revolutionary settlement; and that George III did not have to subvert the constitution to gain control over Parliament because, as in the case of his predecessor and grandfather, George II, his power to choose his own ministers and his control over patronage assured him of considerable influence in determining Parliament's decisions.[82]

What these conclusions mean in terms of the misunderstanding with the colonies, though no one has worked them out in detail, is fairly clear. They reinforce the suggestions of the students of American grievances that British policy was shortsighted and inept. If British political leaders were so preoccupied by the struggle for office and so deeply involved in local matters, it is not difficult to see why they were unable to take a broader view in dealing with the colonies. The engrossment of the ministers and the leaders of Parliament in internal British politics and, prior to 1770, the frequent changes in administration meant, as several recent books have shown,[83] that much of the responsibility for

---

[82]Namier's conclusions have been challenged by Herbert Butterfield, *George III and the Historians* (London, 1957), and others on the grounds that they do not give sufficient weight to the role of ideas and present too atomistic a view of British politics. One of the best replies to Namier's critics is Jacob M. Price, "Party, Purpose and Pattern: Sir Lewis Namier and His Critics," *Journal of British Studies*, I (November, 1961), 71–93.

[83]Especially Dora Mae Clark, *The Rise of the British Treasury: Colonial Administration in the Eighteenth Century* (New Haven, 1960); Franklin B. Wickwire, *British Subministers and Colonial America, 1763–1783* (Princeton, 1966); Sosin, *op. cit.*; and Shy, *op. cit.*

shaping the details of colonial policy devolved upon the bureaucracy, second-line officials in the Treasury, Board of Trade, American Department, and Law Offices who remained in office despite shifts in administration. In *Agents and Merchants: British Colonial Policy and the Origins of the American Revolution, 1763–1775*,[84] Jack M. Sosin has demonstrated that colonial agents and merchants concerned in the colonial trade operated as a kind of rudimentary lobby to present the views of the colonists and actually managed to secure several important concessions from the government. But the agents themselves, and certainly not the merchants, did not always have accurate and up-to-date information about the situation in the colonies and, in any case, most colonial information came to the bureaucracy either from British officials in the colonies, most of whom were unsympathetic to the American cause, or from self-styled experts in both Britain and the colonies who, as John Shy has remarked, often "had some ax to grind or private interest to serve." There was, in short, no sure way for colonial officials to obtain a clear and undistorted version of American views, and this absence of effective channels of communication could lead only to a massive breakdown in understanding in a crisis such as the one that developed after 1773.

Even more important in inhibiting effective action by imperial officials, still other studies have indicated, were their preconceptions about what colonies were and ought to be. Reinforced by the association in the official mind of the opposition in the colonies with the radical and, to many members of the British political nation, profoundly disturbing Wilkite agitation in Britain,[85] those preconceptions, according to recent investigations of four of the key figures in British politics—Townshend, Shelburne, Dartmouth, and Germain[86]—were of the utmost importance in shaping the responses of individuals of every political stripe to the imperial crisis. Similarly, Bernard Donoughue[87] has demonstrated how severely those preconceptions limited the range of choices open to

---

[84]Lincoln, Neb., 1965.

[85]The nature and impact of this agitation has recently been analyzed in Ian R. Christie, *Wilkes, Wyvill and Reform: The Parliamentary Reform Movement in British Politics, 1760–1785* (London, 1962); George Rudé, *Wilkes and Liberty: A Social Study of 1763 to 1774* (Oxford, 1962), and Eugene Charlton Black, *The Association: British Extraparliamentary Political Organization, 1769–1793* (Cambridge, 1963).

[86]Sir Lewis Namier and John Brooke, *Charles Townshend* (London, 1964); John Norris, *Shelburne and Reform* (London, 1963); B. D. Bargar, *Lord Dartmouth and the American Revolution* (Columbia, 1965); and Gerald Saxon Brown, *The American Secretary: The Colonial Policy of Lord George Germain, 1775–1778* (Ann Arbor, 1963).

[87]*British Politics and the American Revolution: The Path to War 1773–75* (London, 1964).

the government in the critical period between the Boston Tea Party in December, 1773 and the outbreak of war in April, 1775. No one either in or out of office, Donoughue found, was able to escape from the oppressive weight of dominant ideas and habits of thinking and to grapple with the possibility that, as Americans were insisting, the empire might be preserved without totally subordinating the colonies to Parliament. The traditional explanation for this failure has been that the men in power lacked vision, magnanimity, and statesmanship. But Donoughue's work pointed to more than a mere series of individual weaknesses. If men could not go beyond the prescribed boundaries of thought and language within which the system required them to work, then perhaps the system itself was incapable of adjustment at that time and the old British Empire may have been less the victim of the men who presided over its dissolution than they were the victims of the system of which the empire was a part. Given his commitment to the revolutionary settlement and to the supremacy of Parliament, George III could not possibly have stood apart from Parliament as a royal symbol of imperial union as the colonists desired.[88]

Revolutionary Consequences

The net effect of the new studies of the coming of the Revolution has been to reestablish the image of the Revolution as a conservative protest movement against what appeared to the men of the Revolution to have been an unconstitutional and vicious assault upon American liberty and property by a tyrannical and corrupt British government. The Revolution, Daniel J. Boorstin argued in *The Genius of American Politics*,[89] had now to be understood as "a victory of constitutionalism." The major issue was "the true constitution of the British Empire," and because the leaders of the Revolution regarded it as an "affirmation of faith in ancient British institutions," the "greater part of the institutional life of the community . . . required no basic change." To Boorstin the Revolution thus appeared a conservative and "prudential decision taken by men of principle," remarkable chiefly because

---

[88]A more detailed and comprehensive analysis of the implications of recent writings on British politics in the eighteenth century for the understanding of the Revolution will be found in Jack P. Greene, "The Plunge of Lemmings: A Consideration of Recent Writings on British Politics and the American Revolution," *South Atlantic Quarterly*, LXVII (Winter, 1968), 141–175.

[89]Chicago, 1953.

"in the modern European sense of the word, it was hardly a revolution at all."

Recent investigations of the concrete political and social changes that accompanied the Revolution have tended to reinforce this image. Detailed studies of the political development of three states after 1776 have indicated that there was virtually no change in the traditional patterns of political leadership and little identifiable interest among any segment of society in achieving a more democratic polity. In a careful examination of Maryland,[90] Philip A. Crowl found that after 1776 "a relatively small class of planters, lawyers, and merchants" dominated the politics of that state without serious challenge from below, just as it had throughout the late colonial period. There was plenty of political conflict in Maryland, much of it over hard economic issues, and a bitter struggle over the emission of cheap paper money in 1785–1787 saw debtors aligned against creditors. But the conflict was not along class lines—the debtors were mostly from the upper classes—and had few democratic overtones. Rather, it consisted of a series of battles over opposing interests, ideas, and personalities between *ad hoc* coalitions of opposing groups of leading men. Richard P. McCormick[91] and John A. Munroe[92] reached similar conclusions about New Jersey and Delaware. "Men of interest" loosely organized into two broad factions deriving from long-standing sectional divisions peculiar to each state played the preponderant role in politics without interference from or unrest among the lower classes. These factions took opposing sides on a variety of issues, including the issuance of more paper money, but democracy per se was not an overt issue.[93]

By contrast, as Robert J. Taylor has shown,[94] the Revolution seems to have served as a much more profound educative and democratizing force among the people of western Massachusetts. Traditionally conservative and deeply suspicious of the commercial east, the westerners were slow in joining the easterners in opposing the British, but once they had thrown in their lot with the

---

[90]*Maryland During and After the Revolution: A Political and Economic Study* (Baltimore, 1943).

[91]*Experiment in Independence: New Jersey in the Critical Period, 1781–1789* (New Brunswick, 1953).

[92]*Federalist Delaware, 1775–1815* (New Brunswick, 1954).

[93]Similarly, Oscar and Mary Handlin found in a survey of Massachusetts politics ("Radicals and Conservatives in Massachusetts after Independence," *New England Quarterly*, XVII [September, 1944], 343–355) that there were not two stable parties, one radical and the other conservative, but a series of shifting alliances that showed little ideological continuity.

[94]*Western Massachusetts in the Revolution* (Providence, 1954).

patriot cause they took the Revolutionary doctrine of popular sovereignty very seriously. In normal situations they were content to leave political leadership where it had always been—in the hands of local gentry. There were unmistakable signs, however, that the people at large now expected to play an expanded role in the polity. Between 1776 and 1780 they were among the most militant supporters of the demand for a state constitution written by a specially-elected convention representing the sovereign authority of the people and then ratified by the people, and the unrest which began in 1781 and culminated in 1786 in Shays' Rebellion dramatically revealed similar tendencies. The unrest was primarily the result of deteriorating economic conditions and was oriented largely toward economic ends, but the fact that western demands for a more equitable tax system and debtor relief were couched in the language of popular sovereignty and made through conventions called by the people on the basis of their "natural right to . . . revise the fundamental law when it became oppressive" served notice that at least in that corner of the new United States the contest with Britain had been accompanied by a potentially powerful revolution in the political expectations of ordinary citizens, a revolution that, to the profound disturbance of political leaders up and down the Atlantic seaboard, might ultimately spread to other regions and other states.

This revolution in expectations did not, however, proceed very far during the period of the Revolution. As Elisha Douglas showed in *Rebels and Democrats*,[95] a study of the process of constitution-making in the states, the internal political revolution that, according to the Progressive historians, had occurred in 1776 was a very modest revolution indeed. There was, Douglass found, an articulate, if not very large, group of "democrats" who viewed the Revolution not as an end in itself but as a means to rebuild society on the principles of the Declaration of Independence, and to that end they demanded "equal rights for all adult males and a government in which the will of the majority of citizens would be the ultimate authority for political decision." Ardently opposed, however, by the dominant Whig leaders, who were suspicious of democracy and wanted governments that would check majority rule and retain the traditional system of political leadership, the democrats scored only limited gains in just three states—North Carolina, Pennsylvania, and Massachusetts—and even in those states they were unable to gain permanent control. A more subtle

---

[95]Chapel Hill, N.C., 1955.

and, ultimately, more important democratizing force was the increase in popular participation in politics described by Jackson Turner Main.[96] By opening up a large number of new political opportunities, the Revolution drew an increasingly greater number of ordinary citizens into politics with the result, Main found, that the social base of both the upper and lower houses of the legislature was much broader after 1776 than it had been in the late colonial period. This development did not, however, lead to either a wholesale turnover in political leadership or immediate repudiation of the ideals of upper-class leadership. Along with the new ideology of popular government fashioned by some of the democrats and described by Douglass and Merrill Jensen,[97] it nevertheless did help to pave the way for the eventual breakdown of the old habits of deference, the ascendency of the belief in a more popular government, and the veneration of majority rule in the early part of the nineteenth century.[98] Although the Revolution contained some powerful democratic tendencies, then, all of these studies seemed to indicate, it was fundamentally, at least insofar as it affected internal politics, an elitist movement with only a modest amount of explicit striving among either the people at large or any of the dominant political factions for a wider diffusion of political power.

Although more work remains to be done before firm conclusions can be drawn, it also seems clear, as Frederick B. Tolles noted in a 1954 survey of recent studies,[99] that the concrete social changes emphasized by Jameson were less sweeping and less significant than he had thought. Louis Hartz presented the most elaborate statement of this theme in *The Liberal Tradition in America*.[100] Taking for his text Tocqueville's observation that the great advantage of Americans lay in the fact that they did not have to "endure a democratic revolution," Hartz argued that "the outstanding thing about the American effort of 1776 was . . . not

---

[96]"Government by the People: The American Revolution and the Democratization of the Legislatures," *William and Mary Quarterly*, 3rd ser., XXIII (July, 1966), 391–407, and "Social Origins of a Political Elite: The Upper House in the Revolutionary Era," *Huntington Library Quarterly*, XXVII (February, 1964), 147–158.

[97]"Democracy and the American Revolution," *ibid.*, XX (August, 1957), 321–341.

[98]In this connection see especially David Hackett Fischer, *The Revolution of American Conservatism: The Federalist Party in the Era of Jeffersonian Democracy* (New York, 1965).

[99]"The American Revolution Considered as a Social Movement: A Re-Evaluation," *American Historical Review*, LX (October, 1954), 1–12.

[100]New York, 1955.

the freedom to which it led, but the established feudal structure it did not have to destroy." Living in "the freest society in the world" in 1776 and taking for granted the continued "reality of atomistic social freedom," the Americans, unlike revolutionaries elsewhere, did not have to destroy an ancient regime. The relics of feudalism abolished during the Revolution were just that, *relics* with no necessary social function, and the success and nature of the Revolution—its "outright conservatism"—were, Hartz insisted, directly attributable to "the social goals *it did not need to achieve.*"

The prevailing view thus came to be that the Revolution was predominantly a conservative Whiggish movement undertaken in defense of American liberty and property, preoccupied throughout with constitutional and political problems, carried on with a minimum of violence—at least when seen in the perspective of other revolutions—and with little change either in the distribution of political power or in the structure and operation of basic social institutions, and reaching its logical culmination with the Federal Constitution. Whatever democratic stirrings may have accompanied it were subordinate and incidental to the main thrust of events and to the central concerns of its leaders.[101] As Benjamin Fletcher Wright insisted,[102] the Spirit of '76 seemed to be represented less accurately by the writings of Thomas Paine—whose ideas, as Cecelia M. Kenyon has shown,[103] were decidedly atypical of the dominant patterns of thought among American Revolutionary leaders—or even the Declaration of Independence than by the state constitutions of 1776, 1777, and 1780, constitutions which were shaped out of traditional materials and revealed the commitment of the men of the Revolution to "order and stability as well as liberty," to the ancient British concept that "liberty required constitutional order." This continuity between the new and the old as well as the amazing "consensus on political and constitutional principles" represented both in the state constitu-

---

[101]This view appears with some variations in most general treatments of the Revolution published in the 1950's and early 1960's. See, for example, John R. Alden, *The American Revolution, 1775–1783* (New York, 1954); Robert E. Brown, "Reinterpretation of the Revolution and Constitution," *Social Education,* XXI (March, 1957), 102–105, 114, and *Reinterpretation of the Formation of the American Constitution* (Boston, 1963); Richard B. Morris, *The American Revolution: A Short History* (New York, 1955), "Class Struggle and the American Revolution," *William and Mary Quarterly,* 3rd ser., XIX (January, 1962), 3–39, and *The American Revolution Reconsidered* (New York, 1967); and Esmond Wright, *Fabric of Freedom, 1763–1800* (New York, 1961).

[102]*Consensus and Continuity, 1776–1787* (Boston, 1958).

[103]"Where Paine Went Wrong," *American Political Science Review,* XLV (December, 1951), 1086–1099.

tions and the Federal Constitution of 1787, Wright argued, cast far more light upon the nature of the American Revolution than the rather narrow range of conflict and disagreement or the relatively minor elements of discontinuity in the Revolutionary experience.

The Revolution, in short, came to be viewed largely from the perspective of the dominant Whig elite which, with very few exceptions, had managed to retain control of political life as well as the confidence of the public throughout the period from 1763 to 1789. The urban mobs and rural populists who so thoroughly fired the imagination of the Progressive historians, according to the new interpretation, for the most part played only supporting parts in the drama of the Revolution, however important the roles they were in the process of creating came to be on the American political stage after 1789. Political conflict thus no longer seemed to have been among classes or discrete and "naturally" antagonistic social and economic groups but among rival elements within the elite which competed against one another within a broad ideological consensus not so much over issues as for power and advantage. To be sure, the Revolution was accompanied, as Edmund S. Morgan has indicated in his masterful survey of the whole period,[104] by a creative search for principles first to defend American constitutional rights and then to build a new nation, but the search, at least during the years of the Revolution, was distinctly less radical in its results than earlier historians had assumed.

This overwhelming stress upon the defensive and preservative character of the Revolution tended to divert attention from any revolutionary or radical implications that may have accompanied it, and not until the early 1960's did a few scholars set out to discover and explain just what was actually revolutionary about the Revolution. The most systematic and thorough exploration of this theme was by Bernard Bailyn in "Political Experience and Enlightenment Ideas in Eighteenth-Century America," *American Historical Review*, LXVII (January, 1962), 339–351, and *The Ideological Origins of the American Revolution*. What "endowed the Revolution with its peculiar force and made of it a transforming event," Bailyn declared, was not the "overthrow of the existing order"— which nowhere occurred—but the "radical idealization and rationalization of the previous century and a half of American experience." Many of the social and political goals of the European

---

[104] *Birth of the Republic, 1763–89* (Chicago, 1956).

Enlightenment, Bailyn pointed out, had already "developed naturally, spontaneously, early in the history of the American colonies, and they existed as simple matters of social and political fact on the eve of the Revolution." Because habits of mind and traditional ways of thinking lagged far behind these fundamental changes in the nature of colonial social and political life, however, there was on the eve of the Revolutionary debate a sharp "divergence between habits of mind and belief on one hand and experience and behavior on the other." By requiring a critical probing of traditional concepts and forcing the colonists to rationalize and explain their experience—"to complete, formalize, systematize, and symbolize what previously had been only partially realized, confused, and disputed matters of fact"—the Revolution helped to end this divergency. Most of the political ideas that emerged from this process—the conceptions of representative bodies as mirrors of their constituents, of human rights as existing above and limiting the law, of constitutions as ideal designs of government, and of sovereignty as divisible—were at once expressive of conditions that had long existed in the colonies and a basic reconception of the traditional notions about the "fundamentals of government and of society's relation to government." By "lifting into consciousness and endowing with high moral purpose" these "inchoate, confused elements of social and political change," the Revolutionary debate thus both released social and political forces that had long existed in the colonies and "vastly increased their power." The movement of thought quickly spilled over into other areas, and the institution of chattel slavery, the principle of the establishment of religion, and even conventional assumptions about the social basis of politics and the constitutional arrangements that followed from those assumptions were called into question. Ultimately, in the decades after the Revolution, these "changes in the realm of belief and attitude" and, more especially, the defiance of traditional order and distrust of authority contained within them affected the very "essentials" of American social organization and, Bailyn pointed out, helped permanently to transform the nature of American life.

Although Cecelia M. Kenyon[105] insisted that independence and the creation and adoption of the Constitution of 1787 were genuinely radical results of the Revolution, the two other consequences that she singled out as radical—the establishment of

---

[105]"Republicanism and Radicalism in the American Revolution: An Old-Fashioned Interpretation," *William and Mary Quarterly*, 3rd ser., XIX (April, 1962), 153–182.

republicanism and the "crystallization of the individualism and equalitarianism of the Declaration of Independence into an operative as well as a formal political philosophy"—also fell largely within the realm of ideas. What was so remarkable and so innovative about the former, she observed, was not the formal institution of republican government, which was accomplished with ease and brought no pervasive or "fundamental changes, either in private or public life," but the sudden development among Americans, who only a short time before had been committed monarchists, of a deep "ideological attachment to republicanism" and the association in the public mind of "all the characteristics of good government with republicanism, and with republicanism only." Far more innovative, she argued, was the radical individualism, the "political and ethical egoism," which was central to the developing philosophy of the Revolution and was symbolized by the substitution in the Declaration of Independence of "the *pursuit of happiness* for *property*" in the traditional trilogy of inviolable rights. Because happiness was "a subjective goal dependent on individual interpretation,' it was, as an end of government, "far more individualistic" than the protection of property and necessarily strongly equalitarian in its implications. Clearly, no individual could decide for another what would promote his happiness, and, as Kenyon pointed out, if all men had by nature an equal right to the pursuit of happiness, it followed "logically that every man should have a voice in the determination of public policy." Although this philosophy of radical individualism was a clear invitation to political relativism and to the acceptance, even idealization, of the pursuit of self-interest as a legitimate form of behavior to be protected, even encouraged, by government, its full effect, Kenyon emphasized, was not realized until well after the Revolutionary era because the men of the Revolution, despite the individualistic trend of their thought, continued to think in terms of an objective common good and "to deplore man's tendency toward self-interest and bias."

Alan Heimert similarly emphasized the radical thrust of the thought of the Revolution in *Religion and the American Mind*. The double focus of the Calvinist Revolutionary crusade, he noted, the emphasis upon both securing the benefits of liberty and achieving an affectionate Christian union free of invidious social and political distinctions, had a millenarian character that made it a potentially "highly radical political movement." The Revolution was expected to inaugurate the moral renovation of man, and once that renovation was under way, Calvinists implied, government—that badge of lost innocence and symbol of man's corruption—could be placed more directly in the hands of the people, who in turn would "persevere in the Christian warfare until all despots, great and petty, had been overthrown." Perhaps because the Calvinist did not, in general, speak for "the more respectable and presumably . . . most powerful elements of colonial society," who, as other writers have shown, retained control of American political life, this movement did not, however, make much headway during the Revolution.

If, then, as most recent writers have indicated, the Revolution was at its center a fundamentally conservative movement concerned primarily with the preservation of American liberty and property, it also had some distinctly radical features, as the works of Bailyn, Kenyon, and Heimert make clear. Its radicalism was to be found, however, less in the relatively modest social and political changes that accompanied it than in the power of its ideas. Some of the immediate and tangible results of the workings of those ideas during the Revolutionary era were discussed by Bailyn and Kenyon. R. R. Palmer[106] has emphasized another. From the broad perspective of general Western European political development, Palmer argued, the "most distinctive work of the Revolution" and its most novel institutional achievement was in devising an institution—the constitutional convention—through which the people could in practice, and not just in theory, exercise their sovereign power to constitute their own governments. Used for the first time in preparing the Massachusetts Constitution of 1780, the convention chosen solely for the purpose of writing a constitution, with the ancillary device of popular ratification of its work, was institutionalized with the Federal Constitution of 1787 and has since served as a model for much of the rest of the world. But the full impact of the radical ideas of the Revolution, their complete expression in the institutions and values of American life, Heimert, Bailyn, and Kenyon all seemed to agree, came not during the Revolution but over the next half century in the political movements associated with Thomas Jefferson and Andrew Jackson. Thus, as William H. Nelson remarked in another essay on "The Revolutionary Character of the American Revolution,"[107] even "if the American revolutionists did not fight for democracy, they contributed to its coming . . . because their individualistic con-

---

[106]*The Age of the Democratic Revolution: A Political History of Europe and America, 1760–1800,* Volume One: *The Challenge* (Princeton, 1959).
[107]*American Historical Review,* LXX (July, 1965), 998–1014.

cepts of government by consent and republican equality led irresistibly in a democratic direction."

The Federal Constitution

The forces for and against the movement for a stronger central government in the 1780's, the nature of the divisions over the Constitution of 1787, and the relationship of the Constitution to the Revolution have also received considerable attention over the past quarter century. Much of this attention has been focused upon Charles A. Beard's economic interpretation of the Constitution, and the clear consensus has been that that interpretation is seriously deficient in almost every respect. In separate articles published in the early 1950's, Richard Hofstadter[108] and Douglass Adair[109] argued that the Beard book was a Progressive tract and showed to what a large extent his interpretation had been warped by his inability to resist viewing eighteenth-century phenomena through Progressive lenses. One of the most serious of the resulting errors was pointed out by Edmund S. Morgan in 1957.[110] By reading back into the Revolution the conflict between property rights and human rights that seemed to him so fundamental to early twentieth-century American politics, Beard and other Progressives had completely distorted and misread the eighteenth-century conception of liberty, which was always coupled with, not set in opposition to, property, and thereby built their whole account upon an anachronism. In the most devastating critique, Robert E. Brown, on the basis of a meticulous paragraph-by-paragraph analysis of the Beard volume,[111] convicted Beard of rank mishandling of his evidence.

The most ambitious analysis of the Beard thesis was presented in 1958 by Forrest McDonald in *We the People: The Economic Origins of the Constitution.*[112] After doing much of the research Beard had said would be necessary to validate his interpretation, McDonald was able to state categorically that Beard's "economic interpretation of the Constitution does not work." Far from being

---

[108]"Beard and the Constitution: the History of an Idea," *American Quarterly,* II (Fall, 1950), 195–212.
[109]"The Tenth Federalist Revisited," *William and Mary Quarterly,* 3rd ser., VIII (January, 1951), 48–67.
[110]"American Revolution: Revisions in Need of Revising," and *Birth of the Republic, op. cit.*
[111]*Charles Beard and the Constitution* (Princeton, 1956).
[112]Chicago, 1958.

as unrepresentative of the American electorate as Beard had inferred, the Philadelphia Convention, McDonald argued, "constituted an almost complete cross-section of the geographical areas" and organized political interest groups "existing in the United States in 1787." Thirty-nine of fifty-five major geographical areas and thirty-one of thirty-four major political factions from twelve of the thirteen states were represented. Neither did the delegates compose a "consolidated economic group" nor did "substantial personalty interests" provide the dynamic element in the movement for the Constitution, as Beard had argued. In both federal and state conventions the amount of real property in land and slaves held by the proponents of the Constitution far exceeded the value of their holdings in public securities and other forms of personal property, wealth in both personal and real property was substantially represented among both Federalists and Antifederalists, and in "no state was the Constitution ratified without the consent of the farmers and a majority of the friends of paper money." Indeed, McDonald implied, such broad categories as those employed by Beard—real property versus personal property, commerce versus agriculture, creditors versus debtors, lower classes versus upper classes—were virtually meaningless when applied to the struggle over the Constitution. With at least six basic forms of capital and "twenty basic occupational groups having distinctly different economic characteristics and needs," there were, obviously, so many diverse and conflicting interests that it was impossible, McDonald concluded, to devise a single set of polar classifications that would adequately explain the alignment over the Constitution.

Although in *We the People* McDonald was primarily concerned with clearing the decks so that he could subsequently write "something meaningful about the making of the Constitution" without constantly stopping to do battle with Beard, the thrust of the book was by no means entirely negative. Scattered throughout the text and in three concluding chapters were conclusions and hypotheses that indicated what McDonald considered the central elements in a more plausible economic interpretation of the Constitution. The whole story, he implied, could be told entirely without reference to class conflict and the struggle for democracy—the two themes that had received most emphasis from Progressive historians. Not class but state, sectional, group, and individual interests and the complex interplay among them comprised the economic forces behind the Constitution. Any economic interpretation of the Constitution would therefore necessarily be pluralistic, but, McDonald indicated, the primary organizing unit would be the individual states. Not only were the activities of most interest groups circumscribed by state boundaries, but those interests that reached across state boundaries, such as the interest in the public debt, "operated under different conditions in the several states, and their attitudes toward the Constitution varied with the internal conditions in their states." The contest over the Constitution was thus "at once *a contest* and *thirteen contests,*" and, McDonald suggested in his most important new general conclusion, the outcome in each state seemed to depend upon how satisfied its citizens were—how well their economic interests were being served—under the Articles of Confederation. "Those states that had done well on their own were inclined to desire to continue on their own," he noted, "and those that found it difficult to survive independently were inclined to desire to cast their several lots with a general government."

That McDonald had overstated his case against Beard and that his focus upon narrow and specific interests tended to obscure the larger, and presumably more significant, divisions over the Constitution was the argument of two formidable critics: Jackson Turner Main and Lee Benson. Main, who had been over much of the same material as McDonald, published a long critical analysis of *We the People*[113] in which he convicted McDonald of a number of factual errors, argued that because "there was not a single delegate who spoke for the small farmers" the Philadelphia Convention was not as representative as McDonald had contended and the delegates were therefore a "consolidated economic group" representing the commercial east coast, and maintained that the Constitution was indeed "written by large property owners and that the division over its acceptance followed, to some extent, class lines" as Beard had affirmed. A year later Main presented the evidence for these propositions and his own explanation of the fight over the Constitution in his book, *The Antifederalists: Critics of the Constitution, 1781–1788.*[114] In some respects Main's conclusions, as McDonald remarked in his rebuttal, appeared to be the same old Progressive story of the rich guys against the poor guys, but there were significant new qualifications and shifts of emphasis. Insisting that there were important ideological and economic differences between Federalist and Antifederalists, Main subscribed to the traditional Progressive view that the ideological

---

[113]"Charles A. Beard and the Constitution: A Critical Review of Forrest McDonald's *We the People* with a Rebuttal by Forrest McDonald," *William and Mary Quarterly*, 3rd ser., XVII (January, 1960), 86–110.
[114]Chapel Hill, N.C., 1961.

split was between advocates of aristocracy and advocates of democracy. He carefully pointed out, however, that not all Antifederalists were democrats. Most Antifederalists leaders were, in fact, well to do and were interested less in democracy than in local self-rule and a weak central government. These leaders, who were the chief spokesmen for antifederalism, tended to mute the democratic voices of rank-and-file Antifederalists, the small property holders who were "fundamentally anti-aristocratic" and "wanted a government dominated by the many rather than the few." Similarly, Main argued that the economic division over the Constitution was in general along class lines with small property holders opposing large property holders, debtors against creditors, and paper money advocates opposed to hard money supporters. As he carefully pointed out, however, there were so many exceptions to his general conclusion that the contest could not possibly be explained "exclusively in terms of class conflict." A far more important division, he suggested, which cut across class lines, was that between the commercial and non-commercial regions, between "the areas, or people, who depended on commerce, and those who were largely self-sufficient." Again there were important exceptions, but, he maintained, this "socio-economic division based on a geographical location" was "the most significant fact" about the ratification struggle, "to which all else is elaboration, amplification, or exception." For Main, then, class conflict and the struggle for democracy were still significant elements in the fight over the Constitution, though neither was nearly so important nor so clearcut as earlier Progressive historians had thought.

In *Turner and Beard: American Historical Writing Reconsidered*,[115] Lee Benson subjected McDonald's work to a different kind of criticism and offered his own hypotheses about the contest over the Constitution. The primary difficulty with McDonald's book, Benson argued, was the assumptions on which it rested. Based upon a "crude version of economic determinism that assumes men behave primarily as members of interest groups that keep a profit-and-loss account of their feelings and calculate the cash value of their political actions," McDonald's interpretive system, Benson charged, was even more grossly distorting than Beard's. That system might conceivably be applicable to the activities of pressure groups in the normal legislative process, but it was clearly inappropriate to the study of a national "Constitutional revolution" like the one that occurred in 1787–1788. Such a revo-

---

[115]Glencoe, Ill., 1960.

lution inevitably involved a conflict of ideology, and ideology, Benson argued, was never the "direct product of self-interest" and "always cuts across the lines of interest groups." On the assumption that "social environment and position in the American social structure mainly determined men's ideologies, and, in turn, their ideologies mainly determined their opinions on the Constitution," Benson proposed to devise a system of interpretation based not on narrow economic interest groups but upon broad symbolic social groups. The principal division in this "social interpretation of the Constitution" was between *agrarian-minded* men and *commercial-minded* men. Ostensibly, the division was over what kind of central government the United States would have, with the agrarian-minded favoring a government of strictly limited powers that was close to the people and the commercial-minded a government that could "function as a creative, powerful instrument" for realizing broad social ends. Agrarians thus tended to be satisfied with the Articles of Confederation while commercialists tended to be supporters of the Constitution. But, Benson insisted in reading back into the ratification struggle the conflict of the 1790's over Hamiltonian finance, the real question at issue was what kind of society—agrarian or commercial—the United States would have, and the struggle over the Constitution, over whether the central government would be weak or strong, was merely a reflection of this larger ideological conflict which had been waged with "great intensity" by the opposing groups and presumably had been behind most political issues ever since 1776. What these hypotheses amounted to, as Benson freely admitted, was a reformulation of Beard's thesis in broader social terms, but they also contained two new, if also highly tentative, propositions: that broad social environment rather than narrow economic interests was the primary determinative force in the struggle over the Constitution and that political behavior in the 1780's was "influenced more strongly by ideas of the Good Society than by ideas of the Good State."

The controversy over Beard's interpretation of the Constitution had thus generated three alternative and partially contradictory sets of hypotheses about the hard social and economic forces behind the Constitution. All three scholars were in general agreement on a number of key points: there were discernible socioeconomic divisions over the Constitution; those divisions exerted a profound, and probably primary, influence in the struggle; their nature and operation were enormously more complicated than Beard had ever imagined; and whether class divisions were important or not, the contest was not a match between the haves and the have-nots. The dispute was mainly over which divisions were most important and what was the precise nature of the divisions. The possibility of achieving some synthesis between Main's "commercial" and "non-commercial" categories on one hand and Benson's "commercial-minded" and "agrarian-minded" on the other was clear enough, but McDonald's insistence that the struggle was between strong (satisfied) states and weak (dissatisfied) states and was shaped by the conflicting ambitions of a multitude of special interest groups seemed completely irreconcilable with the arguments of either Main or Benson. Clearly, as Main pointed out, an enormous amount of work would be required before these competing propositions could be evaluated.

Some of that work has subsequently been performed by E. James Ferguson and McDonald. In *The Power of the Purse: A History of American Public Finance, 1776–1790*,[116] Ferguson explored the relationship between public finance and the movement for constitutional reform. It was Ferguson's thesis that the question of how the public debts incurred during the War for Independence were to be paid, whether by the states or by Congress, was the "pivotal issue in the relations between the states and the nascent central government" during the Confederation period. On this question the alignment was broadly the same as that Main and Benson had seen in the struggle over the Constitution: mercantile capitalists versus agrarians. The former were "nationalists" who favored sound money backed by specie, strong central financial institutions, and the absolute sanctity of contracts and property, while the latter were localists who wanted cheap paper money, state-oriented finance, and easy ways of discharging debts. Seeing in the debt a lever by which they could secure the taxing power for the Congress, the nationalists, led by Robert Morris,[117] endeavored between 1780 and 1786 to vest the debt in Congress and give Congress the taxing power to support it. But these endeavors ran into opposition from the advocates of state-oriented finance, some states began to take care of the interest on the debt, and the nationalist movement, for all practical purposes, collapsed between 1784 and 1786. Except for the foreign debt, on which Congress partially defaulted, the period was not critical in terms of finance, and what produced the nationalist resurgence that led

---

[116]Chapel Hill, N.C., 1961.
[117]Morris' role as superintendent of finance is dealt with at greater length by Clarence L. Ver Steeg, *Robert Morris: Revolutionary Financier* (Philadelphia, 1954).

to the Constitution of 1787 was not public bankruptcy and currency depreciation but the nationalists' "fear of social radicalism" following the flood of paper money emissions in 1785–1786 and Shays' Rebellion. Though it was not entirely clear from Ferguson's account whether the merchants advocated a strong central government so that they could handle the debt or, as he seemed to suggest, the debt was simply a means of achieving the anterior goal of a strong central government, Ferguson had demonstrated, as he later remarked,[118] that the political goals of the nationalists were "interwoven with economic ends, particularly the establishment of a nationwide regime of sound money and contractual obligation."

McDonald, who presented the results of his work in a paper[119] and a book-length essay[120] agreed with Ferguson that the public debt and the public lands were the "material sinews of union," and served as the basis for a national economic interest which formed around Robert Morris and provided the impetus for the movement to give Congress the taxing power in the early 1780's. He also agreed that the virtual collapse of that movement in 1783–1784 did not bring economic disaster. "It was a critical moment only for the United States as United States," for "those who thought the American Republic was worth creating and saving," he wrote, but "not for the several states or their inhabitants," who in general "had it better than they had ever had it before." Where he differed from Ferguson was on the nature of the major political alignments and the central issue that divided them. The debate over whether to augment the powers of Congress, as McDonald saw it, only masked a deeper and much more fundamental issue— whether the United States would be politically one nation or not; and where individuals stood on that question depended on a number of variables, including where they lived, whether their states were thriving, their economic interests, and their ideological commitments. By suggesting that "accessibility to transportation—and

---

[118]Stuart Bruchey, "The Forces Behind the Constitution: A Critical Review of the Framework of E. James Ferguson's *The Power of the Purse* with a Rebuttal by E. James Ferguson," *William and Mary Quarterly*, 3rd ser., XIX (July, 1962), 429–438. For consideration of other economic developments during the Revolution see Clarence L. Ver Steeg, "The American Revolution Considered as an Economic Movement," *Huntington Library Quarterly*, XX (August, 1957), 361–372; Robert A. East, *Business Enterprise in the American Revolutionary Era* (New York, 1938); and Curtis P. Nettels, *The Emergence of a National Economy, 1775–1815* (New York, 1962).

[119]"The Anti-Federalists, 1781–1789," *Wisconsin Magazine of History*, XLVI (Spring, 1963), 206–214.

[120]E Pluribus Unum: *The Formation of the American Republic 1776–1790* (Boston, 1965).

through it to communication—predisposed Americans to be narrow or broad in their loyalties, to oppose or favor the establishment of a national government," McDonald seemed to be adopting categories similar to those earlier used by Main and Benson, albeit with a significant twist in emphasis—for McDonald it was the broad-minded versus the narrow-minded, not the commercial-minded against the agrarian-minded. But McDonald left no doubt that in his mind this division was distinctly secondary to the interplay of competing economic interests. Then, as now, McDonald implied, the primary determinative force in American politics was the pocketbook, the "irresistible and illimitable compulsion to get More," and, although the number of separate interests was vast, the most important division, McDonald contended in an important elaboration of his central conclusion in *We the People,* was between those who thought their interests would best be served by a strong national government and those who had a vested interest in the continued primacy of the state governments. The behavior of some men, however, could not, McDonald admitted, be explained purely in terms of self-interest. Some of the Antifederalists were republican ideologues who would have opposed the Constitution no matter what their interests were. More important, the Constitution was so impressive an achievement—"the miracle of the age . . . and of all ages to come"—that the men who wrote it— McDonald called them "giants"—obviously had to have been inspired by something more than the sordid materialism that normally characterized American politics.

McDonald's admission that the behavior of the men who wrote and pushed through the Constitution, as well as that of *some* of their opponents, could not be explained entirely or even largely in terms of their economic and social interests underlined the fundamental weakness in most of the post-World War II literature on the Confederation and Constitution. McDonald and Ferguson, Benson and Main, have together brought an enlarged and more precise understanding of the tangible economic and social forces at work in the United States during the 1780's and of their relationship to the critical political developments of the decade. They have, in short, succeeded remarkably well in refining Beard's conclusions and categories in such a way as to make them accord much more closely with existing evidence. The very nature of their success, however, only revealed how giant a shadow Beard had cast, how severely constricting his influence had been, even for scholars, like McDonald, who have specifically sought to free themselves from his intellectual domination. In sharp contrast to recent writers on the pre-Revolutionary period, they have not, in other words, advanced very far beyond the Progressive historians in explaining what the ostensible and immediate *political* issues and underlying assumptions were, how men of all political hues saw and reacted to the problems of the Confederation and the issues raised by the Constitution, and how they explained their behavior to themselves, their contemporaries, and posterity, whatever social and economic considerations may have consciously or unconsciously helped to shape their behavior. There seems to be a general agreement that the Constitution was a bold political stroke, but the exact nature of that stroke, what it represented to the people who supported and opposed it, has not been made completely clear.

Though an enormous amount of work still needs to be done on developments within several key states and on the relationship between the states and Congress before the political contours of the 1780's can be fully reconstructed, several recent writers have indicated what the main outlines of that reconstruction may be. Thus, in a suggestive article,[121] John P. Roche emphasized the extent to which the Constitution was at once the product of democratic political procedures and a reflection of the Founders' aspirations for the new country. The Founders, he argued, had to be understood "first and foremost" as "superb democratic politicians" who were spokesmen for "*American* nationalism," a "new and compelling credo" that emerged out of the American Revolution. As they saw it, the Philadelphia Convention was "an all-or-nothing proposition." Either "national salvation or national impotence" would be the result, and to achieve the former they persistently demonstrated a willingness to submerge "their parochial interests in behalf of an ideal which took shape before their eyes and under their ministrations," an ideal that was at best a "patchwork" of compromises over structural details necessary to overcome a variety of differences among the delegates and to make the final document acceptable to the public at large. Far from being an antidemocratic document, as the Progressive historians had claimed, Roche concluded, the Constitution was a "vivid demonstration of effective democratic political action" and a clear indication that the Founding Fathers had to operate, and were aware they had to operate, "with great delicacy and skill in a political cosmos full of enemies to achieve the one definitive goal—popular

---

[121]"The Founding Fathers: A Reform Caucus in Action," *American Political Science Review*, LV (December, 1961), 799–816.

approbation."[122] Implicit in Roche's analysis was the assumption that the Constitution, however much it may have been tailored to fit the fancies of the public, was a striking victory for the "*American* nationalism" represented by the men who wrote it and secured its ratification.[123]

As both Jackson T. Main and, more recently, Robert Allen Rutland[124] have suggested, it was precisely the extreme continental nationalism of the Federalists, and the possibility that they might have sacrificed the libertarian inheritance of the Revolution to it, that so worried their Antifederalist opponents. To the Antifederalists the Constitution seemed not just a threat to local control and state-centered vested interests but, at least to many diehards, an ominous betrayal of the ideals and achievements of the Revolution, the diabolical instrument of a counterrevolutionary conspiracy against American liberty. That the Antifederalists were correct in thinking that they smelled a conspiracy but that they seriously misunderstood its character and intent was the conclusion of Stanley Elkins and Eric McKitrick in "The Founding Fathers: Young Men of the Revolution," *Political Science Quarterly*, LXXVI (June 1961), 181–216, a perceptive analysis of the nature of both the divisions over the Constitution and the nationalistic aspirations of the Federalists. The Federalist conspiracy, Elkins and McKitrick contended, was against not liberty but "particularism and inertia," which in the mid-1780's seemed to the Federalists on the verge of robbing the young nation of its future promise. Significantly younger than their opponents, many leading Federalists, Elkins and McKitrick pointed out, had "quite literally seen their careers launched in the Revolution." In contrast to most Antifederalist leaders, whose careers were already well under way prior to 1776 and who remained largely state-oriented thereafter, the younger Federalists necessarily had been preoccupied with putting together a continental war effort and in the process came to "view the states collectively as a 'country' and to think in continental terms." What made them nationalists, then, what gave them the "dedication, the force and éclat" to attempt to overcome the "urge to rest, to drift, to turn back the clock" that was represented by the Antifederalists and seemed to have a stranglehold on the country from 1783 to 1787, was not "any 'distate' for the

---

[122]Clinton Rossiter expands on this theme in 1787: *The Grand Convention* (New York, 1966).

[123]This point was made more explicitly by Richard B. Morris, "The Confederation Period and the American Historian," *William and Mary Quarterly*, 3rd ser., XIII (April, 1956), 139–156.

[124]*The Ordeal of the Constitution: The Antifederalists and the Ratification Struggle of 1787–1788* (Norman, Okl., 1966).

Revolution . . . but rather their profound and growing involvement in it." Behind "the revolutionary verve and ardor of the Federalists, their resources of will and energy, their willingness to scheme tirelessly, campaign everywhere, and sweat and agonize over every vote" was this inspired vision of what the nation could and should be. Fundamentally, then, Elkins and McKitrick concluded, the struggle was not between rival economic groups, not between competing ideologies, not even between nationalism and localism, but between energy and inertia, and the Constitution was "sufficiently congenial to the underlying commitments of the whole culture—republicanism and capitalism—that" once inertia had been overcome and the basic object of discontent, the absence of a Bill of Rights, removed, opposition to the new government melted away. After a dozen years of anxiety, the men of the Revolution could be reasonably confident in 1788–1789 that "*their* Revolution had been a success." Far from trying to overturn the Revolution, the Federalists were thus trying to bring it to a favorable conclusion.

Beneath the political maneuvering described by Roche and behind the desire for a more energetic government emphasized by Elkins and McKitrick, other writers have recently demonstrated, were certain basic ideas that were central to the state constitutions and indeed to the whole Revolutionary experience. As A. O. Lovejoy has shown,[125] the framers of the Constitution had not changed their mind about human nature as a result of their experience during the Revolution: they still "had few illusions about the rationality of the generality of mankind." Indeed, with the paper money mania of 1785–1786 and Shays' Rebellion in Massachusetts fresh in their minds, they were more fearful than ever of the "giddiness of the multitude." To prevent social anarchy and to guarantee the success of—even to save—the republican experiment in America from the unhappy fate it had suffered everywhere else,[126] they were persuaded, clearly required a stable and vigorous political system that would check such popular excesses.[127] Yet, as Martin Diamond has indicated,[128] they were also

---

[125]*Reflections on Human Nature, op. cit.*

[126]On this point see Douglass G. Adair, " 'Experience Must be Our Only Guide': History, Democratic Theory, and the United States Constitution," in *The Reinterpretation of Early American History,* Ray E. Billington, ed. (San Marino, Calif., 1966), 129–148.

[127]Among several excellent analyses of the relation of Shays' Rebellion to the movement for stronger central government see the discussion in J. R. Pole, *Political Representation in England and the Origins of the American Republic* (London, 1966).

[128]"Democracy and *The Federalist:* A Reconsideration of the Framers' Intent," *American Political Science Review,* LIII (March, 1959), 52–68.

deeply devoted to popular government, to the idea that political authority should be "'derived from the great body of the society, not from . . . [any] favoured class of it.'" However considerable were the roles of economic interests, broad social forces, the personal and social aspirations of the Founders, or the pressures for political compromise, the interaction between these two ideas, between the pessimistic conception of human nature and the commitment to popular government, these writers have argued, exercised a profound shaping influence upon the proceedings of the Philadelphia Convention in 1787. Inspired, as Douglass Adair has shown,[129] by the possibilities that politics might be reduced to a science, they believed, in Lovejoy's words, that it was entirely possible by employing the method of counterpoise, the balancing of harmful elements against one another, "to construct an ideal political society out of bad human materials—to frame a rational scheme of government, in which the general good will be realized, without presupposing that the individuals who exercise ultimate political power will be severally actuated in their use by rational motives, or primarily solicitous about the general good." The Framers were thus trying not just to put together a structure of government that would be acceptable to all of the interests at the convention and to a majority of the public at large, as Roche argued, but also, as Adair remarked, to discover through a "genuinely 'scientific' attempt . . . the 'constant and universal principles' of any republican government in regard to liberty, justice, and stability."[130]

The central problem facing the Framers, then, was, to quote Lovejoy again, "not chiefly one of political ethics but of practical psychology, a need not so much to preach to Americans about what they *ought* to do, as to predict successfully what they *would* do." That the people would behave irrationally and constantly fall under the sway of factions devoted to their own selfish ends rather than to the good of the public was clear enough from the fate of all previous experiments in republican government. To moderate the flightiness of the people and to prevent the formation of a majority faction that would stop at nothing, even tyranny, to

[129]" 'That Politics May Be Reduced to a Science': David Hume, James Madison, and the Tenth *Federalist*," *Huntington Library Quarterly*, XX (August, 1957), 343–360.

[130]The Founders' quest for fame—distinction—and the importance of that quest both in shaping their behavior in 1787 and determining the character of the Philadelphia Convention and the Constitution are discussed by Adair in "Fame and the Founding Fathers," in *Fame and the Founding Fathers*, Edmund P. Willis, ed. (Bethlehem, Pa., 1967), 27–52.

secure its own interest, the Framers agreed, were their primary tasks. The first task they sought to accomplish by the creation of the Senate which, as Diamond has pointed out, was designed to protect property against popular excesses and to provide a check on the popular House of Representatives without in any respect going "beyond the limits" permitted by the " 'genuine principles of republican government.' " The Framers thus rejected the conventional *"mixed* republic," in which the polity was divided into separate and distinct elements and the aristocracy balanced against the democracy, in favor of a *"democratic* republic," in which the body representing stability and moderation was not hereditary but popularly elected, if not directly by the people, by representatives who were elected directly by the people. To prevent the formation of a majority faction, the Framers came up with an equally "republican remedy," a major intellectual breakthrough and the peculiar insight, as Adair has demonstrated, of James Madison. What would save the United States from the tyranny of a majority faction and the fate of earlier republics, Madison argued in applying to the American situation an idea suggested to him by his reading of Scottish philosopher David Hume, was its enormous size and the multiplicity of factions and interests that would necessarily result from that size. With so many separate and diverse interests, Madison contended, there would be no possibility of enough of them submerging their differences and getting together to form a majority faction. In a large republic, then, Madison suggested, the struggle of manifold interests would operate, to quote Diamond, as a "safe, even energizing" force that in itself would guarantee "the safety and stability of society."

It was their inability to accept Madison's contentions, Cecelia M. Kenyon has argued,[131] that constituted the chief ideological difference between Antifederalists and Federalists. An intensive analysis of Antifederalist writings, she argued, revealed that they held the same pessimistic conception of human nature, with the distrust of the masses and fear of factions implied in that conception, as the Federalists. Far from being devoted to simple majoritarianism, as earlier writers had assumed, they were afraid of oppression from all quarters—from the people at large as well as from corrupt factions among the upper classes. So fearful were they of the malignant effects of power from whatever source it emanated, that the proposed federal government would have re-

---

[131]"Men of Little Faith: The Anti-Federalists on the Nature of Representative Government," *William and Mary Quarterly,* 3rd ser., XII (January, 1955), 3–43.

quired "a more rigid system of separation of powers, more numerous and more effective checks and balances" to have met their full approval. But, in fact, they were fundamentally suspicious of any form of a truly "national" government because they were convinced both that no government with such extensive authority could be prevented from yielding to the temptations of power and because, unlike Madison, who thought republican government would work only in a large state, they thought that it would never work except in small polities where the government could be "an exact miniature of the people."

From the perspective of the ideas of those who favored and opposed the Constitution, recent writers have thus indicated, the Federalists were those who were committed to the notion that politics might be reduced to a science, that Americans, despite their imperfections, might be able to devise a workable political mechanism for the entire United States, while the Antifederalists so feared the incapacities of man that they had "little faith" in his ability to construct a national political system which would function efficiently and energetically and still preserve the essences of republican government.

The Constitution has thus come to be seen not as the repudiation of the Revolution but as the fullfillment of the aspirations and ideas of its dominant group of leaders. To the extent it was intended to check the popular excesses that had been one of the incidental, if also entirely logical, results of the Revolution, it was also mildly counterrevolutionary, an attempt to neutralize the radical tendencies of thought and behavior before they threw the young republic into a state of political and social chaos that, the Founders believed, would perforce lead to a tyranny as objectionable as that they had just fought a long and bloody war to escape. Through the Constitution and the powerful central government it created they hoped to reassert and provide the necessary institutional and constitutional framework for achieving the original goals of the oposition to and subsequent break with Britain: a stable and orderly government in which men, despite their imperfections, would be free to enjoy the blessings of liberty and the security of property that was so essential a part of those blessings.

The Nature of the Revolution

What lay behind the manifest events, concrete issues, and manifold interests of the era of the American Revolution, what gave them shape and coherence for the men of the Revolution, scholarship over the past quarter century seems to indicate, were their preconceptions about the nature of man and the function of government. Given the intense preoccupation of American leaders, from the Stamp Act crisis to the adoption of the Constitution of 1787, with human nature and its relationship to the political process, it is now clear that they were grappling with and were fully conscious that they were grappling with the knottiest and most challenging of human problems. The central concern of the men of the American Revolution was not merely the reaffirmation and preservation of their Anglo-colonial heritage and not simply the protection of liberty and property but, as Edmund S. Morgan has put it,[132] the discovery of means "to check the inevitable operation of depravity in men who wielded power." This "great intellectual challenge," Morgan argued, engaged the "best minds of the period" as politics replaced theology as "the most challenging area of human thought and endeavor" and the intellectual leaders in America "addressed themselves to the rescue, not of souls, but of governments, from the perils of corruption." This fear of human nature, Morgan emphasized, lay behind the resistance of the colonists to Britain between 1763 and 1783 and their insistence that "the people of one region ought not to exercise dominion over those of another" unless those subject to that dominion had some control over it; this same fear, Morgan noted, drove them to adopt written constitutions that would, by establishing "the superiority of the people to their government," give the people some protection against "man's tyranny over man."

The meaning of the American Revolution has thus come to be seen primarily in the constitutions it produced and the ideas that lay behind them. Hannah Arendt presented the fullest and most systematic exposition of this view in *On Revolution*,[133] a trenchant analysis of the great revolutions of the late eighteenth century and the revolutionary tradition they spawned. The most significant fact about the American Revolution, Arendt argued, was that armed uprising and the Declaration of Independence were accompanied not by chaos but by a "spontaneous outbreak of constitution-making." And, she contended, the "true culmination" of the Revolutionary process was not the struggle for liberation from Britain but the effort to establish the freedom represented by those

---

[132]"The American Revolution Considered as an Intellectual Movement," in *Paths of American Thought*, Arthur M. Schlesinger, Jr., and Morton White, eds., (Boston, 1963), 11–33.
[133]New York, 1963.

constitutions. Fear of human nature, of the "chartless darkness of the human heart," and the conviction that, in John Adams' phrase, there would be nothing "without a constitution" were initially behind this fever of constitution-making. But it was the possibility of creating a "community, which, even though it was composed of 'sinners,' need not necessarily reflect this 'sinful' side of human nature," the exhilarating hope, as Hamilton expressed it, that men might establish "good government from reflection and choice" and not be forever dependent "for their political constitutions on accident and force," that eventually made them conceive of constitution-making as the "foremost and the noblest of all revolutionary deeds" and emboldened them to try the great experiment in federalism in 1787. To devise a national system which would, as Madison put it, "guard . . . society against the oppression of its rulers" by checking the various powers of government against one another and still have sufficient power to protect "one part of society against the injustice of the other part" was not, and the Founders never understood it to be, an easy task that could be accomplished to perfection. But they had the confidence of the public and a degree of confidence in one another present elsewhere only among conspirators, Arendt contended, and their accomplishment was notable. With the Constitution of 1787 they managed both to consolidate the power of the American Revolution and to provide a foundation for the freedom that was the ultimate concern of the Revolution.

{ II }

BACKGROUND

THE EXTERNAL RELATIONSHIP

The following selections examine two separate aspects of the relations between Great Britain and the colonies in the eighteenth century. The first selection describes the operation and assesses the impact of the navigation system, while the second analyzes political and constitutional relations between imperial officials and their representatives in the colonies, on one hand, and colonial lower houses of assembly on the other. What the nature of those relationships was prior to 1763 and how and why it changed between 1763 and 1776 are the central questions raised by both selections.

CURTIS P. NETTELS (b. 1898) is a noted economic historian, now emeritus at Cornell University.

British Mercantilism and the Economic Development of the Thirteen Colonies

CURTIS P. NETTELS

Mercantilism is defined for this discussion as a policy of government that expressed in the economic sphere the spirit of nationalism that animinated the growth of the national state in early modern times. The policy aimed to gain for the nation a high degree of security or self-sufficiency, especially as regards food supply, raw materials needed for essential industries, and the sinews of war. This end was to be achieved in large measure by

Reprinted with permission from *The Journal of Economic History*, XII, 2 (Spring, 1952), 105–114.

means of an effective control over the external activities and resources upon which the nation was dependent. In turn, that urge impelled the mercantilists to prefer colonial dependencies to independent foreign countries in seeking sources of supply. If the state could not free itself completely from trade with foreign nations, it sought to control that trade in its own interest as much as possible. To realize such objectives, mercantilism embraced three subordinate and related policies. The Corn Laws fostered the nation's agriculture and aimed to realize the ideal of self-sufficiency as regards food supply. State aids to manufacturing industries, such as the protective tariff, sought to provide essential finished goods, including the sinews of war. The Navigation Acts were intended to assure that foreign trade would be carried on in such a way as to yield the maximum advantage to the state concerned.

Since the mercantilist states of Europe lacked the resources for complete self-sufficiency, they could not free themselves from dependence on foreign supplies. Economic growth therefore increased the importance of external trade, and the preference for colonies over foreign countries intensified the struggle for dependent possessions. The importance in mercantilism of a favorable balance of trade and of a large supply of the precious metals is a familiar theme. We need only to remind ourselves that the mercantilists considered it the duty of government to obtain and to retain for the nation both a favorable trade balance and an adequate stock of gold and silver. To this end the state should help to build up a national merchant marine and should foster domestic manufacturing industries. The chief means of procuring raw materials, a favorable trade balance, and an ample supply of the precious metals was that of exporting high-priced manufactured goods and shipping services.

Despite its emphasis on government action, mercantilism was not socialism. In England, the system invoked the initiative and enterprise of private citizens. It encouraged the merchants, shippers, and manufacturers by conferring benefits upon them and by identifying their private interests with the highest needs of the state. So close was this identification that one may properly regard the theory of mercantilism as a rationalization of the special interests of dominant groups of the time. The mercantilist policy was an expression of an accord between landowners and merchant-capitalists in alliance with the Crown.

Is it possible to measure the influence of government on the economic development of an area? Whether such influence be large or small, it must necessarily be only one factor at work in the process of economic change. The range of influence of even the most powerful government is limited, whereas economic activity is world-wide in its scope and ramifications. Thus far no scheme of statecraft has succeeded in bending all the members of the perverse human family to its designs. To many students of economic affairs it may seem futile to attempt to isolate and to measure the effect of only one factor in the immensely intricate, varied, and shifting activities that are involved in the development of a large area, such as the thirteen colonies. But perhaps such an effort may serve a purpose. It at least stimulates thought, which is essential to intellectual growth, and growth—not final answers or ultimate solutions—is all that one can expect to attain in this world of perpetual change.

To begin with, we note that the thirteen colonies experienced a phenomenal development during the 150 years in which they were subject to the regulating policies of English mercantilism. Adam Smith said in 1776:

A nation may import to a greater value than it exports for half a century, perhaps, together; the gold and silver which comes into it during all this time may be all immediately sent out of it; its circulating coin may gradually decay, different sorts of paper money being substituted in its place, and even the debts, too, which it contracts with the principal nations with whom it deals, may be gradually increasing; and yet its real wealth, the exchangeable value of the annual produce of its lands and labor, may, during the same period, have been increasing in a much greater proportion. The state of our North American colonies, and of the trade which they carried on with Great Britain, before the commencement of the present disturbances, may serve as a proof that this is by no means an impossible supposition.

To what extent did English mercantilism contribute to this "real wealth"—this "exchangeable value of the annual produce of . . . lands and labor?" Lands and labor. Two of the most fundamental factors in the growth of the thirteen colonies were the character of the people and the nature of the land and resources to which they applied their labor. The connecting link between the two that gave the thirteen colonies their unique character was the system of small individual holdings that came into being, usually at the start of settlement. It provided a strong incentive to labor and was therefore a major factor in their development. Crèvecoeur spoke of "that restless industry which is the principal characteristic of these colonies," and observed: "Here the rewards of . . . [the farmer's] industry follow with equal steps the progress of his labor; his labor is founded on the basis of nature, self-interest, can it want a stronger allurement . . . ? As farmers they will be careful and anxious to get as much as they can, because what they get is their own."

Although the land system of the thirteen colonies has not usually been considered an element of mercantilism, yet it was not divorced from it. Why did the English Government grant to its colonies a benefit that was not commonly bestowed on settlers by the other colonizing powers? Small holdings inspired the colonists to work; their labor expanded production; and increased production enlarged English commerce. The resulting trade was more susceptible to control by the state than a comparable trade with foreign countries would have been. For this reason, the colonial land system may be regarded as an expression of mercantilist policy. Viewed in this light, mercantilism contributed directly to the growth of the settlements.

Such also was the effect of the policy of England with reference to the peopling of its part of America. The government opened the doors to immigrants of many nationalities and creeds. Its liberality in this respect was unique. It harmonized with the mercantilist doctrine. The Crown admitted dissenters and foreigners in order to expand colonial production and trade. Such immigrants were, to a large extent, industrious, progressive, and energetic. Their productivity was stimulated by the climate of freedom in which they lived—a climate that was made possible in good measure by the indulgence of the government. The resulting growth of English trade served the needs of the state as they were viewed by the mercantilists.

We shall next consider the effects of specific mercantilist laws and government actions on the economic development of the thirteen colonies. It appears at once that such laws and actions did not create or sustain any important industry or trade in Colonial America. The major economic pursuits of the colonies grew out of, and were shaped by, the nature of the resources of the land, the needs of the settlers, and the general state of world trade in the seventeenth century. No important colonial activity owed its birth or existence to English law. The statutes and policies of mercantilism, with an exception or two, sought to control, to regulate, to restrain, to stimulate, or to protect. In the great majority of instances it was not the role of the government to initiate, to originate, to create. All the important mercantilist laws were adopted in response to a development that had occurred. They undertook to encourage, or to regulate, or to suppress some industry, practice, or trade that had been initiated by private citizens and which they had proved to be profitable. When the origins of enterprise in America are considered, it appears that every important industry got its start by reason of the natural resources of an area, by virtue of the demand for a product, or because of such factors of trade as transportation or location. Ordinarily, the government did not subject a colonial activity to regulation by law until it had proved itself to be profitable. In Virginia, for instance, the government did not initiate the tobacco industry or attempt to stimulate its early development. Rather, the Crown sought to discourage it. After it had taken root under the influence of general economic conditions, the government stepped in to regulate it. The major Navigation Act was passed in response to the success of the Dutch in world commerce. The English Government did not legislate against certain industries in the colonies until they had grown of their own accord to the extent that they menaced their English counterparts. The currency policy which England applied to its colonies was worked out not in a vacuum but in answer to practices in which the colonists were engaging.

The effects of mercantilist laws naturally depended upon their enforcement. Since they almost invariably sought to prevent something that the colonists had found to be profitable, the task of enforcement was difficult. It required the exercise of force and vigilance.

In a general way, the government attained a reasonable success in its efforts to enforce the policies that bore directly on the southern mainland colonies, whereas the principal acts which were designed for the Middle Colonies and New England could not be made effective.

The program for the plantation area embraced several policies. The Navigation Act of 1661 excluded from its trade all foreign merchants and foreign vessels. By the terms of the Staple Act of 1663 the planters must buy most of their manufactured goods from England. Slaves must be bought from English slave traders. The area must depend upon English sources for capital and credit, and the planters could not avail themselves of legal devices in order to ease their burdens of debt.

The government made a strenuous effort to enforce these policies. The decisive action centered in the three Dutch wars between 1652 and 1675. The defeat of the Dutch drove them from the southern trade and enabled the English merchants to hold it as in a vise. After 1665 the development of the plantation colonies proceeded in conformity with the tenets of mercantilism.

The effect was to retard that development, since the planters were subjected to a virtual English monopoly and were denied the benefits of competitive bidding for their crops and the privilege of buying foreign goods and shipping services in the cheapest market.

Certain conditions of the period 1675 to 1775 favored the English mercantilists in their efforts to enforce the southern policy. The geography of the Chesapeake country made it easy to exclude foreign vessels, since the English navy had to control only the narrow entrance to the bay in order to keep foreign vessels from reaching the plantations. That the tobacco ships had to move slowly along the rivers made concealment impossible for interlopers. Secondly, there was the factor of debt. Once a planter had become indebted to an English merchant, he was obliged to market his crops through his creditor in order to obtain new supplies. Hence he lost the advantage of competitive bidding for his export produce. And finally, the four wars with France, 1689–1763, served to rivet the plantation area to Britain, as mercantilism intended. The British navy provided convoys for the tobacco ships, and the expenditures of the Crown in America for military purposes provided the planters with additional buying power for English goods, thereby increasing their dependence on British merchants, vessels, and supplies.

By reason of the acts of government, the economic development of the southern colonies exhibited after 1665 about as clear an example of effective political control of economic activity as one can find. The trade of the southern colonies was centered in Britain. They were obliged to employ British shipping, to depend on British merchants, and to look only to British sources for capital and credit. They were not permitted to interfere with the British slave trade. British investments enjoyed a sheltered market in that the Crown excluded the foreign investor from the area and prohibited the colonists from taking any legal steps that would impair the claims of British creditors. The resulting dependence of the plantation country gave it a strongly British character, retarded its development, fostered discontent, and goaded the planters to resistance and revolt.

The initial enforcement of the Navigation Acts in the 1660's reduced the profits of the tobacco planters and forced them to cut the costs of production. Slavery was the answer. Appropriately at this time the English Government undertook to furnish its colonies with an ample supply of slaves. The planters were obliged to buy them on credit—a main factor in reducing them to a state of commercial bondage. The English Government forbade the planters to curtail the nefarious traffic. American slavery was thus one of the outstanding legacies of English mercantilism. That resolute foe of English mercantilist policy, George Washington, subscribed to the following resolve in 1774: "We take this opportunity of declaring our most earnest wishes to see an entire stop forever put to such a wicked, cruel, and unnatural trade."

In another sense the Navigation Act of 1661 had a discernible effect on American development. It stimulated the shipbuilding and shipping industries in New England and the Middle Colonies. It did not, however, create those industries. But the English Government drove the Dutch from the trade of English America before English shipping could meet the full needs of the colonies. The Navigation Act gave to English colonial shipbuilders and shipowners the same privileges that were given to English shipbuilders and shipowners. Undoubtedly this favored treatment spurred on the shipping industries of New England. Shipbuilding flourished there, since the colonial builders were permitted to sell their product to English merchants, and New England shipowners could employ their American-built vessels in the trade of the whole empire. New England benefited directly from the expulsion of the Dutch from the trade of English America. After New England's shipbuilding industry had become fully established (and had proved itself more efficient than its English rival) the British Government refused to heed the pleas of British shipowners who wished to subject it to crippling restraints.

English policy for the plantation area was essentially negative. It did not originate enterprises. With one exception it did not attempt to direct economic development into new channels. The exception appears in the bounty granted for indigo—a form of aid that made the production of that commodity profitable and sustained it in the lower South until the time of the Revolution, when the industry expired with the cessation of the bounty.

The policies that affected the Middle Colonies and New England differed materially in character and effect from the policies that were applied to the South. The northern area received the privilege of exporting its chief surplus products—fish, meats, cereals, livestock, lumber—directly to foreign markets. As already noted, the northern maritime industries flourished under the benefits conferred upon them by the Navigation Acts. Freedom to export the staples of the area in company with vigorous shipbuilding and shipping industries induced the northerners to engage in a varied foreign trade. This outcome, however, was in part a result of certain restrictive measures of the English Government. It prohibited the importation into England of American meats and cereals, thereby forcing the colonists to seek foreign markets for their surplus.

The resulting trade of the northern area—with southern Europe, the Wine Islands, Africa, and the foreign West Indies—did not prove satisfactory to the English mercantilists. It built up in the colonies a mercantile interest that threatened to compete successfully with English traders and shipowners. It carried with it the danger that the northerners might nullify those features of the Navigation Acts which aimed to center most of the trade of English America in England. Nor did their reliance on foreign trade prove to be entirely satisfactory to the colonists. In time of war, their vessels were exposed to the depredations of the French. The English navy could not protect the diverse northern trades with convoys, as it protected the simpler, more concentrated commerce of the plantation area. The wartime disruption of the northern trade deprived the area of the foreign money and products that in peacetime its merchants carried to England for the purpose of buying English goods for the colonial market. The resulting decline of the exportation of English merchandise was then deplored by the English mercantilists. Unable to procure finished goods in England, the northerners were driven to manufacture for themselves. Thence arose what the mercantilists regarded as a fatal danger—the prospect that the colonies would manufacture for themselves, decrease their purchases in England, and produce a surplus of finished goods that would compete with English wares in the markets of the world.

To avoid this danger, the English mercantilists devised their major experiment in state planning of the early eighteenth century. They undertook to foster the production of naval stores in the Middle Colonies and New England. Such products would be sent directly to England as a means of paying for English goods. They would divert the colonists from domestic manufacturing and free them from their dependence on diverse foreign trades. They would transform the commerce of the northern area in such a way that it would resemble that of the plantation area—a simple, direct exchange of American raw products for English finished goods.

The naval-stores program was constructive in intent. The government sought to shape the development of the northern area, thereby solving a serious problem. But the policy failed. It did not stimulate the production of naval stores in the northern area sufficiently to provide it with adequate payments for English goods, or to divert the northerners from their foreign trades, or to halt the trend toward home manufacturing.

This failure led the mercantilists to embrace a purely negative policy. As the trade of the northern area with the foreign West Indies increased, the English Government undertook to stop it altogether. Such was its intent in imposing upon the colonies the Molasses Act of 1733. But that effort did not succeed. Again, a mercantilist policy failed to bear its expected fruit.

The early policies of mercantilism had a marked effect on the growth of the northern area. But the result turned out to be unpleasing to the English authorities. Their endeavors to give a new direction to the development of the area failed completely after 1700. A problem had arisen for which English mercantilism never found a solution.

The main element in this problem was the trend in the northern area toward domestic manufacturing. Since that trend menaced all the essentials of mercantilism, the English Government did its best to thwart it. Thus there was no more important ingredient in English policy than the determined effort to retard or prevent the growth in America of industries that would produce the sort of goods that England could export at the greatest profit. Such, chiefly, were cloth, ironware, hats, and leather goods. The effectiveness of the laws and orders against colonial manufacturing is a subject of dispute. It is difficult to prove why something did not happen. If the colonies were slow in developing manufacturing industries, was it the result of English policy or of other factors? The writer believes that English policies had a strong retarding influence. The barriers erected were extensive and formidable. British statutes restrained the American woolen, iron, and hat industries. The colonies could not impose protective tariffs on imports from England. They could not operate mints, create manufacturing corporations, or establish commercial banks —institutions that are essential to the progress of manufacturing.

It was easier to enforce a policy against American fabricating industries than a policy that aimed to regulate maritime trade. A vessel could slip in and out of the northern ports. A manufacturing plant and its operations could not be concealed, unless, as in later times, it was engaged in mountain moonshining. The exposure of factories to the gaze of officials undoubtedly deterred investors from building them in defiance of the law.

New industries in an economically backward country commonly needed the positive encouragement and protection of government. It was the rule of mercantilism that handicaps to home manufacturing should be overcome by tariffs, bounties, and other forms of state aid. Such stimuli were denied to the colonies while they were subject to English mercantilism. Not only was the imperial government hostile; equally important, the colonial governments were not allowed to extend assistance to American promoters who wished to establish industries on the basis of efficient, large-scale operations.

An important aspect of the influence of state policy is its effect on the attitude of the people who are subjected to its benefits and restraints. The colonists as a whole were not seriously antagonized by the British imperium prior to 1763. Its most detrimental policy—that of the Molasses Act—was not enforced. In time of war (which meant thirty-five years of the period from 1689 to 1763) the military expenditures of the Crown in America helped to solve the most crucial problem of the colonies by supplying them with funds with which they could pay their debts and buy needed supplies in England. The shipbuilders and shipowners of the northern area shared in the national monopoly of imperial trade. Underlying all policy and legislation was the extremely liberal action of the English Government in making land available to settlers on easy terms and of admitting into the colonies immigrants of diverse nationalities, and varied religious faiths.

After 1763 the story is different. The colonies no longer received the sort of easy money that they had obtained from military expenditures during the wars. Instead, they were called upon to support through British taxes the defense establishment that was to be maintained in America after the war. Britain now abandoned its old liberal practice regarding land and immigration and replaced it with restrictive measures suggestive of the colonial policies of France and Spain. The Crown proceeded to enforce with vigor all the restraints it had previously imposed on colonial enterprise. Most of the features of the imperial rule that had placated the colonists were to be done away with. Not only were the old restraints to be more strictly enforced, they were to be accompanied by a host of new ones. The policies of Britain after 1763 merely intensified the central difficulty of the trade of the colonies. How might they find the means of paying for the manufactured goods that they must buy from England? If they could not get adequate returns, they would have to manufacture for themselves.

In its total effect, British policy as it affected the colonies after

1763 was restrictive, injurious, negative. It offered no solutions of problems. In the meantime, the colonists, having lived so long under the rule of mercantilism, had become imbued with mercantilist ideas. If the British imperium would not allow them to grow and expand, if it would not provide a solution of the central problem of the American economy, the colonists would have to take to themselves the right and the power to guide their economic development. They would find it necessary to create a new authority that would foster American shipping and commerce, make possible the continued growth of settlement, and above all stimulate the growth of domestic manufacturing industries. Thus another result of English mercantilism was the American Revolution and the creation thereafter of a new mercantilist state on this side of the Atlantic.

The Role of the Lower Houses of Assembly in Eighteenth-Century Politics

JACK P. GREENE

The rise of the representative assemblies was perhaps the most significant political and constitutional development in the history of Britain's overseas empire before the American Revolution. Crown and proprietary authorities had obviously intended the governor to be the focal point of colonial government with the lower houses merely subordinate bodies called together when necessary to levy taxes and ratify local ordinances proposed by the executive. Consequently, except in the New England charter colonies, where the representative bodies early assumed a leading role, they were dominated by the governors and councils for most of the period down to 1689. But beginning with the Restoration and intensifying their efforts during the years following the Glorious Revolution, the lower houses engaged in a successful quest for power as they set about to restrict the authority of the executive, undermine the system of colonial administration laid down by imperial and proprietary authorities, and make themselves paramount in the affairs of their respective colonies.

Reprinted with substantial additions and with permission from *The Journal of Southern History*, XXVII, 4 (November, 1961), 451–474.

Historians have been fascinated by this phenomenon. For nearly a century after 1776 they interpreted it as a prelude to the American Revolution. In the 1780's the pro-British historian George Chalmers saw it as the early manifestation of a latent desire for independence, an undutiful reaction to the mild policies of the Mother Country.[1] In the middle of the nineteenth century the American nationalist George Bancroft, although more interested in other aspects of colonial history, looked upon it as the natural expression of American democratic principles, simply another chapter in the progress of mankind.[2] The reaction to these sweeping interpretations set in during the last decades of the nineteenth century, when Charles M. Andrews, Edward Channing, Herbert L. Osgood, and others began to investigate in detail and to study in context developments from the Restoration to the end of the Seven Years' War. Osgood put a whole squadron of Columbia students to work examining colonial political institutions, and they produced a series of institutional studies in which the evolution of the lower houses was a central feature. These studies clarified the story of legislative development in each colony, but this necessarily piecemeal approach, as well as the excessive fragmentation that characterized the more general narratives of Osgood and Channing, tended to emphasize the differences rather than the similarities in the rise of the lower houses and failed to produce a general analysis of the common features of their quest for power.[3] Among later scholars, Leonard W. Labaree in his excellent monograph *Royal Government in America* presented a comprehensive survey of the institutional development of the lower houses in the royal colonies and of the specific issues involved in their struggles with the royal govern-

---

[1]George Chalmers, *An Introduction to the History of the Revolt of the American Colonies* (2 vols., Boston, 1845), I, 223–26, and II, 226–28, particularly, for statements of Chalmers' position.

[2]George Bancroft, *History of the United States* (14th ed., 10 vols., Boston, 1854–1875), III, 1–108, 383–98, particularly.

[3]Herbert L. Osgood, *The American Colonies in the Seventeenth Century* (3 vols., New York, 1904–1907) and *The American Colonies in the Eighteenth Century* (4 vols., New York, 1924–1925). For Edward Channing's treatment see *A History of the United States* (6 vols., New York, 1905–1925), II. Representative of the studies of Osgood's students are William R. Shepherd, *History of Proprietary Government in Pennsylvania* (New York, 1896); Newton D. Mereness, *Maryland As a Proprietary Province* (New York, 1901); W. Roy Smith, *South Carolina As a Royal Province, 1719–1776* (New York, 1903); Charles L. Raper, *North Carolina: A Study in English Colonial Government* (New York, 1904); William H. Fry, *New Hampshire As a Royal Province* (New York, 1908); Edwin P. Tanner, *The Province of New Jersey, 1664–1738* (New York, 1908); Edgar J. Fisher, *New Jersey As a Royal Province, 1738–1776* (New York, 1911); and Percy S. Flippin, *The Royal Government in Virginia, 1624–1775* (New York, 1919).

ors, but he did not offer any systematic interpretation of the general process and pattern of legislative development.[4] Charles Andrews promised to tackle this problem and provide a synthesis in the later volumes of his magnum opus, *The Colonial Period of American History,* but he died before completing that part of the project.[5]

As a result, some fundamental questions have never been fully answered, and no one has produced a comprehensive synthesis. No one has satisfactorily worked out the basic pattern of the quest; analyzed the reasons for and the significance of its development; explored its underlying assumptions and theoretical foundations; or assessed the consequences of the success of the lower houses, particularly the relationship between their rise to power and the coming of the American Revolution. This essay is intended to suggest some tentative conclusions about these problems, not to present ultimate solutions. My basic research on the lower houses has been in the Southern royal colonies and in Nova Scotia. One of the present purposes is to test the generalizations I have arrived at about the Southern colonies by applying them to what scholars have learned of the legislatures in the other colonies. This procedure has the advantage of providing perspective on the story of Southern developments. At the same time, it may serve as one guidepost for a general synthesis in the future.

Any student of the eighteenth-century political process will sooner or later be struck by the fact that, although each of the lower houses developed independently and differently, their stories were similar. The elimination of individual variants, which tend to cancel out each other, discloses certain basic regularities, a clearly discernible pattern—or what the late Sir Lewis Namier called a morphology—common to all of them. They all moved along like paths in their drives for increased authority, and although their success on specific issues differed from colony to colony and the rate of their rise varied from time to time, they

---

[4]Leonard W. Labaree, *Royal Government in America* (New Haven, 1930), 172–311, particularly. Two other illuminating studies by Labaree's contemporaries are A. B. Keith, *Constitutional History of the First British Empire* (Oxford, 1930), which is legalistic in emphasis, and John F. Burns, *Controversies Between Royal Governors and Their Assemblies in the Northern American Colonies* (Boston, 1923), which fails to tie together in any satisfactory way developments in the four colonies it treats.

[5]Charles M. Andrews, "On the Writing of Colonial History," *William and Mary Quarterly,* 3rd ser., I (January, 1944), 29–42. The line of interpretation that Andrews would probably have followed is briefly developed in his brilliant *The Colonial Background of the American Revolution* (New Haven, 1924), 3–65.

all ended up at approximately the same destination. They passed successively through certain vaguely defined phases of political development. Through most of the seventeenth century the lower houses were still in a position of subordination, slowly groping for the power to tax and the right to sit separately from the council and to initiate laws. Sometime during the early eighteenth century most of them advanced to a second stage at which they could battle on equal terms with the governors and councils and challenge even the powers in London if necessary. At that point the lower houses began their bid for political supremacy. The violent eruptions that followed usually ended in an accommodation with the governors and councils which paved the way for the ascendancy of the lower houses and saw the virtual eclipse of the colonial executive. By the end of the Seven Years' War, and in some instances considerably earlier, the lower houses had reached the third and final phase of political dominance and were in a position to speak for the colonies in the conflict with the imperial government which ensued after 1763.

By 1763, with the exception of the lower houses in the corporate colonies of Rhode Island and Connecticut, which had virtually complete authority, the Pennsylvania and Massachusetts houses of representatives were probably most powerful. Having succeeded in placing its election on a statutory basis and depriving the Council of direct legislative authority in the Charter of Privileges in 1701, the Pennsylvania House under the astute guidance of David Lloyd secured broad financial and appointive powers during the administrations of Daniel Gookin and Sir William Keith. Building on these foundations, it gained almost complete dominance in the 1730's and 1740's despite the opposition of the governors, whose power and prestige along with that of the Council declined rapidly.[6] The Massachusetts House, having been accorded the unique privilege of sharing in the selection of the Council by the royal charter in 1691, already had a strong tradition of legislative supremacy inherited from a half century

---

[6]Developments in Pennsylvania may be traced in Shepherd, *Proprietary Government, op. cit.*; Benjamin Franklin, *An Historical Review of Pennsylvania* (London, 1759); Roy N. Lokken, *David Lloyd: Colonial Lawmaker* (Seattle, 1959); Sister Joan de Lourdes Leonard, *The Organization and Procedure of the Pennsylvania Assembly, 1682–1772* (Philadelphia, 1949); Winifred T. Root, *The Relation of Pennsylvania with the British Government, 1696–1765* (Philadelphia, 1912); and Theodore Thayer, *Pennsylvania Politics and the Growth of Democracy, 1740–1776* (Harrisburg, Pa., 1953). On Rhode Island and Connecticut see David S. Lovejoy, *Rhode Island Politics and the American Revolution, 1760–1776* (Providence, 1958), and Oscar Zeichner, *Connecticut's Years of Controversy, 1754–1775* (Chapel Hill, N.C., 1949).

of corporate experience. During the first thirty years under the new charter first the benevolent policies of Sir William Phips and William Stoughton and then wartime conditions during the tenures of Joseph Dudley and Samuel Shute enabled the House, led by Elisha Cooke, Jr., to extend its authority greatly. It emerged from the conflicts over the salary question during the 1720's with firm control over finance, and the Crown's abandonment of its demand for a permanent revenue in the early 1730's paved the way for an accommodation with subsequent governors and the eventual dominance of the House under Governor William Shirley after 1740.[7]

The South Carolina Commons and New York House of Assembly were only slightly less powerful. Beginning in the first decade of the eighteenth century, the South Carolina lower house gradually assumed an ironclad control over all aspects of South Carolina government, extending its supervision to the minutest details of local administration after 1730 as a succession of governors, including Francis Nicholson, Robert Johnson, Thomas Broughton, the elder William Bull, and James Glen offered little determined opposition. The Commons continued to grow in stature after 1750 while the Council's standing declined because of the Crown policy of filling it with placemen from England and the Common's successful attacks upon its authority.[8] The New York House of Assembly began to demand greater authority in reaction to the mismanagement of Edward Hyde, Viscount Cornbury, during the first decade of the eighteenth century. Governor Robert Hunter met the challenge squarely during his ten-year administration beginning in 1710, but he and his successors could not check the rising power of the House. During the seven-year tenure of George Clarke beginning in 1736, the House advanced into the final stage of development. Following Clarke,

---

[7]Useful studies on Massachusetts are Robert E. Brown, *Middle-Class Democracy and the Revolution in Massachusetts, 1691–1780* (Ithaca, N.Y., 1955); Martin L. Cole, The Rise of the Legislative Assembly in Provincial Massachusetts (unpublished Ph.D. thesis, State University of Iowa, 1939); Thomas Hutchinson, *The History of the Colony and Province of Massachusetts-Bay*, Lawrence S. Mayo, ed. (3 vols., Cambridge, Mass., 1936); and Henry R. Spencer, *Constitutional Conflict in Provincial Massachusetts* (Columbus, O., 1905).

[8]The best published study on South Carolina is Smith, *South Carolina As a Royal Province*. Also useful are David D. Wallace, *The Life of Henry Laurens* (New York, 1915); Jack P. Greene, The Quest for Power of the Lower Houses of Assembly in the Southern Royal Colonies, 1730–1763 (unpublished Ph.D. thesis, Duke University, 1956); and M. Eugene Sirmans, "The South Carolina Royal Council, 1720–1763," *William and Mary Quarterly*, 3rd ser., XVIII (July, 1961), 373–92.

George Clinton made a vigorous effort to reassert the authority of the executive, but neither he nor any of his successors was able to challenge the power of the House.[9]

The lower houses of North Carolina, New Jersey, and Virginia developed more slowly. The North Carolina lower house was fully capable of protecting its powers and privileges and competing on equal terms with the executive during the last years of proprietary rule and under the early royal governors, George Burrington and Gabriel Johnston. But it was not until Arthur Dobbs' tenure in the 1750's and 1760's that, meeting more regularly, it assumed the upper hand in North Carolina politics under the astute guidance of Speaker Samuel Swann and Treasurers John Starkey and Thomas Barker.[10] In New Jersey the lower house was partially thwarted in its spirited bid for power during the 1740's under the leadership of John Kinsey and Samuel Nevill by the determined opposition of Governor Lewis Morris, and it did not gain superiority until the administrations of Jonathan Belcher, Thomas Pownall, Francis Bernard, and Thomas Boone during the Seven Years' War.[11] Similarly, the Virginia Burgesses vigorously sought to establish its control in the second decade of the century under Alexander Spotswood, but not until the administrations of Sir William Gooch and Robert Dinwiddie, when first the expansion of the colony and then the Seven Years' War required more regular sessions, did the Burgesses finally gain the upper hand under the effective leadership of Speaker John Robinson.[12]

---

[9]Developments in New York can be followed in Carl L. Becker, *The History of Political Parties in the Province of New York, 1760–1776* (Madison, 1909); Milton M. Klein, "Democracy and Politics in Colonial New York," *New York History,* XL (July 1959), 221–46; Lawrence H. Leder, *Robert Livingston, 1654–1728, and the Politics of Colonial New York* (Chapel Hill, N.C., 1961); Beverly McAnear, Politics in Provincial New York, 1689–1761 (unpublished Ph.D. thesis, Stanford University, 1935); Irving Mark, *Agrarian Conflicts in Colonial New York, 1711–1775* (New York, 1940); William Smith, *The History of the Late Province of New York* (2 vols., New York, 1829); and Charles W. Spencer, *Phases of Royal Government in New York, 1691–1719* (Columbus, O., 1905).

[10]Useful analyses of North Carolina are Raper, *North Carolina, op. cit.,* and Desmond Clarke, *Arthur Dobbs Esquire, 1689–1765* (Chapel Hill, N.C., 1957).

[11]New Jersey developments can be traced in Donald L. Kemmerer's excellent study, *Path to Freedom: The Struggle for Self-Government in Colonial New Jersey, 1703–1776* (Princeton, 1940).

[12]Among the more useful secondary works on Virginia are Flippin, *Royal Government, op. cit.;* Bernard Bailyn, "Politics and Social Structure in Virginia," in James M. Smith, ed., *Seventeenth-Century America: Essays on Colonial History* (Chapel Hill, N.C., 1959), 90–115; Lucille Blanche Griffith, *The Virginia House of Burgesses, 1750–1774* (unpublished Ph.D. thesis, Brown University, 1957); Ray Orvin Hummel, Jr., The Virginia House of Burgesses,

Among the lower houses in the older colonies, only the Maryland House of Delegates and the New Hampshire House of Assembly failed to reach the final level of development in the period before 1763. The Maryland body made important advances early in the eighteenth century while under the control of the Crown and aggressively sought to extend its authority in the 1720's under the leadership of the older Daniel Dulany and again in the late 1730's and early 1740's under Dr. Charles Carroll. But the proprietors were usually able to thwart these attempts, and the Delegates failed to pull ahead of the executive despite a concerted effort during the last intercolonial war under the administration of Horatio Sharpe.[13] In New Hampshire, the House had exercised considerable power through the early decades of the eighteenth century, but Governor Benning Wentworth effectively challenged its authority after 1740 and prevented it from attaining the extensive power exercised by its counterparts in other colonies.[14] It should be emphasized, however, that neither the Maryland nor the New Hampshire lower house was in any sense impotent and along with their more youthful equivalent in Georgia gained dominance during the decade of debate with Britain after 1763. Of the lower houses in the continental colonies with pre-1763 political experience, only the Nova Scotia Assembly had not reached the final phase of political dominance by 1776.[15]

The similarities in the process and pattern of legislative development from colony to colony were not entirely accidental. The lower houses faced like problems and drew upon common traditions and imperial precedents for solutions. They all operated in the same broad imperial context and were affected by common historical forces. Moreover, family, cultural, and com-

---

1689–1750 (unpublished Ph.D. thesis, University of Nebraska, 1934); David J. Mays, *Edmund Pendleton, 1721–1803* (2 vols., Cambridge, Mass., 1952); Charles S. Sydnor, *Gentlemen Freeholders: Political Practices in Washington's Virginia* (Chapel Hill, N.C., 1952); Thomas J. Wertenbaker, *Give Me Liberty: The Struggle for Self-Government in Virginia* (Philadelphia, 1958); and David Alan Williams, Political Alignments in Colonial Virginia, 1698–1750 (unpublished Ph.D. thesis, Northwestern University, 1959).

[13]On Maryland see two excellent studies, Charles A. Barker, *The Background of the Revolution in Maryland* (New Haven, 1940), and Aubrey Land, *The Dulanys of Maryland* (Baltimore, 1955).

[14]New Hampshire developments can be followed in Fry, *New Hampshire, op. cit.*, and Jeremy Belknap, *History of New Hampshire* (3 vols., Boston, 1791–1792).

[15]On Georgia see W. W. Abbot, *The Royal Governors of Georgia, 1754–1775* (Chapel Hill, N.C., 1959), and Albert B. Saye, *New Viewpoints in Georgia History* (Atlanta, 1943). John Bartlett Brebner, *The Neutral Yankees of Nova Scotia* (New York, 1937), is the best study of developments in that colony.

mercial ties often extended across colony lines, and newspapers and other printed materials, as well as individuals, often found their way from one colony to another. The result was at least a general awareness of issues and practices in neighboring colonies, and occasionally there was even a conscious borrowing of precedents and traditions. Younger bodies such as the Georgia Commons and Nova Scotia Assembly were particularly indebted to their more mature counterparts in South Carolina and Massachusetts Bay.[16] On the executive side, the similarity in attitudes, assumptions, and policies among the governors can be traced in large measure to the fact that they were all subordinate to the same central authority in London, which pursued a common policy in all the colonies.

Before the Seven Years' War the quest was characterized by a considerable degree of spontaneity, by a lack of awareness that activities of the moment were part of any broad struggle for power. Rather than consciously working out the details of some master plan designed to bring them liberty or self-government, the lower houses moved along from issue to issue and from situation to situation, primarily concerning themselves with the problems at hand and displaying a remarkable capacity for spontaneous action, for seizing any and every opportunity to enlarge their own influence at the executive's expense and for holding tenaciously to powers they had already secured. Conscious of the issues involved in each specific conflict, they were for the most part unaware of and uninterested in the long-range implications of their actions. Virginia Governor Francis Fauquier correctly judged the matter in 1760. "Whoever charges them with acting upon a premeditated concerted plan, don't know them," he wrote of the Virginia burgesses, "for they mean honestly, but are Expedient Mongers in the highest Degree."[17] Still, in retrospect it is obvious that throughout the eighteenth century the lower houses were engaged in a continuous movement to enlarge their sphere of influence. To ignore that continuity would be to miss the meaning of eighteenth-century colonial political development.

One is impressed with the rather prosaic manner in which the lower houses went about the task of extending their authority, with the infrequency of dramatic conflict. They gained much of their power in the course of routine business, quietly and simply extending and consolidating their authority of passing laws and

---

[16] On this point see Abbot, *ibid.*, and Brebner, *ibid.*
[17] "Fauquier to Board of Trade," June 2, 1760, in Colonial Office Papers (London, Public Record Office), Series 5/1330, folios 37–39.

establishing practices, the implications of which escaped both colonial executives and imperial authorities and were not always fully recognized even by the lower houses themselves. In this way they gradually extended their financial authority to include the powers to audit accounts of all public officers, to share in disbursing public funds, and eventually even to appoint officials concerned in collecting and handling local revenues. Precedents thus established soon hardened into fixed principles, "undoubted rights" or "inherent powers," changing the very fabric of their respective constitutions. The notable absence of conflict is perhaps best illustrated by the none too surprising fact that the lower houses made some of their greatest gains under those governors with whom they enjoyed the most harmony, in particular Keith in Pennsylvania, Shirley in Massachusetts, Hunter in New York, and the elder and younger Bull in South Carolina. In Virginia the House of Burgesses made rapid strides during the 1730's and 1740's under the benevolent government of Gooch, who discovered early in his administration that the secret of political success for a Virginia governor was to reach an accord with the plantation gentry.

One should not conclude that the colonies had no exciting legislative-executive conflicts, however. Attempts through the middle decades of the eighteenth century by Clinton to weaken the financial powers of the New York House, Massachusetts Governors Samuel Shute and William Burnet to gain a permanent civil list, Benning Wentworth to extend unilaterally the privilege of representation to new districts in New Hampshire, Johnston to break the extensive power of the Albemarle Counties in the North Carolina lower house, Dinwiddie to establish a fee for issuing land patents without the consent of the Virginia Burgesses, and Boone to reform South Carolina's election laws each provided a storm of controversy that brought local politics to a fever pitch.[18] But such conflicts were the exception and usually arose not out of the lower houses' seeking more authority but from the executives' attempts to restrict powers already won.

---

[18]The details of these disputes can be traced in Smith, *History of New York, op. cit.*, II, 68–151; Hutchinson, *History of Massachusetts Bay, op. cit.*, 163–280; Labaree, *Royal Government*, 180–185; Lawrence F. London, "The Representation Controversy in Colonial North Carolina," *North Carolina Historical Review*, XI (October, 1934), 255–270; Jack P. Greene, ed., "The Case of the Pistole Fee," *Virginia Magazine of History and Biography*, LXVI (October, 1958), 399–422, and "The Gadsden Election Controversy and the Revolutionary Movement in South Carolina," *Mississippi Valley Historical Review*, XLVI (December, 1959), 469–492.

Impatient of restraint and jealous of their rights and privileges, the lower houses responded forcefully and sometimes violently when executive action threatened to deprive them of those rights. Only a few governors, men of the caliber of Henry Ellis in Georgia and to a lesser extent William Henry Lyttelton in South Carolina and Bernard in New Jersey, had the skill to challenge established rights successfully without raising the wrath of the lower houses. Clumsier tacticians—Pennsylvania's William Denny, New York's Clinton, Virginia's Dinwiddie, North Carolina's Dobbs, South Carolina's Boone, Georgia's John Reynolds—failed when pursuing similar goals.

Fundamentally, the quest for power in both the royal and the proprietary colonies was a struggle for political identity, the manifestation of the political ambitions of the leaders of emerging societies within each colony. There is a marked correlation between the appearance of economic and social elites produced by the growth in colonial wealth and population on the one hand and the lower houses' demand for increased authority, dignity, and prestige on the other. In the eighteenth century a group of planters, merchants, and professional men had attained or were rapidly acquiring within the colonies wealth and social position. The lower houses' aggressive drive for power reflects the determination of this new elite to attain through the representative assemblies political influence as well. In another but related sense, the lower houses' efforts represented a movement for autonomy in local affairs, although it is doubtful that many of the members recognized them as such. The lower houses wished to strengthen their authority within the colonies and to reduce to a minimum the amount of supervision, with the uncertainties it involved, that royal or proprietary authorities could exercise. Continuously nourished by the growing desire of American legislators to be masters of their own political fortunes and by the development of a vigorous tradition of legislative superiority in imitation of the imperial House of Commons, this basic principle of local control over local affairs in some cases got part of its impetus from an unsatisfactory experience early in the lower houses' development with a despotic, inefficient, or corrupt governor such as Thomas, Lord Culpeper, or Francis, Lord Howard or Effingham, in Virginia, Lionel Copley in Maryland, Sir Edmund Andros in Massachusetts, Seth Sothell in North Carolina, or the infamous Cornbury in New York and New Jersey.

With most of their contemporaries in Great Britain, colonial Americans were convinced that men were imperfect creatures, perpetually self-deluded, enslaved by their passions, vanities, and interests, confined in their vision and understanding, and incapable of exercising power over each other without abusing it. This cluster of assumptions with the associated ideals of a government of laws rather than of men and of a political structure that restrained the vicious tendencies of man by checking them against each other was at the heart of English constitutionalism. In Britain and in the colonies, wherever Englishmen encountered a seeming abuse of power, they could be expected to insist that it be placed under legal and constitutional restraints. Because the monarchy had been the chief offender in seventeenth-century England, it became conventional for the representative branch to keep an especially wary eye on the executive, and the Glorious Revolution tended to institutionalize this pattern of behavior. The necessity to justify the Revolution ensured both that the specter of Stuart despotism would continue to haunt English political arenas throughout the eighteenth century and that representative bodies and representatives would be expected—indeed obliged—to be constantly on the lookout for any signs of that excess of gubernatorial power that would perforce result in executive tyranny. When colonial lower houses demanded checks on the prerogative and sought to undermine executive authority, they were, then, to some extent, playing out roles created for them by their predecessors in the seventeenth-century English House of Commons and using a rhetoric and a set of ground rules that grew out of the revolutionary conditions of Stuart England. In every debate, and in every political contest, each American legislator was a potential Coke, Pym, or Hampden and each governor, at least in legislators' minds, a potential Charles I or James II.

But the lower houses' quest for power involved more than the extension of legislative authority within the colonies at the expense of the colonial executives. After their initial stage of evolution, the lower houses learned that their real antagonists were not the governors but the proprietors or Crown officials in London. Few governors proved to be a match for the representatives. A governor was almost helpless to prevent a lower house from exercising powers secured under his predecessors, and even the most discerning governor could fall into the trap of assenting to an apparently innocent law that would later prove damaging to the royal or proprietary prerogative. Some governors, for the sake of preserving amicable relations with the representatives or because they thought certain legislation to be in the best interest of a colony, actually conspired with legislative leaders to present the actions of the lower houses in a favorable light in London. Thus, Jonathan Belcher worked with Massachusetts leaders to parry the Crown's demand for a permanent revenue in the 1730's, and Fauquier joined with Speaker John Robinson in Virginia to prevent the separation of the offices of speaker and treasurer during the closing years of the Seven Years' War.

Nor could imperial authorities depend upon the colonial councils to furnish an effective check upon the representatives' advancing influence. Most councilors were drawn from the rising social and economic elites in the colonies. The duality of their role is obvious. Bound by oath to uphold the interests of the Crown or the proprietors, they were also driven by ambition and a variety of local pressures to maintain the status and power of the councils as well as to protect and advance their own individual interests and those of their group within the colonies. These two objectives were not always in harmony, and the councils frequently sided with the lower houses rather than with the governors. With a weakened governor and an unreliable council, the task of restraining the representative assemblies ultimately devolved upon the home government. Probably as much of the struggle for power was played out in Whitehall as in Williamsburg, Charleston, New York, Boston, or Philadelphia.

Behind the struggle between colonial lower houses and the imperial authorities were two divergent, though on the colonial side not wholly articulated, concepts of the constitutions of the colonies and in particular of the status of the lower houses. To the very end of the colonial period, imperial authorities persisted in the views that colonial constitutions were static and that the lower houses were subordinate governmental agencies with only temporary and limited lawmaking powers—in the words of one imperial official, merely "so many Corporations at a distance, invested with an Ability to make Temporary By Laws for themselves, agreeable to their respective Situations and Climates."[19] In working out a political system for the colonies in the later seventeenth century, imperial officials had institutionalized these views in the royal commissions and instructions. Despite the fact that the lower houses were yearly making important changes in their respective constitutions, the Crown never altered either the commissions or instructions to conform with realities of

---

[19]Sir William Keith, "A Short Discourse on the Present State of the Colonies in America with Respect to the Interest of Great Britain," 1729, in Colonial Office Papers (London, Public Record Office), Series 5/4, folios 170–171.

the colonial political situation and continued to maintain throughout the eighteenth century that they were the most vital part of the constitutional structure of the royal colonies. The Pennsylvania and to a lesser extent the Maryland proprietors were less rigid, although they also insisted upon their theoretical constitutional and political supremacy over the lower houses.

Colonial lower houses had little respect for and even less patience with such a doctrinaire position, and whether or not royal and proprietary instructions were absolutely binding upon the colonies was the leading constitutional issue in the period before 1763. As the political instruments of what was probably the most pragmatic society in the eighteenth-century Western World, colonial legislators would not likely be restrained by dogma divorced from reality. They had no fear of innovations and welcomed the chance to experiment with new forms and ideas. All they asked was that a thing work. When the lower houses found that instructions from imperial authorities did not work in the best interests of the colonies, that they were, in fact, antithetic to the very measures they as legislatures were trying to effect, they openly refused to submit to them. Instructions, they argued, applied only to officials appointed by the Crown.

Instructions from his majesty, to his governor, or the council, are binding to them, and esteemed as laws or rules; because if either should disregard them, they might immediately be displaced,

declared a South Carolina writer in 1756 while denying the validity of an instruction that stipulated colonial councils should have equal rights with the lower houses in framing money bills. "But, if instructions should be laws and rules to the people of this province, then there would be no need of assemblies, and all our laws and taxes might be made and levied by an instruction."[20] Clearly, then, instructions might bind governors, but never the elected branch of the legislature.

Even though the lower houses, filled with intensely practical politicians, were concerned largely with practical political considerations, they found it necessary to develop a body of theory with which to oppose unpopular instructions from Britain and to support their claims to greater political power. In those few colonies that had charters, the lower houses relied upon the guarantees in them as their first line of defense, taking the position that the stipulations of the charters were inviolate, despite the fact that some had been invalidated by English courts, and

---

[20]*South Carolina Gazette*, May 13, 1756.

could not be altered by executive order. A more basic premise which was equally applicable to all colonies was that the constituents of the lower houses, as inhabitants of British colonies, were entitled to all the traditional rights of Englishmen. On this foundation the colonial legislatures built their ideological structure. In the early charters the Crown had guaranteed the colonists "all privileges, franchises and liberties of this our kingdom of England . . . any Statute, act, ordinance, or provision to the contrary thereof, notwithstanding."[21] Such guarantees, colonials assumed, merely constituted recognition that their privileges as Englishmen were inherent and unalterable and that it mattered not whether they stayed on the home islands or migrated to the colonies. "His Majesty's Subjects coming over to America," the South Carolina Commons argued in 1739 while asserting its exclusive right to formulate tax laws, "have no more forfeited this their most valuable Inheritance than they have withdrawn their Allegiance." No "Royal Order," the Commons declared, could "qualify or any wise alter a fundamental Right from the Shape in which it was handed down to us from our Ancestors."[22]

One of the most important of these rights was the privilege of representation, on which, of course, depended the very existence of the lower houses. Imperial authorities always maintained that the lower houses existed only through the consent of the Crown,[23] but the houses insisted that an elected assembly was a fundamental right of a colony arising out of an Englishman's privilege to be represented and that they did not owe their existence merely to the King's pleasure.

Our representatives, agreeably to the general sense of their constituents [wrote New York lawyer William Smith in the 1750's] are tena-

---

[21]For instance, see the provision in the Maryland charter conveniently published in Merrill Jensen, ed., *English Historical Documents: American Colonial Documents to 1776* (New York, 1955), 88.

[22]James H. Easterby and Ruth S. Green, eds., *The Colonial Records of South Carolina: The Journals of the Commons House of Assembly* (8 vols., Columbia, 1951–1961), *1736–1739* (June 5, 1739), 720.

[23]This view was implicit in most thinking and writing about the colonies by imperial authorities. For the attitude of John Carteret, Lord Granville, an important figure in colonial affairs through the middle decades of the eighteenth century, see Benjamin Franklin to Isaac Norris, March 19, 1759, as quoted by William S. Mason, "Franklin and Galloway: Some Unpublished Letters," American Antiquarian Society, *Proceedings*, n. s., XXXIV (1925), 245–46. Other examples are Jack P. Greene, ed., "Martin Bladen's Blueprint for a Colonial Union," *William and Mary Quarterly*, 3rd ser., XVII (October, 1960), 516–530, by a prominent member of the Board of Trade, and Archibald Kennedy, *An Essay on the Government of the Colonies* (New York, 1752), 17–18, by an official in the colonies.

cious in their opinion, that the inhabitants of this colony are entitled to all the privileges of Englishmen; that they have a right to participate in the legislative power, and that the session of assemblies here, is wisely substituted instead of a representation in parliament, which, all things considered, would, at this remote distance, be extremely inconvenient and dangerous.[24]

The logical corollary to this argument was that the lower houses were equivalents of the House of Commons and must perforce in their limited spheres be entitled to all the privileges possessed by that body in Great Britain. Hence, in cases where an invocation of fundamental rights was not appropriate, the lower houses frequently defended their actions on the grounds that they were agreeable to the practice of the House of Commons. Thus in 1755 the North Carolina Lower House denied the right of the Council to amend tax bills on the grounds that it was "contrary to Custom and Usage of Parliament."[25] Unintentionally, Crown officials encouraged the lower houses to make this analogy by forbidding them in the instructions to exercise "any power or privilege whatsoever which is not allowed by us to the House of Commons . . . in Great Britain."[26]

Because neither fundamental rights nor imperial precedents could be used to defend practices that were contrary to customs of the mother country or to the British constitution, the lower houses found it necessary to develop still another argument: that local precedents, habits, traditions, and statutes were important parts of their particular constitutions and could not be abridged by a royal or proprietary order. The assumptions were that the legislatures could alter colonial constitutions by their own actions without the active consent of imperial officials and that once the alterations were confirmed by usage they could not be countermanded by the British government. They did not deny the power of the governor to veto or of the Privy Council to disallow their laws but argued that imperial acquiescence over a long period of time was tantamount to consent and that precedents thus established could not be undone without their approval. The implication was that the American colonists saw their constitutions as living, growing, and constantly changing

---

[24]Smith, *op. cit.*, I, 307.

[25]Journals of the Lower House, January 4–6, 1755, William L. Saunders, ed., *The Colonial Records of North Carolina* (10 vols., Raleigh, 1886–1890), V, 287.

[26]Leonard W. Labaree, ed., *Royal Instructions to British Colonial Governors, 1670–1776* (2 vols., New York, 1935), I, 112–113.

organisms, a theory which was directly opposite to the imperial view. To be sure, precedent had always been an important element in shaping the British constitution, but Crown officials were unwilling to concede that it was equally so in determining the fundamental law of the colonies. They willingly granted that colonial statutes, once formally approved by the Privy Council, automatically became part of the constitutions of the colonies, but they officially took the position that both royal instructions and commissions, as well as constitutional traditions of the mother country, took precedence over local practice or unconfirmed statutes.[27] This conflict of views persisted throughout the period after 1689, becoming more and more of an issue in the decades immediately preceding the American Revolution.

In the last analysis it was the imperial denial of the validity of the constitutional defenses of the lower houses that drove colonial lawmakers to seek to extend the power of the lower houses at the very time they were insisting—and, in fact, deeply believed—that no one individual or institution should have a superiority of power in any government. No matter what kind of workable balance of power might be attained within the colonies, there was always the possibility that the home government might unleash the unlimited might of the parent state against the colonies. The chief fear of colonial legislators, then, was not the power of the governors, which they could control, but that of the imperial government, which in the circumstances they could never hope to control, and the whole movement for legislative authority in the colonies can be interpreted as a search for a viable constitutional arrangement in which the rights of the colonists would be secured against the preponderant power of the mother country. The failure of imperial authorities to provide such an arrangement or even to formalize what small concessions they did make, meant, of course, that the search could never be fulfilled, and the resulting anxiety, only partly conscious and finding expression through the classic arguments and ringing phrases of English political struggles of the seventeenth century, impelled the lower houses and the men who composed them relentlessly through the colonial period and was perhaps the most important single factor in the demand of patriot leaders for explicit, written constitutions after the Declaration of Independence.

---

[27]For a classic statement of the imperial argument by a modern scholar see Lawrence H. Gipson, *The British Empire Before the American Revolution* (10 vols., Caldwell, Idaho, and New York, 1936–1961), III (rev.), 275–281.

It is nonetheless true that, if imperial authorities did not grant the validity of the theoretical arguments of the lower houses, neither did they make any systematic or concerted effort to force a rigid compliance with official policies for most of the period after 1689. Repressive measures, at least before 1763, rarely went beyond the occasional disallowance of an offending statute or the official reprimand of a rambunctious lower house. General lack of interest in the routine business of colonial affairs and failure to recognize the potential seriousness of the situation may in part account for this leniency, but it is also true that official policy under both Walpole and the Pelhams called for a light rein on the colonies on the assumption that contented colonies created fewer problems for the administration. "One would not Strain any point," Charles Delafaye, secretary to the lords justices, cautioned South Carolina's Governor Francis Nicholson in 1722, "where it can be of no Service to our King or Country." "In the Plantations," he added, "the Government should be as Easy and Mild as possible to invite people to Settle under it."[28] Three times between 1734 and 1749 the ministry failed to give enthusiastic support to measures introduced into Parliament to insure the supremacy of instructions over colonial laws.[29] Though the Calverts were somewhat more insistent upon preserving their proprietary prerogatives, in general the proprietors were equally lax as long as there was no encroachment upon their land rights or proprietary dues.

Imperial organs of administration were in fact inadequate to deal effectively with all the problems of the empire. Since no special governmental bodies were created in England to deal exclusively with colonial affairs, they were handled through the regular machinery of government—a maze of boards and officials whose main interests and responsibilities were not the supervision of overseas colonies. The only body sufficiently informed and interested to deal competently with colonial matters was the Board of Trade, and it had little authority, except for the brief period from 1748 to 1761 under the presidency of George Dunk, Earl of Halifax. The most useful device for restraining the lower houses was the Privy Council's right to review colonial laws, but even that was only partly effective, because the mass of colonial

---

[28]Delafaye to Nicholson, January 22, 1722, in Papers Concerning the Governorship of South Carolina (Houghton Library, Harvard University, Cambridge, Mass.), bMs Am 1455, Item 9.

[29]For a discussion of these measures see Bernard Knollenberg, *Origin of the American Revolution, 1759–1766* (New York, 1960), 49.

statutes annually coming before the Board of Trade made a thorough scrutiny impossible. Under such arrangements no vigorous colonial policy was likely. The combination of imperial lethargy and colonial aggression virtually guaranteed the success of the lower houses' quest for power. An indication of a growing awareness in imperial circles of the seriousness of the situation was Halifax's spirited, if piecemeal, effort to restrain the growth of the lower houses in the early 1750's. Symptomatic of these efforts was the attempt to make Georgia and Nova Scotia model royal colonies at the institution of royal government by writing into the instructions to their governors provisions designed to insure the continued supremacy of the executive and to prevent the lower houses from going the way of their counterparts in the older colonies. However, the outbreak of the Seven Years' War forced Halifax to suspend his activities and prevented any further reformation until the cessation of hostilities.

Indeed, the war saw a drastic acceleration in the lower houses' bid for authority, and its conclusion found them in possession of many of the powers held less than a century before by the executive. In the realm of finance they had imposed their authority over every phase of raising and distributing public revenue. They had acquired a large measure of independence by winning control over their compositions and proceedings and obtaining guarantees of basic English Parliamentary privileges. Finally, they had pushed their power even beyond that of the English House of Commons by gaining extensive authority in handling executive affairs, including the right to appoint executive officers and to share in formulating executive policy. These specific gains were symptoms of developments of much greater significance. To begin with, they were symbolic of a fundamental shift of the constitutional center of power in the colonies from the executive to the elected branch of the legislature. With the exception of the Georgia and Nova Scotia bodies, both of which had less than a decade of political experience behind them, the houses had by 1763 succeeded in attaining a new status, raising themselves from dependent lawmaking bodies to the center of political authority in their respective colonies.

But the lower houses had done more than simply acquire a new status in colonial politics. They had in a sense altered the structure of the constitution of the British Empire itself by asserting colonial authority against imperial authority and extending the constitutions of the colonies far beyond the limitations of the charters, instructions, or fixed notions of imperial authorities.

The time was ripe for a re-examination and redefinition of the constitutional position of the lower houses. With the rapid economic and territorial expansion of the colonies in the years before 1763 had come a corresponding rise in the responsibilities and prestige of the lower houses and a growing awareness among colonial representatives of their own importance, which had served to strengthen their long-standing, if still imperfectly defined, impression that colonial lower houses were the American counterparts of the British House of Commons. Under the proper stimuli, they would carry this impression to its logical conclusion: that the lower houses enjoyed an equal status under the Crown with Parliament. Here, then, well beyond the embryonic stage, was the theory of colonial equality with the mother country, one of the basic constitutional principles of the American Revolution, waiting to be nourished by the series of crises that beset imperial-colonial relations between 1763 and 1776.

The psychological implications of this new political order were profound. By the 1750's the phenomenal success of the lower houses had generated a soaring self-confidence, a willingness to take on all comers. Called upon to operate on a larger stage during the Seven Years' War, they emerged from that conflict with an increased awareness of their own importance and a growing consciousness of the implications of their activities. Symptomatic of these developments was the spate of bitter controversies that characterized colonial politics during and immediately after the war. The Gadsden election controversy in South Carolina, the dispute over judicial tenure in New York, and the contests over the pistole fee and the two-penny act in Virginia gave abundant evidence of both the lower houses' stubborn determination to preserve their authority and the failure of Crown officials in London and the colonies to gauge accurately their temper or to accept the fact that they had made important changes in the constitutions of the colonies.

With the shift of power to the lower houses also came the development in each colony of an extraordinarily able group of politicians. The lower houses provided excellent training for the leaders of the rapidly maturing colonial societies, and the recurring controversies prepared them for the problems they would be called upon to meet in the dramatic conflicts after 1763. In the decades before Independence there appeared in the colonial statehouses John and Samuel Adams and James Otis in Massachusetts Bay; William Livingston in New York; Benjamin Franklin and John Dickinson in Pennsylvania; Daniel Dulany the younger in Maryland; Richard Bland, Richard Henry Lee, Thomas Jefferson, and Patrick Henry in Virginia; and Christopher Gadsden and John Rutledge in South Carolina. Along with dozens of others, these men guided their colonies through the debate with Britain, assumed direction of the new state governments after 1776, and played conspicuous roles on the national stage as members of the Continental Congress, the Confederation, and, after 1787, the new federal government. By the 1760's, then, almost every colony had an imposing group of native politicians thoroughly schooled in the political arts and primed to meet any challenge to the power and prestige of the lower houses.

Britain's "new colonial policy" after 1763 provided just such a challenge. It precipitated a constitutional crisis in the empire, creating new tensions and setting in motion forces different from those that had shaped earlier developments. The new policy was based upon concepts both unfamiliar and unwelcome to the colonists such as centralization, uniformity, and orderly development. Yet it was a logical culmination of earlier trends and, for the most part, an effort to realize old aspirations. From Edward Randolph in the last decades of the seventeenth century to the Earl of Halifax in the 1750's colonial officials had envisioned a highly centralized empire with a uniform political system in each of the colonies and with the imperial government closely supervising the subordinate governments.[30] But, because they had never made any sustained or systematic attempt to achieve these goals, there had developed during the first half of the eighteenth century a working arrangement permitting the lower houses considerable latitude in shaping colonial constitutions without requiring crown and proprietary officials to give up any of their ideals. That there had been a growing divergence between imperial theory and colonial practice mattered little so long as each refrained from challenging the other. But the new policy threatened to upset this arrangement by implementing the old ideals long after the conditions that produced them had ceased to exist. Aimed at bringing the colonies more closely under imperial control, this policy inevitably sought to curtail the influence of the lower houses, directly challenging many of the powers they had

---

[30]On this point see Charles M. Andrews, *The Colonial Period of American History* (4 vols., New Haven, 1934–1938), IV, 368–425; Michael Garibaldi Hall, *Edward Randolph and the American Colonies, 1676–1703* (Chapel Hill, N.C., 1960); Arthur H. Basye, *Lords Commissioners of Trade and Plantations, 1748–1782* (New Haven, 1925); and Dora Mae Clark, *The Rise of the British Treasury: Colonial Administration in the Eighteenth Century* (New Haven, 1960).

acquired over the previous century. To American legislators accustomed to the lenient policies of Walpole and the Pelhams and impressed with the rising power of their own lower houses, the new program seemed a radical departure from precedent, a frontal assault upon the several constitutions they had been forging over the previous century. To protect gains they had already made and to make good their pretensions to greater political significance, the lower houses thereafter no longer had merely to deal with weak governors or casual imperial administrators; they now faced an aggressive group of officials bent upon using every means at their disposal, including the legislative authority of Parliament, to gain their ends.

Beginning in 1763 one imperial action after another seemed to threaten the position of the lower houses. Between 1764 and 1766 Parliament's attempt to tax the colonists for revenue directly challenged the colonial legislatures' exclusive power to tax, the cornerstone of their authority in America. A variety of other measures, some aimed at particular colonial legislatures and others at general legislative powers and practices, posed serious threats to powers that the lower houses had either long enjoyed or were trying to attain. To meet these challenges, the lower houses had to spell out the implications of the changes they had been making, consciously or not, in the structures of their respective governments. That is, for the first time they had to make clear in their own minds and then to verbalize what they conceived their respective constitutions in fact were or should be. In the process, the spokesmen of the lower houses laid bare the wide gulf between imperial theory and colonial practice. During the Stamp Act crisis in 1764–1766 the lower houses claimed the same authority over taxation in the colonies as Parliament had over that matter in England, and a few of them even asserted an equal right in matters of internal policy.[31] Although justified by the realities of the colonial situation, such a definition of the lower houses' constitutional position within the empire was at

---

[31]See the sweeping claim of the Virginia House of Burgesses to the "Inestimable Right of being governed by such Laws respecting their internal Polity and Taxatior as are devised from their own Consent" in objecting to Grenville's proposed stamp duties. Henry R. McIlwaine and John P. Kennedy (eds.), *Journals of the House of Burgesses in Virginia* (13 vols., Richmond, 1905–1913), *1761–1765*, 302–304 (December 18, 1764). The protests of all the lower houses against the Stamp Act are conveniently collected in Edmund S. Morgan, ed., *Prologue to Revolution: Sources and Documents on the Stamp Act Crisis, 1764–1766* (Chapel Hill, N.C., 1959), 8–17, 46–69.

marked variance with imperial ideals and only served to increase the determination of the home government to take a stricter tone. This determination was manifested after the repeal of the Stamp Act by Parliament's claim in the Declaratory Act of 1766 to "full power and authority" over the colonies "in all cases whatsoever."[32]

The pattern over the next decade was on the part of the home government one of increasing resolution to deal firmly with the colonies and on the part of American lawmakers a heightened consciousness of the implications of the constitutional issue and a continuously rising level of expectation. In addition to their insistence upon the right of Parliament to raise revenue in the colonies, imperial officials also applied, in a way that was increasingly irksome to American legislators, traditional instruments of royal control like restrictive instructions, legislative review, the governors' power to dissolve the lower houses and the suspending clause requiring prior approval of the Crown before laws of an "extraordinary nature" could go into effect. Finally Parliament threatened the very existence of the lower houses by a measure suspending the New York Assembly for refusing to comply with the Quartering Act in 1767 and by another altering the substance of the Massachusetts constitution in the Massachusetts Government Act in 1774. In the process of articulating and defending their constitutional position, the lower houses acquired aspirations well beyond any they had had in the years before 1763. American representatives became convinced in the decade after 1766 not only that they knew best what to do for their constituents and the colonies and that anything interfering with their freedom to adopt whatever course seemed necessary was an intolerable and unconstitutional restraint but also that the only security for their political fortunes was in the abandonment of their attempts to restrict and define Parliamentary authority in America and instead to deny Parliament's jurisdiction over them entirely by asserting their equality with Parliament under the Crown. Suggested by Richard Bland as early as 1766, such a position was openly advocated by James Wilson and Thomas Jefferson in 1774 and was officially adopted by the First Continental Congress when it claimed for Americans in its declarations and resolves "a free and exclusive power of legislation in their several provincial legislatures, where their right of representation

---

[32]Danby Pickering, ed., *The Statutes at Large from Magna Carta to the End of the Eleventh Parliament of Great Britain, Anno 1761, Continued to 1806* (46 vols., Cambridge, Eng., 1762–1807), XXVII, 19–20.

can alone be preserved, in all cases of taxation and internal polity."[33]

Parliament could not accept this claim without giving up the principles it had asserted in the Declaratory Act and, in effect, abandoning the traditional British theory of empire and accepting the colonial constitutional position instead. The First Continental Congress professed that a return to the *status quo* of 1763 would satisfy the colonies, but Parliament in 1774–1776 was unwilling even to go that far, much less to promise them exemption from Parliamentary taxation. Besides, American legislators now aspired to much more. James Chalmers, Maryland planter and later loyalist who was out of sympathy with the proceedings of American patriots between 1774 and 1776, correctly charged that American leaders had "been constantly enlarging their views, and stretching them beyond their first bounds, till at length they have wholly changed their ground."[34] Edward Rutledge, young delegate from South Carolina to the First Continental Congress, was one who recognized that the colonies would not "be satisfied with a restoration of such rights only, as have been violated since the year '63, when we have as many others, as clear and indisputable, that will even then be infringed."[35] The simple fact was that American political leaders, no matter what their professions, would not have been content to return to the old inarticulated and ambiguous pattern of accommodation between imperial theory and colonial practice that had existed through most of the period between 1689 and 1763. They now sought to become masters of their own political fortunes. Rigid guarantees of colonial rights and precise definitions of the constitutional relationship between the mother country and the colonies and between Parliament and the lower houses on American terms—that is, imperial recognition of the autonomy of the lower houses in local affairs and of the equality of the colonies with the mother country—would have been required to satisfy them.

No analysis of the charges in the Declaration of Independence can fail to suggest that the preservation and consolidation of the rights and powers of the lower houses were central in the struggle with Britain from 1763 to 1776, just as they had been the most

---

[33]Worthington C. Ford and others, eds., *Journals of the Continental Congress* (34 vols., Washington, 1904–1937), I, 68–69 (October 14, 1774).

[34]Candidus [James Chalmers], *Plain Truth: Addressed to the Inhabitants of America* (London, 1776), 46.

[35]Rutledge to Ralph Izard, Jr., October 29, 1774, in A. I. Deas, ed., *Correspondence of Mr. Ralph Izard of South Carolina* (New York, 1844), 22–23.

important issue in the political relationship between Britain and the colonies over the previous century and a half. Between 1689 and 1763 the lower houses' contests with royal governors and imperial officials had brought them political maturity, a considerable measure of control over local affairs, capable leaders, and a rationale to support their pretensions to political power within the colonies and in the Empire. The British challenge after 1763 threatened to render their accomplishments meaningless and drove them to demand equal rights with Parliament and autonomy in local affairs and eventually to declare their independence. At issue was the whole political structure forged by the lower houses over the previous century. In this context the American Revolution becomes in form, if not in essence, a war for political survival, a conflict involving not only individual rights as traditionally emphasized by historians of the event but assembly rights as well.

THE INTELLECTUAL
FRAMEWORK

—— ◣◆◢ ——

Two aspects of the ideological and psychological framework from which colonial Americans viewed the critical events occurring after 1763 are discussed in the selections below. The first of these examines the differing uses of the term *British Empire* on opposite sides of the Atlantic in the 1750's and 1760's, shows how these uses reveal a profound divergence between Great Britain and the colonies about the current and future role of the colonies in the British political community, and suggests how that divergence contributed to the breakdown in imperial-colonial communications between 1763 and 1776. The second selection reconstructs and analyzes the implications of many of the more important values, assumptions, and explicit ideas that gave shape and coherence to colonial political life on the eve of the Revolution and conditioned the colonial reaction to both the debate with Britain and the internal political pressures that were by-products of that debate.

Best known for his studies in medieval history and political semantics, RICHARD KOEBNER (1885–1958) was a professor at Breslau University until his expulsion from that post during the Nazi regime. He then became Professor of Modern History at Hebrew University in Jerusalem, a post which he held until he retired in 1955. RICHARD BUEL, JR. (b. 1933) is a member of the Department of History at Wesleyan University.

Two Conceptions of Empire

RICHARD KOEBNER

'Trade, shipping, the Navy—not colonization—were the true imperial interests of Englishmen in the hundred years after the restoration of Charles II.'[1] This statement of C. E. Carrington refers to the time from the second Act of Navigation to 'the Reduction of Quebec', a whole period in the history of British overseas interests. We have seen how, in the course of that century, the name 'British Empire' acquired a place in the English language and in British political consciousness. We have noticed that its main connotation was in fact 'trade, shipping and the Navy', and that the colonies figured only occasionally in its emphatic use. We have finally shown that the failure of the War of Jenkin's Ear adversely influenced its popularity towards the end of the period. From the end of the Seven Years War all this changed. The notion of the British Empire became a main topic of public opinion within the English-speaking world. After the Peace of Paris it had a particular appeal to citizens of the American mainland colonies. To them it had first of all a special bearing on the relations between themselves and the mother country. In the rising conflict the British Empire was felt to be at stake by the apologists of colonial liberty as well as by those of metropolitan authority. The name was to acquire a new attractive power in the course of the events which led to the dismemberment of the Empire that had been built up in America.

In view of these future vicissitudes we should do well to glance at the last decades preceding the Seven Years War. Two attitudes towards the inter-relation of the two concepts, 'the Colonies' (or 'the Plantations') and 'the British Empire', can be seen. The colonies were not 'the Empire' in the eyes of the British officials who dealt with their affairs. To American colonists the two concepts were already linked.

The Board of Trade and Plantations, established in 1696, was concerned, according to its instructions, with 'the plantations, not only with regard to the administration of government, but also in relation to commerce, and the manner in which those colonies

Reprinted with permission from *Empire* (England: Cambridge University Press, 1961), 85–89, 93–94, 101–107, 115, 325–330.
[1]C. E. Carrington, *The British Overseas* (Cambridge, Eng., 1950), p. 68.

could be rendered most beneficial to this Kingdom'. The identification of these interests with that of the British Empire would not have occurred to its members and officials. One of the latter, Thomas Pownall—the 'Governor Pownall' of later years—showed in 1752 that to him the concept of 'empire' was in no way related to his official duties. He defined it anew in some reflections on government in general, which he published under the title: *Principles of Policy, being the Grounds and Reasons of Civil Empire*. The book has nothing to do with colonies. It deals with 'civil empire' in the abstract, meaning the efficient functioning of administration. The expression, as well as the basic theory applied to it, are derived from James Harrington's *Oceana*. To Pownall it is an axiom that 'Property and its influence will always have the Ballance of Power and Authority'. Deviating widely from Harrington, he draws decesive inferences from this principle, not in the sphere of constitutional arrangements, but in that of administrative discipline. Beneficial government depends on the collective wisdom of property owners. They must co-operate 'like some engine and machine, the silk-mills for instance, where a one common great first movement is communicated and distributed thro' the whole'. The idea expressed in this metaphor might be denoted also by a well-known term which still needs to be rightly interpreted—*Imperium* or 'Empire'. 'This modelling the people into various orders, and subordination of orders . . . and acting under that direction as a one whole is what the Romans called by the peculiar word *Imperium,* to express which particular group of ideas we have no word in English but by adopting the word Empire.' The author attempts to support this assertion by classical quotations,[2] but in truth it is wholly his own. He experimented freely with the notion of empire, which he could not have done if his superiors and colleagues at the Board of Trade and Plantations had ever spoken of the British Empire as of the sphere of their authority. There was no such tradition.

---

[2]Pownall, *Principles,* especially pp. 51, 91–4. The author quotes Seneca, *De Clementia,* 1, 4, 1—'Imperium rerum vinculum, per quod republica cohaeret'—but overlooks the fact that the 'cohesive' power is attributed there to the *imperator,* not to some civic *imperium.* At another time he refers to Tacitus, *Agricola* 3, where the original text has 'Nerva Caesar res olim dissociabiles miscuerit, principatum ac libertatem'. Following Bacon and Bolingbroke, Pownall misquotes 'res olim insociabiles, imperium et libertatem'. Disraeli, as is well known, fell into the same trap in his speech on agricultural distress in 1851, and in his Guildhall address of 1879. Cf. W. F. Monypenny and G. E. Buckle, *Life of Disraeli* (6 vols., New York, 1910–1920), 1, p. 1099, II, pp. 855, 1367. On the Ciceronian *imperium et libertas* see above, ch. 1, p. 3.

This could have happened if the central authorities had heeded entreaties which occasionally reached them from overseas. In 1736 the Council and Assembly of South Carolina addressed the King on the grave apprehension aroused in them by the policies of their new southern neighbours, the colonists of Georgia. They humbly asked His Majesty not to let these newcomers encroach on their own colony of more than seventy years' standing, whose founders had been 'moved with a pious and laudable zeal for the propagating of the Christian Faith and knowledge, and enlarging the British Empire and Dominions (at their no small expense and hazard and without any burthen or charge to the Crown or Kingdom)'. They believed that their colony had been 'of some advantage to Great Britain not only in the consumption of their woollen and other manufactures but also in the extension of the British trade and Empire several hundred miles among the native Indians'.[3] By claiming to be pioneers of the British Empire the petitioners manifestly, but vainly, expected to impress their provincial interests on the home authorities. In 1740 and 1743 John Ashley of Barbados[4] addressed to these authorities *Memoirs and Considerations concerning the Trade and Revenues of the British Colonies in America*. While in the first series of these *Memoirs* the author introduced his recommendations only as 'proposals for rendering those colonies more beneficial to Great Britain', he struck a more elevated note on the title-page of the continuation of 1743. Here he undertook to show how 'the Traffick, Wealth and Strength of the whole may thereby be greatly increased'. Having reiterated this assertion in the preface,[5] he closed his *Memoirs* with a chapter 'On the trade, situation and strength of the British Empire, as one body, with a tendency to its colonies'. The reflections introduced by this heading are eulogistic rather than economic. 'No nation in the world is more commodiously situated for trade or war than the British Empire, taking all together as one body, viz. Great Britain, Ireland, and

---

[3] *Calendar of State Papers, Colonial Series, America and West Indies,* 1735–1736; no. 4831, p. 368.

[4] On his former advocacy that sugar should be an 'unenumerated commodity' cf. Richard Pares, *War and Trade in the West Indies 1739–1763* (Oxford, 1936), p. 80 n., *Cal. S.P., Col. Series* 1733, no. 349. On the financial misfortunes between 1735 and 1736 which made him go into hiding and almost cost him his councillorship in Barbados, see *Cal. S.P.* for these years, nos. 183, 188, 395 f., 399, 493 f.

[5] 'And such advantages are here pointed at with remarks on the consequences that may attend the whole British Empire, as well in regard to its naval force as otherwise, from a tender care of its colonies and fisheries in America' (vol. II, pp. Av, A2).

the Plantations and fisheries in America, besides its possessions in the East Indies and Africa.' The mother country with its natural wealth, its maritime power and its industrious people is eloquently praised. Great Britain is presented as the majestic emporium mediating 'between the foreign Dominions of Europe, and the other branches of the British Empire'. As a result of this position the large surplusage that arises from the profits of the junior branches of this great empire, and particularly from its plantations and fisheries in America', cannot but result in 'a large annual addition to the stock and wealth of this elder branch of the whole body.[6] Half a century earlier Edward Littleton of Barbados had complained that the English Empire in America was not fairly appreciated in the mother country. His younger compatriot, John Ashley, writing in 1743, assumed that the idea of one British Empire, with promising younger branches overseas, ought to be an inspiration to the nation at home.

The same conviction had formed in the mind of Benjamin Franklin. It found expression in the enthusiastic predictions of his essay of 1751: the *Observations concerning the Increase of Mankind, Peopling of Countries etc.* 'There are supposed to be now upwards of one million English souls in North America. . . . This million doubling, suppose, but once in twenty-five years will in another century be more than the people of England, and the greatest number of Englishmen will be on this side of the water. What an accession of power to the British Empire by sea as well as land! What increase of trade and navigation! What numbers of ships and seamen.'[7] In this vision, the idea of a greater England growing by colonization is linked to the interpretation of 'the British Empire' proclaimed in the verses of Prior and Thomson—trade, ships and seamen. The maritime interpretation of the term was not reserved for poetry. It was adopted by Franklin, a man of alert common sense, as an adequate expression

---

[6]Vol. II, pp. 94–96. The chapter closes with a renewed discussion of the specific West Indian interest which was earlier treated along with that of the Northern colonies ('ship-building, corn pitch, tar' etc.), adding 'some few remarks on the advantages that would accrue to this empire, if those junior branches of it, the Sugar Islands, should be raised to such a pitch, as to make only double the quantity of sugar, Rum, and molasses, they do now'.

[7]Albert H. Smyth, ed., *Writings of Benjamin Franklin* (New York, 1905–1907), II, pp. 205–208, Sect. 22. Franklin's jealous concern for the English character of the colonies is expressed in Sect. 23, where he objects to the expanding settlements of the Palatine Boers, 'who will shortly be so numerous as to germanize us instead of our anglifying them'. Sect. 24 adds Franklin's curious views on race; the English and the Saxons 'make the principal body of white people on the face of the earth'.

for his Anglo-American national and even racial pride. It had a special appeal to him because his countrymen, 'privateers in the late war', had acquired a share in this maritime glory by their conquest of Louisburg. 'The British Empire by land', which was to win shape in America, was a still more fascinating reality to him, and he expected his feelings to be shared in the mother country.

These single instances of colonials who made the British Empire a symbol of their belief in the future of British America[8] must not be taken as evidence of a literary convention. It was possible fervently to proclaim 'the glory of Britain' on American soil without recourse to the notion of 'empire'.[9] It is only as individual utterances that the few passages to which we can refer have documentary value. They show that to men who took an active part in shaping the future of Anglo-American society the notion of the British Empire became a symbol of the new possibilities to which they looked forward.

• • •

The idea of a greater England, which Benjamin Franklin and other Americans implied when speaking of the British Empire, was borne out by many features of their everyday life which reminded them of their national origin. There were family ties, business relations, and cultural interests; there was jealous pride in the constitutional privileges which were the English birthright. But while British origin was a live issue to many colonists, there was no apparent reason for many Britons to have reciprocal feelings of relationship towards the colonists in general. People living in Britain had less occasion to think of the colonies, and

[8]A fourth testimony, not quite as expressive, may be taken from a statement of 1736 concerning the notorious malpractices of Rhode Island shippers in the West Indian Trade. 'These practices will never be put an end to till Rhode Island is reduced to the subjection of the British Empire; of which at present it is no more a part than the Bahama Islands were, when they were invaded by the Buccaneers.' This sentence has been quoted by M. W. Jernegan, *The American Colonies* 1492–1750, p. 380 (and from there by H. U. Faulkner, *American Economic History*, 7th ed. [1954], p. 78), in a context which makes it appear to be taken from a report of the Board of Trade. There is no such report in the relevant volume of the *Cal. S.P.* Whatever the source, the remark probably originated from an observer in the colonies.

[9]Cf. the phraseology of Archibald Kennedy's fervent warning against French encroachments in North America and further mismanagement of relations with the Indians, written in 1754 for the benefit of the Albany conference; *Serious Considerations on the Present State of the Affairs of the Northern Colonies*, especially pp. 3, 5 f., 15.

in that small minority who had occasion, the number who belonged to refined society was certainly very small. The imaginative effort needed for a sympathetic approach to the colonies was obstructed for many by unpleasant impressions of colonial morals.[10] Such impressions were, in fact, justified only in relation to certain groups of colonists—convicts who had been 'sent to the plantations', smugglers and pirates, cruel slave-drivers, reckless traders, and pioneers of the westward movement who had alienated the native Indians. Actual experience or mere report of these elements was, however, bound to reduce the respectability of colonial society as a whole in the eyes of the many Englishmen who were convinced of their own higher cultural standards. . . .

· · ·

The name of the British Empire was invoked in 1757 . . . by a critic whose strictures also became superseded by the events of the war. Malachi Postlethwayt, the assiduous collector of information and advice for the use of merchants and regulators of mercantile affairs, took stock of 'Britain's Commercial Interests'. While the French in his opinion still held the military ascendancy, he enlarged on suggestions for getting the better of them in commercial rivalry. He hoped first to make Ireland a contributing factor to British productivity. For the American colonies he urged administrative reforms that would help them 'recover their strength and stability, and become a match for our enemies'. Both suggestions implied far-reaching constitutional innovations. His schemes were quite properly summed up as making 'the whole British Empire' 'a complete union'.[11] Postlethwayt was one of the first to elevate the term to the status of a political idea. Nevertheless, his projects of union cannot bear comparison with those of the men of America—Benjamin Franklin, Governor Bernard, and James Otis. He hoped to restore 'the security, the prosperity and the glory of the British Empire' by high-handed administrative measures, none of them built upon a real knowledge of the

---

[10]As is well known, most people wishing to emigrate to the colonies were supposed to be 'a burden to the public' at home, not only by Charles Davenant, who thought them potential criminals, but also still by Joshua Gee, who classed them among 'the poor'. Cf. K. E. Knorr, *British Colonial Theories* (Toronto, 1944), pp. 75 f.

[11]*Britain's Commercial Interest Explained and Improved* (London, 1757), 2nd ed., unchanged (1759), under the title *Great Britain's Commercial Interest*. . . . The following quotations especially refer to 'Dissertations' II, XI, XII, XV, XVI, XVII (vol. 1, pp. 56, 273, 277 f., 287, 289, 328, 420 f., 427 f., 432, 437–440, 461–471).

societies which he wished to unite. He started from the mercantilist obsession that Scotland, Ireland, and the colonies 'do all,
more or less, interfere with England in her native produce and
in some of her staple manufactures, and these distinct parts of
the British Empire do also greatly interfere in their produce and
fabrics with each other'. In the course of his writing, the wish to
'undersell' France won the upper hand over the guiding principle,
which was to 'restrain' Ireland. He thought that this aim might
be achieved if agriculture in Ireland were improved by British
landowners, and if manufactures, especially woollens, were encouraged there by the permission of exports. Both measures
together would make the joint produce of the two kingdoms in-
vincibly cheap on foreign markets. 'An universal spirit of industry
and ingenuity will spread itself through the whole British Empire
and rouse and animate our traders of every rank to vie with and
excel those of the whole world.' The Irish, viewing their improved
position, would gratify the English 'seat of empire' by paying
half their commercial gains into the British exchequer and by
allowing their island to become 'an English Protestant country
like Wales and Scotland'.

As for the North American colonies, the watchwords 'union'
and 'empire' had a different meaning. They did not refer to an
equalization of commercial rights but to an enforcement of strict
discipline. 'The system of Government in America must be regulated by the mother-government system.' The present state of the
colonies showed the reverse of that principle; the author saw
them as 'members lopped from the body politic'. Some of them—
all those which were proprietary or had elected councils or even
elected governors—were constitutionally encouraged in disobedience. In all of them, metropolitan control of provincial legislation
was nullified by the delay in getting reports to London and instructions from it. Governors were guilty of negligence and arbi-
trariness. The colonists had proved 'lukewarm . . . to their own
safety and welfare', and allowed the people of England to be
'encumbered with taxes' on their behalf. They tended 'to hang
forever on the breast of their mother-country'. At the same time
they had been permitted to occupy more land than they could
cultivate, and this impaired the security of their frontiers, whose
fortification they had also neglected. Their greatest sin against
their own safety and British interests generally was that they
had forfeited 'the steady alliance and friendship of the Indian
nations'. They had 'defrauded them by dishonest ways and
measures' and had estranged their better elements by the abomi-

nable practice of 'intoxicating their people with our spirituous liquors . . . the better to deceive them'.

These instances of laxness on the part of the British authorities and of immorality on the part of the colonists were, in Postlethwayt's opinion, responsible for the war and its unlucky course. The French had proved thoughtful and efficient in every respect in which the British had proved wanting. They controlled immigration, 'not permitting any person to take up more land than he shall actually plant and manure within a limited time'. They 'pique themselves on treating the Indians with the strictest regard to truth, integrity, and honour' and 'they treat them with small wines, to preserve their sobriety'. Moreover, they had encircled the disunited British colonies with a unified framework of co-ordinated administration extending from Canada to Louisiana. In their principle of centralised organization, Postlethwayt saw the remedy for all the British deficiencies. 'Let all the colonies . . . be united under a legal, regular and firm establishment, settled and determined by the wisdom of a British legislature . . . after which, why should not a lord lieutenant-general be constituted and appointed, by the crown of England, as supreme governor over these colonies, to act in subordination to the voice of a British parliament?' The governor might be assisted by 'a great council, or general convention of the estates of the colonies', to which each province could annually elect two deputies. In America it meant 'to determine upon such a union in government and constitution of every part of its dominions as may tend to strengthen the whole British Empire'. Such measures 'will in all probability revive the present sinking state of the British Empire'.

There is a faint analogy with the criticisms and demands and suggestions of reform which had been discussed in Albany three years earlier. While that conference discussed concerted organization on the Indian frontier only, Postlethwayt wanted to see established an overruling authority capable in the last resort of executing policies laid down in Westminster. Like his project for Ireland, this was a hazily conceived idea, for whose transformation into administrative reality the author himself would make no suggestion. The circumstances in which it might have appeared practicable to the British authorities and acceptable to the colonies can scarcely be imagined. No moment could have been less auspicious for the scheme than 1759, the year of the re-issue of the book. Pitt's strategy had triumphed; Quebec was taken. The assertion that the British colonial system could not stand up to the French had been refuted. Nobody could believe that the British Empire in America had too many inhabitants. A constitutional project which was so manifestly at variance with colonial self-righteousness and self-reliance was forthwith put out of court. Nevertheless, in its critical passages Postlethwayt's argument contained an element which was later to be given fatal emphasis on the British side. It made colonial society appear to be in need of lessons in disciplinary conduct—not, as the poet Dyer wished to present it, a British offspring of moral promise. The experiences accumulated in North America during the last years of the war and shortly after: haggling about requisitions, smuggling, trading with the enemy, continued maltreatment of Indians which finally provoked them to revolt, all added to the distrust to which the author of *Britain's Commercial Interest* had given vent. British resentment at 'ingratitude' on the one hand, and the buoyant self-confidence which the colonists derived from the conquest of Canada on the other—these were the conflicting ways in which constitutional interpretations of the British Empire revived and found wide acceptance, when those attempted by Malachi Postlethwayt were forgotten.

. . .

At the time when Britain drifted into the war which was to be decisive for its empire overseas, there was one man only for whom the name of empire evoked a vision of new social realities which demanded political wisdom. He was Benjamin Franklin, printer, popular moralist, and amateur scientist of Philadelphia. In his *Observations*, written in 1751 and published in 1753, he tried to create a literary public which would give thought to questions concerning the increase of mankind, the policies of trade, and the distribution of races on the earth. Only in passing did he refer to the political difficulty which interfered with the fulfilment of his dreams: 'How important an affair then to Britain is the present treaty [of Aix-la-Chapelle, 1749] for settling the bounds between the Colonies and the French . . . since on the room depends so much the increase of her people.' He was well aware of the weakness of the frontier beyond the Alleghanies and, like the British governors, understood that only the voluntary co-operation of the colonies concerned could offer a remedy. In 1754 he had the opportunity of making constructive suggestions in this respect. He submitted a plan of concerted action in matters of defence and Indian affairs to the conference of governors and colonial representatives held at Albany, on instructions from

London. His suggestions were welcomed by the participants, but were held to be unacceptable commitments by London, as well as by the colonial assemblies. The idea which matured in Franklin's mind on that occasion was that the home country and the colonies should enter upon far-reaching mutual commitments. His vision of the British Empire transformed itself into a scheme of constitutional reform. We do not know whether he spoke of the Empire at Albany. But his mind was fixed upon that idea when late in the same year Governor Shirley of Massachusetts sought his advice as to the conclusions to be drawn from the failure of the conference. As the military initiative had now clearly become the exclusive responsibility of the British government, Shirley was anxious to make sure that expenses would be repaid by the colonies. He made two suggestions; that the colonies should be taxed by the British central authorities, and that they should have representation in Parliament, in order that taxation should be more tolerable. Franklin sharply deprecated the first suggestion and was very sympathetic to the second. On both points the concept of the British Empire proved essential for his argument.

One cannot but admire the style of his answers. They are calculated to impress the governor by detached objectivity as much as by warm professions of enthusiasm for the common English cause of the Empire. These professions originate in Franklin's sincere feeling; but he suggests that they are also in the hearts of his countrymen. Franklin knows his twofold role—to show himself as a man of enlightened views and at the same time to impersonate the average American. The questions of levying taxes by Act of Parliament was, he told Shirley, to be examined according to what the people 'will be apt to think', apart from 'what they ought to think'. Therefore it mattered 'that it is suppos'd an undoubted right of Englishmen not to be taxed but by their own consent given thro' their representatives'. It was also important to remember that, owing to the regulation of colonial trade, 'our whole centres finally amongst the merchants of Britain.' 'To pay immediate heavy taxes'—in addition to these objectionable 'secondary taxes'—must 'seem hard measure to Englishmen, who cannot conceive, that by hazarding their lives and fortunes in subduing and settling new countries, extending the Dominion, and increasing the commerce of their mother nation, they have forfeited the native rights of Britons. . . .' Significantly it is in connection with this warning that Franklin introduces his favourite topic. The American 'Englishman', he maintains, would tell those of Great Britain 'that the British Colonies bordering on the French are properly frontiers of the British Empire; and the frontiers of an empire are properly defended at the joint expense of the body of the people in such an empire'.

Shirley's second suggestion, that the colonies be directly represented in Parliament, compelled Franklin to concede that his compatriots too had much to learn concerning their obligations to the Empire. 'Such a union', he ventured to say, 'would be very acceptable to the colonies'; but he thought it one of its probable merits that 'the people of Great Britain, and the people of the colonies, would learn to consider themselves, as not belonging to a different community with different interests, but to one community with one interest'. By adding that this outcome would 'greatly lessen the danger of future separations' he allowed his mind to dwell on such awkward contingencies as had sometimes haunted legislators at Westminster, since the Staple Act of 1663.[12] But in contrast with their belief in mercantile restrictions he proposed the daring experiment of putting 'all the old Acts of Parliament restraining the trade or cramping the manufactures of the colonies', together with the new union, to the test of popular consent on the part of the colonies. All these Acts were to be repealed, and 'the new Parliament representing the whole' was to be free to decide whether it was in 'the interest of the whole to re-enact some or all of them'. Combining all these suggestions, he gave his personal opinion:

> Now I look on the Colonies as so many countries gained by Great Britain, . . . and being separated by the ocean, they increase much more its shipping and seamen; and since they are all included in the British Empire, which has only extended itself by their means, . . . what imports it to the general state, whether a merchant, a smith, or a hatter, grow rich in *Old* or *New* England? . . . And if there be any difference, those who have most contributed to enlarge Britain's empire and commerce . . . ought rather to expect some preference.[13]

Again, 'shipping and seamen—empire and commerce'. To Benjamin Franklin the 'British Empire' retained its 'maritime' con-

---

[12]'Firmer dependence' of the plantations upon the kingdom of England was mentioned in the Staple Act (15 Ch. II, c. 7) as one of its intended effects.

[13]*Writings*, Smyth, ed., III, pp. 231–241. Cf. Verner W. Crane, *Benjamin Franklin, Englishman and American* (Baltimore, 1936), pp. 82–85, and *Benjamin Franklin's Letters to the Press, 1758–1775* (Chapel Hill, N.C., 1950), Doc. 32, p. 65.

notation even while he concentrated on its continental future in
America.

. . .

In his *Observations* of 1751, which as often as possible he had
reprinted, he tried to communicate his vision of the new English
world in America which, in foreseeable time, was bound to out-
grow that of the maternal island. This vision was to him almost
identical with a constitutional postulate. In the last resort it was
America, and the America of the future more than that of the
present, which would bring the British Empire into being. The
name of the British Empire stood for that vision. Though grounded
in the English tradition and nationality to which he emphatically
paid allegiance, the British Empire which he wanted to see
respected was an American creation. Englishmen were in duty
bound to prepare for its coming by a reasonable attitude to
current reality. . . .

Democracy and the American Revolution:
A Frame of Reference

RICHARD BUEL, Jr.

American historians have never been famous for agreement,
but in one respect they seem curiously united. All have tried to
measure the significance of the Revolution in relation to the
development of American democracy. However, beyond the limits
of this initial premise their unity dissolves into a rich multiplicity
of interpretations. Such a state of affairs is not necessarily to be
lamented, for the diversity of opinions has helped to illuminate
the complexity of our Revolutionary experience.

There is a point, though, where multiplicity ceases to enlighten
and instead merely creates confusion. We are approaching, though
we may not yet have reached, that point on the question of

Reprinted from *The William and Mary Quarterly*, 3rd ser., XXI, 2 (April,
1964), 165–190. Copyright © 1964 by Richard Buel, Jr. Reprinted with
permission.

whether or not the Revolution was a democratic movement. While it is impossible, and even undesirable, to have complete agreement on the substance of interpretations, to be still debating such a fundamental question indicates a critical weakness in our knowledge. The crux of our confusion lies more in the realm of intellectual history than in institutional history. After almost a century and a half of historical speculation, we are still not agreed on the democratic nature of Revolutionary ideas, let alone on precisely what "democratic" changes took place in American thinking between 1760 and 1789.

The problem transcends simple divergencies in individual points of view and relates more fundamentally to the methods employed. Our confusion in the realm of ideas stems largely from the reluctance of historians to define a point of departure in historical context. Because we have failed to clarify the manner in which mid-eighteenth-century Americans viewed the people's role in the polity, it has been difficult to interpret the significance of institutional and intellectual changes throughout the Revolutionary period.

The institution of representation serves as a useful illustration both because it was subject to rigorous scrutiny during the Revolution and because it has been traditionally associated with democracy. The colonists themselves referred to their representative assemblies as the democratic branch of their constitutions. But were they using the word "democratic" in the same context we use it today? Though modern representative institutions are popularly regarded as the principal mechanism through which the people express their will in politics, this does not mean they were viewed in the same light by the Revolutionary generation almost two centuries ago. If, in fact, representation was conceived to perform quite a different function, then the meaning of such institutional developments as the extension or contraction of the franchise may have to be reassessed.

What we need, then, is an imaginative reconstruction of the values and assumptions as well as the explicit ideas of colonial political thought immediately prior to the Revolution. Generally American historians have dismissed such an enterprise as impractical. They have assumed that American political ideas were unformed or ambiguous at the beginning of the imperial crisis and that colonial thought remained inchoate until the eve of independence. Confirmation for this view has been sought in the instability of the colonists' ideas about the jurisdiction of Parliament throughout the first decade of crisis. The assumption that American thought started from no fixed point and achieved no uniform expression until independence has made it difficult to define with precision the meaning of its development throughout the Revolutionary era.

It is possible, however, that American historians have unduly despaired of defining a point of departure from which to assess the meaning of the Revolutionary experience. Though colonial leaders differed in their initial definitions of Parliament's power, in a more fundamental sense they were in basic agreement. Their agreement sprang from their common experience within the British imperial system which, despite the diffuse heterogeneity of the thirteen colonies, had by 1760 given birth to a surprisingly homogeneous leadership on the provincial scene. During the bitter factional disputes that had infected all the colonial polities throughout the eighteenth century, local political magnates devoid of transatlantic connections had acquired an elaborate conceptual arsenal from the dissenting tradition in English thought[1] with which they sought to protect themselves from the superior power of their adversaries.

Provincial leaders had been attracted to dissenting thought by a combination of circumstances. For one thing a vast majority of them shared a religious affinity with the British dissenters. But of greater importance was the ability of this tradition to interpret unique aspects of the American experience. If the seething factionalism of provincial politics left many colonists disenchanted with the exercise of political power in general, dissenting thought was characterized by a profound distrust of all power, no matter by whom possessed. Most important of all, however, was the fact that these colonists occupied an analogous position to the dissenters in relation to the sovereign power. Because dissenting thought had been developed throughout the seventeenth and eighteenth centuries by men who were excluded from the centers of influence within the state, it had sought to enlist the resources of a virtuous people against the potential aggressions of a hostile

---

[1] By the "dissenting tradition in English thought," I do not mean to refer only to the ideas of English thinkers who were nonconformists, but also to the work of such men as John Trenchard, Thomas Gordon, and Benjamin Hoadly, all of whom were members of the Church of England and whose ideas, for reasons explained below, proved to be especially congenial to the English dissenters. I call it the "dissenting tradition" only because the nonconformists gradually became the exclusive custodians of this strand of thinking in Britain after 1745. For a complete description of the participants in the dissenting tradition, see Caroline Robbins, *The Eighteenth-Century Commonwealthman* . . . (Cambridge, Mass., 1959), *passim*.

sovereign. This, of course, was precisely the same situation local colonial politicians found themselves in during the mid-eighteenth century. In many cases they too possessed no other available resource with which to defend their local autonomy than the united support of the provincial populace.

It was also the situation which confronted all Americans simultaneously when the ministry undertook to reorganize the empire in 1763. Ironically the colonists's initial reaction to parliamentary taxation was not to think radically new thoughts but to apply the familiar political ideas of the English dissenting tradition to an unprecedented situation. If there was any change in the structure of basic concepts, it was one of crystalization and clarification rather than innovation as these ideas were diffused to a wider circle. Many who had been familiar with dissenting notions but had not been accustomed to rely on them were now forced to appropriate them by the common jeopardy in which American rights had been placed. At least in the substratum of fundamental premises, if not in their precise application, the impact of crisis produced uniformity rather than confusion, a uniformity which was only to dissolve under the grueling strain of long years of controversy. Even after independence the ideas and assumptions that were characteristic of dissenting thought continued to dominate the minds of many individuals and were an important influence in the creation of our nation's unique political institutions.

As we have indicated, the dissenting tradition was forced to rely heavily upon the power of the populace. But how was its power to be applied? This paper will explore the colonists' ideas about the contract theory of government, the right of revolution, and representation. These ideas were part of a systematic theory about the role of the people in the polity which lay at the heart of the colonists' initial confrontation with parliamentary taxation.[2] By explicating this theory we can define an initial frame of reference from which the "democratic" significance of subsequent events can be more readily assessed.[3]

---

[2] One facet of the people's power will be omitted from consideration, however, because it was not subject to major revision during or after the Revolution and because it is not germane to the interpretive question of whether or not the American Revolution was a democratic movement. This is the power of the people to participate in the execution of the law through juries.

[3] As the New England clergy were instrumental in disseminating dissenting thought to wide sectors of the population in the northern colonies, much reliance has been placed on their political sermons. Political pamphlets bearing directly on the imperial crisis have been the other major source used. Whenever possible an attempt has been made to refer the reader to relevant English sources from which the colonists derived their ideas.

I

Like all eighteenth-century English thinkers the provincial leadership sought to control power by limiting and dividing it. What was novel in their solutions was not the principle behind their techniques, but the scope with which they were applied. Rather than confine the balance of the constitution to the autonomous composition of the supreme power, to the parliamentary components of King, Lords, and Commons, Americans turned to a conception of balance between two broad, countervailing forces in political society, the rulers and the ruled.[4] In their elaboration of the relationship between rulers and ruled they defined arrangements whereby society might benefit from the exercise of power without suffering from its corresponding abuses.

By enlarging the constitutional balance to embrace not only the rulers but also the ruled, Americans indicated that the real lines of conflict to be anticipated within the polity were not between the constituent parts of the supreme power but between magistrates and people.[5] In doing so they challenged the idea that in a conflict of interests between rulers and ruled the subject should passively acquiesce in the determinations of the magistrate. Though they lamented the existence of such a conflict, they were nonetheless willing to accord the subject's interests a legitimacy which the interests of power did not necessarily possess. Their willingness to reverse the dominant presumptions of eighteenth-century English thought did not proceed from a belief that the people were incapable of mischief. Rather, it proceeded from a theoretical recognition that the ruler's peculiar position made his power even more liable to abuse than was that of the subject.

---

[4] "Dissertation on the Canon and the Feudal Law," in Charles Francis Adams, ed., *The Works of John Adams* . . . (Boston, 1851), III, 542 ff.; Andrew Eliot, *A Sermon Preached Before His Excellency Francis Bernard . . . May 29th 1765* . . . (Boston, 1765), 8; Ebenezer Bridge, *A Sermon Preached Before His Excellency Francis Bernard . . . May 27th 1767* . . . (Boston, 1767), 17, 51; John Tucker, *A Sermon Preached at Cambridge, Before His Excellency Thomas Hutchinson . . . May 29th 1771* . . . (Boston, 1771), 12, 13; Dan Foster, *A Short Essay on Civil Government* . . . (Hartford, 1775), 5; Peter Whitney, *The Transgression of a Land Punished by a Multitude of Rulers* . . . (Boston, 1774), 10; John Trenchard and Thomas Gordon, *Cato's Letters*, 6th ed. (London, 1754), I, 184, hereafter referred to as *Cato's Letters*, all references to volumes I, III, and IV coming from the 6th ed., and all references to volume II coming from the 5th ed. (London, 1748).

[5] By "magistrate" I refer to any civil officer, either legislative or executive, to whom presumptive obedience was due.

By virtue of his office a ruler possessed presumptive control over society's combined resources while the subject's power was confined entirely to his own person, or at most, to the resources of those whose immediate co-operation he could secure. In a predominantly agrarian community where groups of individuals tended to live in isolation from one another, uninformed of each other's needs and opinions, it was difficult enough to get all the people to unite in one common course of action after extensive persuasion and virtually impossible to have them all unite spontaneously. The magistrates, on the other hand, were a compact and potentially disciplined group which constituted a formidable force against a flock of helpless and disunited subjects.[6]

Furthermore, the possession of power exposed the ruler to temptations to which the subject, by virtue of his impotence, was immune. Because of the difficulties obstructing the people's concerted action, history had demonstrated that the populace were usually quiescent under good government and loath to stir even when oppressed with substantial injustices. While the magistrates in full possession of the powers of the state might not only find it within the range of their capabilities but also to their *immediate* interest to erect a tyranny, that is to enhance their own welfare at the expense of the subjects', the people in their naturally unconnected state could rationally desire nothing else but the public welfare in which their own personal welfare would be maximized. Thus the people were not under such temptations to thwart their own interests as powerful rulers were to abuse those of the people. It was precisely because those in power were more likely to pursue interests distinct from the common interest than were those without power that the subject was entitled to some means of influencing the magistrate's actions as security against oppression.[7]

---

[6]See William Livingston and others, *The Independent Reflector*, Milton M. Klein, ed. (Cambridge, Mass., 1963), 188–189.

[7]Samuel Adams to Arthur Lee, April 19, 1771, in Harry Alonzo Cushing, ed., *The Writings of Samuel Adams* (New York, 1904–1908), II, 164; "Novanglus; or, a History of the Dispute with America, from its origin, in 1754, to the present time," in C. F. Adams, ed., *Works*, IV, 14, 17, 83; Charles Turner, *A Sermon Preached Before His Excellency Thomas Hutchinson . . . May 26th 1773 . . .* (Boston, 1773), 17; John Wingate Thornton, *The Pulpit of the American Revolution . . .* (Boston, 1860), 167; *The Farmer's Letters to the Inhabitants of the British Colonies* (Philadelphia, 1767), in *The Political Writings of John Dickinson . . .* (Wilmington, 1801), I, 260–261, 261 *n*; Izrahiah Wetmore, *A Sermon Preached Before the Honorable General Assembly of the Colony of Connecticut . . . May 13th, 1773* (New London, 1773), 24; Peter Laslett, ed., *John Locke: Two Treatises of Government* (Cambridge, Eng., 1960), 428, 432; *Cato's Letters*, I, 80, 178, 250; II, 21–22,

However, in constructing a broad balance between rulers and ruled, all eighteenth-century thinkers had to face the problem of how this balance could be rendered stable. The difficulty of the task was compounded by the apparent absence of a mediating third force, such as the House of Lords in the parliamentary balance, and by the potentially unstable nature of the people's power. If you were willing to give the subject sufficient power to maintain the legitimacy of his interests against the encroachments of the magistrates, how could you in turn render the subject's power incapable of abuse?

Superficially it looked as though this problem could be bypassed. A balance between the rights of the subject and the prerogatives of the magistrate might be stabilized by an agreed on jurisdictional definition of the magistrate's power. Once it was acknowledged that rulers were more likely to violate the common interest than were subjects, was it not reasonable to endow the people with a right to frame a constitution "as the standing measure of the proceedings of government" for their own protection and to solicit their ruler's consent to it?[8] Even if there was no express compact, "yet it has been necessarily implied, and understood, both by governors, and the governed, on their entering into society."[9] In these covenants both rulers and ruled could mark out the fundamental law by which the rights of each would be guaranteed against infringement by the other.[10] If the magistrates transcended the formal boundaries of power delegated to them, then and only then did the people have a right to withdraw their obedience and ultimately to form new governments.[11]

However, Americans took pains to emphasize that slight infringements of the compact would not justify a rebellion. Only when the ruler trampled wholesale upon the rights of the subject and violated the welfare of society was resistance justified, and

---

224; III, 237, 267, 284; J. L. de Lolme, *The Constitution of England* . . . , New ed. (London, 1777), 212; James Burgh, *Political Disquisitions* . . . (London, 1774–1775), I, 272; III, 310, 311, 339, 379, 415.

[8]Eliot, *A Sermon*, 18; Daniel Shute, *A Sermon Preached Before His Excellency Francis Bernard . . . May 25th 1768* . . . (Boston, 1768), 23; Thornton, *Pulpit of the American Revolution*, 159; Tucker, *A Sermon*, 14; quotation in Turner, *A Sermon*, 16; Alexander Hamilton, *The Farmer Refuted* . . . (New York, 1775), 6; Alice M. Baldwin, *The New England Clergy and the American Revolution* (Durham, N.C., 1928), 114.

[9]Gad Hitchcock, *A Sermon Preached Before His Excellency Thomas Gage . . . May 25th, 1774* . . . (Boston, 1774), 7; Whitney, *Transgression*, 10.

[10]Eliot, *A Sermon*, 19 ff.; Tucker, *A Sermon*, 14; Bridge, *A Sermon*, 17.

[11]Jason Haven, *A Sermon Preached Before His Excellency Sir Francis Bernard . . . May 31st 1769* . . . (Boston, 1769), 34, 40; Shute, *A Sermon*, 46–58; Foster, *Short essay*, 5, 55 ff.; Whitney, *Transgression*, 19.

then only insofar as it was necessary to preserve the rights of the people and their welfare from destruction.[12] Until such an emergency occurred the people were morally bound to obey the magistrate's commands as well as it being their interest to do so.[13] Hopefully the existence of such a fundamental law and the ultimate threat of revolution would preclude all emergencies and enable the people to confine their role to obeying their superior's lawful commands.

But the compact theory of government enforced by the sanctions of possible revolution did not provide the subject with practical guarantees against aggression by the magistrates. In the first place, as was often pointed out, the magistrate's office could not be adequately defined by explicit reference to fundamental laws. The extent of the magistrate's power was determined by the ends which his office was designed to realize. He had plenary power for the good of society, but when he used power to society's detriment he was exceeding his lawful commission. What constituted the "good of the society" could not be completely anticipated in a fixed law, but depended upon the changing circumstances in which a society was placed. The plea which was made during the imperial crisis by some of the New England clergy for a clarification of the fundamental law so that neither party could misconstrue it merely indicated the difficulties with which this means of resolving political conflict was beset.[14]

Even had the magistrate's powers been capable of full and complete definition, the basic problem would still have remained of rendering such jurisdictional definitions of equilibrium real, in other words of making these arrangements self-enforcing. Both magistrates and subjects had an interest in guarding their rights against each other's encroachments. But under the compact theory

---

[12]Jonathan Mayhew, *A Discourse Concerning Unlimited Submission and Non-resistance to the Higher Powers* . . . (Boston, 1750), 38 *n*; Eliot, *A Sermon*, 43; Haven, *A Sermon*, 40; *An Essay Upon Government, Adopted by the Americans* . . . (Philadelphia, 1775), 12–14; 68–72, 95; Laslett, ed., *Locke: Two Treatises*, 421.

[13]Eliot, *A Sermon*, 41–43; Stephen White, *Civil Rulers Gods by Office* . . . (New London, 1763), 22; Edward Barnard, *A Sermon Preached Before His Excellency Francis Bernard . . . May 28th. 1766* . . . (Boston, 1766), 38; Haven, *A Sermon*, 37–39; Whitney, *Transgression*, 15, 27; Turner, *A Sermon*, 32–33; Tucker, *A Sermon*, 18–19, 29; James Cogswell, *A Sermon Preached Before the General Assembly, of the Colony of Connecticut . . . May 9, 1771* (New London, 1771), 21; Foster, *Short essay*, 37; Samuel Lockwood, *Civil Rulers an Ordinance of God, for the Good to Mankind* . . . (New London, 1774), 38–39.

[14]Eliot, *A Sermon*, 43; White, *Civil Rulers*, 12; Tucker, *A Sermon*, 18; Hitchcock, *A Sermon, May 25th, 1774*, 32–33.

of government, once encroachments were made, the only remedy was violence which, by obstructing the force of government, placed the very existence of the "social fabric" in jeopardy and threatened to dissolve all into one wild tumult of confusion and anarchy.[15]

The difficulties associated with the compact theory of government were compounded by the fact that according to the premises of dissenting thought, amply reinforced by colonial experience, violations were to be anticipated from one's rulers. But if the magistrate violated the compact, the people were left only with the unpalatable alternatives of submission or resistance by force. Though a people might be perfectly justified in their resistance, this right when exercised could as effectually destroy a free society as would the arbitrary sway of a tyrant. If to enforce the covenant you had to be continually breaking it, you would never derive the benefits of it in the first place.[16] The real problem was to prevent these encroachments from occurring. What was needed was some special power lodged in the people, short of revolution, with which they could peacefully restrain the misuse of political power by their superiors.

One such peaceful restraint might be found in selective as opposed to wholesale or violent disobedience. Eighteenth-century thinkers persisted in emphasizing the co-operative nature of human society. If laws were to be duly executed, the magistrate needed the co-operation of the subject. The exercise of political power was not the autonomous function of the ruler's command, but depended equally on the subject's willingness to obey. Against the possibility of the magistrate issuing oppressive commands the subject always had the choice of yielding or withholding obedience. New England election sermons continually raised the question of when obedience was due and when it was proper to disobey. In telling the people that obedience was a matter of choice and that the subject should not obey the ruler's commands blindly but only in response to his conscience, the New England clergy was advocating a doctrine of selective disobedience

[15]*Farmer's Letters*, in *Political Writings of John Dickinson*, I, 257; Daniel Leonard, *Massachusettensis* (Boston, 1775), 65; for a fuller explication of this point see Richard Buel, Jr., Studies in the Political Ideas of the American Revolution (unpublished Ph.D. dissertation, Harvard University, 1962), 12–13, 16, 34–35.

[16]*Farmer's Letters*, in *Political Writings of John Dickinson*, I, 170; Leonard, *Massachusettensis*, 64; *Essay upon Government*, 73; 77–78, 84; [William Hicks], *The Nature and Extent of Parliamentary Power Considered* . . . (Philadelphia, 1768), 29; John J. Zubly, *The Law of Liberty* . . . (Philadelphia, 1775), 2.

which would not necessarily overturn society. If their rulers persisted in oppressing the people, might not the people withdraw their obedience to such oppressive measures so as to deprive their authors of all benefit from them? And might not this serve as an admonishment to wicked rulers to return to their duty?[17]

Opponents of this school of thought could legitimately object that if obedience to the commands of a political superior was a matter which each member of society could decide for himself, then what security was there that society would not disintegrate in the unrelated disobediences of private men? Such an objection could be leveled equally at admitting the right of revolution, for many felt selective disobedience was the practical consequence of such an admission. Why would not this lead to anarchy?[18]

One could reply that conscience was not an entirely arbitrary standard to which to appeal.[19] Men could agree on questions of conscience, particularly when there was an objective standard by which the lawfulness of authority was to be tested which was independent of the subject's will. It was the subject's duty to resist only when the ruler acted contrary to God's law and the constitution. But when the magistrate remained within the bounds of his commission to rule, his authority was fortified by conscience as well as interest, for the subject's temporal and eternal happiness depended upon obedience to all the ruler's lawful commands.[20]

However, the colonists were willing to admit that in our imperfect condition men with sincere intentions could disagree on matters of conscience. Then there was the added consideration that depraved men unmindful of the dictates of conscience lived in society. But Americans pointed out that the power of the magistrate was so great in proportion to that of the populace that only the united opposition of the people could defeat the magistrate's power. In any conflict an isolated subject would make a very poor match for a magistrate armed with the power of

---

[17]Shute, A Sermon, 43, 46, 47–48, 62–63, 64; Foster, Short Essay, 38, 39, 40, 69; Eliot, A Sermon, 41–43; Tucker, A Sermon, 37, 39, 60; Gad Hitchcock, A Sermon Preached at Plymouth December 22d, 1774 . . . (Boston, 1775), 27–30; Edward Dorr, The Duty of Civil Rulers, To Be Nursing Fathers to the Church of Christ . . . (Hartford, 1765), 33; Essay upon Government, 41.

[18]Essay upon Government, 12, 13–14; Jonathan Boucher, A View of the Causes and Consequences of the American Revolution . . . (London, 1797), 515.

[19]Dorr, Duty of Civil Rulers, 19.

[20]Eliot, A Sermon, 41–43, 45; Barnard, A Sermon, 38; Shute, A Sermon, 46–48; Turner, A Sermon, 28–29; Tucker, A Sermon, 36–37; Hitchcock, A Sermon, May 25th, 1774, 12–13, 27; Whitney, Transgression, 17–18.

the state. To counter the weight of the magistrates' power, subjects had to act in concert, which in itself constituted a substantial check on the people's ability to express their will in politics. When contemporary literature referred to the people as a "rope of sand," the image reflected the obstacles obstructing their effective group action and the tendency of their potential power to dissolve in disunity. The unrelated disobediences of depraved men or the sincere mistakes of a few misguided souls could not disturb the stability of society or the magistrate's power because their opposition, lacking a unifying principle, would not enable them to act in a concerted fashion. Only ordered resistance could successfully challenge the magistrates' power and this could spring only from a general agreement among the individual consciences of the people that the ruler had transcended the legitimate bounds of his authority.[21]

The trouble with the idea of selective disobedience was that it assumed the ruler could not wield the instruments of coercion without the cooperation of the subject. While it was true that the ruler's power to contribute to the public good did depend on the subject's co-operation, and while the notion of selective disobedience might have some remedial effect so far as the operation of oppressive laws was concerned, it could not affect the manner in which the ruler wielded other instruments of power at his disposal such as command of the army or control over the administration of justice. True, the subject might push disobedience to the point where the sinews of government had virtually dissolved in order to destroy some of the advantages the ruler hoped to reap from his oppression, yet when he did so selective disobedience became in effect the right of revolution, and the people were infinitely more vulnerable in a state of anarchy than were their rulers. The fact that by partial resistance the subject could diminish the benefits the ruler sought in oppression provided no guarantee that the ruler would return to a respect for the common interest. The only real sanction which the people possessed in the compact theory of government was the right of revolution for this alone could halt the march of a determined tyrant.

[21]Eliot, A Sermon, 47; Hitchcock, A Sermon, May 25th, 1774, 24; Amos Adams, Religious Liberty an Invaluable Blessing . . . (Boston, 1768), 49; Cato's Letters, I, xxiii, 80, 180, 250; II, 224–225; III, 70, 267, 284, 294; IV, 132; An Historical Essay on the English Constitution . . . (London, 1771), 151; Burgh, Political Disquisitions, I, 272; III, 310–311, 429; Laslett, ed., Locke: Two Treatises, 422; Benjamin Hoadly, The Original and Institution of Civil Government, Discuss'd (London, 1710), 249 (numbered 49), 326 (numbered 126).

While colonial thinkers of the mid-eighteenth century were perfectly aware of the limitations and abuses to which the right of revolution might be put, they continued to affirm it, both as a last resort and because power exercised without the threat of this right was liable to even greater abuse. Acknowledgement of the right of resistance protected rulers as well as subjects because it helped to prevent the evil of the magistrate's encroachments in the first place, and thus ultimately protected rulers from the wrath of the populace.[22] But it provided no guarantee, and as a remedy was likely to prove worse than the disease.[23] For the practical maintenance of a stable constitutional balance between rulers and ruled the people needed subtler and more discriminating means of persuading their superiors to respect their rights. What more acceptable techniques could be devised for protecting the subject from the overwhelming power of the magistrates which were not equally liable to abuse?[24]

II

The contract theory of government was plagued by two essential weaknesses. The first related to the inflexible and unprecise nature of the fundamental law; the second to the procedure of enforcement. Both could be obviated through the institution of representation.

Despite its recognized limitations, eighteenth-century Americans continued to regard the law as an essential device in demarcating the boundary between the rights of the subject and the prerogatives of the magistrate: If power were confined within the channels the law had marked out for its circulation, the subject— provided his behavior conformed to certain pre-established standards—would have security that the power of the magistrate would not affect him.[25] The security that the law might afford in turn

---

[22]Hitchcock, A Sermon, May 25th, 1774, 23, 25; Turner, A Sermon, 28–29; "Novanglus," in C. F. Adams, ed., Works, IV, 83–84; Laslett, ed., Locke: Two Treatises, 433; Cato's Letters, II, 69; Hoadly, Original and Institution of Civil Government, 284 (numbered 84), 326 (numbered 126), 356 (numbered 156).

[23]Farmer's Letters, in Political Writings of John Dickinson, I, 170; Zubly, Law of Liberty, 32; Essay upon Government, 73, 77–78, 84.

[24][Hicks], The Nature and Extent of Parliamentary Power, 29; Essay upon Government, 12–14; see also, Burgh, Political Disquisitions, I, 6–7, 114; de Lolme, The Constitution of England, 33; Cato's Letters, III, 164.

[25]Laslett, ed., Locke: Two Treatises, 371, 376–377, 378; Cato's Letters, II, 254, 259; III, 45.

depended on the character of the laws which were made. The more supple the law was in confronting new situations, the more agile it was in nipping tyranny in the bud, the more effective a barrier it would provide against the potential encroachments of power.

But the possibility still existed that no matter how good the laws were the magistrates would nonetheless overstep them. Against this contingency the colonists invoked a sanction short of revolution which was at the same time calm, gentle, and forceful. This was the power of the purse. Errant rulers could be starved into compliance with the law by the withholding of supplies.[26]

If the people were to be secure from oppression, it seemed necessary that they have a role in the making of laws and levying of taxes. Their role could be either active or passive. They could actively enter into the formation of statutes by framing and enacting them, or they could passively give their consent to what the magistrates proposed. However, both alternatives were open to objection. If the people had the power merely to accept or reject what questions were proposed to them, history demonstrated that in their naturally disconnected state they would prove an easy prey for ambitious rulers, who could divide, deceive, and trick them with impunity into assenting to whatever the magistrate desired. But on the other hand allowing subjects an active voice in policy was liable to all the objections which had been raised about their potential instability and incompetence.[27]

Many observers in the eighteenth century felt that the British constitution had resolved this dilemma through the institution of representation.[28] Similarly, contemporary colonial thinkers

---

[26]James Wilson, *Considerations on the Nature and the Extent of the Legislative Authority of the British Parliament* (Philadelphia, 1774), 13–14; *Farmer's Letters,* in *Political Writings of John Dickinson,* I, 224–226, 234; "To the Inhabitants of Great Britain, Sept. 1774," in Griffith J. McRee, *Life and Correspondence of James Iredell . . .* (New York, 1857–1858), I, 208; Alden Bradford, ed., *Speeches of the Governors of Massachusetts, from 1765 to 1775 . . .* (Boston, 1818), 327; John Dickinson and Arthur Lee, *The Farmer's and Monitor's Letters to the Inhabitants of the British Colonies . . .* (Williamsburg, 1769), 85; *An Historical Essay,* 84–85.

[27]Barnard, *A Sermon,* 13; *Farmer's Letters,* in *Political Writings of John Dickinson,* I, 257; Boucher, *A View,* 100, 313, 379, 391, 393; Sir William Blackstone, *Commentaries on the Laws of England* (Philadelphia, 1771–1772), I, 159; de Lolme, *The Constitution of England,* 54–55, 204–206.

[28]"The Earl of Clarendon to William Pym," in C. F. Adams, ed., *Works,* III, 480–481; James Otis, *The Rights of the British Colonies Asserted and Proved . . .* (Boston, 1764), 13; Hamilton, *The Farmer Refuted,* 10; *Essay upon Government,* 19; *Cato's Letters,* II, 232; Burgh, *Political Disquisitions,* I, 5.

hoped, by providing that the power of the people should be exercised by their representatives, to obviate various objections which were raised against the people's active participation in politics while at the same time providing the people with adequate protection against oppression from their rulers.

The concept of representation specifies the existence of a certain relationship between the representative and the represented. This relationship is one of consensus or agreement.[29] In the modern democratic context we are apt to think of this consensus in a way which was not necessarily congenial to the dominant values of eighteenth-century political science. Democracy means rule by the will of the people, and within a framework of democratic assumptions the representative must place himself in agreement with at least a majority of his constituents if he is to remain a representative. Theoretically, in a democracy agreement is the result of the representative adjusting himself to his constituent's views rather than the constituent adjusting himself to his representative's views.[30]

Such democratic notions had shortcomings from the eighteenth-century point of view. Aside from the practical difficulties the people would confront in making decisions upon all the contingencies of government without access to information and without the leisure to devote their best energies to the problems at hand, theoretically to make the representative nothing more than the obedient lackey of his constituents was the height of folly because it threatened to deprive society of the benefit of its most talented personnel. In a world of radically unequal political competencies, where the least competent would obviously compose the majority of the population, to surrender the power of political decision to a majority of the people would be to surrender this important trust to those in society least capable of executing it, if not to unprincipled demagogues who might control the mob in their own interests.[31] For eighteenth-century thought, representation

[29]Alfred de Grazia, *Public and Republic: Political Representation in America* (New York, 1951), 4.

[30]Elisha P. Douglass, *Rebels and Democrats: The Struggle for Equal Political Rights and Majority Rule during the American Revolution* (Chapel Hill, N.C., 1955), 51, 185; such a definition reflects popular expectations about the democratic process more than it represents the actual operations of a democracy.

[31]On the dangers to be anticipated from demagogues, see Leonard, *Massachusettensis*, 13 ff.; Eliphalet Williams, *The Ruler's Duty and Honor, in Serving his Generation* . . . (Hartford, 1770), 12–13; Robert Prescott, *A Letter from a Veteran, to the Officers of the Army Encamped at Boston* (New York, 1774), 4; Boucher, *A View*, 221, 228, 313–314, 364, 385, 416, 508, 544; *Cato's Letters*, IV, 247–250.

not only solved the obvious difficulties that prevented a whole people from assembling in one place and rationally conducting a debate,[32] it also was an institution which utilized the political *expertise* of the realm in the people's behalf. The representative was not supposed to be an average man who reflected the defects as well as the virtues of his constituents, but in theory he was supposed to be the best man, the wisest and most virtuous.[33]

Far from being the humble servant of his constituents, eighteenth-century thinkers tended to regard the representative as a quasi-magistrate to whose commands constituents owed presumptive obedience. Though rhetorically representation involved a delegation by the people of their powers to the representatives, once the representatives had made laws for the people, the people were expected to obey the decisions of their "delegates." Right down until the crisis of independence the New England clergy proceeded to preach obedience to one's political superiors, and representatives were as much within the category of "political superiors" as were governors and councilors.[34]

Of course, as we have noted, conditions were attached to obedience, and the clergy continued, as the imperial crisis deepened, to confirm to the people their right to judge when the magistrate's power was exercised in violation of the constitution and the public felicity.[35] But the extent of the people's commission was confined to granting or withholding obedience. When the clergy finally urged the people to withdraw their obedience from the royal government, they were not then told to express their will in politics or to riot in a state of nature, but to obey the commands of the

---

[32]See ante n. 28; Blackstone, *Commentaries*, I, 159.

[33]Eliot, *A Sermon*, 7, 9–12, 16, 39–40; Barnard, *A Sermon*, 7; White, *Civil Rulers*, 23; Tucker, *A Sermon*, 23; Levi Hart, *Liberty Described and Recommended* . . . (Hartford, 1775), 12; Benjamin Trumbull, *A Discourse, Delivered at the Anniversary Meeting of the Freemen of the Town of New-Haven, April 12, 1773* (New Haven, 1773), 28; Foster, *Short essay*, 29, 37; "Letter to John Penn, Jan. 1776," in C. F. Adams, ed., *Works*, IV, 205; *An Historical Essay*, 33, 85.

[34]Eliot, *A Sermon*, 7, 41, 58; Mayhew, *Discourse*, 10; White, *Civil Rulers*, 22, 34; Tucker, *A Sermon*, 37; Moses Parsons, *A Sermon Preached at Cambridge, before his Excellency Thomas Hutchinson* . . . *May 27th, 1772* . . . (Boston, 1772), 43; Haven, *A Sermon*, 37–39; Hitchcock, *A Sermon, May 25th, 1774*, 28, 52; Thornton, *Pulpit of the American Revolution*, 276–277; Zubly, *Law of Liberty*, 32; Edward Eells, *Christ, the Foundation of the Salvation of Sinners, and of Civil and Ecclesiastical Government* . . . (Hartford, 1767), 16.

[35]Haven, *A Sermon*, 40–42; Hitchcock, *A Sermon, May 25th, 1774*, 12–13, 21 ff.; Turner, *A Sermon*, 28–29; Whitney, *Transgression*, 17 ff.; Thornton, *Pulpit of the American Revolution*, 284–285.

provincial and continental congresses.[36] John Adams proudly boasted in 1774 that throughout the dispute with the Mother Country the people of Massachusetts had "arranged themselves under their house of representatives and council, with as much order as ever."[37] For the colonial leadership independence was not a democratic movement which dissolved all the ligaments of subordination in colonial society and "liberated" the people. It was much more the orderly transference of allegiance from one set of magistrates to a slightly different set who happened to be called representatives of the people.

If the representative was not the tool of his constituents but the equivalent of a magistrate or political superior, was the consensus which all thinkers anticipated between rulers and ruled, between representative and constituent, to be derived solely from the latter's obedience to the former's commands? Though most colonial thinkers rejected such an extreme position, British proponents of parliamentary power in the colonies were forced to rely on a peculiar notion of virtual representation which implied as much.

Not all British spokesmen rejected the colonists' contention that occording to the constitution no subject might be taxed without his own consent or the consent of his representative. Rather some claimed that the colonists were in fact "represented," or what was more frequently the case, did in fact "consent" to Parliament's acts in exactly the same sense that the nonvoting Briton was virtually represented and consented in Parliament.[38] To this end British pamphleteers attempted to demonstrate that the nonvoting Briton and American occupied identical positions relative to parliamentary power. However, any attempt to convince the colonists that their interests would be considered equally with British interests in Parliament's concern for the common good was foredoomed to failure after the passage of the Stamp Act if not by the

---

[36]John Lathrop, A Discourse Preached December 15th 1774 . . . (Boston, 1774), 18, 20; Whitney, Transgression, 54; Isaac Story, The Love of Our Country Recommended and Enforced . . . (Boston, 1774), 19; Samuel Williams, A Discourse on the Love of Our Country; Delivered on a Day of Thanksgiving, December 15, 1774 (Salem, 1775), 27–28; Turner, A sermon, 44; Zabdiel Adams, The Grounds of Confidence and Success in War, Represented . . . (Boston, 1775), 15–16; see also Burgh, Political Disquisitions, III, 426.

[37]"Novanglus," in C. F. Adams, ed., Works, IV, 68.

[38]Thomas Whately, The regulations Lately Made Concerning the Colonies, and the Taxes Imposed upon Them, Considered (London, 1765), 108, 111; Josiah Tucker, A Letter from a Merchant in London to his Nephew in North America . . . (London, 1766), 19; An Historical Essay, 196.

century of commercial regulation which had preceded it.[39] Therefore, British writers were forced to draw other parallels between the disfranchised in the Mother Country and the colonies in their attempts to prove Americans were in fact virtually represented in Parliament.

Crucial to British logic in this matter was the reception of the Navigation Acts in the colonies. If the colonists could not be taxed by Parliament because they were not represented, neither could they be bound by any parliamentary laws, for the constitution, it was argued, made no distinction between taxation and legislation.[40] On the other hand, since everyone knew the colonists had never disputed the binding force of the Navigation Acts, their reception by the colonists could be taken as presumptive evidence that Americans were represented in Parliament, because "every Argument in support of an Exemption from the Superintendance of the *British* Parliament in the one Case is equally applicable to the others."[41] For the colonists to submit to the Navigation Acts when they nonetheless considered themselves unrepresented in Parliament was inconsistent with their current objections to the constitutionality of taxation without representation, particularly when they claimed that the trade regulations were "a tax" upon them.

Even if one refused to admit that the colonial position was inconsistent, British writers could still claim that by receiving the Navigation Acts in the colonies, Americans had virtually consented to be bound by parliamentary power. For "the reception of any law draws after it by a chain which cannot be broken, the unwelcome necessity of submitting to taxation. . . . We virtually and implicitly allow the institution of any Government of which we enjoy the benefit and solicit the protection."[42]

The crux of the British argument supporting parliamentary power in the colonies remained the same throughout the imperial

[39]Such attempts were made; see Whately, *Regulations Lately Made*, passim. For the colonists' reactions to such pleas, see "Novanglus," in C. F. Adams, ed., *Works*, IV, 49; Thomas Jefferson, *A Summary View of the Rights of British America* . . . (Williamsburg, 1774), 9–10, 16.

[40]Whately, *Regulations Lately Made*, 104–105; Samuel Johnson, *Taxation no Tyranny* . . . (London, 1775), 32; *A Letter to a Member of Parliament Wherein the Power of the British Legislature and the Case of the Colonists, are Briefly and Impartially Considered* (London, 1765), 17–18; *The Right of Parliament Vindicated on the Occasion of the Late Stamp-Act* (London, 1766), 8–9; Leonard, *Massachusettensis*, 78.

[41]Whately, *Regulations Lately Made*, 104.

[42]Johnson, *Taxation No Tyranny*, 33; see also Wiliam Knox, *The Controversy Between Great Britain and Her Colonies Reviewed* (London, 1769), 67–69, 90.

crisis. Americans were bound to obey Parliament's authority for precisely the same reasons that nonvoting Englishmen were bound.[43] However, the colonists felt the only real similarity British writers were able to point to between the virtually represented or consenting American and Briton which they did not share in common with all mankind,[44] was that neither had voted for representatives in Parliament and yet both had obeyed Parliament's statutes.[45] For British thinkers, then, the mark of whether or not one was represented in Parliament lay in whether or not he had obeyed Parliament's commands. Such a logic, which had assumed what it had set out to prove, could only seem plausible to minds which likewise assumed that the consensus existing between the representative and the constituent would invariably depend on the latter's obedience to the former's commands.[46]

The concept of representation which British pamphleteers had advanced seemed to provide no security for the subjects against the oppressions of their representatives, let alone of their other rulers. If obedience were the central ingredient of representation, the subject would have no recourse against the magistrate issuing unlawful commands except the ultimate and unpalatable one of revolution. If representation was to offer the subject practical protection against encroaching power some method of reaching a consensus between the rulers and the ruled had to be devised which did not demand the total compliance of one party to the wishes of the other party, but at least struck a balance between the two.

However, obedience to the commands of a political superior, in this case one's representative, might provide some protection to

---

[43]Whately, *Regulations Lately Made*, 112; Soame Jenyns, *The Objections to the Taxation of Our American Colonies, by the Legislature of Great Britain, Briefly Consider'd* 2d ed. (London, 1765), 8–9; *An Englishman's Answer, to the Address, from the Delegates to the People of Great-Britain, in a Letter to the Several Colonies* . . . (New York, 1775), 8, Tucker, *Letter from a Merchant*, 12 ff.

[44]James Otis, *Considerations on Behalf of the Colonists. In a Letter to a Noble Lord*, 2d ed. (London, 1765), 9.

[45]One could say that Americans and nonvoting Britons also shared in the benefits and protection offered by British power. But so had the Portuguese, and this had not made them liable to parliamentary taxation; see *The Late Regulations Respecting the British Colonies on the Continent of America* . . . (Philadelphia, 1765), in *Political Writings of John Dickinson*, I, 82–83; Jefferson, *Summary View*, 6–7. The benefits and protection argument ultimately resolved itself into a disagreement over whether Parliament was in fact benefiting and protecting the colonies. British spokesmen proposed to resolve this disagreement by exacting obedience from America.

[46] See *Remarks on the New Essay of the Pennsylvania Farmer; and on the Resolves and Instructions Prefixed to that Essay* . . . (London, 1775), 60.

the subject against oppression if the interests of the subject and the representative were so intimately connected if not identical as to preclude the possibility of the one injuring the other without at the same time injurying himself. Moreover, if the consensus which was finally created between the rulers and the ruled proceeded not from the total compliance of one to the arbitrary commands of the other, but was rather the product of an organic unity of interests which would naturally predispose the representative and constituent to agreement, obedience would be more attractive to the subject because it would be his interest as well as his duty to obey. In this sense Americans might be said to consent to laws and taxes framed by their representatives in the legislature.[47]

The basic ingredient of the colonial notion of representation lay in maintaining just such an organic relationship of interest between the representative and the constituent. If such a relationship could be established, it would afford the subject security against the arbitrary decrees of his political superiors without at the same time absolving him from his obligation to obey their commands.[48] Ideally, it would lead to a situation where no law or tax could be passed affecting the liberties or property of the subject which did not directly affect the legislator. Thus every burden which the representative attempted to lay on his constituents would be equally borne by himself. It was to precisely such a circumstance that John Adams and others referred when they said a republic was a government of laws and not of men.[49]

---

[47]See *Farmer's Letters,* in *Political Writings of John Dickinson,* I, 178; Eliot, *A Sermon,* 46.

[48]Ebenezer Devotion, *The Examiner Examined* . . . (New London, 1766), 16–17; Tucker, *A Sermon,* 20–21; Daniel Dulany, *Considerations on the Propriety of Imposing Taxes on the British Colonies* . . . (New York, 1765), 7; James Cogswell, *A Sermon,* 37–38; "The Earl of Clarendon to William Pym," in C. F. Adams, ed., *Works,* III, 481–482; see also Trumbull, *Discourse,* passim.

[49]"Novanglus," and "Thoughts on Government . . . ," in C. F. Adams, ed., *Works,* IV, 106, 194; Dickinson and Lee, *The Farmer's and Monitor's Letters,* 68; Wilson, *Considerations,* 7, 18; Jefferson, *Summary View,* 10; *Farmer's Letters,* in *Political Writings of John Dickinson,* I, 204; Dulany, *Considerations,* 7, 9–10; Otis, *Considerations,* 4; [John Joachim Zubly], *An Humble Enquiry into the Nature of the Dependency of the American Colonies upon the Parliament of Great-Britain* . . . (Charleston?, 1769), 17, 18; Alexander Hamilton, *A Full Vindication of the Measures of the Congress, from the Calumnies of their Enemies* . . . (New York, 1774), 24; Hamilton, *The Farmer Refuted,* 10–11, 17, 22; Josiah Quincy, Jr., *Observations on the Act of Parliament Commonly Caled the Boston Port-Bill* . . . (Boston, 1774), 30; *Cato's Letters,* II, 232–233; Laslett, ed., *Locke: Two Treatises,* 347–348; *An Historical Essay,* 116; Granville Sharp, *A Declaration of the People's Natural Right to a Share in the Legislature* . . . , 2d ed. (London, 1775), 3–4; *An Argument in Defense of the Exclusive Right Claimed by the Colonies to Tax Themselves* . . . (London, 1774), 80, 81.

Nor was an intimate association of interests between rulers and ruled valued solely as security against the abuse of power. It was equally important as a standing incentive to the ruler to promote actively whatever interests he might share in common with his constituents.[50] In binding together the interests of rulers and ruled lay a guarantee of positive advantages to be reaped by all as well as of protection against unreasonable oppression.

It was the realization that the magistrate's power enabled him to pursue interests distinct from those of the community at large and therefore constituted a temptation to do so, from which the ordinary subject was immune, that had ultimately shifted the presumption of distrust from the subject to the magistrate. What a free society really needed, then, was some force to oppose the insidious tendency of power to separate the interests of the rulers from the ruled and thereby preserve the nation from the tyranny to which it was perpetually liable, both from the inherently passionate nature of man and from the rational calculations of a few malignant intelligences. It was precisely this power of keeping the ruler's interest dependent on the interest of the ruled which the provincial leadership was willing to bestow on a populace which they nonetheless considered incompetent to participate directly in the esoteric decisions of government and which they still regarded with suspicion as a potential source of disorder within the polity.[51] But in confiding a power of such importance to the people, colonial thinkers had also to demonstrate that the populace would not misuse their trust.

The device which permitted the people to accomplish their important function was the franchise, the power to choose whom their magistrates or representatives were to be. Their experience as colonials of being subject to an external political authority and of having officials imposed on them from without had taught Americans to value the privilege of electing rulers from among themselves. By virtue of the franchise the people were empowered to choose representatives whose virtues and abilities were known to them and whose interest was organically related to their own.

[50]See by implication references above in n. 49, and in addition, Wilson, *Considerations*, 15, 17; Hamilton, *The Farmer Refuted*, 10; Trumbull, *Discourse*, 22; *The Present State of Liberty in Great Britain and her Colonies . . . By an Englishman* (London, 1769), 10; *Cato's Letters*, II, 322; III, 277; Laslett, ed., *Locke: Two Treatises*, 382.

[51]"The Earl of Clarendon to William Pym," in C. F. Adams, ed., *Works*, III, 480–481; Article Signed "Shippen" from *Boston Gazette*, Jan. 30, 1769, in Cushing, ed., *Writings of Samuel Adams*, I, 305; Trumbull, *Discourse*, 25, 30–31; Isaac Wilkins, *Short Advice to the Counties of New-York* (New York, 1774), 13–14; *An Historical Essay*, 116.

Moreover, the effect of naturally shared interests was reinforced by the very act of choice which bound the representative by ties of honor and gratitude to observe and protect the interests of those who nominated him. While such an identity of interests was maintained the populace could safely be urged to bestow their favor on the leading men in the community with some security that their superior abilities would not be turned against the interests of the people.[52]

However, the power the people possessed to nominate rulers whose interests, at least initially, were intimately related to those over whom they presided did not by itself provide the populace with sufficient security against the potential abuse of the representative's power. Though each representative by himself was endowed with insufficient power to have any incentive but to promote those interests he might share in common with his constituents, even the smallest power possessed for an indefinite length of time gave the possessor opportunities to study the ends to which it might be put, ends which the momentary possession of great power even could not necessarily procure. Prolonged power gave the representative an opportunity to pool his limited resources with other representatives in a general conspiracy against the public. Such a union could not be easily effected in a short time because of the difficulty in reconciling the conflicting interests and passions of any large group of men. However, if once chosen a representative remained in office either permanently or for a long period of time, not only would he be subject to greater temptations to join with his fellow representatives in pursuing interests distinct from those of their constituents, but prolonged tenure would give permanent magistrates, who invariably existed in mixed monarchies, greater incentives as well as opportunities to corrupt the representatives of the nation away from the people's interests.[53]

It was against the operation of forces such as these that colonial

[52]Eliot, A Sermon, 54; White, Civil Rulers, 25; Shute, A Sermon, 55; Haven, A Sermon, 45; Tucker, A Sermon, 44; Thornton, Pulpit of the American Revolution, 301; Wilson, Considerations, 5; Cato's Letters, III, 7, 15 ff.; the New England clergy placed great emphasis on choosing a ruler with personal qualifications which would fortify him against the seductive effects of power; see for example, Bridge, A Sermon, 27; Whitney, Transgression, 30, 58.

[53]Peter Whitney, American Independence Vindicated . . . (Newbury-Port, 1777), 49; "The PEOPLE the best GOVERNORS: or a Plan of Government founded on the just Principles of Natural FREEDOM," in Frederick Chase, A History of Dartmouth College and the Town of Hanover, New Hampshire, John K. Lord, ed. I (Cambridge, Mass., 1891), 655–656; Burgh, Political Disquisitions, I, 82–180 passim, 370; Cato's Letters, II, 233, 239; Algernon Sidney, Discourses Concerning Government (Philadelphia, 1805), II, 373–374.

thinkers invoked an additional power in the people, the power they had periodically to re-elect their representatives. If the representative betrayed his trust and sacrificed the public interest to the gratification of his private appetites, if he disregarded or dissolved the natural ties of interest, which had initially been an incentive for him to pursue his constituent's welfare, by indemnifying himself from their oppression, the subjects still possessed the power to return their representatives to the body of the people.[54]

The power of the people to deny re-election to erring representatives not only involved a mortifying disgrace, it also proved to be a convenient means of subjecting those who were responsible for oppressive measures to the full force of their handiwork. If the representatives participated in the making of oppressive laws from the operation of which they exempted themselves, all immediate restraints upon their power would be dissolved. Through the power of re-election the people could bring oppressive laws to bear upon all by reducing the authors of these laws to the condition of subjects at the next election. Faced with the sustained threat of being made to feel the consequences of their own actions, no representative could contemplate the enslavement of his constituents while the franchise was still effective. An elected ruler had no immediate, rational alternative but to pursue the interests he shared in common with his constituents.[55]

Thus the power of the people to punish their representatives by returning them to the body of the people was an essential technique in binding the interests of rulers and ruled together. However, many colonial thinkers refrained from asserting that a man could not be represented unless he voted for a representative. They were careful to distinguish between the franchise as a technique in achieving the status of being "represented" and the essential attribute of being represented, namely an identity or intimate connection of interests. Thus there was no necessary contradiction between the colonists' insistence that they could be represented only by men chosen within the colonies by themselves and their assertions that the nonvoting Englishman was nonetheless represented in Parliament.[56] However, few Americans would have gone

[54]Wilson, *Considerations*, 8–9.

[55]Hamilton, *The Farmer Refuted*, II; Philip S. Foner, ed., *The Complete Writings of Thomas Paine* (New York, 1945), I, 6; "Thoughts on Government," in C. F. Adams, ed., *Works*, IV, 197; Laslett, ed., *Locke: Two Treatises*, 309; *Cato's Letters*, II, 233, 239; IV, 83–84; *An Historical Essay*, 115, 116, 118, 155.

[56]Devotion, *Examiner Examined*, 16; Dickinson and Lee, *The Farmer's and Monitor's Letters*, 68–69, 83; Oxenbridge Thacher, *The Sentiments of a British American* (Boston, 1764), 5; Dulany, *Considerations*, 6–11; Wilson, *Considerations*, 15; *Considerations upon the Rights of the Colonists to the*

to the other extreme and held that when a whole society was denied the franchise, as indeed the colonists had been so far as Parliament was concerned, it could still be represented. What was a technique with respect to individuals was a necessity for any distinct interests in the community.[57]

Instructions tended to be viewed in the same light as the franchise, as a means to an end but not to be confused with the end itself. They were not considered as the commands of the people with which the representative was bound to comply, but as an aid in preserving a harmony or unity of interests between representative and constituent. If the problem of diverging interests had never arisen, instructions would have been unnecessary. Through instructions the people were able to inform their representatives what their sense of the common interest was in extraordinary circumstances.[58] But the representative relationship did not confine the channels of communication to one direction only.

Privileges of British Subjects . . . (New York, 1766), 17; The Connecticut Resolves, Oct. 25, 1765, in Edmund S. Morgan, ed., *Prologue to Revolution: Sources and Documents on the Stamp Act Crisis, 1764–1766* (Chapel Hill, N.C., 1959), 55; "To the Inhabitants," in McRee, *Life and Correspondence of Iredell*, I, 210; see also J. R. Pole, "Representation and Authority in Virginia from the Revolution to Reform," *Journal of Southern History*, XXIV (1958), 29.

[57]"Thoughts on Government," in C. F. Adams, ed., *Works*, IV, 195; *Boston Evening-Post*, June 24, 1765.

[58]See Dulany, *Considerations*, I; "Instructions of the town of Boston . . . ," in Cushing, ed., *Writings of Samuel Adams*, I, 1-2, 8; *Massachusetts Spy* (Worcester), Apr. 8, 1773; see also Douglass, *Rebels and Democrats*, 85. Strict instructions were open to many objections which had been fully canvassed in European and American thought; see Charles, baron de Montesquieu, *The Spirit of Laws*, trans. Thomas Nugent, 3d ed. (London, 1758), I, 220; Sidney, *Discourses Concerning Government*, II, 368 ff.; *Four Letters on Interesting Subjects* (Philadelphia, 1776), 23. Only the prospect that a legislator was capable of sacrificing the interest of his constituents to his private interest led men to admit the utility of instructions; Dickinson and Lee, *The Farmer's and Monitor's Letters*, 75; Stephen Johnson, *Some Important Observations, Occasioned by, and Adapted to, the Publick Fast* . . . (Newport, 1766), 32. Though the practice of instructing representatives increased throughout the imperial crisis, it did not reflect an insurgent democracy so much as a desire to distribute the burden of onerous responsibilities and to convince the Mother Country that colonial protests reflected the sentiments of a united people; see *Remarks upon a Message, Sent by the Upper to the Lower House of Assembly of Maryland, 1762* . . . (n.p., 1763), 46–47; *Massachusetts Spy*, Mar. 26, 1772; "Pittsfield Addresses the Committee of the General Court, November 1778," in Robert J. Taylor, ed., *Massachusetts, Colony to Commonwealth: Documents on the Formation of Its Constitution 1775–1780* (Chapel Hill, N.C., 1961), 101; Douglass, *Rebels and Democrats*, 61. Even after independence the language of many instructions was not that of insolent command but contained such phrases as, "We therefore entreat you . . ."; see Taylor, ed., *Massachusetts, Colony to Commonwealth*, 40, 117–118.

The representative was equally at liberty to persuade his constituents that their sense of the common interests was wrong, in fact it was his duty to do so if he really thought the people were misled in their judgment.[59] If the people finally refused to re-elect a representative, it was not because he neglected to obey their specific orders, but because he had betrayed their interest. In a society of unequal political abilities the representative was still thought of as a political superior. The mass of the people elected representatives not to order them around like lackeys to do the people's bidding, but to reap benefit from the distinguished abilities of the few upon which the safety of society might in large measure depend.[60]

What power the people actually possessed over their representatives was not easily misused. In the first place the scope of their power was limited and precisely defined. It was not part of their commission to dictate terms to their representatives, but only to apply the brakes when their rulers went off the track. The object of their power was merely to maintain an identity of interests between rulers and ruled, and the means at their disposal to accomplish this end allowed the people a minimum of discretion. They could either accept or reject a delegate, and if they rejected him choose another in his place.[61] As the New England clergy pointed out, the people had no incentive to betray their limited trust for the abuse of their powers would bring civil calamities on them in this world and damnation on them in the next.[62]

Thus representation performed a dual function in refining the people's power through their representatives. On the one hand it enabled a diffuse and unorganized people to make common cause against their oppressors. Through representation their disorderly, uncohesive power could be focused and brought to bear in effectual opposition to the potential tyranny of magistrates not elected by the people. On the other it helped restrain the populace from the

---

[59]See *Speeches of the Governors of Massachusetts,* 43, 341; "Resolves of the Stockbridge Convention, December 15, 1775," in Taylor, ed., *Massachusetts, Colony to Commonwealth,* 16–17; Douglass, *Rebels and Democrats,* 37.

[60]See Daniel Shute, *A Sermon Preached to the Ancient and Honorable Artillery Company in Boston, New-England, June 1, 1767* . . . (Boston, 1767), 29.

[61]"The Earl of Clarendon to William Pym," in C. F. Adams, ed., *Works,* III, 481; see also *Cato's Letters,* I, 87; II, 130; *Essay upon Government,* 109; Montesquieu, *The Spirit of Laws,* I, 13 ff.; William Seal Carpenter, *Democracy and Representation* (Princeton, 1925), 36.

[62]Shute, *A Sermon,* 69; Haven, *A Sermon,* 23, 54–55; Thornton, *Pulpit of the American Revolution,* 186; Tucker, *A Sermon,* 36, 63; Cogswell, *A Sermon,* 9, 24–25; Shute, *A Sermon Preached to the Artillery Company,* 42.

extremes which men dreaded from a united people, even when they acted for legitimate reasons. Here representative devices served a useful function by compartmentalizing the subjects into divisions beneath their representatives. The representative relationship facilitated communication vertically between subject and representative but not horizontally between subjects of different constituencies. Since the constituents' legitimate powers were confined to the election of their particular representatives, the only normal communication they had with their fellow subjects in the political arena was through the medium of their delegates. Representative institutions helped to limit and divide the power of the people as much as they served to restrain the passions of rulers.[63]

III

The complex model of assumptions about the people's power with which Americans entered the imperial crisis bore little relation to American democracy as it is popularly conceived today. What power the people did possess was not designed to facilitate the expression of their will in politics but to defend them from oppression. Nor were such ideas easily abandoned. They lingered on throughout the period of constitutional formation and even into the nineteenth century, helping to account for the many "undemocratic" features of the state constitutions.[64]

However, the jarring effect of the Revolutionary experience administered a series of decisive challenges to this web of undemocratic assumptions which made it impossible to retain the full integrity of the model after independence. As the logic of events thrust rebellion upon the colonists, many were forced to revise their estimate of the people's competence. Moreover, once British authority had been removed from the provincial arena, Americans were explicitly confronted with a problem which before had been

---

[63]See Burgh, *Political Disquisitions*, I, 14; *An Historical Essay*, 3–4; de Lolme, *The Constitution of England*, 33–34, 157, 203–226, 278. The restraints representation imposed on the populace received little discussion in colonial literature during the imperial crisis simply because the provincial leadership was intent upon marshalling a united people to confront British power. Only loyalist writers emphasized these restraints in an effort to inhibit colonial unity. See Samuel Seabury, *An Alarm to the Legislature of the Province of New-York . . .* (New York, 1775), passim.

[64]See Douglass, *Rebels and Democrats*, 68, 70, 198, 211; J. R. Pole, "Historians and the Problem of Early American Democracy," *American Historical Review*, LXVII (1961–1962), 628, 640–641.

only implicit, of protecting themselves from each other. The new danger demanded new solutions which were forever to destroy the notion of virtual representation. Finally the Revolution brought new men into politics who had not been thoroughly schooled in the dissenting tradition. Often these men represented minority groups struggling for recognition within the state. Because the elitist orientation of dissenting theory gave scant support to their aspirations, they turned elsewhere for their ideas.

However, the subversion of dissenting thought was an insidious rather than a dramatic development. It has been difficult to trace precisely because it crept upon many Americans unawares. We today can hardly hope to understand a process which often eluded our forebears without defining the point of departure from which it proceeded.

{ *III* }

CHALLENGE
FROM
WITHOUT

FROM GRIEVANCES
TO PRINCIPLES

In developing a case against British measures that they found objectionable between 1764 and 1776, colonial leaders formulated several precise constitutional principles upon and around which they built their arguments. The nature of two of those principles, the process by which they took shape, their importance in the long debate with Britain, and the extent of the colonists' devotion to them are indicated in the following two pieces. The most important principle developed by the Americans was that Parliament could not tax them because they were not represented in that body, and, as the first selection shows, colonial leaders enunciated that belief fully and explicitly in response to the Stamp Act and consistently held to it in the next decade. A second principle, one that took shape more slowly, claimed that Americans were equal to Englishmen and that Americans were, therefore, entitled to the equal enjoyment, in the colonies, of the same rights and privileges possessed by Englishmen in the home islands. How a secondary grievance—the vice-admiralty courts—contributed to the development of this principle, which found its fullest expression in the general assertion of equality for all men in the Declaration of Independence, is discussed in the second selection.

EDMUND S. MORGAN (b. 1916) is a member of the Department of History at Yale University; DAVID S. LOVEJOY (b. 1919) is a member of the Department of History at the University of Wisconsin.

Colonial Ideas of Parliamentary Power
1764–1766

EDMUND S. MORGAN

I[1]

The distinction between internal and external taxes, said Charles Townshend, was "ridiculous in everybody's opinion except the Americans'."[2] The House of Commons was disposed to agree. Members had declared at the time of the Stamp Act that the distinction was meaningless. Some thought that the Americans were fools for espousing such sophistry; others thought that they were knaves, who would seize any pretext to avoid paying for their own protection. And knaves the Americans certainly appeared to be when they objected to the Townshend Duties almost as vehemently as they had to the Stamp Act. The colonists in fact seemed to be a ridiculous group of hypocrites, who capered from one pious notion of their rights to another. Their conduct was shameful and their efforts to justify it even more so. First they quibbled about external taxes and internal taxes. When this distinction failed them, they talked about taxes for regulating trade as against taxes for revenue. Before long they were denying that Parliament had any authority to tax them, and finally they concluded that they were simply not subject to Parliament at all. The frivolous way in which they skipped from one of these views to the next was sufficient evidence that they had no real devotion to any principle expect that of keeping their pockets full.[3]

Reprinted with permission from *The William and Mary Quarterly*, 3rd ser., V, 3 (July, 1948), 311–341. Copyright © 1948 by Edmund S. Morgan.
[1]This paper, in a shortened version, was read at a meeting of the American Historical Association at Cleveland on December 28, 1947. I wish to express my thanks to the members of the Association who offered comments at that time and to the members of my graduate seminar at Brown University, who criticized the paper at an earlier reading. I also wish to thank Mr. Bernhard Knollenberg, who read the manuscript and made several valuable suggestions.
[2]Quoted in J. C. Miller, *Sam Adams: Pioneer in Propaganda* (Boston, 1936), 115.
[3]See William Knox, *The Controversy between Great-Britain and Her Colonies Reviewed* (London, 1769), 34–35: "When the repeal of the stamp-act was their object, a distinction was set up between internal and external taxes; they pretended not to dispute the right of parliament to impose external taxes, or port duties, upon the Colonies, whatever were the pur-

The modern historian, who has thrown off the mantle of patriotism and Whigism for the more sober garments of impartiality, has tended to accept the Tory analysis of American resistance to taxation. He does not always cast doubt on the sincerity of the successive theories of American constitutional rights, but he agrees with Charles Townshend that it was the Americans who distinguished between internal and external taxes, that they abandoned this distinction for another, which likewise proved untenable, and so on until they reached the Declaration of Independence. Thus in the book which examines the American theories most closely, Doctor Randolph G. Adams' *Political Ideas of the American Revolution*,[4] the American advance toward independence is broken down into three stages:

In the first, the colonies admitted the right of Parliament to levy customs duties (external taxes), but denied the right of Parliament to levy excise taxes (internal taxes) upon them. In the second, the colonies conceded the right of Parliament to regulate the trade of the Empire, and hence exercise a legislative authority over the unrepresented colonies, but denied the right of Parliament to levy taxes of any kind whatever, internal or external. In the third stage of the controversy, the colonies admitted the right of Parliament to act as a quasi-imperial superintending power over them and over all the dominions, but denied that Parliament had any legislative authority over the colonies as a general proposition, on the ground that the colonies were not represented in Parliament.[5]

The first two stages of American Revolutionary thinking, as defined by Doctor Adams, have received less attention and are consequently less well understood than the last stage. My purpose is to examine the colonial ideas of Parliamentary power in the period covered by Doctor Adams' first stage, the period of the Stamp Act crisis.

It will be remembered that the Stamp Act was under discussion in the colonies from the spring of 1764 to the spring of 1766.

---

poses of parliament in laying them on, or however productive of revenue they might be . . . but when parliament seemed to adopt the distinction, and waiving for the present the exercise of its right to impose internal taxes, imposed certain duties on merchandizes imported into the Colonies, . . . the distinction between internal and external taxes is rejected by the colony advocates, and a new one devised between taxes for *the regulation of trade*, and taxes for the *purpose of revenue*."

[4]New York, 1939 (second edition).
[5]P. 69. For similar views by other historians, see C. P. Nettels, *The Roots of American Civilization* (New York, 1940), 634–635; C. L. Becker, *The Declaration of Independence* (New York, 1942, 1945), 80–134; H. J. Eckenrode, *The Revolution in Virginia* (Boston and New York, 1916), 28.

Although it was in force for less than four months before its repeal in February, 1766, the colonists had begun to consider it as soon as they received news of the resolution passed by Parliament on March 10, 1764, the resolution which declared, "That, towards furthur defraying the said Expences, it may be proper to charge certain Stamp Duties in the said Colonies and Plantations."[6] The resolution was one of a series which George Grenville had introduced as the basis of his budget for the ensuing year. The others furnished the substance of the Revenue Act of 1764, the so-called Sugar Act, which became a law two months later. But the resolution for a stamp tax was phrased so as to indicate that no action would be taken on it until the next session, though its ultimate passage was almost a certainty.[7] The colonists were thus presented with two measures which threatened their prosperity and which consequently obliged them to think about the relation which they bore to the body which threatened them. They had to consider the Sugar Act, in which Parliament made use of trade regulations to raise money and which in itself would have been sufficient to set discerning minds at work on the question of Parliamentary taxation. At the same time they had to consider the Stamp Act, an act which would directly affect almost every person in the colonies. Of the two, the Stamp Act appeared to most colonists to be the more dangerous, but in formulating their ideas of Parliamentary power they could not afford to neglect either measure; they had to decide in what way their rights were affected both by the internal taxes of the Stamp Act and by the external taxes of the Sugar Act.

Under the pressure of these two acts colonial ideas reached a remarkable maturity during the period under discussion. In some regions and among some persons the theory of complete colonial autonomy was enunciated. For example a meeting of citizens at New London, Connecticut, on December 10, 1765, adopted resolutions which rehearsed the principles of government by consent, specified that the Stamp Act was a violation of those principles, and finally declared, "That it is the Duty of every Person in the Colonies to oppose by every lawful Means, the Execution of those

---

[6] *Journals of the House of Commons*, XXIX, 935.

[7] Grenville warned the colonial agents that he would bring in a bill for a stamp tax at the next session of Parliament. See the letter from Jasper Mauduit to Massachusetts, May 26, 1764 (Massachusetts Archives, XXII, 375); the letter from Charles Garth to South Carolina, June 5, 1764, *English Historical Review*, LIV, 646–648; and the account by William Knox, agent for Georgia, in *The Claim of the Colonies to an Exemption from Internal Taxes Imposed by Authority of Parliament Examined* (London, 1765), 31–35.

Acts imposed on them,—and if they can in no other way be relieved to reassume their natural Rights, and the Authority the Laws of Nature and of God have vested them with."[8] If there was any confusion in the minds of the colonists as to how to go about reassuming natural rights, newspaper writers were ready with detailed discussions of the technique of revolution.[9] Short of this, other writers expounded the theory which later found more classic expression in the writings of John Adams and James Wilson, the theory that is assumed in the Declaration of Independence, that the colonies owe allegiance only to the king and are not bound in any way by acts of Parliament.[10]

But in the effort to arrive at what may be called the official colonial position during this period, one cannot rely on newspapers and pamphlets nor on the resolutions adopted by informal gatherings of small groups, for these may represent the views of factions or the idiosyncracies of a single man. Fortunately it is not necessary to depend upon such partial statements, for in every colony except Georgia and North Carolina the formally elected representatives of the people produced some official statement of belief. Five of the colonies which later revolted drew up statements in 1764 while the Stamp Act was pending; nine colonies, including all of the first five, did the same in 1765 after the Act was passed; and in the same year at the Stamp Act Congress, nine colonies combined in a declaration which was formally approved by a tenth. These statements, in the form of resolutions, petitions, memorials, and remonstrances, are the safest index of colonial opinion about Parliamentary power. They were carefully phrased by the regularly elected representatives of the voting population and adopted, in many cases unanimously, after deliberation and debate.

In these formal statements it is scarcely possible to discern a trace of the ideas which the Americans are supposed to have adopted during the period under discussion. Almost universally the documents deny the authority of Parliament to tax the colonies at all. Nowhere is there a clear admission of the right of Parliament to levy external taxes rather than internal, and only in three

[8]*Boston Post-Boy and Advertiser,* December 16, 1765.
[9]See, for example,.*Boston Gazette,* December 2, 1765.
[10]*Maryland Gazette,* May 30, 1765; *Providence Gazette,* May 11, 1765; *Boston Gazette,* February 24, March 3, March 17, 1766. Governor Bernard reported to the Lords of Trade, November 30, 1765, that the Massachusetts politicians were claiming that the colonies "have no Superiors upon Earth but the King, and him only in the Person of the Governor, or   according to the terms of the Charter." Bernard Papers, IV, 203, Harvard College Library.

cases does such a right seem to be implied. In at least one of these three, the implication which may be suggested by a partial reading is denied by a full consideration of the document and the circumstances under which it was produced.

II

As might be expected, the statements drawn up in 1764 while the Stamp Act was pending were generally not as explicit as those prepared a year later, when the Act had been passed and the colonists had had more time to think over its implications. The clearest of the early statements was that made by the New York Assembly in three petitions, to the King, the Lords, and the Commons, on October 18, 1764. These petitions, in objecting to both the Sugar Act and the proposed Stamp Act, claimed that the colonists should be exempt "from the Burthen of all Taxes not granted by themselves." Far from singling out internal taxes, the New York Assembly stated pointedly:

. . . since all Impositions, whether they be internal Taxes, or Duties paid, for what we consume, equally diminish the Estates upon which they are charged; what avails it to any People, by which of them they are impoverished? . . . the whole wealth of a country may be as effectually drawn off, by the Exaction of Duties, as by any other Tax upon their Estates.

In accordance with this principle New York admitted the authority of Parliament to regulate the trade of the empire for the good of the mother country, but insisted that

. . . a Freedom to drive all Kinds of Traffick in a Subordination to, and not inconsistent with, the *British* Trade; and an Exemption from all Duties in such a Course of Commerce, is humbly claimed by the Colonies, as the most essential of all the Rights to which they are intitled, as Colonists from, and connected, in the common Bond of Liberty, with the uninslaved Sons of *Great Britain*.[11]

The statement made by Virginia in 1764 was almost as plain as that of New York. The Virginia Council and House of Burgesses in a petition to the King, a memorial to the House of Lords, and a remonstrance to the Commons, claimed an exemption from all Parliamentary taxation. To the King they asserted their "Right of being governed by such laws, respecting their internal Polity and

---

[11]*Journal of the Votes and Proceedings of the General Assembly of the Colony of New York. Began the 8th Day of November, 1743; and Ended the 23d of December, 1765* (New York, 1766), II, 769–779.

Taxation,[12] as are derived from their own Consent"; to the Lords they stated their right as British subjects to be exempt from all taxes, "but as are laid on them by their own Consent, or by those who are legally appointed to represent them"; to the Commons they remonstrated "that laws imposing taxes on the people ought not to be made without the consent of representatives chosen by themselves," and added that they could not discern "by what Distinction they can be deprived of that sacred birthright and most valuable inheritance, by their Fellow Subjects, nor with what Propriety they can be taxed or affected in their estates by the Parliament, wherein they are not and indeed cannot, constitutionally be represented."[13]

Rhode Island, Connecticut, and Massachusetts took a less precise view of their rights in 1764 than did New York and Virginia, although Massachusetts and Connecticut, at least, cleared up the uncertainty of their position in the following year. In Rhode Island the General Assembly deputed Governor Stephen Hopkins to write a statement of the colony's rights and in addition sent a petition to the King, dated November 29, 1764. Both Governor Hopkins' pamphlet and the petition ignored the constitutional question raised by the Sugar Act, the question of external taxes; they argued against the act simply as a trade regulation which would have ruinous economic consequences. Since none of the colonies at this time denied Parliament's right to regulate colonial trade, Rhode Island, in considering the Sugar Act simply as such a regulation, made no attempt to deny Parliament's right to enact it. Against the proposed Stamp Act Hopkins and the Assembly did raise the question of right. This proposal, if carried into execution, would be "a manifest violation of their just and long enjoyed rights. For it must be confessed by all men, that they who are taxed at pleasure by others, cannot possibly have any property, can have nothing to be called their own; they who have no property can have no freedom, but are indeed reduced to the most abject slavery." The petition to the King recited the same objections and concluded with a request

that our trade may be restored to its former condition, and no further limited, restrained and burdened, than becomes necessary for the general good of all your Majesty's subjects; that the courts of vice admi-

---

[12] For the question whether or not the adjective "internal" modifies "taxation" as well as "polity" see the discussion below of the same phrase in the Virginia Resolves of 1765.

[13] *Journals of the House of Burgesses of Virginia 1761–1765* (Richmond, 1907), liv–lvii.

ralty may not be vested with more extensive powers in the colonies than are given them by law in Great Britain; that the colonists may not be taxed but by the consent of their own representatives, as Your Majesty's other free subjects are.[14]

Thus Rhode Island sidestepped the question of external taxes by ignoring the declared intent of the Sugar Act to raise a revenue. She took a stand upon constitutional grounds only against the proposed Stamp Act, only, in other words, against internal taxes. Yet she did not quite admit Parliament's right to levy external taxes, because she considered the Sugar Act, erroneously to be sure, as a regulation of trade and not as a tax. Her position on external taxes was ambiguous: she didn't say yes and she didn't say no.

Connecticut in 1764 was guilty of the same ambiguity. Connecticut's statement took the form of a pamphlet drawn up by a George Wyllys and Jared Ingersoll, deputed by the General Assembly, "to collect and set in the most advantageous light all such arguments and objections as may justly and reasonably [be] advanced against creating and collecting a revenue in America, more particularly in this Colony, and especially against effecting the same by Stamp Duties &c."[15] This committee, of which Governor Fitch was the working member, produced a pamphlet entitled *Reasons why the British Colonies in America should not be charged with Internal Taxes, by Authority of Parliament.*[16] The pamphlet came as close as any American statement to admitting the right of Parliament to levy external taxes. Like the Rhode Island statement, it confined its constitutional objections to internal taxes and failed to consider the problem, raised by the Sugar Act, of whether Parliament could make use of trade regulations as a source of revenue. Instead, it assumed that Parliament would act for the good of the whole in its regulation of trade. "If Restrictions on Navigation, Commerce, or other external Regulations only are established," it said, "the internal Government, Powers of taxing for its Support, an Exemption from being taxed without Consent, and other Immunities, which legally belong to the Subjects of each Colony . . . will be and continue in the Substance of them whole and entire."[17] This was a rather naive view of the situation but it did not necessarily commit the colony to a constitutional acceptance of external taxes.

[14]James R. Bartlett, ed., *Records of the Colony of Rhode Island and Providence Plantations* (Providence, 1861), VI, 414–427.

[15]C. J. Hoadly, ed., *Public Records of the Colony of Connecticut* (Hartford, 1881), XII, 256.

[16]New Haven, 1764. Reprinted in Hoadly, XII, 651–671.

[17]*Ibid.*, 661.

The address of Massachusetts to the House of Commons, dated November 3, 1764, like the pamphlets issued by Rhode Island and Connecticut in this year, was not entirely clear on the question of external taxes. Massachusetts affirmed that the American colonists "have always judged by their representatives both of the way and manner, in which internal taxes should be raised within their respective governments, and of the ability of the inhabitants to pay them." The address concluded with the request that "the privileges of the colonies, relative to their internal taxes, which they have so long enjoyed, may still be continued to them."[18] By specifying internal taxes, the address seemed to imply that the inhabitants of Massachusetts did not object to the idea of an external tax imposed by Parliament. This implication was fortified by the rest of the document, which objected to the Sugar Act on economic rather than constitutional grounds as a measure which would ruin the trade of the colony.

Before this address is interpreted as an implied assent to external taxes the circumstances of its origin must be considered. The General Court adopted the address only because the Council refused to concur in a much more inclusive assertion of rights, originally passed by the lower house. In this version the House affirmed that "we look *upon those Duties as a Tax* [i.e., the duties imposed by the Sugar Act], and which we humbly apprehend ought not to be laid without the Representatives of the People affected by them."[19] The abandonment of this earlier version was regarded in Massachusetts as a victory for the Council under the leadership of Lieutenant-Governor Hutchinson, and the House, even though it acquiesced in the new address, did not consider it a proper statement of colonial rights.[20] Accordingly, when they sent it to their agent in London for presentation, they warned him that it did not represent the views of the House. "The House of Representatives," they said

were clearly for making an example and full declaration of the exclusive Right of the People of the Colonies to tax themselves and that they ought not to be deprived of a right they had so long enjoyed and which they held by Birth and by Charter; but they could not prevail with the Councill, tho they made several Tryalls, to be more explicit than they have been in the Petition sent you. You will therefore collect

[18]Alden Bradford, ed., *Massachusetts State Papers, Speeches of the Governors of Massachusetts from 1765 to 1775, etc.* (Boston, 1818), 21–23.
[19]Massachusetts Archives, XXII, 414.
[20]See the letters by Governor Bernard, November 17 and 18, 1764, to the Earl of Halifax, to John Pownall, and to Richard Jackson, relating the success of the Council in toning down the petition. Bernard Papers, II, 181–187, 189, 260–264.

the sentiments of the Representative Body of People rather from what they have heretofore sent you than from the present Address.[21]

What the House of Representatives had heretofore sent the agent included a long letter instructing him in the doctrine of natural rights and an explicit statement that any attempt by Parliament to tax colonial trade would be "contrary to a fundamentall Principall of our constitution vizt. That all Taxes ought to originate with the people."[22] The House had also approved and sent to the agent a pamphlet written by one of their members, James Otis, entitled *The Rights of the British Colonies asserted and proved.*[23] In this pamphlet Otis had argued against Parliament's right to tax the colonies and had stated in the most unequivocal manner that "there is no foundation for the distinction some make in England, between an internal and an external tax on the colonies."[24] It would hardly seem proper, then, to draw from the Massachusetts Address the inference that the people of the colonies accepted the right of Parliament to levy external as opposed to internal taxes.

III

At the end of the year 1764, when the five initial colonial statements were all on the books, the colonial position was still a little obscure. New York and Virginia had been plain enough, but Rhode

[21]*Collections of the Massachusetts Historical Society,* LXXIV, 170–171.

[22]*Ibid.,* 39–54, 145–146.

[23]Boston, 1764. See *Journal of the Honourable House of Representatives of His Majesty's Province of the Massachusetts-Bay in New-England, Begun and held at Concord, in the county of Middlesex, on Wednesday the Thirtieth Day of May, Annoque Domini, 1764* (Boston, 1764), 66, 77.

[24]P. 42. Strangely enough these were also the private views of Lieutenant-Governor Hutchinson, who was principally responsible for suppressing the original address of the House. In a piece which he wrote in June or July, 1764, but never published, he argued against the Stamp Act on precisely the same line which was later followed by the House. He pointed out that the Sugar Act had been passed, not for the regulation of trade, but "for the sake of the money arising from the Duties," and that the privileges of the people were no less affected by it than they were by an internal tax. (Massachusetts Archives, XXVI, 90–96.) Moreover, on Nov. 9, 1764, just after he had succeeded in getting the Massachusetts Address toned down, Hutchinson wrote to Ebenezer Silliman in Connecticut, criticizing the Connecticut pamphlet for neglecting to object against external taxes. He told Silliman, who was a member of the Connecticut Committee which drew up the pamphlet, that "the fallacy of the argument lies here it is your supposing duties upon trade to be imposed for the sake of regulating trade, whereas the Professed design of the duties by the late Act is to raise a revenue." (Massachusetts Archives, XXVI, 117–118.) Why Hutchinson should have objected to these views when they came from the Massachusetts House of Representatives is not apparent.

Island, Connecticut, and Massachusetts, while denying Parliament's right to levy a stamp tax, had evaded the question of external taxes. By the close of the following year all signs of hesitation had disappeared. The Stamp Act produced an all-but-unanimous reaction: Parliament had no right to tax the colonies.

The first declaration of rights to be made after passage of the Act was the famous set of resolves which Patrick Henry introduced into the Virginia House of Burgesses on May 30, 1765. As recorded on the Journals of the House of Burgesses there were four of these resolves which passed the House. The first two asserted the right of the inhabitants of Virginia to all the privileges of Englishmen. The third declared "that the Taxation of the People by themselves, or by Persons chosen to represent them" was a "distinguishing Characteristick of *British* Freedom, without which the ancient Constitution cannot exist." The fourth stated that the inhabitants of Virginia had always enjoyed and had never forfeited or yielded up "the inestimable Right of being governed by such Laws, respecting their internal Polity and Taxation, as are derived from their own Consent."[25]

Henry had proposed three more resolutions which either failed of passage or later were expunged from the records. The first of these merely repeated what the others had already implied, namely that the General Assembly of Virginia, in its representative capacity, had "the only exclusive right and power to lay taxes and imposts upon the inhabitants of this colony." The second, more radical, stated "That his Majesty's liege people, the inhabitants of this colony, are not bound to yield obedience to any law or ordinance whatever, designed to impose any taxation whatsoever upon them, other than the laws or ordinances of the General Assembly aforesaid." The last provided that anyone who denied the Assembly's exclusive power of taxation should be considered an enemy of the colony.[26]

---

[25]*Journals of the House of Burgesses of Virginia 1761–1765*, 360.

[26]*Ibid.*, lxvii. When the Resolves were printed in the newspapers, the three unsuccessful resolves were included along with the others as though they had been passed. The Resolves, so far as the incomplete newspaper records enable us to tell, were first printed in the *Newport Mercury* on June 24, 1765, and copied in the Boston papers from the version given there. The text printed in the papers, besides including the three unsuccessful resolves, omitted one of those actually passed (the third) and considerably abridged the others. The abridgment did not seriously alter the meaning of the resolves, but the wording was sufficiently changed to suggest that the newspaper text was obtained from an unofficial source, probably from some member of the assembly who had been present when the Resolves were passed. Possibly the source was Henry himself, for the newspaper version,

The Virginia Resolves even without the inclusion of Henry's three additional clauses, constituted a clear denial of Parliament's right to tax. The only phrase which could be interpreted as distinguishing between internal and external taxes was the phrase in the third resolution "internal polity and taxation." Here it was possible to read the adjective "internal" to modify "taxation" as well as "polity." That such a reading would have been incorrect is suggested by the fact that in the version of the Resolves which was printed in the newspapers this phrase was changed to read "taxation and internal police."[27] Furthermore this was also the wording in a copy of the Resolves endorsed on the back in Patrick Henry's handwriting.[28]

The Virginia Resolves served as a model for similar declarations in most of the other colonies. Rhode Island, where the Virginia Resolves were first published, was the first to copy them. In September, 1765, the Rhode Island General Assembly passed six resolutions, three of which were adapted from those passed by the Virginia House of Burgesses, two from Henry's unsuccessful resolutions (which had been printed in the newspapers without any indication that they had failed to pass), and one original resolution which, in effect, called upon officers of government to pay no attention to the Stamp Act.[29] On the question of Parliamentary authority the Rhode Island statements, being copied from those of Virginia, were no less definite: the General Assembly of the colony had always enjoyed control over "taxation and internal police" and possessed "the only exclusive right to lay taxes and imposts upon the inhabitants of this colony."[30] Rhode Island in fact went farther than the Virginia Burgesses had been willing to go and farther than any other colony went in the next eight or nine years, by calling for direct disobedience to Parliament. She passed the measure which Virginia had rejected and declared that her inhabitants need not submit to a Parliamentary tax. Yet in so doing Rhode Island added a qualification which makes her position on the question of external taxes open to suspicion. In the fifth Rhode Island resolution it was stated that the inhabitants of

---

except in its omission of resolution number 3, closely approximates a copy of the resolves which is endorsed on the back in Henry's handwriting. See *Journals of the House of Burgesses*, frontispiece and lxv.

[27]*Newport Mercury*, June 24, 1765; *Boston Post-Boy and Advertiser*, July 1, 1765; *Boston Gazette*, July 1, 1765; *Georgia Gazette*, September 5, 1765.

[28]*Journals of the House of Burgesses of Virginia, 1761–1765*, frontispiece and lxv.

[29]Bartlett, *Records of the Colony of Rhode Island*, VI, 451–452.

[30]*Ibid.*, 452.

the colony were "not bound to yield obedience to any law or ordinance designed to impose any internal taxation whatsoever upon them, other than the laws or ordinances of the General Assembly, aforesaid."[31] In Henry's version the word "internal" had not occurred. Rhode Island by inserting it implied that her citizens could disobey an act of Parliament imposing internal taxes but not one imposing external taxes. It should be noted that this distinction did not appear in the assertions of right contained in the preceding resolutions, where the authority of Parliament to tax the colony was denied without qualification. It was only in the summons to rebellion that the Rhode Island Assembly felt obliged to draw back a little. Though their caution on this score was boldness when compared to the stand of the other colonies, which confined themselves to declarations of right, nevertheless the appearance of the word "internal" makes one wonder whether there may not have been a moderate faction in the assembly which would have allowed Parliament a right over external taxes. If there was such a faction, it was not able to insert its views into the resolutions which defined the rights of the colony but only into the one which proposed open rebellion. Moreover, a few weeks later, on November 6, 1765, Rhode Island's popularly-elected governor, Samuel Ward, wrote to General Conway that the colonists were oppressed, because "duties and taxes" were laid upon them without their knowledge or consent.[32]

If the Rhode Island Resolves of 1765 still left some room for doubt on the question of external taxes, the same was not true of the other colonial statements of that year. The Maryland Assembly, on September 28, passed unanimously resolutions denying Parliament's right to tax, in which the only use of the word "internal" was in the familiar phrase "Taxes, and internal Polity."[33] Meanwhile Pennsylvania, on September 21, had drawn up its own set of Resolves, to much the same effect. The first draught of these resolves, written by John Dickinson, included one clause objecting specifically to internal taxes,[34] but in the version finally adopted by the assembly there was no mention of the word "internal." The crucial item read: "Resolved therefore, N.C.D. That the taxation of the people of this province, by any other persons whatsoever than such their representatives in assembly,

[31] Ibid.
[32] Ibid., 473.
[33] Maryland Gazette, October 3, 1765.
[34] Charles J. Stillé, The Life and Times of John Dickinson, 1732–1808 (Philadelphia, 1891), 339–340.

is UNCONSTITUTIONAL, and subversive of their most valuable rights."[35]

Massachusetts, because of the recess of her assembly, did not take action until October, though the newspapers began to agitate for a more spirited statement of rights as soon as they received news of the Virginia Resolves.[36] Accordingly when the assembly was called together in October, it produced a set of resolutions which defined the rights of British subjects and concluded, "that all acts, made by any power whatever, other than the General Assembly of this province, imposing taxes on the inhabitants, are infringements of our inherent and unalienable rights, as men and British subjects; and render void the most valuable declarations of our charter."[37] The Connecticut Assembly likewise cleared up the ambiguity of its earlier statement by a set of resolves modeled partly on those of Virginia and affirming that an act for raising money in the colonies "by duties or taxes" was beyond the authority of Parliament. Connecticut, like Maryland and Rhode Island, included an item copied after the fourth of the Virginia Resolves, in which once again the questionable phrase was rendered as "taxing and internal police."[38]

South Carolina, on November 29, 1765, denied Parliament's right to tax, in a set of eighteen resolves copied from the declarations of the Stamp Act Congress[39] (see below). New York could scarcely state the colonial position more explicitly than she had done the year before, but nevertheless on December 11, 1765, she adopted three more petitions to King, Lords, and Commons, restating the case with the same clarity.[40] New Jersey in the meantime had adopted eleven resolutions copied principally from those of the Stamp Act Congress, with nothing said about internal taxes;[41] and New Hampshire, which did not participate in the

---

[35]J. Almon, ed., *A Collection of interesting, authentic papers, relative to the dispute between Great Britain and America* (London, 1777), 20–21.

[36]See, for example, the *Boston Gazette* of July 8, 1765: "The People of Virginia have spoke very sensibly, and the frozen Politicians of a more northern Government say they have spoke Treason: Their spirited Resolves do indeed serve as a perfect Contrast for a certain, tame, pusillanimous, daub'd, insipid Thing, delicately touch'd up and call'd an Address; which was lately sent from this Side the Water, to please the Taste of the Tools of Corruption on the other." The reference, of course, was to the Massachusetts Address of 1764.

[37]Bradford, *Massachusetts State Papers*, 50–51.

[38]Hoadly, *Public Records of the Colony of Connecticut*, 421–425.

[39]John Drayton, *Memoirs of the American Revolution* (Charleston, S. C., 1821), I, 39–41.

[40]*Journals of the Votes and Proceedings of the General Assembly of the Colony of New York 1743–1765*, II, 795–802.

[41]*New Jersey Archives*, First Series (Paterson, 1902), XXIV, 683–684.

Congress, had given formal approval to all the resolutions and petitions of that body.[42]

The Stamp Act Congress had met in New York during October, attended by delegates from Massachusetts, Rhode Island, Connecticut, New York, New Jersey, Pennsylvania, Delaware, Maryland, and South Carolina. These delegates had produced a set of resolutions and three petitions, to the King, the Lords, and the Commons, all denying the authority of Parliament to tax the colonies.[43] Here as in the other formal colonial statements of this year there is no distinction made between internal and external taxes. The Stamp Act Congress has frequently been treated by historians as a rather conservative body of men, possibly because it acknowledged "all due subordination" to Parliament. But as conservatives at the time recognized, this phrase was an empty one unless you stated what subordination was due. It is true that the conservatives, in Massachusetts at least, had hoped to gain control of the Stamp Act Congress.[44] They actually succeeded in securing Timothy Ruggles as one of the Massachusetts delegates, and Governor Bernard wrote at least one letter to Ruggles before the convention urging him to secure submission to the Stamp Act pending its probable repeal.[45] Ruggles remained faithfully conservative, but the true character of the Congress is sufficiently indicated by the fact that, as a conservative, he refused to sign the Resolutions it adopted and was later reprimanded for his refusal by the not-so-conservative Massachusetts House of Representatives.[46] The Stamp Act Congress, in other words, was no less "radical" than the colonial assemblies which sent delegates to it.

---

[42]Nathaniel Bouton, ed., *Documents and Records Relating to the Province of New Hampshire* (Nashua, N. H., 1873), VII, 92.

[43]Hezekiah Niles, *Principles and Acts of the Revolution* (Baltimore, 1822), 157–460.

[44]Governor Bernard wrote to the Lords of Trade on July 8, 1765, that in Massachusetts, where the proposal for the congress initiated, "It was impossible to oppose this measure to any good purpose and therefore the friends of government took the lead in it and have kept it in their hands in pursuance of which of the Committee appointed by this House to meet the other Committees at New York on 1st of October next. Two of the three are fast friends to government prudent and discreet men such as I am assured will never consent to any undutiful or improper application to the Government of Great Britain." (Sparks Manuscripts 43: British Manuscripts, IV, Harvard College Library).

[45]Bernard Papers, IV, 72. The letter is dated September 28, 1765.

[46]*Boston Gazette*, Feb. 17, 1766. The membership of the Stamp Act Congress has been analysed in an unpublished paper by Mr. David S. Lovejoy, in which it is indicated that of the twenty-seven members only two are known to have become Tories at the time of the Revolution.

Though it acknowledged due subordination to Parliament, it denied with qualification the right of Parliament to tax the colonies.

In sum, during the period of the Stamp Act crisis, fifteen formal statements of colonial rights had been issued. Of these only the three early statements by Rhode Island, Connecticut, and Massachusetts could be interpreted as implying an assent to the constitutionality of external taxes. The statement by Massachusetts was clearly not representative of official opinion, and both the Massachusetts and the Connecticut statements were clarified the following year by resolutions which unequivocally rejected the authority of Parliament to tax the colonies at all.

IV

The question suggested by all these declarations of right is: what did the Americans mean when they admitted due subordination to Parliament and at the same time denied Parliament's right to tax them? What subordination was due? If they did not distinguish between internal and external taxes, but denied all authority to tax, what authority did they leave to Parliament?

The answer is given clearly enough in the documents: the colonists allowed the right of Parliament to legislate for the whole empire in any way that concerned the common interests of all the members of the empire (as yet they made no claim that the colonial assemblies were entirely coordinate with Parliament in legislative authority), but they denied that Parliament's legislative authority extended either to the internal polity of the colonies or to taxation. Not all the colonies insisted on exclusive control of internal polity, for Parliament at this time was not attempting to interfere in this department. The issue of the day was taxation, and what the colonies insisted on most vigorously was that Parliament's supreme legislative authority did not include the right to tax. Taxation and legislation, they said, were separate functions and historically had always been treated as such. Legislation was a function of sovereignty; and as the sovereign body of the empire, Parliament had absolute legislative authority. Under this authority Parliament was entirely justified in regulating the trade and commerce of the empire. There was, in other words, nothing unconstitutional about the Acts of Trade and Navigation. But taxes were something else. Taxes were the "free gift" of the people who paid them, and as such could be levied only by a body which represented the people. As far as Great Britain was concerned the House of Commons was a representative body and could therefore tax the people of Great Britain; but since the colonists were not, and from their local circumstances could not be, represented in Parliament, they could not be taxed by Parliament. The only body with a constitutional right to tax them was a colonial assembly, in which the people upon whom the tax would fall would be represented. Thus the Connecticut Assembly in October, 1765, resolved,

That, in the opinion of this House, an act for raising money by duties or taxes differs from other acts of legislation, in that it is always considered as a free gift of the people made by their legal and elected representatives; and that we cannot conceive that the people of Great Britain, or their representatives, have right to dispose of our property.[47]

According to this distinction the power to levy taxes even in Great Britain was limited to the House of Commons, the representative part of Parliament. The petition from the General Assembly of New York to the House of Commons, December 11, 1765, while expressing "all due submission to the supreme Authority of the *British* Legislature," affirmed

That all parliamentary Aids in *Great-Britain*, are the free Gifts of the People by their Representatives, consented to by the Lords, and accepted by the Crown, and therefore every Act imposing them, essentially differs from every other Statute, having the Force of a Law in no other Respect than the Manner thereby prescribed for levying the Gift.

That agreeable to this Distinction, the House of Commons has always contended for and enjoyed the constitutional Right of originating all Money Bills, as well in Aid of the Crown, as for other Purposes.

That all Supplies to the Crown being in their Nature free Gifts, it would, as we humbly conceive, be unconstitutional for the People of *Great-Britain*, by their Representatives in Parliament, to dispose of the Property of Millions of his Majesty's Subjects, who are not, and cannot be there represented.[48]

It was this distinction which the members of the Stamp Act Congress had in mind when they acknowledged "due subordination" to Parliament, for they asked in their petition to the House of Commons,

---

[47]*Public Records of the Colony of Connecticut,* XII, 423.
[48]*Journal of the Votes and Proceedings of the General Assembly of the Colony of New York 1743–1765,* II, 800.

[w]hether there be not a material Distinction in Reason and sound Policy, at least, between the necessary Exercise of Parliamentary Jurisdiction in general Acts, for the Amendment of the Common Law, and the Regulation of Trade and Commerce through the whole Empire, and the Exercise of that Jurisdiction by imposing Taxes on the Colonies.[49]

V

Most members of Parliament would have answered this query with a flat denial that the power of taxation could be distinguished from that of legislation. Taxation, they would have said, was inseparable from sovereignty. But there were some members willing to speak in favor of the colonial view. In the debate on the Declaratory Act in the House of Commons the question arose over a motion made by Colonel Barré to omit from the act the phrase "in all cases whatsoever." This motion was intended to exclude Parliament's authority to tax the colonies, and in the debate which followed, Barré and William Pitt the elder argued for the motion in much the same terms as were used in the colonial statements. Visitors were not admitted to Parliament during this session, so that few accounts of the debate have been preserved, but according to Charles Garth, member of Devizes borough, Wiltshire, and agent for several of the southern colonies, the speakers for Barré's motion contended: "That the Principles of Taxation as distinguished from Legislation were as distinct Principles and Powers as any two Propositions under the Sun." The speakers cited the precedent of the counties palatine of Chester and Durham which had been subject to Parliament's legislative authority but had not been taxed until they were represented. The clergy, it was pointed out, taxed themselves separately but did not have separate legislative power. Another indication that the two functions were separate was that taxes were the free gift of the Commons, and tax bills could not be considered by the Lords or the King until the Commons had made a grant. Other bills remained in the Upper House for the King's signature, but tax bills were sent back to the Commons, whose speaker presented them to the King as the free gift of the Commons. All this, it was said,

---

[49]*Proceedings of the Congress at New York* (Annapolis, 1766), 23. The reprint of the proceedings in Niles, *Principles and Acts of the Revolution* is inaccurate at this point.

showed that Parliament might legislate as the supreme authority
of the realm but that it taxed only in its representative capacity.
Since the colonies were not represented in Parliament, they could
not constitutionally be taxed by Parliament.[50] In the House of
Lords, Lord Camden argued the case to the same effect.[51]

In spite of these arguments Parliament decided by an overwhelming majority[52] to include the words "in all cases whatsoever," and thereby, as far as Parliament was concerned, it was
concluded that taxation and legislation were not separate functions and that Parliament's authority over the colonies included
the right to tax. But strangely enough the Declaratory Act did not
include any explicit statement of the right to tax, so that the
colonists could not have recognized that Parliament was denying
their position. What the act said was that the King in Parliament
had "full power and authority to make laws and statutes of sufficient force and validity to bind the colonies and people of *America*,
subjects of the crown of *Great Britain*, in all cases whatsoever."[53]
Though the members of Parliament knew that the words "in all
cases whatsoever" meant in cases of taxation, there is nothing in
the act itself to give the words that meaning. Nor was the ambiguity entirely accidental. When the act was being drawn up,
Charles Yorke, the attorney general, suggested that the crucial
phrase should read "as well in cases of Taxation, as in all other
cases whatsoever." But when he submitted this suggestion to Rockingham, who was then prime minister, Rockingham thought it
impolitic to make any mention of the word "taxation." "I think
I may say," he wrote to Yorke, "that it is our firm Resolution in
the House of Lords—I mean among ourselves—that that word
must be resisted."[54] Thus the omission of any mention of taxation
was deliberate. By supporting the act as it stood, with the resound-
ing but ambiguous phrase "in all cases whatsoever," the Rockingham government could gain support in Parliament by en-

[50]Garth's account is in *Maryland Historical Magazine*, VI, 287–305. Another account is in *American Historical Review*, XVII, 565–574.
[51]*Archives of Maryland* (Baltimore, 1895), XIV, 267–268.
[52]*Maryland Historical Magazine*, VI, 300; *Archives of Maryland*, XIV, 280;
Sir John Fortescue, ed., *The Correspondence of King George the Third*
(London, 1927), I, 254.
[53]Danby Pickering, ed., *The Statutes at Large* (Cambridge, England, 1767),
XXVII, 20.
[54]British Museum Additional Manuscripts 35430, ff. 37–38 (Rockingham's
letter). The exchange of correspondence between Yorke and Rockingham is
printed, in part in George Thomas, Earl of Albemarle, *Memoirs of the Marquis of Rockingham* (London, 1852), I, 285–288. The date of Yorke's letter
is not given. Rockingham's letter is dated January 25, 1766.

couraging the members to beat the drum of Parliamentary power
—behind closed doors—without giving offense to the colonies.

The colonies can hardly be blamed then for not getting the
point of the Declaratory Act. They had not generally been informed of the debate which had taken place over the words "in all
cases whatsoever,"[55] and since the act was accompanied by the
repeal of Parliament's most conspicuous attempt to tax them, they
might very well interpret it as a simple assertion of legislative
authority with no necessary implication of a right to tax. They
knew that the Declaratory Act was a copy of the earlier statute of
6 George I regarding Ireland. And they knew also that in spite of
this statute Ireland had not been taxed by Parliament. The Massachusetts Assembly even before passage of the Stamp Act had
argued from the example of Ireland that the colonies might be
dependent on England without allowing England a right to tax
them.[56] After passage of the Declaratory Act the Massachusetts
agent in London, Richard Jackson, encouraged Massachusetts to
believe that the same reasoning was still valid, for he wrote to
Governor Bernard that the act would probably affect the colonies
as little "as the Power we claim in Ireland, the manner of exercising which you are acquainted with."[57] The same view was expressed by Daniel Dulany of Maryland in a letter to General Conway. According to Dulany the Declaratory Act could not imply a
power to tax, because if it did, then the act of 6 George I must
give authority to tax Ireland, and such authority had never been
claimed or exercised.[58] Thus the fact, so often remarked by historians, that the colonists took little notice of the Declaratory Act
does not mean that the colonists were indifferent to the question
of principle. They simply did not recognize the Act as a challenge
to their views. They could acquiesce in it with a clear conscience
and without inconsistency, unaware that their interpretation differed radically from that held in Parliament.[59]

---

[55]So far as I have been able to discover Garth's account was the only one
sent to the colonies, and it was not published at the time.

[56]Massachusetts Archives, XXII, 415. The argument is made in the petition
to the King passed by the House of Representatives on October 22, 1764,
and non-concurred by the Council.

[57]*Ibid.*, f. 458. The letter is dated March 3, 1766.

[58]Sparks Manuscripts 44, bundle 7, ff. 10–11. The letter is not dated.

[59]George Grenville wrote that the Americans were justified in rejoicing at
the repeal of the Stamp Act "especially if they understand by it, as they
justly may, notwithstanding the Declaratory Bill passed at the same time,
that they are thereby exempted for ever from being taxed by Great Britain
for the public support even of themselves." William J. Smith, ed., *The
Grenville Papers* (London, 1853), III, 250.

VI

Unfortunately this misunderstanding on the part of the Americans was matched by a similar misunderstanding on the part of many people in England with regard to the colonial position. We have seen that the American protests against the Stamp Act did not distinguish between internal and external taxes but denied that Parliament had any right to tax the colonies. Yet some Englishmen, at least, thought that the American protests were directed only against internal taxes. The American misunderstanding of the Declaratory Act is explicable by the vagueness of the act itself, the absence of any official interpretation of it, and the fact that the Parliamentary debate on it had been closed to the public. But the colonial statements had all been communicated to the British government by the beginning of the year 1766, before Parliament began to consider repeal of the Stamp Act. Why then did Englishmen suppose that the Americans distinguished between internal and external taxes?

Of course not all Englishmen did suppose so; those who took the trouble to read the colonial statements knew better. But apparently many Englishmen, including members of Parliament, did not take that trouble. It should be remembered that the colonial petitions were never formally considered by Parliament. Those sent before passage of the Stamp Act were thrown out because of the procedural rule against receiving petitions on money bills. Those sent for repeal of the Act were excluded for other procedural reasons and because they called the authority of Parliament into question. Thus although the contents of the statements could doubtless have been learned by anyone who wished to discover them, they were never given a regular hearing in Parliament.[60]

In the absence of any direct acquaintance with the colonial statements the average member of Parliament must have gained his impressions from one of two sources: either from the multitude of pamphlets dealing with the Stamp Act or from speeches in Parliament. It is possible but not probable that the authors of pamphlets against the Stamp Act were responsible for creating the impression that the Americans did not object to external taxes. We have already observed an ambiguity in the two pamphlets by

---

[60]*Collections of the Connecticut Historical Society,* XVIII, 332–335; *Maryland Historical Magazine,* VI, 282–288.

Stephen Hopkins and John Fitch which received the approval of Rhode Island and Connecticut respectively in 1764. Both these pamphlets used the phrase "internal taxes" in such a way as to suggest that external taxes might be constitutionally acceptable, though neither Hopkins nor Fitch explicitly said as much. Two other pamphlets, which enjoyed a wide circulation though not a formal legislative approval, also used the words "internal taxes" in a way which may have helped to bring about a misunderstanding of the American position. Richard Bland in *An Inquiry into the Rights of the British Colonies*[61] demonstrated that the colonist could not constitutionally be subjected to an internal tax by act of Parliament. Anyone reading Bland's conclusions without reading the argument leading to them might get the impression that Bland would have agreed to Parliament's collection of a revenue from customs duties levied in the colonies; but Bland's demonstration of his conclusion showed that Parliament could not constitutionally charge duties in the colony upon either imports or exports. In fact, he even argued that the Navigation Acts were unconstitutional. Bland evidently included in the phrase "internal taxes" the very duties which other people called "external taxes."

Another pamphlet which objected specially to internal taxes was Daniel Dulany's *Considerations on the Propriety of imposing Taxes in the British Colonies.*[62] This probably had a wider circulation than any other pamphlet against the Stamp Act, and it has frequently been cited as the source of the distinction between internal and external taxes. Although the greater part of Dulany's pamphlet was devoted to general arguments against the constitutionality of Parliamentary taxation, there were a few paragraphs in which he implied that internal taxes alone were unconstitutional. Thus he argued, on page 33, that before the Stamp Act, Parliament had never "imposed an internal Tax upon the Colonies *for the single Purpose of Revenue.*" He went on to deny the contention, which he attributed to the proponents of the Stamp Act, "That no Distinction can be supported between one Kind of Tax and another, an Authority to impose the one extending to the other." Contrary to this erroneous view, he said, "It appears to me, that there is a clear and necessary Distinction between an Act imposing a Tax *for the single Purpose of Revenue,* and those Acts which have been made for the Regulation of Trade, and have produced some Revenue in *Consequence of their Effect* and Op-

---

[61] Williamsburg, 1766.
[62] Annapolis, 1765 (second edition). The succeeding quotations are taken from pp. 30–35.

eration as *Regulations of Trade.*" According to this distinction Parliament had the right to regulate trade by the imposition of duties, even though those duties should incidentally produce some revenue. Dulany closed the discussion of this point by affirming: "a Right to impose an internal Tax on the Colonies without their consent, *for the single Purpose of Revenue,* is denied; a Right to regulate their Trade without their Consent is admitted."

It will be observed that in the course of this discussion, which occupied two pages of the pamphlet, Dulany had not made entirely clear what he regarded as constitutional and what he considered unconstitutional. He said that internal taxes for the purpose of revenue were unconstitutional, and he said that duties on trade for the purpose of regulation were constitutional, even though an incidental revenue might attend them, but he failed to say explicitly how he regarded duties on trade for the single purpose of revenue. He failed, in other words, to say how he stood on external taxes; in fact he did not even use the words "external tax" at any point in the pamphlet. His readers would perhaps have been justified in thinking that Dulany admitted external taxes as constitutional, since he explicitly objected only to internal taxes. Yet, unless Dulany was simply confused about the matter, it would appear that in his use of the phrase "internal tax" he included all duties levied in the colonies for the single purpose of revenue. In no other way does Dulany's argument make sense, for he contrasted what he called an internal tax for the single purpose of revenue with duties for the purpose of regulation from which an incidental revenue might arise. The context indicates clearly that the point of the contrast was not the difference between internal taxes as opposed to duties on trade but the difference between an imposition for the purpose of regulation and one for the purpose of revenue. Dulany emphasized the contrast by italicising the phrases: *single purpose of revenue, incidental Revenue,* and *Regulations of Trade.* The whole force of the contrast is lost unless the phrase "internal tax" is taken to include duties on trade collected in the colonies for the purpose of revenue. That this was Dulany's understanding of the term is further indicated in the two paragraphs which follow those summarized above. Here Dulany demonstrated that the duties on trade which had hitherto been collected in the colony had been levied not for the purpose of revenue but for the purpose of regulating trade. The argument which he used to carry this point was drawn from the fact that the customs duties collected in North America brought only £1,900 a year into the treasury while they cost £7,600 a year to collect. Dulany had taken these figures from a pamphlet by Grenville himself. He concluded with some justice that

[i]t would be ridiculous indeed to suppose that the Parliament would raise a Revenue by Taxes in the Colonies to defray Part of the national Expence, the Collection of which Taxes would increase that Expence to a Sum more than three Times the Amount of the Revenue; but, the Impositions being considered in their true Light, as Regulations of Trade, the Expence arising from an Establishment necessary to carry them into Execution, is so far from being ridiculous, that it may be wisely incurred.

Thus Dulany demonstrated that Parliament could not levy what he called an internal tax for the purpose of revenue by showing that Parliament had never levied an external tax for the purpose of revenue. The conclusion seems inescapable that he used the phrase "internal tax" in a loose sense, to cover all taxes collected in the colonies, whether excise taxes or customs duties levied for the single purpose of revenue. That this was his meaning is also suggested by the remainder of the pamphlet, in which he argued against Parliamentary taxation in general terms, as when he stated that "the Inhabitants of the Colonies claim an Exemption from *all* Taxes not imposed by their own Consent." (The italics are Dulany's.)

Dulany's pamphlet, though it was widely acclaimed as a defense of colonial rights, certainly employed a confusing terminology, and it would not be surprising if Englishmen at the time had gained the impression that there was some sort of distinction in it between the constitutionality of internal taxes as opposed to that of customs duties. Though Dulany never used the phrase "external tax" and though most of the pamphlet will make sense only if his use of the phrase "internal tax" is taken to include all taxes collected in the colonies, yet if American historians have derived the impression that he distinguished between internal and external taxes, it is not unreasonable to suppose that contemporary Englishmen received the same impression.

What does seem unlikely, however, is that British statesmen would have assumed, as American historians frequently seem to do, that Daniel Dulany was the proper spokesman for all the colonies. His pamphlet was only one of many, and the others ranged in attitude from complete submission to the authority of Parliament (as in Martin Howard's *Letter from a Gentleman at*

Halifax, to His friend in Rhode Island[63]) to complete defiance of Parliament (as in the *Considerations upon the Rights of the Colonists to the Privileges of British Subjects*[64]). Most of the pamphlets against the Stamp Act refrained from discussing the question of constitutional right and argued on the grounds of inexpediency or equity.[65] Those which concerned themselves with the constitutional aspects of the question devoted a major part of their attention to the doctrine of virtual representation.[66] This was an easy target, and in centering the constitutional controversy upon it the American protagonists gained a tactical victory; for when their opponents argued that the Americans might be taxed because they were virtually represented, this was tantamount to admitting that the power to tax depended upon representation. Daniel Dulany put his finger on the weakness of the ministerial position when he wrote to General Conway:

> If the right to tax and the right to regulate had been imagined by Mr. Grenville to be inseparable why did he tax his ingenuity to find out a virtual Representation, why did not some able friend intimate to him his Hazard on the slippery ground, he chose, when the all powerful Sovereignty of Parliament might have afforded so safe a footing?[67]

In other words Grenville himself, by arguing for virtual representation (as he did in *The Regulations Lately Made concerning the Colonies, and the Taxes Imposed upon Them, considered*[68]), had

---

[63]Newport, 1765.

[64]New York, 1766.

[65]See for example: John Dickinson's *The Late Regulations Respecting the British Colonies on the Continent of America Considered* (London, 1765); *A Letter to a Member of Parliament, Wherein the Power of the British Legislature, and the Case of the Colonists, Are Briefly and Impartially Considered* (London, 1765); *The True Interest of Great Britain, with Respect to her American Colonies, Stated and Impartially Considered* (London, 1766); *The Importance of the Colonies of North America, and the Interest of Great Britain with Regard to Them, Considered* (London, 1766); *The Necessity of Repealing the American Stamp Act Demonstrated* (London, 1766); *The Late Occurrences in North America, and Policy of Great Britain, Considered* (London, 1766); and Benjamin Franklin's *The General Opposition of the Colonies to the Payment of the Stamp Duty; and the Consequence of Enforcing Obedience by Military Measures; Impartially Considered* (London, 1766).

[66]See for example: Samuel Cooper, *The Crisis. Or, a Full Defense of the Colonies* (London, 1766), 3–30; Maurice Moore, *The Justice and Policy of Taxing the American Colonies, in Great Britain, Considered* (Wilmington, N. C., 1765), 7–14; Richard Bland, *An Inquiry into the Rights of the British Colonies* (Williamsburg, 1766), 5–12. Daniel Dulany, *Considerations on the Propriety of Imposing Taxes in the British Colonies* (Annapolis, Md., 1765), 5–14.

[67]Sparks Manuscripts 44, bundle 7, f.10.

[68]London, 1765.

admitted that taxation was not a function of sovereignty but rather, as the colonies were contending, the prerogative of a representative body.

There was no reason why the pamphleteers on the American side should have made a distinction between internal and external taxes when arguing the case against virtual representation; and it is not surprising that with the possible exception of those discussed above, none of them seems to have employed the distinction for purposes of argument. The distinction did appear in some of the literature in support of the Stamp Act, where it served as a whipping boy. It was attributed to the Americans and then demolished under the heavy gunfire of constitutional history.[69] It hardly seems likely that the defenders of the Stamp Act would have attributed the distinction to the Americans simply in order to discredit the colonial position. It is much more likely that they and the members of Parliament really believed that the colonists did distinguish between internal and external taxes. The question remains as to how they gained this impression.

The source from which, in all probability, it was derived was the speeches made in Parliament by friends of the colonies during the debates on repeal of the Stamp Act and afterwards, not excepting the brilliant interview given at the bar of the House of Commons by Benjamin Franklin. The member of Parliament who heard that carefully rehearsed performance (or who read it afterwards in print) might very justly have concluded that the Americans had no objection to external taxes, for Franklin, the archAmerican, at several points had stated that the Americans objected only to internal taxes.[70] When a member had pointed out that the objection to internal taxes could with equal justice be applied to external taxes, Franklin had replied that the Americans did not reason in that way at present but that they might learn to do so from the English. The wit of Franklin's tongue obscured the fact that he was wrong, but the average member could scarcely have known that. Laughing at Franklin's clever answers, he would probably have forgotten the rather pertinent question put by a member of the opposition: "Do not the resolutions of the Pennsylvania Assembly say, all taxes?" This question was evidently asked by a member who knew something about Pennsylvania's attitude.

[69]See *The Rights of Parliament Vindicated, On Occasion of the Late Stamp-Act. In Which is Exposed the Conduct of the American Colonists* (London, 1766); *An Examination of the Rights of the Colonies upon Principles of Law* (London, 1766).

[70]William Cobbett, ed., *Parliamentary History of England, from the Earliest Period to the Year 1803* (London, 1813), XVI, 137–160.

Franklin's answer to it was not as sprightly as his replies to some of the other questions. The best he could say was that if the Pennsylvania resolutions said all taxes, they meant only internal taxes. Actually it would have been impossible to tell from Franklin's testimony exactly what he thought the constitutional position of the Americans to be. At times he seemed to be saying that the Americans assented to external taxes; at other times he implied that they consented only to the regulation of trade. The performance was a good piece of lobbying for repeal of the Stamp Act, but it gave no clear indication of the American position and certainly could have contributed to the idea that the Americans were willing to accept external taxes.

The speeches of Franklin's friend Richard Jackson, member of Parliament for Weymouth, and agent at various times for Pennsylvania, Connecticut, and Massachusetts, may also have contributed to a false impression of the colonial position. Jackson believed that Parliament had a clear right to tax the colonies by duties on trade. Since Parliament by its admitted right to regulate trade could prohibit any branch of colonial trade, he reasoned, Parliament could also tax any branch of colonial trade.[71] Jackson, moreover, had searched the precedents thoroughly and found that Parliament in the past had imposed external taxes on the trade of Chester and Durham and Wales before those areas were represented in Parliament. At the same time Parliament had refrained from taxing them internally until they were granted representation. When Jackson rehearsed these views before Parliament,[72] he must have been listened to as a man of some authority; for he had the reputation of being extraordinarily learned,[73] and he was, besides, the official agent for several colonies. The average member of Parliament could not have known that he had been elected agent for Massachusetts by the political maneuvers of the royal governor,[74] nor that the Connecticut Assembly had written him a letter deploring his insufficient insistence upon colonial rights,[75] nor that he owed his appointment in Pennsylvania to his friend Benjamin Franklin, who had also misrepresented the colonial position.[76]

---

[71] Carl Van Doren, ed., *Letters and Papers of Benjamin Franklin and Richard Jackson 1753–1785* (Philadelphia, 1947), 123–124, 138–139.

[72] *Ibid.*, 194–196; *Collections of the Connecticut Historical Society*, XVIII, 316; Bradford, *Massachusetts State Papers*, 72–73.

[73] Van Doren, *Letters and Papers of Benjamin Franklin and Richard Jackson*, 1–2.

[74] Bernard Papers, III, 277–283.

[75] *Collections of the Connecticut Historical Society*, XVIII, 366–367.

[76] Van Doren, *Letters and Papers of Benjamin Franklin and Richard Jackson*, 87, 100.

What must also have impressed the uninformed member was the famous speech by William Pitt, when the Great Commoner had come out of his retirement to urge the repeal of the Stamp Act. On this occasion, Pitt had risen to a statement by George Grenville in which the latter had complained that he could not understand the distinction between internal and external taxes. "If the gentleman does not understand the difference between internal and external taxes," said Pitt, "I cannot help it."[77] Pitt's reply, if left there, might have been somewhat misleading. Anyone who listened to the whole of what he had to say would have known that Pitt, like the colonists, was distinguishing, not between internal and external taxes but between taxation and legislation. In an earlier speech he had stated that "Taxation is no part of the governing or legislative power,"[78] and now he went on to argue that "there is a plain distinction between taxes levied for the purpose of raising a revenue, and duties imposed for the regulation of trade, for the accomodation of the subject; although, in the consequences, some revenue might incidentally arise from the latter."[79] Pitt was following the argument of Dulany, whom he had read and admired;[80] and if historians have misunderstood Dulany's argument, it is not unlikely that the members of Parliament may have misunderstood Pitt's. Though there was a manifest difference between Pitt's and Dulany's acceptance of trade regulations which might incidentally produce a revenue and Jackson's and Franklin's acceptance of external taxes as such, nevertheless all four men were arguing in behalf of the colonies. The average member may have lumped them all together and come out with the simple conclusion that Americans accepted external taxes.

This conclusion would have been strengthened a little later by a speech of Thomas Pownall. Pownall, speaking with some authority as the former governor of Massachusetts, said explicitly that the colonists *"never objected to external taxes*—to imposts, subsidies and duties. They know that the express conditions of their settlements and establishments were, that they should pay these—and therefore they never have had any disputes with government on this head—but have always found reason to be satisfied *in the moderation with which government hath exercised this power."*[81]

---

[77] *Parliamentary History*, XVI, 105.
[78] *Ibid.*, 99.
[79] *Ibid.*, 105.
[80] W. S. Taylor and J. H. Pringle, eds., *The Chatham Correspondence* (London, 1838–1840), III, 192; Moses C. Tyler, *The Literary History of the American Revolution 1763–1783* (New York, 1941), 111 and n.
[81] *The Speech of Th-m-s P-n-ll, Esq . . . in the H—se of C—m-ns, in favor of America* (Boston, 1769), 12.

Pownall had apparently never read any of the colonial statements. Perhaps he derived some of his ideas from his friend Benjamin Franklin.[82] Certainly his authority to represent the views of the colonists was long since out of date. But how was the average member to know that? All the friends of America in Parliament seemed to be of opinion that the Americans were resigned to external taxes.

Why the colonial advocates in Parliament should have joined in conveying so false an impression of the colonial position is not entirely clear. A number of reasons might be offered why Pownall or Jackson or Pitt argued as they did: Pownell may have been misinformed;[83] Jackson may have been speaking for himself rather than for the colonies; and Pitt was misunderstood. But Franklin's testimony is more difficult to explain, for Franklin must have been better acquainted with the colonial declarations than he appeared to be. Why should he have contributed to the general misunderstanding? Furthermore why should all the proponents of colonial rights have misrepresented the colonies in the same way?

In the absence of direct information one can only suggest that political circumstances in 1766 required that every friend of the colonies in England refrain from urging the extreme claims put forward by the colonial assemblies and join in representing the colonies as more moderate than they actually were. The immediate object in 1766 was the repeal of the Stamp Act, and repeal was not to be attained by blunt denials of Parliament's authority. Though the colonists seemed to be unaware of this fact and continued on their intransigent course, their friends in England had to seek support where they could find it. They found it in the Rockingham administration, and consequently when they argued for repeal of the Stamp Act, they argued in Rockingham's terms. Now Rockingham's terms, to judge from at least one account, were a recognition of the distinction between internal and external taxes. According to Charles Garth the administration re-

---

[82]Pownall cooperated with Franklin on a scheme for raising money in the colonies by interest-bearing paper currency. This scheme was proposed by Franklin as a substitute for the Stamp Tax. For details see V. W. Crane, "Benjamin Franklin and the Stamp Act" *Publications of the Colonial Society of Massachusetts*, XXXII, 56–78. On Pownall's participation, see Pownall's letter to Hutchinson, Dec. 3, 1765, in Massachusetts Archives, XXV, 113.

[83]That Pownall was an unreliable source of information is suggested by the fact that he himself had suggested a stamp tax in his book *The Administration of the Colonies*. Dennys De Berdt later wrote that he was "as irresolute as the Wind, in one day's debate a friend to America the next quite with the Ministry," *Publications of the Colonial Society of Massachusetts*, XIII, 377–378.

fused to hear the petition of the Stamp Act Congress, because "it tended to question not only the Right of Parliament to impose internal Taxes, but external Duties."[84] Rockingham, it would appear, was prepared to settle the colonial issue by leaving internal taxes to the colonial assemblies. Though this was not as much as the colonies demanded, it was more than the rest of Parliament was willing to give, for most members were as ready to assert Parliament's right to levy all taxes as the colonists were to deny it.[85] Rockingham in fact was unable to repeal the Stamp Act on the basis of the distinction between internal and external taxes. Instead he was obliged to agree to the Declaratory Act, though worded in the ambiguous terms already noticed.[86] Rockingham, it is plain, needed all the support he could get, for he could not carry the rest of Parliament even as far as he and his own group were willing to go. In these circumstances it would have been undiplomatic, not to say reckless, for the friends of the colonies to embarrass him by insisting on the politically impossible claims of the colonial declarations. It seems unlikely that there was any formal agreement between the Rockingham group and the other colonial protagonists, whereby the latter agreed to soft-pedal the colonial claims to exclusive powers of taxation, but the pressure of politics undoubtedly dissuaded the friends of the colonies from giving publicity to the colonial declarations, and probably led them to cooperate with Rockingham in adopting a distinction which the colonists would never have allowed.

One conclusion in any case is clear: it was not the Americans who drew the line between internal and external taxes. It was recognized in America at the time by such diverse political personalities as James Otis and Thomas Hutchinson that the distinction was an English one. Otis, as already noticed, in the pamphlet approved by the Massachusetts assembly in 1764, scouted the distinction as one that "some make in England."[87]

---

[84]*Maryland Historical Magazine*, VI, 285.

[85]This fact was reported to the colonists in several letters. See, for example, that of Jared Ingersoll in *Collections of the Connecticut Historical Society*, XVIII, 317–326, and that of Richard Jackson in *ibid.*, 349–351.

[86]Dennys De Berdt wrote to Samuel White at the time of repeal that there were three parties in Parliament so far as the Stamp Act was concerned, one for enforcing, one for repeal with a declaration of right, and one for repeal without a declaration. According to De Berdt the administration favored the last view but was obliged to take the middle position in order to gain a majority, *Publications of the Colonial Society of Massachusetts*, XIII, 311–312.

[87]*The Rights of the British Colonies asserted and proved* (Boston, 1764), 42.

Hutchinson, in the third volume of his history of Massachusetts, gave credit for it to Pitt. Though it is clear that Pitt did not originate it, Hutchinson evidently thought that he did and was equally certain that the Americans did not accept it; for he averred that in levying the Townshend duties, "government in England too easily presumed, that Mr. Pitt's distinction between internal and external taxes would be favourably received in America."[88] There were members of Parliament in England, too, who realized that the distinction was not an American one, for in the debates on the Declaratory Act, Hans Stanley, the member for Southampton, embarrassed the Rockingham administration by pointing out that "The Americans have not made the futile Distinction between internal and external taxes,"[89] and Lord Lyttelton did the same thing in the House of Lords in the debate on the repeal of the Stamp Act, when he stated that "The Americans themselves make no distinction between external and internal taxes."[90] The colonial agents also realized that the colonists were talking bigger at home than their friends in England would admit, and the agents repeatedly requested their constituents to be less noisy about their rights. The colonists in return instructed the agents to be more noisy about them.[91]

The colonists were bumptious, blunt, and lacking in diplomacy, but they were not guilty of the constitutional frivolity with which they have been charged. When they objected to the Townshend Duties in 1767, they had in no way changed the conception of Parliamentary power which they avowed at the time of the Stamp Act: they still admitted the authority of Parliament to regulate trade and to legislate in other ways for the whole empire; they still denied that Parliament had a right to tax them. These views they continued to affirm until the 1770's when they advanced to the more radical position of denying the authority of Parliament to legislate as well as to tax. Though this denial was generally accompanied by an allowance of Parliamentary legislation as a matter of convenience, there can be no question that the later position was constitutionally different from the earlier one. But that the colonists were guilty of skipping from one constitu-

[88]L. S. Mayo, ed., *History of the Province of Massachusetts Bay* (Cambridge, Mass., 1936), III, 130.
[89]*American Historical Review*, XVII, 566.
[90]*Parliamentary History*, XVI, 167.
[91]*Collections of the Connecticut Historical Society*, XVIII, 349–351, 366–367; *Collections of the Massachusetts Historical Society*, LXXIV, 39–54, 145–146; Massachusetts Archives, XXII, 361–363; *Publications of the Colonial Society of Massachusetts*, XIII, 332–333, 335, 337, 354.

tional theory to another, like so many grasshoppers, is a Tory libel that has too readily been accepted by modern historians. American Revolutionary thought went through two stages, not three; the supposed first stage never existed. If anyone took a more advanced position because of the passage of the Townshend Duties, it was not the colonists. They were already there.

"Rights Imply Equality": The Case Against Admiralty Jurisdiction in America, 1764-1776

DAVID S. LOVEJOY

Equality has become a fundamental principle of American democracy. Although we are frequently reminded that Americans fail to practice altogether what they preach, still, the concept of equality is as much a part of the democratic ideal as manhood suffrage and public education. But the Spirit of '76, although not aristocratic, was not egalitarian either. Despite Thomas Jefferson's eloquent declaration that all men are created equal, most Americans of the Revolutionary generation showed little interest in the broad aspects of human equality which since that time have helped to direct the course of American history.

One very good reason why eighteenth-century Americans did not worry much about equality among themselves was that in America there were not the glaring inequalities between individuals and between groups which obtained in Europe. Colonial society was less stratified than that across the Atlantic. Since land was much easier to acquire here than there, economic opportunity was greater, and wider distribution of land meant wider distribution of suffrage. In this sense the American colonies were generally more democratic by nature both politically and socially than either England or France or any European nation.

What inequality did exist among people in the colonies, whether it was political or social, economic or religious, was secondary

Reprinted with permission from The William and Mary Quarterly, 3rd ser., XVI, 4 (October, 1959), 459-484.

to another kind of inequality which took the colonists' attention in the 1760's and which became a compelling force driving them toward revolution in the years following. This was inequality not among Americans but between Americans and Englishmen as subjects of the same empire, and when Americans became aware of it, they were grateful to the English for pointing it out to them. At the close of the French and Indian War, when Englishmen discovered that their national debt was about as large in pounds sterling as the new empire was in acres of American wilderness, they initiated a new colonial policy which would require Americans to contribute through taxation to the financial responsibilities of this empire. Englishmen were surprised to learn that several generations of salutary neglect of the colonists were accompanied by a striking process of economic and political maturity, changing obedient children into precocious and fractious adolescents. Ambitious Americans regarded Parliamentary taxation as conduct becoming a stepmother's severity rather than parental kindness, and they stubbornly refused to accept it. In justification they argued a theory of empire which denied Parliament's right to tax them without their consent, and, more important, they maintained that Americans were as good as Englishmen and had claim to the same kind of treatment from government.

No one saw more clearly than John Adams the distinction Parliament made between American and British subjects. A few years before his death he wrote to a friend: "However tedious and painful it may be for you to read, or me to transcribe any part of these dull [Parliamentary] statutes, we must endure the task, or we shall never understand the American Revolution."[1] At the age of eighty-three, forty-two years after independence, Adams still bristled and fumed when he thought of the insulting, the degrading attitude of superiority which Parliamentary statutes expressed. What he meant was that the inferior status forced upon the American colonists was an important cause—maybe to Adams, an ambitious man, the most important cause—of the Revolution which, in his mind, was a struggle for equality between American and Englishman.

I

Although Parliamentary taxation was the most celebrated threat to colonial rights in the early years of the Revolutionary move-

---

[1] John Adams to William Tudor, Quincy, Aug. 6, 1818, *The Works of John Adams*, Charles Francis Adams, ed. (Boston, 1850–1856), X, 339.

ment, it was not the only threat, despite the fact that it has received more attention than any other issue by historians since that time. What historians have failed to emphasize is that the means of enforcing the new taxes were as much an innovation in colonial policy and as much a threat to equality of treatment in the empire as the taxes themselves, and, according to the colonists, just as unconstitutional. For Parliament directed that the new tax laws could be enforced in either the regular colony courts where common-law procedures operated or in the courts of admiralty which proceeded without juries according to the civil law.

Admiralty court justice was not new to Americans in 1764, or to the English for that matter. Since medieval times these courts in England had functioned according to the law of nations, and their jurisdiction was limited to disputes occurring on the high seas and traditionally below the first bridge over navigable rivers. The common-law courts and common lawyers constantly kept admiralty jurisdiction in check, and Sir Edward Coke owed some of his reputation as a defender of the common law to frequent trimming of admiralty jurisdiction when it exceeded the limits allowed. Certainly admiralty courts were necessary, and if not popular, they were tolerated since they disposed of disputes, particularly prize cases, which could be settled in no other way. However, Englishmen were jealous of the common law and successfully protected it from unwarranted encroachment by civil courts.[2]

During most of the seventeenth century the colonial governments allowed governors and councils and common-law courts to hear and determine disputes which in England would have been tried before admiralty judges. When it became apparent that Americans were not disposed to enforce the Navigation Acts, Parliament took strong measures. In shoring up the whole imperial structure in 1696, the legislature directed that certain laws of trade could be enforced either in the common-law courts at Westminster or in Ireland or in American courts of admiralty within the colonies where the offenses occurred. Since permanent admiralty courts did not actually exist in the colonies, they were established the next year and judges were appointed. The act of 1696, however, was ambiguously phrased, and it left some doubt whether Parliament meant all forfeitures and penalties under the acts of trade, or just those mentioned in the new act itself, were

---

[2]Helen J. Crump, *Colonial Admiralty Jurisdiction in the Seventeenth Century* (London, 1931), chap. I; Winfred T. Root, *The Relations of Pennsylvania with the British Government, 1696–1765* (New York, 1912), pp. 95–97.

recoverable in admiralty courts in America. (Probably Parliament intended the new courts to enforce all the acts of trade since 1660; otherwise there would have been little sense in extending the jurisdiction to America. In any event, Crown officials came later to regard these courts as suitable for enforcement of all Parliamentary acts which regulated trade in the colonies.)

Regardless of which interpretation was correct, the act of 1696 gave a larger jurisdiction to admiralty courts in America than had ever been given to the same courts in England, thus distinguishing between Americans and Englishmen in matters of justice. His Majesty's courts at Westminster, that is, common-law courts with juries, enforced the acts of trade in England, while admiralty courts, which proceeded under the civil law without juries, could enforce some, if not all, of the same acts in America.[3]

A few people recognized the alarming extension of admiralty jurisdiction in the colonies and protested against it. Among these was William Penn who understood the necessity of trade and commerce for nurturing an infant colony. In 1701 he condemned the comprehensive powers of the new court in Pennsylvania which, he said, "swallowed up a great part of the Government here. . . ." Penn understood, too, that his colonists had not come to America to be deprived of their rights by an arbitrary court: the determining of these causes, he wrote, "without a jury, gives our people the greatest discontent, looking upon themselves as less free here than at home, instead of greater privileges, which were promised."[4]

---

[3]7 & 8 Gul. III, c. 22, sect. VII, *The Statutes at Large* . . . , Danby Pickering, ed. (Cambridge, England, 1762–1866), IX, 432; Crump, *Colonial Admiralty Jurisdiction,* pp. 1, 128–132, 148–149, 163–164, and *passim;* Lawrence A. Harper, *The English Navigation Laws* (New York, 1939), chap. XV; Charles M. Andrews, *The Colonial Period of American History* (New Haven, 1934–1938), IV, 225–229; see also Andrews' Introducion to *Records of the Vice-Admiralty Court of Rhode Island, 1716–1752,* Dorothy S. Towle, ed. (Washington, D. C., 1936), pp. 5–13; Edward Channing, *History of the United States* (New York, 1905–1925), II, 275–277; Root, *The Relations of Pennsylvania,* pp. 95–97.

Crump implies that all acts of trade could come under admiralty jurisdiction in America, while Andrews, although recognizing the momentous change brought about by the act of 1696, seems to think the jurisdiction of the courts was somewhat limited. For confusing judicial opinions on this matter, *see Calendar of State Papers, Colonial Series, America and West Indies, Jan.-Dec. 1, 1702,* Cecil Headlam, ed. (London, 1912), 389, 451, 554–555.

[4]William Penn to Robert Harley [c. 1701], *The Manuscripts of His Grace the Duke of Portland,* IV, Historical Manuscripts Commission, Fifteenth Report, Appendix, Part IV (London, 1897), 31.

Despite the ominous powers given to the new courts by the act of 1696, American merchants and traders were not as badly off as they imagined. It was not long before the common-law courts found ways to circumvent the admiralty courts or at least to limit their effectiveness. The act itself was not as clearly worded as it might have been—"weakly penned," as William Penn[5] put it— and was open to several less rigorous interpretations which the colonists were quick to exploit. The struggle in England between common law and admiralty law, which had helped to push Sir Edward Coke into the limelight in the seventeenth century, was transferred to the colonies in the eighteenth with some of the same results. Courts of common law grew bold, often usurping jurisdiction from admiralty courts by issuing writs of prohibition against their decrees and even discharging prisoners detained by them.[6] The people of Massachusetts generally assumed that their Superior Court exercised locally all the powers of the Court of King's Bench in England and on this basis justified the court's halting admiralty proceedings when the latter got out of line.[7] Jeremiah Dummer defended this conduct as early as 1721 in his *Defence of the New-England Charters . . .* , in which he equated the Massachusetts court not only with the King's Bench, but also with the Courts of Common Pleas and Exchequer in England. If these English courts had a right to restrain admiralty juris-diction, so then did the court in Boston; for, he wrote, if "some bounds are not set to the Jurisdiction of the Admiralty, beyond which it shall not pass, it may in Time, like the Element to which it ought to be confin'd, grow outrageous and overflow the Banks of all the other Courts of Justice." The fact that admiralty judges received only fees and no salaries worried Dummer since they were "strongly tempted to receive all Business that comes before them, however improper for their Cognizance."[8]

Rhode Islanders made life miserable for an admiralty judge appointed there: in 1743, just after his arrival, the legislature enacted a law regulating his fees and reducing them so low, it

---

[5]*Ibid.*

[6]Root, *The Relations of Pennsylvania*, pp. 95–97; Edward Channing, *History*, II, 277–279; Harper, *The English Navigation Laws*, p. 188.

[7]Thomas Hutchinson, *The History of the Colony and Province of Massachusetts-Bay*, Lawrence Shaw Mayo, ed. (Cambridge, Mass., 1936), III, 65, 116.

[8](London, 1721), pp. 50–52, 58, 60. Dummer also argued that an English-man ought not to be deprived of his property by civil law since it is "what he has not consented to himself, or his Representative for him." Therefore, admiralty court justice should cover only transactions which occur on the high seas and not triable at common law (p. 51).

was said, "that the Judge has not a competent Allowance to support the Dignity of the Office." When the ministry in London accused the colony of interfering with the execution of the court's duties, Governor William Greene reassured the Duke of Newcastle that the court enjoyed complete independence in Rhode Island. Surprisingly, in the same letter to His Grace, he admitted that the former deputy judge was then in jail for not paying his debts.[9]

Just about the time Dummer published his *Defence*, Parliament again extended the jurisdiction of the admiralty courts in America, this time, not just beyond the shore line, to which he believed it ought to be confined, but beyond even the banks of the rivers which penetrated the interior. The colonists, it seems, were as careless at times about Parliament's laws reserving particular pine trees for the use of His Majesty as they were about the Navigation Acts. As a consequence, in 1721 Parliament placed enforcement of the white-pine laws in the courts of admiralty where suspected colonists could be tried by a single judge according to the civil law.[10] The extension of admiralty court jurisdiction to include cutting the King's masts does not seem to have caused much complaint. As with the enforcement of the laws of trade, probably the common-law courts frequently interfered and thwarted the efforts of Crown officers and admiralty judges.[11]

Had the Molasses Act of 1733 been enforced, doubtless the American colonists would have added to their complaints about its prohibitive duties the objection that offenses against the act in America were triable in either their own courts of record (common-law courts) or the courts of admiralty. Moreover, the act made clear to those colonists who read it closely just how discriminatory Parliament could be. Besides levying duties on imported goods from the foreign islands, the act prohibited the importation of these same goods into Ireland except when they had been "loaden and shipped in *Great Britain*" in proper vessels. But Parliament specifically directed that offenses committed

---

[9]See letters in *Correspondence of the Colonial Governors of Rhode Island, 1723–1775*, Gertrude S. Kimball, ed. (Cambridge, Mass., 1903), II, 242–245, 251.

[10]8 Geo. I, c. 12, sect. V, Pickering, *The Statutes at Large*, XIV, 387.

[11]This was not always the case. In 1770 William Dean and his sons, who lived in the vicinity of what is now Brattleboro, Vermont, went to jail rather than pay the £800 sterling the admiralty court at New York demanded for cutting sixteen trees on land near their home. *Reports of Cases in the Vice Admiralty of the Province of New York and in the Court of Admiralty of the State of New York, 1715–1788*, Charles M. Hough, ed. (New Haven, 1925), pp. 227–233.

against this section of the act were triable *only* in courts of record at Westminster or Dublin.[12] Since customs officials in America generally avoided enforcement of the Molasses Act[13] and common-law courts were already adept at preventing cases from coming to the admiralty courts, the constitutional issue did not arise.

As long as admiralty courts confined themselves to the condemnation of prizes and problems of salvage, wrecks, and seamen's wages, Americans willingly admitted their jurisdiction. But courts of admiralty were charged with enforcing the acts of trade in America, and when they did so, they were thoroughly disliked.[14] Despite the fact that the seriousness of the colonists' complaints varied in direct proportion to the degree the courts interfered with illegal trade, a constitutional issue was involved. When courts of admiralty exercised all the powers in America that the act of 1696 intended, then Americans were distinguished from their cousins in England and were subject to a different judicial system—one that deprived them, they said, of trial by jury. But Americans escaped any serious difficulty over admiralty jurisdiction until after the French and Indian War when Parliament levied taxes on the colonists and used admiralty courts to see that they were paid.

II

The Sugar and Stamp Acts of 1764 and 1765 inaugurated a major change in British colonial policy. Never before had Parliament directly taxed the American colonists, and their violent reaction to these taxes set in motion a resistance movement which in twelve years culminated in independence. Besides levying a threepence tax on each gallon of molasses imported into the colonies from the foreign West Indies and imposing duties on several other imports, the Sugar Act explicitly directed that forfeitures and penalties imposed by the act and by any of the earlier laws of trade were recoverable at the election of the informer or prosecutor in a court of record or a colonial admiralty court. Any doubt entertained heretofore, owing to the "obscurity, if not inconsistency,"[15] of the 1696 act, that admiralty courts

---

[12]6 Geo. II, c. 13, Pickering, *The Statutes at Large*, XVI, 375–376.

[13]For exceptions, see Andrews, *Colonial Period*, IV, 242–244; also Andrews's Introduction to Towle, *Records of the Vice-Admiralty Court of Rhode Island*, pp. 53–54.

[14]Crump, *Colonial Admiralty Jurisdiction*, pp. 128, 164.

[15]Penn to Harley, *The Manuscripts of the Duke of Portland*, IV, 31.

could try violations of the Navigation Acts was now laid to rest. What is more, in order to put admiralty justice clear of the pressure of colonial common-law courts, the Sugar Act authorized, and an Order in Council established, a vice-admiralty court for all America to be located at Halifax, Nova Scotia, with both appellate and original jurisdiction.[16]

A few months after the Sugar Act became effective, Parliament passed the American Stamp Act which would tax the colonists' use of paper and exact sterling money from most legal and business transactions. Penalties and forfeitures under the Stamp Act were also recoverable in courts of record *or* courts of admiralty in America.[17] At the election of informers or prosecutors the whole British colonial system—Navigation Acts, Sugar Act, and Stamp Act—now came under admiralty court jurisdiction where judges, linked to the prerogative, decided issues according to civil law without benefit of juries.

The documents and pamphlets drafted during the Stamp Act crisis clearly demonstrate that the extension of admiralty court jurisdiction was a major grievance. The Stamp Act Congress listed it prominently in the four documents the members produced.[18] Most colonial legislatures coupled it with Parliamentary taxation in their resolves and complained about the subversion of the rights of Americans.[19] Daniel Dulany in his famous pamphlet declared that the Stamp Act, its power to tax and its substitution of an "arbitrary Civil Law Court, in the Place of . . . the Common-Law-Trial by Jury . . ." left Americans without "even the Shadow of a Privilege."[20] The sacred right of trial by jury, said John Dickinson, was violated "by the erection of arbitrary and unconstitutional jurisdictions."[21] *The Constitutional Courant*, probably the most inflammatory piece of political literature at the time, likened admiralty courts to the "high commission and star chamber courts" and warned Americans that, since the Stamp Act gave these courts "jurisdiction over matters that have no relation to navigation or sea affairs, they may, with equal pro-

---

[16]4 Geo. II, c. 15, sects. LX, LXI, Pickering, *The Statutes at Large*, XXVI, 49; *Acts of the Privy Council of England, Colonial Series*, James Munro, ed. (London, 1908–12), IV, 663–664.

[17]5 Geo. III, c. 12, sects. LVII, LVIII, Pickering, *The Statutes at Large*, XXVI, 202, 203.

[18]*Proceedings of the Congress at New-York* (Annapolis, 1766).

[19]*Prologue to Revolution: Sources . . . on the Stamp Act Crisis*, ed. Edmund S. Morgan (Chapel Hill, 1959), pp. 46–62, *passim*.

[20]*Considerations on the Propriety of Imposing Taxes in the British Colonies* (North America, 1765), p. 25.

[21]*The Late Regulations respecting the British Colonies on the Continent of America, Considered* . . . (Philadelphia, 1765), p. 35.

priety, have jurisdiction in cases of life and death. This is a real representation of the slavish state we are reduced to by the Stamp Act, if we ever suffer it to take place among us."[22] Admiralty courts, said James Otis, "savour more of modern Rome and the Inquisition, than of the common law of England and the constitution of Great-Britain."[23]

In 1765 John Adams, who still lived in Braintree, and whose reputation as a lawyer and patriot was modest, to say the least, compared with that of James Otis, began a series of attacks upon admiralty justice which contributed to his growing stature as a major Revolutionary figure. Adams as much as any colonist hated the Stamp Act and all Parliamentary statutes which discriminated against Americans. But, in the instructions he drafted for Braintree's representatives, he saved his severest condemnation for the "alarming extension" of admiralty court powers, which, he claimed, was the "most grievous innovation of all," for it violated the Great Charter itself and shamelessly distinguished between Americans and English in matters of justice.[24] This was only the opening gun of Adams's attack; he later demonstrated even more forcefully the disgraceful inequalities which Parliament cavalierly established under courts of admiralty in America.

Granted the colonists objected to Parliamentary taxation for very human and self-interested reasons. Granted they objected to admiralty court trials for the same human and selfish reasons —after all, the chances of losing one's shirt would be about a hundred times greater at Halifax or before any admiralty judge than in a local court before a jury of one's peers. Granted, then, the colonists had self-interested motives; their dislike for parting with their property does not vitiate the constitutional arguments they brought to bear against the process used to take it way from them. In the colonists' eyes, the new use of admiralty justice in America compounded Parliament's original error, for these courts would enforce unconstitutional taxes by unconstitutional means.

III

To understand the Tory and English defense of admiralty court jurisdiction in America is to understand in part the growing

[22]Reprinted in a paper by Albert Matthews on the snake devices, 1754–1776, and the *Constitutional Courant*, 1765, in Colonial Society of Massachusetts, *Publications*, XI (Boston, 1910), 429–430.

[23]*The Rights of the British Colonies Asserted and Proved* (Boston, 1764), p. 28.

[24]Adams, *Works*, III, 466–467.

difference between American and English interpretations of the empire and the rights of colonists as British subjects. Justification for admiralty jurisdiction over American trade, said its defenders, was simply its necessity. Juries "in these causes were not to be trusted," said Governor Francis Bernard of Massachusetts. No candid man "will take upon him to declare, that at this time an *American* jury is impartial and indifferent enough, to determine equally upon frauds of trade."[25] Martin Howard, a Newport Tory, came to the same conclusion, and although he admitted that the court at Halifax was a "severity in the method of prosecution," it was a severity Americans had brought upon themselves. Smuggling was so prevalent, he argued, that the "government is justifiable in making laws against it, even like those of *Draco,* which were written in blood."[26]

In 1776 Thomas Hutchinson achieved the dubious honor of answering for Englishmen, article by article, the Declaration of Independence. When he came to the grievance that Americans in many cases were deprived of trial by jury, he demonstrated the same blindness to American argument that had afflicted the ministry for some time. Omitting completely any reference to the fact that admiralty courts in America could enforce Parliamentary taxation, he cited only admiralty court jurisdiction over breaches of the laws of trade and over trespass upon the King's woods as cases in which trial by jury was denied. In both of these, he argued, the "necessity of the case justified the departure from the general rule."[27]

A few years later, George Chalmers, a Tory historian in England, referred to the year 1697 as the era of "memorable change in colonial jurisprudence," which "superseded in some measure the trial by jury, that had been found to be inconvenient in proportion as it was favorable to popular rights." Chalmers cushioned this "memorable change," or so he believed, by informing his readers that John Locke himself had "expressly advised his sovereign 'to settle courts of admiralty under proper officers of his own appointment, in order to prevent illegal trade in those

---

[25]*Select Letters on the Trade and Government of America* (London, 1774), pp. 16–17. Governor Bernard's words were echoed in London by defenders of the Stamp Act. See anon., *The Conduct of the Late Administration Examined,* 2nd ed. (London, 1767), p. 36.

[26]*A Letter from a Gentleman at Halifax, to his Friend in Rhode-Island* (Newport, 1765), pp. 17–20.

[27]*Strictures upon the Declaration of the Congress at Philadelphia; In a Letter to a Noble Lord, &c.* (London, 1776), p. 24, recently reprinted by the Old South Association, *Old South Leaflets,* no. 227, Malcolm Freiberg, ed. (Boston, 1958).

parts.' "[28] Tory argument implied very clearly that Parliament was justified in violating the rights of its subjects so that the Navigation Acts might be enforced.

Justification for admiralty court enforcement of Parliamentary taxation grew in part out of the defense of these courts for the regulation of trade. Enforcement of the Stamp Act in the admiralty courts, said its advocates, was really not a "novel measure" at all, because "a jurisdiction had been assigned to the judges of the court of admiralty, upon the laws of revenue and trade, without juries, for near a century past."[29] This argument goes to the very bottom of the chasm which divided the colonists and the Parliament in these years. Unlike Englishmen, Americans did not speak of trade and revenue in the same breath. They had always accepted regulation of their trade, and although they smuggled on occasion, they seldom doubted Parliament's right to control their commerce. But the colonists distinguished absolutely between statutes which regulated their trade and statutes which taxed their trade and themselves. Members of the Stamp Act Congress and Daniel Dulany, in 1765, and John Dickinson, a few years later, made this distinction clear, and most Americans were disposed to agree with them.[30]

Englishmen, on the other hand, thought this distinction absurd, because to them there was little difference between regulation of trade and taxation, since both brought in revenue to the Crown. Navigation Acts since 1660 had regulated the commerce of the empire, but they had also, when enforced, produced some revenue. For Americans to argue that regulation was right and taxation was wrong made no sense to most members of Parliament and the ministry. According to their argument, Parliament had always taxed American trade; and violations of these laws were

---

[28]Although written during and just after the Revolution, only a part of this work was published in London in 1780 and entitled *Political Annals of the Present United Colonies*. The complete work was published in two volumes in Boston in 1845 and called *An Introduction to the History of the Revolt of the American Colonies*. See I, Introduction and p. 275.

[29]Thomas Pownall, *The Administration of the Colonies, to which is added, an Appendix, No. III, containing, Considerations on the Points lately brought into Question as to the Parliament's Right of taxing the Colonies, and of the Measures necessary to be taken at this Crisis* (London, 1766), pp. 43–44 (of *Considerations*); anon., *Conduct of the Late Administration*, pp. 22–25, 34–37; anon., *Correct Copies of the Two Protests against the Bill to Repeal the American Stamp Act* (Paris, 1766), pp. 16–19.

[30]*Proceedings of the Congress at New-York*, p. 23; Dulany, *Considerations on the Propriety of Imposing Taxes*, p. 34; John Dickinson, *Letters from a Farmer in Pennsylvania, to the Inhabitants of the British Colonies* (Philadelphia, 1768), pp. 29–30.

cognizable in courts of admiralty in America. Most Englishmen saw no reason, then, why admiralty courts were not competent to try cases involving further taxation of Americans under the Sugar and Stamp Acts, particularly since these courts were made necessary by the reluctance of colonial juries to convict Americans.

One can imagine that this argument made no impression whatsoever upon colonists who for some time had questioned admiralty jurisdiction over the trade laws. To extend the jurisdiction of these courts to enforce direct taxation of Americans was intolerable, not merely because the taxes were believed unconstitutional but because the court procedure offended their sense of justice as British subjects.

Englishmen further argued that an admiralty trial for a violation of the Stamp Act in America did not really distinguish Americans from English subjects with respect to trial by jury.[31] And if the issue were trial by jury alone, the Englishmen had the better of the argument. Americans, apparently, were unmindful that Englishmen had paid stamp taxes since 1694. In addition, forfeitures and penalties for several violations of the English acts, specifically for printing or selling pamphlets and newspapers on unstamped paper, had been cognizable since 1711 before two or more justices of the peace only, with appeal to a quarter sessions court, consisting of more justices of the peace, in the county, riding, or shire where the offenses occurred.[32] Actually neither subject enjoyed trial by jury when he disobeyed a stamp act. But the English argument in defense of the American act on these grounds did not go far enough. It failed to point out that the Englishman was brought before a court in his own neighborhood or county where he could count on traditional common-law procedure, while the American might find his trial set in some other colony besides his own or even at Halifax, Nova Scotia, and presided over by a single judge trained in the civil law.

Had Parliament authorized the enforcement of the Stamp Act in the colonies by the same means that similar acts were en-

---

[31]Anon., *Correct Copies of the Two Protests against the Bill,* p. 17; anon., *Conduct of the Late Administration,* p. 36.

[32]For the English stamp acts, see in particular 5 & 6 Gul. III, c. 21; 9 & 10 Gul. III, c. 25; 10 Anne, c. 19, sects. CXIX, CXX, CLXXII; 16 Geo. II, c. 26, sect. V; Pickering, *The Statutes at Large,* IX, 306–321, X, 153–167, XII, 377–378, 388–389, XVIII, 134–135. See also Edward Hughes, "The English Stamp Duties, 1664–1764," *English Historical Review,* LVI (1941), 244–246, 249, 252, 253; Stephen Dowell, *A History of Taxation and Taxes in England* (London, 1884), III, 323–377. Dowell says nothing about enforcement of the stamp acts.

forced in England, the colonists might not have complained as loudly as they did, for justices of the peace were certainly more amenable to the will of the people than were admiralty judges appointed by the Crown. Doubtless members of Parliament were well aware of this when they made enforcement of the American act possible in the courts of admiralty. Experience in England had demonstrated that the stamp acts were not well obeyed there.[33] But Parliament had never dared to enlarge admiralty jurisdiction to assure obedience in England. Parliament did dare to enlarge this jurisdiction in America. This was the distinction: British subjects were under the common law in England but would be under civil law in America for violations of stamp taxes. Although the principle involved, as far as equal treatment was concerned, was not trial by jury, it was equally fundamental. Had the colonists answered the argument regarding equal loss of jury trial, they probably would have exclaimed, and not very respectfully: "If an Englishman was deprived of trial by jury for disobeying a stamp act, he ought not to be!"

The repeal of the Stamp Act in 1766 gave the act's proponents an opportunity to portray their enemies as unsympathetic to American complaints against distant courts and interested judges. Just as the Sugar Act had authorized an over-all vice-admiralty court in America, so the Stamp Act under Grenville had empowered the creation of several more of these courts, with both appellate and original jurisdiction, to be distributed among the thirteen colonies. Once Parliament had passed the act, the Treasury recommended to the Privy Council that the court at Halifax be switched to Boston and two others be established, one at Philadelphia and one at Charlestown, South Carolina—also that dignified salaries be settled on the judges to relieve them of the criticism that poundage and fees tempted them to action.[34] But shortly after they had passed the Stamp Act, George Grenville and his friends went out of government, giving way to the Marquis of Rockingham and his people. Secretary Henry S. Conway, whose duty it would have been under Rockingham to act upon the proposals for new vice-admiralty courts, failed to do so before Parliament, led by his faction, repealed the Stamp Act, thus revoking the authorization for additional courts. The question

---

[33]Hughes, "The English Stamp Duties," *English Historical Review*, LVI, 249, 252, 253.

[34]5 Geo. III, c. 12, sect. LVIII, Pickering, *The Statutes at Large*, XXVI, 203; Munro, *Acts of the Privy Council, Colonial Series*, IV, 664; anon., *Correct Copies of the Two Protests against the Bill*, pp. 17–18; anon., *Conduct of the Late Administration*, pp. 36–37.

of constitutionality, as we have seen, the Stamp Act defenders brushed off with the argument that admiralty courts had always enforced acts of trade and revenue in America and that stamp duties even in England were not enforced by jury trials. Now, they said, the blame for injustice and inconvenience, in dragging a colonist to a court far distant from his home where he was unknown and where the judge was paid in fees, must be laid at the feet of the administration which repealed the Stamp Act.[35]

This was cold comfort for the American colonists. The only complaint against admiralty jurisdiction which seemed to get a hearing in England was that the vice-admiralty court at Halifax was grievous because it was too far removed from the centers of trade. And, as it turned out, relief from this particular grievance was frustrated by the repeal of the very act they protested— an act which taxed Americans without their consent and authorized enforcement of the tax in courts of civil law.

Parliament repealed the Stamp Act, not because it was unconstitutional, as the colonists claimed, but for the sake of expediency, since it was economically unwise and, probably more important, since the colonists generally refused to obey it. Although the courts of admiralty never got the chance to enforce the Stamp Act, the possibility had unsettled a good many people. Moreover, the constitutional issue, according to the colonists, remained unresolved; if Parliament could levy one tax and place its enforcement within the jurisdiction of the admiralty courts, it could levy another and enforce it in the same way. Furthermore, the Sugar Act remained on the statute books—although the tax on molasses was reduced to one penny a gallon—[36] and the court at Halifax was still open for business.

The Stamp Act crisis forced Americans to examine more closely their status within the empire. Probably very few agreed with Benjamin Gale of Connecticut that the Stamp Act had "laid the foundation for Americas being an Independant State."[37] Nevertheless, the people, said John Adams, "even to the lowest ranks, have become more attentive to their liberties, more inquisitive about them, and more determined to defend them, than they were ever before known or had occasion to be."[38]

In defending these liberties, several Americans concluded that

[35]Anon., *Correct Copies of the Two Protests against the Bill*, pp. 16–19; anon., *Conduct of the Late Administration*, pp. 22–25, 37.

[36]6 Geo. III, c. 52, Pickering, *The Statutes at Large*, XXVII, 275–276.

[37]*Extracts from the Itineraries . . . of Ezra Stiles*, Franklin B. Dexter, ed. (New Haven, 1916), p. 494.

[38]Adams, *Works*, II, 154.

British subjects were equal in other matters besides the rights to consent to taxes and to demand the protection of the common law. The Boston town meeting declared that "Britons have been as free on one side of the Atlantic as on the other"; when a people become colonists they are still naturally a part of the state and "intitled to all the essential rights of the mother country."[39] Rhode Islanders petitioned the King and reminded him of their "equal freedom" with their fellow subjects in Great Britain.[40] Their governor, Stephen Hopkins, besides declaring that colonists anywhere throughout history had always enjoyed the same rights as subjects who remained at home, boldly argued that the separate American colonies and England constituted a commonwealth of nations, each with its own government—the colonies were subject to the superintendence of Parliament only for such general matters as the regulation of trade.[41] A pamphleteer in North Carolina admitted that "the more closely united the Mother Country and the Colonies are, the happier it will be for both"; but, he cautioned, "such an union will never take effect, but upon a foundation of equality."[42] Richard Bland of Virginia complained bitterly of Parliamentary acts which put heavier restrictions on American than on English commerce. Such acts, he declared, "constituted an unnatural Difference between Men under the same Allegiance, born equally free, and entitled to the same civil Rights." I am speaking of the "*Rights* of a People," and "*Rights* imply *Equality* in the Instances to which they belong. . . ." Colonists, he concluded, "were not sent out to be the Slaves but to be the Equals of those that remain behind."[43]

The crisis over taxation provoked among a number of Americans the doctrine that British subjects, regardless of where they lived, ought to be treated as equals. Americans, it seems, were content to be colonials as long as their status as colonists was in no way inferior to that of subjects within the realm—an interpretation of the British Empire which was a slap in the face to most eighteenth-century Englishmen. If Americans believed this

---

[39]"Substance of a Memorial presented the House," May 1764, bound in Otis, *Rights of the British Colonies*, p. 70, John Carter Brown Library, Brown University.

[40]*Records of the Colony of Rhode Island*, John R. Bartlett, ed. (Providence, 1856–1865), VI, 415.

[41]*The Rights of Colonies Examined* (Providence, 1764), reprinted *ibid.*, VI, 424–425.

[42]Maurice Moore, *The Justice and Policy of Taxing the American Colonies, in Great-Britain, Considered* (Wilmington, N. C., 1765), p. 15.

[43]*An Inquiry into the Rights of the British Colonies* (Williamsburg, 1766), pp. 23, 27.

in the 1760's, and there is certainly evidence that a number of them did, then Benjamin Gale's conclusion, although extreme for the time, was not very far from the truth. An empire in which all subjects were "born equally free" and live upon a "foundation of equality" was no empire at all, as both Englishmen and Americans came to see in the next few years.

IV

Just how hollow a victory the Americans won in the repeal of the Stamp Act became clear the next year when Charles Townshend persuaded Parliament to levy more taxes on the colonists, this time on certain goods imported from England: glass, lead, paper, paint, and tea. Again, suits for recovery of forfeitures and penalties inflicted by the new taxes were cognizable in the courts of admiralty. The Townshend Acts set up elaborate machinery for rigorous enforcement not merely of import taxes but of all the laws of trade as well. An American Board of Customs was created with headquarters in Boston where it could keep an eye on colonial ships and merchants and where its members soon earned unenviable reputations as racketeers and pirates.[44]

Americans learned, too, that what Parliament had intended to do under the Stamp Act, but did not do because of the act's sudden repeal, it accomplished under the Townshend Acts. The new legislation authorized several vice-admiralty courts distributed in America, and the Privy Council eventually established four —one at Halifax (recommissioning the court already there) and one each at Boston, Philadelphia, and Charlestown, South Carolina—giving them original and appellate jurisdiction over the areas under their control. To meet the complaint that the judges' profits increased in proportion to the number of condemnations they made, salaries of £600 per annum were fixed upon them, and they were forbidden to accept fees or gratuities of any kind.[45] The establishment of more courts in America with better opportunities for their use by customs collectors only antagonized the colonists and provoked louder complaints. The constitutional issues were the same; and as far as convenience was concerned, a Connecticut merchant, instead of following his

---

[44] 7 Geo. III, c. 46; 7 Geo. III, c. 41; 8 Geo. III, c. 22; Pickering, *The Statutes at Large*, XXVII, 505–512, 447–449, XXVIII, 70–71.

[45] 8 Geo. III, c. 22, *ibid.*, XXVIII, 70–71; Munro, *Acts of the Privy Council, Colonial Series*, V, 151–153.

vessel to Halifax to see it condemned, might now have to go only as far as Boston, or a Virginian to Philadelphia, for the same privilege.

The choice of judges for these new courts did not make the pill any easier for the colonists to swallow. Jonathan Sewall accepted a commission for the court at Halifax without relinquishing his post as King's attorney in Massachusetts, while the Boston judgeship went to Robert Auchmuty, already well established as judge of the Bay Colony's admiralty court.[46] The two remaining positions at Philadelphia and Charlestown were given to former Stamp Masters Jared Ingersoll of Connecticut and Augustus Johnston of Rhode Island, obviously in compensation for their trying experiences during the Stamp Act riots when both were hanged in effigy, threatened in person, and forced to resign.[47]

V

Before the government had quite established the new vice-admiralty courts, the commissioners of customs and the local admiralty courts combined in the late 1760's to give American merchants and traders the roughest handling they had ever received from the customs people. By a calculated system alternating between deliberate negligence and utmost severity, the Crown officials inaugurated what Oliver M. Dickerson has called an "era of customs racketeering" which pushed many a neutral merchant into the patriot camp.

Customs collectors could seize vessels and libel cargoes, but it took admiralty courts to condemn them and legalize the division of spoils. The two most notorious instances occurred in Charlestown and Boston in 1767 and 1768; both demonstrated the obvious intent of customs officials to destroy influential merchants, and both provoked violent attacks upon the admiralty courts, increasing the hatred already felt for them. The first involved Henry Laurens, wealthy merchant and planter and popular figure in South Carolina. Within twelve months the customs collector and his deputy at Charlestown seized on frivolous charges three of Laurens's vessels and a fourth in which he

---

[46]Josiah Quincy, Jr., *Reports of Cases Argued and Adjudged in the Superior Court of Judicature of the Province of Massachusetts Bay, 1761–1772* (Boston, 1865), pp. 300, 311–312n.

[47]Lawrence H. Gipson, *Jared Ingersoll* (New Haven, 1920), pp. 294–297, 299n; *Newport* [Rhode Island] *Mercury*, Dec. 5, 1768, May 15, 1769.

had part interest, immediately taking the cases to the colony's admiralty court for trial and condemnation. The cases were heard before Egerton Leigh who was not only judge of the admiralty court, but also attorney general of the colony, surveyor-general of His Majesty's customs, a member of the colony's council appointed by the King, and a prominent practicing lawyer. Each case, whether he won it or not, cost Laurens a good deal of money in costs of court and fees for the judge. The last case, involving the packet *Ann* caused so much adverse publicity for Judge Leigh and his court that he was obliged to dismiss the charge—not, however, before Laurens had exposed and declared to the world by newspaper articles, letters, and pamphlets the infamous conduct of both customs people and the court.[48]

Laurens disclosed what he called the "amazing Accession of Jurisdiction given to Courts of Admiralty" in America. British subjects, he declared, quoting William Blackstone, had always asserted, " 'That it is the most transcendent Privilege which any Subject can enjoy or wish for, that he cannot be affected either in his Property, his Liberty, or his Person, but by the unanimous Consent of twelve of his Neighbours and Equals.' " Like other ambitious Americans who had accumulated property and reputation and who intended to go right on accumulating both, Laurens was struck by the discriminatory treatment admiralty courts gave the colonists. How were causes relating to the revenue decided in England, or even in Ireland, he asked. Are they tried before the Admiral? Laurens answered with a thumping NO! America was the "only Place where Cognizance of such Causes is given to the Admiralty." Why are Americans so "particularised, to be disfranchised and stript of so invaluable a Privilege as the Trial by Jury?" Are the liberties of an American less dear or of smaller consequence "than those of any other Subject of the *British* Empire?" Laurens presumed they were not.[49]

Judge Leigh fought back with a dreary discourse of over 150 pages, scrupulously avoiding any discussion of the constitutional issues at stake. He focused his attack on Laurens, who, he said, thirsted "after the phantom Popularity," and whose libelous writings demonstrated the "evil workings of a *cruel* and *malignant* heart." Besides defending himself at the other's expense, Leigh

---

[48]Oliver M. Dickerson, *The Navigation Acts and the American Revolution* (Philadelphia, 1951), pp. 224–231; Laurens, *Extracts from the Proceedings of the High Court of Vice-Admiralty, in Charlestown, South-Carolina . . .* (Charlestown, 1769).

[49]"A Few General Observations on American Custom-House Officers, and Courts of Vice-Admiralty," appended to *Extracts from the Proceedings of the High Court of Vice-Admiralty*, p. 3.

held up to ridicule Laurens's "unlettered judgment" in the law and declared him clearly out of his depth in an inquiry completely foreign to the "whole study and labour of his life."[50]

Henry Laurens answered shortly, defending his character, his conduct, and his recent publication of the admiralty court proceedings which had followed the seizure of his vessels. He reproduced a good deal of the correspondence involved in the controversy which, along with the court proceedings, was particularly damaging to the reputation of Judge Leigh. Again he drove home for all the world to see the major grievance he and other Americans suffered: "the Disadvantages to which a *British* Subject, whose Property, perhaps his ALL, and his Reputation into the Bargain, is exposed by a Trial in an *American* Court of Vice-Admiralty before a *Volunteer* sole Judge." Any doubt in Laurens's mind up to this time as to where his allegiance belonged was soundly resolved.[51]

Laurens and his friends received some satisfaction from their long drawn-out struggle: both the collector and his deputy were replaced, and the government in England gave Egerton Leigh his choice of keeping the judgeship or his post as the King's attorney. He chose to remain as attorney general probably because of the larger fees, although Laurens doubtless would have testified that the fees as judge were nothing to sneeze at since for the past year or so Laurens himself had paid most of them out of his own pocket. Laurens received a measure of satisfaction he may not have counted on, for he managed, during the course of one of the trials, after a *"by your leave,* in the phrase and manner of a London porter," to pull the collector by the nose.[52]

Henry Laurens's counterpart in Massachusetts was the wealthy merchant and recognized patriot, John Hancock, who had never got along well with customs people and disliked in particular the commissioners who descended on Boston in 1768. Hancock's dislike was bountifully returned, and at the same time the customs officials in Charlestown were ganging up on Laurens, the commissioners, the collectors, and Governor Bernard himself launched an attack on Hancock unprecedented for its illegality and greed.

In June of 1768 the customs officials seized Hancock's sloop

---

[50]*The Man Unmasked: or, the World Undeceived, in the Author of a Late Pamphlet, Intitled, "Extracts from the Proceedings . . ."* (Charlestown, 1769), pp. 13, 22, 26, 40, and *passim.*

[51]*An Appendix to the Extracts from the Proceedings of the High Court of Vice-Admiralty . . . containing Strictures upon, and proper Answers to . . . The Man Unmask'd* (Charlestown, 1769), p. 24 and *passim.*

[52]Dickerson, *The Navigation Acts,* p. 231; Leigh, *The Man Unmasked,* pp. 35–36, 100–101, 102–103; Laurens, *An Appendix to the Extracts,* p. 11.

Liberty for loading whale oil and tar without first giving bond that the cargo's destination was within the limits of the laws of trade. Despite the fact that Hancock and all other Boston traders, with full knowledge of the customs people, had always loaded first and given bond later before clearance, the letter of the law in this instance was enforced, and Hancock stood by helpless while the King's men sailed the sloop out into the harbor and anchored it under the covering guns of a man-of-war. He was not entirely alone, however; a number of sympathizers met and rioted throughout Boston in reaction to what they believed to be outright plunder. During the summer months the admiralty court met, condemned, and confiscated both vessel and cargo and divided the proceeds according to law: one-third to the colony, one-third to Governor Bernard, and one-third to the informers, in this case, the customs officials.

Although Hancock lost both vessel and cargo, the action did not impair his fortune, his prestige, or his influence in Massachusetts. The customs officials tried again and in the fall of 1768 brought suit in the admiralty court, this time against Hancock himself, for smuggling wine in the *Liberty* several months earlier. His vessel, it seems, had arrived at Boston in May of that year with a cargo from the islands; the tax was paid on the declared amount of wine and the cargo unloaded. But in the fall the customs commissioners, partly on the evidence of a perjured witness, claimed that Hancock had actually unloaded in May large quantities of undeclared wine valued at £3,000 and therefore, according to the Sugar Act, was liable to a penalty of treble the costs of the cargo. Moreover, the law said, anyone who aided in unloading contraband was also guilty of the offense, and the customs people claimed that five of Hancock's friends had assisted him. The government filed suit against six Boston merchants for £9,000 each or a total of over £50,000 sterling for allegedly smuggling one hundred pipes of wine into the port. The admiralty court accepted the case against Hancock *in Personam*, issued a warrant for his arrest, and demanded and got bail of £3,000, an exorbitant amount for a case of this kind. Obviously the commissioners of customs and Governor Bernard, each of whom would benefit handsomely from a conviction, had plotted and planned at some length for Hancock's demise.[53]

---

[53]For information about the events leading to Hancock's trial, I have relied upon Dickerson, *The Navigation Acts*, pp. 231–250; Quincy, *Reports of Cases*, pp. 456–457, 459; George G. Wolkins, "The Seizure of John Hancock's Sloop *Liberty*," Massachusetts Historical Society, *Proceedings*, LV (1921–1922), 260–261.

When Hancock appeared in court before Judge Auchmuty in November 1768, he happily brought John Adams with him as counsel. The Braintree lawyer, now moved to Boston, was by this time of wider reputation as both lawyer and patriot than when he began his siege against admiralty jurisdiction at the time of the Stamp Act. Not content merely to defend Hancock against a smuggling charge, Adams, like James Otis seven years earlier in the famous writs of assistance case, transcended the immediate issue and defined fundamental principles which were to become stock in trade in the Revolutionary movement. But while Otis attacked the writs and general warrants in 1761 as contrary to natural law and the natural rights of Americans, Adams stuck to the rights of subjects under the British constitution. In what was doubtless for Adams his best opportunity to date, he attacked with considerable eloquence the legislative authority of Parliament and in particular, admiralty court jurisdiction in America.

Adams, who has left his defense laboriously transcribed in his "Admiralty Notebook," was much more interested in the validity of the Sugar Act itself than in the specific charge of its violation (although he defied the court to prove that Hancock was aware that any undeclared wine had been removed from the *Liberty*). Three years earlier the colonists, almost to a man, had denied Parliament's right to tax them without their consent. Since that time Parliament had done nothing to convince them they were wrong. In fact, between 1765 and 1774 Americans enlarged their attack from taxes without consent to laws without consent, and by the latter date they denied Parliament any authority in America. John Adams contributed generously to this shift in American opinion, and in Hancock's trial before the court of admiralty, he harangued at length about subjection to laws which the colonists had not approved. In words which must have maddened and at the same time amused the ministry and Parliament when they read them, he boldly remarked of the statute in question: "My Clyant Mr Hancock never consented to it."[54]

Not only, argued Adams, was the Sugar Act passed without the colonists' approval; not only were the penalties inflicted by it— that is, treble the value of the smuggled cargo—out of all proportion to the severity of the crime; but, added Adams, violations of this act, these penalties and forfeitures are "to be heard and

---

[54]For information about Hancock's trial, I have relied upon John Adams, "Admiralty Notebook," in Adams Family Papers, Miscellany, Legal Papers (microfilm, reel 184, Brown University Library); Quincy, *Reports of Cases*, pp. 457, 459.

try'd.—how? Not by a Jury, not by the Law of the Land," but by the civil law before a single judge, contrary to the will of the ancient barons who, in similar circumstances, had answered in one voice: "We will not that the laws of England be changed, which of old have been used and approved." The barons of modern times, Adams went on, were quite willing that the laws of England should be changed, at least as far as America was concerned, and, more important, "in the most tender Point, the most fundamental Principle." But the crowning insult to Americans was that this statute, on the same page that it deprived Americans of trial by jury and the law of the land, directed that the penalties and forfeitures incurred under the act in Great Britain be prosecuted, sued for, and recovered in His Majesty's courts of record which proceeded under the common law.

John Adams's next remarks demand a full hearing, because they go to the core of a fundamental cause of the American Revolution, a cause which has been only partly appreciated and not specifically demonstrated. Here, said Adams, "is the Contrast that stares us in the Face!"

The Parliament in one Clause guarding the People of the Realm, and securing to them the Benefit of a Tryal by the Law of the Land, and by the next Clause, depriving all Americans of that Priviledge.— What shall we say to this Distinction? Is there not in this Clause, a Brand of Infamy, of Degradation, and Disgrace, fixed upon every American? Is he not degraded below the Rank of an Englishman: Is it not directly, a Repeal of Magna Charta, as far as America is concerned . . . [and here Adams quoted in Latin: No freeman shall be taken or imprisoned or disseised of his freehold or liberties or free customs or outlawed or exiled or any otherwise destroyed, nor will we pass upon him nor condemn him, but by lawful judgment of his peers or the law of the land.] This 29. Chap. of Magna Charta has for many Centuries been esteemed by Englishmen, as one of the noblest Monuments one of the firmest Bulwarks of their Liberties. . . . The Stat 4 G. 3 [Sugar Act] takes from Mr Hancock this precious Tryal Per Legem Terra, and gives it to a single Judge. However respectable the Judge may be, it is however an Hardship and Severity, which distinguishs my Clyent from the rest of Englishmen. . . .[55]

After challenging the authority of Parliament and the constitutionality of the court, Adams proceeded to tear to shreds the court's use of evidence and examination of witnesses, claiming that the court had so mixed up the rules of civil and common

---

[55]John Adams, "Admiralty Notebook."

law, using favorable parts of each for the benefit of the government alone, that no one could tell under which system of law his client was being unfairly tried. This last impressed the judge, or so it seemed, and after an interlocutory decree in March 1769, pronouncing that the Crown's method of examination was improper, the attorney general stopped proceedings and withdrew the case.[56]

It would be easy to conclude that Hancock owed the happy outcome of the trial to Adams alone, but there was more involved here than Adams's eloquent persuasiveness. Several things occurred in the spring of 1769 which convinced the customs people that they would be better off out of the business. Governor Bernard, it was learned, was soon to be recalled; the government in England became suspicious of the motives of the commissioners and curious as to just what the customs people had done with all the revenue. Meanwhile, Auchmuty and the attorney general were promoted to vice-admiralty judgeships in Boston and Halifax with fixed salaries of £600 apiece, a fact which may have reduced the necessity of plundering Hancock. In any event the case was dropped.[57]

Unlike James Otis's attack against writs of assistance in 1761, which received little publicity then or later,[58] Adams's speech before the admiralty court did not long lie hidden from public view. During and after the extended trial, from November 1768 well into the spring of the next year, the colonial presses, adept at the use of propaganda, were fed a running account of what occurred behind the closed doors of the court.[59] Not two months after his final appearance before the court, Adams lifted from the "Admiralty Notebook" whole sections of his argument against admiralty courts and incorporated them into Boston's instructions

[56]*Ibid.*

[57]Dickerson, *The Navigation Acts*, pp. 245–246; *Boston under Military Rule, 1768–1769*, as revealed in *A Journal of the Times*, Oliver M. Dickerson ed., (Boston, 1936), pp. 83–84.

[58]For a discussion of Otis's speech, see Oliver M. Dickerson, "Writs of Assistance as a Cause of the Revolution," in *The Era of the American Revolution*, Richard B. Morris ed., (New York, 1939), pp. 40, 42–43.

[59]During the winter and spring, 1768–1769, *The New-York Journal* printed, and several other colonial newspapers reprinted in whole or part, what was called a "Journal of the Times," describing contemporary events in Boston including Hancock's trial. These articles, some of which appeared later in English journals, have been collected and published in Dickerson, *Boston under Military Rule.* For an account of Hancock's trial, see pp. 18–84, *passim.* For further discussion of the "Journal," see Arthur M. Schlesinger, *Prelude to Independence, the Newspaper War on Britain, 1764–1776* (New York, 1958), pp. 100–103, 312–313.

to its representatives in the General Court where they would receive wide currency and again prompt printing in the newspapers.[60] The next year the Massachusetts House of Representatives digested Adams's argument including the quotation from Magna Charta—this time in English—and sent it to Benjamin Franklin, its agent in London.[61] The fate which befell the speech of James Otis was not repeated in the case of John Adams. The vigorous attack on admiralty justice and on the authority of Parliament and the clear denunciation of Parliamentary statutes, which, he said, fixed upon every American a "Brand of Infamy, of Degredation, and Disgrace," received wide publicity at home and abroad through his own efforts.

VI

Adams, Hancock, Laurens, and other Americans were not to be degraded below the rank of Englishmen. A government in London which by Parliamentary statute relegated Americans to an inferior position within the empire was not long to be tolerated. Inferiority was galling to an ambitious people, and inferiority was never more explicitly demonstrated than in the extension of admiralty court jurisdiction in America. Enactments, which deprived colonists of trial by jury and the law of the land, denied them that equality of treatment they insisted was their birthright as British subjects. John Adams sooner than most Americans recognized that mere denial of Parliament's power to tax Americans was a feeble defense of American rights; for it was the legislative authority of Parliament over America which was doing the damage, and one had to go no further than the extension of admiralty court jurisdiction to see just how much damage this authority had done. The concerted attack on Hancock, Laurens, and their property was sufficient warning of what might follow. And despite the slight easing of tension owing to the repeal of most of the Townshend taxes, the colonists did not let up in their complaints against the extending to "so

---

[60]May 15, 1769, Adams, *Works*, III, 507–510. Half of the content of these instructions is devoted to admiralty court justice as a major grievance. On June 29, 1769, *The New-York Journal, Supplement*, printed an attack on admiralty court jurisdiction using many of Adams's own words and phrases. See Dickerson, *Boston under Military Rule*, pp. 97, n. 2, and 98–99.

[61]Nov. 6, 1770, *Papers Relating to Public Events in Massachusetts Preceding the American Revolution*, III, *Massachusetts Papers*, Seventy Six Society (Philadelphia, 1856), p. 174.

enormous a degree" the powers of these courts. Sam Adams included the grievance in his "List of Infringements and Violations of Rights" which he persuaded the Boston town meeting—John Hancock, moderator—to adopt in the fall of 1772.[62] And wily old Benjamin Franklin the next year vexed the English in London with the biting explanation that depriving Americans of trial by jury and subjecting them to arbitrary judges—the "lowest characters in the country"—was one of the *Rules by which a Great Empire may be Reduced to a Small One.*[63]

In five short years after Hancock's trial, a majority of Americans had caught up with John Adams; a series of events, beginning with the Boston Massacre and ending with the Coercive Acts of 1774, convinced Americans that the sooner they got out from under Parliament the better. They sent to the Continental Congress in September of that year delegates who fashioned a theory of empire which admitted allegiance to the King but denied Parliament any authority whatever in America except when the colonists consented. The Resolves of the Congress were a declaration of equality, announcing that Americans and Englishmen were equally subject to the same King and to their local legislatures, Parliament in England and the colonial assemblies in America. The Congress also declared, as had most protests since 1764, that the American colonies were "entitled to the common law of England, and more especially to the great and inestimable privilege of being tried by their peers. . . ." Any statutes denying these rights—and the Congress suggested several—Parliament must immediately repeal.[64]

The only trouble with the concept of empire which Americans formulated in the fall of 1774 was that its acceptance was limited to one side of the Atlantic. King, Parliament, and ministry scoffed at such ideas and stirred their troops in America to see to it that the colonists remained subject to the authority of Parliament. Within a year hostilities commenced.

Unable to establish themselves equal to the English within the empire, Americans in July 1776 cast off and declared themselves equal to the English as members of the human race; for, said Jefferson, *all* men are created equal. The appeal to the law of nature above the constitution was not so much a stroke of genius

---

[62]*Sources and Documents Illustrating the American Revolution, 1764–1788,* Samuel Eliot Morison, ed. (Oxford, 1929), p. 94.

[63]*The Writings of Benjamin Franklin,* Albert H. Smyth, ed. (New York, 1905–1907), VI, 132.

[64]*Journals of the Continental Congress, 1774–1789,* Worthington C. Ford, ed. (Washington, D. C., 1904–1937), I, 69.

in 1776 as it was a stark necessity. The home government's refusal to accept the colonists' terms and the outbreak of fighting dissolved the hope of Americans' being equal on any other grounds. Despite the fact that Jefferson's magnificent declaration of human equality has come to mean many things to many men since 1776, it had only a particular meaning at the time it was written. Americans were not yet interested in the rights of all men. They had been interested in the rights of British subjects and particularly American subjects, and these rights, they said, implied equality. When the government in London repeatedly offended their sense of equality, as it did when meddling with the common law and trial by jury, the Americans called a halt and set up for themselves. John Adams knew what he was talking about when he advised his friend to read the statutes if he wanted to understand the American Revolution.

FROM ANXIETIES
TO DISAFFECTION

———— ◆·◆———◆◈◆———◆·◆ ————

Behind the concrete issues and explicit arguments of
the American protest against British policies between
1763 and 1776 lay a cluster of deepseated anxieties that
were brought to the surface of colonial consciousness by
those policies. The nature of those anxieties, and the
ways in which they determined the American response
to the developing Revolutionary situation, are discussed
in the first selection in this chapter. This selection illustrates how the colonists' fear of power and British corruption convinced them that the new British measures
were part of a malignant conspiracy among men in
power in Britain against colonial, and ultimately all
British, liberty. The second and third pieces suggest how
the colonists' fear of their own internal corruption colored their reaction to the crucial events after 1764.

BERNARD BAILYN (b. 1922) is a member of the Department of History at Harvard University; PERRY MILLER
(1905–1964) was, for most of his scholarly career, a
member of the Department of English at the same
university.

The Logic of Rebellion

BERNARD BAILYN

It is the meaning imparted to the events after 1763 by this integrated group of attitudes and ideas that lies behind the colonists' rebellion. In the context of these ideas, the controversial issues centering on the question of Parliament's jurisdiction in America acquired as a group new and overwhelming significance. The colonists believed they saw emerging from the welter of events during the decade after the Stamp Act a pattern whose meaning was unmistakable. They saw in the measures taken by the British government and in the actions of officials in the colonies something for which their peculiar inheritance of thought had prepared them only too well, something they had long conceived to be a possibility in view of the known tendencies of history and of the present state of affairs in England. They saw about them, with increasing clarity, not merely mistaken, or even evil, policies violating the principles upon which freedom rested, but what appeared to be evidence of nothing less than a deliberate conspiracy launched surreptitiously by plotters against liberty both in England and in America. The danger to America, it was believed, was in fact only the small, immediately visible part of the greater whole whose ultimate manifestation would be nothing less than the destruction of the English constitution with all the rights and privileges embedded in it.

This belief transformed the meaning of the colonists' struggle, and it added an inner accelerator to the movement of opposition. For, once grasped, it could not be easily dispelled: denial only confirmed it, since what conspirators profess is not what they believe; the ostensible, for them, is not the real; and the real is deliberately malign.

It was this—the overwhelming evidence, as they saw it, that they were faced with conspirators against liberty determined at all costs to gain ends which their words dissembled—that was signaled to the colonists after 1763, and it was this above all else that in the end propelled them into Revolution.

Reprinted with permission of the publishers from *Pamphlets of the American Revolution, 1750–1776*, Volume I: 1775–1765 (Cambridge, Mass.: Harvard University Press, 1965), 60–85. Copyright, 1965, by the President and Fellows of Harvard College.

Suspicion that an active conspiracy of power against liberty existed and involved the colonies directly was deeply rooted in the consciousness of a large segment of the American population; it had assumed specific form before any of the famous political events of the struggle with England took place. No adherent of a nonconformist church or sect in the eighteenth century was free from suspicion that the Church of England, an arm of the English state, was working to bring all subjects of the crown into the community of the Church; and since toleration was official and nonconformist influence in English politics formidable, it was doing so by stealth, disguising its efforts, turning to improper uses devices that had been created for benign purposes. In particular, the Society for the Propagation of the Gospel in Foreign Parts, an arm of the Church created in 1701 to aid in bringing the Gospel to the pagan Indians, was said by 1763 to have "long had a formal design to root out Presbyterianism, etc., and to establishing both episcopacy and bishops."[1]

This suspicion, which had smoldered in the breasts of New Englanders and nonconformists throughout the colonies for half a century or more, had burst into flame repeatedly, but never so violently as in 1763, in the Mayhew-Apthorp controversy which climaxed years of growing anxiety that plans were being made secretly to establish an American episcopate. To Mayhew, as to Presbyterian and Congregational leaders throughout the colonies, there could be little doubt that the threat was real. Many of the facts were known, facts concerning maneuvers in London and in America. Anglican leaders in New York and New Jersey had met almost publicly to petition England for an American episcopate, and there could be little doubt also of the role of the Society for the Propagation of the Gospel in this undercover operation. For if the ostensible goal of the Society was the gospelizing of the pagan Indians and Negroes, its true goal was manifestly revealed when it established missions in places like Cambridge, Massachusetts, which had not had a resident Indian since the seventeenth century and was well equipped with "orthodox" preachers. Such missions, Mayhew wrote, have "all the appearance of entering wedges . . . carrying on the crusade, or spiritual siege of our churches, with the hope that they will one day submit to an episcopal sovereign." Bishops, he wrote unblinkingly in reply to

---

[1] Jonathan Mayhew, *Observations on the Charter and Conduct of the Society for the Propagation of the Gospel in Foreign Parts . . .* (Boston, 1763), pp. 103–108.

the Archbishop of Canterbury, have commonly been instruments in arbitrary reigns of "establishing a tyranny over the bodies and souls of men," and their establishment in America would mark the end of liberty in Massachusetts and elsewhere. By 1765, when the final exchanges in this pamphlet war were published, it was commonly understood in New England and elsewhere that "the stamping and episcopizing [of] our colonies were . . . *only different branches of the same plan of power*."[2]

Fear of an ecclesiastical conspiracy against American liberties, latent among nonconformists through all of colonial history, thus erupted into public controversy at the very same time that the first impact of new British policies in civil affairs was being felt. And though it was, in an obvious sense, a limited fear (for large parts of the population identified themselves with the Anglican church and were not easily convinced that liberty was being threatened by a plot of Churchmen) it nevertheless had a profound indirect effect everywhere, for it stimulated among highly articulate leaders of public opinion, who would soon be called upon to interpret the tendency of civil affairs, a general sense that they lived in a conspiratorial world in which what the highest officials professed was not what they in fact intended, and that their words masked a malevolent design.[3]

Reinforcement for this belief came quickly. Even for those who had in no way been concerned with the threat of an episcopal establishment, the passage of the Stamp Act was not merely an impolitic and unjust law that threatened the priceless right of the individual to retain possession of his property until he or his chosen representative voluntarily gave it up to another; it was to many, also, a danger signal indicating that a more general threat existed. For though it could be argued, and in a sense proved by the swift repeal of the act, that nothing more was involved than ignorance or confusion on the part of people in

[2]Mayhew, *Observations,* p. 57; Jonathan Mayhew, *Remarks on an Anonymous Tract . . . Being a Second Defence . . .* (Boston, 1764), p. 12; Alden Bradford, *Memoir of the Life and Writings of Rev. Jonathan Mayhew . . .* (Boston, 1838), p. 372. For a full account of "the Anglican Plot," see Carl Bridenbaugh, *Mitre and Sceptre* (New York, 1962), chaps. vii–ix. See also Introduction to [John Aplin], *Verses on Doctor Mayhew's Book of Observations* (Providence, 1763: JHL Pamphlet 3).

[3]Thus John Adams drew the theme of his *Dissertation on the Canon and Feudal Law* (1765) from the association of the episcopal "plot" and the Stamp Act; see especially the concluding section ("there seems to be a direct and formal design on foot to enslave all America") in Charles Francis Adams, ed., *The Works of John Adams . . .* (Boston, 1850–1856), III, 464. On this association in general, see Bridenbaugh, *Mitre and Sceptre,* chap. ix: "Bishops and Stamps, 1764–1766."

power who really knew better and who, once warned by the reaction of the colonists, would not repeat the mistake—though this could be, and by many was, concluded, there nevertheless appeared to be good reason to suspect that more was involved. For from whom had the false information and evil advice come that had so misled the English government? From officials in the colonies, said John Adams, said Oxenbridge Thacher, James Otis, and Stephen Hopkins—from officials bent on overthrowing the constituted forms of government in order to satisfy their own lust for power, and not likely to relent in their passion. Some of these local plotters were easily identified. To John Adams, Josiah Quincy, and others the key figure in Massachusetts from the beginning to the end was Thomas Hutchinson who by "serpentine wiles" was befuddling and victimizing the weak, the avaricious, and the incautious in order to increase his notorious engrossment of public office. In Rhode Island it was, to James Otis, that "little, dirty, drinking, drabbing, contaminated knot of thieves, beggars, and transports . . . made up of Turks, Jews, and other infidels, with a few renegado Christians and Catholics"—the Newport junto, led by Martin Howard, Jr., which had already been accused by Stephen Hopkins and others in Providence of "conspiring against the liberties of the colony."[4]

But even if local leaders associated with power elements in England had not been so suspect, there were grounds for seeing

---

[4]For a succinct explanation of the manifest threat of the Stamp Act, see Stephen Hopkins, *Rights of Colonies Examined* (Providence, 1765: JHL Pamphlet 9), pp. 16–17. Adams' almost paranoiac suspicions of Hutchinson's hidden motives run through his *Diary and Autobiography* (L. H. Butterfield, ed., Cambridge, Mass., 1961); e.g., I, 306; II, 39; III, 430. See also *Novanglus and Massachusettensis* . . . (Boston, 1819), pp. 49–50, 68; *Works*, X, 285–286, 298. It is the generality of such suspicions that accounts for the furor caused by the publication in 1773 of Hutchinson's innocuous letters of 1768—letters in which, the publishers wrote in the pamphlet's title, *"the Judicious Reader Will Discover the Fatal Source of the Confusion and Bloodshed."* Josiah Quincy thought he saw the final proof of Hutchinson's conspiratorial efforts in his maneuverings with the North administration in London in 1774 and 1775: "Journal of Josiah Quincy Jun. . . . in England . . . ," *Proceedings of the Massachusetts Historical Society*, 50 (1916–1917), 444, 446, 447, 450, 452. Thacher's suspicions of Hutchinson (whom he called "Summa Potestatis," or "Summa" for short), are traced in the Introduction to his *Sentiments of a British American* (Boston, 1764: JHL Pamphlet 8). Otis' phrase is quoted from his abusive pamphlet, *Brief Remarks on the Defence of the Halifax Libel* . . . (Boston, 1765), p. 5. The charge against Howard appeared in the *Providence Gazette*, Sept. 15, 1764, and is part of the intense antipathy that built up in Providence against the royalist group in Newport. See, in general, Edmund S. and Helen M. Morgan, *The Stamp Act Crisis* . . . (Chapel Hill, N.C., 1953), chap. iv; and Introduction to Howard's *Letter from a Gentleman at Halifax* (Newport, 1765: JHL Pamphlet 10).

more behind the Stamp Act than its ostensible purpose. The
official aim of the act was, of course, to bring in revenue to the
English treasury. But the sums involved were in fact quite small,
and "some persons . . . may be inclined to acquiesce under it."
But that would be to fall directly into the trap, for the smaller
the taxes, John Dickinson wrote in the most influential pamphlet
published in America before 1776, the more dangerous they were,
since they would the more easily be found acceptable by the
incautious, with the result that a precedent would be established
for making still greater inroads on liberty and property.

> Nothing is wanted at home but a PRECEDENT, the force of which
> shall be established by the tacit submission of the colonies. . . . If the
> Parliament succeeds in this attempt, other statutes will impose other
> duties . . . and thus the Parliament will levy upon us such sums of
> money as they choose to take, *without any other* LIMITATION *than their*
> PLEASURE.[5]

But by then, in 1768, when Dickinson's *Farmer's Letters* were
published as a pamphlet, more explicit evidence of a wide-ranging
plot was accumulating rapidly. Not only had another revenue
act, the Townshend Duties, been passed by Parliament despite
all the violence of the colonists' reaction to the Stamp Act, but
it was a measure that enhanced the influence of the customs
administration, which for other reasons had already come under
suspicion. There had been, it was realized by the late 1760's, a
sudden expansion in the number of "posts in the [colonial]
'government' . . . worth the attention of persons of influence in
Great Britain"—posts, Franklin explained, like the governorships,
filled by persons who were

> generally strangers to the provinces they are sent to govern, have no
> estate, natural connection, or relation there to give them an affection
> for the country . . . they come only to make money as fast as they
> can; are sometimes men of vicious characters and broken fortunes,
> sent by a minister merely to get them out of the way.[6]

By the late 1760's, in the perspective of recent events, one could
see that the invasion of customs officers "born with long claws

[5]*Letters from a Farmer in Pennsylvania* . . . (Philadelphia, 1768), in
Paul L. Ford, ed., *Writings of John Dickinson* (*Memoirs of the Historical
Society of Pennsylvania*, XIV, Philadelphia, 1895), 382.

[6]Dickinson, *Farmer's Letters*, in Ford, *Writings*, p. 380; Albert H. Smyth,
ed., *Writings of Benjamin Franklin* (New York, 1905–1907), V, 83. Cf.
Verner W. Crane, *Benjamin Franklin's Letters to the Press, 1758–1775*
(Chapel Hill, 1950), pp. 106–107, 277.

like eagles," had begun as far back as the last years of the Seven Years' War and was now being reinforced by the new tax measures. The wartime Orders in Council demanding stricter enforcement of the Navigation Laws; the Sugar Act of 1764, which had multiplied the customs personnel; and the American Board of Customs Commissioners created in 1767 with "power," Americans said, "to constitute as many under officers as they please"—all of these developments could be seen to have provided for an "almost incredible number of inferior officers," most of whom the colonists believed to be "wretches . . . of such infamous characters that the merchants cannot possibly think their interest safe under their care." More important by far, however, was their influence on government.

For there was an obvious political and constitutional danger in having such "a set of *idle drones*," such "lazy, proud, worthless *pensioners* and *placemen*," in one's midst. It was nothing less than "a general maxim," James Wilson wrote,

that the crown will take advantage of every opportunity of extending its prerogative in opposition to the privileges of the people, [and] that it is the interest of those who have *pensions* or *offices at will* from the crown to concur in all its measures.

These "baneful harpies" were instruments of power, of prerogative. They would upset the balance of the constitution by extending "*ministerial influence* as much beyond its former bounds as the late war did the *British* dominions." Parasitic officeholders, thoroughly corrupted by their obligations to those who had appointed them, would strive to "*distinguish themselves* by their sordid zeal in defending and promoting measures which *they know beyond all questionsi* to be *destructive* to the *just rights* and *true interest* of their country." Seeking to "*serve the ambitious purposes of great men* at home," these "*base-spirited wretches*" would urge— were already urging—as they logically had to, the specious attractions of "SUBMISSIVE behavior." They were arguing

with a plausible affection of *wisdom* and *concern* how *prudent* it is to please the *powerful*—how *dangerous* to provoke them—and then comes in the perpetual incantation that freezes up every generous purpose of the soul in cold, inactive expectation—"that if there is any request to be made, compliance will obtain a favorable attention."

In the end, this extension of executive patronage, based on a limitless support of government through colonial taxation, would make the whole of government "merely a ministerial engine"; by throwing off the balance of its parts, it would destroy the protective machinery of the constitution.[7]

But even this did not exhaust the evidence that a design against liberty was unfolding. During the same years the independence of the judiciary, so crucial a part of the constitution, was suddenly seen to be under heavy attack, and by the mid-1760's to have succumbed in many places.[8]

This too was not a new problem. The status of the colonial judiciary had been a controversial question throughout the century. The Parliamentary statute of 1701 which guaranteed judges in England life tenure in their posts had been denied to the colonies, in part because properly trained lawyers were scarce in the colonies, especially in the early years, and appointments for life would prevent the replacement of ill-qualified judges by their betters, when they appeared; and in part because, judicial salaries being provided for by temporary legislative appropriations, the removal of all executive control from the judiciary, it was feared, would result in the hopeless subordination of the courts to popular influences. The status of the judiciary in the eighteenth century was therefore left open to political maneuvering in which, more often than not, the home government managed to carry its point and to make the tenure of judges as temporary as their salaries. Then suddenly, in the early 1760's, the whole issue exploded. In 1759 the Pennsylvania Assembly declared that the judges of that province would thereafter hold their offices by the same permanence of tenure that had been guaranteed English judges after the Glorious Revolution. But the law was disallowed forthwith

---

[7][Silas Downer], Discourse Delivered in Providence . . . at the Dedication of the Tree of Liberty . . . (Providence, 1768), p. 10; Ebenezer Baldwin, An Appendix Stating the Heavy Grievances . . . , published in Samuel Sherwood, A Sermon Containing Scriptural Instructions to Civil Rulers . . . (New Haven, [1774]), pp. 52–53; Observations on Several Acts of Parliament . . . and Also on the Conduct of the Officers of the Customs . . . ([Boston], 1769), p. 15; William Gordon, Discourse Preached December 15th 1774 . . . (Boston, 1775), p. 11; [James Wilson], Considerations on the . . . Legislative Authority of the British Parliament (Philadelphia, 1774), pp. 6–7; Dickinson, Farmer's Letters, in Ford, Writings, pp. 382, 398n, 399–400; Votes and Proceedings of . . . Boston . . . (Boston, [1772]), p. 21. See also, among the voluminous expressions of resentment and fear of petty officeholders in the colonies, [Henry Laurens], Extracts from the Proceedings of the High Court of Vice-Admiralty in Charlestown . . . with . . . Observations on American Custom-House Officers . . . (Charleston, 1769); and A Ministerial Catechise, Suitable To Be Learned by All . . . Pensioners, Placemen . . . (Boston, 1771).

[8]For further details on the problem of the judiciary, and for documentation of the paragraphs that follow, see the Introduction and notes to A Letter to the People of Pennsylvania (Philadelphia, 1760: JHL Pamphlet 2).

by the crown. Opposition newspapers boiled with resentment; angry speeches were made in the Assembly; and a pamphlet appeared explaining in the fullest detail the bearing of judicial independence on constitutional freedom.

In New York the issue was even more inflamed and had wider repercussions. There, the judges of the Supreme Court, by a political maneuver of 1750, had managed to secure their appointments for life. But this tenure was interrupted by the death of George II in 1760 which required the reissuance of all crown commissions. An unpopular and politically weak lieutenant governor, determined to prevent his enemies from controlling the courts, refused to recommission the judges on life tenure. The result was a ferocious battle in which the opposition asserted New York's "*undoubted right* of having the judges of our courts on a constitutional basis," and demanded the "liberties and privileges" of Englishmen in this connection as in all others. But they were defeated, though not by the governor. In December 1761 orders were sent out from the King in Council to all the colonies, permanently forbidding the issuance of judges' commissions anywhere on any tenure but that of "the pleasure of the crown."[9]

All the colonies were affected. In some, like New Jersey, where the governor's incautious violation of the new royal order led to his removal from office, or like North Carolina, where opposition forces refused to concede and managed to keep up the fight for permanent judicial tenure throughout the entire period from 1760 to 1776, the issue was directly joined. In others, as in Massachusetts, where specific supreme court appointments were vehemently opposed by anti-administration interests, the force of the policy was indirect. But everywhere there was bitterness at the decree and fear of its implications, for everywhere it was known that judicial tenure "at the will of the crown" was "dangerous to the liberty and property of the subject," and that if the bench were occupied by "men who depended upon the smiles of the crown for their daily bread," the possibility of having an independent judiciary as an effective check upon executive power would be wholly lost.[10]

---

[9] Milton M. Klein, "Prelude to Revolution in New York: Jury Trials and Judicial Tenure," *William and Mary Quarterly*, 3d ser., 17 (1960), 452.

[10] [William H. Drayton], *A Letter from Freeman of South-Carolina . . .* (Charleston, 1774), pp. 10, 20. For other characteristic expressions of the fear of a corrupt judiciary, see [John Allen], *An Oration upon the Beauties of Liberty . . .* (Boston, 1773), pp. 21 ff.: *The Conduct of Cadwallader Colden . . .* ([New York], 1767), reprinted in *Collections of the New-York Historical Society*, X (New York, 1877), 433–467; [John Allen], *The Ameri-*

This fear was magnified by the rumor, which was circulating vigorously as early as 1768, that it was part of the administration's policy to have the salaries of the colonial judges "appointed for them by the crown, independent of the people." If this ever happened, the Boston Town Meeting asserted when the rumor was becoming actuality, it would "complete our slavery." The reasoning was simple and straightforward:

if taxes are to be raised from us by the Parliament of Great Britain without our consent, and the men on whose opinions and decisions our properties, liberties, and lives in a great measure depend receive their support from the revenues arising from these taxes, we cannot, when we think of the depravity of mankind, avoid looking with horror on the danger to which we are exposed!

"More and more," as the people contemplated the significance of crown salaries for a judiciary that served "at pleasure," was it clear that "the designs of administration [were] totally to subvert the constitution." Any judge, the House in Massachusetts ultimately stated, who accepted such salaries would thereby declare "that he has not a due sense of the importance of an impartial administration of justice, that he is an enemy to the constitution, and has it in his heart to promote the establishment of an arbitrary government in the province."[11]

Long before this, however, another aspect of the judicial system was believed also to have come under deliberate attack. The jury system, it was said, in New York particularly but elsewhere as well, was being systematically undermined. In New York the same executive who had fought the permanent tenure of judges insisted on the legality of allowing jury decisions, on matters of fact as well as of law, to be appealed to the governor and Council. This effort, though defeated within a year by action of the Board of Trade in England, had a lasting impact on the political consciousness of New Yorkers. It was publicly assailed, in the year of the Stamp Act, as "arbitrary" and "scandalous" in its deliberate subversion of the British constitution.[12]

Associated with this but more important because more widespread in its effect was the extension and enforcement of the

---

can Alarm . . . (Boston, 1773), 1st sec., pp. 17, 20, 27, 28; *Votes and Proceedings of Boston*, pp. 37–38; Adams, *Diary and Autobiography*, II, 36, 65–67; III, 297 ff.

[11]*Votes and Proceedings of Boston*, p. 20; Thomas Hutchinson, *History of . . . Massachusetts-Bay* (Lawrence S. Mayo, ed., Cambridge, 1936), III, 278, 279.

[12]Klein, "Prelude to Revolution in New York," pp. 453–459.

jurisdiction of the vice-admiralty courts—"prerogative" courts composed not of juries but of single judges whose posts were "political offices in the hands of the royal governors, to be bestowed upon deserving friends and supporters." Since these courts had jurisdiction over the enforcement of all laws of trade and navigation as well as over ordinary marine matters, they had always been potentially threatening to the interests of the colonists. But in the past, by one means or another, they had been curtailed in their effect, and much of their business had been shunted off to common law courts dominated by juries. Suddenly in the 1760's they acquired a great new importance, for it was into their hands that the burden of judicial enforcement of the new Parliamentary legislation fell. It was upon them, consequently, and upon the whole principle of "prerogative" courts that abuse was hurled as the effect of their enhanced power was felt. "What has America done," victims of the decisions of these courts asked, "to be thus particularized, to be disfranchised and stripped of so invaluable a privilege as the trial by jury?" The operations of the vice-admiralty courts, it was felt, especially after their administrative reorganization in 1767, denied Americans a crucial measure of the protection of the British constitution. "However respectable the judge may be, it is however an hardship and severity which distinguishes [defendants before this court] from the rest of Englishmen." The evils of such prerogative invasion of the judiciary could hardly be exaggerated: their "enormous created powers . . . threatens future generations in America with a curse tenfold worse than the Stamp Act."[13]

The more one looked the more one found evidences of deliberate malevolence. In Massachusetts, Thomas Hutchinson's elaborate patronage machine, long in existence but fully organized only after the arrival of Governor Francis Bernard in 1760, appeared to suspicious tribunes like Oxenbridge Thacher and John Adams to constitute a serious threat to liberty. The Hutchinsons and the Olivers and their ambitious allies, it was said (and the view was widely circulated through the colonies), had managed, by accumulating a massive plurality of offices, to engross the power of all branches of the Massachusetts government thereby building a "foundation sufficient on which to erect a tyranny."

---

[13]Carl Ubbelohde, *The Vice-Admiralty Courts and the American Revolution* (Chapel Hill, 1960), pp. 112, 125–126. For further expressions of antipathy to the admiralty courts, see especially the Laurens pamphlet cited in note 7 above, and . . . Adams, *Works*, III, 466–467; *Votes and Proceedings of Boston*, p. 24.

Bernard had all the executive, and a negative of the legislative; Hutchinson and Oliver, by their popular arts and secret intrigues, had elevated to the [Council] such a collection of crown officers, and their own relations, as to have too much influence there; and they had three of a family on the superior bench. . . . This junto therefore had the legislative and executive in their control, and more natural influence over the judicial than is ever to be trusted to any set of men in the world.

With encouragement, no doubt, from England, they were stretching their power beyond all proper bounds, becoming "conspirators against the public liberty."[14]

The same evil of plural officeholding, tending to destroy the protective mechanism of the separation of powers, was observed to be at work in South Carolina. In both cases the filiation between the engrossing of offices in England and in America could be said to be direct. The self-seeking monopolists of office in the colonies, advancing themselves and their faithful adherents "to the exclusion of much better men," Adams wrote somewhat plaintively, were as cravenly obedient to their masters in power in England as their own despicable "creatures" were to them.[15] How deep this issue ran, how powerful its threat, could be seen best when one noted the degree to which it paralleled cognate developments in England.

John Wilkes's career was crucial to the colonists' understanding of what was happening to them; his fate, the colonists came to believe, was intimately involved with their own.[16] Not only was he associated in their minds with general opposition to the government that passed the Stamp Act and the Townshend Duties, that was flooding the colonies with parasitic placemen, and that appeared to be making inroads into the constitution by weakening the judiciary and bestowing monopolies of public offices on pliant puppets—not only was he believed to be a national leader of opposition to such a government, but he had entered the public arena first as a victim and then as the suc-

---

[14]John Adams ("Novanglus"), *Novanglus and Massachusettensis*, pp. 49–50; Ellen E. Brennan, *Plural Office-Holding in Massachusetts 1760–1780* (Chapel Hill, 1945), chaps. i, ii. See also references to Hutchinson, above, note 4.

[15]Drayton, *Letter from Freeman*, pp. 9, 18–19, 32–33; Edward McCrady, *The History of South Carolina Under the Royal Government 1719–1776* (New York, 1899), pp. 533–535, 710–713; Adams, *Diary and Autobiography*, I, 306; II, 39.

[16]For a detailed discussion of the Wilkes affair in the context of the present discussion, see Pauline Maier, "John Wilkes and American Disillusionment with Britain," *William and Mary Quarterly*, 3d ser., 20 (1963), 373–395.

cessful antagonist of general warrants, which, in the form of writs of assistance, the colonists too had fought in heroic episodes known throughout the land. He had, moreover, defended the sanctity of private property against confiscation by the government. His cause was their cause. His *Number 45 North Briton* was as celebrated in the colonies at it was in England, and more generally approved of; its symbolism became part of the iconography of liberty in the colonies. His return from exile in 1768 and subsequent election to Parliament were major events to Americans. Toasts were offered to him throughout the colonies, and substantial contributions to his cause as well as adulatory letters were sent by Sons of Liberty in Virginia, Maryland, and South Carolina. A stalwart, independent opponent of encroaching government power and a believer in the true principles of the constitution, he was expected to do much in Parliament for the good of all: so the Bostonians wrote him in June 1768 "your perseverance in the *good old cause* may still prevent the great system from dashing to pieces. 'Tis from your endeavors we hope for a royal 'Pascite, ut ante, boves,' and from our attachment to 'peace and good order' we wait for a constitutional redress: being determined that the King of Great Britain shall have subjects but not slaves in these remote parts of his dominions."[17]

By February 1769 it was well known that "*the fate of Wilkes and America must stand or fall together.*"[18] The news, therefore, that by the maneuvers of the court party Wilkes had been denied the seat in Parliament to which he had been duly elected came as a profound shock to Americans. It shattered the hopes of many that the evils they saw around them had been the result not of design but of inadvertence, and it portended darker days ahead. When again, and then for a second, a third, and a fourth time Wilkes was re-elected to Parliament and still denied his seat, Americans could only watch with horror and agree with him that the rights of the Commons, like those of the colonial Houses, were being denied by a power-hungry government that assumed to itself the privilege of deciding who should speak for the people in their own branch of the legislature. Power had reached directly and brutally into the main agency of liberty. Surely Wilkes was right: the constitution was being deliberately, not inadvertently, torn up by its roots.

---

[17]Boston Sons of Liberty to Wilkes, June 6, 1768, *Proceedings of the Massachusetts Historical Society,* 47 (1913–1914), 191. The quotation is from Virgil, *Eclogues* i, 45: "pasture your cattle as of old."

[18]William Palfrey to Wilkes, February 21, 1769, *Proceedings of the Massachusetts Historical Society,* 47 (1913–1914), 197.

Meanwhile an event even more sinister in its implications had taken place in the colonies themselves. On October 1, 1768, two regiments of regular infantry, with artillery, disembarked in Boston. For many months the harassed Governor Bernard had sought some legal means or excuse for summoning military help in his vain efforts to maintain if not an effective administration then at least order in the face of Stamp Act riots, circular letters, tumultuous town meetings, and assaults on customs officials. But the arrival of troops in Boston increased rather than decreased his troubles. For to a populace steeped in the literature of English radicalism the presence of troops in a peaceful town had such portentous meaning that resistance instantly stiffened. It was not the physical threat of the troops that affected the attitudes of the Bostonians; it was the bearing their arrival had on the likely tendency of events. Viewed in the perspective of Trenchard's writings, these were not simply soldiers assembled for police duties; they were precisely what history had proved over and over again to be prime movers of the process by which unwary nations lose "that precious jewel *liberty*." Here, in bold, stark actuality, was a standing army—just such a standing army as had snuffed out freedom in Denmark. True, British regulars had been introduced into the colonies on a permanent basis at the end of the Seven Years' War; that in itself had been disquieting. But it could then be argued that troops were needed to police the newly acquired territories, and that they were not in any case to be regularly garrisoned in peaceful, populous towns.[19] No such defense could be made of the troops sent to Boston in 1768. No simple, ingenuous explanation would suffice. The true motive was only too apparent for those with eyes to see. One of the classic stages in the process of destroying free constitutions of government had been reached.

And again significant corroboration could be found in developments in England, and support furnished for the belief that events in America were only part of a larger whole. On May 10, 1768, a mob assembled in St. George's Fields, London, in support of the imprisoned Wilkes was fired upon by the regiment of Foot Guards that had been summoned by the nervous magistrates. Several deaths resulted, the most dramatic being that of a boy, wrongly identified as a leader of the mob, who was tracked down

---

[19]L. H. Gipson, *The British Empire Before the American Revolution* . . . (New York, 1936–   ), X, 200–201, 328–329, 408; cf. Bernhard Knollenberg, *Origin of the American Revolution, 1759–1766* (New York, 1960), pp. 87–96.

and shot to death on orders of the commander. The political capital made of this misfortune by the Wilkesites and other anti-government groups in London was echoed loudly in the colonies, the more so when it appeared that convictions of the guilty soldiers by normal processes of the law courts were being quashed by the government. Could it be believed to be a coincidence that in February 1770 a young Bostonian was also shot to death by officers of the state? This was more than a parallel to what had happened in London: the two events were two effects of the same cause.[20]

And then, a few weeks later, came the Boston Massacre. Doubts that the troops in Boston constituted a standing army and that it was the purpose of standing armies to terrify a populace into compliance with tyrannical wills were silenced by that event. The narrative of the Massacre written by James Bowdoin and others, which was distributed everywhere in the English-speaking world, stressed the deliberateness of the shooting and the clarity of the design that lay behind the lurid event; nor was the parallel to the St. George's Fields murders neglected. The acquittal of the indicted soldiers did not alter the conviction that the Massacre was the logical work of a standing army, for it accentuated the parallel with the English case which also had concluded with acquittal; and in Boston too there was suspicion of judicial irregularities. How the murderers managed to escape was known to some, it was said, but was "too dark to explain."[21]

Unconstitutional taxing, the invasion of placemen, the weakening of the judiciary, plural officeholding, Wilkes, standing armies—these were major evidences of a deliberate assault of

---

[20]George Rudé, *Wilkes and Liberty* (Oxford, 1962), pp. 49 ff.; Maier, "Wilkes and American Disillusionment," pp. 386–387.

[21]Allen, *Oration upon the Beauties of Liberty*, p. xiii. [Bowdoin, et al.], *Short Narrative of the Horrid Massacre in Boston* . . . (Boston, 1770), reprinted within the year three times in Boston, three times in London and once (retitled) in Dublin, appears also in Frederic Kidder, *History of the Boston Massacre* . . . (Albany, 1870); for the direct association of the Massacre with the problem of standing armies, see Kidder, *History*, p. 27. The annual Massacre Day orators played up this association in lurid detail: see, for example, Joseph Warren, *An Oration* . . . (Boston, 1772), pp. 11–12; John Hancock, *An Oration* . . . (Boston, 1774), pp. 13–15. The view of the Massacre held by John Adams and Josiah Quincy, Jr., the lawyers who successfully defended the soldiers in court, is especially important. Both thought the Massacre was "the strongest of proofs of the danger of standing armies" despite their efforts on the soldiers' behalf; Adams saw nothing incompatible between the verdict of the jury and his being invited to deliver one of the orations commemorating the Massacre. Josiah Quincy, *Memoir of the Life of Josiah Quincy Jun.* . . . (Boston, 1825), p. 67; Adams, *Diary and Autobiography*, II, 74, 79.

power upon liberty. Lesser testimonies were also accumulating at the same time: small episodes in themselves, they took on a large significance in the context in which they were received. Writs of assistance in support of custom officials were working their expected evil: "our houses, and even our bedchambers, are exposed to be ransacked, our boxes, trunks, and chests broke open, ravaged and plundered by wretches whom no prudent man would venture to employ even as menial servants." Legally convened legislatures had been "adjourned . . . to a place highly inconvenient to the members and greatly disadvantageous to the interest of the province"; they had been prorogued and dissolved at executive whim. Even the boundaries of colonies had been tampered with, whereby *rights of soil* had been eliminated at a stroke. When in 1772 the Boston Town Meeting met to draw up a full catalogue of the "infringements and violations" of the "rights of the colonists, and of this province in particular, as men, as Christians, and as subjects," it approved a list of twelve items, which took seventeen pamphlet pages to describe.[22]

But then, for a two-year period, there was a *détente* of sorts created by the repeal of the Townshend Duties, the withdrawal of troops from Boston, and the failure of other provocative measures to be taken. It ended abruptly, however, in the fall and winter of 1773, when, with a terrifying rush, the tendencies earlier noted were brought to fulfillment. In the space of a few weeks, all the dark, twisted roots of malevolence were finally revealed, plainly, for all to see.

The turning point was the Boston Tea Party in December 1773. Faced by this defiant resistance to intimidation, the powers at work in England, it was believed, gave up all pretense of legality —"threw off the mask," John Adams said—and moved swiftly to complete their design. In a period of two months in the spring of 1774 Parliament took its revenge in a series of coercive actions no liberty-loving people could tolerate: the Boston Port Act, intended, it was believed, to snuff out the economic life of the Massachusetts metropolis; the Administration of Justice Act, aimed at crippling judicial processes once and for all by permitting trials to be held in England for offenses committed in Massachusetts; the Massachusetts Government Act, which stripped from the people of Massachusetts the protection of the British constitution by giving over all the "democratic" elements of the province's government—even popularly elected juries and town meetings—

---

[22] *Votes and Proceedings of Boston*, pp. 13–30.

into the hands of the executive power; the Quebec Act, which, while not devised as a part of the coercive program, fitted it nicely, in the eyes of the colonists, by extending the boundaries of a "papist" province, and one governed wholly by prerogative, south into territory claimed by Virginia, Connecticut, and Massachusetts; finally, the Quartering Act, to take effect in all colonies, which permitted the seizure for the use of troops of all buildings, public and private, deserted and occupied.

Once these coercive acts were passed there could be little doubt that "the system of slavery fabricated against America . . . is the offspring of mature deliberation." To the leaders of the Revolutionary movement there was, beyond question, "a settled, fixed plan for *enslaving* the colonies, or bringing them under arbitrary government, and indeed the nation too." By 1774 the idea "that the British government—the *King, Lords,* and *Commons*—have laid a regular plan to enslave America, and that they are now deliberately putting it in execution" had been asserted, Samuel Seabury wrote wearily but accurately, "over, and over, and over again." The less inhibited of the colonial orators were quick to point out that "the MONSTER of a standing ARMY" had sprung directly from "a PLAN . . . systematically laid and pursued by the British ministry near twelve years for enslaving America"; the Boston Massacre, it was claimed, had been "planned by Hillsborough and a knot of treacherous knaves in Boston." Careful analysts like Jefferson agreed on the major point; in one of the most closely reasoned of the pamphlets of 1774 the Virginian stated unambiguously that though "single acts of tyranny may be ascribed to the accidental opinion of a day . . . a series of oppressions begun at a distinguished period and pursued unalterably through every change of ministers too plainly prove a deliberate and systematical plan of reducing us to slavery." And the fastidious and scholarly John Dickinson, though in 1774 he still clung to the hope that inadvertence, at least on the part of the King, was involved, believed that "a plan had been deliberately framed and pertinaciously adhered to, unchanged even by frequent changes of ministers, unchecked by any intervening gleam of humanity, to sacrifice to a passion for arbitrary dominion the universal property, liberty, safety, honor, happiness, and prosperity of us unoffending yet devoted Americans." Some sought to date the origins of the plot. Josiah Quincy found it in the Restoration of Charles II; and though John Adams, with one eye on Thomas Hutchinson, wrote in 1774 that "the conspiracy was first regularly formed and begun to be executed in 1763 or 4," later he traced it back to the 1750's and forties and the administration of Governor Shirley of Massachusetts. Nor were the stages of its development neglected. They could be traced, if in no other place then in the notorious Hutchinson letters of 1768–1769, those "profoundly secret, dark, and deep" letters which, published in 1773, totally exposed Hutchinson's "machiavellian dissimulation," John Adams wrote, and convicted him of "junto conspiracy"; they gave proof, the Boston Committee of Correspondence wrote, that God had "wonderfully interposed to bring to light the plot that has been laid for us by our malicious and invidious enemies."[23]

But who, specifically, were these enemies, and what were their goals? Local plotters like Hutchinson were clearly only "creatures" of greater figures in England coordinating and impelling forward the whole effort. There were a number of specific identifications of these master influences. One, which appeared in 1773, claimed that at the root of the evil stood the venerable John Stuart, Lord Bute, whose apparent absence from politics during the previous decade could be seen as one of his more successful dissimulations: "he has been aiming for years . . . to destroy the ancient right of the subjects," and now was finally taking steps to "overthrow both . . . King and state; to bring on a revolution, and to place another whom he [is] more nearly allied to upon the throne." Believing the people to "have too much liberty," he intended to reduce them to the "spiritless SLAVES" they had been "in the reign of the *Stuarts*."[24] A more general version of this view was that a

[23][Alexander Hamilton], *A Full Vindication of the Measures of the Congress* . . . (New York, 1774), in H. C. Lodge, ed., *Works* (New York and London, 1904), I, 10; Baldwin, *Appendix*, p. 67; [Samuel Seabury], *A View of the Controversy* . . . (New York, 1774), in Clarence H. Vance, ed., *Letters of a Westchester Farmer* . . . (1774–1775) (*Publications of the Westchester County Historical Society*, VIII, White Plains, 1930), p. 123; Oliver Noble, *Some Strictures upon the . . . Book of Esther* . . . (Newburyport, 1775), pp. 28, 26; Hancock, *Oration*, p. 9; [Jefferson], *A Summary View* . . . (Williamsburg, 1774), in Paul L. Ford, ed., *Writings of Thomas Jefferson* (New York, 1892–1899), I, 435; on the development of Dickinson's understanding of the cause of the crisis, see Introduction to his *Late Regulations* (Philadelphia, 1765: JHL Pamphlet 14); Quincy, *Observations on the . . . Boston Port-Bill with Thoughts on . . . Standing Armies* (Boston, 1774), in Quincy, *Memoir*, p. 446 (cf. pp. 464–465); Adams, *Works*, X, 242–243 (for Adams' full elaboration of the ministry's "dark intrigues and wicked machinations" so clearly dovetailed with the Hutchinson clique's maneuverings, see *Novanglus and Massachusettensis*, pp. 15 ff., 49–50, 55, 71–72; *Diary and Autobiography*, II, 80, 90, 119); John C. Miller, *Origins of the American Revolution* (Boston, 1943), p. 332. For other expressions of the fear of "a constant, unremitted, uniform aim to enslave us," see *Votes and Proceedings of Boston*, pp. 30, 37; Allen, *American Alarm*, 1st sec., pp. 8–9, 17, 18, 33; Edmund S. Morgan, *The Gentle Puritan* (New Haven, 1962), pp. 263–265.

[24]Allen, *American Alarm*, 1st sec., pp. 18–19; cf. the same author's reference to "Scotch barbarian troops" at the St. George's Fields riot, in *Oration upon the Beauties of Liberty*, p. xiii.

Stuart-Tory party, the "corrupt, Frenchified party in the nation," as it was described in 1766, was at work seeking to reverse the consequences of the Glorious Revolution. It was this notion that led to the republication of Rapin's *Dissertation on . . . the Whigs and Tories* in Boston in 1773; and it was this notion that furnished Jefferson with his ultimate understanding of the "system" that sought to destroy liberty in America.[25] Still another explanation emphasized the greed of a "monied interest" created by the crown's financial necessities during the Seven Years' War. The creation of this group was accompanied "by levying of taxes, by a host of tax gatherers, and a long train of dependents of the crown. The practice grew into system, till at length the crown found means to break down those barriers which the constitution had assigned to each branch of the legislature, and effectually destroyed the independence of both Lords and Commons."[26]

The most common explanation, however—an explanation almost universally accepted even after the Declaration of Independence placed responsibility officially on the King himself— located "the spring and cause of all the distresses and complaints of the people in England or in America" in "a kind of fourth power that the constitution knows nothing of, or has not provided against." This "overruling arbitrary power, which absolutely controls the King, Lords, and Commons," was composed, it was said, of the "ministers and favorites" of the King, who, in defiance of God and man alike, "extend their usurped authority infinitely too

---

[25] [Stephen Johnson], *Some Important Observations . . .* (Newport, 1766), p. 15. Jefferson's explanation appeared first as notes he jotted down on reading François Soulé's *Histoire des troubles de l'Amérique anglaise* (London, 1785) at the point where George III's education is mentioned: "The education of the present King was Tory. He gave decisive victories to the Tories. To these were added sundry rich persons sprung up in the E. I. America would have been too formidable a weight in the scale of the Whigs. It was necessary therefore to reduce them by force to concur with the Tories." Later he wrote more formally to Soulé: "The seeds of the war are here traced to their true source. The Tory education of the King was the first preparation for that change in the British government which that party never ceases to wish. This naturally ensured Tory administrations during his life. At the moment he came to the throne and cleared his hands of his enemies by the peace of Paris, the assumptions of unwarrantable right over America commenced; they were so signal, and followed one another so close as to prove they were part of a system either to reduce it under absolute subjection and thereby make it an instrument for attempts on Britain itself, or to sever it from Britain so that it might not be a weight in the Whig scale. This latter alternative however was not considered as the one which would take place. They knew so little of America that they thought it unable to encounter the little finger of Great Britain." *The Papers of Thomas Jefferson*, Julian P. Boyd, ed. (Princeton, 1950–), X, 373n2, 369.

[26] [Carter Braxton], *An Address to . . . Virginia; on the Subject of Government . . .* (Philadelphia, 1776), p. 10.

far," and, throwing off the balance of the constitution, make their "despotic will" the authority of the nation.

For their power and interest is so great that they can and do procure whatever laws they please, having (by power, interest, and the application of the people's money to *placemen* and *pensioners*) the whole legislative authority at their command. So that it is plain (not to say a word of a particular reigning arbitrary *Stuarchal* power among them) that the rights of the people are ruined and destroyed by ministerial *tyrannical* authority, and thereby . . . become a kind of slaves to the ministers of state.

This "junto of courtiers and state-jobbers," these "court-locusts," whispering in the royal ear, "instill in the King's mind a divine right of authority to command his subjects" at the same time as they advance their "detestable scheme" by misinforming and misleading the people.[27]
It was a familiar notion that had served in England for generations to justify opposition to a crown that could do no wrong, and it had recently been revived by both Pitt and Burke echoing the earlier eloquence of Bolingbroke. It had, moreover, a particular familiarity in New England, and elsewhere in the colonies, where people generally were acquainted with the Book of Esther and hence had a model for a ministerial conspiracy in the story of that "tyrannic *bloodthirsty* MINISTER OF STATE," Haman, at the court of Ahasuerus. There he was, wrote the Newbury, Massachusetts, minister Oliver Noble in 1775, "*Haman* the *Premier*, and his junto of court *favorites*, *flatterers*, and *dependents* in the royal city, together with *governors* of the provinces, *councilors*, *boards of trade*, *commissioners* and their *creatures*, *officers* and *collectors* of REVENUE, *solicitors*, assistants, *searchers*, and *inspectors*, down to tide-waiters and their *scribes*, and the good Lord knows whom and how many of them, together with the coachmen and servants of the whole . . ."—[*footnote:*] "Not that I am certain the *Persian* state had all these *officers* . . . or that the underofficers of state rode in *coaches* or chariots . . . But as the Persian monarchy was despotic . . . it is highly probable . . ." The story was so well known: ". . . now behold the DECREE obtained! The *bloody* PLAN ripened!" The "*cruel perpetrators of the horrid* PLOT and a *banditti* of ministerial tools through the provinces" had everything in readiness. "But behold! . . . A merciful GOD heard the cries of this oppressed people . . ." The parallels were closely drawn; Haman:

---

[27] Allen, *American Alarm*, 1st sec., pp. 8–9; Noble, *Some Strictures*, p. 6; Allen, *Oration upon the Beauties of Liberty*, p. 29.

Lord North; Esther and the Jews: the colonists; and Mordicai: Franklin.[28]

But why were not these manipulators of prerogative satisfied with amassing power at home? Why the attention to faraway provinces in America? Several answers were offered, besides the general one that power naturally seeks to drive itself everywhere, into every pocket of freedom. One explanation was that the court, having reached a limit in the possibilities of patronage and spoils in the British Isles, sought a quarrel with the colonies as an excuse for confiscating their wealth. "The long and scandalous list of placemen and pensioners and the general profligacy and prodigality of the present reign exceed the annual supplies. England is drained by taxes, and Ireland impoverished to almost the last farthing . . . America was the only remaining spot to which their oppression and extortion had not fully reached, and they considered her as a fallow field from which a large income might be drawn . . ." When the colonists' reaction to the Stamp Act proved that "raising a revenue in America quietly" was out of the question, it was decided to destroy their power to resist: the colonies were to be "politically broken up." And so the Tea Act was passed, not to gain a revenue but to provoke a quarrel. The ministry wished "to see America in arms . . . because it furnished them with a pretense for declaring us rebels; and persons conquered under that character forfeit their all, be it where it will or what it will, to the crown." England did not desire an accommodation of any sort, Lord North's conciliatory plan notwithstanding. "From motives of political avarice," she sought an excuse for conquest: "it is on this ground only that the continued obstinacy of her conduct can be accounted for."[29]

But perhaps the most explicit and detailed explanation of the assault upon America by a conspiratorial ministry came from the pen of a country parson in Connecticut writing "to enlighten the people of a country town not under the best advantages for information from the newspapers and other pieces wrote upon the controversy." Seeking to rouse the villagers "to a sense of the danger to which their liberties are now involved," the Rev. Ebenezer Baldwin of Danbury explained that during the last war "the

[28]Archibald S. Foord, *His Majesty's Opposition, 1714–1830* (Oxford, 1964), pp. 37–38, 51, 53–54, 147–148, 170, 291, 318–319; Noble, *Some Strictures,* pp. 10, 17–18, 12. See also Richard Salter, *A Sermon* . . . (New London, 1768); Johnson, *Some Important Observations,* pp. 39, 55–56; Elisha Fish, *Joy and Gladness* . . . (Providence, 1767).

[29]*Four Letters on Interesting Subjects* (Philadelphia, 1776), p. 5.

state of the colonies was much more attended to than it had been in times past," and "a very exalted idea of the riches of this country" had been conveyed back to England by the returning officers and soldiers. This exciting information fitted the plans of the ministry neatly, for

notwithstanding the excellency of the British constitution, if the ministry can secure a majority in Parliament who will come into all their measures [and] will vote as they bid them, they may rule as absolutely as they do in *France* or *Spain*, yea as in *Turkey* or *India*. And this seems to be the present plan: to secure a majority of Parliament, and thus enslave the nation with their own consent. The more places or pensions the ministry have in their gift the more easily they can *bribe* a majority of Parliament by bestowing those places on them or their friends. This makes them erect so many new and unnecessary offices in America, even so as to swallow up the whole of the revenue . . . by bestowing these places—places of considerable profit and no labor—upon the children or friends or dependents of the members of Parliament, the ministry can secure them in their interest. This doubtless is the great thing the ministry are driving at, to establish arbitrary government with the consent of Parliament. And to keep the people of England still, the first exertions of this power are upon the colonies.[30]

Thus the balance of the constitution had been thrown off by a gluttonous ministry usurping the prerogatives of the crown and systematically corrupting the independence of the Commons. Corruption was at the heart of it—the political corruption built on the general dissoluteness of the populace, so familiar in the history of tyranny and so shocking to observers of mid-eighteenth-century England. The evil, public and private, that had appalled Dickinson in 1754 had ripened, it seemed clear, in the subsequent decade. As early as 1766 there had been nervous speculation in the colonies about what would happen

if the British empire should have filled up the measure of its iniquity and become ripe for ruin: . . . if a proud, arbitrary, selfish, and venal spirit of corruption should ever reign in the British court and diffuse itself through all ranks in the nation; if lucrative posts be multiplied without necessity, and pensioners multiplied without bounds; if the policy of governing be by bribery and corruption, and the trade and manufactures of the nation be disregarded and trampled under foot; if all offices be bought and sold at a high and extravagant price . . . and if, to support these shocking enormities and corruptions, the subjects in all quarters must be hard squeezed with the iron arms of oppression.

---

[30]Baldwin, *Appendix*, p. 51, 67–68.

Two years later it was stated that

> The present involved state of the British nation, the rapacity and profuseness of many of her great men, the prodigious number of their dependents who want to be gratified with some office which may enable them to live lazily upon the labor of others, must convince us that we shall be taxed so long as we have a penny to pay, and that new offices will be constituted and new officers palmed upon us until the number is so great that we cannot by our constant labor and toil maintain any more.

By 1769 a Boston correspondent of Wilkes commented on "that torrent of corruption which 'like a general flood, has deluged all' to the eternal disgrace of the British nation," and suggested that the reason the "arbitrary and despotic" English government had "extended their ravages to America" was because they had found the British Isles too restricted an area for the full gratification of their "incessant cravings of luxury, extravagance and dissipation."[31]

That by 1774 the final crisis of the constitution, brought on by political and social corruption, had been reached was, to most informed colonists, evident; but if they had not realized it themselves they would soon have discovered it from the flood of newspapers, pamphlets, and letters that poured in on them from radical sources in England. Again and again reports from the home country proclaimed that the English nation had departed, once and for all and completely, from the true principles of liberty: the principles not of "certain modern Whigs," as one English pamphlet of 1774, reprinted in the colonies seven times within the year of its first appearance, explained, but of "Whigs before the [Glorious] Revolution and at the time of it; I mean the principles which such men as Mr. Locke, Lord Molesworth, and Mr. Trenchard maintained with their pens, Mr. Hampden and Lord [William] Russell with their blood, and Mr. Algernon Sidney with both." To those Englishmen who in the 1770's most directly inherited and most forcefully propagated these radical principles—Richard Price, Joseph Priestley, James Burgh—the situation at home if not abroad justified, even exaggerated, the worst fears for the future of liberty that their predecessors had expressed. For these latter-day radicals had witnessed personally the threatening rise of

[31]Johnson, *Some Important Observations*, p. 20; Thomas Bradbury, *The Ass, or, the Serpent . . .* (1712: reprinted in Boston, 1768), p. 12n; William Palfrey to Wilkes, February 21 and April 12, 1769, *Proceedings of the Massachusetts Historical Society*, 47 (1913–1914), 197, 199.

prerogative influence in the English government and its dramatic manifestation in the Wilkes affair; and they had seen revealed the rapacity and bankruptcy of the swollen East India Company, a revelation which illuminated to them the corruption of their era as dramatically as the collapse of the South Sea Company had revealed the rottenness of the era of George I to Trenchard and Gordon. Everywhere there was cynicism and gluttonous self-seeking. What more was needed to convince one that affairs in Britain were plummeting toward complete and irrecoverable collapse? The long-awaited signs of the total degeneration of the moral qualities necessary to preserve liberty were unmistakable, and these English radicals said so, vigorously, convincingly, in a series of increasingly shrill pamphlets and letters that were read avidly, circulated, published and republished, in America.[32]

There, these ideas carried conviction to a far larger part of the population, and bore more dramatic implications than they did in England. "Liberty," John Adams wrote, "can no more exist without virtue and independence than the body can live and move without a soul," and what liberty can be expected to flow from England where "luxury, effeminacy, and venality are arrived at such a shocking pitch" and where "both electors and elected are become one mass of corruption"? It was not hard to see where England stood: it was, Adams declared, precisely at the point "where the Roman republic was when Jugurtha left it and pronounced it a venal city ripe for destruction, if it can only find a purchaser." The analogy to the decline and fall of Rome and its empire was intriguing and informative; others carried it further and became more specific. Like Rome in its decline, England, "from being the nursery of heroes, became the residence of musicians, pimps, panders, and catamites." The swift decline of her empire, which, it was observed, had reached its peak only between

---

[32][Matthew Robinson-Morris, Lord Rokeby], *Considerations on the Measures Carrying on with Respect to the British Colonies in North America*, 2d ed. (London, 1774), p. 10. This pamphlet was reprinted three times in Boston, twice in Philadelphia, and once in New York and Hartford in 1774 and 1775. For Abigail Adams' awareness of the identity between Rokeby's views and those of her husband writing as "Novanglus," see her letter of May 22, 1775, in L. H. Butterfield, *et al.*, eds., *Adams Family Correspondence* (Cambridge, 1963), I, 202, 203n11. See also [Joseph Priestley], *An Address to Protestant Dissenters* (Boston, 1774), p. 6; this pamphlet, first published in London in 1773, appeared in three American editions in 1774. And see, in general, Oscar and Mary F. Handlin, "James Burgh and American Revolutionary Theory," *Proceedings of the Massachusetts Historical Society*, 73 (1961), 38–57; H. Trevor Colbourn, "John Dickinson, Historical Revolutionary," *Pa. Mag.*, 83 (1959), 284; Caroline Robbins, *The Eighteenth-Century Commonwealthman* (Cambridge, 1959), chap. ix.

1758 and the Stamp Act, resulted from the same poison that had proved so fatal to free states in classical antiquity: the corruption, effeminacy, and languor that came from "the riches and luxuries of the East" and led to a calamitous "decay of virtue" and the collapse of the constitution. So often, so stridently, and so convincingly was it said in the colonies that in England "luxury has arrived to a great pitch; and it is a universal maxim that luxury indicates the declension of a state"—so often was it argued that vigor was gone, exhaustion and poverty approaching, that those who would defend British policy were obliged to debate the point: to assert the health and strength of English society, arguing, as Samuel Seabury did, that England was a "vigorous matron, just approaching a green old age; and with spirit and strength sufficient to chastise her undutiful and rebellious children" and not at all, as his adversary Alexander Hamilton had pictured her, "an old, wrinkled, withered, worn-out hag."[33]

The fact that the ministerial conspiracy against liberty had risen from corruption was of the utmost importance to the colonists. It gave a radical new meaning to their claims: it transformed them from constitutional arguments to expressions of a world regenerative creed. For they knew that England was one of the last refuges of the ancient gothic constitution that had once flourished everywhere in the civilized world. By far "the greatest part of the human race," it was known, already lies in "total subjection to their rulers." Throughout the whole continent of Asia people are reduced "to such a degree of abusement and degradation"

that the very idea of liberty is unknown among them. In *Africa,* scarce any human beings are to be found but barbarians, tyrants, and slaves: all equally remote from the true dignity of human nature and from a well-regulated state of society. Nor is *Europe* free from the curse. Most of her nations are forced to drink deep of the bitter cup. And in those in which freedom seems to have been established, the vital flame is going out. Two kingdoms, those of *Sweden* and *Poland,* have been betrayed and enslaved in the course of one year. The free towns of *Germany* can remain free no longer than their potent neighbors shall please to let them. *Holland* has got the forms if she has lost the spirit of a free country. *Switzerland* alone is in the full and safe possession of her freedom.

---

[33]Adams ("Novanglus"), *Novanglus and Massachusettensis,* pp. 25, 22, 43; William Hooper of North Carolina, quoted in Charles F. Mullett, "Classical Influences on the American Revolution," *Classical Journal,* 35 (1939–1940), 103; William H. Drayton, *A Charge on the Rise of the American Empire* . . . (Charleston, 1776), pp. 2–3; Seabury, *A View of the Controversy,* in Vance, *Letters of a Westchester Farmer,* p. 140.

And if now, in this deepening gloom, the light of liberty went out in Britain too—in Britain, where next to "self-preservation, political liberty is the main aim and end of her constitution"—if, as events clearly portended and as "senators and historians are repeatedly predicting . . . continued corruption and standing armies will prove mortal distempers in her constitution"—what then? What refuge will liberty find?

"To our own country," it was answered, "must we look for the biggest part of that liberty and freedom that yet remains, or is to be expected, among mankind. . . . For while the greatest part of the nations of the earth are held together under the yoke of universal slavery, the North American provinces yet remain *the country of freemen:* the *asylum,* and the last, to which such may yet flee from the common deluge." More than that: "our native country . . . bids the fairest of any to promote *the perfection and happiness of mankind.*" No one, of course, can predict "the state of mankind in future ages." But insofar as one can judge the ultimate "designs of providence by the number and power of the causes that are already at work, we shall be led to think that the perfection and happiness of mankind is to be carried further in America than it has ever yet been in any place." Consider the growth the colonies had enjoyed in so short a time—growth in all ways, but especially in population: a great natural increase it had been, supplemented by multitudes from Europe, "tired out with the miseries they are doomed to at home," migrating to America "as the only country in which they can find food, raiment, and rest." Consider also the physical vigor of the people. But above all consider the moral health of the people and of the body politic.

The fatal arts of luxury and corruption are but comparatively beginning among us . . . Nor is corruption yet established as the common principle in public affairs. Our representatives are not chosen by bribing, corrupting, or buying the votes of the electors. Nor does it take one half of the revenue of a province to manage her house of commons . . . We have been free also from the burden and danger of standing armies . . . Our defenses has been our *militia* . . . the general operation of things among ourselves indicate strong tendencies towards a state of greater perfection and happiness than mankind has yet seen.

No one, therefore, can conceive of the cause of America as "the cause of a mob, of a party, or a faction." The cause of America "is the cause of *self-defense,* of *public faith,* and of the *liberties of mankind.* . . . 'In our destruction, liberty itself expires, and human nature will despair of evermore regaining its first and original dignity.' "[34]

This theme, elaborately orchestrated by the colonial writers, marked the fulfillment of the ancient idea, deeply embedded in the colonists' awareness, that America had from the start been destined to play a special role in history. The controversy with England, from its beginning in the early 1760's, had lent support to that belief, so long nourished by so many different sources: the covenant theories of the Puritans, certain strands of Enlightenment thought, the arguments of the English radicals, the condition of life in the colonies, even the conquest of Canada. It had been the Stamp Act that had led John Adams to see in the original settlement of the colonies "the opening of a grand scene and design in providence for the illumination of the ignorant and the emancipation of the slavish part of mankind all over the earth." And Jonathan Mayhew, celebrating the conclusion of the same episode, had envisioned future streams of refugees escaping from a Europe sunk in "luxury, debauchery, venality, intestine quarrels, or other vices." It was even possible, Mayhew had added, "who knows?" that "our liberties being thus established, . . . on some future occasion . . . we or our posterity may even have the great felicity and honor to . . . keep Britain herself from ruin."[35]

Now, in 1774, that "future occasion" was believed to be at hand. After the passage of the Coercive Acts it could be said that "all the spirit of patriotism or of liberty now left in England" was no more than "the last snuff of an expiring lamp," while "the same sacred flame . . . which once showed forth such wonders in Greece and in Rome . . . burns brightly and strongly in America." Who ought then to suppress as "whimsical and enthusiastical" the belief that the colonies were to become "the foundation of a great and mighty empire, the largest the world ever saw to be founded on such principles of liberty and freedom, both civil and religious . . . [and] which shall be the principal seat of that glorious kingdom which Christ shall erect upon earth in the latter days"? It was the hand of God that was "in America now giving a new epocha to the history of the world."[36]

---

[34]Samuel Williams, *A Discourse on the Love of our Country* . . . (Salem, 1775), pp. 21, 22, 23, 25, 26. Cf., e.g., Thomas Coombe, *A Sermon Preached* . . . (Philadelphia, 1775), pp. 19–20; [Richard Wells], *A Few Political Reflections* . . . (Philadelphia, 1774), pp. 38–40, 50.

[35]Adams, *Dissertation*, in *Works*, III, 452n; Jonathan Mayhew, *The Snare Broken* . . . (Boston, 1766), pp. 36, 38.

[36]Rokeby, *Considerations*, p. 148; Ebenezer Baldwin, *The Duty of Rejoicing under Calamities and Afflictions* . . . (New York, 1776), p. 38.

In the invigorating atmosphere of such thoughts, the final conclusion of the colonists' logic could be drawn not with regret but with joy. For while everyone knew that when tyranny is abroad "submission is a crime"; while they readily acknowledged that "no obedience is due to arbitrary, unconstitutional edicts calculated to enslave a free people"; and while they knew that the invasion of the liberties of the people "constitutes a state of war with the people" who may properly use "all the power which God has given them" to protect themselves—nevertheless they hesitated to come to a final separation even after Lexington and Bunker Hill. They hesitated, moving slowly and reluctantly, protesting "before God and the world that the utmost of [our] wish is that things may return to their old channel." They hesitated because their *"sentiments of duty and affection"* were sincere; they hesitated because their respect for constituted authority was great; and they hesitated too because their future as an independent people was a matter of doubt, full of the fear of the unknown.[37]

What would an independent American nation be? A republic, necessarily—and properly, considering the character and circumstances of the people. But history clearly taught that republics were delicate polities, quickly degenerating into anarchy and tyranny; it was impossible, some said, to "recollect a single instance of a nation who supported this form of government for any length of time or with any degree of greatness." Others felt that independence might "split and divide the empire into a number of petty, insignificant states" that would easily fall subject to the will of "some foreign tyrant, or the more intolerable despotism of a few American demogogues"; the colonies might end by being "parceled out, Poland-like."

But if what the faint-hearted called "the ill-shapen, diminutive brat *independency*" contained within it all that remained of freedom; if it gave promise of growing great and strong and becoming the protector and propagator of liberty everywhere; if it were indeed true that "the cause of America is in a great measure the cause of all mankind"; if " 'Tis not the concern of a day, a year, or an age; posterity are virtually involved in the contest, and will be more or less affected even to the end of time by our proceedings now"—if all of this were true, ways would be found by men inspired by such prospects to solve the problems of a new society

---

[37]Johnson, *Some Important Observations,* pp. 21, 23; [Robert Carter Nicholas], *Considerations on the Present State of Virginia Examined* ([Williamsburg], 1774), in Earl G. Swem reprint (New York, 1919), pp. 68, 42.

and government. And so let every lover of mankind, every hater of tyranny,

stand forth! Every spot of the old world is overrun with oppression. Freedom hath been hunted round the globe. Asia and Africa have long expelled her. Europe regards her like a stranger, and England hath given her warning to depart. O! receive the fugitive, and prepare in time an asylum for mankind.[38]

The Puritan Ethic and the Coming of the American Revolution

EDMUND S. MORGAN

The American Revolution, we have been told, was radical and conservative, a movement for home rule and a contest for rule at home, the product of a rising nationality and the cause of that nationality, the work of designing demagogues and a triumph of statesmanship. John Adams said it took place in the minds and hearts of the people before 1776; Benjamin Rush thought it had scarcely begun in 1787. There were evidently many revolutions, many contests, divisions, and developments that deserve to be considered as part of the American Revolution. This paper deals in a preliminary, exploratory way with an aspect of the subject that has hitherto received little attention.[1] Without pretending to explain the whole exciting variety of the Revolution, I should like to suggest that the movement in all its phases, from the resistance against Parliamentary taxation in the 1760's to the establishment of a national government and national policies in the 1790's was

Reprinted with additions and permission from *The William and Mary Quarterly*, 3rd ser., XXIV (January, 1967), 3–18. Copyright © 1967 by Edmund S. Morgan.

[38]Braxton, *Address*, p. 19; Seabury, *View*, in Vance, *Letters of a Westchester Farmer*, p. 112; Daniel Leonard ("Massachusettensis"), in *Novanglus and Massachusettensis*, p. 185; [Joseph Galloway], *A Candid Examination of the Mutual Claims of Great-Britain and the Colonies* . . . (New York, 1775), p. 31; [Thomas Paine], *Common Sense* . . . (Philadelphia, 1776), in Moncure D. Conway, ed., *The Writings of Thomas Paine* (New York, 1894–1896), I, 68, 84–85, 100–101.

[1]The author is engaged in a full-scale study of this theme. The present essay is interpretative, and citations have for the most part been limited to identifying the sources of quotations.

affected, not to say guided, by a set of values inherited from the age of Puritanism.

These values or ideas, which I will call collectively the Puritan Ethic,[2] were not unconscious or subconscious, but were deliberately and openly expressed by men of the time. The men who expressed them were not Puritans, and few of the ideas included in the Puritan Ethic were actually new. Many of them had existed in other intellectual contexts before Puritanism was heard of, and many of them continue to exist today, as they did in the Revolutionary period, without the support of Puritanism. But Puritanism wove them together in a single rational pattern, and Puritans planted the pattern in America. It may be instructive, therefore, to identify the ideas as the Puritans defined and explained them before going on to the way in which they were applied in Revolutionary America after they had emerged from the Puritan mesh.

The values, ideas, and attitudes of the Puritan Ethic, as the term will be used here, clustered around the familiar idea of "calling." God, the Puritans believed, called every man to serve Him by serving society and himself in some useful, productive occupation. Before entering on a trade or profession, a man must determine whether he had a calling to undertake it. If he had talents for it, if it was useful to society, if it was appropriate to his station in life, he could feel confident that God called him to it. God called no one to a life of prayer or to a life of ease or to any life that added nothing to the common good. It was a "foul disorder in any Commonwealth that there should be suffered rogues, beggars, vagabonds." The life of a monk or nun was no calling because prayer must be the daily exercise of every man, not a way for particular men to make a living. And perhaps most important, the life of the carefree aristocrat was no calling: "miserable and damnable is the estate of those that being enriched with great livings and revenues, do spend their days in eating and drinking, in sports and pastimes, not employing themselves in service for Church or Commonwealth."[3]

Once called to an occupation, a man's duty to the Maker Who called him demanded that he labor assiduously at it. He must

---

[2] I have chosen this term rather than the familiar "Protestant Ethic" of Max Weber, partly because I mean something slightly different and partly because Weber confined his phrase to attitudes prevailing while the religious impulse was paramount. The attitudes that survived the decline of religion he designated as the "spirit of capitalism." In this essay I have not attempted to distinguish earlier from later, though I am concerned with a period when the attitudes were no longer dictated primarily by religion.

[3] William Perkins, *Workes* (London, 1626–1631), I, 755–756.

shun both idleness, or neglect of his calling, and sloth, or slack-
ness in it. Recreation was legitimate, because body and mind
sometimes needed a release in order to return to work with renewed vigor. But recreation must not become an end in itself.
One of the Puritans' objections to the stage was that professional
players made recreation an occupation and thereby robbed the
commonwealth of productive labor. The emphasis throughout was
on productivity for the benefit of society.

In addition to working diligently at productive tasks, a man
was supposed to be thrifty and frugal. It was good to produce but
bad to consume any more than necessity required. A man was
but the steward of the possessions he accumulated. If he indulged
himself in luxurious living, he would have that much less with
which to support church and society. If he needlessly consumed
his substance, either from carelessness or from sensuality, he
failed to honor the God who furnished him with it.

In this atmosphere the tolerance accorded to merchants was
grudging. The merchant was suspect because he tended to encourage unnecessary consumption and because he did not actually
produce anything; he simply moved things about. It was formally
recognized that making exchanges could be a useful service, but
it was a less essential one than that performed by the farmer, the
shoemaker, or the weaver. Moreover, the merchant sometimes de-
meaned his calling by practicing it to the detriment rather than
the benefit of society: he took advantage of his position to collect
more than the value of his services, to charge what the market
would bear. In short, he sometimes engaged in what a later generation would call speculation.

As the Puritan Ethic induced a suspicion of merchants, it also
induced, for different reasons, a suspicion of prosperity. Super-
ficial readers of Max Weber have often leapt to the conclusion
that Puritans viewed economic success as a sign of salvation. In
fact, Puritans were always uncomfortable in the presence of
prosperity. Although they constantly sought it, although hard
work combined with frugality could scarcely fail in the New World
to bring it, the Puritans always felt more at ease when adversity
made them tighten their belts. They knew that they must be
thankful for prosperity, that like everything good in the world it
came from God. But they also knew that God could use it as a
temptation, that it could lead to idleness, sloth, and extravagance.
These were vices, not simply because they in turn led to poverty,
but because God forbade them. Adversity, on the other hand,
though a sign of God's temporary displeasure, and therefore a

cause for worry, was also God's means of recalling a people to Him. When God showed anger man knew he must repent and do something about it. In times of drought, disease, and disaster a man could renew his faith by exercising frugality and industry, which were good not simply because they would lead to a restoration of prosperity, but because God demanded them.

The ambivalence of this attitude toward prosperity and adversity was characteristic of the Puritans: it was their lot to be forever improving the world, in full knowledge that every improvement would in the end prove illusory. While rejoicing at the superior purity of the churches they founded in New England, they had to tell themselves that they had often enjoyed more godliness while striving against heavy odds in England. The experience caused Nathaniel Ward, the "simple cobbler of Aggawam," to lament the declension that he was sure would overtake the Puritans in England after they gained the upper hand in the 1640's: "my heart hath mourned, and mine eyes wept in secret, to consider what will become of multitudes of my dear Countrymen [in England], when they shall enjoy what they now covet."[4] Human flesh was too proud to stand success; it needed the discipline of adversity to keep it in line. And Puritans accordingly relished every difficulty and worried over every success.

This thirst for adversity found expression in a special kind of sermon, the Jeremiad, which was a lament for the loss of virtue and a warning of divine displeasure and desolation to come. The Jeremiad was a rhetorical substitute for adversity, designed to stiffen the virtue of the prosperous and successful by assuring them that they had failed. Nowhere was the Puritan Ethic more assiduously inculcated than in these laments, and it accordingly became a characteristic of the virtues which that ethic demanded that they were always seen to be expiring, if not already dead. Industry and frugality in their full vigor belonged always to an earlier generation, which the existing one must learn to emulate if it would avoid the wrath of God.

These ideas and attitudes were not peculiar to Puritans. The voluminous critiques of the Weber thesis have shown that similar attitudes prevailed widely among many groups and at many times. But the Puritans did have them, and so did their descendants in the time of the Revolution and indeed for long after it. It matters little by what name we call them or where they came from. "The

[4]Nathaniel Ward, *The Simple Cobbler of Aggawam in America* (London, 1647), 41.

Puritan Ethic" is used here simply as an appropriate shorthand phrase to designate them, and should not be taken to imply that the American Revolutionists were Puritans.

The Puritan Ethic as it existed among the Revolutionary generation had in fact lost for most men the endorsement of an omnipresent angry God. The element of divinity had not entirely departed, but it was a good deal diluted. The values and precepts derived from it, however, remained intact and were reinforced by a reading of history that attributed the rise and fall of empires to the acquisition and loss of the same virtues that God had demanded of the founders of New England. Rome, it was learned, had risen while its citizens worked at their callings and led lives of simplicity and frugality. Success as usual had resulted in extravagance and luxury. "The ancient, regular, and laborious life was relaxed and sunk in Idleness," and the torrent of vices thus let loose had overwhelmed the empire. In modern times the frugal Dutch had overthrown the extravagant Spanish.[5] The lesson of history carried the same imperatives that were intoned from the pulpit.

Whether they derived their ideas from history thus interpreted or from the Puritan tradition or elsewhere, Americans of the Revolutionary period in every colony and state paid tribute to the Puritan Ethic and repeated its injunctions. Although it was probably strongest among Presbyterians and Congregationalists like Benjamin Rush and Samuel Adams, it is evident enough among Anglicans like Henry Laurens and Richard Henry Lee and even among deists like Franklin and Jefferson. Jefferson's letters to his daughters sometimes sound as though they had been written by Cotton Mather: "It is your future happiness which interests me, and nothing can contribute more to it (moral rectitude always excepted) than the contracting a habit of industry and activity. Of all the cankers of human happiness, none corrodes it with so silent, yet so baneful a tooth, as indolence." "Determine never to be idle. No person will have occasion to complain of the want of time, who never loses any. It is wonderful how much may be done, if we are always doing."[6] And Jefferson of course followed his own injunction: a more methodically industrious man never lived.

The Puritan Ethic whether enjoined by God, by history, or by

---

[5]Purdie and Dixon's *Virginia Gazette* (Williamsburg), Sept. 5, 1771. Cf. *Pennsylvania Chronicle* (Philadelphia), Feb. 9–16, May 4–11, 1767; *Newport Mercury*, Mar. 7, 1774; and *Boston Evening Post*, Nov. 30, 1767.

[6]To Martha Jefferson, Mar. 28, May 5, 1787, in Julian Boyd *et al.*, eds., *The Papers of Thomas Jefferson* (Princeton, 1950–), XI, 250, 349.

philosophy, called for diligence in a productive calling, beneficial both to society and to the individual. It encouraged frugality and frowned on extravagance. It viewed the merchant with suspicion and speculation with horror. It distrusted prosperity and gathered strength from adversity. It prevailed widely among Americans of different times and places, but those who urged it most vigorously always believed it to be on the point of expiring and in need of renewal.

The role of these ideas in the American Revolution—during the period, say, roughly from 1764 to 1789—was not explicitly causative. That is, the important events of the time can seldom be seen as the result of these ideas and never as the result solely of these ideas. Yet the major developments, the resistance to Great Britain, independence, the divisions among the successful Revolutionists, and the formulation of policies for the new nation, were all discussed and understood by men of the time in terms derived from the Puritan Ethic. And the way men understood and defined the issues before them frequently influenced their decisions.

The Origins of American Independence

In the first phase of the American Revolution, the period of agitation between the passage of the Sugar Act in 1764 and the outbreak of hostilities at Lexington in 1775, Americans were primarily concerned with finding ways to prevent British authority from infringing what they considered to be their rights. The principal point of contention was Parliament's attempt to tax them; and their efforts to prevent taxation, short of outright resistance, took two forms: economic pressure through boycotts and political pressure through the assertion of political and constitutional principles. Neither form of protest required the application of the Puritan Ethic, but both in the end were affected by it.

The boycott movements were a means of getting British merchants to bring their weight to bear on Parliament for the specific purpose of repealing tax laws. In each case the boycotts began with extralegal voluntary agreements among citizens not to consume British goods. In 1764–1765, for instance, artisans agreed to wear only leather working clothes. Students forbore imported beer. Fire companies pledged themselves to eat no mutton in order to increase the supply of local wool. Backed by the nonconsumers, merchants of New York, Philadelphia, and Boston agreed to import no British goods until the repeal of the Stamp Act. The pressure had the desired effect: The Stamp Act was repealed and the Sugar Act revised. When the Townshend Acts and later the Coercive Acts were passed, new nonconsumption and nonimportation agreements were launched.[7]

From the outset these colonial boycott movements were more than a means of bringing pressure on Parliament. That is to say, they were not simply negative in intent. They were also a positive end in themselves, a way of reaffirming and rehabilitating the virtues of the Puritan Ethic. Parliamentary taxation offered Americans the prospect of poverty and adversity, and, as of old, adversity provided a spur to virtue. In 1764, when Richard Henry Lee got news of the Sugar Act, he wrote to a friend in London: "Possibly this step of the mother country, though intended to oppress and keep us low, in order to secure our dependence, may be subversive of this end. Poverty and oppression, among those whose minds are filled with ideas of British liberty, may introduce a virtuous industry, with a train of generous and manly sentiments. . . ."[8] And so it proved in the years that followed: as their Puritan forefathers had met providential disasters with a renewal of the virtue that would restore God's favor, the Revolutionary generation met taxation with a self-denial and industry that would hopefully restore their accustomed freedom and simultaneously enable them to identify with their virtuous ancestors.

The advocates of nonconsumption and nonimportation, in urging austerity on their countrymen, made very little of the effect that self-denial would have on the British government. Nonimportation and nonconsumption were preached as means of renewing ancestral virtues. Americans were reminded that they had been "of late years insensibly drawn into too great a degree of *luxury* and *dissipation*."[9] Parliamentary taxation was a blessing in disguise, because it produced the nonimportation and nonconsumption agreements. "Luxury," the people of the colonies were told, "has taken deep root among us, and to cure a people of luxury were an Herculean task indeed; what perhaps no power on earth but a British Parliament, in the very method they are taking with us, could possibly execute."[10] Parliamentary taxation,

---

[7]Arthur M. Schlesinger, *The Colonial Merchants and the American Revolution, 1763–1776* (New York, 1918), remains the best account of these movements.

[8]To [Unknown], May 31, 1764, in James C. Ballagh, ed., *The Letters of Richard Henry Lee* (New York, 1911), I, 7.

[9]*Boston Evening Post*, November 16, 1767.

[10]*Virginia Gazette* (Purdie and Dixon), June 1, 1769 (reprinted from *New York Chronicle*).

like an Indian attack in earlier years, was thus both a danger to be resisted and an act of providence to recall Americans from declension: "The Americans have plentifully enjoyed the delights and comforts, as well as the necessaries of life, and it is well known that an increase of wealth and affluence paves the way to an increase of luxury, immorality and profaneness, and here kind providence interposes; and as it were, obliges them to forsake the use of one of their delights, to preserve their liberty."[11] The principal object of this last homily was tea, which, upon being subjected to a Parliamentary duty, became luxurious and enervating. Physicians even discovered that it was bad for the health.[12] Importations, it now appeared, were mainly luxuries, "Baubles of Britain," "foreign trifles."[13]

In these appeals for self-denial, the Puritan Ethic acquired a value that had been only loosely associated with it hitherto: it became an essential condition of political liberty. Americans like Englishmen had long associated liberty with property. They now concluded that both rested on virtue. An author who signed himself "Frugality" advised the readers of the *Newport Mercury* that "We may talk and boast of liberty; but after all, the industrious and frugal only will be free,"[14] free not merely because their self-denial would secure repeal of Parliamentary taxes, but because freedom was inseparable from virtue, and frugality and industry were the most conspicuous public virtues. Bostonians were told that "by consuming *less* of what we are not really in want of, and by industriously cultivating and improving the natural advantages of our own country, we might save our *substance, even our lands,* from becoming the property of others, and we might effectually preserve our *virtue* and our *liberty,* to the latest posterity." Liberty, virtue, and property offered a powerful rallying call to Americans. Each supported the others; but virtue was the sine qua non of the trio, for while liberty would expire without the support of property, property itself could not exist without industry and frugality. Expounding this point, the *Pennsylvania Journal* assured its readers that "Our enemies very well know that dominion and property are closely connected; and that to impoverish us, is the surest way to enslave us. Therefore, if we mean still to be

---

[11]*Newport Mercury,* December 13, 1773.
[12]*Ibid.,* November 9, 1767, November 29, 1773, February 14, 28, 1774.
[13]*Boston Evening Post,* November 9, 16, 1767; To Arthur Lee, October 31, 1771, in H. A. Cushing, ed., *The Writings of Samuel Adams* (New York, 1904–1908) II, 267.
[14]February 28, 1774.

free, let us unanimously lay aside foreign superfluities, and encourage our own manufacture. SAVE YOUR MONEY AND YOU WILL SAVE YOUR COUNTRY!"[15]

There was one class of Americans who could take no comfort in this motto. The merchants, on whom nonimportation depended, stood to lose by the campaign for austerity, and it is not surprising that they showed less enthusiasm for it than the rest of the population. Their lukewarmness only served to heighten the suspicion with which their calling was still viewed. "Merchants have no country," Jefferson once remarked. "The mere spot they stand on does not constitute so strong an attachment as that from which they draw their gains."[16] And John Adams at the Continental Congress was warned by his wife's uncle that merchants "have no Object but their own particular Interest and they must be Contrould or they will ruin any State under Heaven."[17]

Such attitudes had been nourished by the merchants behavior in the 1760's and 1770's. After repeal of the Stamp Act, Silas Downer, secretary of the Sons of Liberty in Providence, Rhode Island, wrote to the New York Sons of Liberty that "From many observations when the Stamp Act was new, I found that the Merchants in general would have quietly submitted, and many were zealous for it, always reciting the Difficulties their Trade would be cast into on Non Compliance, and never regarding the Interest of the whole Community . . ."[18] When the Townshend Acts were passed, it was not the merchants but the Boston town meeting that took the lead in promoting nonimportation, and after the repeal of the Acts the merchants broke down and began importing while the duty on tea still remained. Samuel Adams had expected their defection to come much sooner for he recognized that the nonimportation agreements had "pressed hard upon their private Interest" while the majority of consumers could participate under the "happy Consideration that while they are most effectually serving their Country they are adding to their private fortunes."[19]

The merchants actually had more than a short-range interest at

[15]*Boston Evening Post*, November 16, 1767; *Pennsylvania Journal* (Philadelphia), December 10, 1767.
[16]To Horatio Spafford, March 17, 1817, quoted in Boyd, ed., *Jefferson Papers*, XIV, 221.
[17]Cotton Tufts to John Adams, April 26, 1776, in L. H. Butterfield *et al.*, eds., *Adams Family Correspondence* (Cambridge, Mass., 1963–), I, 395.
[18]Letter dated July 21, 1766, Peck Manuscripts, III, 3, Rhode Island Historical Society, Providence.
[19]To Stephen Sayre, November 16, 1770, in Cushing, ed., *Writings of Samuel Adams*, II, 58.

stake in their reluctance to undertake nonimportation. The movement, as we have seen, was not simply a means of securing repeal of the taxes to which merchants along with other colonists were opposed. The movement was in fact anticommercial, a repudiation of the merchant's calling. Merchants, it was said, encouraged men to go into debt. Merchants pandered to luxury. Since they made more on the sale of superfluous baubles than on necessities, they therefore pressed the sale of them to a weak and gullible public. What the advocates of nonimportation demanded was not merely an interruption of commerce but a permanent reduction, not to say elimination, of it. In its place they called for manufacturing, a palpably productive, useful calling.

The encouragement of manufacturing was an accompaniment to all the nonimportation, nonconsumption movements. New Yorkers organized a society specifically for that purpose, which offered bounties for the production of native textiles and other necessaries. The nonconsumption of mutton provided new supplies of wool, which housewives turned into thread in spinning matches (wheelwrights did a land-office business in spinning wheels). Stores began selling American cloth, and college students appeared at commencement in homespun. Tories ridiculed these efforts, and the total production was doubtless small, but it would be difficult to underestimate the importance of the attitude toward manufacturing that originated at this time. In a letter of Abigail Adams can be seen the way in which the Puritan Ethic was creating out of a Revolutionary protest movement the conception of a self-sufficient American economy. Abigail was writing to her husband, who was at the First Continental Congress, helping to frame the Continental Association for nonimportation, nonexportation, and nonconsumption:

If we expect to inherit the blessings of our Fathers, we should return a little more to their primitive Simplicity of Manners, and not sink into inglorious ease. We have too many high sounding words, and too few actions that correspond with them. I have spent one Sabbeth in Town since you left me. I saw no difference in respect to ornaments, etc. etc. but in the Country you must look for that virtue, of which you find but small Glimerings in the Metropolis. Indeed they have not the advantages, nor the resolution to encourage their own Manufactories which people in the country have. To the Mercantile part, tis considered as throwing away their own Bread; but they must retrench their expenses and be content with a small share of gain for they will find but few who will wear their Livery. As for me I will seek wool and flax and work willingly with my Hands, and indeed there is occasion for all our industry and economy.[20]

In 1774 manufacture retained its primitive meaning of something made by hand, and making things by hand seemed a fitting occupation for frugal country people who had always exhibited more of the Puritan Ethic than high-living city folk. Abigail's espousal of manufactures, with its defiant rejection of dependence on the merchants of the city, marks a step away from the traditional notion that America because of its empty lands and scarcity of people was unsuited to manufactures and must therefore obtain them from the Old World. Through the nonimportation movements the colonists discovered that manufacturing was a calling not beyond the capacities of a frugal, industrious people, however few in number, and that importation of British manufactures actually menaced frugality and industry. The result of the discovery was to make a connection with Britain seem neither wholly necessary nor wholly desirable, so that when the thought of independence at last came, it was greeted with less apprehension that it might otherwise have been.

Nonimportation had produced in effect a trial run in economic self-sufficiency. The trial was inconclusive as a demonstration of American economic capacity, but it carried immense significance intellectually, for it obliged the colonists to think about the possibility of an economy that would not be colonial. At the same time it confirmed them in the notion that liberty was the companion not only of property but of frugality and industry, two virtues that in turn fostered manufactures. By invoking the Puritan Ethic on behalf of a protest movement Americans had led themselves into affirmations of value in which can be seen the glimmerings of a future national economic policy.

While engaged in their campaign of patriotic frugality, Americans were also articulating the political principles that they thought should govern free countries and that should bar Parliament from taxing them. The front line of defense against Parliament was the ancient maxim that a man could not be taxed except by his own consent given in person or by his representative. The colonists believed this to be an acknowledged principle of free government, indelibly stamped on the British Constitution, and

---

[20]October 16, 1774, in Butterfield, ed., *Adams Family Correspondence*, I, 173.

they wrote hundreds of pages affirming it. In those pages the Puritan Ethic was revealed at the very root of the constitutional principle when taxation without representation was condemned as an assault on every man's calling. To tax a man without his consent, Samuel Adams said, was "against the plain and obvious rule of equity, whereby the industrious man is intitled to the fruits of his industry."[21] And the New York Assembly referred to the Puritan Ethic when it told Parliament that the effect of the sugar and stamp taxes would be to "dispirit the People, abate their Industry, discourage Trade, introduce Discord, Poverty, and Slavery."[22] Slavery, of course, meant no liberty and no property; and without these, men had no motive for frugality and industry. In other words, the New York protest was pointing out that uncontrolled Parliamentary taxation, like luxury and extravagance, was an attack not merely on property but on industry and frugality, for which liberty and property must be the expected rewards. With every protest that British taxation was reducing them to slavery, Americans reaffirmed their devotion to industry and frugality and their readiness to defy the British threat to them. Students of the American Revolution have often found it difficult to believe that the colonists were willing to fight about an abstract principle and have sometimes dismissed the constitutional arguments of the time as mere rhetoric. But the constitutional principle on which the colonists rested their case was not the product either of abstract political philosophy or of the needs of the moment. In the colonists' view, the principle of no taxation without representation was a means, hallowed by history, of protecting property and of maintaining those virtues, associated with property, without which no people could be free. Through the rhetoric, if it may be called that, of the Puritan Ethic, the colonists reached behind the constitutional principle to the enduring human needs that had brought the principle into being.

We may perhaps understand better the urgency both of the constitutional argument and of the drive toward independence that it ultimately generated, if we observe the growing suspicion among the colonists that the British government had betrayed its own constitution and the values which that constitution protected. In an earlier generation the colonists had vied with one another

---

[21][*Boston Gazette*, December 19, 1768] in Cushing, ed., *Writings of Samuel Adams*, I, 271.

[22]E. S. Morgan, ed., *Prologue to Revolution: Sources and Documents on the Stamp Act Crisis, 1764–1776* (Chapel Hill, 1959), 13.

in praising the government of England. Englishmen, they believed, had suffered again and again from invasion and tyranny, had each time recovered control of their government, and in the course of centuries had developed unparalleled constitutional safeguards to keep rulers true to their callings. The calling of a ruler, as the colonists and their Puritan forbears saw it, was like any other calling: it must serve the common good; it must be useful, productive; and it must be assiduously pursued. After the Glorious Revolution of 1688, Englishmen had fashioned what seemed a nearly perfect instrument of government, a constitution that blended monarchy, aristocracy, and democracy in a mixture designed to avoid the defects and secure the benefits of each. But something had gone wrong. The human capacity for corruption had transformed the balanced government of King, Lords, and Commons into a single-minded body of rulers bent on their own enrichment and heedless of the public good.

A principal means of corruption had been the multiplication of office-holders who served no useful purpose but fattened on the labors of those who did the country's work. Even before the dispute over taxation began, few colonists who undertook trips to England failed to make unflattering comparisons between the simplicity, frugality, and industry that prevailed in the colonies and the extravagance, luxury, idleness, drunkenness, poverty, and crime that they saw in the mother country. To Americans bred on the values of the Puritan Ethic, England seemed to have fallen prey to her own opulence, and the government shared heavily in the corruption. In England, the most powerful country in the world, the visitors found the people laboring under a heavy load of taxes, levied by a government that swarmed with functionless placeholders and pensioners. The cost of government in the colonies, as Professor Gipson has shown, was vastly lower than in England, with the per capita burden of taxation only a fraction of that which Englishmen bore.[23] And whatever the costs of maintaining the empire may have contributed to the British burden, it was clear that the English taxpayers supported a large band of men who lived well from offices that existed only to pay their holders. Even an American like George Croghan, who journeyed to London to promote dubious speculative schemes of his own, felt uncomfortable in the presence of English corruption: "I am Nott

---

[23]L. H. Gipson, *The British Empire Before the American Revolution* . . . (New York, 1936–), X, 53–110; Gipson, *The Coming of the Revolution 1763–1775* (New York, 1954), 116–161.

Sorry I came hear," he wrote, "as it will Larn Me to be Contented on a Litle farm in amerrica. . . . I am Sick of London and heartily Tierd of the pride and pompe. . . ."[24]

In the 1760's Americans were given the opportunity to gain the perspective of a Croghan without the need for a trip abroad. The Townshend Acts called for a reorganization of the customs service with a new set of higher officials, who would perforce be paid out of the duties they extracted from the colonists. In the establishment of this American Board of Customs Commissioners, Americans saw the extension of England's corrupt system of officeholding to America. As Professor Dickerson has shown, the Commissioners were indeed corrupt.[25] They engaged in extensive "customs racketeering" and they were involved in many of the episodes that heightened the tension between England and the colonies: it was on their request that troops were sent to Boston; the Boston Massacre took place before their headquarters; the *Gaspée* was operating under their orders. But it was not merely the official actions of the Commissioners that offended Americans. Their very existence seemed to pose a threat both to the Puritan Ethic and to the conscientious, frugal kind of government that went with it. Hitherto colonial government had been relatively free of the evils that had overtaken England. But now the horde of placeholders was descending on America.

From the time the Commissioners arrived in Boston in November 1767, the newspapers were filled with complaints that "there can be no such thing as common good or common cause where mens estates are ravaged at pleasure to lavish on parasitical minions."[26] Samuel Adams remarked that the commissioners were "a useless and very expensive set of officers" and that they had power to appoint "as many officers under them as they please, for whose Support it is said they may sink the whole revenue."[27] American writers protested against the "legions of idle, lazy, and to say no worse, altogether useless customs house locusts, catterpillars, flies and lice."[28] They were "a parcel of dependant tools of arbitrary power, sent hither to enrich themselves and their Masters, on the Spoil of the honest and industrious of these

---

[24]Quoted in T. P. Abernethy, *Western Lands and the American Revolution* (New York, 1937), 24.

[25]O. M. Dickerson, *The Navigation Acts and the American Revolution* (Philadelphia, 1951), 208–265.

[26]*Boston Evening Post,* November 30, 1767.

[27]To Dennys De Berdt, May 14, 1768, in Cushing, ed., *Writings of Samuel Adams,* I, 216.

[28]*Newport Mercury,* June 21, 1773.

colonies."[29] By 1774, when the debate between colonies and Parliament was moving into its final stages, town meetings could state it as an intolerable grievance "that so many unnecessary officers are supported by the earnings of honest industry, in a life of dissipation and ease; who, by being *properly* employed, might be useful members of society."[30]

The coming of the Customs Commissioners showed the colonists that the ocean barrier which had hitherto isolated them from the corruption of Britain was no longer adequate. Eventually, perhaps, Englishmen would again arise, turn out the scoundrels, and recall their government to its proper tasks. And Americans did not fail to support Englishmen like John Wilkes whom they thought to be working toward this end. But meanwhile they could not ignore the dangers on their own shores. There would henceforth be in their midst a growing enclave of men whose lives and values denied the Puritan Ethic; and there would be an increasing number of lucrative offices to tempt Americans to desert ancestral standards and join the ranks of the "parasitical minions." No American was sure that his countrymen would be able to resist the temptation. In 1766, after repeal of the Stamp Act, George Mason had advised the merchants of London that Americans were "not yet debauched by wealth, luxury, venality and corruption."[31] But who could say how long their virtue would withstand the closer subjection to British control that Whitehall seemed to be designing? Some Americans believed that the British were deliberately attempting to undermine the Puritan Ethic. In Boston Samuel Adams observed in 1771 that "the Conspirators against our Liberties are employing all their Influence to divide the people, . . . introducing Levity Luxury and Indolence and assuring them that if they are quiet the Ministry will alter their Measures."[32] And in 1772 Henry Marchant, a Rhode Island traveler in England wrote to his friend Ezra Stiles: "You will often hear the following Language—Damn those Fellows we shall never do any Thing with Them till we root out that cursed puritanick Spirit— How is this to be done?—keep Soldiers amongst Them, not so much to awe Them, as to debauch their Morals—Toss off to them all the Toies and Baubles that genius can invent to weaken their Minds, fill Them with Pride and Vanity, and beget in them all

[29]*Ibid.*, July 13, 1772.
[30]Resolves of Bristol, R. I., *ibid.*, March 21, 1774.
[31]Morgan, *Prologue to Revolution*, 160.
[32]To Arthur Lee, October 31, 1771, in Cushing, ed., *Writings of Samuel Adams*, II, 266–267.

possible Extravagance in Dress and Living, that They may be kept poor and made wretched. . . ."[33]

By the time the First Continental Congress came together in 1774, large numbers of leading Americans had come to identify Great Britain with vice and America with virtue, yet with the fearful recognition that virtue stands in perennial danger from the onslaughts of vice. Patrick Henry gave voice to the feeling when he denounced Galloway's plan for an intercolonial American legislature that would stand between the colonies and Parliament. "We shall liberate our Constituents," he warned, "from a corrupt House of Commons, but thro[w] them into the Arms of an American Legislature that may be bribed by that Nation which avows in the Face of the World, that Bribery is a Part of her System of Government."[34] A government that had succeeded in taxing seven million Englishmen (with the consent of their supposed representatives), to support an army of placeholders, would have no hesitation in using every means to corrupt the representatives of two and one half million Americans.

When the Second Congress met in 1775, Benjamin Franklin, fresh from London, could assure the members that their contrast of England and America was justified. Writing back to Joseph Priestley, he said it would "scarce be credited in Britain, that men can be as diligent with us from zeal for the public good, as with you for thousands per annum. Such is the difference between uncorrupted new states, and corrupted old ones."[35] Thomas Jefferson drew the contrast even more bluntly in an answer rejecting Lord North's Conciliatory Proposal of February 20, 1775, which had suggested that Parliament could make provisions for the government of the colonies. "The provisions we have made," said Jefferson, "are such as please our selves, and are agreeable to our own circumstances; they answer the substantial purposes of government and of justice, and other purposes than these should not be answered. We do not mean that our people shall be burthened with oppressive taxes to provide sinecures for the idle or the wicked. . . ."[36]

When Congress finally dissolved the political bands that had connected America with England, the act was rendered less

---

[33]Quoted in E. S. Morgan, *The Gentle Puritan: A Life of Ezra Stiles, 1727–1795* (New Haven, 1962), 265.

[34]September 28, 1774, in L. H. Butterfield *et al.*, eds., *Diary and Autobiography of John Adams* (Cambridge, Mass., 1961), II, 143.

[35]July 6, 1775, in E. C. Burnett, ed., *Letters of Members of The Continental Congress*, Washington, 1921–1936), I, 156.

[36]July 31, 1775, in Boyd, ed., *Jefferson Papers*, I, 232.

painful by the colonial conviction that America and England were already separated as virtue is from vice. The British Constitution had foundered, and the British government had fallen into the hands of a luxurious and corrupt ruling class. There remained no way of preserving American virtue unless the connection with Britain was severed. The meaning of virtue in this context embraced somewhat more than the values of the Puritan Ethic, but those values were pre-eminent in it. In the eyes of many Americans the Revolution was a defense of industry and frugality, whether in rulers or people, from the assaults of British vice. It is unnecessary to assess the weight of the Puritan Ethic among the many revolutionary factors that scholars argue about. It is enough simply to recognize that the Puritan Ethic prepared the colonists both in their political and in their economic thinking to embrace the idea of independence.

The Moral and Psychological Roots of American Resistance

PERRY MILLER

I

On June 12, 1775, the Continental Congress dispatched from Philadelphia to the thirteen colonies (and to insure a hearing, ordered the document to be published in newspapers and in handbills) a "recommendation" that July 20 be universally observed as "a day of publick humiliation, fasting, and prayer." The Congress prefaced the request with a statement of reasons. Because the great "Governor" not only conducts by His Providence the course of nations "but frequently influences the minds of men to serve the wise and gracious purposes of his providential government," and also it being our duty to acknowledge his superintendency, "especially in time of impending danger and publick calamity"—therefore the Congress acts.

Reprinted with permission from "From the Covenant to the Revival," in James Ward Smith and A. Leland Jamison, eds., *The Shaping of American Religion* (Princeton, 1961), I, 322–350. Copyright © 1961 by Princeton University Press.

What may elude the secular historian—what in fact has eluded him—is the mechanism by which the Congress proposed that the operation be conducted:

. . . that we may with united hearts and voices unfeignedly confess and deplore our many sins, and offer up our joint supplications to the all-wise, omnipotent, and merciful Disposer of all events; humbly beseeching him to forgive our iniquities, to remove our present calamities, to avert those desolating judgments with which we are threatened. . . .

The essential point is that the Congress asks for, first, a national confession of sin and iniquity, then a promise of repentance, that only *thereafter* may God be moved so to influence Britain as to allow America to behold "a gracious interposition of Heaven for the redress of her many grievances."[1] The subtle emphasis can be detected once it is compared with the formula used by the Virginia House of Burgesses in the previous month, on May 14:

". . . devoutly to implore the Divine interposition for averting the heavy calamity which threatens destruction to our civil rights, and the evils of civil war, to give us one heart and one mind firmly to oppose, by all just and proper means, every injury to *American* rights. . . ."

Jefferson testifies that in Virginia this measure was efficacious. The people met with alarm in their countenances, "and the effect of the day through the whole colony was like a shock of electricity, arousing every man and placing him erect and solidly on his centre."[2] However gratifying the local results might be, it should be noted that this predominantly Anglican House of Burgesses, confronted with calamity, made no preliminary detour through any confession of their iniquities, but went directly to the throne of God, urging that He enlist on their side. The Virginia delegation in Philadelphia (which, let us remember, included Patrick Henry but *not* Jefferson) concurred in the unanimous adoption of the Congress's much more complicated—some were to say more devious—ritualistic project. Was this merely a diplomatic concession? Or could it be that, once the threatened calamity was confronted on a national scale, the assembled representatives of all the peoples instinctively realized that some deeper, some more atavistic, search of their own souls was indeed the indispensable prologue to exertion?

---

[1]B. F. Morris, *Christian Life and Character of the Civil Institutions of the United States,* Philadelphia, 1864, p. 525.
[2]*Ibid.,* pp. 526–527.

The question is eminently worth asking, if only because conscientious historians have seen no difference between the two
patterns, and have assumed that the Congressional followed the
Virginian.[3] And there are other historians, who may or may not be
cynical, but who have in either case been corrupted by the twentieth century, who perceive in this and subsequent summonses to
national repentance only a clever device in "propaganda."[4] It
was bound, they point out, to cut across class and regional lines,
to unite a predominantly Protestant people; wherefore the rationalist or deistical leaders could hold their tongues and silently
acquiesce in the stratagem, calculating its pragmatic worth. In
this view, the fact that virtually all the "dissenting" clergy, and
a fair number of Anglicans, mounted their pulpits on July 20 and
preached patriotic self-abnegation, is offered as a proof that they
had joined with the upper middle-class in a scheme to bamboozle
the lower orders and simple-minded rustics.

This interpretation attributes, in short, a diabolical cunning to
the more sophisticated leaders of the Revolution, who, being themselves no believers in divine providence, fastened onto the form
of invocation which would most work upon a majority who did
believe passionately in it. This reading may, I suggest, be as much
a commentary on the mentality of modern sociology as upon the
Continental Congress, but there is a further observation that has
been more cogently made by a few who have noted the striking
differences in phraseology: the Congressional version is substantially the form that for a century and a half had been employed
in New England. There, since the first years of Plymouth and the
first decade of Massachusetts Bay and Connecticut, the official
response in the face of affliction had been to set aside a day for
public confession of transgression and a promise of communal
repentance as the only method for beseeching the favor of
Jehovah.[5] Hence some analysts surmise that the action of the
Congress, if it was not quite a Machiavellian ruse for hood-wink-
ing the pious, was at best a Yankee trick foisted on Virginia and
New York. Leaving aside the question of whether, should this
explanation be true, it might just as well have been a Virginian
fraud, one which cost Patrick Henry and Peyton Randolph nothing,
perpetrated to keep the New Englanders active, the simple fact

---

[3]Cf., for instance, Arthur M. Schlesinger, *Prelude to Independence,* New
York, 1958, pp. 31–32.
   [4]Philip Davidson, *Propaganda and the American Revolution,* Chapel Hill,
N.C., 1941, passim.
   [5]Perry Miller, *The New England Mind: From Colony to Province,* Cambridge, Mass., 1953, pp. 19–26.

is that unprejudiced examination of the records of 1775 and 1776 shows that New England enjoyed no monopoly on the procedure. The House of Burgesses might suppose it enough to petition Almighty God to redress their wrongs; the churches of the dissenters, and indeed most Anglican communities already knew, whether in Georgia, Pennsylvania, or Connecticut, that this was not the proper way to go about obtaining heavenly assistance. The Biblical conception of a people standing in direct daily relation to God, upon covenanted terms and therefore responsible for their moral conduct, was a common possession of the Protestant peoples.

However, there can be no doubt that New England had done much more than the other regions toward articulating colonial experience within the providential dialectic. Because, also, presses were more efficient there than elsewhere, and Boston imprints circulated down the coast, it is probable that the classic utterances of Massachusetts served as models for Presbyterians and Baptists as well as for "low-church" Anglicans. For many decades the Puritan colonies had been geographically set apart; the people had been thoroughly accustomed to conceiving of themselves as a chosen race, entered into specific covenant with God, by the terms of which they would be proportionately punished for their sins. Their afflictions were divine appointments, not the hazards of natural and impersonal forces.[6] Furthermore, the homogeneity of the Puritan communities enabled their parsons to speak in the name of the whole body—even when these were internally riven by strife over land banks, the Great Awakening, or baptism. Finally, this same isolation of the New England colonies encouraged a proliferation of the "federal theology" to a point where the individual's relation with God, his hope of salvation through a personal covenant, could be explicitly merged with the society's covenant. Hence in New England was most highly elaborated the theorem that the sins of individuals brought calamity upon the commonwealth.

In that sense, then, we may say that the Congressional recommendation of June 12, 1775, virtually took over the New England thesis that these colonial peoples stood in a contractual relation to the "great Governor" over and above that enjoyed by other groups; in effect, Congress added the other nine colonies (about whose status New Englanders had hitherto been dubious) to New

[6] Perry Miller, *The New England Mind; The Seventeenth Century*, New York, 1954, pp. 464–484.

England's covenant. Still, for most of the population in these nine, no novelty was being imposed. The federal theology, in general terms, was an integral part of the Westminster Confession and so had long figured in the rhetoric of Presbyterians of New Jersey and Pennsylvania. The covenant doctrine, including that of the society as well as of the individual, had been preached in the founding of Virginia,[7] and still informed the phraseology of ordinary Anglican sermonizing. The Baptists, even into Georgia, were aware of the concept of church covenant, for theirs were essentially "congregational" polities; they could easily rise from that philosophy to the analogous one of the state. Therefore the people had little difficulty reacting to the Congressional appeal. They knew precisely what to do: they were to gather in their assemblies on July 20, inform themselves that the afflictions brought upon them in the dispute with Great Britain were not hardships suffered in some irrational political strife but intelligible ordeals divinely brought about because of their own abominations. This being the situation, they were to resolve, not only separately but in unison, to mend their ways, restore primitive piety, suppress vice, curtail luxury. Then, and only thereafter, if they were sincere, if they proved that they meant their vow, God would reward them by raising up instruments for the deflection of, or if necessary, destruction of, Lord North.

Since the New Englanders were such old hands at this business —by exactly this method they had been overcoming, from the days of the Pequot War through King Philip's War, such difficulties as the tyranny of Andros, small-pox epidemics, and parching droughts—they went to work at once. For the clergy the task was already clear: beginning with the Stamp Act of 1765, the clerical orator who spoke at every election day, in May, conveyed the respects in which relations with England should be subsumed under the over-all covenant of the people with God. Charles Chauncy's *A Discourse on the good News from a far Country,* delivered upon a day of "thanksgiving" (the logical sequel to several previous days of humiliation) to the General Court in 1766, explained that repeal of the odious Stamp Act was a consequence not of any mercantile resistance but of New England's special position within the Covenant of Grace.[8] As the crisis in Boston grew more and more acute, successive election orators

---

[7]Perry Miller, *Errand into the Wilderness,* Cambridge, Mass., 1956, pp. 119–122.

[8]John Wingate Thornton, *The Pulpit of the American Revolution,* Boston, 1860, pp. 105 ff.

had an annual opportunity to develop in greater detail proof that any vindication of provincial privileges was inextricably dependent upon a moral renovation. Following the "Boston Massacre" of 1770, anniversaries of this atrocity furnished every preacher an occasion for spreading the idea among the people. The form of these discourses was still that of the traditional "jeremiad"— a threatening of further visitation upon the covenanted people until they returned to their bond by confession and reformation— but by the time the Congress issued its wholesale invitation, the New England clergy had so merged the call to repentance with a stiffening of the patriotic spine that no power on earth, least of all the government of George III, could separate the acknowledgment of depravity from the resolution to fight.

Everything the Congress hoped would be said in 1775 had already been declared by the Reverend Samuel Cooke of the Second Church in Boston at the election of 1770.[9] If that were not precedent enough, the General Court on October 22, 1774, confronting General Gage and the Boston Port Bill, showed how double-edged was the sword by proclaiming not a fast day but one of thanksgiving; it was illuminated by the sermon of William Gordon, from the Third Church in Roxbury, which was all the more memorable because Gordon had been English-born.[10] On May 31, 1775, six weeks after Lexington and Concord, Samuel Langdon, President of Harvard, put the theory of religious revolution so completely before the Court (then obliged to meet in Watertown) that the doctrine of political resistance yet to be formulated in the Declaration seems but an afterthought.[11] A few weeks before that assertion, on May 29, 1776, Samuel West of Dartmouth made clear to the General Court that what was included within the divine covenant as a subsidiary but essential portion had been not simply "British liberties" but the whole social teaching of John Locke.[12] After the evacuation of Boston, both Massachusetts and Connecticut were able to assemble as of old, and comfortably listen to a recital of their shortcomings, secure in the knowledge that as long as jeremiads denounced them, their courage could not fail. The fluctuations of the conflict called for many days of humiliation and a few for thanksgiving; in Massachusetts, the framing of the state constitution in 1780 evoked another spate of clerical lectures on the direct connection

[9]*Ibid.*, pp. 147–186.
[10]*Ibid.*, pp. 187–226.
[11]*Ibid.*, pp. 227–258.
[12]*Ibid.*, pp. 259–322.

between piety and politics. Out of the years between the Stamp Act and the Treaty of Paris emerged a formidable, exhaustive (in general, a repetitious) enunciation of the unique necessity for America to win her way by reiterated acts of repentance. The jeremiad, which in origin had been an engine of Jehovah, thus became temporarily a service department of the Continental army.

The student of New England's literature is not astonished to find this venerable machine there put to patriotic use; what has not been appreciated is how readily it could be set to work in other sections. On this day of humiliation, July 20, 1775, Thomas Coombe, an Anglican minister at Christ's Church and St. Peter's in Philadelphia, who once had been chaplain to the Marquis of Rockingham, explained, in language which would at once have been recognized in Connecticut, that our fast will prove ineffectual unless we execute a genuine reformation of manners (interestingly enough, the printed text is dedicated to Franklin):

We must return to that decent simplicity of manners, that sober regard to ordinances, that strict morality of demeanor, which characterized our plain forefathers; and for the decay of which, their sons are but poorly compensated by all the superfluities of commerce. We must *associate* to give a new tone and vigor to the drooping state of religion among ourselves. We must support justice, both public and private, give an open and severe check to vices of every sort, and by our example discourage those luxurious customs and fashions, which serve but to enervate the mind and bodies of our children; drawing them off from such manly studies and attainments, as alone can render them amiable in youth or respectable in age.[13]

This Philadelphia Anglican combined as neatly as any Yankee the call for patriotic resistance and the old cry of Cotton Mather that the people respond to a jeremiad by implementing *Essays To Do Good*. By Coombe's standard, Quaker Philadelphia would appear to be a Babylon, but the opportunity for salvation was at last providentially offered: "Let such persons, however, now be told, that patriotism without piety is mere grimace."[14]

Thus we should not be surprised that Jacob Duché, preaching on this same July 20 before not only his Anglican parish but the assembled Congress, portrayed the whole trouble as "a national punishment" inflicted on "national guilt." He surveyed, as did all "Puritan" speakers, the manifest favors God had shown the colonies, and then diagnosed their present affliction as centering

[13]Thomas Coombe, *A Sermon*, Philadelphia, 1775, pp. 11–12.
[14]*Ibid.*, p. 15.

not on the iniquity of the British Cabinet (iniquitous as it undoubtedly was) but rather on the infidelity of Americans:

. . . have we not rather been so far carried away by the stream of
prosperity, as to be forgetful of the source from whence it was derived?
So elevated by the prospect, which peace and a successful commerce
have opened to us, as to neglect those impressions of goodness, which
former affections had left upon our hearts.

Was it not palpably for this reason, and this alone, "that the
Almighty hath bared his arm against us?" If so, the answer for
Duché, as for President Langdon, was clear: by reformation of
manners, by a return to primitive piety, we would, as a united
people, win the cause of American liberty. "Go on, ye chosen band
of Christians," he cried to the Congress.[15] The fact that after the
Declaration Duché lost heart and turned Loyalist does not make
his *The American Vine* any less a spiritual jeremiad of the sort
that most invigorated Patriot courage.

The way the War went, and especially the British occupation
of Philadelphia, prevented among the middle states the copious
displays that flowed from the presses of Boston and Worcester.
Even so, there was some sort of printing shop in Lancaster, and
there in 1778 Hugh Henry Brackenridge brought out *Six Political
Discourses Founded on the Scripture*. Known to fame—such fame
as he has—for his picaresque novel of the 1790's, *Modern Chiv-
alry*, Brackenridge figures in our histories as a Jeffersonian rationalist. So profound is the spirit of the Enlightenment displayed in
this work that we are convinced that he could not have later
imbibed it, but must have learned it at Princeton, where he was
classmate and friend of Madison and Freneau. In 1778, however,
he was an ordained Presbyterian minister; hence this fugitive
publication is of more than passing interest as illustrating the
continuation, three years after the first day of national humiliation, of the religious conception of the struggle. George III, declares
Brackenridge, was instigated by Satan; divine providence must
perforce be on the patriot side. "Heaven hath taken an active part,
and waged war for us." This he can say, even when the British
hold Philadelphia! However, he can produce Saratoga for evidence. Hence it is clear that "Heaven knows nothing of neutrality,"
providence is the agency of God, and "there is not one tory to be
found amongst the order of the seraphim." For our reverses we
must have only our own sins to blame, and the surest way to
victory is our conversion: "it becomes every one in the day of

---

[15]Jacob Duché, *The American Vine*, Philadelphia, 1775, pp. 24–26.

storm and sore commotion, to fly swiftly to the rock of Christ Jesus!" Granted that a man like Brackenridge might cleverly play upon these stops to excite a pious auditory, still it is evident that these were the appeals even a rational patriot would need to sound.[16]

To glance for a moment at the other end of the geographical spectrum: the people of Georgia had so far in their brief history found few opportunities to promote themselves into the role of an elected community; certainly the saints of Connecticut would never suppose Georgians equal in standing before the Lord with themselves. Still, when the Provincial Congress of Georgia met in 1775, before proceeding to support the Revolution they first listened to a clerical address—for all the world as though they were in Connecticut—by the Reverend John J. Zubly. It was printed in Philadelphia as *The Law of Liberty*.

Zubly reproduces the pattern of New England argumentation, though perhaps with somewhat less provincial egotism. These Americans are the result of a consecutive unfolding of God's covenant with mankind, now come to a climax on this continent; for Americans, the exercise of liberty becomes simply the one true obedience to God. This is not license, but resistance to sin; those who do not combat depravity will be judged:

> We are not to imagine because the gospel is a law of liberty, therefore men will not be judged; on the contrary judgment will be the more severe against all who have heard and professed the gospel, and yet walked contrary to its precepts and doctrines.

By this logic, once more, patriotic resistance to England is a way —the only way—to avert the wrath of Jehovah.[17]

If anywhere among the states the lineaments of Puritan federal theology would be dim, one might suppose that place to be Charleston, South Carolina. Legend continually obscures for us, however, how profoundly Protestant the culture of that region was at this time and for several decades afterwards. In 1774 William Tennent, son of the great William of Log College, expounded to planters and merchants that they were threatened with slavery because of their transgressions. The first dictate of natural passion is to imprecate vengeance upon the instruments of our torment, to resolve to endure hardships rather than surrender the privileges of our ancestors. But this, Tennent ex-

---

[16]H. H. Brackenridge, *Six Political Discourses Founded on the Scripture*, Lancaster, 1778, pp. 50–61.
[17]John J. Zubly, *The Law of Liberty*, Philadelphia, 1775, p. 6.

plained, is the wrong procedure. The first duty of good men is to find out and bewail "the Iniquities of our Nation and country," which are the true causes of the dismal catastrophe about to befall us.[18]

Though by now the Revolution has been voluminously, and one might suppose exhaustively, studied, we still do not realize how effective were generations of Protestant preaching in evoking patriotic enthusiasm. No interpretation of the religious utterances as being merely sanctimonious window-dressing will do justice to the facts or to the character of the populace. Circumstances and the nature of the dominant opinion in Europe made it necessary for the official statement to be released in primarily "political" terms—the social compact, inalienable rights, the right of revolution. But those terms, in and by themselves, would never have supplied the drive to victory, however mightily they weighed with the literate minority. What carried the ranks of militia and citizens was the universal persuasion that they, by administering to themselves a spiritual purge, acquired the energies God had always, in the manner of the Old Testament, been ready to impart to His repentant children. Their first responsibility was not to shoot redcoats but to cleanse themselves; only thereafter to take aim. Notwithstanding the chastisements we have already received, proclaimed the Congress on March 20, 1779—they no longer limited themselves to mere recommending—"too few have been sufficiently awakened to a sense of their guilt, or warmed with gratitude, or taught to amend their lives and turn from their sins, so He might turn from His wrath." They call for still another fast in April, 1780: "To make us sincerely penitent for our transgressions; to prepare us for deliverance, and to remove the evil with which he hath been pleased to visit us; to banish vice and irreligion from among us, and establish virtue and piety by his Divine grace." And when there did come a cause for rejoicing (almost the only one in four or five years that might justify their using other vestibule, the surrender of Burgoyne), patriots gave little thought to lengthening lines of supply or the physical obstacles of logistics; instead, they beheld Providence at work again, welcomed Louis XVI as their "Christian ally," and congratulated themselves upon that which had really produced vic-

---

[18]William Tennent, *An Address, Occasioned by the Late Invasion of the Liberties of the American Colonies by the British Parliament,* Philadelphia, 1774, p. 11. Tennent must have charmed his Carolinian audience by exclaiming (p. 17) that if these judgments have begun in New England, the bulwark of piety, those awaiting the profane South would be "more dreadful calamities."

tory—their success in remodeling themselves. Now more than ever, asserted the Congress on October 31, 1777, we should "implore the mercy and forgiveness of God, and beseech him that vice, profaneness, extortion and every evil may be done away, and that we may be a reformed and a happy people."[19]

II

Historians of English political thought have reduced to a commonplace of inevitable progression the shift of Puritan political philosophy from the radical extreme of 1649 to the genial universals of 1689. John Locke so codified the later versions as to make the "Glorious Revolution" seem a conservative reaction. As we know, Locke was studied with avidity in the colonies; hence the Congress used consummate strategy in presenting their case to a candid world through the language of Locke.

Nevertheless, we do know that well before the Civil War began in England, Parliamentarians—and these include virtually all Puritans—had asserted that societies are founded upon covenant; that the forms of a particular society, even though dictated by utilitarian factors, are of divine ordination; that rulers who violate the agreed-upon forms are usurpers and so to be legitimately resisted. This complex of doctrine was transported bodily to early Virginia and most explicitly to Puritan New England. The turmoils of Massachusetts Bay—the expulsion of Roger Williams and Anne Hutchinson, the exile of Robert Child, the disciplining of the Hingham militia, and the first trials of the Quakers— whatever other issues were involved in them, were crises in the political creed. Governor Winthrop was not much troubled, though possibly a bit, when he told the men of Hingham that in signing the covenant they had agreed to submit to rulers set over them for their own good—unless they could positively prove that their rulers were the violators!

The development of New England, however, steadily encouraged the citizens to deduce that they themselves, in framing the compact, had enumerated the items which made up their good. John Cotton and John Winthrop, having entirely accepted the contractual idea, were still making within it a last-ditch stand for medieval scholasticism by contending that the positive content of the magisterial function had been prescribed by God long before any

---

[19]Morris, pp. 533–536.

specific covenant, whether of Israel or of Massachusetts, was drawn up. By the mid-eighteenth century, even in "semi-Presbyterial" Connecticut, good Christians were certain they could designate both the duties and the limitations of magistrates. In basically similar fashion, though not so easily traceable, the same transformation was wrought among the Protestant, or at least among the "Calvinistic," elements of all the communities. To put the matter bluntly, the agitation which resulted in the War for American Independence commenced after an immense change had imperceptibly been wrought in the minds of the people. That they needed from 1765 to 1776 to realize this was not because they had, under stress, to acquire the doctrine from abroad, but because they did have to search their souls in order to discover what actually had happened within themselves.

Consequently, every preacher of patriotism was obliged to complicate his revolutionary jeremiad by careful demonstrations of exactly how the will of almighty God had itself always operated through the voluntary self-imposition of a compact, how it had provided for legitimate, conservative resistance to tyrants. Early in the eighteenth century, John Wise prophesied how this union of concepts would be achieved, but he seems to have had no direct effect on the patriot argument. Jonathan Mayhew was far ahead of his fellows; after his death in 1766 the others required hard work to catch up. In general it may be said that they started off serenely confident that of course the philosophy of the jeremiad, which required abject confession of unworthiness from an afflicted people, and that of the social compact, which called for immediate and vigorous action against an intruding magistrate, were one and the same. Then, discovering that the joining required more carpentry than they had anticipated, they labored for all they were worth at the task. Finally, by 1776, they triumphantly asserted that they had indeed succeeded, that the day of humiliation was demonstrably one with the summons to battle.

Political historians and secular students of theory are apt to extract from the context those paragraphs devoted solely to the social position, to discuss these as comprising the only contribution of the "black regiment" to Revolutionary argument.[20] To read

---

[20]For example, Alice Baldwin, *The New England Clergy and the American Revolution*, Durham, N.C., 1928, a pioneer work of great value, but upon which later historians have unhappily depended. In this view, I should take Clinton Rossiter, *Seedtime of the Republic*, New York, 1953, as representing the strain of obtuse secularism.

these passages in isolation is to miss the point. They were effective with the masses not as sociological lectures but because, being embedded in the jeremiads, they made comprehensible the otherwise troubling double injunction of humiliation and exertion. In this complicated pattern (which could be offered as the ultimate both in right reason and in true piety), the mentality of American Protestantism became so reconciled to itself, so joyfully convinced that it had at last found its long-sought identity, that for the time being it forgot that it had ever had any other reason for existing.

A few examples out of thousands will suffice. Gordon's *Discourse* of December 15, 1774, runs for page after page in the standardized jeremiad vein: "Is not this people strangely degenerated, so as to possess but a faint resemblance of that godliness for which their forefathers were eminent?" Is it not horrible beyond all imagination that *this* people should degenerate, seeing how scrupulously God has befriended them according to the stipulations of their covenant with Him? Yet the ghastly fact is "that while there is much outward show of respect to the Deity, there is but little inward heart conformity to him." And so on and on, until abruptly, with hardly a perceptible shift, we are hearing a recital of the many palpable evidences that Divine Providence is already actively engaged in the work. Only by the direct "inspiration of the Most High" could the unanimity of the colonies have been brought about. From this point Gordon's cheerful jeremiad comes down to the utilitarian calculation that Americans are expert riflemen, wherefore "the waste of amunition will be greatly prevented"; after which he concludes by urging the people to "accept our punishment at his hands without murmuring or complaining"![21]

The elements woven together in this and other speeches can, of course, be separated one from another in the antiseptic calm of the historian's study, and the whole proved to be an unstable compound of incompatible propositions. What may be left out of account is the impact of the entire argument, the wonderful fusion of political doctrine with the traditional rite of self-abasement which, out of colonial experience, had become not what it might seem on the surface, a failure of will, but a dynamo for generating action.

President Langdon's sermon of May, 1775, played a slight variation on the theme by suggesting that the notorious crimes of England had brought these troubles as a divine visitation on *her!*

---

[21]Thornton, pp. 208, 212, 225.

Other preachers occasionally toyed with this device, but obviously it was not the full-throated note the populace expected and wanted. Langdon returned to the really effective music when he justified the afflictions of America:

> But alas! have not the sins of America, and of New England in particular, had a hand in bringing down upon us the righteous judgments of Heaven? Wherefore is all this evil come upon us? Is it not because we have forsaken the Lord? Can we say we are innocent of crimes against God? No surely.

After several pages of such conventional self-accusation, the moral emerges as easily in 1775 as it used to flow from the mouth of Cotton Mather: "However unjustly and cruelly we have been treated by man, we certainly deserve, at the hand of God, all the calamities in which we are now involved."[22]

Then follows a turn which is indeed novel, which reveals the subtle yet largely unconscious transformation that the Revolution was actually working in the hearts of the people. Langdon concludes his jeremiad by calling upon Americans to repent and reform, because *if* true religion can be revived, "we may hope for the direction and blessing of the most High, while we are using our best endeavors to preserve and restore the civil government of this colony, and defend America from slavery."[23]

Here, in exquisite precision, is the logic of the clerical exhortation which, though it may seem to defy logic, gives a vivid insight into what had happened to the pious mentality of the communities. For, Langdon's argument runs, once we have purged ourselves and recovered our energies in the act of contrition, how then do we go about proving the sincerity of our repentance (and insuring that Divine Providence will assist us)? We hereupon act upon the principles of John Locke! At this point, and not until after these essential preliminaries, Langdon turns to his exposition of Whig doctrine:

> Thanks be to God that he has given us, as men, natural rights, independent of all human laws whatever, and that these rights are recognized by the grand charter of British liberties. By the law of nature, any body of people, destitute of order and government, may form themselves into a civil society according to their best prudence, and so provide for their common safety and advantage. When one form is found by the majority not to answer the grand purpose in any

---

[22]*Ibid.*, p. 247.
[23]*Ibid.*, p. 249.

tolerable degree, they may, by common consent, put an end to it and set up another.[24]

The next year, Samuel West of Dartmouth persuaded the General Court of Massachusetts, not to mention readers elsewhere in the colonies, that the inner coherence of the thesis was maintained by these two combined doctrines: while, because of our abysmally sinful condition, we must obey magistrates for conscience' sake, we also find "that when rulers become oppressive to the subject and injurious to the state, their authority, their respect, their maintenance, and the duty of submitting to them, must immediately cease; they are then to be considered as the ministers of Satan, and as such, it becomes our indispensable duty to resist and oppose them."[25] What we today have to grasp is that for the masses this coalescence of abnegation and assertion, this identification of Protestant self-distrust with confidence in divine aid, erected a frame for the natural-rights philosophy wherein it could work with infinitely more power than if it had been propounded exclusively in the language of political rationalism.

There were, it should be pointed out, a few clerics who could become patriots without having to go through this labyrinth of national humiliation. But in the colonies they were a minority, and they came from a Protestantism which had never been permeated by the federal theology—which is to say, they were generally Anglicans. The most conspicuous was William Smith, later Provost of the College of Philadelphia. When he responded to the Congressional recommendation, on July 20, 1775, at All-Saints in Philadelphia, he emphasized his dissent from the covenantal conception at once:

I would, therefore, cherish these good dispositions; and what may, peradventure, have begun through Fear, I would ripen into maturity by the more cheering beams of Love. Instead of increasing your afflictions, I would convey a dawn of comfort to your souls; rather striving to woo and to win you to Religion and Happiness, from a consideration of what God hath promised to the Virtuous, than of what He hath denounced against the Wicked, both through Time and in Eternity.[26]

A historian not versed in the discriminations of theology may see little difference, considered as propaganda, between Provost Smith's form of Christian exhortation and President Langdon's,

---

[24]*Ibid.*, p. 250.
[25]*Ibid.*, p. 296.
[26]*The Works of William Smith, D.D.*, Philadelphia, 1803, 11, 119.

since Smith also aligns the Providence of God on the side of resistance. But for men of 1775—that is for most of them—there was a vast gulf between Smith's conception and that of the New Englanders, of Coombe, of Duché, of Zubly. The really effective work of the "black regiment" was not an optimistic appeal to the rising glory of America, but their imparting a sense of crisis by revivifying Old Testament condemnations of a degenerate people.

Smith's method, however, did have one advantage: more readily than the Puritans and Presbyterians, he could promise that God would bless a victorious America with prosperity, with that "happiness" which the Declaration said all men had a natural right to pursue. Smith did note in passing that we must repent and sincerely reform our naughty manners,[27] but his recruiting sermons pay much more attention than do those of New England or of the back-country to the strictly legal contention. These generally conclude, as did one to a battalion of militia on June 25, 1775, with the earthly rewards in prospect:

> Illiberal or mistaken plans of policy may distress us for a while, and perhaps sorely check our growth; but if we maintain our own virtue; if we cultivate the spirit of Liberty among our children; if we guard against the snares of luxury, venality and corruption; the Genius of America will still rise triumphant, and that with a power at last too mighty for opposition. This country will be free—nay, for ages to come a chosen seat of Freedom, Arts, and Heavenly Knowledge; which are now either drooping or dead in those countries of the old world.[28]

Surely Smith's logic is straightforward. On December 28, 1778, he preached before a Masonic chapter and dedicated the sermon to Washington. There is no mention in it of affliction; hardships, even unto death, are to be borne in a spirit of Christian fortitude, and Christians are simply to fight the good fight, confident that when they die they shall have full scope for the exercise of charity.[29] But, though Smith's form of Christianity, with its piety hardly more than a species of Stoicism, might appeal to Washington and prove unobjectionable even to Jefferson, and though Smith delivered a heartfelt eulogy on Benjamin Franklin,[30] it was neither Smith's genial Anglicanism nor the urbane rationalism of these statesmen which brought the rank and file of American

---

[27]*Ibid.*, pp. 123, 138.
[28]*Ibid.*, pp. 283–284.
[29]*Ibid.*, p. 67.
[30]*Ibid.*, 1, 44–92.

Protestants into the War. What aroused a Christian patriotism that needed staying power was a realization of the vengeance God denounced against the wicked; what fed their hopes was not what God promised as a recompense to virtue, but what dreary fortunes would overwhelm those who persisted in sloth; what kept them going was an assurance that by exerting themselves they were fighting for a victory thus providentially predestined.

To examine the Revolutionary mind from the side of its religious emotion is to gain a perspective that cannot be acquired from the ordinary study of the papers of the Congresses, the letters of Washington, the writings of Dickinson, Paine, Freneau, or John Adams. The "decent respect" that these Founders entertained for the opinion of mankind caused them to put their case before the civilized world in the restricted language of the rational century. A successful revolution, however, requires not only leadership but receptivity. Ideas in the minds of the foremost gentlemen may not be fully shared by their followers, but these followers will accept the ideas, even adopt them, if such abstractions can be presented in an acceptable context. To accommodate the principles of a purely secular social compact and a right to resist taxation—even to the point of declaring political independence to a provincial community where the reigning beliefs were still original sin and the need of grace—this was the immense task performed by the patriotic clergy.

Our mental image of the religious patriot is distorted because modern accounts do treat the political paragraphs as a series of theoretical expositions of Locke, separated from what precedes and follows. When these orations are read as wholes, they immediately reveal that the sociological sections are structural parts of a rhetorical pattern. Embedded in their contexts, these are not abstractions but inherent parts of a theology. It was for this reason that they had so energizing an effect upon their religious auditors. The American situation, as the preachers saw it, was not what Paine presented in *Common Sense*—a community of hardworking, rational creatures being put upon by an irrational tyrant —but was more like the recurrent predicament of the chosen people in the Bible. As Samuel Cooper declared on October 25, 1780, upon the inauguration of the Constitution of Massachusetts, America was a new Israel, selected to be "a theatre for the display of some of the most astonishing dispensations of his Providence." The Jews originally were a free republic founded on a covenant over which God "in peculiar favor to that people, was pleased to

preside." When they offended Him, He punished them by destroying their republic, subjecting them to a king. Thus while we today
need no revelation to inform us that we are all born free and
equal and that sovereignty resides in the people—"these are the
plain dictates of that reason and common sense with which the
common parent has informed the human bosom"—still Scripture
also makes these truths explicit. Hence when we angered our
God, a king was also inflicted upon us; happily, Americans have
succeeded, where the Jews did not, in recovering something of
pristine virtue, whereupon Heaven redressed America's earthly
grievances. Only as we today appreciate the formal unity of the
two cosmologies, the rational and the Biblical, do we take in
the full import of Cooper's closing salute to the new Constitution:
"How nicely it poises the powers of government, in order to render
them as far as human foresight can, what God ever designed
they should be, power only to do good."[31]

Once this light is allowed to play on the scene, we perceive the
shallowness of that view which would treat the religious appeal
as a calculated propaganda maneuver. The ministers did not have
to "sell" the Revolution to a public sluggish to "buy." They were
spelling out what both they and the people sincerely believed, nor
were they distracted by worries about the probability that Jefferson held all their constructions to be nonsense. A pure rationalism such as his might have declared the independence of these
folk, but it could never have inspired them to fight for it.

This assertion may seem too sweeping, but without our making
it we can hardly comprehend the state in which American Protestantism found itself when the victory was won. A theology
which for almost two centuries had assumed that men would
persistently sin, and so would have to be recurrently summoned
to communal repentance, had for the first time identified its
basic conception with a specific political action. Then, for the
first time in the life of the conception, the cause was totally
gained. Did not a startling inference follow: these people must
have reformed themselves completely, must now dwell on a pin-
nacle of virtuousness? But there was no place in the theology of
the covenant for a people to congratulate themselves. There was
a station only for degenerates in need of regeneration, who occasionally might thank God for this or that mercy He granted them,
forgiving their imperfections. Where could Protestantism turn,

[31]Samuel Cooper, *A Sermon Preached* . . . October 25, 1780, Boston, 1780,
pp. 2, 8, 11, 14, 15, 29.

what could it employ, in order still to hold the religious respect of this now victorious society?

III

An Anglican rationalist, as we have seen with William Smith, would have no difficulty about the sequence of statements which said that by resisting England we would assure the future prosperity of the republic. The patriotic Jeremiahs also employed the argument, but they had to be more circumspect. Protestant political thinking had never doubted, of course, that God instituted government among men as a means toward their temporal felicity —or, at least toward their "safety." But it always based its philosophy upon the premise of original sin. Since the Fall, had men been left in a pure state of nature, all would have been Ishmaels; no man's life, family, or property would be secure. So, government was primarily a check on evil impulses; its function was negative rather than positive; it was to restrain violence, not to advance arts, sciences, technology. Yet, as Governor John Winthrop agreed during the first years of Massachusetts Bay, because *"salus populi suprema lex,"* there was a corollary (lurking out of sight) that government ought, once it restrained the lusts of these people, to do something more creative about making them comfortable.

In the negativistic emphasis of Protestant teachings, the reason for King George's violence and the consequent righteousness of resisting him were easy to make out. He and his ministers were violating the compact, so that he had become Ishmael. Law-abiding subjects were defending social barriers which, if once broken through, would cease to confine all social passions. By defying Britain they were preserving mankind from a descent into chaos. Resistance to a madman is not revolution; it is, in obedience to God, an exercise of the police power.

Yet what happens to particles of this logic when to it is joined the contention that by such resistance the righteous not only obey God but acquire wealth for themselves and their children? How can the soldier venture everything in the holy cause, after having confessed his depravity, if all the time he has a secret suspicion that by going through this performance he in fact is not so much repenting as gaining affluence for his society?

In most of the patriotic jeremiads the material inducement is entered—sometimes, we may say, smuggled in. It could not be left out. Yet once the machinery of national humiliation proved effective in producing the providential victory of the Americans, were they not bound to the prophecy that by their utilization of the form, they, and they alone, would bring about a reign of national bliss? But in that case how could a confession of unworthiness be sincere?

An uneasy awareness of the dilemma was present even in the early stages of agitation. Listen, for instance, to Samuel Williams, pastor of the Church in Bradford, delivering *A Discourse on the Love of Country*, December 15, 1774:

> As what should further confirm our attachment to our native country, it bids the fairest of any to promote the *perfection and happiness of mankind*. We have but few principles from which we can argue with certainty, what will be the state of mankind in future ages. But if we may judge the designs of providence, by the number and power of the causes that are already at work, we shall be led to think that the perfection and happiness of mankind is to be carried further in America, than it has ever yet been in any place.[32]

This passage is only one of hundreds in the same vein, and all wrestle with the same dubious contention: we have sinned, therefore we are afflicted by the tyranny of a corrupt Britain; we must repent and reform, in order to win the irresistible aid of Providence; once we have wholeheartedly performed this act, we shall be able to exert our freedom by expelling the violators of the compact; when we succeed we shall enter upon a prosperity and temporal happiness beyond anything the world has hitherto seen. But always implicit in this chain of reasoning was a vague suggestion that the people were being bribed into patriotism. And by universal admission, the occasion for a nation's deserting its Maker and surrendering to sensuality was always an excess of material comforts. So, was not the whole machinery an ironic device for bringing upon the children of the victors judgments still more awful than any that had previously been imposed?

The clergy had, in short, simplified the once massive complexity of the process of social regeneration by concentrating its terrorizing appeal upon a single hardship, the British government. Seventeenth-century theologians would have been more wary. They took pains to keep the list so long—draught, fires, earthquakes, insects, small-pox, shipwrecks—that while the people by their holy exertions might be let off this or that misery,

---

[32]Samuel Williams, *A Discourse on the Love of Country*, Salem, 1775, p. 22.

they were sure to be tormented by some other. The Revolutionary divines, in their zeal for liberty, committed themselves unwittingly to the proposition that in this case expulsion of the British would automatically leave America a pure society. In their righteous anger, they painted gorier and gorier pictures of the depravity of England. Said President Langdon, "The general prevalence of vice has changed the whole face of things in the British government";[33] wherefore it had to follow that the sins of the colonial peoples, which brought down the Intolerable Acts, were in great part "infections" received from "the corruption of European courts." But then, once we innoculated ourselves against these contagions, would we not become a people washed white in the Blood of the Lamb?

The progress of events which led the patriots from their initial defense of "British liberties" to the radical plunge into independence also led them to this doctrinaire identification of religious exertion with the political aim. By 1776 Samuel West made it crystal clear:

Our cause is so just and good that nothing can prevent our success but only our sins. Could I see a spirit of repentance and reformation prevail through the land, I should not have the least apprehension or fear of being brought under the iron rod of slavery, even though all the powers of the globe were combined against us. And though I confess that the irreligion and profaneness which are so common among us gives something of a damp to my spirits, yet I cannot help hoping, and even believing, that Providence has designed this continent for to be the asylum of liberty and true religion; for can we suppose that the God who created us free agents, and designed that we should glorify and serve him in this world that we might enjoy him forever hereafter, will suffer liberty and true religion to be banished from off the face of the earth?[34]

What else, then, could President Ezra Stiles of Yale College preach upon, before the General Assembly of Connecticut, on May 8, 1783, but *The United States Elevated to Glory and Honor?*

This will be a great, a very great nation, nearly equal to half Europe. . . . Before the millennium the English settlements in America may become more numerous millions than the greatest dominion on earth, the Chinese Empire. Should this prove a future fact, how applicable would be the text, when the Lord shall have made his American Israel high above all nations which he has made, in numbers, and in praise, and in name, and in honor![35]

---

[33]Thornton, p. 243.
[34]*Ibid.*, p. 311.
[35]*Ibid.*, p. 440.

Still, the more closely we study this literature of exultation, the more we suspect that the New Englanders were dismayed by the very magnitude of their success. The Middle States were less inhibited. Most revelatory is George Duffield's *A Sermon Preached in the Third Presbyterian Church* of Philadelphia on December 11, 1783—the day that Congress could at long last conscientiously appoint a "Thanksgiving." It was now abundantly clear, said Duffield, that from the beginning the Revolution had been under providential direction. We have created a nation which shall receive the poor and oppressed: "here shall the husbandman enjoy the fruits of his labor; the merchant trade, secure of his gain; the mechanic indulge his inventive genius; and the sons of science pursue their delightful employment, till the light of knowledge pervade yonder yet uncultivated western wilds, and form the savage inhabitants into men." In the exuberance of triumph, Duffield permitted himself to say, in effect, that the jeremiad had also triumphed, and that we, being a completely reformed nation, need no longer be summoned to humiliation!

A *day* whose evening shall not terminate in night; but introduce that joyful period, when the outcasts of Israel, and the dispersed of Judah, shall be restored; and with them, the fulness of the Gentile world shall flow to the standard of redeeming love: And the nations of the earth, become the kingdom of our Lord and Saviour. Under whose auspicious reign holiness shall universally prevail; and the noise and alarm of war be heard no more.[36]

In this situation—if all the nation participated, as most of it did, in the assurances of Duffield's *te Deum*—there would be, at least for the moment, no further use for the jeremiad. A few New Englanders, along with President Witherspoon of Princeton, cautioned the people that while indeed God had blessed them beyond all expectation, they now had the further responsibility of perpetuating the reformation, but theirs were but feeble admonitions compared with the compulsions of the dark days of 1775. Because the program of salvation had been combined with the struggle for nationhood, American Protestants were obliged to see in the Treaty of Paris the fulfillment of prophecies. Ezra Stiles took as his text Deuteronomy xxvi. 19, a verse that long had done yeoman's service as a club for beating backsliders, and then explained that on this occasion he selected it "only as introductory to a discourse upon the political welfare of God's Ameri-

---

[36]George Duffield, *A Sermon Preached in the Third Presbyterian Church,* Philadelphia, 1784, pp. 16–17, 18.

can Israel, and as allusively prophetic of the future prosperity and splendor of the United States."[37] This by implication does pretend that the reformation had been entirely successful. So, with some reluctance, Stiles suggests that with the finish of the colonial era we have come also to the close of the jeremiad:

And while we have to lament our Laodiceanism, deficient morals, and incidental errors, yet the collective system of evangelical doctrines, the instituted ordinances, and the true ecclesiastical polity, may be found here in a great degree of purity.[38]

Whereupon a chill strikes the exulting heart. If this be so, are we not, under the Providence of God, on leaving the exciting scenes both of war and spiritual conflict, now headed for a monotonous, an uninteresting prosperity, the flatness of universal virtue?

These people, however, had for a long time been disciplined to the expectation of woe. The government of the Confederacy became mired in confusion, thus clouding once more any reading of God's design. While the States were devising a Constitution to correct this affliction, the blow was struck; but not in America —in Paris. At first, of course, the fall of the Bastille seemed to strengthen the alliance of social doctrine and religious hope. Shortly the fallacy became evident. Not that there was any serious threat in America of a reversion to the depraved state of nature which engulfed France in 1793; yet in this glorious republic the French Revolution brought home to the devout an immediate realization of the need for dissociating the Christian conception of life from any blind commitment to the philosophy of that Revolution. Indeed, they had no choice ultimately but to abandon the whole political contention of either of the two revolutions, and to seek at once some other program for Christian solidarity. They did not need to renounce the Declaration, nor even to denounce the Constitution, but only henceforth to take those principles for granted, yield government to the secular concept of the social compact, accept the First Amendment, and so to concentrate, in order to resist Deism and to save their souls, upon that other mechanism of cohesion developed out of their colonial experience, the Revival.

It took them until about the year 1800 to recast—or, as they believed, to recover—their history. Amid the great revivals which swept over Connecticut, Kentucky, and Tennessee in that year,

---

[37]Thornton, p. 403.
[38]*Ibid.*, p. 473.

which expanded into Georgia, Illinois, and for decades burned over northern New York, the Revolution was again and again presented as having been itself a majestic Revival. The leadership of Jefferson, Paine, and the rationalists was either ignored or explained away. The "Second Great Awakening" engendered the denominational forms of American Protestantism which still endure, but perhaps equally important was its work in confirming the American belief that the Revolution had not been at all revolutionary, but simply a protest of native piety against foreign impiety.

{ *IV* }

TRANSFORMATION

THE REVOLUTION IN IDEALS

If the Revolution was in origin and at its center basically a conservative protest movement against what appeared to the men of the Revolution to have been a tyrannical assault upon American liberty and property by Britain's government, it also contained, as several recent works have emphasized, significant radical elements. The two selections that follow strongly suggest that it was the implications of Revolutionary thought—the radical thrust of its ideals—that made the Revolution something more than a defensive war for independence and gave it a truly revolutionary character. The first selection argues that the Revolution brought about a "radical idealization and rationalization of the previous century and a half" of what, by European standards, had been an extremely radical experience and, thereby, unleashed a set of ideas that, as the author has emphasized elsewhere, ultimately helped to transform many of the essentials of American life. The second selection considers what the author regards as the four principal achievements of the Revolution and analyzes the radical nature of each. The two achievements given primary emphasis—the sudden and permanent commitment to republicanism after 1776 and the philosophy of radical individualism that was implicit in much of Revolutionary political thought—lie primarily within the realms of ideals and beliefs.

CECELIA M. KENYON (b. 1922) is a member of the Department of Government at Smith College.

Political Experience and Enlightenment Ideas in Eighteenth-Century America

BERNARD BAILYN

The political and social ideas of the European Enlightenment have had a peculiar importance in American history. More universally accepted in eighteenth-century America than in Europe, they were more completely and more permanently embodied in the formal arrangements of state and society; and, less controverted, less subject to criticism and dispute, they have lived on more vigorously into later periods, more continuous and more intact. The peculiar force of these ideas in America resulted from many causes. But originally, and basically, it resulted from the circumstances of the prerevolutionary period and from the bearing of these ideas on the political experience of the American colonists.

What this bearing was—the nature of the relationship between Enlightenment ideas and early American political experience— is a matter of particular interest at the present time because it is centrally involved in what amounts to a fundamental revision of early American history now under way. By implication if not direct evidence and argument, a number of recent writings have undermined much of the structure of historical thought by which, for a generation or more, we have understood our eighteenth-century origins, and in particular have placed new and insupportable pressures on its central assumption concerning the political significance of Enlightenment thought. Yet the need for rather extensive rebuilding has not been felt, in part because the architecture has not commonly been seen as a whole—as a unit, that is, of mutually dependent parts related to a central premise —in part because the damage has been piecemeal and uncoordinated: here a beam destroyed, there a stone dislodged, the inner supports only slowly weakened and the balance only gradually thrown off. The edifice still stands, mainly, it seems, by habit and by the force of inertia. A brief consideration of the whole, conse-

Reprinted with permission from *American Historical Review*, LXVII, 2 (January, 1962), 339–351.

Note: This paper was presented in a briefer form to the 11th International Congress of Historical Sciences, Stockholm, 1960. As printed here, it was read at the Massachusetts Historical Society, January 12, 1961.

quently, a survey from a position far enough above the details to see the outlines of the over-all architecture, and an attempt, however tentative, to sketch a line—a principle—of reconstruction would seem to be in order.

A basic, organizing assumption of the group of ideas that dominated the earlier interpretation of eighteenth-century American history is the belief that previous to the Revolution the political experience of the colonial Americans had been roughly analogous to that of the English. Control of public authority had been firmly held by a native aristocracy—merchants and landlords in the North, planters in the South—allied, commonly, with British officialdom. By restricting representation in the provincial assemblies, limiting the franchise, and invoking the restrictive power of the English state, this aristocracy had dominated the governmental machinery of the mainland colonies. Their political control, together with legal devices such as primogeniture and entail, had allowed them to dominate the economy as well. Not only were they successful in engrossing landed estates and mercantile fortunes, but they were for the most part able also to fight off the clamor of yeoman debtors for cheap paper currency, and of depressed tenants for freehold property. But the control of this colonial counterpart of a traditional aristocracy, with its Old World ideas of privilege and hierarchy, orthodoxy in religious establishment, and economic inequality, was progressively threatened by the growing strength of a native, frontier-bred democracy that expressed itself most forcefully in the lower houses of the "rising" provincial assemblies. A conflict between the two groups and ways of life was building up, and it broke out in fury after 1765.

The outbreak of the Revolution, the argument runs, fundamentally altered the old regime. The Revolution destroyed the power of this traditional aristocracy, for the movement of opposition to parliamentary taxation, 1760–1776, originally controlled by conservative elements, had been taken over by extremists nourished on Enlightenment radicalism, and the once dominant conservative groups had gradually been alienated. The break with England over the question of home rule was part of a general struggle, as Carl Becker put it, over who shall rule at home. Independence gave control to the radicals, who, imposing their advanced doctrines on a traditional society, transformed a rebellious secession into a social revolution. They created a new regime, a reformed society, based on enlightened political and social theory.

But that is not the end of the story; the sequel is important. The success of the enlightened radicals during the early years of the Revolution was notable; but, the argument continues, it was not wholly unqualified. The remnants of the earlier aristocracy, though defeated, had not been eliminated: they were able to reassert themselves in the postwar years. In the 1780's they gradually regained power until, in what amounted to a counter-revolution, they impressed their views indelibly on history in the new federal Constitution, in the revocation of some of the more enthusiastic actions of the earlier revolutionary period, and in the Hamiltonian program for the new government. This was not, of course, merely the old regime resurrected. In a new age whose institutions and ideals had been born of revolutionary radicalism, the old conservative elements made adjustments and concessions by which to survive and periodically to flourish as a force in American life.

The importance of this formulation derived not merely from its usefulness in interpreting eighteenth-century history. It provided a key also for understanding the entire course of American politics. By its light, politics in America, from the very beginning, could be seen to have been a dialectical process in which an aristocracy of wealth and power struggled with the People, who, ordinarily ill-organized and inarticulate, rose upon provocation armed with powerful institutional and ideological weapons, to reform a periodically corrupt and oppressive polity.

In all of this the underlying assumption is the belief that Enlightenment thought—the reforming ideas of advanced thinkers in eighteenth-century England and on the Continent—had been the effective lever by which native American radicals had turned a dispute on imperial relations into a sweeping reformation of public institutions and thereby laid the basis for American democracy.

For some time now, and particularly during the last decade, this interpretation has been fundamentally weakened by the work of many scholars working from different approaches and on different problems. Almost every important point has been challenged in one way or another.[1] All arguments concerning politics during

---

[1] Recent revisionist writings on eighteenth-century America are voluminous. The main points of reinterpretation will be found in the following books and articles, to which specific reference is made in the paragraphs that follow: Robert E. Brown, *Middle-Class Democracy and the Revolution in Massachusetts, 1691–1780* (Ithaca, N. Y., 1955); E. James Ferguson, "Currency

the prerevolutionary years have been affected by an exhaustive demonstration for one colony, which might well be duplicated for others, that the franchise, far from having been restricted in behalf of a borough-mongering aristocracy, was widely available for popular use. Indeed, it was more widespread than the desire to use it—a fact which in itself calls into question a whole range of traditional arguments and assumptions. Similarly, the Populist terms in which economic elements of prerevolutionary history have most often been discussed may no longer be used with the same confidence. For it has been shown that paper money, long believed to have been the inflationary instrument of a depressed and desperate debtor yeomanry, was in general a fiscally sound and successful means—whether issued directly by the governments or through land banks—not only of providing a medium of exchange but also of creating sources of credit necessary for the growth of an underdeveloped economy and a stable system of public finance for otherwise resourceless governments. Merchants and creditors commonly supported the issuance of paper, and many of the debtors who did so turn out to have been substantial property owners.

Equally, the key writings extending the interpretation into the revolutionary years have come under question. The first and still classic monograph detailing the inner social struggle of the decade before 1776—Carl Becker's *History of Political Parties in*

Finance: An Interpretation of Colonial Monetary Practices," *William and Mary Quarterly*, X (April, 1953), 153–180; Theodore Thayer, "The Land Bank System in the American Colonies," *Journal of Economic History*, XIII (Spring, 1953), 145–159; Bray Hammond, *Banks and Politics in America from the Revolution to the Civil War* (Princeton, N. J., 1957); George A. Billias, *The Massachusetts Land Bankers of 1740* (Orono, Me., 1959); Milton M. Klein, "Democracy and Politics in Colonial New York," *New York History*, XL (July, 1959), 221–246; Oscar and Mary F. Handlin, "Radicals and Conservatives in Massachusetts after Independence," *New England Quarterly*, XVII (September, 1944), 343–355; Bernard Bailyn, "The Blount Papers: Notes on the Merchant 'Class' in the Revolutionary Period," *William and Mary Quarterly*, XI (January, 1954), 98–104; Frederick B. Tolles, "The American Revolution Considered as a Social Movement: A Re-Evaluation," *American Historical Review*, LX (October, 1954), 1–12; Robert E. Brown, *Charles Beard and the Constitution: A Critical Analysis of "An Economic Interpretation of the Constitution"* (Princeton, N. J., 1956); Forrest McDonald, *We the People: The Economic Origins of the Constitution* (Chicago, 1958); Daniel J. Boorstin, *The Genius of American Politics* (Chicago, 1953), and *The Americans: The Colonial Experience* (New York, 1958). References to other writings and other viewpoints will be found in Edmund S. Morgan. "The American Revolution: Revisions in Need of Revising," *William and Mary Quarterly*, XIV (January, 1957), 3–15; and Richard B. Morris, "The Confederation Period and the American Historian," *ibid.*, XIII (April, 1956), 139–156.

the Province of New York, 1760–1776 (1909)—has been subjected to sharp criticism on points of validation and consistency. And, because Becker's book, like other studies of the movement toward revolution, rests upon a belief in the continuity of "radical" and "conservative" groupings, it has been weakened by an analysis proving such terminology to be deceptive in that it fails to define consistently identifiable groups of people. Similarly, the "class" characteristic of the merchant group in the northern colonies, a presupposition of important studies of the merchants in the revolutionary movement, has been questioned, and along with it the belief that there was an economic or occupational basis for positions taken on the revolutionary controversy. More important, a recent survey of the writings following up J. F. Jameson's classic essay, *The American Revolution Considered as a Social Movement* (1926), has shown how little has been written in the last twenty-five years to substantiate that famous statement of the Revolution as a movement of social reform. Most dramatic of all has been the demolition of Charles Beard's *Economic Interpretation of the Constitution* (1913), which stood solidly for over forty years as the central pillar of the counterrevolution argument: the idea, that is, that the Constitution was a "conservative" document, the polar opposite of the "radical" Articles of Confederation, embodying the interests and desires of public creditors and other moneyed conservatives, and marking the Thermidorian conclusion to the enlightened radicalism of the early revolutionary years.

Finally, there are arguments of another sort, assertions to the effect that not only did Enlightenment ideas not provoke native American radicals to undertake serious reform during the Revolution, but that ideas have never played an important role in American public life, in the eighteenth century or after, and that the political "genius" of the American people, during the Revolution as later, has lain in their brute pragmatism, their successful resistance to the "distant example and teachings of the European Enlightenment," the maunderings of "garret-spawned European illuminati."

Thus from several directions at once have come evidence and arguments that cloud if they do not totally obscure the picture of eighteenth-century American history composed by a generation of scholars. These recent critical writings are of course of unequal weight and validity; but few of them are totally unsubstantiated, almost all of them have some point and substance, and taken together they are sufficient to raise serious doubts about the organization of thought within which we have become accustomed to view the eighteenth century. A full reconsideration of the problems raised by these findings and ideas would of course be out of the question here even if sufficient facts were now available. But one might make at least an approach to the task and a first approximation to some answers to the problems by isolating the central premise concerning the relationship between Enlightenment ideas and political experience and reconsidering it in view of the evidence that is now available.

Considering the material at hand, old and new, that bears on this question, one discovers an apparent paradox. There appear to be two primary and contradictory sets of facts. The first and more obvious is the undeniable evidence of the seriousness with which colonial and revolutionary leaders took ideas, and the deliberateness of their efforts during the Revolution to reshape institutions in their pattern. The more we know about these American provincials the clearer it is that among them were remarkably well-informed students of contemporary social and political theory. There never was a dark age that destroyed the cultural contacts between Europe and America. The sources of transmission had been numerous in the seventeenth century; they increased in the eighteenth. There were not only the impersonal agencies of newspapers, books, and pamphlets, but also continuous personal contact through travel and correspondence. Above all, there were Pan-Atlantic, mainly Anglo-American, interest groups that occasioned a continuous flow of fresh information and ideas between Europe and the mainland colonies in America. Of these, the most important were the English dissenters and their numerous codenominationalists in America. Located perforce on the left of the English political spectrum, acutely alive to ideas of reform that might increase their security in England, they were, for the almost endemically nonconformist colonists, a rich source of political and social theory. It was largely through nonconformist connections, as Caroline Robbins' recent book, *The Eighteenth-Century Commonwealthman* (1959), suggests, that the commonwealth radicalism of seventeenth-century England continued to flow to the colonists, blending, ultimately, with other strains of thought to form a common body of advanced theory.

In every colony and in every legislature there were people who knew Locke and Beccaria, Montesquieu and Voltaire; but perhaps more important, there was in every village of every colony someone who knew such transmitters of English nonconformist

thought as Watts, Neal, and Burgh; later Priestley and Price—
lesser writers, no doubt, but staunch opponents of traditional
authority, and they spoke in a familiar idiom. In the bitterly
contentious pamphlet literature of mid-eighteenth-century American politics, the most frequently cited authority on matters of
principle and theory was not Locke or Montesquieu but *Cato's
Letters*, a series of radically libertarian essays written in London
in 1720–1723 by two supporters of the dissenting interest, John
Trenchard and Thomas Gordon. Through such writers, as well
as through the major authors, leading colonists kept contact with
a powerful tradition of enlightened thought.

This body of doctrine fell naturally into play in the controversy
over the power of the imperial government. For the revolutionary
leaders it supplied a common vocabulary and a common pattern
of thought, and, when the time came, common principles of
political reform. That reform was sought and seriously if unevenly
undertaken, there can be no doubt. Institutions were remodeled,
laws altered, practices questioned all in accordance with advanced
doctrine on the nature of liberty and of the institutions needed to
achieve it. The Americans were acutely aware of being inno-
vators, of bringing mankind a long step forward. They believed
that they had so far succeeded in their effort to reshape circumstances to conform to enlightened ideas and ideals that they had
introduced a new era in human affairs. And they were supported
in this by the opinion of informed thinkers in Europe. The contemporary image of the American Revolution at home and abroad
was complex; but no one doubted that a revolution that threatened
the existing order and portended new social and political arrangements had been made, and made in the name of reason.

Thus, throughout the eighteenth century there were prominent,
politically active Americans who were well aware of the development of European thinking, took ideas seriously, and during the
Revolution deliberately used them in an effort to reform the institutional basis of society. This much seems obvious. But, paradoxically, and less obviously, it is equally true that many, indeed
most, of what these leaders considered to be their greatest achievements during the Revolution—reforms that made America seem
to half the world like the veritable heavenly city of the eighteenth-
century philosophers—had been matters of fact before they were
matters of theory and revolutionary doctrine.

No reform in the entire Revolution appeared of greater importance to Jefferson than the Virginia acts abolishing primogeniture and entail. This action, he later wrote, was part of "a

system by which every fibre would be eradicated of antient or future aristocracy; and a foundation laid for a government truly republican." But primogeniture and entail had never taken deep roots in America, not even in tidewater Virginia. Where land was cheap and easily available such legal restrictions proved to be encumbrances profiting few. Often they tended to threaten rather than secure the survival of the family, as Jefferson himself realized when in 1774 he petitioned the Assembly to break an entail on his wife's estate on the very practical, untheoretical, and common ground that to do so would be "greatly to their [the petitioners'] Interest and that of their Families." The legal abolition of primogeniture and entail during and after the Revolution was of little material consequence. Their demise had been effectively decreed years before by the circumstances of life in a wilderness environment.

Similarly, the disestablishment of religion—a major goal of revolutionary reform—was carried out, to the extent that it was, in circumstances so favorable to it that one wonders not how it was done but why it was not done more thoroughly. There is no more eloquent, moving testimony to revolutionary idealism than the Virginia Act for Establishing Religious Freedom: it is the essence of Enlightenment faith. But what did it, and the disestablishment legislation that had preceded it, reform? What had the establishment of religion meant in prerevolutionary Virginia? The Church of England was the state church, but dissent was tolerated well beyond the limits of the English Acts of Toleration. The law required nonconformist organizations to be licensed by the government, but dissenters were not barred from their own worship nor penalized for failure to attend the Anglican communion, and they were commonly exempted from parish taxes. Nonconformity excluded no one from voting and only the very few Catholics from enjoying public office. And when the itineracy of revivalist preachers led the establishment to contemplate more restrictive measures, the Baptists and Presbyterians advanced to the point of arguing publicly, and pragmatically, that the toleration they had so far enjoyed was an encumbrance, and that the only proper solution was total liberty: in effect, disestablishment.

Virginia was if anything more conservative than most colonies. The legal establishment of the Church of England was in fact no more rigorous in South Carolina and Georgia: it was considerably weaker in North Carolina. It hardly existed at all in the middle colonies (there was of course no vestige of it in

Pennsylvania), and where it did, as in four counties of New York, it was either ignored or had become embattled by violent opposition well before the Revolution. And in Massachusetts and Connecticut, where the establishment, being nonconformist according to English law, was legally tenuous to begin with, tolerance in worship and relief from church taxation had been extended to the major dissenting groups early in the century, resulting well before the Revolution in what was, in effect if not in law, a multiple establishment. And this had been further weakened by the splintering effect of the Great Awakening. Almost everywhere the Church of England, the established church of the highest state authority, was embattled and defensive— driven to rely more and more on its missionary arm, the Society for the Propagation of the Gospel, to sustain it against the cohorts of dissent.

None of this had resulted from Enlightenment theory. It had been created by the mundane exigencies of the situation: by the distance that separated Americans from ecclesiastical centers in England and the Continent; by the never-ending need to encourage immigration to the colonies; by the variety, the mere numbers, of religious groups, each by itself a minority, forced to live together; and by the weakness of the coercive powers of the state, its inability to control the social forces within it.

Even more gradual and less contested had been the process by which government in the colonies had become government by the consent of the governed. What has been proved about the franchise in early Massachusetts—that it was open for practically the entire free adult male population—can be proved to a lesser or greater extent for all the colonies. But the extraordinary breadth of the franchise in the American colonies had not resulted from popular demands: there had been no cries for universal manhood suffrage, nor were there popular theories claiming, or even justifying, general participation in politics. Nowhere in eighteenth-century America was there "democracy"—middle-class or otherwise—as we use the term. The main reason for the wide franchise was that the traditional English laws limiting suffrage to freeholders of certain competences proved in the colonies, where freehold property was almost universal, to be not restrictive but widely permissive.

Representation would seem to be different, since before the Revolution complaints had been voiced against the inequity of its apportioning, especially in the Pennsylvania and North Carolina assemblies. But these complaints were based on an assumption that would have seemed natural and reasonable almost nowhere else in the Western world: the assumption that representation in governing assemblages was a proper and rightful attribute of people as such—of regular units of population, or of populated land—rather than the privilege of particular groups, institutions, or regions. Complaints there were, bitter ones. But they were complaints claiming injury and deprivation, not abstract ideals or unfamiliar desires. They assumed from common experience the normalcy of regular and systematic representation. And how should it have been otherwise? The colonial assemblies had not, like ancient parliaments, grown to satisfy a monarch's need for the support of particular groups or individuals or to protect the interests of a social order, and they had not developed insensibly from precedent to precedent. They had been created at a stroke, and they were in their composition necessarily regular and systematic. Nor did the process, the character, of representation as it was known in the colonies derive from theory. For colonial Americans, representation had none of the symbolic and little of the purely deliberative qualities which, as a result of the revolutionary debates and of Burke's speeches, would become celebrated as "virtual." To the colonists it was direct and actual: it was, most often, a kind of agency, a delegation of powers, to individuals commonly required to be residents of their constituencies and, often, bound by instructions from them—with the result that eighteenth-century American legislatures frequently resembled, in spirit if not otherwise, those "ancient assemblies" of New York, composed, the contemporary historian William Smith wrote, "of plain, illiterate husbandmen, whose views seldom extended farther than to the regulation of highways, the destruction of wolves, wild cats, and foxes, and the advancement of the other little interests of the particular counties which they were chosen to represent." There was no theoretical basis for such direct and actual representation. It had been created and was continuously reinforced by the pressure of local politics in the colonies and by the political circumstances in England, to which the colonists had found it necessary to send closely instructed, paid representatives—agents, so called—from the very beginning.

But franchise and representation are mere mechanisms of government by consent. At its heart lies freedom from executive power, from the independent action of state authority, and the concentration of power in representative bodies and elected officials. The greatest achievement of the Revolution was of course the repudiation of just such state authority and the transfer of power to popular legislatures. No one will deny that this action was taken in accordance with the highest principles of Enlightenment theory. But the way had been paved by fifty years of grinding factionalism in colonial politics. In the details of prerevolutionary American politics, in the complicated maneuverings of provincial politicians seeking the benefits of government, in the patterns of local patronage and the forms of factional groupings, there lies a history of progressive alienation from the state which resulted, at least by the 1750's, in what Professor Robert Palmer has lucidly described as a revolutionary situation: a condition

. . . in which confidence in the justice or reasonableness of existing authority is undermined; where old loyalties fade, obligations are felt as impositions, law seems arbitrary, and respect for superiors is felt as a form of humiliation; where existing sources of prestige seem undeserved . . . and government is sensed as distant, apart from the governed and not really "representing" them.

Such a situation had developed in mid-eighteenth-century America, not from theories of government or Enlightenment ideas but from the factional opposition that had grown up against a succession of legally powerful, but often cynically self-seeking, inept, and above all politically weak officers of state.

Surrounding all of these circumstances and in various ways controlling them is the fact that that great goal of the European revolutions of the late eighteenth century, equality of status before the law—the abolition of legal privilege—had been reached almost everywhere in the American colonies at least by the early years of the eighteenth century. Analogies between the upper strata of colonial society and the European aristocrats are misleading. Social stratification existed, of course; but the difference between aristocracies in eighteenth-century Europe and in America are more important than the similarities. So far was legal privilege, or even distinction, absent in the colonies that where it existed it was an open sore of festering discontent, leading not merely, as in the case of the Penn family's hereditary claims to tax exemption, to formal protests, but, as in the case of the powers enjoyed by the Hudson River land magnates, to violent opposition as well. More important, the colonial aristocracy, such as it was, had no formal, institutional role in government. No public office or function was legally a prerogative of birth. As there were no social orders in the eyes of the law, so there were no governmental bodies to represent them. The only claim that has been made to the contrary is that, in effect, the governors'

Councils constituted political institutions in the service of the aristocracy. But this claim—of dubious value in any case because of the steadily declining political importance of the Councils in the eighteenth century—cannot be substantiated. It is true that certain families tended to dominate the Councils, but they had less legal claim to places in those bodies than certain royal officials who, though hardly members of an American aristocracy, sat on the Councils by virtue of their office. Councilors could be and were removed by simple political maneuver. Council seats were filled either by appointment or election: when appointive, they were vulnerable to political pressure in England; when elective, to the vagaries of public opinion at home. Thus on the one hand it took William Byrd II three years of maneuvering in London to get himself appointed to the seat on the Virginia Council vacated by his father's death in 1704, and on the other, when in 1766 the Hutchinson faction's control of the Massachusetts Council proved unpopular, it was simply removed wholesale by being voted out of office at the next election. As there were no special privileges, no peculiar group possessions, manners, or attitudes to distinguish councilors from other affluent Americans, so there were no separate political interests expressed in the Councils as such. Councilors joined as directly as others in the factional disputes of the time, associating with groups of all sorts, from minute and transient American opposition parties to massive English-centered political syndicates. A century before the Revolution and not as the result of anti-aristocratic ideas, the colonial aristocracy had become a vaguely defined, fluid group whose power—in no way guaranteed, buttressed, or even recognized in law—was competitively maintained and dependent on continuous, popular support.

Other examples could be given. Were written constitutions felt to be particular guarantees of liberty in enlightened states? Americans had known them in the form of colonial charters and governors' instructions for a century before the Revolution; and after 1763, seeking a basis for their claims against the constitutionality of specific acts of Parliament, they had been driven, out of sheer logical necessity and not out of principle, to generalize that experience. But the point is perhaps clear enough. Major attributes of enlightened polities had developed naturally, spontaneously, early in the history of the American colonies, and they existed as simple matters of social and political fact on the eve of the Revolution.

But if all this is true, what did the Revolution accomplish? Of what real significance were the ideals and ideas? What was the bearing of Enlightenment thought on the political experience of eighteenth-century Americans?

Perhaps this much may be said. What had evolved spontaneously from the demands of place and time was not self-justifying, nor was it universally welcomed. New developments, however gradual, were suspect by some, resisted in part, and confined in their effects. If it was true that the establishment of religion was everywhere weak in the colonies and that in some places it was even difficult to know what was orthodoxy and what was not, it was nevertheless also true that faith in the idea of orthodoxy persisted and with it belief in the propriety of a privileged state religion. If, as a matter of fact, the spread of freehold tenure qualified large populations for voting, it did not create new reasons for using that power nor make the victims of its use content with what, in terms of the dominant ideal of balance in the state, seemed a disproportionate influence of "the democracy." If many colonists came naturally to assume that representation should be direct and actual, growing with the population and bearing some relation to its distribution, crown officials did not, and they had the weight of precedent and theory as well as of authority with them and hence justification for resistance. If state authority was seen increasingly as alien and hostile and was forced to fight for survival within an abrasive, kaleidoscopic factionalism, the traditional idea nevertheless persisted that the common good was somehow defined by the state and that political parties or factions— organized opposition to established government—were seditious. A traditional aristocracy did not in fact exist; but the assumption that superiority was indivisible, that social eminence and political influence had a natural affinity to each other, did. The colonists instinctively conceded to the claims of the well-born and rich to exercise public office, and in this sense politics remained aristocratic. Behavior had changed—had had to change—with the circumstances of everyday life; but habits of mind and the sense of rightness lagged behind. Many felt the changes to be *away from*, not *toward*, something: that they represented deviance; that they lacked, in a word, legitimacy.

This divergence between habits of mind and belief on the one hand and experience and behavior on the other was ended at the Revolution. A rebellion that destroyed the traditional sources of public authority called forth the full range of advanced ideas. Long-settled attitudes were jolted and loosened. The grounds of legitimacy suddenly shifted. What had happened was seen to have been good and proper, steps in the right direction. The glass was half full, not half empty; and to complete the work of fate and nature, further thought must be taken, theories tested, ideas applied. Precisely because so many social and institutional reforms had already taken place in America, the revolutionary movement there, more than elsewhere, was a matter of doctrine, ideas, and comprehension.

And so it remained. Social change and social conflict of course took place during the revolutionary years; but the essential developments of the period lay elsewhere, in the effort to think through and to apply under the most favorable, permissive, circumstances enlightened ideas of government and society. The problems were many, often unexpected and difficult; some were only gradually perceived. Social and personal privilege, for example, could easily be eliminated—it hardly existed; but what of the impersonal privileges of corporate bodies? Legal orders and ranks within society could be outlawed without creating the slightest tremor, and executive power with equal ease subordinated to the legislative: but how was balance within a polity to be achieved? What were the elements to be balanced and how were they to be separated? It was not even necessary formally to abolish the interest of state as a symbol and determinant of the common good; it was simply dissolved: but what was left to keep clashing factions from tearing a government apart? The problems were pressing, and the efforts to solve them mark the stages of revolutionary history.

In behalf of Enlightenment liberalism the revolutionary leaders undertook to complete, formalize, systematize and symbolize what previously had been only partially realized, confused, and disputed matters of fact. Enlightenment ideas were not instruments of a particular social group, nor did they destroy a social order. They did not create new social and political forces in America. They released those that had long existed, and vastly increased their power. This completion, this rationalization, this symbolization, this lifting into consciousness and endowing with high moral purpose inchoate, confused elements of social and political change— this was the American Revolution.

Republicanism and Radicalism
in the American Revolution:
An Old-Fashioned Interpretation
CECELIA M. KENYON

I

Although the American Revolution was a central and decisive phenomenon in the national life of the American people, taken comfortably for granted by its heirs and nominally commemorated by a convenient summer holiday, its nature and significance continue to puzzle historians who seek to know it well. From the very beginning, it was believed by those who participated in it—on the western side of the Atlantic—to be a quite remarkable event, not merely because it was their revolution, but because it seemed to them to introduce a new phase in the political evolution of mankind, and therefore to be touched with universal significance. This native estimate was not entirely parochial. There was considerable interest in the American experiment among contemporary Europeans, and the volumes of commentary written by visitors in the nineteenth century indicate that this interest was not merely ephemeral. In more recent times, Americans have been reminded of their Revolutionary heritage by later rebels against colonial rule, who have sometimes seemed to find the America of 1776 more inspiring than the America of 1962. Thus the Revolution was, and continues to be, an event of enduring importance. And yet, in spite of generations of study, its essential nature remains obscure. In fact, as its two-hundredth anniversary approaches, there seems to be more uncertainty about its meaning, more diversity in interpretation, than ever before. For the last two generations, scholars have debated such questions as the relationship between the Declaration of Independence and the Constitution, what the real causes of the Revolution were, whether it was essen-

Reprinted with permission from *The William and Mary Quarterly*, 3rd ser., XIX (April, 1962), 153–182 and the Institute of Early American History and Culture.

Note: An earlier version of this article was presented at the Seminar on the American Revolution, sponsored by Colonial Williamsburg, Inc., Williamsburg, Virginia, September 9, 1960.

tially a colonial revolt or an internal struggle for power, whether it was radical or conservative—indeed, whether, in fact, it was actually a revolution. Among these and other issues, a crucial one over which there has been much confusion is whether the Revolution was radical or conservative. The purpose of this article is to consider some of the intellectual forces which have contributed to this confusion, to suggest a way by which some of this confusion may be resolved, and to analyze the Revolution with respect to its radical and conservative immediate aspects and long-range implications.

II

Among the factors responsible for this confusion, one of the most important is sheer lack of accurate and precise knowledge. Not until very recently, for example, have we really known much about the suffrage or about actual participation in politics.[1] It has taken nearly two centuries for historians to learn the historiographical lessons implicit in Madison's Tenth *Federalist* and to begin to dig out the extraordinarily complex interest groups involved in the ratification of the Constitution.[2] As more knowledge accumulates, so should our understanding of the total Revolutionary situation increase in both depth and breadth.

Yet the facts do not reveal themselves spontaneously, nor do they always speak for themselves. A second factor which has contributed to confusion has been the attempt to impose upon the Revolution too simple a pattern of interpretation. It is natural and inevitable for historians and political scientists to fit the ideas, the institutions, the political, social, and economic developments of the period into a unified and coherent whole. No mere listing of these elements, without classification and an effort to see their various interrelationships, would be intelligible. The hazard of this process of intellectual construction is as natural and familiar as

---

[1]See, for example, Robert E. Brown, *Middle-Class Democracy and the Revolution in Massachusetts, 1691–1780* (Ithaca, N. Y., 1955); Richard P. McCormick, *Experiment in Independence: New Jersey in the Critical Period, 1781–1789* (New Brunswick, N. J., 1950), and *The History of Voting in New Jersey* . . . (New Brunswick, N. J., 1953); J. R. Pole, "Suffrage Reform and the American Revolution in New Jersey," New Jersey Historical Society, *Proceedings*, LXXIV (Newark, 1956), 173–194; "Suffrage and Representation in Massachusetts: A Statistical Note," *William and Mary Quarterly*, 3d Ser., XIV (1957), 560–592.

[2]See Forrest McDonald, *We the People: The Economic Origins of the Constitution* (Chicago, 1958), esp. iv.

the process itself. It is that the pattern may distort reality even as it illuminates it. Such has been the result of the inclination to view the conflicts and debates of the Revolution as if the parties to them were divided naturally into pairs of opposites. We speak of the American and British position, of Loyalists and Patriots, of radicals and conservatives, of democrats and aristocrats, of Federalists and Anti-Federalists. There is much validity in this categorization, because there were times during the period between 1765 and 1789 when the alternative choices of action were reduced to two: one did or did not sign the Declaration of Independence; one voted for or against the Constitution of 1787. Furthermore, there was some degree of consistency and continuity in the positions taken by various men over an extended period of time. Yet I believe that it is a mistake to see the Revolution from its early stages to its later ones as a movement involving issues over which men divided naturally into two clearly defined groups, radical and conservative, more or less constant in composition.

Among the intellectual forces which have operated to incline American historians toward this dichotomous analysis of the Revolutionary period are two, one conscious, one perhaps unconscious. The first is that inspired by the Populist critique of the Constitution during the 1890's, and later elaborated into a full-blown interpretation according to which the Declaration of Independence represented and embodied the spirit of democracy which characterized the early stages of the Revolution, while the Constitution was the product of a successful conservative and antidemocratic reaction.[3] Charles A. Beard's *Economic Interpretation of the Constitution*[4] was not identical with this interpretation, but it tended to absorb and reinforce it by seeming to present impressive evidence for its validity. An economic interpretation does not necessarily have to be dichotomous, but Beard's was, and it was Beard who exercised a dominant influence over more than a generation of American historians. Why Beard and his followers should have accepted a Hamiltonian rather than a Madisonian view of politics is not easy to explain, but the results of this acceptance do seem reasonably clear. It has exercised an enormous influence both in the selection and interpretation of facts, and has tended to create a simplified pattern to describe and explain what was in reality a very complex set of political phenomena.

[3]See C. Edward Merriam, *A History of American Political Theories* (New York and London, 1903), and J. Allen Smith, *The Spirit of American Government* . . . (New York, 1907).

[4]Charles A. Beard, *An Economic Interpretation of the Constitution of the United States* (New York, 1913).

This historiographical factor has probably been reinforced by a second one, much less visible, and probably impossible to document. It is the unconscious conditioning effect on Americans of a two-party political system. Only twice within a century has a third party threatened the dominance of the two major parties, and each was strictly a one-shot flash never repeated. To be sure, each of the major parties has its internal cleavages, of which informed students of politics as well as politicians are well aware. Still, Americans do think of politics in terms of two parties, and this conception, I suspect, has had its influence on the way in which we visualize our past. A dualistic party system seems to us so normal that we tend to think of it as part of a natural political order.

It was not so for the men of the Revolution. We do not yet have sufficient evidence to know to what extent their aversion to parties was negated by their tendency to form and use them. The attitude of the most articulate spokesmen is unequivocal and unmistakable, and it appears to have been rather pervasive. As such, it was itself a factor in Revolutionary politics and must be taken into consideration. What I am proposing is that in analyzing the Revolution, we adopt something of the intellectual habit of its makers and consider the implications of their dislike and distrust of parties. One such implication is obvious; they thought of parties as reflecting or magnifying selfish interests. Another is equally obvious and for our purposes perhaps more significant. Their ideal of politics appears to have involved not the division of the body of citizens into more or less permanent groupings held together by similar views on a composite cluster of principles and/or interests, but rather *ex tempore* majorities and minorities formed by the issue of the moment and undistorted by pre-existing organization not related to the instant issue. This ideal was matched and perhaps countered by a recognition of economic and other factors which tended to divide society into relatively stable, though not necessarily politically organized or active, groups, whose influence might, nonetheless, be felt in politics. Some of the new constitutions adopted during the period specifically recognized an economic class division in their property qualifications for office-holding. Similarly, in several of the states, and certainly in the national debate of 1787–1788, there was present an awareness of two major classes, and it was assumed by both sides that these classes would sometimes have different economic and political interests. At the same time, the pre-Revolutionary arguments against the British theory of virtual representation, and the later debates over the ratification of the Constitution, expressed the necessity of making the representative assembly reflect a multiplicity of interests and opinions among the voters rather than a dualistic division along party or factional lines. Thus it seems quite clear that the Americans of the Revolutionary period did not have a consistent, systematic theory of the political process, and especially not of political parties. It seems a safe hypothesis to suggest that in this respect there would very likely be a reciprocal relationship between political thought and political behavior. We should not read the pattern of later political divisions back into the eighteenth century, any more than we should read their substance.

It would be remarkable indeed if a simple dichotomous pattern could really fit so complex a phenomenon as the Revolution. It was, as revolutions go, a rather peculiar one. In the first place, no revolution was intended; the colonists wanted merely a redress of grievances as British subjects and had no plans either for independence or for the formation of republican government. In the second place, there were thirteen separate colonies or states involved, and, though they may not have been as different from one another as their members believed them to be, the differences were sufficient to make the impact and the aftermath of the Revolution far from identical in each of them. In the third place, the Revolution was both the creator of and the fruit of the emergence of first a growing consciousness that the British continental colonies constituted a separate community with interests different from those of the mother country and later a spirit of nationalism and eventually of national unity. In the fourth place, the Revolution was accomplished with remarkably little internal coercion and remarkably great decentralization of leadership. No central committee, party, government, or army ever possessed or exercised a preponderance either of power or authority at any time during the period from 1765 to 1789. In short, Americans found themselves in 1776 in a position for which they were not prepared and for which they had no plans. When the decision for independence was taken, they had been in armed revolt for over a year and, during this period, had been living either without formal, recognized governments or with governments of dubious legitimacy and authority. It is necessary to understand this combination of a complex situation and complex political attitudes before proceeding to an analysis of republicanism and radicalism during the American Revolution.

A third factor contributing to the confusion over the nature of the Revolution has been our inability to achieve a precise and meaningful terminology with which to analyze and categorize the phenomena we have sought to describe. There has been no general agreement among scholars about the meaning of words such as radical, conservative, liberal, or democratic, and there has been a notable lack of rigor in the way we have applied them to the Revolutionary era. In particular, I would object that the common use of the terms *radical* and *conservative* to denote respectively populist and anti-populist divisions within the Revolutionary party has tended to obscure the nature of the changes which took place in America during the last quarter of the eighteenth century.

There are several major difficulties involved in an identification of *democratic* and *radical*. In the first place, the word *democratic* is too loose. It is not easy to get a precise yardstick for democracy in the Revolutionary period, or to find among the articulate men of the age one whose views were purely and consistently democratic by any standard. Benjamin Franklin, for example, is usually associated with the radical democrats of Pennsylvania because he was a believer in unicameralism. In the Philadelphia Convention, Franklin was opposed to a salary in excess of expenses for the President, and this arrangement in effect would have restricted that office to the relatively wealthy. James Wilson and Gouverneur Morris both advocated the direct, popular election of the President —on its face a radically democratic proposal—but neither was identified with the populist party in his state, and Morris was very closely associated with Alexander Hamilton. Thomas Jefferson devised a comprehensive plan of reform for the state of Virginia, aimed, as he said, at uprooting the last remnants of aristocracy there. But Jefferson was a staunch believer in separation of powers and therefore can scarcely qualify as a democrat for those who tend to identify democracy with the absence of separation of powers or the concentration of power in the legislative branch of the government. Similarly, Jefferson's objections to the Constitution of 1787 did not touch the distribution of powers between the central government and the states, and he cannot therefore fit into the association of democracy with localism. In short, the identification of radicalism with democracy or localism fails to provide a clear and precise definition as a tool for analyzing the Revolution.

In the second place, such an identification involves a chain of assumptions of dubious validity. The definition of radical in terms of democracy assumes that the latter was the central issue of the period, that it operated as a primary determinative force in lining up men on other issues which were derivative from it and which were therefore of secondary importance, that its effect, in short, was to produce a polarization of opinion. Was democracy an ideological and dynamic force which operated in this manner? I think not, or at least not consistently. For example, the separation of church and state was a fundamental change. If democracy and radicalism were identical, then the more democratic party should have been in favor of this separation. The opposition to the clause in the Constitution which prohibited religious tests for officeholding suggests that such was not the case. The legal effect of this clause was to establish equality of eligibility for all men, regardless of their religious or nonreligious beliefs or associations. It also, by implication, broadened the potential choice of the electorate, in comparison with the situation in a number of the state governments. In other words, it prohibited a religious monopoly of officeholding, and it prohibited restraints on the free choice of the electorate. These factors are frequently associated with democratic government, yet they were not desired by some of the opponents of the Constitution who criticized that document, on other grounds, as having an aristocratic bias. I submit that these opponents were not democratic on this issue and that the association of radicalism with Revolutionary democracy assumes a unity, consistency, and rationality in political thought which is rarely found even in the most sophisticated and systematic of theorists.

This is not to deny that the association of *radical* with *democratic* has considerable historical justification. In America, as elsewhere, one element of political evolution in the eighteenth and nineteenth centuries was the extension of power and privilege to the majority of the population. With respect to this element, the populist parties of the Revolution may be called radical, though the recent studies of the suffrage requirements indicate that reformist would be more accurate. There were other movements, however, in the direction of nationalism, of individualism, of industralization that were certainly in the literal sense radical, though none of them was by necessary and exclusive logic connected with democracy. In fact, the advocates of nationalism and industrialism during the last quarter of the eighteenth century in America were frequently in opposition to the advocates of populism and/or democracy. If one accepts the identification of radicalism with the latter, then it would seem to follow that nationalism and industralism were conservative movements. Put in these general terms, this sounds like a ridiculous conclusion, for both were to become major movements of the nineteenth and twentieth centuries, both produced radical changes, and both have been called "revolutions." Similarly, we are accustomed to having the Constitution described as the product of a conservative reaction, although it was unquestionably a great step in the direction of nationalism. Hamilton's financial program had industrialization as one of its purposes, and, though there are probably few historians who would call him a conservative on this particular matter, there is still considerable reluctance to associate him with Revolutionary radicalism. It is men like Thomas Paine and the authors of the Pennsylvania constitution whom that term is more likely to bring to mind. The tendency to define *radical* purely in terms of populist groups makes it difficult to classify changes which were fundamental but not overtly or immediately democratic. If we are to continue to accept this kind of terminology, then we must recognize that it is a very parochial kind of history we write, one which foreign students of America must find difficult to translate into terms which are meaningful to them. And we must recognize that such terminology does not lend itself to precise comparative and analytical studies.

A third major difficulty stemming from the identification of radicalism and democracy is that it inhibits a precise analysis of the issues which arose during the period and of the groups who divided over them. Once a group is labeled democratic or radical on one issue, there is a tendency to assume that whatever stand it took on others was also democratic or radical. Conversely, once a particular policy is associated with a democratic or radical group, it may take on the coloring of that group. Both tendencies may result in distortion, confusion, or a limited presentation of reality. Consider the latter, with respect to the issue of paper money. There must be thousands of graduates of American history courses who associate paper money during the Revolution with radicalism, and radicalism with the *demos*. Yet it is perfectly clear that paper money was supported in some states by the upper classes also. Were the South Carolina planters who supported paper money radicals and democrats? Or was paper money radical only when supported by some groups and opposed by others? Radical in Rhode Island but not in South Carolina? The former tendency, the labeling of ideas and institutions in terms of the assumed character of their advocates or opponents, makes objective analysis and comparison awkward if not impossible.

Two examples may serve to make this difficulty clear. It has been a common interpretation of the Revolutionary period to associate democracy with opposition to separation of powers and checks and balances, partly because the Pennsylvania insurgents of 1776 were a populist group who seized power from a former privileged group and who then established a constitution which did not follow the principle of separation of powers. If this and other similar groups opposed this principle and favored instead a concentration of authority in the legislature, then the latter form must be democratic and the former not. But if this categorization is accepted, then how are we to describe the changes which took place in state constitutions in the period from about 1820 to 1860? An almost universal trend was the creation of an independent executive, popularly elected; the election of other administrative officers was also common and, to a lesser extent, so was the election of judges. These changes were made partly in the name of democracy, and we are familiar with them under the label of the "long ballot." It is perfectly obvious, though not so frequently noted, that they meant a relative decrease in the authority of the legislature and—especially the independent executive—an increase in separation of powers. Were these later constitutions, then, antidemocratic, or at least less democratic than those of the Revolutionary period which did not have an executive independent of the legislature, elected directly by the people? Such a conclusion is certainly possible, but it does involve difficulties. One of them is that not only have our state and federal constitutions continued to be undemocratic, but that there has been no substantial popular demand to have them otherwise. The fundamental methodological point is that a definition of radical in terms of Revolutionary democracy does not provide an adequate tool for comparative analysis of ideas and institutions during different periods in our own political evolution, or of similar ones in different countries. For that, we need a more objective and less relativistic concept.

My second example illustrates another facet of the same need. The Constitution of 1787 was opposed by groups who have been commonly regarded as more democratic than its advocates, and this interpretation has been partly responsible for the opinion that the Constitution itself was undemocratic. One specific argument against ratification was that the proposed system of representation would prejudice the election of men of "the people" and that the lower house of the national legislature would not truly represent the people. In short, the Constitution, even in its then most democratic feature, would not really be democratic at all. Are we to accept this contemporary opinion and conclude that the Constitution was undemocratic in this most fundamental and simple respect? The reasoning back of this opinion was the belief that large constituencies would necessitate pre-election organization and that the organized electoral majority would not return a legislative majority which faithfully reflected the real, unorganized constituent majority. If we accept the reasoning and the conclusions of the Anti-Federalists on this point, then we must conclude that the House of Representatives is not and has never been democratic; that the Senate, since the Seventeenth Amendment, has been even less democratic (since the constituencies of Senators are entire states); and that the Presidency (with the entire nation as its constituency) is and has been least democratic of all. If the two-thirds of our government which is constituted by popular election is not democratic, then it must of course follow that the United States is not a democracy, has never been one since 1789, and can never be one. Again, this is a perfectly possible and reasonable conclusion. But I do not think that it is a very useful one. We ought not to accept as historiographical tools the opinions of Revolutionary polemicists. The prediction of the Anti-Federalists on this particular point, even in terms of their own conception of democracy, may have been wrong; the election of 1800 suggests the distinct possibility that it was. More importantly, their conception of democracy may be one which cannot be appropriately applied to the study of the whole range of American history. If Revolutionary democracy has these limitations as a definitional tool, then surely it is folly to define *radical* by associating it with this *democracy*.

It is for this reason that I have chosen to use the term *radical* in its strict and formal sense, unassociated with any substantive concept such as democracy, majoritarianism, unicameralism, or localism. Similarly, I would use the term *conservative* in a comparable sense, to refer to an attitude, position, tendency, or policy involving or favoring preservation or continuation of some element or elements in the existing situation, but not identifying it exclusively with any of those elements. The Revolution was not a monolithic or even a dualistic affair. It precipitated the one great creative period in the political and constitutional history of the United States, and its ramifications were not limited to the single theme of more or less democratization of political structure. It was a pluralistic phenomenon involving different sectors of change. Men and groups might be opposed to some changes and in favor of others. Men who were in favor of democracy in the sense of majority rule were not always in favor of such liberal and individualistic measures as complete freedom of religion. Men who sided with what appeared to be the populist party on some issues did not do so on others. Men who joined together on some particular issue, such as adoption or rejection of the Constitution, did so for different reasons and with different motives. In order to analyze all of these issues and their interrelationships, we need a terminology which is capable of expressing subtle as well as gross distinctions, nonsubstantive as well as substantive concepts. Thus I would use *radical* to indicate a fundamental change; *democratic* to denote a political system in which authority is derived from the majority of adult inhabitants, all of whom enjoy the suffrage and may use it at regular and reasonably frequent intervals and all of whom are legally eligible for office; *populist* to indicate a more or less self-conscious group, movement, attitude, or achievement on behalf of the majority conceived of in terms of the mass of the people; and *liberal* to indicate the values of individual rights, freedom, or happiness.[5] Accordingly, there could be radical democrats, radical populists, radical liberals, or any combination of these three substantive positions or their opposites. Similarly, a man or group can be radical on one issue, conservative on another. Or a particular policy or set of institutions can be partly radical, partly conservative. Such a terminology, like many definitions, reflects the outlook of the user. In this case, it reflects a conception of the Revolution as composed of pluralistic factors which do not fall together in a dichotomous pattern. Its parts were diverse, and its major ideological and institutional results were eclectic composites. Very few of the ingredients were totally new, and none of the finished products had that rational symmetry characteristic of systematic political philosophy. They were the products of compromise, of adaptation, sometimes of improvisation. Nevertheless, the Revolution did shape the future development of American politics and government. It selected and accentuated certain ingredients in the British and colonial heritage, rejected others, and made of the whole something that was fundamentally new and different. For all its pluralistic diversity, the American Revolution was still a *revolution,* and it was radical.

---

[5]It may be objected that these definitions, especially that of *democratic* or *democracy,* do not correspond to the meanings the words conveyed in America at the time of the Revolution. I would agree that one should be aware of contemporary usage. Otherwise the ideas expressed in a given age will be misunderstood. However, if the historian himself uses words only and always in their historical sense, he will find it difficult to analyze, compare, and evaluate different but similar ideas and institutions in different countries and in different periods. I do not offer the above definitions as absolutes, but as functional tools for the purposes of analysis and comparison.

III

In the later years of their lives, John Adams and Thomas Jefferson both had occasion to comment on the nature of the Revolution, in which each had played a major role. Both left no doubt that after nearly fifty years they still regarded it, as they had in the beginning, as the fundamental change in the history of the American people. Adams emphasized the death of loyalty, affection, and allegiance toward the King of England and toward England itself. *"This radical change in the principles, opinions, sentiments, and affections of the people was the real American Revolution."*[6] Jefferson expressed a hope for the universal realization of the principles of the Declaration of Independence: "May it be to the world, what I believe it will be, (to some parts sooner, to others later, but finally to all,) the signal of arousing men to burst the chains under which monkish ignorance and superstition had persuaded them to bind themselves, and to assume the blessings and security of self-government."[7] Both men were in their eighties at the time of these remarks, and one may be tempted to make some allowance for the inclination of old men to exaggerate the importance of an event which they had helped to bring about. I am prepared to accept their opinion, and have accordingly described this article as an old-fashioned interpretation. The Revolution was radical in its four principal achievements: independence; the establishment of republican government and the identification of republicanism with political right; the crystallization of the individualism and equalitarianism of the Declaration of Independence into an operative as well as a formal political philosophy; the extension of the principle and practice of republicanism to a large and heterogeneous population by combination with a new form of federalism.

Of these four results, the first was prior to all the rest and the one most consciously and immediately felt to be radical. The decision to declare formal separation from Great Britain was a difficult one, taken only after a long period of deliberation and after the colonies had been in armed revolt against the mother

---

[6]Letter to Hezekiah Niles, Feb. 13, 1818, in Adrienne Koch and William Peden, eds., *The Selected Writings of John and John Quincy Adams* (New York, 1946), 204.

[7]Letter to Roger C. Weightman, June 24, 1826, in Paul Leicester Ford, ed., *The Works of Thomas Jefferson* (New York and London, 1904–1905), XII, 477.

country for more than a year. Nearly three-quarters of the colonists were of British descent, and the vast majority of these were accustomed to thinking of themselves as Englishmen. Their resistance to the Stamp Act and subsequent colonial regulations had not been motivated by a desire for independence, but by a desire to maintain their rights as Englishmen. Independence was a last resort, a means to secure these rights as men, and as Americans. Once accepted as the only means to get what they wanted, the decision for independence inexorably produced consequences other than the achievement of their original goal. The United States developed as an independent nation, not as British colonies nor as a constituent member of the British Commonwealth. We take this fact so much for granted today that it is difficult to conceive of what our political, economic, social, and even geographical development might have been had the colonists achieved their goals within the Empire, or had the Revolution been unsuccessful. It is tempting to speculate about the possible "might-have-beens" had the long years of protest resulted in either of these eventualities. But the facts are that we did win our independence, and that we did so with revolutionary violence. Colonial political ideas and practice had already deviated to some extent from British patterns; the institution of independent governments widened the gap and produced a markedly different political tradition.

IV

The most important, as well as the most immediate, change was the formal establishment of republican governments. Throughout most of the period of colonial protest, there had been little criticism of the British constitution or of its aristocratic and monarchical elements as such. The main thrust of American argument had been directed toward Parliament rather than the King, and primarily toward the House of Commons rather than the House of Lords. It was almost inevitable that Americans would not carry their arguments further, given the fact that the issue of taxation was at the heart of colonial opposition. The habitual professions of allegiance, devotion, and loyalty to their gracious Sovereign which accompanied colonial petitions, resolutions, and acts of defiance were both formal and traditional, but they were not completely insincere. As long as Americans believed that the crux of their problem was legislative and not administrative, they could not but consider Parliament as the central opponent; as long as they believed that their aims could be achieved within the Empire, there was no reason for hostility to the institution of the Crown. The Americans were not republicans in either a formal or an ideological sense before 1776. Within a few months, they were, and have remained so ever since. Once the decision for independence was made, there seems to have been no serious question that any other form of government was either possible or desirable. Certainly it would have been difficult for all thirteen states to agree on a single monarch for them all, and the spectacle of thirteen separate embassies touring Europe and interviewing prospective candidates suggests that common sense as well as *Common Sense* had something to do with the American choice of republicanism.

This quick transition from monarchy to republic in form and belief was accomplished with relative ease. The question whether it was a radical change is difficult to answer. In its actual and immediate effect on the general poulation, it was not. Almost from the very beginning, with some exceptions of time and place, monarchy had rested lightly upon the colonists. George III and his predecessors were weeks away by sea, and in most of the colonies most of the time, the royal governors were effectively limited in the exercise of their authority by the power of the purse and the difficulty of enforcing unpopular measures in the face of concerted opposition without adequate and reliable military forces. Above all, there had been the long years of salutary neglect. It would be too much to say that the American colonies were autonomous republics before 1776, but their governments had been far more republican than that of the home country, and they had long been accustomed to governing themselves with relatively little interference or assistance from the other side of the Atlantic. The transition from monarchy to republic did not therefore bring with it pervasive and fundamental changes, either in private or public life. In this sense, the establishment of republican governments was not a radical change, and it is not remarkable that it took place so quickly and easily.

What is more remarkable is the rapid shift in attitude and belief. Within a very short period of time, Americans developed an ideological attachment to republicanism, and this change was a radical one, with radical and far-reaching consequences. Before 1776, the prevailing opinion in America had been that the ends of government—liberty, justice, happiness, and the public good— could be secured within the framework of monarchy. To be sure, they meant a limited or mixed monarchy, and they emphasized the central importance of constitutionalism. Still, they assumed the compatibility of monarchy with good government. After 1776, they tended to associate all the characteristics of good government with republicanism, and with republicanism only. To be sure, there were dissenters, of whom Alexander Hamilton was the most illustrious. But the preponderant opinion, the genius, to use Madison's word,[8] was clear and unambiguous: good government meant republican government. Thus there emerged an element of rigidity in American political thinking which has never disappeared and scarcely, if ever, been relaxed. The idea was so central and so fixed in the public mind, and the fear and distrust of other forms of government so great (perhaps inconsistently), that a guarantee of republican government to each state was written into the Constitution of 1787. More important, the idea has continued to dominate the American attitude toward politics and has been an important element in the formation of foreign policy. This identification of republican or democratic government with political right was a change both in substance and in intellectual outlook from pre-Revolutionary thought, and its consequences have been radical and far-reaching. Americans have regarded themselves, and have been regarded, as an essentially pragmatic people, but the preference for republicanism which crystallized at the time of the Revolution has constituted an ideological, doctrinaire element in their political outlook which has rarely been questioned. It may also be suggested that the ideological habit thus acquired has been extended to other areas and has become a major factor in American political thinking. Like republicanism, socialism, imperialism, and colonialism are all terms which have become stereotypes for Americans, frequently exercising a powerful ideological force at odds with our alleged pragmatism.

Thus I would suggest that the actual establishment of republican governments in 1776–1780 was not a radical change, but that its intellectual consequences were. What is puzzling is the reason for the sudden and virtually complete revolution in attitude. There was, of course, the influence of Paine's critique of monarchy in *Common Sense*. There was the fact that the potential

---

[8]Alexander Hamilton, James Madison, and John Jay, *The Federalist*, Benjamin Fletcher Wright, ed. (Cambridge, Mass., 1961): "The first question that offers itself is, whether the general form and aspect of the government be strictly republican? It is evident that no other form would be reconcilable with the genius of the people of America; with the fundamental principles of the Revolution; or with that honorable determination which animates every votary of freedom, to rest all our political experiments on the capacity of mankind for self-government." The Thirty-ninth Essay, p. 280.

counterinfluence of the losing Loyalists was virtually eliminated by their exodus during and after the war. There was the psychological necessity in the midst of war for an ideal that would inspire, sustain, and justify the participants and their actions. None of these reasons seems quite adequate, but the last was probably the most important. For the concept of republicanism, linked with the modified Lockeian ideals of the Declaration of Independence, provided a truly revolutionary doctrine with universal significance. Had the Revolution been merely a fight for independence, it would have remained a parochial affair of interest only to Great Britain and possibly to her continental rivals as convenient material for troublemaking. It was the genius of the Americans to see this, and once committed, to transform what might have remained a petty rebellion within the Empire into a symbol for the liberation of all mankind. Republicanism was an integral part of the symbol, and both contributed to and drew strength from it. The Revolution in its origins was a conservative movement to resist what were believed to be the pernicious innovations of George III and his Parliament. After 1776 it was, and was believed to be by its makers, truly radical.

V

The philosophy associated with republicanism and with the Revolution was also radical. It was the philosophy drawn from Locke's *Second Treatise,* but it was Lockeianism with an American gloss. A survey of Revolutionary literature both before and after 1776 reveals a number of modifications in and deviations from the original treatise which the Americans made as they used the great philosopher for their polemical purposes. The most familiar was the substitution in the Declaration of Independence of the *pursuit of happiness* for *property.* Another somewhat less familiar and certainly less clearly defined change was the American refusal to make a sharp distinction between the state of nature and civil society. These and other differences were apparent before the final break with England. The establishment of republican governments induced still other differences, of which the most important were an emphasis on equality, an intensification of individualism, and the identification of Locke with republicanism. The result was a subtle but substantial simplification and radicalization of the doctrine of the *Second Treatise.*

None of the separate changes was radical in the sense of being completely new or unrooted in the original *Treatise* or in the seventeenth-century body of thought upon which Locke drew. Nor was their sum more radical than the ideas set forth by the Levellers of the Civil War or their English heirs. Furthermore, the ideas were rooted in the colonial past and were therefore not unfamiliar. Yet the total complex was radical in implication and operation, especially when linked with the belief in, as well as the practice of, republicanism.

The most important of the changes was the American tendency to blur the differences which Locke had either stated or implied between the state of nature and the state of civil society. The concept of a state of nature was familiar to American thinkers before Locke wrote the *Second Treatise,* and, in American Puritan thought, it more closely resembled the Hobbesian version than the Lockeian. Americans emphasized the innate selfishness of man and the consequently hostile competition of a society in which men lived without the external restraints of law and government. Like Hobbes and Locke, they used the concept as a justification of government. What they did not do was to accept the idea that government could or would provide a completely impartial judge.[9] Their long experience in colonial self-government had taught them the inevitability of factious disputes and the difficulty if not the impossibility of securing impartial legislators and governors. Furthermore, the basis of their case against Parliamentary taxation and against the British theory of virtual representation had been the assumption that men in politics pursue their selfish interests and, in doing so, influence governmental policy. Accordingly, long before Madison's famous Tenth *Federalist,* Americans had questioned the likelihood, though not the ideal, of government as an impartial judge. Perhaps because their governments were already more republican than anything Locke knew, they were more acutely aware of "the people" as a collectivity of different and sometimes competitive groups and individuals than he was.

Similarly, because they expected men to behave selfishly in civil society, whether in or out of the government, they were also more rigorous than Locke was in attempting to insure that the rights men were entitled to in the state of nature were actually enjoyed in civil society. Locke had left the rights of the individual in an am-

---

[9]James Otis, "The Rights of the British Colonies Asserted and Proved" (1764), in Charles F. Mullett, ed., *Some Political Writings of James Otis* (Columbia, Mo., 1929), I, 54: "The necessity of a common, indifferent and impartial judge, makes all men seek one; though few find him in the *sovereign power,* of their respective states or any where else in *subordination* to it."

biguous if not precarious position. He stated that the consent of the majority could be taken for the consent of the individual and that, for generations other than the original contracting one, consent might be no more than tacit acceptance of the status quo. Locke also said that the original contractors might select hereditary monarchy or aristocracy as the form of government. Furthermore, the only kind of revolution Locke defined as a legitimate one was a revolution by the majority of the people. Thus, although he provided for protection of majority rights against monarchical or aristocratic infringement, he did not provide, either in the ordinary operation of government or through revolutionary means, for the protection of individual or minority rights against a majority or against a government supported by a majority. These rights would be secure only if the majority acted in accordance with the dictates of natural law. Locke seems to have assumed that it would so act, though he did not assume that individuals would always do so. The Americans were more consistent and more pessimistic. They did not assume that the behavior of groups of men, whether minorities or majorities, would be more virtuous than that of individuals. In the decade of constitutional protest before Lexington and Concord, the Americans found Locke very congenial and useful, for in the *Second Treatise* the problem of securing liberty is treated almost entirely in terms of the people against the government. Since the colonists were not represented in Parliament, their position was more or less that of Locke's "people," while Parliament's was that of Locke's "government." But the Americans did not ignore the fact that Parliament also represented the people of England and thus was, in another sense, a Lockeian "majority." James Wilson's case against Parliamentary authority over the colonies rested not only on the argument that the members of Parliament were not bound to Americans by mutual or identical interests, but on the assumption that members of Parliament *were* bound in this way to their English constituents and could therefore be held accountable by the latter.[10] It followed

---

[10]See the emphatic statement to this effect in Wilson's "On the Legislative Authority of the British Parliament" (1774), in Bird Wilson, ed., *The Works of the Honorable James Wilson, L.L.D.* . . . (Philadelphia, 1804), III, 211: "The interest of the representatives is the same with that of their constituents. Every measure, that is prejudicial to the nation, must be prejudicial to them and their posterity. They cannot betray their electors, without, at the same time, injuring themselves. They must join in bearing the burthen of every oppressive act; and participate in the happy effects of every wise and good law. Influenced by these considerations, they will seriously and with attention examine every measure proposed to them; they will behold it in every light, and extend their views to its most distant consequences."

that the interests of Americans and of Englishmen were different. By implication, therefore, the people of England were responsible for Parliamentary oppression, not just Parliament itself. Americans constituted a minority in the Empire of which they regarded themselves members, and their demand for legislative autonomy under the Crown was, in one sense, a means to protect their minority rights and interests.

Thus, in their collective relationship to Parliament, the colonists had had some experience with governmental policies which represented, from their point of view, a self-interested and dominant faction of the Empire. Far more important in determining their political attitudes, however, was their long experience in internal colonial politics. Long before the natural rights doctrine of the *Second Treatise* was generally accepted, the existence of factions had been recognized and deplored, and eventually accepted.[11] The Americans had advanced far beyond the point where they could view the problems of liberty and its opposite *simply* in terms of the people against the government. Their political ideas reflected not only the influence of Locke, but also the lessons of their greater experience in self-government. Accordingly, while Locke himself was ambiguous as to how and to what extent the rights of the individual or of minorities would be protected in civil society, his avowed disciples were not. They emphasized the necessity of securing the rights derived from the state of nature

---

[11]The development of American colonial thought on this subject is reflected in various of the Election Sermons given in New England in the latter part of the 17th century and the first two-thirds of the 18th. Note the variety as well as the similarity of views expressed in these three sermons: "Take heed of any Sinister Aims in whatsoever Laws do pass: Laws made to strengthen a particular separate Interest, never did Good, but Hurt to a Body-Politick: that which may serve the present turn, may in a little time prove more Mischievous, than ever it was Advantageous." (Samuel Willard, *The Character of a Good Ruler* . . . [Boston, 1694], 27.) "*Where there are Envyings and Strifes*, Animosities and Divisions, *there is Confusion and every Evil Work*. Where these Govern, if men can but Obtain their particular Ends and Desires, Advance their Party, Confound their Opposers, they are Content, what Prejudices soever the Publick Suffers: Then all the good Offices that make Society Valuable are Intercepted, and Fierceness, and Provocations, and Injuries Succeed." (Timothy Cutler, *The Firm Union of a People Represented* . . . [New London, 1717], 33.) "Every large community is constituted of a number of little societies, in which there will be different branches of business. These, whatever pains are taken to prevent it, will have their different connections, and form separate interests; it is vastly difficult for those who govern, to keep the balance so exactly poized that neither part may be injured; but much more, to prevent jealousies and suspicions that things are carried by favor and affection." (Andrew Eliot, *A Sermon Preached before His Excellency Francis Bernard* . . . [Boston, 1765], 14.)

against both a monarch and a legislative majority in a civil society. The fear of majority oppression, which has been so persistent and pervasive a factor in American politics, was thus firmly rooted in colonial experience and in the movement of protest which resulted in revolution and independence. When combined with another major modification in the original Locke, this position led the Revolutionists to a radical individualism.

This modification was the substitution of the *pursuit of happiness* for *property* in the Lockeian trilogy of rights. The substitution was not a mere linguistic one made in the Declaration of Independence for rhetorical effect. The colonists had included happiness as one of the natural and fundamental rights in polemical literature of the preceding decade. John Dickinson, for example, had gone so far as to suggest that the constitutionality of Parliamentary statutes be measured by their tendency to make the people of America happy.[12] So indefinite a concept was obviously impossible as a legal test, but the idea of happiness as an end of government was firmly rooted in colonial attitudes before 1776. It was, furthermore, a far more individualistic end than the protection of property.[13] Property was a tangible, objective ele-

---

[12]See John Dickinson, *The Political Writings of John Dickinson* . . . (Wilmington, Del., 1801), I, 332, 395.

[13]I do not mean to imply that the exclusion of *property* from the Declaration of Independence meant that Americans had ceased to regard it as a natural right to be secured by government. They had not; many of them probably continued to regard it as superior or prior to that of the pursuit of happiness, while the majority saw no conflict between the two. The line of reasoning to which I would call attention is exemplified in John Dickinson's *An Address to the Committee of Correspondence in Barbados* (Philadelphia, 1766), and in his *Letters from a Farmer in Pennsylvania to the Inhabitants of the British Colonies* (Boston, 1768). From the former: "KINGS or parliaments could not *give* the *rights essential to happiness,* as you confess those invaded by the Stamp Act to be. We claim them from a higher source—from the King of kings, and Lord of all the earth. . . . It would be an insult on the divine Majesty to say, that he has given or allowed any man or body of men a *right to make me miserable.* If no man or body of men has *such a right,* I have a *right to be happy.* If there can be no happiness without freedom, I have a *right to be free.* If I cannot enjoy freedom without security of property, I have a *right to be thus secured.*" pp. 4–5. From the *Letters from a Farmer:* "Let these truths be indelibly impressed on our minds—that we cannot be happy without being free—that we cannot be free, without being secure in our property—that we cannot be secure in our property, if, without our consent, others may, as by right, take it away—that taxes imposed on us by Parliament, do thus take it away. . . ." p. 137. Dickinson is here clearly placing happiness as a right logically prior to property and even to liberty, which stand in relation to it as means to end. James Wilson also emphasized happiness rather than property, stating that, "the happiness of the society is the *first* law of every government." Wilson, *Works,* III, 206.

By placing the *pursuit of happiness* in the Declaration, and omitting

ment, while happiness was a subjective goal dependent on individual interpretation. Also, the assertion of a right to happiness had strong equalitarian implications. The concept of property as a right to be protected and fostered by government may be and has been interpreted to mean the protection of property already vested in individuals. It may therefore mean the preservation of the *status quo,* and the *status quo* may be an aristocratic one. This seems to have been Locke's intention, for there is nothing in the *Second Treatise* to suggest that he had an economic or social revolution in mind. The idea of the pursuit of happiness necessarily had both dynamic and equalitarian implications, and these have played a substantial role in American politics. The situation at the time of the Revolution was not such as to lead to an explosive implementation of these implications, but the implications were there, and to some extent recognized and acted upon. Since happiness is a subjective state, no individual can decide for another what will promote his happiness. If happiness is really an end of government, and if all men have by nature an equal right to the pursuit of it, then it follows logically that every man should have a voice in the determination of public policy. Thus the two American modifications—the emphasis on happiness rather than property, and the greater concern for the actual implementation of rights in civil society—led to a democratization of Locke as well as to an unequivocal individualism.

The relationship between the ideal of individual happiness and the recognition of factions in society was an important one. As I have indicated before, the Americans had become thoroughly familiar with the existence and operation of factious divisions in society, and they had come to accept with considerable equanimity the fact that self-interest was a primary political motive. They therefore could not, as Locke for the most part did, think and write of "the people" as a corporate whole more or less distinct from the government. Such a dichotomy was not absent from their thought, but because they had already had experience with a relatively high degree of representative government, they were

property, Jefferson gave official sanction to these views. If the Declaration had lapsed into obscurity, this departure from Locke's trilogy might not have been particularly important, except for the historical record. But the Declaration did not become an historian's document merely. It became an ideological force, and this helped to make Jefferson's substitution operative in actual political life. Of course one may also raise the question whether the Declaration would have had the influence that it has had, if the substitution had not been made. Needless to say, the omission of *property* from the Declaration did not keep it from becoming a dominant, if not the dominant, right during certain periods of United States history.

aware of government as a tool of the stronger faction among the people. This realistic or pessimistic attitude toward human nature has come to be associated with conservatism, but it had a logical connection with the radical implications of the Declaration of Independence. It embodied the American view that the same defects of human nature which Locke and Hobbes had used to explain the transition from the state of nature to civil society would still jeopardize the ends for which government was instituted. The connection was succinctly stated in Jefferson's First Inaugural Address: "Some times it is said that Man cannot be trusted with the government of himself. Can he then be trusted with the government of others? Or have we found angels in the form of kings to govern him?"[14] In other words, the imperfection of man was itself an argument for republican government. By logical extension, it was also an argument for a democratic republic. For if all men were equally entitled to the rights of life, liberty, and the pursuit of happiness, and if self-interest was a universal characteristic of human nature, then all men must be given the opportunity of defending their rights against encroachment by others. Thus, although the colonists had not set out with the intention of establishing republicanism, once they had done so, as a corollary of independence, the pessimistic strain in their thought provided ideological reinforcement for practical accomplishment. Similarly, the establishment of republican governments served to accentuate the equalitarian and individualistic content of their official philosophy.

This philosophy was one of radical individualism, and it was accepted, I think, by the majority of Americans at the time, including many of those who are frequently regarded as conservatives. Without abandoning completely the concept of a common good or public interest or justice, they tended to regard the pursuit of self-interest as legitimate and sought primarily to avoid an overwhelming concentration of power behind a single interest, whether it be upper or lower class, urban, rural, northern, southern, or other. It was the refusal of Thomas Paine and Alexander Hamilton to accept this individualism which made both of them alien to the prevailing political attitude. Paine was a radical democrat, but he could not stomach the rough and tumble politics of his colleagues in Pennsylvania, who pursued what he regarded as selfish interests with little restraint. Similarly, Hamilton could not recognize opposition to his policies as legitimate because he

---

[14]Ford, ed., *Works of Jefferson*, IX, 196.

interpreted the national interest in terms of corporate greatness, while his opponents interpreted it in terms of individual satisfaction. Paine and Hamilton, therefore, were both conservative in their attitude toward the proper ends of government and the proper political behavior of individual citizens. The individualism which they rejected was not new in theory. It was clearly explicit in *The Leviathan*, present though somewhat obscured in the *Second Treatise*, and had been an increasing element in both colonial thought and practice. With the coming of the Revolution it became manifestly operative, and has continued to exert a decisive influence in American politics.

This individualism, rooted in colonial experience but transformed by the break with Britain and the establishment of republican governments, had ramifications which influenced the nature of our political tradition and served further to set it apart from that of the mother country. These ramifications, though some of them did not become apparent until much later, help to illuminate the radical effects of the Revolution.

As I have suggested in the preceding pages, the individualism of the early republic was associated with equalitarianism in civil society as well as in the state of nature. Of this, the Revolutionists were themselves aware. They were less aware of the relativistic implications of the theory summarized in the Declaration, and of the extent to which that theory gave philosophical justification to the egoism which they so frequently and habitually deplored, but which they accepted as an ordinary ingredient of politics. The relativism of the Declaration can be summarized briefly. Two of the central rights, to which all men are entitled, are not amenable to objective definition or delimitation. The *liberty* of the trilogy was to some extent defined in the specific terms of traditional procedural liberties associated with the British constitution or common law, and in the newer substantive terms of freedom of speech, press, and religion. There were also attempts, by Jefferson and Paine, for example, to classify rights into primary and secondary categories, the latter being subject to social or political regulation. Except for the allegedly absolute rights of the first order, a man's liberty was commonly said to extend so far as it did not interfere with or jeopardize the similar liberties of other men. This sounds like a good enough common-sense definition. However, the Revolutionary American conception of society as composed of selfish individuals and groups whose interests would frequently be in conflict, suggests the impossibility of using that common-sense definition in practice with any degree of precision. If, that is to say, men's interests habitually and *normally* come into conflict, then this formula is not altogether relevant or applicable. Somewhat the same thing is true of the third right in the trilogy, the pursuit of happiness. It is an even more subjective right than liberty. And unless one assumes a very harmonious society, the happiness of different individuals are likely to come in conflict with each other. If all individuals possess these rights equally, and if they are an integral end of government, then there is no logical criterion by which such conflicts can be adjudicated. There is no way to define justice objectively, and there is great difficulty in defining the substantive common good objectively, except perhaps in some obvious crisis of national preservation. What is left is political relativism, combined with a philosophy of natural rights which tended to provide a justification of political and ethical egoism.

I do not think the men of the Revolution were fully aware of the trend of their thought. They continued to think in terms of justice and the general welfare and to deplore man's tendency toward self-interest and bias. Their hostility to parties is in itself an indication of their belief in a common good to which all men owed their allegiance. Nevertheless, the relativism implicit in natural rights doctrine had undermined the operative force of the common good by making it difficult if not impossible to define. This difficulty of defining justice or the common interest would, paradoxically and ironically, encourage the propensity to use ideological stereotypes in political debate.

Had the Americans been imbued with a strong sense of nationalism, or had their security not been so easily achieved by the happy windfall of Louisiana and the physical barrier of the Atlantic Ocean, this relativism might have been balanced by a concern for national defense or perhaps national glory. As it was, the same individualism which produced the relativism contributed to the really profound inclination toward isolation and withdrawal from international affairs. It is perhaps ironical that the Declaration of Independence, written partly for the purpose of securing foreign aid, should have had so strong an influence in the direction of concentration on domestic affairs. Yet I think it did. If the primary function of government is believed to be the protection of individual rights, and if by the grace of history and geography this can be done in the absence of serious and continuous threats from abroad, then it is natural that the people involved should be primarily occupied with immediate and domestic concerns. If, furthermore, they have another ocean to aim at, with nothing much in between but a few savages, and if they regard themselves as the world's torchbearers for a great ideal, whatever ambitions they may have for national and imperial greatness may be satisfied with a minimum awareness of or involvement in the affairs of other nations. There was very little to keep Americans constantly aware of one of the traditional functions of statehood—defense against external danger. This fact, plus the nature of our federal system, inhibited the emergence of a sense of national interest transcendent of individual, group, and sectional interests which would supply content for the concept of the common good. There was thus no strong compensatory factor, such as the mystique of the British Empire, to offset the relativism and individualism implicit in Revolutionary doctrine.

These factors, combined with the Revolutionary acceptance of egoism, gradually brought about a major divergence in the American attitude toward politics from the heritage which the colonists had shared with the home country. At the time of the Revolution, in America as in Britain, politics was an occupation regarded with respect and engaged in by men of distinguished qualities. It was, to use modern sociological terminology, a prestige occupation. To be sure, this condition was due in part to the property qualifications for officeholding, in some colonies and states considerably stiffer than those for voting. But far more important, both ambition and a sense of responsibility drew men of wealth and learning into colonial, state, and federal office. It was Jefferson's intention and hope that his scheme of education would, among other things, provide a reservoir of political leaders —a kind of aristocracy of talent. This concept of aristocratic leadership was undermined in a number of ways. Historically as well as philosophically, it had been linked with belief in an objective good, and it was this link which the idea of happiness as an end of government tended to negate. For if individual happiness—or self-interest—is an end of government, then one man's opinion is as good as another. Thus, though the concept of the public good as a composite of individual and group interests does not require the rejection of wisdom and virtue as a qualification for the exercise of political authority, it does promote a powerful alternative—identity of opinion and interest, or the willingness to give the voter what he wants. To be sure, this was not a peculiarly American phenomenon, as Burke's experience with the electors of Bristol indicates. Furthermore, there was a touch of the Burkeian theory of representation in that of the authors of the Constitution, especially in their attitude toward the Senate. Nevertheless, the realism concerning political motivation and behavior which characterized the American attitude, as it was summarized in the Tenth *Federalist,* expressed something very close to a theory of pressure group politics. And it is this kind of politics which, by and large, has dominated the American tradition. However, Americans have never been completely comfortable with it, and their uneasiness has produced a reliable scapegoat. At the time of the Revolution, dissatisfaction found expression and release in the almost universal dislike and distrust of parties, a tribute to the lost ideal of a transcendent public good. Gradually, this antipathy was extended to the men who manned and ran the parties, the politicians. There has thus been a peculiar schizophrenia in the American political mind. On the one hand, we have engaged in pressure and partisan politics continuously and with vigor; on the other, we despise the men who act as brokers to carry out our demands, whether honestly or corruptly. Even now, a sure way of winning popular approval is to create the image that one is not a politician. Something of the same attitude is involved in the American reaction to the word and the fact of bipartisanship; it gives a comfortable sense of satisfied virtue. This distrust and contempt for politicians is no doubt partially attributable to the personal corruption of individuals, but it has more profound causes, and one of these is the somewhat obscurely felt dissatisfaction with the relativism and its consequent pressure group politics which have as their basis the radical individualism of the Declaration of Independence.

VI

Equally radical was the Revolution's culmination, the creation and adoption of the Constitution of 1787. There had been federations of states before, both in ancient and modern times, and the idea of a central government had become familiar in America with the Albany Plan, the first two Continental Congresses, and the Articles of Confederation. What was new was the direct control over the central government exercised by the electorate, the relative independence of that government with respect to the governments of the constituent states, and its direct authority over the individual citizens of those states. This was a government so new that, as its critics gibed, it lacked a name. It was, in the strict meaning of the word, radical.

Its opponents perceived this fact from the very beginning, and both the spirit and substance of their polemics provide evidence of a typically conservative stance. They argued that the Philadelphia Convention had gone too far, that they had exceeded their instructions, that there was no necessity for an entirely new frame of government, and that a little patching up of the Articles of Confederation would have been sufficient. They pointed out that what was proposed had never been done before and bewailed the loss of resistance to innovation which the Revolution itself had induced in the people. They paraded a succession of imaginary horribles, and they said that the authors of the Constitution had based their scheme of government on too optimistic a view of human nature. Furthermore, they saw quite clearly that the Constitution, if adopted, would bring about a new kind of politics in which large-scale organization would be a major factor, and they identified the old, familiar, personal politics with liberty and responsible government. Most important and most significant, they denied that the principle and practice of republicanism could be made operative over the area and population then embraced by the thirteen separate states. Their position, both with respect to the *status quo* of 1776–87 and with that of the pre-Revolutionary experience of self-government, was the conservative one in the great debate over ratification.[15]

It was the Founding Fathers who were the true radicals. In the very first number of *The Federalist,* Hamilton struck a radical stance when he stated that the question for decision was whether mankind could determine its government by deliberate choice or must continue to be subject to the forces of accident and chance.[16] Indeed, the whole idea of drafting a constitution for an entire nation and then submitting it to conventions chosen by the people for ratification or rejection was radical in the extreme, though the example of Massachusetts had provided a precedent for a similar procedure on a much smaller scale. Scholars may argue until doomsday as to whether the Constitution was democratic or not, but they are less likely to argue as to whether it was a new departure in political institutions. It must rank with the establishment of republican government and the philosophy of the Declaration of Independence as one of the great and radical achievements of the Revolution.

---

[15]This interpretation is presented at some length in my article, "Men of Little Faith: The Anti-Federalists on the Nature of Representative Government," *William and Mary Quarterly,* 3d Ser., XII (1955), 3–43.

[16]Hamilton, Madison, and Jay, *The Federalist,* Wright, ed., 89.

VII

The establishment of a new nation, the initiation of the first great modern experiment in republican government, the combination of this experiment with an entirely new kind of federalism, the crystallization in operative form of a political philosophy of individualism and equality—these were the results of the American Revolution. Together with the Revolutionary experience itself, they gave decisive shape to the American political tradition and, in particular, operated to differentiate it from that of the mother country and from those of the older British Commonwealths which won their independence in a later period and without revolution. The relatively short period of intensive opposition and resistance to imperial impositions, the realistic recognition of egoism as a general cause of these, the emphasis in the Declaration on the rights of the individual combined to fix in the American mind an ineradicable fear and distrust of government and government officials, even when popularly elected. This general fear was more profound and more enduring than the specific fear of the executive which stemmed from colonial experience with nonelective governors, and helped to sustain the system of separation of powers, which was also rooted in colonial institutions. Later, the individualist relativism implicit in the Declaration. added to this recognition of egoism, accentuated the distrust of politicians, and reduced the prestige of government as a career. To fear and distrust of government, there was thus added contempt. The American attitude toward government as a necessary evil (and probably more evil than necessary) goes back to the Revolution. It has, perhaps paradoxically, continued to find expression in the strong localist conservatism which helped precipitate the Revolution and later provided much of the opposition to the Constitution. Our Revolutionary experience also both embodied and encouraged that peculiar combination of pragmatism and appeal to ideological principles which has characterized American political thinking. The men of 1776 did not set out to establish republicanism, but once they had done so as a means of securing the rights of life, liberty, and the pursuit of happiness, republicanism itself became a principle of political right. So it has been with later concepts. We have not asked only whether policies would or would not contribute to the realization of these rights; we have asked whether the policies were democratic or antidemocratic, socialist or laissez-faire. Our political tradition has involved the interaction of pragmatic and ideological attitudes and thus has reflected the spirit of 1776.

That spirit was not a particularly radical one, certainly not when compared with that of the French Revolution, the Soviet Revolution of 1917, or the nationalist revolutions of the present time. It had a profoundly conservative aspect, and the radicalism it involved was of a very sober variety. Apart from the recent revival of conservatism and the consequent desire to establish its roots in the political foundation of the nation, there are excellent reasons for regarding the American Revolution as conservative—at least in some respects.

It was a limited revolution, and it was primarily a political movement. There were some social and economic repercussions, but there was no concerted, deliberate attempt at wholesale reconstruction of society or of the habits and everyday lives of the people. There was no American Robespierre or Lenin; Thomas Paine, who looked like a radical in the American context, was imprisoned in France because of the moderate position he took there. The American leaders, even while initiating radical changes, acted with sobriety and, with some exceptions, exhibited a political sophistication based on experience in politics other than as revolutionists.

Most important of all, the Revolution began as a movement of conservative protest, and none of its results represented a total break with the colonial past. Independence had been preceded by a long enjoyment of considerable autonomy; long before Paul Revere ordered lanterns hung in the Old North Church, John Winthrop had mounted a cannon on Beacon Hill to repel any British attempt to seize the Charter of the Colony. Before Thomas Paine ridiculed the British Monarchy in *Common Sense*, the colonists had put a bridle on their governors. The ideas expressed in the second paragraph of the Declaration of Independence were not quite so firmly rooted in colonial experience, and the fact of their formal acceptance gave them an operative force they had previously lacked. But if we are to believe Thomas Jefferson, even they had become embedded in the American mind. The one thing which was most truly radical was the new federalism of the Constitution of 1787. Even it had been preceded by the lesser authority of the Empire and the experience of intercolonial co-operation preceding the war and under the Articles of Confederation. And it was combined with a structure of government, many of whose elements were familiar, because they, too, were rooted in colonial institutions.

So it seems to me that we must conclude that the American Revolution was partly radical and partly conservative. If I may borrow a figure from the great Greek so despised by the author of the Declaration of Independence, the character of the Revolution was the character of the men who made it writ large.[17] Their attitude toward the past was selective. Part of it they wished to preserve, part of it they wished to abandon. They were quite self-conscious about the newness of their enterprise and referred to it frequently as an experiment, but they never had the slightest inclination to repudiate the whole of their British heritage or of their colonial past. They had some fine old bricks to start with, and they knew it. Nevertheless, what they designed and partly built from these bricks was not Georgian. It was American, and they knew that too.

[17]In a letter to John Adams in 1814, Jefferson criticized *The Republic* severely and speculated as to the reasons for Plato's reputation. His general estimate of the great philosopher is suggested by these references scattered throughout a lengthy passage: "the whimsies, the puerilities, and unintelligible jargon of this work," "nonsense," "foggy mind;" he also concluded that Plato's dialogues "are libels on Socrates." Jefferson to John Adams, July 5, 1814, in Ford, ed., *Works of Jefferson*, XI, 396–398.

THE REVOLUTION
IN PRACTICE

———— ◆ ————

Many of the more important tangible results of the application of the Revolutionary ideals described in the last two articles came well after the Revolutionary era, in the closing years of the eighteenth and in the early decades of the nineteenth cenutry. Two more immediate concrete results of the Revolution that were genuinely radical are discussed in the next two selections. The first describes the process by which the Revolution led to a broadening of the base of popular political participation by drawing many men of modest wealth into politics and assesses the long-range significance of that development. The second article describes the constitution-making process in the states, beginning in 1776. It shows how the political community in Massachusetts discovered and worked out a procedure by which the traditional notion of the people as constituent power could be put into practical effect and analyzes the importance of that novel institutional achievement in Western political development. By calling attention to the high seriousness with which Americans approached the task of constitution-making, the second selection also testifies to the continuing importance of constitutionalism to the Revolution after the Declaration of Independence.

JACKSON TURNER MAIN (b. 1917) is a member of the Department of History at the State University of New York at Stony Brook; R. R. PALMER (b. 1909) is an administrative officer at Princeton University.

Government by the People:
The American Revolution and the
Democratization of the Legislatures

JACKSON TURNER MAIN

An article with "democracy" in its title, these days, must account for itself. This essay holds that few colonials in British North America believed in a government by the people, and that they were content to be ruled by local elites; but that during the Revolution two interacting developments occurred simultaneously: ordinary citizens increasingly took part in politics, and American political theorists began to defend popular government. The ideological shift can be traced most easily in the newspapers, while evidence for the change in the structure of power will be found in the make-up of the lower houses during the revolutionary years.

Truly democratic ideas, defending a concentration of power in the hands of the people, are difficult to find prior to about 1774. Most articulate colonials accepted the Whig theory in which a modicum of democracy was balanced by equal parts of aristocracy and monarchy. An unchecked democracy was uniformly condemned.[1] For example, a contributor to the *Newport Mercury* in 1764 felt that when a state was in its infancy, "when its members are few and virtuous, and united together by some peculiar ideas of freedom or religion; the whole power may be lodged with the people, and the government be purely democratical"; but when the state had matured, power must be removed from popular control because history demonstrated that the people "have been incapable, collectively, of acting with any degree of moderation or wisdom."[2] Therefore while colonial theorists

---

Reprinted with permission from *The William and Mary Quarterly*, 3rd ser., XXIII (July, 1966), 391–407.

[1] See Richard Buel, Jr., "Democracy and the American Revolution: A Frame of Reference," *William and Mary Quarterly*, XXI (1964), 165–190.

[2] "Z. Y.," April 23, 1764. Other characteristic newspaper articles praising a balanced government and disparaging a democratic one are, "A Son of Liberty," *Providence Gazette, and Country Journal*, October 26, 1771; *Pennsylvania Chronicle, and Universal Advertiser* (Philadelphia), August 29, September 26, 1768, August 14, 1769; *New-York Gazette: and the Weekly*

recognized the need for some democratic element in the government, they did not intend that the ordinary people—the *demos*—should participate. The poorer men were not allowed to vote at all, and that part of the populace which did vote was expected to elect the better sort of people to represent them. "Fabricus" defended the "democratic principle," warned that "liberty, when once lost, is scarce ever recovered," and declared that laws were "made for the people, and not people for the laws." But he did not propose that ordinary citizens should govern. Rather, "it is right that men of *birth and fortune,* in every government that is free, should be invested with power, and enjoy higher honours than the people."[3] According to William Smith of New York, offices should be held by "the better Class of People" in order that they might introduce that "Spirit of Subordination essential to good Government."[4] A Marylander urged that members of the Assembly should be "ABLE in ESTATE, ABLE in KNOWLEDGE AND LEARNING," and mourned that so many "little upstart insignificant Pretenders" tried to obtain an office. "The *Creature* that is able to keep a little Shop, rate the Price of an Ell of Osnabrigs, or, at most, to judge of the Quality of a Leaf of Tobacco" was not a fit statesman, regardless of his own opinion.[5] So also in South Carolina, where William Henry Drayton warned the artisans that mechanical ability did not entitle them to hold office.[6] This conviction that most men were incompetent to rule, and that the elite should govern for them, proved a vital element in Whig thought and was its most antidemocratic quality. The assumption was almost never openly challenged during the colonial period.

Whether the majority whose capacity was thus maligned accepted the insulting assumption is another question. They were not asked, and as they were unable to speak or write on the subject, their opinions are uncertain. But the voters themselves seem to have adhered, in practice at least, to the traditional view, for when the people were asked to choose their representatives they seldom elected common farmers and artisans. Instead they put their trust in men of the upper class. In the colonies as a whole, about 30 per cent of the adult white men owned property

Mercury, April 23, May 14, 1770; Purdie and Dixon's *Virginia Gazette* (Williamsburg), October 27, 1768; *Connecticut Journal* (New Haven), March 17, 1769; *Newport Mercury,* November 21, 1763.

[3]Rind's *Va. Gazette* (Williamsburg), June 9, 1768.

[4]December 30, 1768, in *Journal of the Legislative Council of the Colony of New-York . . . 1743 . . . 1775* (Albany, 1861).

[5]*Maryland Gazette* (Annapolis), December 3, 1767.

[6]*South Carolina Gazette* (Charleston), September 21, 1769.

worth £500 or more. About two thirds of these colonials of means had property worth £500 to £2,000; their economic status is here called *moderate*. The other third were worth over £2,000. Those worth £2,000 to £5,000 are called *well-to-do,* and those whose property was valued at more than £5,000 are called *wealthy.*[7] The overwhelming majority of the representatives belonged to that ten per cent who were well-to-do or wealthy. Government may have been for the people, but it was not administered by them. For evidence we turn to the legislatures of New Hampshire, New York, New Jersey, Maryland, Virginia, and South Carolina.

In 1765 New Hampshire elected thirty-four men to its House of Representatives.[8] Practically all of them lived within a few miles of the coast; the frontier settlements could not yet send deputies, and the Merrimack Valley towns in the south-central part of the colony, though populous, were allotted only seven. New Hampshire was not a rich colony. Most of its inhabitants were small farmers with property enough for an adequate living but no more. There were a few large agricultural estates, and the Portsmouth area had developed a prosperous commerce which supported some wealthy merchants and professional men; but judging from probate records not more than one man in forty was well-to-do, and true wealth was very rare. Merchants, professional men, and the like comprised about one tenth of the total population, though in Portsmouth, obviously, the proportion was much larger. Probably at least two thirds of the inhabitants were farmers or farm laborers and one in ten was an artisan. But New Hampshire voters did not call on farmers or men of average property to represent them. Only about one third of the representatives in the 1765 House were yeomen. Merchants and lawyers were just as numerous, and the rest followed a variety of occupations: there were four doctors and several millers and manufacturers. One third of the delegates were wealthy men and more than two thirds were at least well-to-do. The relatively small upper class of the colony, concentrated in the southeast, furnished ten of the members. They did not, of course, constitute a majority, and the family background of most of the representatives, like that

---

[7] A discussion of the distribution of property and income is contained in Jackson Turner Main, *The Social Structure of Revolutionary America* (Princeton, 1965).

[8] Biographical information is reasonably complete for 30 of the 34. Genealogies and town histories were the principal sources. The *New Hampshire Provincial and State Papers* contain much useful information, especially probate records, and the *New England Historical and Genealogical Register* is valuable.

of most colonials, was undistinguished. Probably nearly one half had acquired more property and prestige than their parents. In another age New Hampshire's lower house would have been considered democratic—compared with England's House of Commons it certainly was—but this was a new society, and the voters preferred the prosperous urban upper class and the more substantial farmers.

New York was a much richer colony than New Hampshire. Although most of its population were small farmers and tenants, there were many large landed estates and New York City was incomparably wealthier than Portsmouth. In general the west bank of the Hudson and the northern frontier were usually controlled by the yeomanry, as was Suffolk County on Long Island, but the east bank from Albany to the City was dominated by great "manor lords" and merchants. The great landowners and the merchants held almost all of the twenty-eight seats in the Assembly.[9] In 1769 the voters elected only seven farmers. Five others including Frederick Philipse and Pierre Van Cortland, the wealthy manor lords from Westchester, were owners of large tenanted estates. But a majority of New York's legislators were townspeople. Merchants were almost as numerous as farmers, and together with lawyers they furnished one half of the membership. The legislators were no more representative in their property than in their occupation. At most, five men, and probably fewer, belonged to the middle class of moderate means. At least 43 per cent were wealthy and an equal number were well-to-do. The members' social background was also exceptional. Ten came from the colony's foremost families who had, for the times, a distinguished ancestry, and two thirds or more were born of well-to-do parents. Taken as a whole the legislators, far from reflecting New York's social structure, had either always belonged to or had successfully entered the colony's economic and social upper class.

New Jersey's Assembly was even smaller than that of New York. The body chosen in 1761, and which sat until 1769, contained but twenty men.[10] Half of these represented the East

[9]Especially important for New York biographies are the volumes of wills included among the *Collections* of the New York Historical Society, and the *New York Biographical Record*.

[10]In 1769 four new members were added, and six more were chosen in 1772. The *New Jersey Archives* include several volumes of wills. Tax records, the earliest of which date from 1773, supply data on real estate but not on nonfarm property. They have been microfilmed from originals in the New Jersey State Library, Trenton.

Jersey counties (near New York City) which were in general occupied by small farmers, but only three of the ten members came from that class. The others were merchants, lawyers, and large proprietors. Although several of these had started as yeomen they had all acquired large properties. West Jersey, which had a greater number of sizable landed estates, especially in the Delaware Valley region, sent the same sort of men as did East Jersey: three farmers, an equal number of large landowners, and an even larger number of prosperous townsmen, some of whom also owned valuable real estate. Merchants and lawyers made up one half of the membership. As usual, a considerable proportion—perhaps forty per cent—were self-made men, but the colony's prominent old families furnished at least 30 per cent of the representatives. Four out of five members were either well-to-do or wealthy.

In contrast to the legislatures of New Hampshire, New York, and New Jersey, Maryland's House of Delegates was a large body and one dominated by the agricultural interest. Like its northern equivalents, however, its members belonged to the upper class of the colony—in Maryland, the planter aristocracy. The 1765 House supposedly contained over sixty members, but only fifty-four appear in the records.[11] About one half of these came from the Eastern Shore, an almost entirely rural area. Except for Col. Thomas Cresap who lived on Maryland's small frontier, the remainder came from the Potomac River and western Chesapeake Bay counties, where agriculture was the principal occupation but where a number of towns also existed. About one sixth of the Delegates belonged to the yeoman farmer class. Most of these lived on the Eastern Shore. Incidentally they did not vote with the antiproprietary, or "popular," party, but rather followed some of the great planters in the conservative "court" party. As in the northern colonies, a number of the Delegates were *nouveaux riches,* but in Maryland's stable and primarily "Tidewater" society, fewer than one fifth had surpassed their parents in wealth. The overwhelming majority came from the lesser or the great planter class, and probably one third belonged to the colony's elite families. Four fifths were well-to-do or wealthy. Lawyers and merchants (among whom were several of the self-made men) furnished about one sixth of the principally rural membership.

Virginia's Burgesses resembled Maryland's Delegates, but they

---

[11]The *Maryland Historical Magazine* contains a great deal of biographical data. Essential are the unpublished tax lists in the Maryland State Archives, Annapolis, and the Maryland Historical Society, Baltimore.

were even richer and of even more distinguished ancestry. The Old Dominion's much larger west helped to make the House of Burgesses twice as large a body, with 122 members in 1773.[12] Small property holders, though they formed a great majority of the voters, held only one out of six seats. Half of the Burgesses were wealthy and four fifths were at least well-to-do. Merchants and lawyers contributed one fifth of the members, much more than their proper share, but most of them were also large landholders and the legislature was firmly in control of the great planters. Indeed the median property owned was 1,800 acres and 40 slaves. Virginia's social structure was quite fluid, especially in the newly-settled areas, but between five sixths and seven eighths of the delegates had inherited their property. A roll call of the Burgesses would recite the names of most of the colony's elite families, who held nearly one half of the seats.

The planters of South Carolina, unlike the Virginians, were unwilling to grant representation to the upcountry, and its House of Commons was an exclusively eastern body.[13] The colony was newer and its society may have been more fluid, for in 1765 between 20 and 40 per cent of the representatives were self-made men. The legislature also differed from its southern equivalents in Maryland and Virginia in that nearly half of its members were merchants, lawyers, or doctors. But these figures are deceptive, for in reality most of these men were also great landowners, as were almost all of the representatives; and prominent old families contributed one half of the members of the House. All were at least well-to-do and over two thirds were wealthy. The rich planters of South Carolina's coastal parishes held a monopoly of power in the Assembly.

These six legislatures, from New Hampshire to South Carolina, shared the same qualities. Although farmers and artisans comprised probably between two thirds and three fourths of the voters in the six colonies, they seldom selected men from their own ranks to represent them. Not more than one out of five representatives were of that class. Fully one third were merchants

---

[12]The 1773 legislature was chosen for study because the tax records of 1782, which are the earliest available, would be most nearly valid in determining the property of the members. The Virginia State Library, Richmond, contains the tax records as well as a remarkable collection of local records on microfilm. E. G. Swem, comp., *Virginia Historical Index* (Roanoke, 1934–1936), I–II, is useful.

[13]The *South Carolina Historical Magazine* is essential, as is Emily Bellinger Reynolds and Joan Reynolds Faunt, eds., *Biographical Directory of the Senate of South Carolina* 1776–1964 (Columbia, 1964). There are some quit rent and probate records in the State Archives building at Columbia.

and lawyers or other professionals, and most of the rest were large landowners. Although only about 10 per cent of the colonials were well-to-do or wealthy, this economic elite furnished at least 85 per cent of the assemblymen. The mobile character of colonial society meant that perhaps 30 per cent had achieved their high status by their own efforts; but an even larger percentage were from prominent, long-established families.

Collectively these "representatives of the people" comprised not a cross section of the electorate but a segment of the upper class. Although the colonials cherished the democratic branch of their governments, and although a majority may have hoped to make the lower house all powerful, they did not yet conceive that the *demos* should actually govern. The idea of a government by as well as for the people was a product of the Revolution. It should be noted here that Rhode Island and Connecticut are exceptions to this general pattern, though the upper house of Connecticut was composed entirely of well-to-do men. As for Massachusetts, the number of representatives with moderate properties exceeded that in the royal and proprietary colonies; but the Massachusetts legislature was still controlled by the well-to-do. Of the 117 men in the House in 1765, at least fifty-six were not farmers and thirteen were large landowners; of the remaining forty-eight, thirty-seven were ordinary farmers and the occupations of eleven are unknown. Among those representatives whose economic status can be discovered (about nine tenths), well over one half were well-to-do or wealthy and two fifths of these had inherited their property.

Widespread popular participation in politics began during 1774 with the various provincial congresses and other extralegal organizations. Although the majority of these bodies seem to have been made up of men of standing, both artisans and farmers appeared in greater numbers than they had in the colonial legislatures. There were several reasons for this. Whereas heretofore the more recently settled areas of most colonies had been underrepresented—at times seriously so—the legal prohibitions on their sending representatives to the colonial assemblies did not apply to the extralegal congresses, and they chose delegates when they wished. Moreover the congresses were much larger than the colonial assemblies, and consequently the over-all number of men who could be elected was greatly increased. For instance, South Carolina's House of Commons contained forty-eight men in 1772, but almost twice that number attended the first Provincial Congress in December 1774 and four times as many were present in January 1775. By 1775 the western districts were sending about one third of the members. Similarly, nothing now prevented New Hampshire's country villages from choosing representatives, and they seized the opportunity. By the time the fourth Provincial Congress met in New Hampshire, four times as many men attended as had been admitted to the 1773 legislature, and nearly one half of them came from the inland counties.

Perhaps an even more important reason for the greater participation in politics by men of moderate means than simply the enlarged and broadened membership of the Provincial Congresses was that the interior areas often contained no real upper class. They had no choice but to send men of moderate property. Furthermore, many men of the upper classes who had previously held political power were not sympathetic with the resistance movement and either withdrew from politics or did not participate in the extralegal Congresses. At the same time events thrust new men forward, as for example in Charleston where the artisans became increasingly active. As the Revolution ran its course, many new men came to fill the much larger number of civil offices, and new men won fame in battle. These developments were quickly reflected in the composition of the legislatures, and by the time the war ended the legislatures were far different bodies from what they had been in colonial days. At the same time democratic ideas spread rapidly, justifying and encouraging the new order.[14]

With the overthrow of royal government, the previously unrepresented New Hampshire villages hastened to choose representatives to the state legislature. The number of men present in the lower house varied considerably, for small communities were too poor to send a man every year, while others combined to finance the sending of a single delegate; but during the 1780's between two and three times as many attended as before the war. The House chosen in 1786 had eighty-eight members. The balance of power had shifted into the Merrimack Valley, for fewer than half of the delegates came from the two counties near the coast, and even these included frontier settlements.[15]

The socio-economic composition of the New Hampshire legis-

---

[14]For the development of democratic ideas after 1774, see Merrill Jensen, "Democracy and the American Revolution," *Huntington Library Quarterly*, XX (1957), 321–341. The entrance of many new men into the upper house, and their transformation into more nearly democratic institutions, is emphasized in Main, "Social Origins of a Political Elite: The Upper House in the Revolutionary Era," *ibid.*, XXVII (1964), 147–158. The point will be elaborated in a forthcoming book.

[15]Strafford County, which contained the commercial center of Dover, extended north through what are now Belknap and Carroll Counties, then just under settlement.

lature also changed. All but four of the 1765 legislators can be identified, but more than one fifth of the post-war representatives are obscure, and the parentage of very few can be established despite the existence of many town histories, genealogies, and published records. Before the war fewer than one third were farmers, exclusive of large landowners but including the men whose occupation is doubtful; by 1786 at least 50 per cent were yeomen and if those whose occupations are unknown are added, as most of them should be, the proportion rises to over 70 per cent. Merchants and lawyers, who had furnished about one third of the members of the 1765 legislature, now comprised only one tenth of the membership. Similarly men of wealth totalled one third of the former legislature but less than one tenth of the latter. The well-to-do element who had dominated the prewar Assembly with 70 per cent of the seats were now reduced to a minority of about 30 per cent. Thus a very large majority of the new legislature consisted of ordinary farmers who had only moderate properties. Ten members of the prominent old families had seats in the 1765 house; by 1786 there were only four in a body two and one half times as large. Even if the newly-represented towns are eliminated, the trend toward the election of less wealthy and less distinguished representatives remains the same, though the degree of change was less. If only the towns which sent men to both legislatures are considered, one finds that whereas farmers formed between 20 and 30 per cent in 1765, they accounted for 55 to 67 per cent twenty years later. Similarly, in these towns the proportion of representatives having moderate properties rose from 30 per cent to more than twice that. Thus the economic and social character of the members in the lower house had been radically changed.

The pattern of change was much the same in other states. New York's society was fundamentally less egalitarian than that of New Hampshire, having more men with large estates and proportionately fewer areas dominated by small farmers. The agricultural upcountry had not yet extended much beyond Albany to the north and Schenectady to the west, so that most New Yorkers still lived in the older counties. As might be expected the changes which occurred in New York were not as striking as in New Hampshire but they were still obvious. By 1785 the counties west of the Hudson, together with those north of Westchester, increased their representation from about one third to nearly two thirds of the total. That fact alone might not have guaranteed a social or economic change in the composition of the Assembly, for every county had its upper class, but the new legislature differed from the old in many respects. The voters selected far fewer townspeople. In the 1769 Assembly some 57 per cent of the members had been engaged primarily in a nonagricultural occupation; by 1785 the proportion had been halved. Farmers, exclusive of large landowners, had made up 25 per cent of the total in 1769; now they furnished about 42 per cent.[16] In contrast, one half of the 1769 legislators had been merchants and lawyers, but now such men held less than one third of the seats. Similarly the proportion of wealthy members dropped from 43 per cent to 15 per cent, whereas the ratio of men of moderate means increased from probably one seventh to nearly one half. New York's elite families, which had contributed ten out of twenty-eight Assemblymen in 1769, contributed the same number in 1785, but in a House twice as large. Meanwhile the number of men who had started without any local family background, newcomers to New York, increased from two to twenty-three. In general, the yeoman-artisan "middle class," which in colonial days had furnished a half-dozen members, now actually had a majority in the legislature. Under the leadership of George Clinton and others of higher economic and social rank, they controlled the state during the entire decade of the eighties.[17] In New York, as in New Hampshire, the trend was the same even within those counties which had been represented before the Revolution. If Washington and Montgomery counties are eliminated, the proportion of delegates who were well-to-do declines from 86 per cent to 60 per cent.

New Jersey's lower house, the size of which had increased in stages from twenty members to thirty-nine after the Revolution, retained equal distribution of seats between East and West Jersey. As in New Hampshire and New York, the economic upper class of well-to-do men, which in New Jersey had held three fourths of the seats before the war, saw its control vanish; indeed two thirds of the states' representatives in 1785 had only moderate

---

[16]So many men in the 1785 legislature are obscure that the figure cannot be exact, but it is a safe assumption that those who lived in the country and whose occupations are not given in local histories, genealogies, or other published sources, were farmers. Ordinarily men of importance, or business and professional men, are discussed in such sources, so that if one conscientiously searches the published materials, including of course the wills, most of those men who remain unidentified can be confidently termed farmers of moderate property.

[17]As far as the fathers of these legislators could be identified, 12 of the prewar 28 were merchants, lawyers, and large landowners, as were 12 or possibly 13 of the postwar 66.

properties. The typical legislator before the war held at least 1,000 acres; in 1785 the median was about 300 acres. Merchants and lawyers were all but eliminated from the legislature, retaining only a half-dozen seats. The colonial elite, once controlling one third of the votes of the house, now had one eighth; the overwhelming majority of the new legislators were men who had been unknown before the war and whose ancestry, where ascertainable, was uniformly undistinguished. Fully two thirds of the representatives were ordinary farmers, presumably men of more than average ability and sometimes with military experience, but clearly part of the common people. Again these changes occurred not just because new areas were represented but because the counties which had sent delegates in the prewar years now chose different sort of men. In New Jersey, the counties of Cumberland, Salem, Hunterdon, Morris, and Sussex had previously been underrepresented. If these are eliminated, we find that the proportion of men of moderate property rose from 20 per cent to 73 per cent and of farmers (exclusive of large landowners) from 23.5 per cent to 60 per cent.[18]

Southern legislatures were also democratized. Maryland's House of Delegates expanded to seventy-four by 1785, with the addition of a few members from the western counties. As had been true before the war, most of the representatives were engaged in agriculture, the proportion of those with a nonfarm occupation remaining constant at about 20 per cent. The most obvious change in economic composition was the replacement of planters by farmers, of large property owners by men with moderate estates. If the planter is defined as one who held at least twenty slaves or 500 acres, then they formed 57 per cent of the House in 1765 and only 36.5 per cent in 1785, while the farmers increased from 18.5 to 28 per cent. Wealthy men occupied about two fifths of the seats in the pre-Revolutionary period, one sixth after the war, while delegates with moderate property, who had previously formed only one fifth of the total, now comprised one third. The yeoman farmer class, though still lacking a majority, had doubled in numbers while members of the old ruling families, in turn, saw their strength halved.[19] By com-

---

[18]Those of unknown property or occupation are excluded.

[19]The proportion of self-made men in the House seems to have increased from one fifth to one fourth, but information on the delegates' fathers is too incomplete for precision. Material on land and slave ownership is drawn from manuscript census and tax records as well as from the usual secondary materials. The median acreage declined from 1,400 acres to 1,000 acres; the median number of slaves owned decreased from about 40 to 20. My figures

parison with the northern states the shift of power was decidedly less radical, but the change was considerable. It was made more obvious, incidentally, by the great contrast between the postwar House of Delegates and the postwar Senate, for the large majority of the Senators were wealthy merchants, lawyers, and planters, who fought bitterly with the popular branch.

The planter class of Virginia, like that of Maryland, did not intend that the Revolution should encourage democracy, but it was unable to prevent some erosion of its power. The great landowners still controlled the lower house, though their strength was reduced from 60 per cent to 50 per cent, while that of ordinary farmers rose from perhaps 13 per cent in 1773 to 26 per cent in 1785. An important change was the decline in the number of wealthy members, who now held one quarter instead of one half of the seats. Power thus shifted into the hands of the lesser planters, the well-to-do rather than the wealthy. Meanwhile men with moderate properties doubled their share, almost equaling in number the wealthy Burgesses. Similarly the sons of the First Families lost their commanding position, while an even larger fraction of delegates were of humble origins. The general magnitude of the change is suggested by the decline in the median property held from 1,800 acres to about 1,100, and from forty slaves to twenty.[20]

Thus, although the planter class retained control of the Burgesses, the people were now sending well-to-do rather than wealthy men, and at least one out of four representatives was an ordinary citizen. A roll call of the House would still recite the familiar names of many elite families, but it would also pronounce some never heard before. The alteration in the composition of the Virginia legislature undoubtedly sprang in part from the growing influence of westerners, for counties beyond the Blue Ridge sent many more representatives in 1785 than before the war, while the representation from the Piedmont also increased in size. However, the same shift downward also occurred within the older counties, those which had been represented in 1773. If we eliminate from consideration all of the newly-formed counties, we find that delegates with moderate property increased from 13.5 per

---

are on two thirds of the men. Charles A. Barker gives 2,400 acres as the average for the 1771 legislature. *The Background of the Revolution in Maryland* (New Haven, 1940), 384.

[20]Data for land was obtained on 78 per cent of the 1773 Burgesses and 83 per cent of the delegates in the 1785 house. Percentages for slaves are 70 and 86 respectively. Tax lists beginning in 1782 were the most important source, supplemented by probate records and statements in secondary sources.

cent, and that wealthy ones declined from 48 to 30 per cent, while the proportion of farmers rose from 13 to about 25 per cent.

The South Carolina constitution of 1778 is noted as an expression of conservatism. Its conservatism, however, was much more evident with respect to the Senate than to the House of Representatives, which was now nearly four times as large. Although the eastern upper class refused to grant westerners as many seats in the House as were warranted by their population, the upcountry did increase its share from not more than 6 or 8 per cent (depending on one's definition of where the upcountry started) to nearly 40 per cent. The urban upper class of merchants, lawyers, and doctors dropped to 20 per cent of the total membership in 1785, as compared to 36 per cent in 1765. The agricultural interest greatly increased its influence, the principal gain being made by farmers rather than by planters. A significant change was a reduction in the strength of wealthy representatives, who made up four fifths of those whose property is known in 1765 and but one third twenty years later. The pre-Revolutionary House of Commons seems to have contained not a single man of moderate property, but the postwar representatives included more than fifty such—probably over 30 per cent of the membership. The median acreage held by the 1765 members was certainly over 2,000 and probably a majority owned over 100 slaves each. The lack of tax records makes it impossible to determine what land the 1785 representatives held, but they obviously owned much less; while the median number of slaves was about twenty-five. The scarcity of such records as well as of genealogies and other historical materials also makes it exceedingly difficult to identify any but fairly prominent men. This situation in itself lends significance to the fact that whereas before the Revolution the desired information is available for seven out of eight representatives and even for over two thirds of their parents, data are incomplete concerning 30 per cent of the postwar delegates and most of their parents. Equally significant is the different social make-up of the two bodies. The long-established upper class of the province controlled half of the 1765 house, but less than one fourth of the 1785 legislature. Although most of the representatives were well-to-do, the house was no longer an exclusively aristocratic body, but contained a sizable element of democracy. It should be pointed out that South Carolina was peculiar in that the change in the House was due almost entirely to the admission of new delegates from the west. In those parishes which elected representatives both before and after the war, the proportion of wealthy delegates decreased very slightly, while that of men with moderate property rose from zero to between 7 and 14 per cent.

All of the six legislatures had been greatly changed as a result of the Revolution. The extent of that change varied from moderate in Virginia and Maryland to radical in New Hampshire and New Jersey, but everywhere the same process occurred. Voters were choosing many more representatives than before the war, and the newly settled areas gained considerably in representatives. The locus of power had shifted from the coast into the interior. Voters were ceasing to elect only men of wealth and family. The proportion of the wealthy in these legislatures dropped from 46 per cent to 22 per cent; members of the prominent old families declined from 40 per cent to 16 per cent. Most of these came from the long-established towns or commercial farm areas. Of course many men who were well-to-do or better continued to gain office, but their share decreased from four fifths to just one half. Even in Massachusetts the percentage of legislators who were wealthy or well-to-do dropped from 50 per cent in 1765 to 21.5 per cent in 1784.[21]

Significantly, the people more and more often chose ordinary yeomen or artisans. Before the Revolution fewer than one out of five legislators had been men of that sort; after independence they more than doubled their strength, achieving in fact a majority in the northern houses and constituting over 40 per cent generally. The magnitude of the change is suggested by the fact that the legislators of the postwar South owned only about one half as much property as their predecessors. Also suggestive is the great increase in the proportion of men of humble origin, which seems to have more than doubled. Therefore men who were or had once been a part of the *demos* totalled about two thirds

---

[21]*Economic status of Massachusetts Representatives (percentages)*

	1765	1784 duplicate towns	1784 total
wealthy	17	8	6.5
well-to-do	33	17	15
moderate	40	55	51.5
unknown	10	20	27

Probably most of those whose property is unknown had only moderate incomes. Similarly the proportion of men from prominent old families dropped from 22 per cent to 6 per cent, college educated delegates from 27 per cent to 9 per cent, and representatives whose fathers were well-to-do from 30 per cent to 10 per cent, the change being greatest in the new towns but occurring everywhere.

TABLE I. ECONOMIC STATUS OF THE REPRESENTATIVES[a]

	N.H., N.Y., and N.J.		Md., Va., and S.C.	
	Prewar (percentages)	Postwar (percentages)	Prewar (percentages)	Postwar (percentages)
Wealthy	36	12	52	28
Well-to-do	47	26	36	42
Moderate	17	62	12	30
Merchants & lawyers	43	18	22.5	17
Farmers	23	55	12	26

[a] This table analyzes the property of about 900 representatives. The economic status of 85 per cent was discovered with reasonable certainty. Most of the rest were dealt with by informed guesswork. No one was admitted to the wealthy category unless their property was certainly known. Lawyers were assumed to be well-to-do, for almost all of them were. Merchants were also considered well-to-do if they lived in an important urban center, but inland shopkeepers were not. Doctors and judges were distributed on similar principles. Artisans were almost always of moderate property. Farmers and those whose occupation was unknown composed the two largest groups. Those who came from the inland, semi-subsistence communities were almost never well-to-do, the exceptions being conspicuous men, so that if nothing was discovered about them they were almost certainly of moderate means. On the other hand those who lived in the well-developed commercial farm areas were often well-to-do, so they were not assigned to any category unless other information was available. The basis for this procedure was derived from extensive study of property holdings as discussed in my *Social Structure of Revolutionary America*. By such an analysis the proportion of unknowns was reduced to 3½ per cent, most of whom were probably of moderate property. They are eliminated in the table. Percentages for occupation are less accurate, especially those for the postwar South.

of the whole number of representatives. Clearly the voters had ceased to confine themselves to an elite, but were selecting instead men like themselves. The tendency to do so had started during the colonial period, especially in the North, and had now increased so dramatically as almost to revolutionize the legislatures. The process occurred also in those areas which were represented both before and after the Revolution, as compared with those which were allowed to choose delegates for the first time after the war.

Although a similar change may not have taken place in Connecticut or Rhode Island, it surely did so in the states of Pennsylvania, Delaware, North Carolina, and Georgia, which have not been analyzed here.

TABLE II. ECONOMIC STATUS OF THE REPRESENTATIVES FROM PRE-REVOLUTIONARY DISTRICTS

	N.H., N.Y., and N.J.		Md., Va., and S.C.	
	Prewar	Postwar	Prewar	Postwar
Wealthy	35	18	50	38
Well-to-do	45	37	38	42
Moderate	20	45	12	20
Merchants & lawyers	41	24	22	18.5
Farmers	25	50	12	22

The significance of the change may be more obvious to historians than it was to men of the Revolutionary era. Adherents of the Whig philosophy deplored the trend. They continued to demand a government run by the elite in which the democratic element, while admitted, was carefully checked. Such men were basically conservatives who conceived themselves as struggling for liberty against British tyranny, and who did not propose to substitute a democratical tyranny for a monarchical one.[22] The states, observed a philosophical New Englander in 1786, were "worse governed" than they had been because "men of sense and property have lost much of their influence by the popular spirit of the war." The people had once respected and obeyed their governors, senators, judges, and clergy. But "since the war, blustering ignorant men, who started into notice during the troubles and confusion of that critical period, have been attempting to push themselves into office."[23]

On the other hand democratic spokesmen now rose to defend this new government by the people. A writer in a Georgia newspaper rejoiced in 1789 that the state's representatives were "taken from a class of citizens who hitherto have thought it more for their interest to be contented with a humbler walk in life," and hoped that men of large property would not enter the state, for Georgia had "perhaps the most *compleat* democracy in the known world," which could be preserved only by economic equality.[24] In Massachusetts as early as 1775 "Democritus" urged the voters to "choose men that have learnt to get their living by honest industry, and that will be content with as small an income as the generality of those who pay them for their service. If you would be well represented," he continued, "choose a man in middling circumstances as to worldly estate, if he has got it by his industry so much the better, he knows the wants of the poor, and can judge pretty well what the community can bear of public burdens, if he be a man of good common understanding."[25] "A Farmer"

---

[22]Illustrations of this antidemocratic bias among Whig spokesmen are numerous, e.g., "A faithful Friend to his Country," *Independent Chronicle* (Boston), August 7, 1777; "The Free Republican," *Boston Magazine*, August 1784, pp. 420–423; "Constitutionalist," *Connecticut Courant* (Hartford), April 10, 1786; "Honestus," *Vermont Gazette* (Bennington), September 18, 1786; "Lycurgus," *Massachusetts Spy* (Worcester), July 12, 26, August 2, 1775; Samuel Chase, *Md. Gazette*, December 11, 1777; "Agricola," *Pennsylvania Packet* (Philadelphia), February 6, 1779; "A Citizen of New Jersey," *New Jersey Gazette* (Trenton), October 10, 1785; and *Falmouth Gazette*, September 17, 1785.

[23]*American Herald* (Boston), December 11, 1786.

[24]*Gazette of the State of Georgia* (Savannah), January 1, 1789.

[25]*Massachusetts Spy*, July 5, 1775.

in Connecticut boldly declared it a maxim that the people usually judged rightly, insisted that politics was not so difficult but that common sense could comprehend it, and argued that every free-man could be a legislator.[26]

The change in men might be deprecated or applauded, but it could not be denied, and some found it good. To Jedidiah Morse the government of Virginia still seemed to be "oligarchical or aristocratical,"[27] but to a Virginian a revolution had taken place. The newly-chosen House of Burgesses, wrote Roger Atkinson in 1776, was admirable. It was "composed of men not quite so well dressed, nor so politely educated, nor so highly born as some Assemblies I have formerly seen," yet on the whole he liked it better. "They are the People's men (and the People in general are right). They are plain and of consequence less disguised, but I believe to the full as honest, less intriguing, more sincere. I wish the People may always have Virtue enough and Wisdom enough to chuse such plain men."[28] Democracy, for a moment at least, seemed to have come to Virginia.

The American Revolution:
The People as Constituent Power

R. R. PALMER

If it be asked what the American Revolution distinctively contributed to the world's stock of ideas, the answer might go somewhat along these lines. It did not contribute primarily a social doctrine—for although a certain skepticism toward social rank was an old American attitude, and possibly even a gift to man-

---

[26]*Weekly Monitor* (Litchfield), August 6, 1787. For two more examples see "A Watchman," *Pa. Packet*, June 10, 17, 1776; and *Maryland Journal, and Baltimore Advertiser*, February 18, 1777.

[27]Jedidiah Morse, *The American Geography* . . . (2d ed., London, 1792), 387.

[28]To Samuel Pleasants, Nov. 23, 1776, *Virginia Magazine of History and Biography*, XV (1908), 357.

Reprinted with permission from *The Age of the Democratic Revolution: A Political History of Europe and America, 1760–1800*. Volume One: *The Challenge* (Princeton, 1959), 213–235. Copyright © 1959 by Princeton University Press.

kind, it long antedated the Revolution, which did not so much cut down, as prevent the growth of, an aristocracy of European type. It did not especially contribute economic ideas—for the Revolution had nothing to teach on the production or distribution of goods, and the most advanced parties objected to private wealth only when it became too closely associated with government. They aimed at a separation of economic and political spheres, by which men of wealth, while free to get rich, should not have a disproportionate influence on government, and, on the other hand, government and public emoluments should not be used as a means of livelihood for an otherwise impecunious and unproductive upper class.

The American Revolution was a political movement, concerned with liberty, and with power. Most of the ideas involved were by no means distinctively American. There was nothing peculiarly American in the concepts, purely as concepts, of natural liberty and equality. They were admitted by conservatives, and were taught in the theological faculty at the Sorbonne.[1] Nor could Americans claim any exclusive understanding of the ideas of government by contract or consent, or the sovereignty of the people, or political representation, or the desirability of independence from foreign rule, or natural rights, or the difference between natural law and positive law, or between certain fundamental laws and ordinary legislation, or the separation of powers, or the federal union of separate states. All these ideas were perfectly familiar in Europe, and that is why the American Revolution was of such interest to Europeans.

THE DISTINCTIVENESS OF AMERICAN POLITICAL IDEAS

The most distinctive work of the Revolution was in finding a method, and furnishing a model, for putting these ideas into practical effect. It was in the implementation of similar ideas

---

[1]See on Réal de Curban my *Catholics and Unbelievers in Eighteenth Century France* (Princeton, 1939), 126, quoting L. J. Hooke, *Religionis naturalis et moralis philosophiae principia, methodo scholastica digesta* (Paris, 1752–1754), I, 623–624: "Status is a permanent condition of man, involving various rights and a long series of obligations. It is either *natural,* constituted by nature itself, or *adventitious,* arising from some human act or institution. . . . By the *status of nature* we understand that in which men would be who were subject to no government but joined only by similarity of nature or by private pacts. . . . In the status of nature all men are equal and enjoy the same rights. For in that state they are distinguished only by the gifts of mind or body by which some excel others." Italics are the Abbé Hooke's.

that Americans were more successful than Europeans. "In the last fifty years," wrote General Bonaparte to Citizen Talleyrand in 1797, "there is only one thing that I can see that we have really defined, and that is the sovereignty of the people. But we have had no more success in determining what is constitutional, than in allocating the different powers of government." And he said more peremptorily, on becoming Emperor in 1804, that the time had come "to constitute the Nation." He added: "I am the constituent power."[2]

The problem throughout much of America and Europe, for half a century, was to "constitute" new government, and in a measure new societies. The problem was to find a constituent power. Napoleon offered himself to Europe in this guise. The Americans solved the problem by the device of the constitutional convention, which, revolutionary in origin, soon became institutionalized in the public law of the United States.[3]

The constitutional convention in theory embodied the sovereignty of the people. The people chose it for a specific purpose, not to govern, but to set up institutions of government. The convention, acting as the sovereign people, proceeded to draft a constitution and a declaration of rights. Certain "natural" or "inalienable" rights of the citizen were thus laid down at the same time as the powers of government. It was the constitution that created the powers of government, defined their scope, gave them legality, and balanced them one against another. The constitution was written and comprised in a single document. The constitution and accompanying declaration, drafted by the convention, must, in the developed theory, be ratified by the people. The convention thereupon disbanded and disappeared, lest its members have a vested interest in the offices they created. The constituent power went into abeyance, leaving the work of government to the authorities now constituted. The people, having exercised sovereignty, now came under government. Having made law, they came under law. They put themselves voluntarily under restraint. At the same time, they put restraint upon government. All government was limited government; all public authority must keep within the bounds of the constitution and of the declared rights. There were two levels of law, a higher law or constitution

---

[2]*Correspondance de Napoleon I,* III (Paris, 1859), 314; R. M. Johnston, *The Corsican* (N.Y., 1910), 182.
[3]See, for example, J. A. Jameson, *The Constitutional Convention: Its History, Powers and Modes of Proceeding,* (N.Y., 1867); H. C. Hockett, *The Constitutional History of the United States, 1776–1826* (N.Y., 1939).

that only the people could make or amend, through constitutional conventions or bodies similarly empowered; and a statutory law, to be made and unmade, within the assigned limits, by legislators to whom the constitution gave this function.

Such was the theory, and it was a distinctively American one. European thinkers, in all their discussion of a political or social contract, of government by consent and of sovereignty of the people, had not clearly imagined the people as actually contriving a constitution and creating the organs of government. They lacked the idea of the people as a constituent power. Even in the French Revolution the idea developed slowly; members of the French National Assembly, long after the Tennis Court oath, continued to feel that the constitution which they were writing, to be valid, had to be accepted by the King as a kind of equal with whom the nation had to negotiate. Nor, indeed, would the King tolerate any other view. On the other hand, we have seen how at Geneva in 1767 the democrats advanced an extreme version of citizen sovereignty, holding that the people created the constitution and the public offices by an act of will; but they failed to get beyond a simple direct democracy; they had no idea of two levels of law, or of limited government, or of a delegated and representative legislative authority, or of a sovereign people which, after acting as a god from the machine in a constituent convention, retired to the more modest status of an electorate, and let its theoretical sovereignty become inactive.

The difficulty with the theory was that the conditions under which it could work were seldom present. No people really starts *de novo;* some political institutions always already exist; there is never a *tabula rasa,* or state of nature, or Chart Blanche as Galloway posited for conservative purposes. Also, it is difficult for a convention engaged in writing a constitution not to be embroiled in daily politics and problems of government. And it is hard to live voluntarily under restraint. In complex societies, or in times of crisis, either government or people or some part of the people may feel obliged to go beyond the limits that a constitution has laid down.

In reality, the idea of the people as a constituent power, with its corollaries, developed unclearly, gradually, and sporadically during the American Revolution. It was adumbrated in the Declaration of Independence: the people may "institute new government." Jefferson, among the leaders, perhaps conceived the idea most clearly. It is of especial interest, however, to see how the "people" themselves, that is, certain lesser and unknown or poorer or unsatisfied persons, contributed to these distinctive American ideas by their opposition to the Revolutionary elite.

There were naturally many Americans who felt that no change was needed except expulsion of the British. With the disappearance of the British governors, and collapse of the old governor's councils, the kind of men who had been active in the colonial assemblies, and who now sat as provincial congresses or other *de facto* revolutionary bodies, were easily inclined to think that they should keep the management of affairs in their own hands. Some parallel can be seen with what happened in Europe. There was a revolution, or protest, of constituted bodies against authorities set above them, and a more popular form of revolution, or protest, which aimed at changing the character or membership of these constituted bodies themselves. As at Geneva the General Council rebelled against the patriciate, without wishing to admit new citizens to the General Council; as in Britain the Whigs asserted the powers of Parliament against the King, without wishing to change the composition of Parliament; as in Belgium, in 1789, the Estates party declared independence from the Emperor, while maintaining the preexisting estates; as in France, also in 1789, the nobility insisted that the King govern through the Estates-General, but objected to the transformation of the three estates into a new kind of national body; as in the Dutch provinces in 1795 the Estates-General, after expelling the Prince of Orange, tried to remain itself unchanged, and resisted the election of a "convention"; so, in America in 1776, the assemblies that drove out the officers of the King, and governed their respective states under revolutionary conditions, sought to keep control of affairs in their own hands, and to avoid reconstitution at the hands of the "people."

Ten states gave themselves new constitutions in 1776 and 1777. In nine of these states, however, it was the ordinary assembly, that is, the revolutionary government of the day, that drafted and proclaimed the constitution. In the tenth, Pennsylvania, a constituent convention met, but it soon had to take on the burden of daily government in addition. In Connecticut and Rhode Island the colonial charters remained in force, and the authorities constituted in colonial times (when governors and councils had already been elected) remained unchanged in principle for half a century. In Massachusetts the colonial charter remained in effect until 1780.

Thus in no state, when independence was declared, did a true constituent convention meet, and, as it were, calmly and rationally devise government out of a state of nature. There was already, however, some recognition of the principle that constitutions cannot be made merely by governments, that a more fundamental power is needed to produce a constitution than to pass ordinary laws or carry on ordinary executive duties. Thus, in New Hampshire, New York, Delaware, Maryland, North Carolina, and Georgia, the assemblies drew up constitutions only after soliciting authority for that purpose from the voters. In Maryland and North Carolina there was a measure of popular ratification.

CONSTITUTION-MAKING IN NORTH CAROLINA, PENNSYLVANIA AND MASSACHUSETTS

The popular pressures that helped to form American political doctrine are best illustrated from North Carolina, Pennsylvania, and Massachusetts.[4]

In North Carolina class lines had been sharply drawn by the Regulator movement and its suppression. The people of the back-country even inclined to be loyalist, not eager for an independence that might only throw them into the hands of the county gentry. In the turbulent election of October 1776 the voters knew that the assembly which they elected would draft a state constitution. There was no demand for a convention to act exclusively and temporarily as a constituent power. But several counties drew up instructions for the deputies, in which the emerging doctrine was set forth clearly.

Orange and Mecklenburg counties used identical language. This is a sign, as in the case of identical phrasing in the French *cahiers* of 1789, where the matter has been carefully studied, that some person of influence and education, and not some poor farmer ruminating in his cabin, had probably written out a draft. Still, the public meetings of both counties found it to their taste. "Political power," they said, "is of two kinds, one principal and superior, the other derived and inferior. . . . The principal supreme power is possessed only by the people at large. . . . The derived and inferior power by the servants which they employ. . . . The rules by which the inferior power is exercised are to be con-

---

[4]Here I am indebted, without sharing all his conclusions, to E. P. Douglass, *Rebels and Democrats: the Struggle for Equal Political Rights and Majority Rule during the American Revolution* (Chapel Hill, N.C., 1955).

stituted by the principal supreme power. . . ."[5] In other words, government was not a form of guardianship. Office was to be no longer a perquisite of the gentry, or "an aristocracy of power in the hands of the rich," to use their own language, but a form of employment by the people, whom they did not hesitate to call "the poor." Mecklenburg favored a unicameral legislature, Orange a bicameral one, but both called for a separation of powers. It was not that any organ of government should enjoy independence from the electorate (the essence of balance-of-power theory in the European, British, and loyalist view), but rather that the various functions of government should be defined and distributed among different men, to prevent what had happened in colonial times. The fact that before 1776 the council had possessed executive, legislative, and judicial functions, and that members of the assembly had served as justices of the peace, or had their relatives appointed judges and sheriffs, was the basis on which North Carolina had been dominated by small groups of gentry. It was popular objection to this situation, probably more than a reading of European books, that made the separation of powers a principal American doctrine.

The North Carolina constitution, as written and adopted, enlarged the electorate by granting all taxpayers the right to vote for members of the lower house. It equalized the representation by giving more deputies to the western counties. It required a freehold of 100 acres for members of the lower house, and of 300 acres for those of the upper house, who were to be elected only by voters possessing 50 acres. The governor, elected by the two houses, had to have a freehold worth £1,000. The constitution was a compromise between populace and landed gentry. It lasted until the Civil War.[6]

The situation in Pennsylvania was complex. The Quaker colony, idealized by European intellectuals as the heaven of innocent equality and idyllic peace, had long been plagued by some of the most acrimonious politics in America. Quaker bigwigs had long clashed with the non-Quaker lesser orders of Philadelphia and the West. In the spring of 1776 Pennsylvania was the only colony in which the assembly was still legal under the old law. It still showed a desire for reconciliation with England, and, with it, maintenance of the old social and political system. This persist-

---

[5]*Ibid.,* 126.

[6]For the text of the constitutions, see F. N. Thorpe, *Federal and State Constitutions, Colonial Charters and Other Organic Laws of the . . . United States of America* (Washington, 7 vols., 1909).

ence of conservatism in high places made a great many people all the more radical. A year of open war with Britain had aroused the determination for independence, and in May 1776 a mass meeting of 4,000 people in Philadelphia demanded the calling of a constitutional convention. Various local committees got to work, and a convention was elected by irregular methods. Where the three eastern counties had formerly been heavily over-represented, the situation was now not equalized, but reversed. The West, with the same population as the three eastern counties, had 64 delegates in the convention to only 24 for the East. "The Convention in Pennsylvania was a political expedient, and not, as in Massachusetts, the cornerstone of constitutional government."[7] Its real function was to promote the Revolution, and assure independence from England, by circumventing the assembly and all other opposition. Like the more famous French Convention elected in 1792, it rested on a kind of popular mandate which did not reflect an actual majority of the population; like it, it became the government of the country during war and revolution; like it, it behaved dictatorially. The constitutions drafted in Pennsylvania in 1776, and in France in 1793, were, in their formal provisions, by far the most democratic of any produced in the eighteenth century. The Pennsylvania constitution of 1776, unlike the French constitution of the Year I, was never submitted even to the formalities of popular ratification. But the two constitutions became a symbol of what democrats meant by democracy.

The Pennsylvania constitution vested legislative power in a single house. For the executive it avoided the name and office of governor, entrusting executive power to a council and "president," a word which then meant no more than chairman. All male taxpayers twenty-one years of age had the vote, and were eligible for any office. To sit in the assembly, however, it was necessary publicly to acknowledge the divine inspiration of the Old and New Testaments. Voters elected the legislators, the executive councillors, sheriffs, coroners, tax-assessors, and justices of the peace. Voting was by ballot. The president was chosen by the legislature and the executive council; he had no veto or appointive powers, and what powers he did have he could exercise only in agreement with his council. All officers were elected for one year, except that councillors served for three. Rotation of office was provided for; legislators, councillors, president, and sheriffs could be reelected only a certain number of times. Doors of the legislative assembly

---

[7]Douglass, op. cit., 260.

must always be open to the public. There was a kind of referendum, in that no bill passed by the assembly, short of emergency, became law until submitted for public consideration and enacted in the assembly of the following year, if there was no public objection. Officeholders received pay, but if revenues of any office became too large the assembly could reduce them. All officers and judges could be impeached by the assembly. Judges of the Supreme Court could be removed by the assembly for "misbehavior." There was an elected council of censors, or board of review, which every seven years ascertained whether the constitution had been preserved inviolate, and called a convention if amendment seemed necessary.

The Pennsylvania constitution represented the doctrine of a single party, namely the democrats, people of the kind who had formerly had little to do with government, and whose main principle was that government should never become a separate or vested interest within the state. This was indeed an understandable principle, at a time when government, in all countries in varying degree, had in fact become the entrenched interest of a largely hereditary governing class. The Pennsylvania constitution substituted almost a direct democracy, in which no one in government could carry any responsibility or pursue any sustained program of his own. Many people in Pennsylvania objected to it from the beginning. It must be remembered that the democratic constitution did not signify that Pennsylvania was really more democratic than some of the other states; it signified, rather, that Pennsylvania was more divided, and that conservatism was stronger, certain upper-class and politically experienced elements, which elsewhere took a leading part in the Revolution, being in Pennsylvania tainted with Anglophilism. Whether the constitution of 1776 was workable or not, these people soon put an end to it. It lasted only until 1790.[8]

The most interesting case is that of Massachusetts. Here the great political thinker was John Adams, who became the main author of the Massachusetts constitution of 1780, which in turn had an influence on the Constitution of the United States. In his own time Adams was denounced as an Anglomaniac and a Monocrat. In our own time some sympathizers with the eighteenth-century democrats have considered him very conservative, while on the other hand theorists of the "new conservatism" would

---

[8]*Ibid.*, 214–286; J. P. Selsam, *The Pennsylvania Constitution of 1776: a Study in Revolutionary Democracy* (Philadelphia, 1936).

persuade us that John Adams was in truth the American Edmund Burke. I confess that I see very little in any of these allegations.

Adams in January 1776 published some *Thoughts on Government*, for the guidance of those in the various colonies who were soon to declare independence and begin to govern themselves. This was in some ways a conservative tract. Adams thought it best, during the war, for the new states simply to keep the forms of government that they had. He obviously approved the arrangement under the Massachusetts charter of 1691, by which the popular assembly elected an upper house or council. In other ways he was not very conservative. He declared, like Jefferson, that the aim of government is welfare or happiness, that republican institutions must rest on "virtue," and that the people should support a universal system of public schools. He wanted one-year terms for governors and officials (the alternative would be "slavery"), and he favored rotation of office. He quite agreed that someday the state governors and councillors might be popularly elected, as they were in Connecticut already. He gave six reasons for having a bicameral legislature, but in none of these six reasons did he show any fear of the people, or belief that, with a unicameral legislature, the people would plunder property or degenerate into anarchy. He was afraid of the one-house legislature itself. He never committed the folly of identifying the deputies with the deputizers. He was afraid that a single house would be arbitrary or capricious, or make itself perpetual, or "make laws for their own interest, and adjudge all controversies in their own favor."[9] He himself cited the cases of Holland and the Long Parliament. The fear of a self-perpetuating political body, gathering privileges to itself, was certainly better grounded in common observation than vague alarms about anarchy or pillage.

The *Thoughts* of 1776 were conservative in another way, if conservatism be the word. Adams had not yet conceived the idea of a constitutional convention. He lacked the notion of the people as constituent power. He had in mind that existing assemblies would draft the new constitutions, when and if any were drafted. Adams was familiar with all the high-level political theory of England and Europe. But the idea of the people as the constituent power arose locally, from the grass roots.

The revolutionary leadership in Massachusetts, including both Adamses, was quite satisfied to be rid of the British, and otherwise

---

[9]*Works* (1851), IV, 196.

to keep the Bay State as it had always been. They therefore "resumed" the charter of 1691. They simply undid the Massachusetts Government Act of 1774. Some of the commonalty of Boston, and farmers of Concord and the western towns, envisaged further changes. It is hard to say what they wanted, except that they wanted a new constitution. Experts in Massachusetts history contradict each other flatly; some say that debtors, poor men, and Baptists were dissatisfied; others that all kinds of diverse people naturally owed money anyway, that practically no one was too poor to vote, and that Baptists were an infinitesimal splinter group in a solidly Congregationalist population. It may be that the trouble was basically psychological; that many people of fairly low station, even though they had long had the right to vote, had never until the Revolution participated in politics, were aroused by the Revolution, the war, and excitement of soldiering, and, feeling that affairs had always been managed by people socially above them, wanted now to act politically on their own.

Demands were heard for a new constitution. It was said that the charter of 1691 was of no force, since the royal power that had issued it was no longer valid. It was said that no one could be governed without his consent, and that no living person had really consented to this charter. Some Berkshire towns even hinted that they did not belong to Massachusetts at all until they shared in constituting the new commonwealth. They talked of "setting themselves apart," or being welcomed by a neighboring state. Echoes of the social contract floated through the western air. "The law to bind all must be assented to by all," declared the farmers of Sutton. "The Great Secret of Government is governing all by all," said those of Spencer.[10] It began to seem that a constitution was necessary not only to secure liberty but to establish authority, not only to protect the individual but to found the state.

The house of representatives proposed that it and the council, that is, the two houses of legislation sitting together, should be authorized by the people to draw up a constitution. All adult males were to vote on the granting of this authorization, not merely those possessing the customary property qualification. In a sense, this was to recognize Rousseau's principle that there must be "unanimity at least once": that everyone must consent to the law under which he was to live, even if later, when constitutional arrangements were made, a qualification was required for ordinary voting. The council objected to a plan whereby it would lose its identity by merging with the house. A little dispute occurred, not

[10]Douglass, op. cit., 178.

unlike that in France in 1789 between "vote by head" and "vote by order." The plan nevertheless went through. The two houses, sitting as one, and authorized by the people, produced a constitution in 1778. It was submitted for popular ratification. The voters repudiated it. Apparently both democrats and conservatives were dissatisfied. This is precisely what happened in Holland in 1797, when the first constitution of the Dutch revolution was rejected by a coalition of opposite-minded voters.

A special election was therefore held, in which all towns chose delegates to a state convention, "for the sole purpose of forming a new Constitution." John Adams, delegate from Braintree, was put on the drafting committee. He wrote a draft, which the convention modified only in detail. The resulting document reflected many influences. It is worth while to suggest a few.

There is a modern fashion for believing that Rousseau had little influence in America, particularly on such sensible characters as John Adams. I do not think that he had very much. Adams, however, had read the *Social Contract* as early as 1765, and ultimately had four copies of it in his library. I suspect that, like others, he found much of it unintelligible or fantastic, and some of it a brilliant expression of his own beliefs. He himself said of the Massachusetts constitution: "It is Locke, Sidney, Rousseau, and de Mably reduced to practice."[11]

Adams wrote in the preamble: "The body politic is formed by a voluntary association of individuals. It is a social compact, by which the whole people covenants with each citizen, and each citizen with the whole people, that all shall be governed by certain laws for the common good."[12] The thought here, and the use of the word "covenant," go back to the Mayflower compact. But whence comes the "social" in *social* compact? And whence comes the word "citizen"? There were no "citizens" under the British constitution, except in the sense of freemen of the few towns known as cities. In the English language the word "citizen" in its modern sense is an Americanism, dating from the American Revolution.[13] It is entirely possible that Jean-Jacques Rousseau had deposited these terms in Adams' mind. The whole passage suggests Chapter

---

[11]*Works* (1851), IV, 216. Adams also, in 1787, cited Rousseau's *Discourse on Inequality and Considerations on Poland* with approval, recommending the former for its picture of the evil in civilized men, the latter for its view that Poland was dominated exclusively by nobles. *Works*, IV, 409 and 367.

[12]*Ibid.*, 219; Thorpe, *op. cit.*, III, 1889.

[13]This may be readily confirmed from the Oxford Dictionary, or by comparison of definitions of "citizen" in British and American dictionaries, or by tracing the article "citizen" through successive editions of the Encyclopaedia Britannica, where the modern meaning does not appear until the eleventh edition in 1910.

vi, Book 1, of the *Social Contract*. The convention adopted this part of Adams' preamble without change.

In the enacting clause of the preamble Adams wrote: "We, therefore, the delegates of the people of Massachusetts . . . agree upon the following . . . Constitution of the Commonwealth of Massachusetts." The convention made a significant emendation: "We, therefore, the people of Massachusetts . . . agree upon, ordain and establish . . ." The formula, *We the people ordain and establish*, expressing the developed theory of the people as constituent power, was used for the first time in the Massachusetts constitution of 1780, whence it passed into the preamble of the United States constitution of 1787 and the new Pennsylvania constitution of 1790, after which it became common in the constitutions of the new states, and in new constitutions of the old states. Adams did not invent the formula. He was content with the matter-of-fact or purely empirical statement that the "delegates" had "agreed." It was the popularly elected convention that rose to more abstract heights. Providing in advance for popular ratification, it imputed the creation of government to the people.

Adams wrote, as the first article of the Declaration of Rights: "All men are born equally free and independent, and have certain natural, essential and unalienable rights," which included defense of their lives, liberties, and property, and the seeking of "safety and happiness." The Virginia Declaration of Rights, drafted by George Mason in June 1776, was almost identical, and Adams certainly had it in mind. The Massachusetts convention made only one change in the sentence. It declared: "All men are born free and equal." The convention, obviously, was thinking of the Declaration of Independence, that is, Jefferson's more incisive rewording of Mason's Virginia declaration.

The convention had been elected by a true universal male suffrage, but it adopted, following Adams' draft, a restriction on the franchise. To vote, under the constitution, it was necessary to own real estate worth £3 a year, or real and personal property of a value of £60. The charter of 1691 had specified only £2 and £40 respectively. The state constitution was thus in this respect more conservative than the charter. How much more conservative? Here we run into the difference between experts already mentioned.[14] A whole school of thought, pointing to a 50 per cent

---

[14]For emphasis on the conservative or reactionary character of the Massachusetts constitution, see Douglass, *op. cit.*, 189–213, and more specialized writers cited there; for the opposite view, which I follow in part, see R. E. Brown, *Middle-Class Democracy and the Revolution in Massachusetts, 1691–1780* (Ithaca, N. Y., 1955), 384–400.

increase in the voting qualification, has seen a reaction of property-owners against dangers from below. Closer examination of the values of money reveals that the £3 and £60 of 1780 represent an increase of only one-eighth over the figures of 1691. Even if half the people of Boston were unfranchised, all Boston then had only a twentieth of the population of the state. In the rural areas, where farm ownership was usual, it was mainly grown sons living for a few years with their parents who lacked the vote. There seems to have been only sporadic objection to the suffrage provision.

Adams put into the constitution, and the convention retained it, that ghost of King, Lords, and Commons that now assumed the form of governor, senate, and house of representatives. Partisans of the British system, in England or America, would surely find this ghost highly attenuated. The point about King and Lords, in the British system, was precisely that they were not elected by anyone, that they were immune to popular pressure, or any pressure, through their enjoyment of life tenure and hereditary personal rights to political position. Governor and senators in Massachusetts, like representatives, both in Adams' draft and in the final document, were all elected, all by the same electorate, and all for one-year terms. To Adams (as, for example, to Delolme), it was of the utmost importance to prevent the executive from becoming the mere creature of the legislature. He even wished the governor to have an absolute veto, which the convention changed to a veto that could be overridden by a two-thirds majority of both houses. Adams continued to prefer a final veto. Jeffersonians and their numerous progeny found this highly undemocratic. In all states south of New York, at the end of the Revolution, governors were elected by the legislative houses, and none had any veto. Adams justified the veto as a means "to preserve the independence of the executive and judicial departments."[15] And since governors could no longer be appointed by the crown, an obvious way to prevent their dependence on legislatures was to have them issue, like legislators, from the new sovereign, the people. It was legislative oligarchy that Adams thought the most imminent danger. As he wrote to Jefferson in 1787: "You are afraid of the one—1, of the few."[16]

As for the phantom "lords," or senators, though they were directly elected by the ordinary voters for one-year terms, they were in a way supposed to represent property rather than numbers. They were apportioned among the counties of Massachusetts

---

[15]Adams, *Works* (1851), IV, 231, and 232 note.
[16]*Papers of Thomas Jefferson*, XII (Princeton, 1955), 396.

not according to population but according to taxes paid, that is, according to assessed value of taxable wealth. Suffolk County, which included Boston, thus received 6 senators out of 40, where on a purely numerical basis it would have received only four. The Maine districts, Cape Cod, and the western counties were numerically somewhat underrepresented. The three central and western counties received 11 senators, where a representation in proportion to numbers would have given them 12 or 13. Inequalities in wealth in Massachusetts, as between individuals or as between city and country, were not yet great enough to make a senate apportioned according to "property" (which included the small man's property as well as the rich man's) very different from a senate apportioned according to numbers.[17]

The Massachusetts constitution prescribed certain qualifications for eligibility. The governor was required to have a freehold worth at least £1,000, senators a freehold of £300 or £600 total estate, representatives a freehold of £100 or £200 total estate. (British law at this time required £300 or £600 *annual income* from land to qualify for the House of Commons.) These Massachusetts requirements resembled those in North Carolina, where the governor had to have a £1,000 freehold, and members of the upper and lower houses freeholds of 300 or 100 acres respectively. In the absence of comparative statistics on land values and distribution of land ownership in the two states, it is impossible to compare the real impact of these legal qualifications for office. In Massachusetts, however, whatever may have been true in North Carolina, the average 100-acre one-family farm was worth well over £300, and there were a great many such farms, so that the ordinary successful farmer could qualify for either house of the legislature, and a few well-to-do ones in almost every village might if they chose have aspired to the office of governor.[18] The requirements in Massachusetts, as set forth by John Adams, were, if anything, Jeffersonian or agrarian in their tendency, since they favored the farm population, and made it even harder for middle-class townspeople, who might own no land, to occupy public office. The aim was clearly to limit office to the substantial segment of the population, but the substantial segment was broadly defined.

---

[17]Compare the apportionment of senators in the Massachusetts constitution with the population of counties in the census of 1790. The fact that the senate represented property rather than numbers is stressed by those who see the Massachusetts constitution of 1780 as a very conservative or reactionary document. I confess to sharing the impatience of Professor Brown at academic theories which dissolve under a little grade-school computation.
[18]Brown, *op. cit.*, 18, 394.

Still, there were people who by this definition were not "substantial," and some of them objected to these provisions, though not many would in any case have ventured to run for office or been elected if they did, in the Massachusetts of 1780.

It was Article III of the Declaration of Rights, both in Adams' draft and in the finished constitution, that caused most debate in the convention and most disagreement among the voters during ratification. This article, declaring religion to be the foundation of morality and of the state, authorized the legislature to "enjoin" people to go to church, and required the use of public funds to maintain the churches, while allowing any "subject" to have his own contribution paid to the denomination of his choice. While it received a large majority of the popular vote, 8,885 to 6,225, it was the one article which most clearly failed to obtain a two-thirds majority, and the one which may have never been legally ratified, though declared so by the convention. Those voting against it expressed a desire to separate church and state. These, in turn, included perhaps a few Baptists who favored such separation on religious principle, a great many Protestants who feared that the article might legalize Roman Catholicism, and an unknown number of people, one suspects, who were no longer very regular in attending any church at all.

The Massachusetts constitution of 1780 was adopted by a two-thirds majority in a popular referendum from which no free adult male was excluded. The vote was light, for opinion on the matter seems not to have been excited.[19] It was six years since the rebellion against King George, and four years since the British army had left Massachusetts; doubtless many people wished to be bothered no longer. The action of the people as constituent power is, after all, a legal concept, or even a necessary legal fiction where the sovereignty of any concrete person or government is denied. It does not signify that everyone is actually engrossed in

[19]About 23 per cent of adult males voted on ratification of the constitution of 1780, a figure which may be compared with 30 per cent of adult males voting on ratification of the French constitution of 1793, with the difference that in the France of 1793 only those voting "yes" took the trouble to vote at all (1,801,918 "ayes" to 11,610 "no's" with some 4,300,000 abstentions). It is a question whether a vote by 23 per cent of the population should be considered "light." This percentage may have been a good measure of the politically interested population; in the annual elections of the governor the ratio of persons actually casting a vote to the total of adult white males ranged between 9 per cent and 28 per cent until it began to rise with the election of 1800. See J. R. Pole, "Suffrage and Representation in Massachusetts: A Statistical Note," in *William and Mary Quarterly*, XIV (October, 1957), 590–592, and J. Godechot, *Les institutions de la France sous la Révolution et l'Empire* (Paris, 1951), 252.

the fabrication of constitutions. On the other hand, it does not seem necessary to believe that the convention, when it declared the constitution ratified, put something over on an innocent or apathetic or reluctant people. The people of Massachusetts had rejected the constitution proposed in 1778. They could have rejected the one proposed in 1780. It was adopted, not because it was thought perfect or final by everyone, but because it offered a frame of government, or basis of agreement, within which people could still lawfully disagree. It has lasted, with many amendments, until the present day.

A WORD ON THE CONSTITUTION OF THE UNITED STATES

The idea that sovereignty lay with the people, and not with states or their governments, made possible in America a new kind of federal structure unknown in Europe. The Dutch and Swiss federations were unions of component parts, close permanent alliances between disparate corporate members. For them no other structure was possible, because there was as yet no Dutch or Swiss people except in a cultural sense. It was in the Dutch revolution of 1795 and the Swiss revolution of 1798 that these two bundles of provinces or cantons were first proclaimed as political nations. In America it was easier to make the transition from a league of states, set up during the Revolution, to a more integral union set up in the United States constitution of 1787. The new idea was that, instead of the central government drawing its powers from the states, both central and state governments should draw their powers from the same source; the question was the limit between these two sets of derived powers. The citizen, contrariwise, was simultaneously a citizen both of the United States and of his own state. He was the sovereign, not they. He chose to live under two constitutions, two sets of laws, two sets of courts and officials; theoretically, he had created them all, reserving to himself, under each set, certain liberties specified in declarations of rights.

It has been widely believed, since the publication in 1913 of Charles A. Beard's *Economic Interpretation of the Constitution,* that the federal constitution of 1787 marked a reaction against democratic impulses of the Revolution, and was a device by which men of property, particularly those holding securities of the state or continental governments, sought to protect themselves and their financial holdings against the dangers of popular rule. The Philadelphia convention has been represented as an almost clandestine body, which exceeded its powers, and which managed (as has also been said of the Massachusetts convention of 1780) to impose a conservative constitution on a confused or apathetic people. Recently the flimsiness of the evidence for this famous thesis has been shown by Professor Robert Brown.[20] The thesis takes its place in the history of historical writing, as a product of that Progressive and post-Progressive era in which the common man could be viewed as the dupe or plaything of private interests.

It seems likely enough that there was a conservative reaction after the American Revolution, and even a movement among the upper class (minus the old loyalists) not wholly unlike the "aristocratic resurgence" which I shall soon describe in the Europe of the 1780's. The difference is that these neo-aristocrats of America were less obstinate and less caste-conscious than in Europe. They did not agree with each other, and they knew they could not rule alone. The men at Philadelphia in 1787 were too accomplished as politicians to be motivated by anything so impractical as ideology or mere self-interest. They hoped, while solving concrete problems, to arouse as little opposition as possible. They lacked also the European sense of the permanency of class status. Thinking of an upper class as something that individuals might move into or out of, they allowed for social mobility both upward and downward. The wealthy Virginian, George Mason, at the Philadelphia convention, on urging that the upper class should take care to give adequate representation to the lower, offered it as one of his reasons that, however affluent they might be now, "the course of a few years not only might, but certainly would, distribute their posterity through the lowest classes of society."[21] No one seems to have disputed this prognostication. Such acceptance of future downward mobility for one's own grandchildren, if by no means universal in America, was far more common than in Europe. Without such downward mobility there could not long remain much room for newcomers at the top, or much assurance of a fluid society. With it, there could not be a permanent aristocracy in the European sense.

It was the state legislatures that chose the delegates to the

---

[20]R. E. Brown, *Charles Beard and the Constitution: a Critical Analysis of "An Economic Interpretation of the Constitution"* (Princeton, 1956). The critique of Beard is carried even further in a more recent work, Forrest McDonald, *We the People: The Economic Origins of the Constitution* (Chicago, 1958).

[21]*Writings* of James Madison, 9 vols. (New York, 1902–1910), III, 47.

Philadelphia convention, in answer to a widely expressed demand for strengthening the federal government under the Articles of Confederation. The Philadelphia convention proceeded, not to amend the Articles, but to ignore and discard them. It repudiated the union which the thirteen states had made. Beard in 1913 found it satisfying to call this operation a revolution, a revolution from above to be sure, which he compared to a *coup d'état* of Napoleon. His critic, Professor Brown, in 1956, found it satisfying and important to deny any revolutionary action in what happened.

What did really happen? The men at Philadelphia did circumvent the state governments, and in a sense they betrayed those who sent them. They did so by adopting the revolutionary principle of the American Revolution, which had already become less purely revolutionary and more institutionalized as an accepted routine, as shown in the Massachusetts convention of 1780, which had been followed by a New Hampshire convention, and new constitution for New Hampshire in 1784. The Philadelphia convention went beyond the existing constituted bodies, that is, the state governments and the Congress under the Articles, by appealing for support directly to the people, who in each state elected, for this purpose only, conventions to discuss, ratify, or refuse to ratify the document proposed by the convention at Philadelphia. The authors of the proposed federal constitution needed a principle of authority; they conceived that "the people were the fountain of all power," and that if popularly chosen conventions ratified their work "all disputes and doubt concerning [its] legitimacy" would be removed.[22] In each state, in voting for ratifying conventions, the voters voted according to the franchise as given by their state constitutions. No use was made of the more truly revolutionary idea, still alive in Massachusetts in 1780, that on the acceptance of a government *every* man should have a vote. In some states the authorized voters were a great majority; in none were they a small minority. The actual vote for the ratifying conventions was light, despite protracted public discussion, because most people lost interest, or never had any, in abstract debates concerning governmental structure at the distant federal level. Eleven states ratified within a few months, and the constitution went into effect for the people of those eleven states. The remaining two states came in within three years. The whole procedure was revolutionary in a sense, but revolution had already become domesticated in America. The idea of the people as the

---

[22]Quoted by Brown, *op. cit.*, 140.

constituent power, acting through special conventions, was so generally accepted and understood that a mere mention of the word "convention," in the final article of the proposed constitution, was thought sufficient explanation of the process of popular endorsement.

Nevertheless, men of popular principles, those who would soon be called democrats, and who preferred the arrangements of the Pennsylvania constitution, with its single-house legislature to which the executive was subordinated, found much in the new federal constitution not to their liking, at least at first sight. The new instrument reproduced the main features of the Massachusetts constitution of 1780: the strong president, the senate, the house of representatives, the partial executive veto, the independent judiciary, the separation and balance of powers. In fact, the longer tenure of offices—four years for the president, six for senators, two for representatives, in place of the annual terms for corresponding functionaries in Massachusetts—shows a reaction away from revolutionary democracy and toward the giving of more adequate authority to those entrusted with public power. The president was not popularly elected, like the governor in Massachusetts; but neither was he designated by the legislative assembly, like the president in Pennsylvania and governors in the Southern states. He was elected by an electoral college, with each state free to determine how its own share of these electors should be chosen. Although as early as 1788 almost half the states provided for popular election of presidential electors, it was not until 1828 that this became the general and permanent rule. In the federal constitution the unique feature, and key to the main compromise, was the senate. Not only did large and small states have the same number of senators, but it was the state legislatures that chose them. Since it was the state legislatures that conservative or hard-money men mainly feared in the 1780's, this provision can hardly have been introduced in the hope of assuring economic conservatism. It was introduced to mollify the states as states. In the senate the new union was a league of preexisting corporate entities. In the house of representatives it rested more directly on the people. Anyone who had the right to vote in his state could vote for a member of the lower house of Congress. In one respect the federal constitution, by its silence, was more democratic in a modern sense than any of the state constitutions. No pecuniary or religious qualification was specified for any office.

The new constitution was a compromise, but that it produced a less popular federal government, less close to the people, than that of the Articles of Confederation, seems actually contrary to the facts. It created a national arena for political controversy. There were now, for the first time, national elections in which voters could dispute over national issues. One result was the rise, on a national scale, of the Jeffersonian democratic movement in the 1790's.

AMBIVALENCE OF THE AMERICAN REVOLUTION

In conclusion, the American Revolution was really a revolution, in that certain Americans subverted their legitimate government, ousted the contrary-minded and confiscated their property, and set the example of a revolutionary program, through mechanisms by which the people was deemed to act as the constituent power. This much being said, it must be admitted that the Americans, when they constituted their new states, tended to reconstitute much of what they already had. They were as fortunate and satisfied a people as any the world has known. They thus offered both the best and the worst example, the most successful and the least pertinent precedent, for less fortunate or more dissatisfied peoples who in other parts of the world might hope to realize the same principles.

Pennsylvania and Georgia gave themselves one-chamber legislatures, but both had had one-chamber legislatures before the Revolution. All states set up weak governors; they had been undermining the authority of royal governors for generations. South Carolina remained a planter oligarchy before and after independence, but even in South Carolina fifty-acre freeholders had a vote. New York set up one of the most conservative of the state constitutions, but this was the first constitution under which Jews received equality of civil rights—not a very revolutionary departure, since Jews had been prospering in New York since 1654.[23] The Anglican Church was disestablished, but it had had few roots in the colonies anyway. In New England the sects obtained a little more recognition, but Congregationalism remained favored by law. The American revolutionaries made no change in the laws of indentured servitude. They deplored, but avoided, the matter of Negro slavery. Quitrents were generally abolished, but they had been nominal anyway, and a kind of manorial system remained long after the Revolution in New York. Laws favoring primogeni-

---

[23] J. R. Marcus, *Early American Jewry* (Philadelphia, 1953), II, 530.

ture and entail were done away with, but apparently they had been little used by landowners in any case. No general or statistical estimate is yet possible on the disposition of loyalist property. Some of the confiscated estates went to strengthen a new propertied class, some passed through the hands of speculators, and some either immediately or eventually came into the possession of small owners. There was enough change of ownership to create a material interest in the Revolution, but obviously no such upheaval in property relations as in France after 1789.

Even the apparently simple question of how many people received the right to vote because of the Revolution cannot be satisfactorily answered. There was some extension of democracy in this sense, but the more we examine colonial voting practices the smaller the change appears. The Virginia constitution of 1776 simply gave the vote to those "at present" qualified. By one estimate the number of persons voting in Virginia actually declined from 1741 to 1843, and those casting a vote in the 1780's were about a quarter of the free male population over twenty-one years of age.[24] The advance of political democracy, at the time of the Revolution, was most evident in the range of officers for whom voters could vote. In the South the voters generally voted only for members of the state legislatures; in Pennsylvania and New England they voted also for local officials, and in New England for governors as well.

In 1796, at the time of the revolution in Europe, and when the movement of Jeffersonian democracy was gathering strength in America, seven of the sixteen states then in the union had no property qualification for voters in the choice of the lower legislative house, and half of them provided for popular election of governors, only the seaboard South, and New Jersey, persisting in legislative designation of the executive.[25] The best European historians underestimate the extent of political democracy in America at this time. They stress the restrictions on voting rights in America, as in the French constitution of 1791.[26] They do so because they have read the best American historians on the sub-

---

[24]C. S. Sydnor, *Gentlemen Freeholders: Political practices in Washington's Virginia* (Williamsburg, 1952), 138–139, 143.

[25]W. L. Smith, *A Comparative View of the Several States with Each Other . . .* (Philadelphia, 1796). There are six tables showing comparisons.

[26]See, for example, G. Lefebvre, *La Révolution française* (Paris, 1951), 99, and *Coming of the French Revolution*, Eng. trans. (Princeton, 1947), 180–181; P. Sagnac, *La fin de l'ancien régime et la Révolution américaine 1763–1789* (Paris, 1947), 386–393, where the Beard view of issues involved in the writing and ratification of the federal constitution is clearly expounded.

ject and have in particular followed the school of Charles Beard and others. The truth seems to be that America was a good deal more democratic than Europe in the 1790's. It had been so, within limits, long before the revolutionary era began.

Nor in broad political philosophy did the American Revolution require a violent break with customary ideas. For Englishmen it was impossible to maintain, in the eighteenth century or after, that the British constitution placed any limits on the powers of Parliament. Not so for Americans; they constantly appealed, to block the authority of Parliament or other agencies of the British government, to their rights as Englishmen under the British constitution. The idea of limited government, the habit of thinking in terms of two levels of law, of an ordinary law checked by a higher constitutional law, thus came out of the realities of colonial experience. The colonial Americans believed also, like Blackstone for that matter, that the rights of Englishmen were somehow the rights of all mankind. When the highest English authorities disagreed on what Americans claimed as English rights, and when the Americans ceased to be English by abjuring their King, they were obliged to find another and less ethnocentric or merely historical principle of justification. They now called their rights the rights of man. Apart from abstract assertions of natural liberty and equality, which were not so much new and alarming as conceptual statements as in the use to which they were applied, the rights claimed by Americans were the old rights of Englishmen— trial by jury, *habeas corpus*, freedom of the press, freedom of religion, freedom of elections, no taxation without representation. The content of rights was broadened, but the content changed less than the form, for the form now became universal.[27] Rights were demanded for human beings as such. It was not necessary to be English, or even American, to have an ethical claim to them. The form also became more concrete, less speculative and metaphysical, more positive and merely legal. Natural rights were numbered, listed, written down, and embodied in or annexed to constitutions, in the foundations of the state itself.

So the American Revolution remains ambivalent. If it was conservative, it was also revolutionary, and vice versa. It was conservative because colonial Americans had long been radical by general standards of Western Civilization. It was, or appeared, conservative because the deepest conservatives, those most at-

[27] For a European view, see O. Vossler, "Studien zur Erklärung der Menschenrechte," *Historische Zeitschrift*, vol. 142 (1930), 536–539.

tached to King and empire, conveniently left the scene. It was conservative because the colonies had never known oppression, excepting always for slavery—because, as human institutions go, America had always been free. It was revolutionary because the colonists took the risk of rebellion, because they could not avoid a conflict among themselves, and because they checkmated those Americans who, as the country developed, most admired the aristocratic society of England and Europe. Henceforth the United States, in Louis Hartz's phrase, would be the land of the frustrated aristocrat, not of the frustrated democrat; for to be an aristocrat it is not enough to think of oneself as such, it is necessary to be thought so by others; and never again would deference for social rank be a characteristic American attitude. Elites, for better or for worse, would henceforth be on the defensive against popular values. Moreover the Americans in the 1770's, not content merely to throw off an outside authority, insisted on transmuting the theory of their political institutions. Their revolution was revolutionary because it showed how certain abstract doctrines, such as the rights of man and the sovereignty of the people, could be "reduced to practice," as Adams put it, by assemblages of fairly levelheaded gentlemen exercising constituent power in the name of the people. And, quite apart from its more distant repercussions, it was certainly revolutionary in its impact on the contemporary world across the Atlantic.

{ V }

BETWEEN
FEAR
AND HOPE

THE FORCES IN CONTENTION

———— ◆◆ ◆◆◆ ◆◆ ————

After the American victory in the War for Independence the major political question facing the American nation was whether the Articles of Confederation provided a strong enough central government to enable the young republic to fulfill its potentialities, to achieve, in the view of the advocates of change, the promises of the Revolution. The forces of contention in the struggle over this question are described in the following two selections. The first piece emphasizes the material interests and concrete forces that distinguished the proponents of a stronger central government from their antagonists, while the second stresses the differences in age, experience, psychology, and aspirations that divided the two groups.

FORREST MCDONALD (b. 1927) is a member of the Department of History at Wayne State University; STANLEY ELKINS (b. 1925) is a member of the Department of History at Smith College; and ERIC MCKITRICK (b. 1919) of the Department of History at Columbia University.

The Anti-Federalists,
1781-1789

FORREST MCDONALD

The term anti-Federalists[1] means those persons who opposed the establishment of a national government under the Constitution. Anti-Federalists did not use the term to designate themselves; it was coined by Federalists as a term of opprobrium, and was used much as one might today denounce a conservative by calling him a reactionary or a fascist, or denounce a liberal as a radical left-winger or communist. Because the label stuck, however, it can be used here as a convenient term for purposes of communication, without conveying disapproval, at least not in the sense in which it originally conveyed disapproval.

Indeed, the most important point to be made about the anti-Federalists is that they were not, as they were sometimes depicted by the Federalists, uniformly unintelligent, uninformed, and unprincipled; and neither were they the downtrodden masses, the

---

Reprinted with permission from *The Wisconsin Magazine of History*, XLVI, 3 (Spring, 1963), 206–214.

Author's Note: This paper, in slightly different form, was delivered as an address before the annual meeting of the American Historical Association in New York, December 28, 1960. It is published here without any pretensions that it is definitive; rather, it is a condensed forecast of one of the major portions of a forthcoming book on the establishment of the American governmental system, 1781–1792. Nor are the factual data or the documentation represented as adequate to "prove" the thesis; rather, the factual data are only illustrative, and the footnotes only document the illustrative matter. Finally, I am familiar with the several books relating to the subject —including one, Jackson T. Main's *The Antifederalists* (Chapel Hill, 1961), which has the same main title as this paper—that have been published since the delivery of my address; and am aware that this paper, and the forthcoming book that underlies it, disagree with those works in almost every salient.

[1]Spellings of the term vary. Mr. Main, cited above, uses a single, unhyphenated word with a capital "A": Antifederalists. This and "Antifœderalists" were as commonly used by Federalist writers as were "Anti-federalists" and "anti-Federalists" and their variants with the "œ" character. Historians have used all these spellings. The single capitalized word, Antifederalists, suggest that the wearers of the term had something positive in common that would justify thinking of them as a group—in general, cohesiveness, organization, self-consciousness, and some existence pre-dating the contest over the Constitution. The term anti-Federalists has a different connotation: it only designates those persons who, on the single issue of the ratification of the Constitution, opposed the persons calling themselves Federalists. It is thus the more neutral term and, in my judgment, the preferable term.

exploited farmers, or the debtor class; nor yet the "agrarian-minded," the old Whigs, or the radicals, as they have been depicted by various twentieth-century historians. Their leadership matched that of the Federalists for intelligence, education, experience, and political savoir faire, and they comprehended a similar assortment of rich men, poor men, virtuous men, and thieves. In short, they can not be ordered with any rigid or simple system of classification.

Answering the question, Who were the anti-Federalists and how did they come to be that way? involves answering, in large measure, the same question about their opposite number, the Federalists, and neither is an easy undertaking. A suitable point of departure, I think, is a comment made by Edmund Morgan: "The most radical change produced in Americans by the Revolution was in fact not a division at all"—for they began divided—"but the union of three million cantankerous colonists into a new nation."[2] It is explaining why so many people espoused more perfect union through the Constitution, and not why so many people opposed it, that is the difficult task.

This point will be illustrated, and the first basis of division established, by recalling certain facts of life, as life was lived in the eighteenth century, that are so obvious as to be almost invisible. Given the existing technology of communication and transportation—which dictated that these functions be synonymous, and that travel by water was far easier and faster than travel by land—it took about the same amount of time to move men, goods, money, or ideas and information from Portsmouth, New Hampshire, to Liverpool as it did to move them to, say, Augusta, Georgia. Similarly, in point of time Philadelphia—possibly the second largest English-speaking city in the world—was little further from London, the largest, than it was from Pittsburgh, and it was closer to London than was Vienna. Norfolk was closer to the Azores than to the furthermost Virginia town; Charleston was closer to any island in the British West Indies than it was to Raleigh.

It was thus far more natural for most Americans to think in local terms than in national terms, and, when they thought about it at all, to prefer local authority to national authority. If distance made unreasonable the notion that the thirteen colonies could be well governed from London, distance made almost equally far-

---

[2]Edmund S. Morgan, *The Birth of the Republic, 1763–1789* (Chicago, 1956), 100.

fetched the notion that the thirteen states could be well governed by a single national government. In short, for most people the natural thing to be was an anti-Federalist, and it took something special to make them think otherwise. Too, simply by virtue of living in one place instead of another, Americans were less or more prone to think nationally: to be aware of the existence of national problems, and to think of themselves as Americans before thinking of themselves as citizens of their states or towns. An inhabitant of, say, Jaffrey, New Hampshire, would normally not have direct contact with the government of the United States from one year to the next, would deal with his state government only through the annual visit of the tax collector, and would come into direct contact with information, ideas, or people from the outside world only two or three times a year. On the other hand, in the normal course of events an inhabitant of Philadelphia would, irrespective of his occupation, wealth, education, or station in life, come into daily contact with persons and news and ideas from the other states and, indeed, from Europe as well.[3]

These were the first and most important factors predisposing Americans towards national or provincial loyalties during the postwar decade, and towards corresponding loyalties during the contest over ratification—and their preponderating weight was on the side of localism. Several other sets of predisposing factors worked the other way: particularly, the wartime experience of some people, the peacetime experience of others, and the economic interests of still others.

Among those who became devoted to the national cause as a result of the war, three groups are most important. First, those who learned at first-hand the idiocy of attempting to wage a war without a government, which would include particularly members of Congress and important administrative officials who served between 1778 and 1782.[4] Second, those who fought in the war, particularly those in the continental line and most particularly

---

[3]Said Alexander Hamilton: "Man is very much a creature of habit. A thing that rarely strikes his senses will generally have but little influence upon his mind. A government continually at a distance and out of sight, can hardly be expected to interest the sensations of the people." *The Federalist* (Modern Library Edition, 1941), 168.

[4]This generalization, like all generalizations made here, is only partially valid; an effort will be made later to account for the exceptions. The striking exception to the generalization about Congress is the members of the so-called Lee-Adams Junto—delegates from Virginia and Massachusetts and certain of their allies, especially in New England—who were in Congress for part of the years cited, and some of whom later opposed the Constitution.

those officers who served close to Washington. Third, those who inhabited areas which suffered great devastation or long occupation at the hands of the British during the war.

The peacetime experience (1783–1787) likewise convinced some that a national government was necessary, but its effect was upon whole populations of whole states—that is, on those states in which the experiments in independence convinced most people that their states could not make a go of it alone. Making a go of it appeared impossible for a variety of reasons: in Connecticut because of a hopelessly ensnarled fiscal system that blocked the successful working of both government and economy; in Maryland because of a political movement that portended great social upheaval; in Georgia because of an Indian uprising that threatened the very survival of the inhabitants; and so on.[5]

As to the role of economic interests, I have previously devoted 435 pages of a book to an effort to delineate how these worked in winning friends for the Constitution, and apart from repeating that they were complex, subtle, and variable, I shall not reiterate the effort here.[6] But I shall return to economic interests that worked for anti-Federalism in a moment.

Now, if one applies to the contest over ratification the several considerations just mentioned, one comes up with a remarkable picture of it. I invite you to try it. Begin with an outline map of the United States, vintage 1787, with counties and towns indicated. Then color in red (for Federalist) all places which had regular intercourse with other states, and color the remainder blue (for anti-Federalist). Then erase and change from blue to red all areas which were occupied by British armies for more than a year, or in which the ascertainable destruction from warfare exceeded, say,

---

[5]These generalizations are drawn largely from manuscript volumes 2, "Industry," and 5, "Finance and Currency," in the Connecticut Archives, Hartford; Hartford *Connecticut Courant,* New London *Connecticut Gazette,* Middletown *Middlesex Gazette,* and New Haven *Connecticut Journal,* 1785–1787, *passim;* Records of the Loan of 1790, especially volumes 174A, 491, 495, and 498, and the New Haven Port Records, all manuscripts in the Fiscal Section of the National Archives; Philip A. Crowl, "Anti-Federalism in Maryland, 1787–1788," *William and Mary Quarterly,* 3d Series, IV (October, 1947), 446–469 and the same author's *Maryland during and after the Revolution* (Baltimore, 1943); Baltimore *Maryland Journal;* Annapolis *Maryland Gazette,* 1785–1787, *passim;* Savannah *Gazette of the State of Georgia,* July–December, 1787; Journal of the Assembly of the State of Georgia, September Session, 1787, manuscript in the Georgia Department of Archives and History, Atlanta; and Kenneth Coleman, *The American Revolution in Georgia, 1763–1789* (Athens, Ga., 1958).

[6]Forrest McDonald, *We The People: The Economic Origins of the Constitution* (Chicago, 1958).

25 percent of the total value of property other than land. Then repeat the operation for places which furnished members of Congress between 1778 and 1782, and men who served in the continental line with the rank of lieutenant colonel or higher; and do so again for places in which the place itself or three of its half-dozen richest inhabitants stood to profit directly by the adoption of the Constitution. Finally, repeat the operation for the entirety of the five states which, given the objective conditions prevailing under the Articles of Confederation, considered themselves the weakest: Connecticut, New Jersey, Maryland, Delaware, and Georgia. The map you end up with will, at a glance, seem scarcely distinguishable from Orin G. Libby's maps showing the geographical distribution of the vote on the ratification of the Constitution.[7]

But only at a glance. Closer inspection will reveal discrepancies, *e.g.*, that thirteen of the fourteen delegates from counties in the Trans-Alleghany region of Virginia, which you have as blue (anti-Federalist) actually voted for ratification; or that the Connecticut Valley and Cape Cod come out as checkerboards, whereas you have them definitely one way or the other. In all, perhaps a fourth or a fifth of the votes are as yet unaccounted for.

And that is as far as a general analysis of the contest can go. For the remainder of the analysis, one must look to individuals and to vested interests in local politics. When the microscope is thus applied, the leaders of anti-Federalism, as well as the most important dynamic elements in their opposition to the Constitution, stand revealed.

Individuals first. For one kind of person, at least, it was possible to be well educated, well informed, disinterested, and genuinely concerned over the national welfare, and yet opposed to ratification. This was the ideologue, the doctrinaire republican in the classical sense, who could oppose the Constitution on the grounds that it contained many imperfections from the point of view of republican principles of political theory. Now, what makes a man a doctrinaire—republican or any other kind—I can not say, but who these men were and what they believed and how they behaved is easily enough pointed out. In the Constitutional Convention, they were Elbridge Gerry, Edmund Randolph, John Francis Mercer, George Mason, and perhaps others; in the country at large, they were such prominent anti-Federalists as Joshua Atherton of New Hampshire, Rawlins Lowndes of South Carolina,

---

[7]Orin Grant Libby, *Geographical Distribution of the Vote of the Thirteen States on the Ratification of the Federal Constitution, 1787–1788* (Madison, 1894).

George Bryan of Pennsylvania, Timothy Bloodworth of North Carolina, and a host of Virginians. They were men in the rationalist tradition, men who reasoned from principles to particulars, men whose views were the precise opposite of that so well expressed by John Dickinson in the Constitutional Convention: "Experience," said Dickinson, "must be our only guide. Reason may mislead us."[8] Such men viewed Harrington, Locke, and Montesquieu much as a fundamentalist views the Holy Bible; to them, political salvation lay in the difficult but possible task of devising a perfect system. Inasmuch as reason would show that any imperfect form (whether democratic, aristocratic, or monarchistic) would inevitably degenerate into tyranny, it was better to make do without a national government than to create an imperfect one.[9]

With the ideologues the Federalists could argue, through the facile pens and dexterous wits of such skilled theoreticians as Hamilton, Madison, Wilson, Coxe, and Webster. Vested interest groups were another matter, and Federalists could cope with them only by hurling derisive epithets—"pretended patriots," "ambitious and interested men," "artful and designing men," "anti-Federalists" —or by attempting to offer contrary interests. A part of the opposition to the Constitution by vested interest groups has long since been recognized: in the very first number of The Federalist, Hamilton predicted that "men in every State" would "resist all changes which may hazard a diminution of the power, emolument and consequence of the offices they hold under the State-establishments"; and in 1924 Allan Nevins made it clear that holders of important state offices generally were, in fact, anti-Federalists. But we are dealing here with a much larger field. Lucrative and prestigious state offices were few, and men with vested interests in state primacy were legion.[10]

It is impossible to delineate all such vested-interest groups here,

---

[8]Madison's Journal, August 13, 1787, in Charles C. Tansill, ed., *Documents Illustrative of the Formation of the Union* (Washington, 1927), 533.

[9]For an elaboration and further development of these comments on the doctrinaire republican mentality, see the introduction to Forrest McDonald, ed., *Empire and Nation: Letters from a Farmer in Pennsylvania by John Dickinson and Letters from the Federal Farmer by Richard Henry Lee* (New York, 1962). For a clear example of how it worked, see Lee's *Letters* in that volume. A lengthy analysis of it, tentatively titled "The Anti-Federalist Papers," is the subject of a forthcoming book by Professor Morton Borden of Montana State University (a preview of which was given in a provocative paper delivered by Professor Borden at the Mississippi Valley Historical Association meeting in Milwaukee, April, 1962).

[10]*The Federalist* (Modern Library Edition, 1941), 4; Allan Nevins, *The American States during and after the Revolution* (New York, 1924).

but it is possible to draw lines around enough of them to afford abundant illustration of the point. New York offers a prime example. Governor George Clinton, aspiring to make his the Empire State and to establish a dynasty to rule it, had the good sense to realize that doing so involved the use of political power both to govern well and to buy the loyalties of people through their ambition or avarice.[11]

This was not a simple task, and should not be regarded as such. That is, most modern devices which we associate with the welding of political organizations were not available to Clinton. The functions of government were yet too limited to permit building power through patronage; public works were too few to permit building power through graft in the construction business; and so on. One will search in vain for evidence of modern manifestations of machine politics.

But one can hold to this maxim: wherein lies the profit in dealing with government, there also lies the greatest source of power. In New York, as in most states, profit in dealing with government lay in public lands and the public debt. Salable public lands in New York consisted primarily of confiscated loyalist estates, the total market value of which was some £750,000 New York current, or almost $2,000,000. The unimaginative stirrer of these ingredients might have been disposed simply to sell the estates, pay the debts, and be done with it. Not so with Clinton; no dullard was he. On the theory that one wins friends among the well-to-do by making them better-to-do, he arranged, through a series of acts and administrative decisions, that the confiscated estates be disposed of according to a careful design. So as to insure that the field of buyers would not be cluttered with small purchasers, the lands were sold in large blocs at public auction. So as to insure profits to all speculators, it was provided in 1780 that purchases could be made on the installment plan and in certain kinds of public securities, at par. Since these securities had not yet been provided for, they could be bought on the open market at prices which returned handsome profits to purchasers of confiscated estates. In effect, such operators were enabled to buy on

---

[11]There is only one full-length biography of Clinton, E. Wilder Spaulding's *His Excellency George Clinton, Critic of the Constitution* (New York, 1938); the same author's *New York in the Critical Period* (New York, 1932) is also useful. See also the *Public Papers of George Clinton* (New York and Albany, 1900), and Hamilton's comments about Clinton and his supporters in Harold C. Syrett and Jacob E. Cooke, eds., *The Papers of Alexander Hamilton,* vols. 2 and 3 (New York, 1962).

the market at prices ranging from three shillings nine pence to four shillings on the pound, and sell to the state (for confiscated estates) at twenty shillings.[12]

The speculative orgy thus engendered lasted from the latter part of the war to 1786, until a number of rich people had become political friends and a larger number of political friends had become rich people. Then it was time for the next step. It was time to do justice to the suffering public creditors. But not quite all of them. Clinton's chief financial advisor, state treasurer Gerard Bancker, first reckoned how much debt could be supported with the income from the state's lucrative import duties, and then combed the lists of security holders and came up with tables of the various combinations of securities in which a minimum expenditure could result in largesse for a maximum number of voters. In what was offered to the public as a generous, responsible, and patriotic action, the Clintonians decided to fund not only all the state debts but about $1,400,000 of continental debts as well. Two forms of continental debts were assumed: Loan Office Certificates and so-called Barber's Notes, certificates issued by the United States for supplies furnished the continental army. Some 5,000 holders of continental securities—about half the number of voters in a normal election—were provided for under this act. As the system was devised, these securities were neither paid off nor funded; they were simply lent to the state, and the state punctually paid interest on them. Note that the system created, in effect, a list of 5,000 pensioners. Note also that the action could hardly have been inspired by either patriotism or responsibility, for $3,600,000 in other kinds of continental debts held in the state, which were politically less potent because they were concentrated in the hands of only a couple of hundred persons, remained unfunded. This scheme was, as one critic charged, "a studied design to divide the interests of the public creditors."[13]

But it was even more than that. It was also a method for doubly rewarding the faithful and punishing those who had been so

---

[12]For an excellent description of speculation in confiscated estates in New York, see Harry B. Yoshpe, *The Disposition of Loyalist Estates in the Southern District of the State of New York* (New York, 1939), 59–60, 63–78, 114–115, and elsewhere. Prices of public securities have been taken from occasional notices in New York newspapers.

[13]*Laws of the State of New York Passed at the Sessions of the Legislature* (3 vols., Albany, 1886–1888), 2:253ff.; Report of the Committee on the Treasury to the House of Assembly, January 16, 1788, published in the *New York Journal* of January 31, 1788; "Gustavus," in the *New York Packet* of April 13, 1786; and Records of the Loan of 1790, vols. 22, 545, 548, 549, 551, in the National Archives.

wicked as to fail to appreciate past favors. The rise in security prices which quickly followed the funding act caught the speculators in confiscated estates as bears in a bull market. That is, they were in effect short sellers, whose profits depended upon keeping the security market low; they were heavily extended for installment delivery of securities against purchases of confiscated estates. When the securities market rose, they found themselves having to pay roughly 300 per cent as much as they had expected to pay for the securities with which to make their payments. Not surprisingly, many of them were broken.

Those who had appreciated Clinton's generosity, however, those who had given him unreserved political support, were protected. They were informed in advance (1) that the funding would take place, (2) the precise securities which would be funded, and (3) when the operations would occur. Accordingly, they were able to cover their positions and even make a tidy sum by going long in appropriate securities.[14]

These were merely among the more spectacular of Clinton's devices. There were others, and they all worked. Small wonder, then, that when the Constitution came along and threatened to undermine Clinton by transferring control of the more lucrative devices from the state to a general government, as well as similarly transferring that great source of revenue, the tariff, Clinton greeted the document with less than enthusiasm. Small wonder, too, that when he vigorously opposed ratification, the people of the state voted against it, 14,000 to 6,500.[15]

Before proceeding with an effort to outline the development of major vested-interested groups in other states, it is well to pause and observe that by no means all vested interests created during the period were economic interests. Greed may have been the quickest motive to which politicians could appeal, but lust for prestige and power drove most of the managers themselves and, when properly utilized, could provide a continuing basis of strength among the followers. This is clearly seen in a contrasting view of Clinton himself and of the two Clintonian delegates to the

---

[14]The statements in the two foregoing paragraphs are inferences drawn from the sources cited in notes 12, 13, and 14, and from the *Votes and Proceedings of the Assembly of the State of New York, 1786–1787,* and New York newspapers for the same period.

[15]A summary of election returns for five counties appears in the *New York Journal* of June 5, 1788; for Orange County, see the *Daily Advertiser,* June 14, 1788; for Queens County (incorrectly called Suffolk therein), *ibid.,* June 7, 1788; for Dutchess County, the Poughkeepsie *Country Journal,* June 3, 1788; and for Westchester County, the *Daily Advertiser,* June 3, 1788. The popular votes in two counties, Washington and Suffolk, are unknown.

Philadelphia Convention, John Lansing and Robert Yates. Clinton was clearly driven by desire for power, and it does not alter the case that he exercised his power judiciously and, for the most part, in the interest of the state. Lansing, on the other hand, liked money. He was a rich man when he began his association with Clinton, and because he capitalized on the opportunities his party afforded, he became a much richer man. He also became a perpetually loyal party adherent. Yates, on the contrary, was incorruptible—at least, he was not corruptible by the love of money. His biographer, writing soon after his death, gives us a moving picture: "He was often urged to unite with some of his friends in speculating in forfeited estates during the war, by which he might easily have enriched himself and his connections without censure or suspicion—and although such speculations were common, yet he would not consent to become wealthy upon the ruin of others." (The biographer adds a touching footnote: "Chief Justice Yates died poor.")[16]

Nor was Yates particularly ambitious for power. But where avarice and ambition were absent, vanity was abundantly and fatally present. Yates was induced to become a loyal Clintonian by the simple expedient of giving him an extremely prestigious position, albeit one which was neither particularly powerful nor remunerative, that of chief justice of the state supreme court. Interestingly, New York Federalists won him away from Clinton in 1789 by offering him their support for governor in a campaign against Clinton himself.[17]

It should be noted that in regard to non-economic vested interests the weight of advantages favored the anti-Federalists, but in individual instances of particular strategic importance, the Federalists were invariably in a position to gain. Two well-known examples illustrate this matter. Massachusetts Federalists won the indispensible support of Governor John Hancock by promising him the vice-presidency, a promise they subsequently felt no obligation to fulfill; and Virginia Federalists won the indispensible support of Governor Edmund Randolph by promising him the attorney-generalship, which he was actually awarded.[18]

---

[16]On Lansing, see the sketch in the *Dictionary of American Biography;* Spaulding's *New York in the Critical Period,* 237; and scattered references in vol. 3 of Syrett and Cooke, eds., *The Papers of Alexander Hamilton,* especially III: 139–140. On Yates, see the sketch in the *Dictionary of American Biography* and the biography appended to Senate Document 728, 60th Congress, 2d Session, p. 205.

[17]*Ibid.;* see also the several New York newspapers, April–June, 1789.

[18]Moncure D. Conway, *Omitted Chapters in History Disclosed in the Life and Papers of Edmund Randolph* (New York, 1888), 385ff.; Rufus King to Henry Knox, February 1, 1788, in Charles R. King, *Life and Correspondence*

Now let us return to a survey of the development of vested interests in the states of the Confederation. The most fruitful soil
for such development existed when a policy designed for the over-
all, best interests of the state as a whole could be combined with
policies that worked to the particular advantage of particular
individuals. Such was the case with New York, and in this respect
the history of Virginia during the period strikingly resembles that
of New York, though it was different in every detail. The tangle
of interests in Virginia—state, regional, local, and personal—was
so involved that any attempt to discuss them in full here would be
folly. Let us, then, take notice of such matters as confiscated
estates, western lands, navigation of the Mississippi, and the nebu-
lous but vital questions of personal prides and prestiges, but pass
over them and focus on but a single aspect of the problem, Virginia's commercial policy.[19]

Virginia had, at least in considerable measure, been moved to
join the revolutionary movement as a means of dissolving the
credit bands which had bound planters to British and Scotch
merchants. The sequestration acts by which prewar private indebtedness, amounting to some £2,000,000, was wiped out are well
known. As Isaac Harrell has so well shown, hordes of planters
seized the opportunity to pay nominal sums into the state treasury
and thereby legally expunge their debts to foreign merchants.[20]
What is less known is that Virginia's postwar commercial policy,
whose principal architects were Patrick Henry and the Lees, was
carefully designed to preserve the economic independence so un-
scrupulously won.

To oversimplify considerably, that program was as follows. In
the view of the framers of the program, merchants had been able
to enshackle Virginia planters before the war only because they
operated in an artificially created oligopolistic (or semi-monopo-
listic) marketing system. To prevent the reforging of the chains,
all that was necessary was to create, artificially, a system of excessive competition. The method chosen was to develop a Virginia
mercantile class to conduct about a third of the tobacco business,
and to underwrite it with a system of bounties, drawbacks, and

of Rufus King (6 vols., New York, 1894–1900), 1:319; and Samuel B.
Harding, The Contest over the Ratification of the Federal Constitution in
the State of Massachusetts (New York, 1896), 85–87.

[19]There is no published general history of Virginia during the period;
useful secondary sources include the several biographies of Washington,
Henry, Madison, and Jefferson; Freeman H. Hart, The Valley of Virginia in
the American Revolution, 1763–1789 (Chapel Hill, N.C., 1942); and W. A. Low,
"Merchant and Planter Relations in Post-Revolutionary Virginia, 1783–1789,"
in the Virginia Magazine of History and Biography, LXI (1953) 308–318.

[20]Isaac S. Harrell, Loyalism in Virginia (Philadelphia, 1926).

so on, that enabled it to operate far more cheaply than foreigners. This and many nicer refinements of the state's commercial policy produced intense competition between British, Scotch, French, and other American carriers and merchants for a share of the business, for there was not enough business to go around. As a result, in the 1780's, *relative to the prewar years*, credit was easy, money was abundant, freight rates were low, and tobacco prices, despite Robert Morris' efforts to drive them down so as to fill his contract with the French Farmers' General, were high.[21] In short, because of its political independence, Virginia had been able to liberate a vast number of its inhabitants from the clutches of their foreign creditors, and bring about a prosperity rarely matched in the preceding century.[22]

The ensuing vested interests in Virginia's continued sovereignty are thus obvious. Equally obvious is the fact that the Constitution ran directly counter to these interests in every way. Again, the intense opposition to ratification on the part of state leaders, and the near-success of their efforts, are hardly surprising.[23]

While public policy in these states worked to the advantage of the states as well as to that of rapacious individuals, it was not so in all places. In Massachusetts, for example, public creditors loaded an insupportable burden upon the taxpayers when they succeeded in having all their public paper funded at par in 1784. Private advantage here was contrary to public advantage, and the result was first the weakening of a state whose economy had already been totally disrupted, then in increasing popular discontent, and finally a brief civil war.[24] In Pennsylvania the most important public actions that enriched special groups had a neutral effect upon the welfare of the whole, and consequently won only such friends of state sovereignty as could profit directly from it. In 1785, for ex-

---

[21]The Farmers' General was an organization of French financiers, to whom collection of many indirect taxes had been farmed out, and who had been granted a monopoly on the importation of tobacco.

[22]The development of the program can be traced in the *Journal of the House of Delegates of the State of Virginia* (Richmond, 1828) and in the published statutes. Its operations have been studied in the manuscript Naval Officer Returns in the Virginia State Library, Richmond, and in the quotations of prices and freight rates in the Alexandria *Virginia Journal*, Richmond *Independent Chronicle*, Richmond *Weekly Advertiser*, Richmond *American Advertiser*, *Fredericksburg Advertiser*, Philadelphia *Evening Herald*, and New York *Daily Advertiser*.

[23]The vote of the Virginia convention was 89 to 79 in favor of ratification. The best account of the struggle in the convention is Hugh Blair Grigsby's *The History of the Virginia Federal Convention of 1788*, edited by R. A. Brock (2 vols., Richmond, 1890–1891).

[24]On Massachusetts finance, see Whitney K. Bates, "State Finances of Massachusetts, 1780–1789" (Unpublished master's thesis, University of Wisconsin, 1948).

ample, that state's Constitutionalist Party (those who became anti-Federalists) caused the passage of an act simultaneously funding the state debt and that portion of the national debt owned in the state, and issuing £150,000 ($400,000) in paper money. The Bank of North America opposed this action and offered to lend the state $300,000 if it would not go through with the scheme, but the Constitutionalist majority refused. As one writer said of the entire program, "to unravel the code of policy which it contains, requires no small amount of sagacity and Machiavelian shrewdness." The principal elements in the code of policy it contained, however, are clearly visible: a calculated appeal to an existing interest group and a scheme for enriching the politicians who devised the program. The existing interest group was the public creditors, to whom the program was made immediately palatable by the payment of £100,000 of the new money to them for back interest on their holdings of national debt. The remainder of the paper was issued on loan. Constitutionalist insiders borrowed the paper from the state on long-term, easy credit, and invested in the securities being funded. Thus such Constitutionalists as Charles Pettit, William Moore, John Bayard, Frederick Kuhl, William Will, John Steinmetz, and William Irvine, all holders of several thousand pounds of public securities, profited; and such Constitutionalists as Joseph Heister, John Bishop, Nicholas Lotz, John Hanna, William Brown, William Findley, James Martin, and Robert Whitehill, most of them back-country politicians who had not previously owned any securities, suddenly emerged with profits of several thousand dollars apiece from the rise in security prices.[25]

In 1787, Constitutionalist Party leaders formed a strong phalanx against ratification, but, not surprisingly, they were grossly lacking in public support.[26]

If space permitted, similar developments in virtually all other

---

[25] Merrill Jensen, *The New Nation* (New York, 1950), 316–317; Philadelphia *Evening Herald*, March 8, 1785; Philadelphia *Pennsylvania Packet*, throughout January, 1784, March 31, April 1, 1785; New Loan Certificates, vol. A, accounts 1, 2, 3, 60, 225, 230, 262, 1775–1802, 1954–1958, 2718–2724, 4915, 4919–4925, 5381, vol. B, accounts 10, 391, 6177–6184, 10525–10526, 10528, vol. C, accounts 37, 54, 120, 126, vol. D, 19235–19241, all manuscript volumes in the Public Records Division of the Pennsylvania Historical and Museum Commission; Records of the Loan of 1790, vol. 54, no. 2, folio 330, vol. 610, folios 23, 24, 39, 43, 45, vol. 611, folios 21, 23, 25, 114–115, vol. 612, accounts 8693, 8976–9025, vol. 624, folio 40, vol. 630, folios 48, 49, 122, 309, vol. 631, folios 223, 250, 298.

[26] The Pennsylvania convention ratified the Constitution by a vote of 46 to 23. The standard work on ratification in Pennsylvania is John Bach McMaster and Frederick D. Stone, eds., *Pennsylvania and the Federal Constitution, 1787–1788* (Philadelphia, 1888).

states could be described. In Rhode Island the habit of mixing public policy and private gain was perhaps deepest rooted and highest developed; interestingly, this was also the state that offered the greatest resistance to the Constitution. But the existence of strong vested interest groups in Connecticut, Maryland, and North Carolina—all of whom became anti-Federalists—is abundantly evident, and traces of the phenomenon are visible elsewhere.

I would leave you, not with a summary or a conclusion, but with a question. The foregoing data, all of which are profusely documentable, smack strongly of a knaves-and-fools interpretation of anti-Federalism. Knaves and fools is precisely what Federalists charged their opponents were—the knaves, in their view, being the groups with vested interests in state governments, and the fools being both the ideologues and the uninformed or misinformed. The anti-Federalists, on the other hand, regularly charged that Federalists were knaves, but rarely accused them of being fools. Federalists viewed themselves as friends of the nation; anti-Federalists depicted themselves as friends of the people.

My question is this: if it is true, as I believe it to be, that as a general rule the verdict of history has been the view held by the winner—that of the Patriots over that of the Loyalists, of Jefferson over Hamilton, of Jackson over Biddle, of Franklin Roosevelt over Sam Insull—then how did it happen that historians have, in the main, preferred the anti-Federalists' description of themselves and of their opponents?

The Founding Fathers:
Young Men of the Revolution

STANLEY ELKINS and ERIC MCKITRICK

The intelligent American of today may know a great deal about his history, but the chances are that he feels none too secure about the Founding Fathers and the framing and ratification of the Federal Constitution. He is no longer certain what the "enlight-

Reprinted from *The Political Science Quarterly*, LXXVI, 2 (June, 1961), 181–183, 200–216. Reprinted with permission of the authors.

ened" version of that story is, or even whether there is one. This is because, in the century and three quarters since the Constitution was written, our best thinking on that subject has gone through two dramatically different phases and is at this moment about to enter a third.

Americans in the nineteenth century, whenever they reviewed the events of the founding, made reference to an Olympian gathering of wise and virtuous men who stood splendidly above all faction, ignored petty self-interests, and concerned themselves only with the freedom and well-being of their fellow-countrymen. This attitude toward the Fathers has actually never died out; it still tends to prevail in American history curricula right up through most of the secondary schools. But bright young people arriving at college have been regularly discovering, for nearly the last fifty years, that in the innermost circle this was regarded as an old-fashioned, immensely oversimplified, and rather dewey-eyed view of the Founding Fathers and their work. Ever since J. Allen Smith and Charles Beard wrote in the early years of the twentieth century, the "educated" picture of the Fathers has been that of a group not of disinterested patriots but of hardfisted conservatives who were looking out for their own interests and those of their class. According to this worldlier view, the document which they wrote—and in which they embodied these interests— was hardly intended as a thrust toward popular and democratic government. On the contrary, its centralizing tendencies all reflected the Fathers' distrust of the local and popular rule which had been too little restrained under the Articles of Confederation. The authors of the Constitution represented the privileged part of society. Naturally, then, their desire for a strong central government was, among other things, an effort to achieve solid national guarantees for the rights of property—rights not adequately protected under the Articles—and to obtain for the propertied class (their own) a favored position under the new government.

This "revisionist" point of view—that of the Founding Fathers as self-interested conservatives—has had immeasurable influence in the upper reaches of American historical thought. Much of what at first seemed audacious to the point of lèse majesté came ultimately to be taken as commonplace. The Tory-like, almost backward-turning quality which this approach has imparted to the picture of constitution-making even renders it plausible to think of the Philadelphia Convention of 1787 as a counter-revolutionary conspiracy, which is just the way a number of writers have actually described it. That is, since the Articles of Confederation were the product of the Revolution, to overthrow the Articles was —at least symbolically—to repudiate the Revolution. The Declaration of Independence and the Constitution represented two very different, and in some ways opposing, sets of aspirations; and (so the reasoning goes) the Philadelphia Convention was thus a significant turning-away from, rather than an adherence to, the spirit of the Declaration.

In very recent years, however, a whole new cycle of writing and thinking and research has been under way; the revisionists of the previous generation are themselves being revised. The economic ideas of the late Professor Beard, which dominated this field for so long, have been partially if not wholly discredited. And yet many of the old impressions, intermingled with still older ones, persist. Much of the new work, moreover, though excellent and systematic, is still in progress. Consequently the entire subject of the Constitution and its creation has become a little murky; new notions having the clarity and assuredness of the old have not as yet fully emerged; and meanwhile one is not altogether certain what to think.

Before the significance of all this new work can be justly assessed, and before consistent themes in it may be identified with any assurance, an effort should be made to retrace somewhat the psychology of previous conceptions. At the same time, it should be recognized that any amount of fresh writing on this subject will continue to lack something until it can present us with a clear new symbolic image of the Fathers themselves. The importance of this point lies in the function that symbols have for organizing the historical imagination, and the old ones are a little tired. The "father" image is well and good, and so also in certain respects is the "conservative" one. But we may suppose that these men saw themselves at the time as playing other rôles too, rôles that did not partake so much of retrospection, age, and restraint as those which would come to be assigned to them in after years. The Republic is now very old, as republics go, yet it *was* young once, and so were its founders. With youth goes energy, and the "energy" principle may be more suggestive now, in reviewing the experience of the founding, than the principle of paternal conservatism.

• • •

The work of Merrill Jensen, done in the 1930's and 1940's, has suffered somewhat in reputation due to the sweep and vehemence of the anti-Beardian reaction. Yet that work contains perceptions which ought not to be written off in the general shuffle. They derive not so much from the over-all Beardian traditions and influences amid which Jensen wrote, as from that particular sector of the subject which he marked off and preempted for his own. Simply by committing himself—alone among Beardians and non-Beardians—to presenting the Confederation era as a legitimate phase of American history, entitled to be taken seriously like any other and having a positive side as well as a negative one, he has forced upon us a peculiar point of view which, by the same token, yields its own special budget of insights. For example, Jensen has been profoundly impressed by the sheer force, determination, and drive of such nationalist leaders as Hamilton, Madison, Jay, Knox, and the Morrises. This energy, he feels, created the central problem of the Confederation and was the major cause of its collapse. He deplores this, seeing in the Confederation "democratic" virtues which it probably never had, finding in the Federalists an "aristocratic" character which in actual fact was as much or more to be found in the Anti-Federalists, smelling plots everywhere, and in general shaping his nomenclature to fit his own values and preferences. But if Professor Jensen seems to have called everything by the wrong name, it is well to remember that nomenclature is not everything. The important thing—what does ring true—is that this driving "nationalist" energy was, in all probability, central to the movement that gave the United States a new government.

The other side of the picture, which does not seem to have engaged Jensen's mind half so much, was the peculiar sloth and inertia of the Anti-Federalists. Cecelia Kenyon, in a brilliant essay on these men,[1] has shown them as an amazingly reactionary lot. They were transfixed by the specter of power. It was not the power of the aristocracy that they feared, but power of any kind, democratic or otherwise, that they could not control for themselves. Their chief concern was to keep governments as limited and as closely tied to local interests as possible. Their minds could not embrace the concept of a national interest which they themselves might share and which could transcend their own parochial concerns. Republican government that went beyond the compass of state boundaries was something they could not imagine. Thus the chief difference between Federalists and Anti-Federalists had little to do with "democracy" (George Clinton and Patrick Henry were

---

[1]"Men of Little Faith: The Anti-Federalists on the Nature of Representative Government," *William and Mary Quarterly*, XII, 3rd ser. (January, 1955), 3–43.

no more willing than Gouverneur Morris to trust the innate virtue of the people), but rather in the Federalists' conviction that there was such a thing as national interest and that a government could be established to care for it which was fully in keeping with republican principles. To the Federalists this was not only possible but absolutely necessary, if the nation was to avoid a future of political impotence, internal discord, and in the end foreign intervention. So far so good. But still, exactly how did such convictions get themselves generated?

Merrill Jensen has argued that the Federalists, by and large, were reluctant revolutionaries who had feared the consequences of a break with England and had joined the Revolution only when it was clear that independence was inevitable. The argument is plausible; few of the men most prominent later on as Federalists had been quite so hot for revolution in the very beginning as Patrick Henry and Samuel Adams. But this may not be altogether fair; Adams and Henry were already veteran political campaigners at the outbreak of hostilities, while the most vigorous of the future Federalists were still mere youngsters. The argument, indeed, could be turned entirely around: the source of Federalist, or nationalist, energy was not any "distaste" for the Revolution on these men's part, but rather their profound and growing involvement in it.

Much depends here on the way one pictures the Revolution. In the beginning it simply consisted of a number of state revolts loosely directed by the Continental Congress; and for many men, absorbed in their effort to preserve the independence of their own states, it never progressed much beyond that stage even in the face of invasion. But the Revolution had another aspect, one which developed with time and left a deep imprint on those connected with it, and this was its character as a continental war effort. If there is any one feature that most unites the future leading supporters of the Constitution, it was their close engagement with this continental aspect of the Revolution. A remarkably large number of these someday Federalists were in the Continental Army, served as diplomats or key administrative officers of the Confederation government, or, as members of Congress, played leading roles on those committees primarily responsible for the conduct of the war.

Merrill Jensen has compiled two lists, with nine names in each, of the men whom he considers to have been the leading spirits of the Federalists and Anti-Federalists respectively. It would be well to have a good look at this sample. The Federalists—Jensen calls them "nationalists"—were Robert Morris, John Jay, James Wilson, Alexander Hamilton, Henry Knox, James Duane, George Washington, James Madison, and Gouverneur Morris. Washington, Knox, and Hamilton were deeply involved in Continental military affairs; Robert Morris was Superintendent of Finance; Jay was president of the Continental Congress and minister plenipotentiary to Spain (he would later be appointed Secretary for Foreign Affairs); Wilson, Duane, and Gouverneur Morris were members of Congress, all three being active members of the war committees. The Anti-Federalist group presents a very different picture. It consisted of Samuel Adams, Patrick Henry, Richard Henry Lee, George Clinton, James Warren, Samuel Bryan, George Bryan, George Mason, and Elbridge Gerry. Only three of these—Gerry, Lee, and Adams—served in Congress, and the latter two fought consistently against any effort to give Congress executive powers. Their constant preoccupation was state sovereignty rather than national efficiency. Henry and Clinton were active war governors, concerned primarily with state rather than national problems, while Warren, Mason, and the two Bryans were essentially state politicians.

The age difference between these two groups is especially striking. The Federalists were on the average ten to twelve years younger than the Anti-Federalists. At the outbreak of the Revolution George Washington, at 44, was the oldest of the lot; six were under 35 and four were in their twenties. Of the Anti-Federalists, only three were under 40 in 1776, and one of these, Samuel Bryan, the son of George Bryan, was a boy of 16.

This age differential takes on a special significance when it is related to the career profiles of the men concerned. Nearly half of the Federalist group—Gouverneur Morris, Madison, Hamilton, and Knox—quite literally saw their careers launched in the Revolution. The remaining five—Washington, Jay, Duane, Wilson, and Robert Morris—though established in public affairs beforehand, became nationally known after 1776 and the wide public recognition which they subsequently achieved came first and foremost through their identification with the continental war effort. All of them had been united in an experience, and had formed commitments, which dissolved provincial boundaries; they had come to full public maturity in a setting which enabled ambition, public service, leadership, and self-fulfillment to be conceived, for each in his way, with a grandeur of scope unknown to any previous generation. The careers of the Anti-Federalists, on the other hand, were not only state-centered but—aside from those of

Clinton, Gerry, and the young Bryan—rested heavily on events that preceded rather than followed 1776.

As exemplars of nationalist energy, two names in Professor Jensen's sample that come most readily to mind are those of Madison and Hamilton. The story of each shows a wonderfully pure line of consistency. James Madison, of an influential Virginia family but with no apparent career plans prior to 1774, assumed his first public role as a member of the Orange County Revolutionary Committee, of which his father was chairman. As a delegate from Orange County he went to the Virginia convention in 1776 and served on the committee that drafted Virginia's new constitution and bill of rights. He served in the Virginia Assembly in 1776 and 1777 but failed of re-election partly because he refused to treat his constituents to whisky. (He obviously did not have the right talents for a state politician.) In recognition of Madison's services, however, the Assembly elected him to the Governor's Council, where he served from 1778 to 1780. Patrick Henry was then Governor; the two men did not get on well and in time became bitter political enemies. At this period Madison's primary concern was with supplying and equipping the Continental Army, a concern not shared to his satisfaction by enough of his colleagues. It was then, too, that he had his first experience with finance and the problems of paper money. He was elected to the Continental Congress in 1780, and as a member of the Southern Committee was constantly preoccupied with the military operations of Nathanael Greene. The inefficiency and impotence of Congress pained him unbearably. The Virginia Assembly took a strong stand against federal taxation which Madison ignored, joining Hamilton in the unsuccessful effort to persuade the states to accept the impost of 1783. From the day he entered politics up to that time, the energies of James Madison were involved in continental rather than state problems—problems of supply, enlistment, and finance—and at every point his chief difficulties came from state parochialism, selfishness, and lack of imagination. His nationalism was hardly accidental.

The career line of Alexander Hamilton, *mutatis mutandis,* is functionally interchangeable with that of James Madison. Ambitious, full of ability, but a young man of no family and no money, Hamilton arrived in New York from the provinces at the age of 17 and in only two years would be catapulted into a brilliant career by the Revolution. At 19 he became a highly effective pamphleteer while still a student at King's College, was captain of an artillery company at 21, serving with distinction in the New York and New Jersey campaigns, and in 1777 was invited to join Washington's staff as a lieutenant-colonel. He was quickly accepted by as brilliant and aristocratic a set of youths as could be found in the country. As a staff officer he became all too familiar with the endless difficulties of keeping the Continental Army in the field from 1777 to 1780. With his marriage to Elizabeth Schuyler in 1780 he was delightedly welcomed into one of New York's leading families, and his sage advice to his father-in-law and Robert Morris on matters of finance and paper money won him the reputation of a financial expert with men who knew an expert when they saw one. He had an independent command at Yorktown. He became Treasury representative in New York in 1781, was elected to Congress in 1782, and worked closely with Madison in the fruitless and discouraging effort to create a national revenue in the face of state particularism. In the summer of 1783 he quit in despair and went back to New York. Never once throughout all this period had Alexander Hamilton been involved in purely state affairs. His career had been a continental one, and as long as the state-centered George Clinton remained a power in New York, it was clear that this was the only kind that could have any real meaning for him. As with James Madison, Hamilton's nationalism was fully consistent with all the experience he had ever had in public life, experience whose sole meaning had been derived from the Revolution. The experience of the others—for instance that of John Jay and Henry Knox—had had much the same quality; Knox had moved from his bookstore to the command of Washington's artillery in little more than a year, while Jay's public career began with the agitation just prior to the Revolution and was a story of steady advancement in continental affairs from that time forward.

The logic of these careers, then, was in large measure tied to a chronology which did not apply in the same way to all the men in public life during the two decades of the 1770's and 1780's. A significant proportion of relative newcomers, with prospects initially modest, happened to have their careers opened up at a particular time and in such a way that their very public personalities came to be staked upon the national quality of the experience which had formed them. In a number of outstanding cases energy, initiative, talent, and ambition had combined with a conception of affairs which had grown immense in scope and promise by the close of the Revolution. There is every reason to think that a contraction of this scope, in the years that immediately followed, operated as a powerful challenge.

The stages through which the constitutional movement proceeded in the 1780's add up to a fascinating story in political management, marked by no little élan and dash. That movement, viewed in the light of the Federalist leaders' commitment to the Revolution, raises some nice points as to who were the "conservatives" and who were the "radicals." The spirit of unity generated by the struggle for independence had, in the eyes of those most closely involved in coördinating the effort, lapsed; provincial factions were reverting to the old provincial ways. The impulse to arrest disorder and to revive the flame of revolutionary unity may be pictured in "conservative" terms, but this becomes quite awkward when we look for terms with which to picture the other impulse, so different in nature: the urge to rest, to drift, to turn back the clock.

Various writers have said that the activities of the Federalists during this period had in them a clear element of the conspiratorial. Insofar as this refers to a strong line of political strategy, it correctly locates a key element in the movement. Yet without a growing base of popular dissatisfaction with the status quo, the Federalists could have skulked and plotted forever without accomplishing anything. We now know, thanks to recent scholarship, that numerous elements of the public were only too ripe for change. But the work of organizing such a sentiment was quite another matter; it took an immense effort of will just to get it off the ground. Though it would be wrong to think of the Constitution as something that had to be carried in the face of deep and basic popular opposition, it certainly required a series of brilliant maneuvers to escape the deadening clutch of particularism and inertia. An Anti-Federalist "no" could register on exactly the same plane as a Federalist "yes" while requiring a fraction of the energy. It was for this reason that the Federalists, even though they cannot be said to have circumvented the popular will, did have to use techniques which in their sustained drive, tactical mobility, and risk-taking smacked more than a little of the revolutionary.

By 1781, nearly five years of intimate experience with the war effort had already convinced such men as Washington, Madison, Hamilton, Duane, and Wilson that something had to be done to strengthen the Continental government, at least to the point of providing it with an independent income. The ratification of the Articles of Confederation early in the year (before Yorktown) seemed to offer a new chance, and several promising steps were taken at that time. Congress organized executive departments of war, foreign affairs, and finance to replace unwieldy and inefficient committees; Robert Morris was appointed Superintendent of Finance; and a 5 percent impost was passed which Congress urged the states to accept.

By the fall of 1782, however, the surge for increased efficiency had lost the greater part of its momentum. Virginia had changed its mind about accepting the impost, Rhode Island having been flatly opposed all along, and it became apparent that as soon as the treaty with England (then being completed) was ratified, the sense of common purpose which the war had created would be drained of its urgency. At this point Hamilton and the Morrises, desperate for a solution, would have been quite willing to use the discontent of an unpaid army as a threat to coerce the states out of their obstructionism, had not Washington refused to lend himself to any such scheme. Madison and Hamilton thereupon joined forces in Congress to work out a revenue bill whose subsidiary benefits would be sufficiently diffuse to gain it general support among the states. But in the end the best that could be managed was a new plan for a 5 percent impost, the revenues of which would be collected by state-appointed officials. Once more an appeal, drafted by Madison, was sent to the states urging them to accept the new impost, and Washington wrote a circular in support of it. The effort was in vain. The army, given one month's pay in cash and three in certificates, reluctantly dispersed, and the Confederation government, with no sanctions of coercion and no assured revenues, now reached a new level of impotence. In June, 1783, Alexander Hamilton, preparing to leave Congress to go back to private life, wrote in discouragement and humiliation to Nathanael Greene:

There is so little disposition either in or out of Congress to give solidity to our national system that there is no motive to a man to lose his time in the public service, who has no other view than to promote its welfare. Experience must convince us that our present establishments are Utopian before we shall be ready to part with them for better.

Whether or not the years between 1783 and 1786 should be viewed as a "critical period" depends very much on whose angle they are viewed from. Although it was a time of economic depression, the depressed conditions were not felt in all areas of economic life with the same force, nor were they nearly as damaging in some localities as in others; the interdependence of economic enterprise was not then what it would become later on, and a depression in Massachusetts did not necessarily imply one in Virginia, or even in New York. Moreover, there were definite signs of improvement by 1786. Nor can it necessarily be said that government on the state level lacked vitality. Most of the states were addressing their problems with energy and decision. There were problems everywhere, of course, many of them very grave, and in some cases (those of New Jersey and Connecticut in particular) solutions seemed almost beyond the individual state's resources. Yet it would be wrong, as Merrill Jensen points out, to assume that no solutions were possible within the framework which then existed. It is especially important to remember that when most people thought of "the government" they were not thinking of Congress at all, but of their own state legislature. For them, therefore, it was by no means self-evident that the period through which they were living was one of drift and governmental impotence.

But through the eyes of men who had come to view the states collectively as a "country" and to think in continental terms, things looked altogether different. From their viewpoint the Confederation was fast approaching the point of ruin. Fewer and fewer states were meeting their requisition payments, and Congress could not even pay its bills. The states refused to accept any impost which they themselves could not control, and even if all the rest accepted, the continued refusal of New York (which was not likely to change) would render any impost all but valueless. Local fears and jealousies blocked all efforts to establish uniform regulation of commerce, even though some such regulation seemed indispensable. A number of the states, New York in particular, openly ignored the peace treaty with England and passed discriminatory legislation against former Loyalists; consequently England, using as a pretext Congress' inability to enforce the treaty, refused to surrender the northwest posts. Morale in Congress was very low as members complained that lack of a quorum prevented them most of the time from transacting any business; even when a quorum was present, a few negative votes could block important legislation indefinitely. Any significant change, or any substantial increase in the power of Congress, required unanimous approval by the states, and as things then stood this had become very remote. Finally, major states such as New York and Virginia were simply paying less and less attention to Congress. The danger was not so much that of a split with the Confederation—Congress lacked the strength that would make any such "split" seem very urgent—but rather a policy of neglect that would just allow Congress to wither away from inactivity.

These were the conditions that set the stage for a fresh effort —the Annapolis Convention of 1786—to strengthen the continental government. The year before, Madison had arranged a conference between Maryland and Virginia for the regulation of commerce on the Potomac, and its success had led John Tyler and Madison to propose a measure in the Virginia Assembly that would give Congress power to regulate commerce throughout the Confederation. Though nothing came of it, a plan was devised in its place whereby the several states would be invited to take part in a convention to be held at Annapolis in September, 1786, for the purpose of discussing commercial problems. The snapping-point came when delegates from only five states appeared. The rest either distrusted one another's intentions (the northeastern states doubted the southerners' interest in commerce) or else suspected a trick to strengthen the Confederation government at their expense. It was apparent that no serious action could be taken at that time. But the dozen delegates who did come (Hamilton and Madison being in their forefront) were by definition those most concerned over the state of the national government, and they soon concluded that their only hope of saving it lay in some audacious plenary gesture. It was at this meeting, amid the mortification of still another failure, that they planned the Philadelphia Convention.

The revolutionary character of this move—though some writers have correctly perceived it—has been obscured both by the stateliness of historical retrospection and by certain legal peculiarities which allowed the proceeding to appear a good deal less subversive than it actually was. The "report" of the Annapolis meeting was actually a call, drafted by Hamilton and carefully edited by Madison, for delegates of all the states to meet in convention at Philadelphia the following May for the purpose of revising the Articles of Confederation. Congress itself transmitted the call, and in so doing was in effect being brought to by-pass its own constituted limits. On the one hand, any effort to change the government within the rules laid down by the Articles would have required a unanimous approval which could never be obtained. But on the other hand, the very helplessness which the several states had imposed upon the central government meant in practice that the states were sovereign and could do anything they pleased with it. It was precisely this that the nationalists now prepared to exploit: this legal paradox had hitherto prevented the growth of strong loyalty to the existing Confederation and could presently allow that same Confederation, through the action of the states, to be undermined in the deceptive odor of legitimacy. Thus the Beardian school of constitutional thought, for all its errors of economic analysis and its transposing of ideological semantics, has called attention to one element—the element of subversion—that is actually entitled to some consideration.

But if the movement had its plotters, balance requires us to add that the "plot" now had a considerable measure of potential support, and that the authority against which the plot was aimed had become little more than a husk. Up to this time every nationalist move, including the Annapolis Convention, had been easily blocked. But things were now happening in such a way as to tip the balance and to offer the nationalists for the first time a better-than-even chance of success. There had been a marked improvement in business, but shippers in Boston, New York, and Philadelphia were still in serious trouble. Retaliatory measures against Great Britain through state legislation had proved ineffective and useless; there was danger, at the same time, that local manufacturing interests might be successful in pushing through high state tariffs. In the second place, New York's refusal to reconsider a national impost, except on terms that would have removed its effectiveness, cut the ground from under the moderates who had argued that, given only a little time, everything could be worked out. This did not leave much alternative to a major revision of the national government. Then there were Rhode Island's difficulties with inflationary paper money. Although that state's financial schemes actually made a certain amount of sense, they provided the nationalists with wonderful propaganda and helped to create an image of parochial irresponsibility.

The most decisive event of all was Shays' Rebellion in the fall and winter of 1786–1787. It was this uprising of hard-pressed rural debtors in western Massachusetts that frightened moderate people everywhere and convinced them of the need for drastic remedies against what looked like anarchy. The important thing was not so much the facts of the case as the impression which it created outside Massachusetts. The Shaysites had no intention of destroying legitimate government or of redistributing property, but the fact that large numbers of people could very well imagine them doing such things added a note of crisis which was all to the Federalists' advantage. Even the levelheaded Washington was disturbed, and his apprehensions were played upon quite knowingly by Madison, Hamilton, and Knox in persuading him to attend the Philadelphia Convention. Actually the Federalists and the Shaysites had been driven to action by much the same conditions; in Massachusetts their concern with the depressed state of trade and the tax burden placed them for all practical purposes on the same side, and there they remained from first to last.

Once the balance had been tipped in enough states, to the point of a working consensus on the desirability of change, a second principle came into effect. Unless a state were absolutely opposed—as in the extreme case of Rhode Island—to any change in the Articles of Confederation, it was difficult to ignore the approaching Philadelphia Convention as had been done with the Annapolis Convention: the occasion was taking on too much importance. There was thus the danger, for such a state, of seeing significant decisions made without having its interests consulted. New York, with strong Anti-Federalist biases but also with a strong nationalist undercurrent, was not quite willing to boycott the convention. Governor Clinton's solution was to send as delegates two rigid state particularists, John Yates and Robert Lansing, along with the nationalist Hamilton, to make sure that Hamilton would not accomplish anything.

We have already seen that nineteenth century habits of thought created a ponderous array of stereotypes around the historic Philadelphia conclave of 1787. Twentieth century thought and scholarship, on the other hand, had the task of breaking free from them, and to have done so is a noteworthy achievement. And yet one must return to the point that stereotypes themselves require some form of explanation. The legend of a transcendent effort of statesmanship, issuing forth in a miraculously perfect instrument of government, emerges again and again despite all efforts either to conjure it out of existence or to give it some sort of rational linkage with mortal affairs. Why should the legend be so extraordinarily durable, and was there anything so special about the circumstances that set it on its way so unerringly and so soon?

The circumstances *were,* in fact, special; given a set of delegates of well over average ability, the Philadelphia meeting provides a really classic study in the sociology of intellect. Divine accident, though in some measure present in men's doings always, is not required as a part of this particular equation. The key conditions were all present in a pattern that virtually guaranteed for the meeting an optimum of effectiveness. A sufficient number of states were represented so that the delegates could, without strain, realistically picture themselves as thinking, acting, and making decisions in the name of the entire nation. They themselves, moreover, represented interests throughout the country that were diverse enough, and they had enough personal prestige at home, that they could act in the assurance of having their decisions treated at least with respectful attention. There had also been at work a remarkably effective process of self-selection, as to both men and states. Rhode Island ignored the convention, and as a result its position was not even considered there. There were leading state particularists such as Patrick Henry and Richard Henry Lee who were elected as delegates but refused to serve. The Anti-Federalist position, indeed, was hardly represented at all, and the few men who did represent it had surprisingly little to say. Yates and Lansing simply left before the convention was over. Thus a group already predisposed in a national direction could proceed unhampered by the friction of basic opposition in its midst. This made it possible for the delegates to "try on" various alternatives without having to remain accountable for everything they said. At the same time, being relieved from all outside pressures meant that the only way a man could expect to make a real difference in the convention's deliberations was to reach, through main persuasion, other men of considerable ability and experience. Participants and audience were therefore one, and this in itself imposed standards of debate which were quite exacting. In such a setting the best minds in the convention were accorded an authority which they would not have had in political debates aimed at an indiscriminate public.

Thus the elements of secrecy, the general inclination for a national government, and the process whereby the delegates came to terms with their colleagues—appreciating their requirements and adjusting to their interests—all combined to produce a growing esprit de corps. As initial agreements were worked out, it became exceedingly difficult for the Philadelphia delegates not to grow more and more committed to the product of their joint efforts. Indeed, this was in all likelihood the key mechanism, more important than any other in explaining not only the peculiar genius of the main compromises but also the general fitness of the document as a whole. That is, a group of two or more intelligent men who are subject to no cross-pressures and whose principal commitment is to the success of an idea, are perfectly

capable—as in our scientific communities of today—of perform-
ing what appear to be prodigies of intellect. Moving, as it were,
in the same direction with a specific purpose, they can function
at maximum efficiency. It was this that the historians of the nineteenth century did in their way see, and celebrated with sweeping
rhetorical flourishes, when they took for granted that if an occasion of this sort could not call forth the highest level of statesmanship available, then it was impossible to imagine another
that could.

Once the Philadelphia Convention had been allowed to meet
and the delegates had managed, after more than three months
of work, to hammer out a document that the great majority of
them could sign, the political position of the Federalists changed
dramatically. Despite the major battles still impending, for practical purposes they now had the initiative. The principal weapon
of the Anti-Federalists—inertia—had greatly declined in effectiveness, for with the new program in motion it was no longer enough
simply to argue that a new federal government was unnecessary.
They would have to take positive steps in blocking it; they would
have to arouse the people and convince them that the Constitution
represented a positive danger.

Moreover, the Federalists had set the terms of ratification in
such a way as to give the maximum advantage to energy and
purpose; the key choices, this time, had been so arranged that
they would fall right. Only nine states had to ratify before the
Constitution would go into effect. Not only would this rule out
the possibility of one or two states holding up the entire effort,
but it meant that the Confederation would be automatically destroyed as an alternative before the difficult battles in New York
and Virginia had to be faced. (By then, Patrick Henry in Virginia
would have nothing but a vague alliance with North Carolina
to offer as a counter-choice.) Besides, there was good reason to
believe that at least four or five states, and possibly as many as
seven, could be counted as safe, which meant that serious fighting
in the first phase would be limited to two or three states. And
finally, conditions were so set that the "snowball" principle would
at each successive point favor the Federalists.

As for the actual process of acceptance, ratification would be
done through state conventions elected for the purpose. Not only
would this circumvent the vested interests of the legislatures
and the ruling coteries that frequented the state capitals, but
it gave the Federalists two separate chances to make their case—
once to the people and once to the conventions. If the elected

delegates were not initially disposed to do the desired thing, there was still a chance, after the convention met, of persuading them. Due partly to the hampering factor of transportation and distance, delegates had to have considerable leeway of choice and what amounted to quasi-plenipotentiary powers. Thus there could be no such thing as a fully "instructed" delegation, and members might meanwhile remain susceptible to argument and conversion. The convention device, moreover, enabled the Federalists to run as delegates men who would not normally take part in state politics.

The revolutionary verve and ardor of the Federalists, their resources of will and energy, their willingness to scheme tirelessly, campaign everywhere, and sweat and agonize over every vote meant in effect that despite all the hairbreadth squeezes and rigors of the struggle, the Anti-Federalists would lose every crucial test. There was, to be sure, an Anti-Federalist effort. But with no program, no really viable commitments, and little purposeful organization, the Anti-Federalists somehow always managed to move too late and with too little. They would sit and watch their great stronghold, New York, being snatched away from them despite a two-to-one Anti-Federalists majority in a convention presided over by their own chief, George Clinton. To them, the New York Federalists must have seemed possessed of the devil. The Federalists' convention men included Alexander Hamilton, James Duane, John Jay, and Robert Livingston—who knew, as did everyone else, that the new government was doomed unless Virginia and New York joined it. They insisted on debating the Constitution section by section instead of as a whole, which meant that they could out-argue the Anti-Federalists on every substantive issue and meanwhile delay the vote until New Hampshire and Virginia had had a chance to ratify. (Madison and Hamilton had a horse relay system in readiness to rush the Virginia news northward as quickly as possible.) By the time the New York convention was ready to act, ten others had ratified, and at the final moment Hamilton and his allies spread the chilling rumor that New York City was about to secede from the state. The Anti-Federalists, who had had enough, directed a chosen number of their delegates to cross over, and solemnly capitulated.

In the end, of course, everyone "crossed over." The speed with which this occurred once the continental revolutionists had made their point, and the ease with which the Constitution so soon became an object of universal veneration, still stands as one of the minor marvels of American history. But the document did contain certain implications, of a quasi-philosophical nature, that make the reasons for this ready consensus not so very difficult to find. It established a national government whose basic outlines were sufficiently congenial to the underlying commitments of the whole culture—republicanism and capitalism—that the likelihood of its being the subject of a true ideological clash was never very real. That the Constitution should mount guard over the rights of property—"realty," "personalty," or any other kind—was questioned by nobody. There had certainly been a struggle, a long and exhausting one, but we should not be deceived as to its nature. It was not fought on economic grounds; it was not a matter of ideology; it was not, in the fullest and most fundamental sense, even a struggle between nationalism and localism. The key struggle was between inertia and energy; with inertia overcome, everything changed.

There were, of course, lingering objections and misgivings; many of the problems involved had been genuinely puzzling and difficult; and there remained doubters who had to be converted. But then the perfect bridge whereby all could become Federalists within a year was the addition of a Bill of Rights. After the French Revolution, anti-constitutionalism in France would be a burning issue for generations; in America, an anti-constitutional party was undreamed of after 1789. With the Bill of Rights, the remaining opponents of the new system could say that, ever watchful of tyranny, they had now got what they wanted. Moreover, the Young Men of the Revolution might at last imagine, after a dozen years of anxiety, that *their* Revolution had been a success.

THE SPECTER OF FAILURE

The roots and nature of the anxieties that caused a sizable number of the American political community to fear for the success of the Revolution during the Confederation period are explored in the two selections that follow. The first selection demonstrates to what an extraordinary extent the Founding Fathers' reading of history and, more specifically, their awareness and interpretation of the long record of failure of republican government in both classical and modern times shaped their responses to developments of the mid-1780's. They became convinced, as a result, that an excess of democracy was the most serious danger confronting the United States. Their theories and interpretations, moreover, gave the clamor for paper money in 1785–1786 and Shays' Rebellion an especially frightening aspect. Shays' Rebellion, in particular, seemed to portend not just social anarchy but the failure of the whole American experiment in republicanism. That it should have occurred because a large body of the citizenry could not obtain redress of grievances through normal constitutional processes in, of all places, Massachusetts—the only state in which the people lived under a constitution that they themselves had made through specially-elected representatives and to which they had given their collective approval— was, as the second selection makes clear, an especially ominous sign, a certain indication of the eventful degeneration of the young republic into either a popular or aristocratic tyranny. To solve the basic problem, to achieve a government that was more sensitive to the grievances of the public, required, as the author of the second piece points out, the development of some mechanism—the political party, for example—through which public opinion could be mobilized. In the 1780's, however, alarmed observers tended to pin their hopes upon the creation of a central government with sufficient strength to provide both a stable environment within which the sensitive republican plant could be properly nourished and some check on any petty tyrannies that might arise in the individual states.

DOUGLASS G. ADAIR (1912–1968) was a member of the
Department of History at the Clarement Graduate School;
J. R. POLE (b. 1922) is Reader in American History at
Churchill College, Cambridge.

Experience Must Be Our Only Guide: History, Democratic Theory, and the United States Constitution

DOUGLASS G. ADAIR

"The history of Greece," John Adams wrote in 1786, "should
be to our countrymen what is called in many families on the
Continent, a *boudoir*, an octagonal apartment in a house, with
a full-length mirror on every side, and another in the ceiling.
The use of it is, when any of the young ladies, or gentlemen
if you will, are at any time a little out of humour, they may
retire to a place where, in whatever direction they turn their
eyes, they see their own faces and figures multiplied without
end. By thus beholding their own beautiful persons, and seeing,
at the same time, the deformity brought upon them by their
anger, they may recover their tempers and their charms together."[1]

Adams' injunction that his countrymen should study the history
of ancient Greece in order to amend their political behavior
suggests two points for our consideration. First, John Adams
assumed without question that history did offer lessons and
precepts which statesmen could use in solving immediate problems. Secondly, Adams urged the study of the classical Greek
republics as the particular history especially relevant, most full
of useful lessons and precepts for Americans in 1787.

Adams, as is well known, practiced what he preached. Working

Reprinted with permission from Ray A. Billington, ed., *The Reinterpretation of Early American History: Essays in Honor of John Edwin Pomfret*
(San Marino, Calif., 1966), 129–148.

[1]John Adams, *Defence of the Constitutions of the United States of America* (1787), in Charles F. Adams, ed., *The Works of John Adams* (10 vols.,
Boston, 1850–1856), IV, 469. Hereafter cited as *Defence, IV.*

at high speed between October 1786 and January 1787, in time stolen from his duties as United States Minister to Great Britain, he composed his *Defence of the Constitutions of the United States* —a 300-page book exhibiting for his countrymen the lessons of history. And though he included material from all periods of western civilization, a large part of his data was collected from the classical republics of antiquity.

Nor did his American audience who read Adams' work in the weeks immediately prior to the meeting of the Philadelphia Convention deny his assumptions or purposes in urging them to study the lessons of Greek history. Benjamin Rush, for example, reporting to the Reverend Richard Price in England on the attitude of the Pennsylvania delegation to the Convention, gave Adams' study the highest praise. "Mr. Adams' book," he wrote, "has diffused such excellent principles among us that there is little doubt of our adopting a vigorous and compounded federal legislature. Our illustrious Minister in this gift to his country has done us more service than if he had obtained alliances for us with all the nations of Europe."[2]

Do Adams and Rush in their view on the utility of history for the constitutional reforms of 1787 represent the typical attitude of the members of the Convention? Did the fifty-five men gathered to create a more perfect union consciously turn to past history for lessons and precepts that were generalized into theories about the correct organization of the new government? Did lessons from the antique past, applied to their present situation, concretely affect their actions at Philadelphia? The evidence is overwhelming that they did, although the weight of modern commentary on the Constitution either ignores the Fathers' conscious and deliberate use of history and theory or denies that it played any important part in their deliberations.

Max Farrand, for example, after years of study of the debates in the Convention concluded that the members were anything but historically oriented. Almost all had served (Farrand noted) in the Continental Congress and had tried to govern under the impotent Articles of Confederation. There is little of importance in the Constitution (Farrand felt) that did not arise from the effort to correct specific defects of the Confederation.

Robert L. Schuyler, an able and careful student of the Constitution, goes even further in denying the Convention's depend-

---

[2]Lyman H. Butterfield, ed., *Letters of Benjamin Rush* (2 vols., Princeton, 1951), I, 418; to Richard Price, Philadelphia, June 2, 1787.

ence upon history. "The Fathers were practical men. They lived at a time when a decent respect for the proprieties of political discussion required at least occasional reference to Locke and Montesquieu . . . but . . . such excursions into political philosophy as were made are to be regarded rather as purple patches than as integral parts of the proceedings. The scholarly Madison had gone extensively into the subject of Greek federalism . . . but it was his experience in public life and his wide knowledge of the conditions of his day, not his classical lucubrations that bore fruit at Philadelphia. . . . The debate . . . did not proceed along theoretical lines. John Dickinson expressed the prevailing point of view when he said in the Convention: 'Experience must be our only guide. Reason may mislead us.' "[3]

Dickinson's statement on August 13th: "Experience must be our only guide" does indeed express the mood of the delegates; no word was used more often; time after time "experience" was appealed to as the clinching argument for a controverted opinion. But "experience" as used in the Convention, more often than not, referred to the precepts of history. This is Dickinson's sense of the word when he warned the Convention that "reason" might mislead. "It was not reason," Dickinson continued, "that discovered the singular and admirable mechanism of the English Constitution . . . [or the] mode of trial by jury. Accidents probably produced these discoveries, and experience has given a sanction to them." And then Dickinson, turning to James Wilson and Madison who had argued that vesting the power to initiate revenue bills exclusively in the lower house of the Legislature had proved "pregnant with altercation in every [American] State where the [revolutionary] Constitution had established it," denied that the short "experience" of the American States carried as weighty a sanction as the long historic "experience" of the English House of Commons. "Shall we oppose to this long [English] experience," Dickinson asked, "the short experience of 11 years which we had ourselves, on this subject."[4] Dickinson's words actually point to

---

[3]Robert L. Schuyler, *The Constitution of the United States* (New York, 1923), 90–91.

[4]Max Farrand, ed., *Records of the Federal Convention of 1787* (4 vols., New Haven, 1911–1937), II, under date of August 13, 1787. Unless otherwise noted, quotations from the Debates are from Madison's "Notes." Dickinson, in noting that the English Constitution was not the result of "reason" but of "accident," is referring to the commonly held belief in the eighteenth century that the most successful republican constitutions of antiquity had almost without exception been drafted single-handed by a semi-divine legislator at one creative moment in time: Moses, Lycurgus, Minos, Zaleueus. For a discussion of this tradition see *The Federalist*, No.

the fact that theories grounded in historical research are indeed integral parts of the debate on the Constitution.

For Dickinson is not alone in using "experience" in this dual fashion to refer both to political wisdom gained by participation in events, and wisdom gained by studying past events. Franklin and Madison, Butler and Mason, Wilson and Hamilton all appeal to historical "experience" in exactly the same way. "Experience shows" or "history proves" are expressions that are used interchangeably throughout the Convention by members from all sections of the United States.[5] Pure reason not verified by history might be a false guide; the mass of mankind might indeed be the slave of passion and unreason, but the fifty-five men who gathered at Philadelphia in 1787 labored in the faith of the enlightenment that experience-as-history provided "the least fallible guide of human opinions,"[6] that historical experience is "the oracle of truth, and where its responses are unequivocal they ought to be conclusive and sacred."[7]

Schuyler's insistence that the Fathers were "practical men" who abhorred theory, associates him with a standard theme of American anti-intellectualism that honors unsystematic "practicality" and distrusts systematic theoretical thought. His argument, undoubtedly too, reflects nineteenth-century theories of "progress-evolution" that assume the quantitative lapse in time between 400 B.C. and 1787 A.D. *a priori* makes the earlier period irrelevant for understanding a modern and different age. And, of course, what came to be called "sound history" after 1880 when the

---

38. The two striking exceptions of constitutions not born in the brain of one great lawgiver were the English constitution and the Roman. On the latter see Machiavelli's statement in *Discourses on Livy* (which Adams quotes in his *Defence*, IV, 419): "Though that city [Rome] had not a Lycurgus to model its constitution at first . . . yet so many were the accidents which happened in the contests betwixt the patricians and the plebians, that chance effected what the lawgiver had not provided for."

[5]Farrand, ed., *Records of the Federal Convention:* Franklin, September 7, "Experience shewed"; Mason, June 4, "Experience, the best of all tests"; Hamilton, June 18, "Theory is in this case fully confirmed by experience"; Madison, June 28, "Experience . . . that instinctive monitor"; Butler, June 22 (Yates), "We have no way of judging of mankind but by experience. Look at the history of Great Britain. . . ." H. Trevor Colbourn uses a quotation from Patrick Henry's 1765 oration, "The Lamp of Experience," as the title of his able and suggestive study of the way in which historical interpretation helped transform a three-penny tax on molasses and a two-penny tax on tea into revolutionary constitutional principles that Americans would die to defend. H. Trevor Colbourn, *'The Lamp of Experience!' Whig History and the Intellectual Origins of the American Revolution* (Chapel Hill, 1965).

[6]Alexander Hamilton, *The Federalist*, No. 6.
[7]James Madison, *ibid.*, No. 20.

discipline came to roost in academic groves, is quite different itself from the "history" that eighteenth-century statesmen found most significant and useful. Modern historians have tended to insist that the unique and the particular is the essence of "real history"; in contrast the eighteenth-century historian was most concerned and put the highest value on what was universal and constant through time.

Eighteenth-century historians believed "that there is a great uniformity among the actions of men, in all nations and ages, and that human nature remains still the same, in its principles and operations. The same motives always produce the same actions; the same events follow from the same causes. Ambition, avarice, self-love, vanity, friendship, generosity, public spirit; these passions, mixed in various degrees, and distributed through society, have been from the beginning of the world, and still are the source of all the actions and enterprizes, which have ever been observed among mankind. Would you know the sentiments, inclinations, and course of life of the Greeks and Romans? Study well the temper and actions of the French and English." Thus David Hume, distinguished eighteenth-century historian and philosopher.[8]

The method of eighteenth-century history for those who would gain political wisdom from it followed from this primary assumption—it was historical-comparative synthesis. Again Hume speaks: "Mankind are so much the same, in all times and places, that history informs us of nothing new or strange, in this particular. *Its chief use is only to discover the constant and universal principles of human nature,* by showing men in all varieties of circumstances and situations, and furnishing us with materials, from which we may form our observations and become acquainted with the regular springs of human action and behavior. These records . . . are so many collections of experiments, by which the politician or moral philosopher fixes the principles of his science, in the same manner as the physician or natural philosopher becomes acquainted with the nature of plants, minerals, and other external objects, by the experiments which he forms concerning them."

---

[8]David Hume, one of the most penetrating intellects of the age and famed as a great contemporary historian, used "experience" in the same fashion as Dickinson, Madison, et al., and offered analytic proof to show why the two kinds of experience together might provide the highest measure of practical wisdom. See Hume's *Inquiry Concerning Human Understanding,* Section VIII, "Of Liberty and Necessity," from which this and the following quotations are taken.

John Adams would echo Hume's argument and use the identical metaphor in the preface to his *Defence*. "The system of legislators are experiments made on human life, and manners, society and government. Zoroaster, Confucius, Mithras, Odin, Thor, Mohamet, Lycurgus, Solon, Romulus and a thousand others may be compared to philosophers making experiments on the elements." Adams was too discreet to list his own name with the Great Legislators of the past, but in his own mind, we know from his *Diary* and letters to his wife, he identified himself with Moses, Lycurgus, and Solon as the Lawgiver of his state, Massachusetts, whose republican constitution, based on his study of history, he had written almost singlehanded in October 1779. Now eight years later his *Defence* both justified the form of government he had prepared for his own state and "fixed the principles"—to use Hume's words—of the science of government that ought to be followed in modeling a more perfect union of the states. Adams' book, in complete accord with eighteenth-century canons, was a comparative-historical survey of constitutions reaching back to Minos, Lycurgus, and Solon.

History proved, Adams felt sure, "that there can be no free government without a democratical branch in the constitution." But he was equally sure that "Democracy, simple democracy, never had a patron among men of letters." Rousseau, indeed, had argued, as Adams pointed out, that "a society of Gods would govern themselves democratically," but this is really an ironic admission by "the eloquent philosopher of Geneva that it is not practicable to govern *Men* in this way." For very short periods of time pure democracy had existed in antiquity, but "from the frightful pictures of a democratical city, drawn by the masterly pencils of ancient philosophers and historians, it may be conjectured that such governments existed in Greece and Italy . . . [only] for short spaces of time."[9] Such is the nature of pure democracy, or simple democracy, that this form of government carries in its very constitution, infirmities and vices that doom it to speedy disaster. Adams agreed completely with Jonathan Swift's pronouncement that if the populace of a country actually attempted to rule and establish a government by the people they would soon become their "own dupe, a mere underworker and a purchaser in trust for some single tyrant whose state and power they advance to their own ruin, with as blind an instinct as those

---

[9]The following quotations, unless otherwise noted, are all from the preface to Adams' *Defence*, IV, 283–298, and Chapter I of "Democratic Republics," IV, 303–327.

worms that die with weaving magnificent habits for beings of a superior order to their own." It was not surprising then to Adams that when he surveyed contemporary Europe he found no functioning democracy. Indeed, governments that had even the slightest "democratical mixture" in their constitutions "are annihilated all over Europe, except on a barren rock, a paltry fen, an inaccessible mountain, or an impenetrable forest." The one great exception outside of the American states where a democratic element was part of the constitution was Britain, the great monarchical or regal republic. And as Adams contemplated the English Constitution, he felt it to be "the most stupendous fabric of human invention. . . . Not the formation of languages, not the whole art of navigation and shipbuilding does more honor to the human understanding than this system of government."[10]

The problem for Americans in 1787 was to recognize the principles exemplified in Britain, Adams thought, and to frame governments to give the people "a legal, constitutional" *share* in the process of government—it should operate through representation; there should be a balance in the legislature of lower house and upper house; and there should be a total separation of the executive from the legislative power, and of the judicial from both. Above all, if the popular principles of government were to be preserved in America it was necessary to maintain an independent and powerful executive: "If there is one certain truth to be collected from the history of all ages, it is this; that the people's rights and liberties, and the democratical mixture in a constitution, can never be preserved without a strong executive, or, in other words, without separating the executive from the legislative power. If the executive power . . . is left in the hands either of an aristocratical or democratical assembly, it will corrupt the legislature as necessarily as rust corrupts iron, or as arsenic poisons the human body; and when the legislature is corrupted, the people are undone."

And then John Adams took on the role of scientific prophet. If Americans learned the lessons that history taught, their properly limited democratic constitutions would last for ages. Only long in the future when "the present states become . . . rich, powerful, and luxurious, as well as numerous, [will] their . . . good sense . . . dictate to them what to do; they may [then] make transitions to a nearer resemblance of the British constitution," and presumably make their first magistrates and their senators hereditary.

---

[10]Quoted in Adams' *Defence*, IV, 388.

But note the ambiguity which underlies Adams' historical thinking. Science, whether political or natural, traditionally has implied determinism—scientific prediction is possible only because what was, is, and ever shall be. Reason thus might be free to discover the fixed pattern of social phenomena, but the phenomena themselves follow a pre-destined course of development. The seventeenth-century reason of Isaac Newton discovered the laws of the solar system, but no man could change those laws or the pattern of the planets' orbits; Karl Marx might in the nineteenth century discover the scientific laws of economic institutions, but no man could reform them or change the pattern in which the feudal economy inevitably degenerated into bourgeois economy, which in its turn worked inexorably toward its predetermined and proletarian end.

In the same fashion Adams' scientific reading of history committed him and his contemporaries in varying degrees of rigidity to a species of *political determinism*. History showed, so they believed, that there were only three basic types of government: monarchy, aristocracy, and democracy, or government of the one, the few, or the many. Moreover history showed, so they believed, that each of these three types when once established had particular and terrible defects—"mortal diseases," Madison was to call these defects—that made each pure type quickly degenerate: Every monarchy tended to degenerate into a tyranny. Every aristocracy, or government of the few, by its very nature, was predestined to evolve into a corrupt and unjust oligarchy. And the democratic form, as past experience proved, inevitably worked toward anarchy, class conflict, and social disorder of such virulence that it normally ended in dictatorship.[11]

On this deterministic theory of a uniform and constant human nature, inevitably operating inside a fixed pattern of limited political forms, producing a predictable series of evil political results, John Adams based his invitation to Americans to study

---

[11]The classification of the three pure forms of government with their corrupt counterparts is a legacy from Greek political theory first stated by Herodotus (c. 495–425 B.C.), which reached its most penetrating and comprehensive statement in Aristotle's (384–322 B.C.) *Politics*. It was Polybius (201–120 B.C.), however, who first froze the earlier flexible analysis into a doctrinaire theory of cyclical change in Book VI of his *History*. This classical theory was "rediscovered" and popularized by various Renaissance thinkers, among them Machiavelli. It became important in English history in the seventeenth century when republican thinkers like Harrington, Milton, and Sidney became converts. See Zera Fink, *The Classical Republicans* (Evanston, 1945). Adams' *Defence* reprints Polybius, in Adams, *Works*, IV, 435 ff.

the classical republics. This assumption of determinism explains the constant and reiterated appeal to Greek and Roman "experience," both during the Philadelphia Convention and in the State ratifying conventions. At the beginning of the Revolution Adams had invited his rebellious compatriots to study English history, for from 1765 to 1776 the immediate and pressing questions of practical politics related to the vices and corruption of the English monarchy.[12] But after 1776 at which time Americans committed their political destinies to thirteen democratic frames of government loosely joined in a Confederation, English monarchical history became temporarily less relevant to American problems. The American States of 1776 in gambling on democratic republics stood alone in the political world. Nowhere in contemporary Europe or Asia could Americans turn for reassuring precedents showing functioning republican government. So, increasingly from 1776 to 1787, as Americans learned in practice the difficulties of making republican systems work, the leaders among the Revolutionary generation turned for counsel to classical history. They were *obliged* to study Greece and Rome if they would gain "experimental" wisdom on the dangers and potentialities of the republican form. Only in classical history could they observe the long-range predictable tendencies of those very "vices" of their democratic Confederacy that they were now enduring day by day.

It was these frightening lessons from classical history added to their own present difficulties under the Confederation that produced the total dimension of the crisis of 1787.[13] Standing, as it were, in John Adams' hall of magic mirrors where past and present merged in a succession of terrifying images, the Founding Fathers could not conceal from themselves that republicanism in

---

[12]Adams, *Essay on the Federal and Canon Law* (1765), in *Works*, III, 464–465.

[13]American historians have praised one scholarly research memorandum that Madison prepared for use at Philadelphia. This is his study, running to eight printed pages, entitled "Notes on the Confederacy:—April 1787. Vices of the Political System of the United States," in *Letters and Other Writings of James Madison* (4 vols., Philadelphia, 1867), I, 293–328. Historians in contrast have generally ignored the twenty-two page historical research memorandum, "Notes of Ancient and Modern Confederacies, Preparatory to the Federal Convention of 1787," in *ibid.*, I, 293–315, which Madison rated of equal weight in reaching the conclusions that he voiced at Philadelphia. These two memos which provided the theoretical foundation for the Virginia Plan and hence for the completed Constitution are the most strikingly successful examples of the enlightenment ideal of a rational attempt to reduce politics to a science put into practice. See my essay, " 'That Politics May be Reduced to a Science:' David Hume, James Madison, and the *Tenth Federalist*," *Huntington Library Quarterly*, XX (1957), 343–360.

America might already be doomed. Was it indeed possible to maintain stable republican government in any of the thirteen American States? And even if some of the States units could maintain republicanism, could union be maintained in a republican confederation?

The answer of history to both of these questions seemed to be an emphatic "no." As Alexander Hamilton reminded the Convention June 18th and later reminded the country speaking as Publius, "It is impossible to read the history of the petty Republics of Greece and Italy without feeling sensations of horror and disgust at the distractions with which they were continually agitated, and at the rapid succession of revolutions, by which they were kept in a state of perpetual vibration between the extremes of tyranny and anarchy. If they exhibit occasional calms, these only serve as short-lived contrasts to the furious storms that are to succeed. If now and then intervals of felicity open themselves to view, we behold them with a mixture of regret, arising from the reflection, that the pleasing scenes before us are soon to be overwhelmed by the tempestuous waves of sedition and party rage."[14]

Hamilton along with Madison, Adams, Jefferson, and every educated eighteenth-century statesman thus knew from history that the mortal disease of democratical republics was and always would be the class struggle that had eventually destroyed every republican state in history.[15] And *now* with the "desperate debtor" Daniel Shays, an American Cataline—an American Alcibiades— proving only ten years after independence, the class struggle was raising monitory death's-heads among the barely united republican States of America. If potential class war was implicit in every republic, so too did war characterize the interstate relations of adjacent republics. The only union that proved adequate to unite Athens and Sparta, Thebes and Corinth in one functioning peaceful whole was the monarchical power of Philip of Macedon; Rome, after conquering her neighbor city states, it is true, had maintained republican liberty for a relatively long period, in spite of internal conflict of plebes and patricians, but when the Empire increased in extent, when her geographical boundaries were

[14]Hamilton, *The Federalist*, No. 9.

[15]Major William Pierce, one of the Georgia delegates to the Convention, wrote character sketches of all the delegates. It is significant that he consistently singles out those who have a "compleat classical education" as being particularly well qualified for the role of American Solons and Lycurguses. Note his comments on Baldwin, Dayton, Hamilton, Ingersoll, Johnson, King, Livingston, Madison, G. Morris, Patterson, C. Pinckney, Randolph, Wilson, and Wythe.

enlarged, Roman liberty died and an Emperor displaced the Senate as the center of Roman authority. In 1787 the authority of scholars, philosophers, and statesmen was all but unanimous in arguing (from the experience of history) that no republic ever could be established in a territory as extended as the United States—that even if established for a moment, class war must eventually destroy every democratic republic.[16]

These were the two lessons that Hamilton insisted in his great speech of June 18 the Constitutional Convention must remember. These were the lessons that were stressed in John Adams' morbid anatomy of fifty historic republican constitutions. This was the theme of Madison's arguments (which the Convention accepted) for junking entirely the feeble Articles of the Confederation in favor of a government that would, it was hoped, neutralize interstate conflict and class war. It was because these lessons were accepted by so many educated men in America that the commercial crisis of 1784–1785 had become a political crisis by 1786, and a moral crisis by 1787.

Had the Revolution been a mistake from the beginning? Had the blood and treasure of Americans spent in seven years of war against England ironically produced republican systems in which rich and poor New Englanders must engage in bloody class war among themselves? Had independence merely guaranteed a structure in which Virginians and Pennsylvanians would cut each others' throats until one conquered the other or some foreign crown conquered both?[17]

---

[16]One of the chief arguments of the Anti-Federalists against the Constitution was that the country was too large for unified national government which in an extensive area could function efficiently only as a despotism. See the covering letter of Senators R. H. Lee and William Grayson, September 28, 1789, submitting proposed amendments to the Constitution to the Virginia legislature: "We know of no instances in History that shew a people ruled in Freedom when subject to an individual Government, and inhabiting a Territory so extensive as that of the United States." "Agrippa" (*Massachusetts Gazette*, December 3, 1787) along with dozens of other spokesmen had made the same point over and over in 1787–1788: "It is the opinion of the ablest writers on the subject [of government] that no extensive empire can be governed upon republican principles." For a brilliant analysis of the sterile and essentially undemocratic nature of the Anti-Federalist attacks on the Constitution see Cecelia Kenyon, "Men of Little Faith: The Anti-Federalists on the Nature of Representative Government," *William and Mary Quarterly*, XII (1955), 3–43, and the introduction to *The Antifederalists* (Indianapolis, 1966).

[17]Note Franklin's speech on the final day of the Convention, September, 17, urging all members to sign the Constitution even if they disapproved of parts: "I think it will astonish our enemies, who are waiting with confidence to hear that our councils are confounded like those of the builders of Babel; and that our States are on the point of separation, only to meet hereafter for the purpose of cutting one another's throats."

From our perspective, 179 years later, this may appear an hysterical and distorted analysis of the situation of the United States in 1787, but we, of course, are the beneficiaries of the Fathers' practical solution to this problem that *their* reading of history forced upon them. Americans today have the historic experience of living peacefully in the republic stabilized by their Constitution. History has reassured us concerning what only the wisest among them dared to hope in 1787: that the republican form could indeed be adapted to a continental territory. Priestley, a sympathetic friend of the American Revolution was speaking the exact truth in 1791 when he said: "It was taken for granted that the moment America had thrown off the yoke of Great Britain, the different states would go to war among themselves."

When Hamilton presented his analysis of the vices of republicanism to his acceptant audience in Philadelphia, he also offered the traditional remedy which statesmen and philosophers from antiquity on had proposed as the ONLY cure for the evils of the three types of pure government. This remedy was to "mix" or "compound" elements of monarchy, aristocracy, and democracy into one balanced structure.[18] There was, Hamilton reasoned, little danger of class war in a state which had a king vested with more power than the political organs of government representing either the rich or the poor. The "size of the country" and the "amazing turbulence" of American democracy made him despair of republicanism in the United States, without an elective monarch who once in office could not be voted out by majority rule. The people, *i.e.*, the multitudinous poor, would directly elect the lower house of the legislature; a Senate to represent the rich would be elected for life; and to guard against the poison of democracy in the separate States, they would be transformed into administrative districts with their governors appointed by the elected King.

We mistake the significance of Hamilton's proposal of an elective monarch as a solution of the crisis of 1787 if we think of his plan as either *original* or *unrepresentative* of the thought of important segments of American opinion in 1787. The strength of Hamilton's logical position lay in the fact that his proposal was the traditional, the standard, indeed, as history showed the *only* solution for the specific dangers of interclass and interstate

---

[18]For the theory of the ideal mixed or compounded government, sometimes called balanced government, see Stanley Pargellis, "The Theory of Balanced Government," in Conyers Read, *The Constitution Reconsidered* (New York, 1938), 37–49; John Adams, *Defence, passim;* Hamilton, Speech of June 18.

conflict that were destroying the imperfect Union. As early as 1776 Carter Braxton had offered almost this identical plan as the ideal constitution for Virginia.[19] In May, 1782, reasoning parallel to Hamilton's had emboldened Colonel Lewis Nicola to invite Washington to use the Army to set himself up as a King.[20] And after Shays' rebellion voices grew louder, particularly in the New England and the Middle States, proposing two cures for the ills of America. One cure was to divide the unwieldy Confederation into two or three small units; the other was the creation of an American throne.[21] We have Washington's word for it that the most alarming feature of this revival of monarchial sentiment was its appearance among staunch "republican characters"—men who like Hamilton had favored independence in 1776 but who had become disillusioned about ever achieving order and security in a republic. Add to this group of new converts the large bloc of old Tories who had never forsaken their allegiance to monarchy, and it is easy to see why Washington, Madison, and other leaders were seriously alarmed that Union would break up and that kings would reappear in the Balkanized segments.

Furthermore, at the very time the Philadelphia Convention was rejecting Hamilton's mixed-monarchy as a present solution for the vices of American democracy, leading members of the Convention most tenacious of republicanism accepted the fact that an American monarchy was inevitable at some future date. As Mr. Williamson of North Carolina remarked, on July 24, "it was pretty certain . . . that we should at some time or other have a king; but he wished no precaution to be omitted that might postpone the event as long as possible."[22] There is a curious statistical study of Madison's which points to his certainty also, along with the precise prophecy that the end of republicanism in the United States would come approximately 142 years after 1787—about the decade of the 1930's.[23] John Adams' *Defence*

[19]*Address to the Convention . . . of Virginia . . . By a Native of the Colony* (June, 1776), in Peter Force, ed., *American Archives* (Washington, 1837–1853), 4th Ser., 747–754.

[20]Colonel Lewis Nicola, in *Dictionary of American Biography* (21 vols., New York, 1928–1937), XIII, 509–510.

[21]Madison to Pendleton, February 24, 1787, in *Letters and Other Writings of James Madison*, I, 280; Louise Dunbar, *A Study of Monarchial Tendencies in the United States from 1776 to 1801* (Urbana, 1922). The latter collects a mass of contemporary material on this topic, including the Braxton pamphlet and the Nicola letter.

[22]Williamson in the Convention, July 24.

[23]*Letters and Other Writings of James Madison*, IV, 21, 29–30. The statistical estimate was of probable American population growth which Madison thought, in 1829, would by 1929 be 192,000,000. This would end

contains the same sort of prophecy. "In future ages," Adams remarked, "if the present States become great nations, rich, powerful, and luxurious, as well as numerous," the "feelings and good sense" of Americans "will dictate to them" reform of their governments "to a nearer resemblance of the British Constitution," complete with a hereditary king and a hereditary Senate.[24] Gouverneur Morris is reported to have argued during the Convention "we must have a Monarch sooner or later . . . and the sooner we take him while we are able to make a Bargain with him, the better." Nor did the actual functioning of the Constitution during its first decade of existence lighten Morris' pessimism; in 1804 he was arguing that the crisis would come sooner rather than later.[25] Even Franklin, the least doctrinaire of the Fathers—perhaps with Jefferson the most hopeful among the whole Revolutionary generation regarding the potentialities of American democracy—accepted the long-range pessimism of the Hamiltonian analysis. Sadly the aged philosopher noted, June 2, "There is a natural inclination in mankind to kingly government. . . . I am apprehensive, therefore,—perhaps too apprehensive,—that the government of these States may in future time end in monarchy. But this catastrophe, I think may be long delayed. . . ."[26]

The "precious advantage" that the United States had in 1787 that offered hope for a "republican remedy for the diseases most incident to republican government"—the circumstance which would delay the necessity of accepting Hamilton's favored form of mixed monarchy—lay in the predominance of small free-hold farmers among the American population. Since the time of Aristotle, it had been recognized that yeoman farmers—a middle class between the greedy rich and the envious poor—provided

the nation's "precious advantage" both of wide distribution of landed property and "universal hope of acquiring property." At that time, being "nearly as crowded" as England or France, with a society increasingly polarized between "wealthy capitalists and indigent laborers," Madison feared an amended Constitution more like England's would be required.

[24]John Adams, *Defence*, IV, 358–359.

[25]Mason in 1792 reported this remark of Morris quoted in Dunbar, *Monarchial Tendencies*, p. 91. In 1804, writing to Aaron Ogden, Morris, like Adams and Madison, related the appearance of an American monarchy to the growth of population and poverty. Jared Sparks, ed., *The Life of Gouverneur Morris, with Selections from his Correspondence* (3 vols, Boston, 1832), III, 217.

[26]Franklin, June 2. It should be noted that acceptance of the deterministic theory of the unmixed democratic form swinging inevitably to the opposite extreme of despotism explains the number of prophets—Hamilton, Morris in America; Burke in England—who foretold the eventual advent of Napoleon almost as soon as the French Revolution began.

the most stable foundation upon which to erect a popular government. This factor, commented on by Madison, Pinckney, Adams and others, helps explain why the Convention did not feel it necessary to sacrifice either majority rule or popular responsibility in their new Constitution.

Of equal importance was the factor of expedience. Less doctrinaire than Alexander Hamilton, the leaders of the Convention realized that a theoretical best—and member after member went on record praising the British Constitution as *the best* ever created by man—a theoretical best might be the enemy of a possible good. As Pierce Butler insisted, in a different context, "The people will not bear such innovations. . . . Supposing such an establishment to be useful, we must not venture on it. We must follow the example of Solon who gave the Athenians not the best government he could devise, but the best they would receive."[27]

Consequently the Constitution that emerged from the Convention's debates was, as Madison described it a "novelty in the political world"—a "fabric" of government which had "no model on the face of the globe."[28] It was an attempt to approximate in a structure of balanced republican government the advantages of stability that such mixed governments as Great Britain's had derived from hereditary monarchy and a hereditary House of Lords.

It was an "experiment" as members of the Convention frankly admitted, but one about which most of the Fathers could be hopeful because it adapted to the concrete circumstances of the United States of 1787, the experience of mankind through all ages as revealed by history. Driven by the collapse of the Confederation, the depression of 1785–1786, and Shays' Rebellion to take stock of their political situation six years after Yorktown had won for Americans the opportunity for self-government, the Fathers had turned to history, especially classical history, to help them analyze their current difficulties. Their reading of history, equally with their immediate experience, defined for them both the short-range and the long-range potentialities for evil inherent in a uniform human nature operating in a republican government. But their reading of history also suggested a specific type of government that would remedy the evils they already knew and those worse evils they expected to come. Utilizing this knowl-

---

[27]Butler in debate on June 5. Compare Bedford of Delaware's use of the same phrase from Plutarch's *Life of Solon* in debate of June 30.
[28]Madison, *The Federalist*, No. 14.

edge, building on the solid core of agreement which historical wisdom had helped supply, they created, by mutual concession and compromise, a governmental structure as nearly like mixed government as it was possible to approach while maintaining the republican principle of majority rule. And this they offered the American people *hoping* it would be ratified, *hoping* that after ratification their "experiment" with all its compromises of theory and interest would provide a more perfect union.

If there is substance in the argument offered in the foregoing paragraphs, it should throw some light, at least, on the intellectual confusion exhibited during the last half-century by many learned commentators in discussing the nature of our Constitution. This confused and confusing debate has focused in part on the question: "did the Fathers write a 'democratic' Constitution?"[29] The

---

[29]In view of the number of able historiographical essays on the recent revisionist literature about the "critical period" and the writings of the Constitution, it seemed superfluous to add merely another. Two pamphlets printed by the Service Center for Teachers of History that survey the current historical literature on the theme, through 1962, are recommended for those who wish to stand in the most modern historiographical *boudoir*—the contemporary historian's hall-of-mirrors. The first, Edmund S. Morgan's *The American Revolution, A Review of Changing Interpretations* (Washington, 1958), relates the monographic studies dealing with the period 1783–1787 to the general problem of interpreting the whole American Revolution; the second, Stanley Elkins and Eric McKitrick's *The Founding Fathers: Young Men of the Revolution* (Washington, 1962), not only surveys critically historians' commentaries on the framing of the Constitution, but also makes the point that the group of young men who worked most intensely to achieve a stronger national government and a more perfect union had staked their political careers on the national rather than the state scene and thus mingled their self-interest in status and power with a patriotic concern for the national welfare.

Two books and two significant essays have also been published, since 1962, that must be considered by any serious student of the "critical period." Forrest McDonald, in *E Pluribus Unum* (Boston, 1965), continues his analysis, begun in *We The People* (Chicago, 1958), of the multiple economic groups and burgeoning local economic appetites that existed in the United States, post 1783. His most persuasive chapters show how selfish regional and state parties and economic groups—in politics these normally became Anti-Federalists in 1787–1788—had strained the tenuous Union to the extreme by 1787, so much so, in fact, that the success of the countervailing movement of the men who wrote and got the Constitution ratified was, in McDonald's view, a "miracle." In a ninety-page introduction to an anthology of Anti-Federalist tracts, (see footnote 16 *supra*), Cecelia M. Kenyon provides the most thorough and wise analysis of the ideological stance of the men who opposed ratification of the Constitution, in 1787–1788; and she makes it clear that the Anti-Federalists were not majoritarian "democrats" in any sense of the term.

Finally, two recent important articles in the *William and Mary Quarterly* throw light on the problem of "democracy" and our Revolution. Richard Buel, Jr., "Democracy and the American Revolution: A Frame of Reference,"

answers given have been almost as "mixed" as the theory to which the Framers subscribed.

Part of the bother lies in the lack of precision with which the word *democracy* was used then, and the even more unprecise way that we use it now. The more a word is used the less exact its meaning becomes, and in our day *democratic/democracy* has been extended to describe art, foreign policy, literature, etc., etc. Thus, from being a somewhat technical word of political discourse, in 1787, it has become a perfect sponge of squashy vagueness. Luckily, the context of formal theory that mixed government did imply in 1787 does allow us to recognize certain rather concrete and specific features usually associated, then, with the democratic form of government. In the first place, the very concept of "mixture" implies a relativism that modern doctrinaire democrats often forget: a political system, in 1787, was thought of as more-or-less democratic, as possessing few or many democratic features. Only in the pure form was democracy an either/or type of polity. In the second place, the simple democratic form was almost always thought of as appropriate only for a tiny territorial area—Madison in *Federalist 10*, for instance, would only equate the word with the direct democracy of the classical city-state. Thirdly, the functional advantages and disadvantages of the pure democratic form of government were almost universally agreed upon. A government *by* the people (so it was thought) always possessed *fidelity* to the common good; it was impossible for a people not to *desire* and to *intend* to promote the general welfare. However, the vices of democracy

---

(3rd ser., XXI [1964], 165–190) makes the point that although Whig theory before 1776 in British-America consistently defended the right of the people to share in government, at the same time an unchecked, "simple," or "pure" democracy was uniformly condemned by all American spokesmen. Jackson Turner Main, in an essay in the same journal, "Government by the People: The American Revolution and the Democratization of the Legislatures" (3rd ser., XXIII [1966], 391–407), shows how, after 1776, "two interacting developments occurred simultaneously: ordinary citizens increasingly took part in politics, and American political theorists began to defend popular government [*i.e.*, simple democracy]." As my essay has argued, the Constitutional Convention was dominated by men who rejected the idea that "simple" democracy was either a desirable or a safe form for the American people. To a certain extent their ideas exemplify a limited, but definite, reaction against both the institutional and theoretical "democratic" developments that Professor Main charts. This shift and change in one leader's estimate of "democracy"—a vague and non-critical view of the American peoples' virtue before 1776, a positive praise of this virtue in 1776, and then reservations about the wisdom and virtue of Americans, 1779 ff.—has been ably analyzed by John R. Howe Jr., *The Changing Political Thought of John Adams* (Princeton, 1966).

were that the people, collectively, were not *wise* about the correct measures to serve this great end and that the people could be easily duped by demagogues, who, flattering their good hearts and muddled heads, would worm their way to unlimited power. It was this well-meaning stupidity, the capacity for thoughtless injustice, the fickle instability of the popular will, that led the classical theorists, who the Fathers were familiar with, to designate "pure democracy" as a form doomed to a short existence that tended to eventuate, with a pendulum swing, in the opposite extreme of tyranny and dictatorship.

In dark contrast to this *fidelity* of the democratic many was the vice afflicting both monarchy and aristocracy: an inveterate and incorrigible tendency to use the apparatus of government to serve the special selfish interests of the one or the few. However, the aristocratic form offered, so it was believed, the best possibility of *wisdom,* in planning public measures, while monarchy promised the necessary *energy, secrecy,* and *dispatch* for executing policy.[30]

It is in this ideological context that one can deduce some of the intentions of the authors of our Constitution. It is clear, I think, that the office and power of the President was consciously designed to provide the *energy, secrecy,* and *dispatch* traditionally associated with the monarchical form. Thus Patrick Henry, considering the proposed Chief Executive and recognizing that the President was not unlike an elective king, could cry with reason that the Constitution "squints toward monarchy." But it was equally possible for Richard Henry Lee, focusing on the Senate, to complain that the document had a "strong tendency to aristocracy." This was said by Lee six months before Madison, in *Federalists 62–63,* explicitly defended the Senate as providing the *wisdom* and the *stability*—"aristocratic virtues"—needed to check the fickle lack of wisdom that Madison predicted would characterize the people's branch of the new government, the Lower House. Nor were there other critics lacking who, recognizing that the Constitution ultimately rested on popular consent, who, seeing that despite the ingenious apparatus designed to temper the pop-

---

[30]Most of the modern discussion of the framing of the Constitution has concerned itself with the domestic consequences of ratification. This, I suspect, springs from the century of military security and isolation that so deeply colored American thinking from 1815 to 1940. The dangers of the international jungle we live in, that now makes foreign policy our primary concern, has helped some of us recognize why a statesman like Hamilton was obsessed with the need for a strong chief executive as a prime measure of defense and security in the world of 1787, where foreign policy showed the same jungle characteristics that frighten us.

ular will by introducing into the compound modified monarchical/
aristocratic ingredients, could argue that the new Constitution
was too democratic to operate effectively as a national government
in a country as large and with a population as heterogeneous as
the Americans'. One such was William Grayson, who doubted the
need of *any* national government, but who felt, if one was to be
established, it ought to provide a President and a Senate elected
for life terms, these to be balanced by a House of Representatives
elected triennially.[31]

It is, thus, significant that if modern scholars are confused and
disagreed about the nature of the Constitution today, so, too, in
1787–1788, contemporary observers were also confused and also
disagreed as to whether it was monarchical, aristocratic, or democratic in its essence.[32]

My own opinion is that the Constitution of 1787 is probably
best described in a term John Adams used in 1806. Writing to
Benjamin Rush, September 19, 1806, Adams, disapproving
strongly of Jefferson's style as President, bemoaned the fact that
Jefferson and his gang had now made the national government
"to all intents and purposes, in virtue, spirit, and effect a democracy."—Alas! "I once thought," said Adams, "our Constitution was
quasi or mixed government,"—but alas![33]

"Quasi," or better still "quasi-mixed"—for, given the American
people's antipathy to monarchy after 1776, and given the non-
aristocratic nature (in a European sense) of the American upper
class of 1787, the Constitution at best, or worst, could only be
"*quasi*-mixed,"[34] since there were not "ingredients" available in
the United States to compose a genuine mixture in the classic
sense. So what the Fathers fashioned was a "quasi-mixed" Constitution that, given the "genius" of the American people, had a

[31]For convenience of reference, see Kenyon, *The Antifederalists:* Henry,
257; Lee, 205; and Grayson, 282–283.

[32]Madison, in *Federalist 38,* mocked (somewhat unfairly, under the circumstances) the Anti-Federalists for exactly this disagreement and confusion. "This politician," Madison wrote, "discovers in the constitution a
direct and irresistible tendency to monarchy [Henry]; that is equally sure
it will end in aristocracy [Lee]. Another is puzzled to say which of these
shapes it will ultimately assume, but sees clearly it must be one or other
of them [George Mason]; whilst a fourth [Grayson] . . . affirms that . . .
the weight on that side [*i.e.,* monarchical/aristocratic] will not be sufficient
to keep it upright and firm against its opposite [*i.e.,* democratic] tendencies."

[33]John Adams to Benjamin Rush, 19 September 1806. J. A. Schutz and
D. Adair, eds., *The Spur of Fame: Dialogues of John Adams and Benjamin
Rush, 1805–1813* (San Marino, 1966), 66.

[34]Quasi, [Latin = as if] seemingly, not real(ly), practical(ly), half-, almost.
Concise Oxford Dictionary (1963).

strong and inevitable tendency that "squinted" from the very beginning towards the national democracy that would finally develop
in the nineteenth century.

Shays's Rebellion:
A Political Interpretation

J. R. POLE

A constitutional historian of Massachusetts, after bringing his
subject safely through the year 1780, might feel entitled to lay
down his pen and contemplate a work well done. Few were disposed to deny that the Constitution had been adopted with the
general consent of the governed or that the annually elected legislators conformed to the accepted notion of true representatives.
This impression of consent is made stronger by the tacit admission of the rebels and malcontents who within a year had begun
to challenge the General Court by holding county conventions.
Their numerous demands for constitutional revision were not advanced on the grounds that the ratification of the Constitution
had been a mere legal fiction; the justice of the Constitution was
impugned, but not its legality.

Within six years, longstanding discontent throughout much of
the Commonwealth had been fanned into organised riots, and
these in turn were raised, under the hesitant leadership of Captain
Daniel Shays, into a minor rebellion. The rebellion, a strangely dis-
jointed, aimless affair, was crushed with slight loss. The State
Constitution not only emerged unshaken, but proved itself capable
of absorbing the impetus of discontent through the normal elective
system; at the ensuing elections, in April 1787, both Governor
James Bowdoin and a great majority of representatives lost their
seats. Within a few months, and particularly after the ratification
of the Federal Constitution, it was easy to believe that the whole
episode had been greatly over-rated; but before it was over it had
given the legislators and many substantial citizens, in Massachusetts and in other states, a severe fright. If a truly republican

Reprinted with permission from *Political Representation in England and
the Origins of the American Republic* (New York, St. Martin's Press, Inc.,
Macmillan & Co., Ltd., 1966), 227–244.

government could not hold the allegiance of the people, was the American experiment destined to fail?

The question gave rise to some of the animus against 'democracy' expressed in the opening days of the Philadelphia Convention. Shays's Rebellion thus has a peculiar stature, much out of proportion to its local character. The history of Europe is dotted with minor peasant revolts, local, wild, and hopeless, which barely attract the attention of the historian; Richelieu would have made short work of Shays and his friends. But the rising of 1786 demonstrated with cruel violence that something had gone wrong with the very institutions of representation which the people of the Bay Colony had fought to defend and had agreed, by conference, to maintain.

The grievances underlying the county conventions of 1786 and the rebellion itself were repeatedly expounded at the time. They may be summarised as economic distress, arising from the aftermath of war and from legislative policies, administered through, and exacerbated by, the courts, the legal profession, and the county officials. The burden of taxation to meet State debts was compounded by the burden of private debt, and both were made terrifying by the practice, or the threat, of the imprisonment of debtors. The exorbitant expenses of court action often precluded the poorer victims from seeking relief through litigation, even when they had the better case. The petty tyrannies of sheriffs and constables aroused bitter hatred.

No administration could entirely have averted the post-war economic crisis; but the form it took in Massachusetts was in large measure a product of the policies of the General Court, a point firmly grasped by the more articulate and better informed spokesmen of the protest movements.

As early as 1777, the General Court had initiated the hard-money policy which it pursued, with much tacking and veering but with unwavering purpose, right down to the crisis. By Acts of 1780 and 1781, all legal tender except gold and silver was abolished and heavy taxes were imposed. Further measures in the following years constantly proclaimed the dedication of successive legislatures to the principle of redeeming the State's obligations to its creditors at whatever cost to the overburdened and the poor. And the poll tax, the most consistently used means of raising money, being levied at a flat rate, had a most unequal operation.[1]

---

[1] Oscar and Mary Handlin, "Revolutionary Economic Policy in Massachusetts," *William and Mary Quarterly*, IV (January, 1947), 3–26. Robert A. East, "Massachusetts Conservatives in the Critical Period," in Richard B. Morris, ed., *The Era of the American Revolution* (New York, 1939), 349–391;

It seemed by the early spring of 1786 that the hard struggles of the Revolutionary War were to produce, for those who had fought or endured them, nothing better than a dwindling lifetime of debt, poverty, and even imprisonment. What made this intolerable was that every officer of government was engaged as a matter of duty in forcing home the exactions, inflicting the hardships.

The General Court was not unaware of the plight of the country. Several towns instructed their representatives to procure remedies; a graphic statement coming from the town of Palmer, in which the removal of the General Court from Boston and the establishment of a 'bank of paper money' were asked for—'Considering the great desperateness of the Inhabitants of this commonwealth (and the said Town of Palmer in particular) labours under by reason of the great scarcity of surculating medeam'.[2] A few measures of relief were passed in 1786, but in general the legislature did not allow itself to be deflected from its main objectives either by the evidence of economic crisis or by the fact that its own policies were not working. As late as January, 1787, the import and excise were renewed for three years and outstanding taxes ordered to be collected 'instantly'.[3]

When every allowance has been made for the imperfections of economic science and the humanity of the legislators, their course on the one hand, and on the other the county conventions and the outbreak of rebellion, raise questions which cannot be answered by examining either economic statistics or the provisions of the Constitution of 1780. The question is why a government consisting solely of duly elected representatives should have pursued a policy capable of alienating a large section of the people and driving the remnant to despair and revolt; the question is also why, under a representative government, the opposition should have been able to find no means of attaining redress, both constitutional and effective.

It is clear that, despite occasional hesitations and tackings, the Assembly majority did pursue a definable policy. It is also clear that this policy conformed in general to the objective of the lead-

---

Robert J. Taylor, *Western Massachusetts in the Revolution* (Providence, 1954), 27–33, gives the best modern account of the court system, which is vividly described in J. E. A. Smith, *History of Pittsfield, Massachusetts* (Boston, 1869–1876), i, chap. 23.

[2] House documents, no. 2234, 4 February 1786, Mass. Archives, Boston.

[3] House of Representatives Journal, 1786–7, vol. 7, 26 October 1786, Mass. Archives; *Acts and Resolves of the Province of Massachusetts Bay* (Boston, 1869–1922), May session 1786, chaps. 28, 29, 100, 113; January session 1787, chap. 29.

ing economic interest of the seaboard, and that it aroused heated and widespread opposition.

The appointment of representatives was still determined under the Act of May, 1776,[4] which will be recalled as the first to depart from the pure principle of the corporate equality of the towns.

The larger numbers of members from the eastern towns were, of course, within much easier reach of the capital than their colleagues from the interior; their attendance could therefore always be more regular. Their position also gave them the opportunity of seeing each other and conferring in ways denied to the interior. The county conventions so popular in the west, though hotly denounced as unconstitutional and subversive, may reasonably be considered an organised counterpart to this unofficial but immensely useful seaboard advantage, which had originated so many years before in the private caucus meetings in Boston.

The Speakers of the House continued to be Representatives either of Boston or of other towns in the seaboard area, right through the war and the Confederation period, with the single and interesting exception of the critical year 1786–1787 when the Speaker came from Shrewsbury in Worcester County. For most of the same period the clerk of the House was also a Boston man.

The significance of this unauthorised system was understood by the opposition. Few demands of the protest movement were more insistently repeated than that for the removal of the General Court out of Boston; and Massachusetts was a noteworthy exception to the general tendency to remove the capital in a westerly direction soon after the Revolution. This was frequently linked with demands for a reform in the basis of representation and, significantly, for the abolition of the Senate.[5] These three measures were aimed at the machinery by which the seaboard kept its grip; but it is doubtful whether they would ever have made a permanent

---

[4]See Pole, *Political Representation*, p. 175.

[5]Resolutions of Worcester County Convention, 17 August 1786, *Worcester Magazine*, 4th week, August 1786; Resolutions of Hampshire County Convention, *Worcester Magazine*, 3rd week, September 1786; town instructions to Representatives, East Sudbury, May 1786, House Documents, no. 2305; Watertown (which itself was adjacent to Boston and probably jealous of its power), 29 May 1786, House Documents, no. 2281; Framingham, 22 September 1786, House Documents, no. 2279; Salisbury, 25 September 1786, House Documents, no. 2278; Freetown, 14 May 1787, House Documents, no. 2698; Mansfield, 14 May 1787, House Documents, no. 2706; Dracut, 16–26 May 1787, House Documents, no. 2709; Wendover, 28 May 1787, House Documents, no. 2708; Hardwick, 21 May 1787, House Documents, no. 2705; Douglass, 28 May 1787, House Documents, no. 2702; Harvard, 28 May 1787, House Documents, no. 2696; Watertown (again), 28 May 1787, House Documents, no. 2695, Mass. Archives.

difference without the aid of some standing political organisation.

Opposition demands for reform of the basis of representation were usually general, and failed to specify precisely what reform was desired. A clue seems to lie in a statement from the town of Greenwich, suggesting (in reply to a letter from Boston town meeting) that each town should send two members as of old, under the Charter.[6] This letter included another point of greater importance than seems to have been appreciated by many of the protesters: that members of the General Court should be paid from the state treasury since their service was to the whole community. Had this been adopted in the Constitution, the chronic non-representation of the poorer towns could have been remedied.[7]

The mere existence of the Senate was a grievance. The conservatism of that body consisted partly in its tendency to reject reforms emanating from the House,[8] partly in the mere presence of a constitutional body based on property rather than persons. The election of James Bowdoin as Governor in 1785, which took place in the General Court owing to the lack of a popular majority for any candidate, was carried with the aid of a senatorial majority of commercial interests.[9] Economic distress and the policies of the General Court had begun to make this principle seem more objectionable than it had seemed in theory in 1780. The young John Quincy Adams noted in 1787 that the Senate had several times within the last eighteen months 'saved the commonwealth from complete anarchy, and perhaps from destruction'; but he observed with earnest exaggeration that its hands were tied, that the 'democratical branch' of the government was 'quite unrival'd'; and that the people were too generally disposed to abolish the Senate as 'a useless body.'[10]

The actual distribution of senators on the basis of taxes paid, rather than numbers, did not make a great difference.[11] Suffolk

---

[6]*Worcester Magazine*, 4th week, November 1786.

[7]The provision in the Constitution was that the treasury should pay members their expenses but that their towns were then assessed for the amount in taxes.

[8]As late as October 1786 the Senate rejected a committee report for simplifying legal procedure by requiring all original processes in civil cases to be opened before Justices of the Peace, and that in cases of default executions should issue without further delay. *Essex Journal*, 1 November 1786.

[9]Richard B. Morris, 'Insurrection in Massachusetts', in Daniel Aaron, ed., *America in Crisis* (New York, 1952), 35.

[10]*Life in a New England Town: 1787, 1788* (Boston, 1903), 120. Being the Diary of John Quincy Adams.

[11]R. R. Palmer, *The Age of the Democratic Revolution*, I, *The Challenge* (Princeton, 1959), 226.

County, with Boston, had six senators instead of the four to which it would have been entitled on a numerical basis; the central and western counties were short by one or two senators; but it is a mistake to assess representation in merely arithmetical terms. All the senators, from whatever counties, were required to be men of substance; and it is important to note that because they represented counties, not towns, the senators were free from the restrictions imposed by the prevalent and very strongly held doctrine of the right of constituency instruction.[12] The Senate, indeed, retained its character long after the fires of Shays's Rebellion had burned out and its political cast was generally Federalist in the 1790s.[13]

The better informed commentators who contributed essays on economic policy to the newspapers showed much understanding and often a fund of knowledge; but this was brought out only by the crisis and the usual situation in the towns showed little change since the days before the Revolution. Newspapers very seldom reported Assembly debates—the *Hampshire Gazette* was roused to do so as late as November, 1786, and it did not become a habit.[14] The House itself did nothing to inform the people either of its measures or the reason for them; even when it had acted to redress grievances it failed to explain its actions.[15] A contributor sympathetic to the demonstrators pointed out that it would be well if the General Court would inform their constituents more particularly of the state of public affairs; especially of the state's part of the national debt, the amount of the domestic debt, the annual charge for the support of government, and the interest paid annually; the takings of the treasury by imposts, excise, licenses and auctions, and taxes; and many other matters of political economy which were later to become the currency of political discussion.[16] Other glimpses of the curiously episodic state of information about public affairs are caught from the instructions of Douglass in May 1787, which remarked to the representative that as he would have better information in that capacity than the town he might make all reasonable alterations; a remark by the chief justice that the representatives were better informed than

---

[12]Taylor, *Western Massachusetts*, 140. Thus the senators were much less tied by local opinion than the representatives, and occupied a position analogous with that of the provincial councillors.

[13]Anson E. Morse, *The Federalist Party in Massachusetts to 1800* (Princeton, 1909), 64 (hereafter referred to as *Federalist Party*).

[14]*Hampshire Gazette*, 1 November 1786.

[15]Taylor, *Western Massachusetts*, 136.

[16]'From a Friend . . .', *Hampshire Gazette*, 11 October 1786.

the towns, and a remark by another town that it 'believed' laws had been passed contrary to the peace treaty—plainly admitting to uncertainty about legislative history.[17]

These deficiencies were admitted by the General Court to be part of the reason for the prevailing dissatisfaction—or rather they were proclaimed on the ground that better information would have led to fairer appreciation of the efforts of the legislators. In October 1786 a committee of both branches of the legislature brought in a long report directly designed to answer recent complaints and to provide public information, and several measures of redress were ordained; one of which, the introduction of a new institution to take the place of the unpopular court of Common Pleas, was later rejected by the Senate.[18] Soon afterwards, a formal Address to the People by the General Court gave an account of public revenues, spending, expectations from land sales, and the state of the debt. This was necessary because, it was stated, discontent had arisen largely from misinformation.[19]

The great increase in the numbers of newspapers that had taken place since before the Revolution might have been expected to alter this situation for the better. Yet the Press remained a medium for episodic and often disconnected information. Acts of the General Court were frequently reported, often being reproduced in full; at the end of the session the papers sometimes regaled their readers with a complete list of Acts passed. News from Europe was given great prominence as often as it arrived by the packet. But state and continental news came in for very inconsistent treatment; and it is probable that much that was known in the tavern was not thought worth reproducing in the Press. What, in general, this Press system represented by contrast with the later development of the Press, was a lack of any organised newsgathering service—something only vaguely felt by the printereditors as they solicited news and contributions.

In constitutional theory the towns were represented through their right to instruct representatives. Through them the General Court would possess all the information it needed for legislative purposes. The difficulties experienced not only by Massachusetts but by the American economy after the end of the war might have been expected to provide the legislators with all the information

---

[17]House Documents, nos. 2702, 2705, Mass. Archives; *Hampshire Gazette,* 29 November 1786.

[18]*Hampshire Gazette,* 18 October 1786; *Essex Journal,* 1 November 1786.

[19]*Worcester Magazine,* November–December 1786; *Hampshire Gazette,* 13 December 1786.

they needed. Yet the months before the outbreak of violence in Western Massachusetts present a curiously mixed picture. On 2 June 1786 Governor Bowdoin addressed the legislature on matters requiring their attention. He remarked on the importance of paying the revenue due to Congress and observed that appropriate tax Acts would be necessary to raise the funds to meet the domestic debt; he alluded also to the question of the Commonwealth's boundary with New York and the need to support Harvard College. No one would have guessed from this speech that the western counties seethed with discontented elements on the point of revolt.[20]

Why then, had not the afflicted areas themselves made better use of their constitutional rights to instruct their representatives and to apply for redress? If the instructions and petitions for relief lying in the state archives are grouped together the cries of distress sound insistent and impressive. None speaks clearer than the plea of Ludlow:

We humbly Conceve that your honours are well acquainted with the distresses of the people of this Commonwealth and are possessed of Bowels of pitty and tenderness.[21]

Not all these petitions agreed with each other. Most demanded paper money, and a few denounced it:[22] but the curious thing is that, from the period January to June 1786, the total number surviving is 15 out of a total of instructions and petitions numbering some 220.[23] The other factor of great significance is the chronic non-representation of the smaller towns.

May 1786 began a session at which, in view of the growing discontent, a large delegation might have been expected from the western counties. In fact, of 314 towns entitled to representation no fewer than 145 failed to elect a member. The three western and central counties of Hampshire, Worcester, and Berkshire—entitled between them to 130 representatives—could send only 67. This figure probably represented a strenuous exertion, for it com-

---

[20]*Acts and Resolves, 1786–1787*, 2 June 1786.

[21]6 February 1786, House Documents, no. 2033, Mass. Archives.

[22]Newburyport asked for a stronger Congress and support for agriculture, as well as drawing attention to unemployment in the shipbuilding industry. Paper money was rejected as a bad remedy. *Worcester Magazine*, 3rd week, June 1786.

[23]The serial numbers run from 2,009 to 2,231 for this period. But the arrangement of the documents does not make this a conclusive guide. Between late 1785 and early 1788 there appear to be some 5,000 petitions. The number of these bearing reference to economic distress is surprisingly small.

pared favourably with the percentage of the state as a whole. But where Hampshire, Worcester, and Berkshire achieved a representation of about 51 per cent against a state average of about 53, the eastern counties of Suffolk, Essex, and Middlesex sent delegations from 46 of their 78 towns—almost 60 per cent; and if the count is confined to Essex and Suffolk, which between them concentrated most of the seaboard population and mercantile property, the contrast becomes still more striking: 29 out of 40 towns, or 72 per cent.[24] When all the unofficial advantages of the seaboard are weighed in, and the lack of unity, previous consultation, or even uniformity of interest of the interior counties is considered, the political influence of the east becomes almost a tangible thing.

The basic reason for this non-representation was economic. The town records show again and again that when the cost of being assessed for the support of a member throughout the legislative sessions was considered by a community, the gains to be had from representation frequently did not seem worth the price. But the very factors which made representation urgent also made it more burdensome. The harder the times, the more inducement to the towns to cut their costs. That any one town's one or two representatives would be able to make an effective impression on the general policies of the Court or on the condition of the Commonwealth always seemed improbable. It was easier to risk the fine for non-representation and hope for the success of a plea of poverty. The worse the crisis, the worse the representation of the state as a whole at the seat of government; and this was a weakness that applied particularly to the areas of greatest distress. The times thus gave great force to the argument of Greenwich, that all representatives should be paid from the public chest—a view which only some dozen towns had thought worth advancing in their returns on the Constitution of 1780.

But the unwillingness of the dissatisfied towns to make an instrument of reform of the General Court is not fully explained by their poverty. It must be recognised that there occurred a dangerous breakdown of confidence between the General Court and a large body of citizens—a much larger body, to judge by the county conventions, than eventually took part in the disturbances. Against the strangely small number of petitions seeking redress from the

---

[24]*Acts and Resolves*, May 1786. The state average is computed with the omission of Duke's, Nantucket, and York, which for geographical reasons were untypical. The low representation of Middlesex County, in which only 17 of 38 towns sent delegates, is evidence of the difficulties of the times. It was not only in the west that these were true.

legislature, the conventions brought together and gave vent to an impressive volume of indignation.

The link between the county conventions and the Shays disorders is obscure. The chief justice, William Cushing, charged that every county to have held a convention also produced a rebellion; the others had not.[25] Hostile critics heaped mountains of abuse on the conventions, repeating incessantly that they were unconstitutional bodies led by desperate men; it was also alleged that the leaders were old partisans of Britain, still acting under her guidance; and it was occasionally said that they aimed at complete levelling and the seizure and division of property. Whether or not the Convention leaders were possessed with the frenzy of class hatred and the purpose of class war, such motives were freely attributed to them by their enemies.[26]

Much of the frenzy was worked up by the 'conservatives', who convinced themselves that a new social revolution was in the making, although there is no evidence of rebel plans against the state government; it was on western ground that the rival forces met, and hardly anyone on either side was hurt.

Not all conventions were radical. During the strange earlier interlude of Berkshire's semi-independence, the conservatives, those who adhered to the central government and styled themselves 'friends of order', held a convention in Stockbridge;[27] on one occasion at least the legislature actually ordained a county convention in Berkshire, to settle a dispute about the site of a new county court house.[28] But it was of course perfectly true that the Convention movement which revived even before the end of the War and gathered momentum in the post-war crisis was a movement of protest.

The conventions were composed of delegates from the towns, regularly elected in town meetings. It was open to each town to decide whether or not to send a delegation, and those in which a majority—or the leading citizens—opposed the whole practice sometimes gave their reasons for declining. Thus Medford, refusing to attend the Worcester Convention of August 1786, declared it an unwarrantable attempt to take the public business out of the hands of those (i.e. the General Court) to whom the Con-

---

[25] *Hampshire Gazette*, 29 November 1786.

[26] These attacks were carried widely in the newspapers through the summer and winter of 1786–1787.

[27] Theodore Sedgwick to James Sullivan, 16 May 1779. Sedgwick Papers, Mass. Hist. Soc., Boston.

[28] In September 1784. Smith, *History of Pittsfield*, i. 429.

stitution had confided it. The proper procedure was to lay grievances before the General Court through instructions to representatives; but the call did not specify any grievances. The Convention,
this statement sharply added, was likely to create more grievances
by making parties and counteracting the proceedings of the General Court. Medford believed the state debts to be debts of honour,
the price of victory in war. If the states repudiated it, the prediction of their enemies that the Americans were incapable of governing themselves would be completely verified.[29]

The biggest gain from the conventions may well have been that
by causing excitement and public debate they attracted attention
to the widespread nature of the grievances which called them
forth. But as a means of concerting opposition, they were not very
effective. The complaints listed in the resolves of the conventions
frequently reappeared in the instructions or petitions of the towns
which had sent delegations. But the repetition of these demands
made little impression on the General Court. As early as 1782, a
Convention in Worcester County demanded that the treasury make
out an annual account to be circulated among the towns, asked
for the removal of the General Court from Boston, and attacked
the problem of the jurisdiction of the civil courts.[30] The chief
justice, in his comprehensive indictment delivered in 1786, charged
the conventions, two or three years previously, with having drawn
up a list of nominees recommended for election to the House and
Senate;[31] and this is just the step that the conventions might be
expected to have taken in view of the need for an organised opposition, representing the discontented elements in the country.

This step was taken after the defeat of Shays. A Convention in
Worcester County then drew up and caused to be circulated a list
of proposed senatorial candidates—a fact made public by the
denunciation of the practice by a newspaper correspondent. It
appeared that a town meeting, called by the malcontents, had
written inviting other towns to send delegates to Patch's tavern
in Worcester. 'Their ultimate dependence', said the writer, 'is on a
new General Court; and their greatest wishes are, to have men
of their own character and sentiments elected into the legislature,
that they may have a pardon enacted for all their treasonable practices, and laws passed whereby they may be absolved from all
obligations to pay their debts, or be allowed to cheat their creditors
out of their dues, under sanction and colour of law.'[32] Another

---

[29]*Worcester Magazine*, last week, August 1786.
[30]*Massachusetts Spy*, 23 May 1782.
[31]*Hampshire Gazette*, 29 November 1786.
[32]*Worcester Magazine*, 3rd week, March 1787.

letter in the same number, by a correspondent who had caught wind of the scheme, hoped that the report was without foundation, asserting that every measure of that kind 'to INFLUENCE Elections, is a violation of the CONSTITUTION'. The news was confirmed one week later, however, by a letter calling for the meeting, and signed by the three committee members from the town of Lunenburg.[33]

The fate of this initiative is extremely interesting. Two letters in the same issue, one from the town of Athol and one from an individual, denounced the plan. The Constitution, said the Athol reply, had wisely provided that senators be chosen by the free suffrage of the people, 'and anything that gives an undue influence on the election of Senators is unconstitutional, and therefore criminal . . .' So hostile was the response of the county that the chairman of the meeting at Patch's actually published, in the same issue, a notice stating that the lists being handed about had not emanated from his meeting; no person for senator or any other government office was agreed on; 'We thought it best not to do any business of that kind, and dispersed without doing any'.

This reaction was quite characteristic of the times. In Massachusetts, electioneering was still held in that sort of disfavour which makes a practice impossible to admit in public. But in other states this tradition was already crumbling and could not last long.

The attack on the plan to prepare lists was not a mere trick by the other side. The governing conception was that the election was an occasion on which every freeholder voted his own mind; and any attempt to influence him, by temptation or pressure, was an attempt to corrupt the essential freedom of the election. Massachusetts, before the rise of political parties, was on the whole singularly free from complaints of improper electoral tactics, and the tickets which had so long been prepared by the Quakers in Pennsylvania, the lavish treating in New York, and the gentlemanly canvassing, not by the candidates so much as by their hospitable friends in the South, would still, at this date, have seemed grossly corrupt in New England, except perhaps in Rhode Island.

It was the general policy of the conventions to correspond with each other on views, grievances, and remedies. Their meetings became more frequent as the crisis developed. It is not surprising that by early in the new year they should have begun to plan for the forthcoming elections. Their whole procedure, indeed their

---

[33]*Worcester Magazine*, 4th week, March 1787.

existence, was disagreeably reminiscent, in the opinion of their opponents, of the measures by which the province had been rallied against the Crown. Then, at least from about 1774, there had been a rising degree of unity; it could be argued that the Charter, under attack by the British, was being defended by the people. But once the Constitution of 1780 had gone into force, conventions challenged the legitimacy of the government of the state. It was therefore consistently argued by all their opponents that since the Constitution made no provision for them, but had provided adequate means of representation, they lay outside the Constitution and were illegal.

The charge of illegality can best be understood as an implied counterassertion that the Constitution, having been established by the consent of the governed, comprehended all possible modes of legitimate political action. That instrument, as Chief Justice Cushing observed, had parcelled out all the power to be exercised under it; no delegated power remained to give to the county conventions, unless it were to counteract the General Court and compel or over-awe them. What then was to be done about real grievances? The answer was plain: follow the ancient usage by applying at regular town meetings to lawful representatives, either by petition or instruction. The Constitution expressly protected the right of instruction and the right of assembly.[34]

This counsel, however, ignored the core of the dissidents' problem. In legislative divisions the instructed members might simply be defeated. It was inherently unlikely that instructions could overturn set legislative policies unless the opposing members had had the opportunity of concerting their own measures. Here and there a specific mistake or grievance might be corrected; but that was not at all the same thing as reversing the entire direction of economic policy. Yet the whole system under which the General Court operated tended to preclude such previous consultation; the country members came together from all over the state; and the very steps by which some co-ordinated policy might have been devised were denounced by all the agents and supporters of central government as unconstitutional. Within the formal constitution of government was an informal but no less powerful system by which the government was carried on. There was no lack of opportunity for concerting policy by the men who were always on the spot and who anyway held most of the strings of power and influence. The county conventions must be understood as the

---

[34]*Hampshire Gazette*, 29 November 1786.

natural—indeed, the normal—response of the discontented elements to the effective exercise of power, through the control of
the 'system', by their opponents.

The county convention, springing directly from the towns, upon
particular occasions and derived from the popular resistance of
revolutionary times, seemed to its supporters to be nearer to the
people than did the General Court. The Court was of course made
up of representatives, no one denied that; but they were chosen on
a basis that was now found to be unsatisfactory, they were subject to the check of a Senate chosen on a different basis and free
from the great control of instruction, and they were governed by
detailed rules of procedure not the least significant of which—as
some towns had noticed in 1780—was the rule that only sixty
members were required to make a quorum; this provision gave a
standing advantage to the nearby coastal and eastern towns. The
conventions seemed to claim to be an 'anti-Court' in the same way
that the association which convened almost contemporaneously
in England seemed to its opponents to be an 'anti-Parliament';
and they, too, denounced the body as unconstitutional.

The conventions, then, emerged as an old way of meeting new
problems. They reflected not so much the power as the lack of
effective instruments in the hands of a gravely discontented section of the people. It is this sense of lack which offers us a clearer
view of them—though one that was not available to them. The conventions were the only mode of collective protest, of the concerting of policies, which the dissidents could hit on before the rise of
the organized political party. Conventions disappeared when parties arose, until in due course the parties revived them for party
purposes; but after this they acquired a national, and lost their
local, character.

The upheaval of the spring elections of 1787 was all the more
remarkable. It was reflected in the sheer scale of participation by
the voters. In 1786, some 8,000 of them took part in the election
for Governor, being about 11 per cent of the adult white males
of the state; this, though slightly low, was not much below the
average for such elections since 1780. But 1787 produced a turn-
out of over 24,000; about 32 per cent and nearly twice as high as
any before.[35] The *Worcester Magazine* reported the election of
sixteen new senators. The towns made an unprecedented effort to
return representatives. No fewer than 228 made elections, leaving

---

[35]See Pole, *Political Representation,* Appendix II, p. 542.

only 87 as absentees. (Next year an ebbing of this exertion was already to be noticed, with 108 towns unrepresented.) In Hampshire 41 of 59 towns, in Berkshire 21 of 25, and in Worcester, by a magnificent effort, every one of the 46 towns, returned representatives. Essex also achieved 100 per cent representation of its 18 towns, Suffolk 18 out of 22, and Middlesex 32 out of 38. An extraordinary proportion of the representatives were new; no fewer than 159 out of 253 were counted by the *Worcester Magazine*.[36]

The social composition of the House of Representatives had already begun to change by 1786, if the rank claimed by members can be considered as a guide. The dignity of an 'esquire' still told in such matters, but the 'esquires' had begun to yield place, particularly to members bearing a military rank dating from the Revolutionary War.[37] In policy, the results of the elections were felt more in relief of distress than in a fundamental change of direction. The former legislature had acted to suspend the collection of debts in specie, and this Act was periodically renewed; and a measure was passed for the relief of poor prisoners committed for debt. Acts were also passed postponing the payment of taxes.[38] The new legislature also showed notable leniency towards the Shaysites, who had been subjected to certain disabilities by the preceding body. To those who had been disfranchised, the suffrage franchise was restored in June 1787 after the disqualification had been in effect for only four months and had applied only to the election of April 1787.[39]

These measures do not disclose a basic reorientation of economic policy. The encouragement and protection of Massachusetts production and commerce, which was already legislative policy under the Confederation, was continued; but the new legislature did not initiate the paper money policy, or the establishment of a 'bank of paper money', which were demanded by so many of the stricken towns.[40] It should be recognised that even at the height of discontent, the opposition to these measures was strong and highly articulate, even in the west. The articulateness, the grasp

---

[36] *Acts and Resolves,* May session 1787; May session 1788. *Worcester Magazine,* 1st week, June 1787.

[37] East, 'Massachusetts Conservatives', 358, 367.

[38] *Acts and Resolves,* May session 1787, chap. 6; October session 1787, chap. 20, chap. 29; February session 1788, chap. 53.

[39] *Acts and Resolves,* 1787, chap. 21, approved 15 June 1787.

[40] A Bank of Massachusetts had been founded in 1784 (M. Jensen, *The New Nation* [New York, 1950], 232) but it was an enterprise of the Boston merchants and did not respond to the demands of the loose money interests.

of political language of the economic conservatives, especially when combined with their social position, gave them an advantage that could not easily be outswayed. In the election which turned out the old General Court, even the insurgent county of Berkshire returned two of the staunchest conservatives in America: Henry Van Schaack and Theodore Sedgwick. The authority of men of their social pre-eminence outweighed adverse political opinions.

When the new legislature met, the Philadelphia Convention had already begun its sessions. In considering the course of state economic policy by that time, it is well to remember that the expectation of a new and stronger central government must have influenced all deliberations.[41]

The seaboard party of merchant leadership, the creditor interest which is generally—though somewhat mistakenly—described as 'conservative', was the party of Federalism. They supported the new Constitution and they immediately appeared as friends of the attitudes that would soon be identified with Hamilton. They no longer felt, after the elections of 1787, that they could be sure of controlling the state, but they took great comfort in the superior power of the Federal Congress. 'In my opinion', wrote one of them, 'we never had a worse House of Reps—I thank God that we have a federal Govt.' Another observed that the Massachusetts House was said to be the worse that had ever sat, and added pungently, 'I desire to thank God, it is not in their power to make paper money or to take many other disgraceful measures which we should undoubtedly be obliged to submit to but for that sovereign balm the Federal Constitution.'[42] Theodore Sedgwick, on his election to the state legislature in 1787, received the congratulations of Rufus King, who hoped there would be enough of his sentiments 'to check the madness of Democracy'.[43]

---

[41]However, the General Court was still debating modes of paying the state debt as late as June 1789, though Federalists had reason to doubt whether the majority had any real intention of providing for it. Thomas Dwight to Theodore Sedgwick, 19 June 1789, Sedgwick papers.

[42]S. Henshaw to Sedgwick, 14 June 1789; Thomas Dwight to Sedgwick, 9 July 1789, Sedgwick Papers. As early as May 1788 Sedgwick, reporting on the new legislature, assured his friend Van Schaack that at least two-thirds of both Houses were 'federal'. Clearly the word had already been translated from its reference to the controversy over the Constitution, which had been ratified by Massachusetts but had not yet been adopted, to a description of interests represented by groups in the legislature. Sedgwick to Van Schaack, 29 May 1788, Sedgwick Papers.

[43]Rufus King to Sedgwick, 10 June 1787, Sedgwick Papers. King, writing from Philadelphia, where he was a member of the Convention, remarked that he was precluded from communicating, 'even confidentially', any particular of the proceedings. One may wonder how many politicians could be relied on to observe such a pledge in the conditions of modern democracy.

The year 1780 established the Constitution of Massachusetts but did not bring any change in the conduct of its politics. The province had long been used to political factions, to the struggle for prominence of energetic men, to the caucus and the manipulation of the town meeting; from about 1774, something like a united front was brought into being against British tyranny, but this front did not hold the government of the Bay Province together. When, soon after the adoption of the new state Constitution, the policy of the legislature began to provoke renewed discontent, the opposition resorted to the use of the county convention, the only form of effective organisation it knew.

Though effective as an expression of grievance, it was less useful for securing redress. The persistent weakness of the opposition was a phenomenon of some complexity. There were real difficulties about the working out of a satisfactory economic policy, and these difficulties were multiplied for those who, being in a permanent minority and not standing at the centre of information and authority, were never in a position to formulate a clear policy of their own. The merchant party did not handle the economic affairs of the state with great success, and were ready to permit modifications and to alleviate undue hardships when the need was pointed out to them: but they did in effect work as a political party. Their strategic position, their opportunities of mutual consultation, and the quorum rule in the House of Representatives gave them all the advantages of a party without the distasteful formality of organisation; nor were they required to face the extremely arduous task, which gave much trouble to later party organisers, of keeping the machinery of a party in existence between elections.

The organisation of opposition through committees of correspondence had worked splendidly during the Revolution because of the essential unity of purpose between the towns and the provincial Congress, which soon became the Assembly of the state; but it was a different matter when the opposition was to the policy of the state's own legislature. Americans politicians had not learned to differentiate between opposing the policy of the majority and opposing the Constitution itself; it was a distinction which until very lately had been delicate in Britain, where the idea of a 'formed' opposition was officially held to imply disloyalty to the Crown. Supporters of majority policies could easily denounce the efforts of their opponents as unconstitutional—as 'disloyal', in the American sense.

What the opposition needed, instead of a series of county conventions, was a state-wide political party. The need was urgent, a fact which can be seen very clearly in retrospect; but the idea was inchoate, and when it began to take shape it reeked of those signs of conspiracy, of dissent from the agreed will of the sovereign people, of the attempt to interfere with the elemental freedom of the choice made by the voter on the spot at the time of the election, which the managers of the system always found so easy to discern and denounce.

The amount of public information carried by the newspapers increased through the period; and during the Shays troubles they fairly groaned with political and economic argument; that none of them was sympathetic to the malcontents was a factor which diminished their utility as organs of a possible organised opposition; but some of them gave both sides a hearing, and they could always be used to announce meetings and to sound opinion.

After the recent excitements, and the struggle over the adoption of the Constitution, the townsmen watched their representatives with keen and suspicious attention. A particularly bad impression was created by the Act of the new Congress establishing the salaries of members. The husbandmen of Massachusetts were not prepared to acquiesce in letting politics become a remunerative career; and the Act caused great anxiety to the Federalists, who had the job of explaining and justifying the Congress to the electorate. 'The idea of making money out of the public *at this time*', wrote Van Schaack, from Pittsfield, to Sedgwick, now in Congress, 'ought to be expunged.' If the report of the committee on this matter were adopted it would lessen the confidence of 'a considerable number of the yeomanry of the country'.[44] The frugal people of New England were not impressed by the explanation that the Congress had to pay regard to the habits of Southern gentlemen; gentlemen and yeomen were unanimously against it.[45] A year later the defeat of a respected member was attributed to his support of this measure.[46]

Nothing could more persuasively demonstrate the system of personal influence by which the Federalists maintained their leadership than the correspondence between Sedgwick, the leading Federalist of Western Massachusetts and one of the leaders in Congress, and his close associates at home. It was as a result of a militia matter that Van Schaack was able to confirm the accuracy of his impressions about the remuneration of federal representa-

[44]Van Schaack to Sedgwick, 5 July 1789, Sedgwick Papers.
[45]Van Schaack to Sedgwick, 26 July 1789, Sedgwick Papers.
[46]Thomas Dwight to Theodore Sedgwick, 13 July 1790, Sedgwick Papers.

tives and officers of government; while Sedgwick was urged to tell other members of Congress to 'take every opportunity to write to their country friends' about every beneficial measure; no pains should be spared to make a favourable impression among the great body of people.[47]

The language of this correspondence is that of a network of distinguished men who, understanding each other well, expected to be able through the exercise of traditional influence to lead the yeomanry. These were the gentlemen, and they knew it; the yeomanry were expected to follow. To maintain their leadership by this time required hard work: it meant making sure that people attended town meetings, and even making sure that votes, once cast, were returned to the secretary of state's office within the proper time.

'I am persuaded by recent experience', wrote another of Sedgwick's friends, 'that we can do infinitely more by private Letters than by News paper publications'.[48]

This was the old system, and it was not played out yet. But in order to make it work, the Federalists would soon have to admit the necessity for a more permanent and even a more professional form of organisation; and it would not be long before they proclaimed—or admitted—themselves to be a political party.

[47] Van Schaack to Sedgwick, 19 July 1789, 7 February 1790, Sedgwick Papers.

[48] S. Henshaw to Sedgwick, 15 April 1789, Sedgwick Papers.

{VI}

THE
TRIUMPH
OF HOPE

FROM PROBLEMS TO
SOLUTIONS

———— ◂▸ ◂●▸ ◂▸ ————

Given the political rivalries, conflicting material interests, and divergent social outlooks within the United States, as well as the frailties of human nature and the long and dismal history of failure of experiments in republican government, the problems that confronted the men who met in Philadelphia in the summer of 1787 would seem to have been almost insurmountable. How they diagnosed those problems, the practical political considerations and psychological and philosophical imperatives that drove and emboldened them to try to solve them, and the solutions they reached are described in the three selections below. The first selection emphasizes the concrete political problems with which the Framers had to grapple, their nationalistic orientation, their skill at compromise and improvisation, their commitment to democratic political procedures, and the "patchwork" quality of the resulting Constitution. The second selection analyzes the Framers' pessimistic conception of man and the assumptions about the function, nature, and form of government that flowed from it; it also assesses the importance of that conception and those assumptions in shaping the work of the Convention. The third selection discusses James Madison's solution to the historic problems of republican governments and traces that solution to Madison's reading of the Scottish philosopher, David Hume. Though neither of the last two selections in any way suggests that the practical and tangible considerations emphasized by the first selection did not play a major role in determining the behavior of the Framers, they both call attention to the devotion of many of the Framers to the ideal of making a genuinely scientific attempt to discover the "true" principles of republican government and to devise ways to put these principles into practical operation.

JOHN P. ROCHE (b. 1923) is a member of the Politics Department at Brandeis University and currently special assistant to President LYNDON B. JOHNSON; ARTHUR O. LOVEJOY (1873–1963), pioneer in the study of the history of ideas, was a member of the Department of Philosophy at The Johns Hopkins University.

The Founding Fathers: A Reform Caucus in Action

JOHN P. ROCHE

Over the last century and a half, the work of the Constitutional Convention and the motives of the Founding Fathers have been analyzed under a number of different ideological auspices. To one generation of historians, the hand of God was moving in the assembly; under a later dispensation, the dialectic (at various levels of philosophical sophistication) replaced the Deity: "relationships of production" moved into the niche previously reserved for Love of Country. Thus in counterpoint to the Zeitgeist, the Framers have undergone miraculous metamorphoses: at one time acclaimed as liberals and bold social engineers, today they appear in the guise of sound Burkean conservatives, men who in our time would subscribe to *Fortune*, look to Walter Lippmann for political theory, and chuckle patronizingly at the antics of Barry Goldwater. The implicit assumption is that if James Madison were among us, he would be President of the Ford Foundation, while Alexander Hamilton would chair the Committee for Economic Development.

The "Fathers" have thus been admitted to our best circles; the revolutionary ferocity which confiscated all Tory property in reach and populated New Brunswick with outlaws has been converted by the "Miltown School" of American historians into a benign dedication to "consensus" and "prescriptive rights." The Daughters of the American Revolution have, through the ministrations of Professors Boorstin, Hartz, and Rossiter, at last found ancestors

Reprinted with permission from *The American Political Science Review*, LV (December, 1961), 799–816.

worthy of their descendants. It is not my purpose here to argue that the "Fathers" were, in fact, radical revolutionaries; that proposition has been brilliantly demonstrated by Robert R. Palmer in his *Age of the Democratic Revolution*. My concern is with the further position that not only were they revolutionaries, but also they were democrats. Indeed, in my view, there is one fundamental truth about the Founding Fathers that *every* generation of Zeitgeisters has done its best to obscure: they were first and foremost superb democratic politicians. I suspect that in a contemporary setting, James Madison would be speaker of the House of Representatives and Hamilton would be the *eminence grise* dominating (*pace* Theodore Sorenson or Sherman Adams) the Executive Office of the President. They were, with their colleagues, *political men*— not metaphysicians, disembodied conservatives or Agents of History—and as recent research into the nature of American politics in the 1780s confirms,[1] they were committed (perhaps willy-nilly) to working within the democratic framework, within a universe of public approval. Charles Beard *and* the filiopietists to the contrary notwithstanding, the Philadelphia Convention was not a College of Cardinals or a council of Platonic guardians working within a manipulative, pre-democratic framework; it was a *nationalist* reform caucus which had to operate with great delicacy and skill in a political cosmos full of enemies to achieve the one definitive goal—popular approbation.

Perhaps the time has come, to borrow Walton Hamilton's fine phrase, to raise the Framers from immortality to mortality, to give them credit for their magnificent demonstration of the art of democratic politics. The point must be reemphasized; they *made* history and did it within the limits of consensus. There was nothing inevitable about the future in 1787; the *Zeitgeist*, that fine Hegelian technique of begging causal questions, could only be discerned in retrospect. What they did was to hammer out a pragmatic compromise which would both bolster the "National interest" and be acceptable to the people. What inspiration they got came from their collective experience as professional politicians

[1] The view that the right to vote in the states was severely circumscribed by property qualifications has been thoroughly discredited in recent years. See Chilton Williamson, *American Suffrage from Property to Democracy, 1760–1860* (Princeton, 1960). The contemporary position is that John Dickinson actually knew what he was talking about when he argued that there would be little opposition to vesting the right of suffrage in freeholders since "The great mass of our Citizens is composed at this time of freeholders, and will be pleased with it." Max Farrand, *Records of the Federal Convention*, Vol. 2 (New Haven, 1911), p. 202. (Henceforth cited as *Farrand.*)

in a democratic society. As John Dickinson put it to his fellow delegates on August 13, "Experience must be our guide. Reason may mislead us."

In this context, let us examine the problems they confronted and the solutions they evolved. The Convention has been described picturesquely as a counter-revolutionary junta and the Constitution as a *coup d'état*,[2] but this has been accomplished by withdrawing the whole history of the movement for constitutional reform from its true context. No doubt the goals of the constitutional elite were "subversive" to the existing political order, but it is overlooked that their subversion could only have succeeded if the people of the United States endorsed it by regularized procedures. Indubitably they were "plotting" to establish a much stronger central government than existed under the Articles, but only in the sense in which one could argue equally well that John F. Kennedy was, from 1956 to 1960, "plotting" to become President. In short, on the fundamental *procedural* level, the Constitutionalists had to work according to the prevailing rules of the game. Whether they liked it or not is a topic for spiritualists—and is irrelevant: one may be quite certain that had Washington agreed to play the de Gaulle (as the Cincinnati once urged), Hamilton would willingly have held his horse, but such fertile speculation in no way alters the actual context in which events took place.

I

When the Constitutionalists went forth to subvert the Confederation, they utilized the mechanisms of political legitimacy. And the roadblocks which confronted them were formidable. At the same time, they were endowed with certain potent political assets. The history of the United States from 1786 to 1790 was largely one of a masterful employment of political expertise by the Constitutionalists as against bumbling, erratic behavior by the opponents of reform. Effectively, the Constitutionalists had to induce

---

[2]The classic statement of the *coup d'état* theory is, of course, Charles A. Beard, *An Economic Interpretation of the United States* (New York, 1913), and this theme was echoed by Vernon L. Parrington, Merrill Jensen and others in "populist" historiographical tradition. For a sharp critique of this thesis see Robert E. Brown, *Charles Beard and the Constitution* (Princeton, 1956). See also Forrest McDonald, *We the People* (Chicago, 1958); the trailblazing work in this genre was Douglas Adair, "The Tenth Federalist Revisited," *William and Mary Quarterly*, 3rd ser., Vol. VIII (1951), pp. 48–67.

the states, by democratic techniques of coercion, to emasculate themselves. To be specific, if New York had refused to join the new Union, the project was doomed; yet before New York was safely in, the reluctant state legislature had *sua sponte* to take the following steps: (1) agree to send delegates to the Philadelphia Convention; (2) provide maintenance for these delegates (these were distinct stages: New Hampshire was early in naming delegates, but did not provide for their maintenance until July); (3) set up the special *ad hoc* convention to decide on ratification; and (4) concede to the decision of the *ad hoc* convention that New York should participate. New York admittedly was a tricky state, with a strong interest in a *status quo* which permitted her to exploit New Jersey and Connecticut, but the same legal hurdles existed in every state. And at the risk of becoming boring, it must be reiterated that the *only* weapon in the Constitutionalist arsenal was an effective mobilization of public opinion.

The group which undertook this struggle was an interesting amalgam of a few dedicated nationalists with the self-interested spokesmen of various parochial bailiwicks. The Georgians, for example, wanted a strong central authority to provide military protection for their huge, underpopulated state against the Creek Confederacy; Jerseymen and Connecticuters wanted to escape from economic bondage to New York; the Virginians hoped to establish a system which would give that great state its rightful place in the councils of the republic. The dominant figures in the politics of these states therefore cooperated in the call for the Convention.[3] In other states, the thrust towards national reform was taken up by opposition groups who added the "national interest" to their weapons system; in Pennsylvania, for instance, the group fighting to revise the Constitution of 1776 came out foursquare behind the Constitutionalists, and in New York, Hamilton and the Schuyler *ambiance* took the same tack against George Clinton.[4] There was, of course, a large element of personality in the affair: there is reason to suspect that Patrick Henry's opposition to the Convention and the Constitution was founded on his

[3] A basic volume, which, like other works by Warren, provides evidence with which one can evaluate the author's own opinions, is Charles Warren, *The Making of the Constitution* (Boston, 1928). The best brief summary of the forces behind the movement for centralization is ch. 1 of *Warren* (as it will be cited hereafter).

[4] On Pennsylvania see Robert L. Brunhouse, *Counter-Revolution in Pennsylvania* (Harrisburg, 1942) and Charles P. Smith, *James Wilson* (Chapel Hill, 1956), ch. 15; for New York, which needs the same sort of microanalysis Pennsylvania has received, the best study is E. Wilder Spaulding, *New York in the Critical Period, 1783–1789* (New York, 1932).

conviction that Jefferson was behind both, and a close study of local politics elsewhere would surely reveal that others supported the Constitution for the simple (and politically quite sufficient) reason that the "wrong" people were against it.

To say this is not to suggest that the Constitution rested on a foundation of impure or base motives. It is rather to argue that in politics there are no immaculate conceptions, and that in the drive for a stronger general government, motives of all sorts played a part. Few men in the history of mankind have espoused a view of the "common good" or "public interest" that militated against their private status; even Plato with all his reverence for disembodied reason managed to put philosophers on top of the pile. Thus it is not surprising that a number of diversified private interests joined to push the nationalist public interest; what would have been surprising was the absence of such a pragmatic united front. And the fact remains that, however motivated, these men did demonstrate a willingness to compromise their parochial interests in behalf of an ideal which took shape before their eyes and under their ministrations.

As Stanley Elkins and Eric McKitrick have suggested in a perceptive essay,[5] what distinguished the leaders of the Constitutionalist caucus from their enemies was a "Continental" approach to political, economic and military issues. To the extent that they shared an institutional base of operations, it was the Continental Congress (thirty-nine of the delegates to the Federal Convention had served in Congress[6]), and this was hardly a locale which inspired respect for the state governments. Robert de Jouvenal observed French politics half a century ago and noted that a revolutionary Deputy had had more in common with a non-revolutionary Deputy than he had with a revolutionary non-Deputy;[7] similarly one can surmise that membership in the Congress under the Articles of Confederation worked to establish a continental frame of reference, that a Congressman from Pennsylvania and one from North Carolina would share a universe of discourse which provided them with a conceptual common denominator vis à vis their respective state legislatures. This was particularly true with respect to external affairs: the average state legislator was probably about as concerned with foreign policy then as he is today, but Congressmen were constantly forced to take the broad

---

[5]Stanley Elkins and Eric McKitrick, "The Founding Fathers: Young Men of the Revolution," *Political Science Quarterly*, Vol. 76 (1961), p. 181.

[6]*Warren*, p. 55.

[7]In *La République des Camarades* (Paris, 1914).

view of American prestige, were compelled to listen to the reports of Secretary John Jay and to the dispatches and pleas from their frustrated envoys in Britain, France and Spain.[8] From considerations such as these, a "Continental" ideology developed which seems to have demanded a revision of our domestic institutions primarily on the ground that only by invigorating our general government could we assume our rightful place in the international arena. Indeed, an argument with great force—particularly since Washington was its incarnation—urged that our very survival in the Hobbesian jungle of world politics depended upon a reordering and strengthening of our national sovereignty.[9]

Note that I am not endorsing the "Critical Period" thesis; on the contrary, Merrill Jensen seems to me quite sound in his view that for most Americans, engaged as they were in self-sustaining agriculture, the "Critical Period" was not particularly critical.[10] In fact, the great achievement of the Constitutionalists was their ultimate success in convincing the elected representatives of a majority of the white male population that change was imperative. A small group of political leaders with a Continental vision and essentially a consciousness of the United States' *international impotence,* provided the matrix of the movement. To their standard other leaders rallied with their own parallel ambitions. Their great assets were (1) the presence in their caucus of the one authentic American "father figure," George Washington, whose prestige was enormous;[11] (2) the energy and talent of their leadership (in which one must include the towering intellectuals of the time, John Adams and Thomas Jefferson, despite their absence abroad), and their communications "network," which was far superior to anything on the opposition side;[12] (3) the preemptive skill which made "their" issue The Issue and kept the locally oriented opposi-

---

[8]See Frank Monaghan, *John Jay* (New York, 1935), ch. 13.

[9]"[T]he situation of the general government, if it can be called a government, is shaken to its foundation, and liable to be overturned by every blast. In a word, it is at an end; and, unless a remedy is soon applied, anarchy and confusion will inevitably ensue." Washington to Jefferson, May 30, 1787, *Farrand,* III, 31. See also Irving Brant, *James Madison, The Nationalist* (New York, 1948), ch. 25.

[10]Merrill Jensen, *The New Nation* (New York, 1950). Interestingly enough, Prof. Jensen virtually ignores international relations in his laudatory treatment of the government under the Articles of Confederation.

[11]The story of James Madison's cultivation of Washington is told by Brant, *op. cit.,* pp. 394–397.

[12]The "message center" being the Congress; nineteen members of Congress were simultaneously delegates to the Convention. One gets a sense of this coordination of effort from Broadus Mitchell, *Alexander Hamilton, Youth to Maturity* (New York, 1957), ch. 22.

tion permanently on the defensive; and (4) the subjective consideration that these men were spokesmen of a new and compelling credo: *American* nationalism, that ill-defined but nonetheless potent sense of collective purpose that emerged from the American Revolution.

Despite great institutional handicaps, the Constitutionalists managed in the mid-1780s to mount an offensive which gained momentum as years went by. Their greatest problem was lethargy, and paradoxically, the number of barriers in their path may have proved an advantage in the long run. Beginning with the initial battle to get the Constitutional Convention called and delegates appointed, they could never relax, never let up the pressure. In practical terms, this meant that the local "organizations" created by the Constitutionalists were perpetually in movement building up their cadres for the next fight. (The word organization has to be used with great caution: a political organization in the United States—as in contemporary England[13]—generally consisted of a magnate and his following, or a coalition of magnates. This did not necessarily mean that it was "undemocratic" or "aristocratic," in the Aristotelian sense of the word: while a few magnates such as the Livingstons could draft their followings, most exercised their leadership without coercion on the basis of popular endorsement. The absence of organized opposition did not imply the impossibility of competition any more than low public participation in elections necessarily indicated an undemocratic suffrage.)

The Constitutionalists got the jump on the "opposition" (a collective noun: oppositions would be more correct) at the outset with the demand for a Convention. Their opponents were caught in an old political trap: they were not being asked to approve any specific program of reform, but only to endorse a meeting to discuss and recommend needed reforms. If they took a hard line at the first stage, they were put in the position of glorifying the *status quo* and of denying the need for *any* changes. Moreover, the Constitutionalists could go to the people with a persuasive argument for "fair play"—"How can you condemn reform before you know precisely what is involved?" Since the state legislatures obviously would have the final say on any proposals that might emerge from the Convention, the Constitutionalists were merely reasonable men asking for a chance. Besides, since they did not make any concrete proposals at that stage, they were in a position

---

[13]See Sir Lewis Namier, *The Structure of Politics at the Accession of George III*, 2d ed. (New York, 1957); *England in the Age of the American Revolution* (London, 1930).

to capitalize on every sort of generalized discontent with the Confederation.

Perhaps because of their poor intelligence system, perhaps because of over-confidence generated by the failure of all previous efforts to alter the Articles,[14] the opposition awoke too late to the dangers that confronted them in 1787. Not only did the Constitutionalists manage to get every state but Rhode Island (where politics was enlivened by a party system reminiscent of the "Blues" and the "Greens" in the Byzantine Empire)[15] to appoint delegates to Philadelphia, but when the results were in, it appeared that they dominated the delegations. Given the apathy of the opposition, this was a natural phenomenon: in an ideologically nonpolarized political atmosphere those who get appointed to a special committee are likely to be the men who supported the movement for its creation. Even George Clinton, who seems to have been the first opposition leader to awake to the possibility of trouble, could not prevent the New York legislature from appointing Alexander Hamilton—though he did have the foresight to send two of his henchmen to dominate the delegation. Incidentally, much has been made of the fact that the delegates to Philadelphia were not elected by the people; some have adduced this fact as evidence of the "undemocratic" character of the gathering. But put in the context of the time, this argument is wholly specious: the central government under the Articles was considered a creature of the component states and in all the states but Rhode Island, Connecticut and New Hampshire, members of the national Congress were chosen by the state legislatures. This was not a consequence of elitism or fear of the mob; it was a logical extension of states'-rights doctrine to guarantee that the national institution did not end-run the state legislatures and make direct contact with the people.[16]

---

[14]The Annapolis Convention, called for the previous year, turned into a shambles: only five states sent commissioners, only three states were legally represented, and the instructions to delegates named varied quite widely from state to state. Clinton and others of his persuasion may have thought this disaster would put an end to the drive for reform. See Mitchell, *op. cit.*, pp. 362–367; Brant, *op. cit.*, pp. 375–387.

[15]See Hamilton M. Bishop, *Why Rhode Island Opposed the Federal Constitution* (Providence, 1950) for a careful analysis of the labyrinthine political course of Rhode Island. For background see David S. Lovejoy, *Rhode Island Politics and the American Revolution* (Providence, 1958).

[16]The terms "radical" and "conservative" have been bandied about a good deal in connection with the Constitution. This usage is nonsense if it is employed to distinguish between two economic "classes"—*e.g.*, radical debtors versus conservative creditors, radical farmers versus conservative capitalists, etc.—because there was no polarization along this line of division;

II

With delegations safely named, the focus shifted to Philadelphia. While waiting for a quorum to assemble, James Madison got busy and drafted the so-called Randolph or Virginia Plan with the aid of the Virginia delegation. This was a political master-stroke. Its consequence was that once business got under way, the framework of discussion was established on Madison's terms. There was no interminable argument over agenda; instead the delegates took the Virginia Resolutions—"just for purposes of discussion"— as their point of departure. And along with Madison's proposals, many of which were buried in the course of the summer, went his major premise: a new start on a Constitution rather than piecemeal amendment. This was not necessarily revolutionary—a little exegesis could demonstrate that a new Constitution might be formulated as "amendments" to the Articles of Confederation— but Madison's proposal that this "lump sum" amendment go into effect after approval by nine states (the Articles required unanimous state approval for any amendment) was thoroughly subversive.[17]

Standard treatments of the Convention divide the delegates into "nationalists" and "states'-righters" with various improvised shadings ("moderate nationalists," etc.), but these are *a posteriori* categories which obfuscate more than they clarify. What is striking to one who analyzes the Convention as a case-study in democratic politics is the lack of clear-cut ideological divisions in the Convention. Indeed, I submit that the evidence—Madison's *Notes*, the correspondence of the delegates, and debates on ratification—indicates that this was a *remarkably homogeneous body on the ideological level*. Yates and Lansing, Clinton's two chaperones for Hamilton, left in disgust on July 10. (Is there anything more

---

the same types of people turned up on both sides. And many were hard to place in these terms: does one treat Robert Morris as a debtor or a creditor? or James Wilson? See Brown, *op. cit., passim*. The one line of division that holds up is between those deeply attached to states' rights and those who felt that the Confederation was bankrupt. Thus, curiously, some of the most narrow-minded, parochial spokesmen of the time have earned the designation "radical" while those most willing to experiment and alter the *status quo* have been dubbed "conservative"! See Cecelia Kenyon, "Men of Little Faith," *William and Mary Quarterly*, Vol. 12 (1955), p. 3.

[17]Yet, there was little objection to this crucial modification from any quarter—there almost seems to have been a gentlemen's agreement that Rhode Island's *liberum veto* had to be destroyed.

tedious than sitting through endless disputes on matters one deems fundamentally misconceived? It takes an iron will to spend a hot summer as an ideological *agent provocateur*.) Luther Martin, Maryland's bibulous narcissist, left on September 4 in a huff when he discovered that others did not share his self-esteem; others went home for personal reasons. But the hard core of delegates accepted a grinding regimen throughout the attrition of a Philadelphia summer precisely because they shared the Constitutionalist goal.

Basic differences of opinion emerged, of course, but these were not ideological; they were *structural*. If the so-called "states'-rights" group had not accepted the fundamental purposes of the Convention, they could simply have pulled out and by doing so have aborted the whole enterprise. Instead of bolting, they returned day after day to argue and to compromise. An interesting symbol of this basic homogeneity was the initial agreement on secrecy: these professional politicians did not want to become prisoners of publicity; they wanted to retain that freedom of maneuver which is only possible when men are not forced to take public stands in the preliminary stages of negotiation.[18] There was no legal means of binding the tongues of the delegates: at any stage in the game a delegate with basic principled objections to the emerging project could have taken the stump (as Luther Martin did after his exit) and denounced the convention to the skies. Yet Madison did not even inform Thomas Jefferson in Paris of the course of the deliberations[19] and available correspondence indicates that the delegates generally observed the injunction. Secrecy is certainly uncharacteristic of any assembly marked by strong ideological polarization. This was noted at the time: the *New York Daily Advertiser,* August 14, 1787, commented that the ". . . profound secrecy hitherto observed by the convention [we consider] a happy omen, as it demonstrates that the spirit of party on any great and essential point cannot have arisen to any height."[20]

Commentators on the Constitution who have read *The Federalist* in lieu of reading the actual debates have credited the Fathers with

[18]See Mason's letter to his son, May 27, 1787, in which he endorsed secrecy as "a proper precaution to prevent mistakes and misrepresentation until the business shall have been completed, when the whole may have a very different complexion from that in which the several crude and indigested parts might in their first shape appear if submitted to the public eye." *Farrand,* III, 28.

[19]See Madison to Jefferson, June 6, 1787, *Farrand,* III, 35.

[20]Cited in *Warren,* p. 138.

the invention of a sublime concept called "Federalism."[21] Unfortunately *The Federalist* is probative evidence for only one proposition: that Hamilton and Madison were inspired propagandists with a genius for retrospective symmetry. Federalism, as the theory is generally defined, was an improvisation which was later promoted into a political theory. Experts on "federalism" should take to heart the advice of David Hume, who warned in his *Of the Rise and Progress of the Arts and Sciences* that ". . . there is no subject in which we must proceed with more caution than in [history], lest we assign causes which never existed and reduce what is merely contingent to stable and universal principles." In any event, the final balance in the Constitution between the states and the nation must have come as a great disappointment to Madison, while Hamilton's unitary views are too well known to need elucidation.

It is indeed astonishing how those who have glibly designated James Madison the "father" of Federalism have overlooked the solid body of fact which indicates that he shared Hamilton's quest for a unitary central government. To be specific, they have avoided examining the clear import of the Madison-Virginia Plan,[22] and have disregarded Madison's dogged inch-by-inch retreat from the bastions of centralization. The Virginia Plan envisioned a unitary national government effectively freed from and dominant over the states. The lower house of the national legislature was to be elected directly by the people of the states with membership proportional to population. The upper house was to be selected by the lower and the two chambers would elect the executive and choose the judges. The national government would be thus cut completely loose from the states.[23]

---

[21]See, *e.g.*, Gottfried Dietze, *The Federalist, A Classic on Federalism and Free Government* (Baltimore, 1960); Richard Hofstadter, *The American Political Tradition* (New York, 1948); and John P. Roche, "American Liberty," in M. Konvitz and C. Rossiter, eds., *Aspects of Liberty* (Ithaca, 1958).

[22]"I hold it for a fundamental point, that an individual independence of the states is utterly irreconcilable with the idea of an aggregate sovereignty," Madison to Randolph, cited in Brant, *op. cit.*, p. 416.

[23]The Randolph Plan was presented on May 29, see *Farrand*, I, 18–23; the state legislatures retained only the power to *nominate* candidates for the upper chamber. Madison's view of the appropriate position of the states emerged even more strikingly in Yates' record of his speech on June 29: "Some contend that states are sovereign when in fact they are only political societies. There is a gradation of power in all societies, from the lowest corporation to the highest sovereign. The states never possessed the essential rights of sovereignty. . . . The states, at present, are only great corporations, having the power of making by-laws, and these are effectual only if they are not contradictory to the general confederation. The states ought to be placed under the control of the general government—at least as much so as they formerly were under the king and British parliament." *Farrand,*

The structure of the general government was freed from state control in a truly radical fashion, but the scope of the authority of the national sovereign as Madison initially formulated it was breathtaking—it was a formulation worthy of the Sage of Malmesbury himself. The national legislature was to be empowered to disallow the acts of state legislatures,[24] and the central government was vested, in addition to the powers of the nation under the Articles of Confederation, with plenary authority wherever ". . . the separate States are incompetent or in which the harmony of the United States may be interrupted by the exercise of individual legislation."[25] Finally, just to lock the door against state intrusion, the national Congress was to be given the power to use military force on recalcitrant states.[26] This was Madison's "model" of an ideal national government, though it later received little publicity in *The Federalist*.

The interesting thing was the reaction of the Convention to this militant program for a strong autonomous central government. Some delegates were startled, some obviously leery of so comprehensive a project of reform,[27] but nobody set off any fireworks and nobody walked out. Moreover, in the two weeks that followed, the Virginia Plan received substantial endorsement *en principe;* the initial temper of the gathering can be deduced from the approval "without debate or dissent," on May 31, of the Sixth Resolution which granted Congress the authority to disallow state legislation ". . . contravening *in its opinion* the Articles of Union." Indeed, an amendment was included to bar states from contravening national treaties.[28]

The Virginia Plan may therefore be considered, in ideological terms, as the delegates' Utopia, but as the discussions continued

---

I, 471. Forty-six years later, after Yates' "Notes" had been published, Madison tried to explain this statement away as a misinterpretation: he did not flatly deny the authenticity of Yates' record, but attempted a defense that was half justification and half evasion. Madison to W. C. Rives, Oct. 21, 1833. *Farrand*, III, 521–524.

[24]Resolution 6 gave the National Legislature this power subject to review by the Council of Revision proposed in Resolution 8.

[25]Resolution 6.

[26]*Ibid.*

[27]See the discussions on May 30 and 31. "Mr. Charles Pinkney wished to know of Mr. Randolph whether he meant to abolish the State Governts. altogether . . . Mr. Butler said he had not made up his mind on the subject and was open to the light which discussion might throw on it . . . Genl. Pinkney expressed a doubt . . . Mr. Gerry seemed to entertain the same doubt." *Farrand*, I, 33–34. There were no denunciations—though it should perhaps be added that Luther Martin had not yet arrived.

[28]*Farrand*, I, 54. (Italics added.)

and became more specific, many of those present began to have second thoughts. After all, they were not residents of Utopia or guardians in Plato's Republic who could simply impose a philosophical ideal on subordinate strata of the population. They were practical politicians in a democratic society, and no matter what their private dreams might be, they had to take home an acceptable package and defend it—and their own political futures—against predictable attack. On June 14 the breaking point between dream and reality took place. Apparently realizing that under the Virginia Plan, Massachusetts, Virginia and Pennsylvania could virtually dominate the national government—and probably appreciating that to sell this program to "the folks back home" would be impossible—the delegates from the small states dug in their heels and demanded time for a consideration of alternatives. One gets a graphic sense of the inner politics from John Dickinson's reproach to Madison: "You see the consequences of pushing things too far. Some of the members from the small States wish for two branches in the General Legislature and are friends to a good National Government; but we would sooner submit to a foreign power than . . . be deprived of an equality of suffrage in both branches of the Legislature, and thereby be thrown under the domination of the large States."[29]

The bare outline of the Journal entry for Tuesday, June 14, is suggestive to anyone with extensive experience in deliberative bodies. "It was moved by Mr. Patterson [*sic*, Paterson's name was one of those consistently misspelled by Madison and everybody else] seconded by Mr. Randolph that the further consideration of the report from the Committee of the whole House [endorsing the Virginia Plan] be postponed til tomorrow, and before the question for postponement was taken, it was moved by Mr. Randolph seconded by Mr. Patterson that the House adjourn."[30] The House adjourned by obvious prearrangement of the two principals: since the preceding Saturday when Brearley and Paterson of New Jersey had announced their fundamental discontent with the representational features of the Virginia Plan, the informal pressure had certainly been building up to slow down the streamroller. Doubtless there were extended arguments at the Indian Queen between Madison and Paterson, the latter insisting that events were moving rapidly towards a probably disastrous conclusion, towards a poli-

---

[29]*Ibid.*, p. 242. Delaware's delegates had been instructed by their general assembly to maintain in any new system the voting equality of the states. *Farrand*, III, 574.

[30]*Ibid.*, p. 240.

tical suicide pact. Now the process of accommodation was put into action smoothly—and wisely, given the character and strength of the doubters. Madison had the votes, but this was one of those situations where the enforcement of mechanical majoritarianism could easily have destroyed the objectives of the majority: the Constitutionalists were in quest of a qualitative as well as a quantitative consensus. This was hardly from deference to local Quaker custom; it was a political imperative if they were to attain ratification.

III

According to the standard script, at this point the "states'-rights" group intervened in force behind the New Jersey Plan, which has been characteristically portrayed as a revision to the *status quo* under the Articles of Confederation with but minor modifications. A careful examination of the evidence indicates that only in a marginal sense is this an accurate description. It is true that the New Jersey Plan put the states back into the institutional picture, but one could argue that to do so was a recognition of political reality rather than an affirmation of states'-rights. A serious case can be made that the advocates of the New Jersey Plan, far from being ideological addicts of states'-rights, intended to substitute for the Virginia Plan a system which would both retain strong national power and have a chance of adoption in the states. The leading spokesman for the project asserted quite clearly that his views were based more on counsels of expediency than on principle; said Paterson on June 16: "I came here not to speak my own sentiments, but the sentiments of those who sent me. Our object is not such a Governmt. as may be best in itself, but such a one as our Constituents have authorized us to prepare, and as they will approve."[31] This is Madison's version; in Yates' transcription, there is a crucial sentence following the remarks above: "I believe that a little practical virtue is to be preferred to the finest theoretical principles, which cannot be carried into effect."[32] In his preliminary speech on June 9, Paterson had stated ". . . to the public mind we must accommodate ourselves,"[33] and in his notes for this and his later effort as well, the emphasis is the same. The *structure* of government under the Articles should be retained:

[31]*Ibid.*, p. 250.
[32]*Ibid.*, p. 258.
[33]*Ibid.*, p. 178.

2. Because it accords with the Sentiments of the People

[Proof:] 1. Coms. [Commissions from state legislatures defining the jurisdiction of the delegates]

    2. News-papers—Political Barometer. Jersey never would have sent Delegates under the first [Virginia] Plan—

Not here to sport Opinions of my own. Wt. [What] can be done. A little practicable Virtue preferrable to Theory.[34]

This was a defense of political acumen, not of states'-rights. In fact, Paterson's notes of his speech can easily be construed as an argument for attaining the substantive objectives of the Virginia Plan by a sound political route, *i.e.*, pouring the new wine in the old bottles. With a shrewd eye, Paterson queried:

Will the Operation and Force of the [central] Govt. depend upon the mode of Representn.—No—it will depend upon the Quantum of Power lodged in the leg. ex. and judy. Departments—Give [the existing] Congress the same powers that you intend to give the two Branches, [under the Virginia Plan] and I apprehend they will act with as much Propriety and more Energy . . .[35]

In other words, the advocates of the New Jersey Plan concentrated their fire on what they held to be the *political liabilities* of the Virginia Plan—which were matters of institutional structure—rather than on the proposed scope of national authority. Indeed, the Supremacy Clause of the Constitution first saw the light of day in Paterson's Sixth Resolution; the New Jersey Plan contemplated the use of military force to secure compliance with national law; and finally Paterson made clear his view that under either the Virginia or the New Jersey systems, the general government would ". . . act on individuals and not on states."[36] From the states'-rights viewpoint, this was heresy: the fundament of that doctrine was the proposition that any central government had as its constituents the states, not the people, and could only reach the people through the agency of the state government.

Paterson then reopened the agenda of the Convention, but he did so within a distinctly nationalist framework. Paterson's position was one of favoring a strong central government in principle, but opposing one which in fact *put the big states in the saddle*. (The Virginia Plan, for all its abstract merits, did very well by Virginia.) As evidence for this speculation, there is a curious and

---

[34]*Ibid.*, p. 274.

[35]*Ibid.*, pp. 275–276.

[36]"But it is said that this national government is to act on individuals and not on states; and cannot a federal government be so framed as to operate in the same way? It surely may." *Ibid.*, pp. 182–183; also *ibid.* at p. 276.

intriguing proposal among Paterson's preliminary drafts of the New Jersey Plan:

> Whereas it is necessary in Order to form the People of the U.S. of America in to a Nation, that the States should be consolidated, by which means all the Citizens thereof will become equally intitled to and will equally participate in the same Privileges and Rights . . . it is therefore resolved, that all the Lands contained within the Limits of each state individually, and of the U.S. generally be considered as constituting one Body or Mass, and be divided into thirteen or more integral parts.
>
> Resolved, That such Divisions or integral Parts shall be styled Districts.[37]

This makes it sound as though Paterson was prepared to accept a strong unified central government along the lines of the Virginia Plan if the existing states were eliminated. He may have gotten the idea from his New Jersey colleague Judge David Brearley, who on June 9 had commented that the only remedy to the dilemma over representation was ". . . that a map of the U.S. be spread out, that all the existing boundaries be erased, and that a new partition of the whole be made into 13 equal parts."[38] According to Yates, Brearley added at this point, ". . . then a government on the present [Virginia Plan] system will be just."[39]

This proposition was never pushed—it was patently unrealistic —but one can appreciate its purpose: it would have separated the men from the boys in the large-state delegations. How attached would the Virginians have been to their reform principles if Virginia were to disappear as a component geographical unit (the largest) for representational purposes? Up to this point, the Virginians had been in the happy position of supporting high ideals with that inner confidence born of knowledge that the "public interest" they endorsed would nourish their private interest. Worse, they had shown little willingness to compromise. Now the delegates from the small states announced that they were unprepared to be offered up as sacrificial victims to a "national interest" which reflected Virginia's parochial ambition. Caustic Charles Pinckney was not far off when he remarked sardonically that ". . . the whole [conflict] comes to this": "Give N. Jersey an equal vote, and she will dismiss her scruples, and concur in the Natil. system."[40] What he rather unfairly did not add was that the Jersey delegates were

---

[37]*Farrand*, III, 613.
[38]*Farrand*, I, 177.
[39]*Ibid.*, p. 182.
[40]*Ibid.*, p. 255.

not free agents who could adhere to their private convictions; they had to take back, sponsor and risk their reputations on the reforms approved by the Convention—and in New Jersey, not in Virginia.

Paterson spoke on Saturday, and one can surmise that over the weekend there was a good deal of consultation, argument, and caucusing among the delegates. One member at least prepared a full length address: on Monday Alexander Hamilton, previously mute, rose and delivered a six-hour oration.[41] It was a remarkably apolitical speech; the gist of his position was that *both* the Virginia and New Jersey Plans were inadequately centralist, and he detailed a reform program which was reminiscent of the Protectorate under the Cromwellian *Instrument of Government* of 1653. It has been suggested that Hamilton did this in the best political tradition to emphasize the moderate character of the Virginia Plan,[42] to give the cautious delegates something *really* to worry about; but this interpretation seems somehow too clever. Particularly since the sentiments Hamilton expressed happened to be completely consistent with those he privately—and sometimes publicly—expressed throughout his life. He wanted, to take a striking phrase from a letter to George Washington, a "strong well mounted government";[43] in essence, the Hamilton Plan contemplated an elected life monarch, virtually free of public control, on the Hobbesian ground that only in this fashion could strength and stability be achieved. The other alternatives, he argued, would put policy-making at the mercy of the passions of the mob; only if the sovereign was beyond the reach of selfish influence would it be possible to have government in the interests of the whole community.[44]

From all accounts, this was a masterful and compelling speech, but (aside from furnishing John Lansing and Luther Martin with ammunition for later use against the Constitution) it made little impact. Hamilton was simply transmitting on a different wavelength from the rest of the delegates; the latter adjourned after his great effort, admired his rhetoric, and then returned to business.[45] It was rather as if they had taken a day off to attend the opera. Hamilton, never a particularly patient man or much of a

---

[41]J. C. Hamilton, cited *ibid.*, p. 293.
[42]See, *e.g.*, Mitchell, *op. cit.*, p. 381.
[43]Hamilton to Washington, July 3, 1787, *Farrand*, III, 53.
[44]A reconstruction of the Hamilton Plan is found in *Farrand*, III, 617–630.
[45]Said William Samuel Johnson on June 21: "A gentleman from New-York, with boldness and decision, proposed a system totally different from both [Virginia and New Jersey]; and though he has been praised by every body, he has been supported by none." *Farrand*, I, 363.

negotiator, stayed for another ten days and then left, in considerable disgust, for New York.[46] Although he came back to Philadelphia sporadically and attended the last two weeks of the Convention, Hamilton played no part in the laborious task of hammering out the Constitution. His day came later when he led the New York Constitutionalists into the savage imbroglio over ratification —an arena in which his unmatched talent for dirty political infighting may well have won the day. For instance, in the New York Ratifying Convention, Lansing threw back into Hamilton's teeth the sentiments the latter had expressed in his June 18 oration in the Convention. However, having since retreated to the fine defensive positions immortalized in *The Federalist,* the Colonel flatly denied that he had ever been an enemy of the states, or had believed that conflict between states and nation was inexorable! As Madison's authoritative *Notes* did not appear until 1840, and there had been no press coverage, there was no way to verify his assertions, so in the words of the reporter, ". . . a warm personal altercation between [Lansing and Hamilton] engrossed the remainder of the day [June 28, 1788]."[47]

IV

On Tuesday morning, June 19, the vacation was over. James Madison led off with a long, carefully reasoned speech analyzing the New Jersey Plan which, while intellectually vigorous in its criticisms, was quite concilliatory in mood. "The great difficulty," he observed, "lies in the affair of Representation; and if this could be adjusted, all others would be surmountable."[48] (As events were to demonstrate, this diagnosis was correct.) When he finished, a vote was taken on whether to continue with the Virginia Plan as the nucleus for a new constitution: seven states voted "Yes"; New York, New Jersey, and Delaware voted "No"; and Maryland, whose position often depended on which delegates happened to be on the floor, divided.[49] Paterson, it seems, lost

---

[46]See his letter to Washington cited *supra* note 43.

[47]*Farrand,* III, 338.

[48]*Farrand,* I, 321.

[49]Maryland's politics in this period were only a bit less intricate than Rhode Island's: the rural gentry, in much the same fashion that Namier described in England, divided up among families—Chases, Carrolls, Pacas, Lloyds, Tilghmans, etc.—and engaged in what seemed, to the outsider, elaborate political Morris dances. See Philip A. Crowl, *Maryland During and After the Revolution* (Baltimore, 1943). The Maryland General Assembly named five delegates to the Convention and provided that "the said

decisively; yet in a fundamental sense he and his allies had achieved their purpose: from that day onward, it could never be forgotten that the state governments loomed ominously in the background and that no verbal incantations could exorcise their power. Moreover, nobody bolted the convention: Paterson and his colleagues took their defeat in stride and set to work to modify the Virginia Plan, particularly with respect to its provisions on representation in the national legislature. Indeed, they won an immediate rhetorical bonus; when Oliver Ellsworth of Connecticut rose to move that the word "national" be expunged from the Third Virginia Resolution ("Resolved that a *national* Government ought to be established consisting of a *supreme* Legislative, Executive and Judiciary"[50]), Randolph agreed and the motion passed unanimously.[51] The process of compromise had begun.

For the next two weeks, the delegates circled around the problem of legislative representation. The Connecticut delegation appears to have evolved a possible compromise quite early in the debates, but the Virginians and particularly Madison (unaware that he would later be acclaimed as the prophet of "federalism") fought obdurately against providing for equal representation of states in the second chamber. There was a good deal of acrimony and at one point Benjamin Franklin—of all people—proposed the institution of a daily prayer; practical politicians in the gathering however, were mediating more on the merits of a good committee than on the utility of Divine intervention. On July 2, the ice began to break when through a number of fortuitous events[52]—and one

---

Deputies or such of them as shall attend . . . shall have full Power to represent this State," *Farrand*, III, 586. The interesting circumstance was that three of the delegates were Constitutionalists (Carroll, McHenry and Jenifer), while two were opposed (Martin and Mercer); and this led to an *ad hoc* determination of where Maryland would stand when votes were taken. The vote on equality of representation, to be described *infra*, was an important instance of this eccentricity.

[50]This formulation was voted into the Randolph Plan on May 30, 1787, by a vote of six states to none, with one divided. *Farrand*, I, 30.

[51]*Farrand*, I, 335–336. In agreeing, Randolph stipulated his disagreement with Ellsworth's rationale, but said he did not object to merely changing an "expression." Those who subject the Constitution to minute semantic analysis might do well to keep this instance in mind; if Randolph could so concede the deletion of "national," one may wonder if any word changes can be given much weight.

[52]According to Luther Martin, he was alone on the floor and cast Maryland's vote for equality of representation. Shortly thereafter, Jenifer came on the floor and "Mr. King, from Massachusetts, valuing himself on Mr. Jenifer to divide the State of Maryland on this question . . . requested of the President that the question might be put again; however, the motion was too extraordinary in its nature to meet with success." Cited from "The Genuine Information . . ." *Farrand*, III, 188.

that seems deliberate[53]—the majority against equality of representation was converted into a dead tie. The Convention had reached the stage where it was "ripe" for a solution (presumably all the therapeutic speeches had been made), and the South Carolinians proposed a committee. Madison and James Wilson wanted none of it, but with only Pennsylvania dissenting, the body voted to establish a working party on the problem of representation.

The members of this committee, one from each state, were elected by the delegates—and a very interesting committee it was. Despite the fact that the Virginia Plan had held majority support up to that date, neither Madison nor Randolph was selected (Mason was the Virginian) and Baldwin of Georgia, whose shift in position had resulted in the tie, was chosen. From the composition, it was clear that this was not to be a "fighting" committee: the emphasis in membership was on what might be described as "second-level political entrepreneurs." On the basis of the discussions up to that time, only Luther Martin of Maryland could be described as a "bitter-ender." Admittedly, some divination enters into this sort of analysis, but one does get a sense of the mood of the delegates from these choices—including the interesting selection of Benjamin Franklin, despite his age and intellectual wobbliness, over the brilliant and incisive Wilson or the sharp, polemical Gouverneur Morris, to represent Pennsylvania. His passion for conciliation was more valuable at this juncture than Wilson's logical genius, or Morris' acerbic wit.

There is a common rumor that the Framers divided their time between philosophical discussions of government and reading the classics in political theory. Perhaps this is as good a time as any to note that their concerns were highly practical, that they spent little time canvassing abstractions. A number of them had some acquaintance with the history of political theory (probably gained from reading John Adams' monumental compilation *A Defense of the Constitutions of Government,*[54] the first volume of which ap-

---

[53]Namely Baldwin's vote *for* equality of representation which divided Georgia—with Few absent and Pierce in New York fighting a duel, Houston voted against equality and Baldwin shifted to tie the state. Baldwin was originally from Connecticut and attended and tutored at Yale, facts which have led to much speculation about the pressures the Connecticut delegation may have brought on him to save the day (Georgia was the last state to vote) and open the way to compromise. To employ a good Russian phrase, it was certainly not an accident that Baldwin voted the way he did. See *Warren,* p. 262.

[54]For various contemporary comments, see *Warren,* pp. 814–818. On Adams' technique, see Zoltan Haraszti, "The Composition of Adams' *Defense,*" in *John Adams and the Prophets of Progress* (Cambridge, 1952),

peared in 1786), and it was a poor rhetorician indeed who could not cite Locke, Montesquieu, or Harrington *in support* of a desired goal. Yet up to this point in the deliberations, no one had expounded a defense of states'-rights or the "separation of powers" on anything resembling a theoretical basis. It should be reiterated that the Madison model had no room either for the states or for the "separation of powers": effectively *all* governmental power was vested in the national legislature. The merits of Montesquieu did not turn up until *The Federalist;* and although a perverse argument could be made that Madison's ideal was truly in the tradition of John Locke's *Second Treatise of Government,*[55] the Locke whom the American rebels treated as an honorary president was a pluralistic defender of vested rights,[56] not of parliamentary supremacy.

It would be tedious to continue a blow-by-blow analysis of the work of the delegates; the critical fight was over representation of the states and once the Connecticut Compromise was adopted on July 17, the Convention was over the hump. Madison, James Wilson, and Gouverneur Morris of New York (who was there representing Pennsylvania!) fought the compromise all the way in a last-ditch effort to get a unitary state with parliamentary supremacy. But their allies deserted them and they demonstrated after their defeat the essentially opportunist character of their objections—using "opportunist" here in a non-pejorative sense, to indicate a willingness to swallow their objections and get on with the business. Moreover, once the compromise had carried (by five states to four, with one state divided), its advocates

---

ch. 9. In this connection it is interesting to check the Convention discussions for references to the authority of Locke, Montesquieu and Harrington, the theorists who have been assigned various degrees of paternal responsibility. There are no explicit references to James Harrington; one to John Locke (Luther Martin cited him on the state of nature, *Farrand,* I, 437); and seven to Montesquieu, only one of which related to the "separation of powers" (Madison in an odd speech, which he explained in a footnote was given to help a friend rather than advance his own views, cited Montesquieu on the separation of the executive and legislative branches, *Farrand,* II, 34). This, of course, does not prove that Locke and Co. were without influence; it shifts the burden of proof, however, to those who assert ideological causality. See Benjamin F. Wright, "The Origins of the Separation of Powers in America," *Economica,* Vol. 13 (1933), p. 184.

[55] I share Willmoore Kendall's interpretation of Locke as a supporter of parliamentary supremacy and majoritarianism; see Kendall, *John Locke and the Doctrine of Majority Rule* (Urbana, 1941). Kendall's general position has recently received strong support in the definitive edition and commentary of Peter Laslett, *Locke's Two Treatises of Government* (Cambridge, 1960).

[56] The American Locke is best delineated in Carl Becker, *The Declaration of Independence* (New York, 1948).

threw themselves vigorously into the job of strengthening the general government's substantive powers—as might have been predicted, indeed, from Paterson's early statements. It nourishes an increased respect for Madison's devotion to the art of politics, to realize that this dogged fighter could sit down six months later and prepare essays for *The Federalist* in contradiction to his basic convictions about the true course the Convention should have taken.

V

Two tricky issues will serve to illustrate the later process of accommodation. The first was the institutional position of the Executive. Madison argued for an executive chosen by the National Legislature and on May 29 this had been adopted with a provision that after his seven-year term was concluded, the chief magistrate should not be eligible for reelection. In late July this was reopened and for a week the matter was argued from several different points of view. A good deal of desultory speechmaking ensued, but the gist of the problem was the opposition from two sources to election by the legislature. One group felt that the states should have a hand in the process; another small but influential circle urged direct election by the people. There were a number of proposals: election by the people, election by state governors, by electors chosen by state legislatures, by the National Legislature (James Wilson, perhaps ironically, proposed at one point that an Electoral College be chosen by lot from the National Legislature!), and there was some resemblance to three-dimensional chess in the dispute because of the presence of two other variables, length of tenure and reeligibility. Finally, after opening, reopening, and re-reopening the debate, the thorny problem was consigned to a committee for resolution.

The Brearley Committee on Postponed Matters was a superb aggregation of talent and its compromise on the Executive was a masterpiece of political improvisation. (The Electoral College, its creation, however, had little in its favor as an *institution*—as the delegates well appreciated.) The point of departure for all discussion about the presidency in the Convention was that in immediate terms, the problem was non-existent; in other words, everybody present knew that under any system devised, George Washington would be President. Thus they were dealing in the future tense and to a body of working politicians the merits of the Brearley proposal were obvious: everybody got a piece of cake. (Or to put it more academically, each viewpoint could leave the Convention and argue to its constituents that it had *really* won the day.) First, the state legislatures had the right to determine the mode of selection of the electors; second, the small states received a bonus in the Electoral College in the form of a guaranteed minimum of three votes while the big states got acceptance of the principle of proportional power; third, if the state legislatures agreed (as six did in the first presidential election), the people could be involved directly in the choice of electors; and finally, if no candidate received a majority in the College, the right of decision passed to the National Legislature with each state exercising equal strength. (In the Brearley recommendation, the election went to the Senate, but a motion from the floor substituted the House; this was accepted on the ground that the Senate already had enough authority over the executive in its treaty and appointment powers.)

This compromise was almost too good to be true, and the Framers snapped it up with little debate or controversy. No one seemed to think well of the College as an *institution;* indeed, what evidence there is suggests that there was an assumption that once Washington had finished his tenure as President, the electors would cease to produce majorities and the chief executive would usually be chosen in the House. George Mason observed casually that the selection would be made in the House nineteen times in twenty and no one seriously disputed this point. The vital aspect of the Electoral College was that it got the Convention over the hurdle and protected everybody's interests. The future was left to cope with the problem of what to do with this Rube Goldberg mechanism.

In short, the Framers did not in their wisdom endow the United States with a College of Cardinals—the Electoral College was neither an exercise in applied Platonism nor an experiment in indirect government based on elitist distrust of the masses. It was merely a jerry-rigged improvisation which has subsequently been endowed with a high theoretical content. When an elector from Oklahoma in 1960 refused to cast his vote for Nixon (naming Byrd and Goldwater instead) on the ground that the Founding Fathers intended him to exercise his great independent wisdom he was indulging in historical fantasy. If one were to indulge in counter-fantasy, he would be tempted to suggest that the Fathers would be startled to find the College still in operation—and perhaps even dismayed at their descendants' lack of judgment or inventiveness.[57]

The second issue on which some substantial practical bargaining took place was slavery. The morality of slavery was, by design, not at issue;[58] but in its other concrete aspects, slavery colored the arguments over taxation, commerce, and representation. The "Three-Fifths Compromise," that three-fifths of the slaves would be counted both for representation and for purposes of direct taxation (which was drawn from the past—it was a formula of Madison's utilized by Congress in 1783 to establish the basis of state contributions to the Confederation treasury) had allayed some Northern fears about Southern over-representation (no one then foresaw the trivial role that direct taxation would play in later federal financial policy), but doubts still remained. The Southerners, on the other hand, were afraid that Congressional control over commerce would lead to the exclusion of slaves or to their excessive taxation as imports. Moreover, the Southerners were disturbed over "navigation acts," *i.e.*, tariffs or special legislation providing, for example, that exports be carried only in American ships; as a section depending upon exports, they wanted protection from the potential voracity of their commercial brethren of the Eastern states. To achieve this end, Mason and others urged that the Constitution include a proviso that navigation and commercial laws should require a two-thirds vote in Congress.

These problems came to a head in late August and, as usual were handed to a committee in the hope that, in Gouverneur Morris' words, ". . . these things may form a bargain among the Northern and Southern states."[59] The Committee reported its measures of reconciliation on August 25, and on August 29 the package was wrapped up and delivered. What occurred can best be described in George Mason's dour version (he anticipated Calhoun in his conviction that permitting navigation acts to pass by majority vote would put the South in economic bondage to the North—it was mainly on this ground that he refused to sign the Constitution):

---

[57]See John P. Roche, "The Electoral College: A Note on American Political Mythology," *Dissent* (Spring, 1961), pp. 197–199. The relevant debates took place July 19–26, 1787, *Farrand*, II, 50–128, and September 5–6, 1787, *ibid.*, pp. 505–531.

[58]See the discussion on August 22, 1787, *Farrand*, II, 366–375; King seems to have expressed the sense of the Convention when he said, "the subject should be considered in a political light only." *Ibid.* at 373.

[59]*Farrand*, II, 374. Randolph echoed his sentiment in different words.

The Constitution as agreed to till a fortnight before the Convention rose was such a one as he would have set his hand and heart to. . . . [Until that time] The 3 New England States were constantly with us in all questions . . . so that it was these three States with the 5 Southern ones against Pennsylvania, Jersey and Delaware. With respect to the importation of slaves, [decision-making] was left to Congress. This disturbed the two Southernmost States who knew that Congress would immediately suppress the importation of slaves. Those two States therefore struck up a bargain with the three New England States. If they would join to admit slaves for some years, the two Southern-most States would join in changing the clause which required the ⅔ of the Legislature in any vote [on navigation acts]. It was done.[60]

On the floor of the Convention there was a virtual love-feast on this happy occasion. Charles Pinckney of South Carolina attempted to overturn the committee's decision, when the compromise was reported to the Convention, by insisting that the South needed protection from the imperialism of the Northern states. But his Southern colleagues were not prepared to rock the boat and General C. C. Pinckney arose to spread oil on the suddenly ruffled waters; he admitted that:

It was in the true interest of the S[outhern] States to have no regulation of commerce; but considering the loss brought on the commerce of the Eastern States by the Revolution, their liberal conduct towards the views of South Carolina [on the regulation of the slave trade] and the interests the weak Southn. States had in being united with the strong Eastern states, he thought it proper that no fetters should be imposed on the power of making commercial regulations; *and that his constituents, though prejudiced against the Eastern States, would be reconciled to this liberality.* He had himself prejudices agst the Eastern States before he came here, but would acknowledge that he had found them as liberal and candid as any men whatever. (Italics added.)[61]

Pierce Butler took the same tack, essentially arguing that he was not too happy about the possible consequences, but that a deal was a deal.[62] Many Southern leaders were later—in the wake of

---

[60]Mason to Jefferson, cited in Warren, p. 584.

[61]August 29, 1787, *Farrand*, II, 449–450.

[62]*Ibid.*, p. 451. The plainest statement of the matter was put by the three North Carolina delegates (Blount, Spaight and Williamson) in their report to Governor Caswell, September 18, 1787. After noting that "no exertions have been wanting on our part to guard and promote the particular interest of North Carolina," they went on to explain the basis of the negotiations in cold-blooded fashion: "While we were taking so much care to guard ourselves against being over reached and to form rules of Taxation that might operate in our favour, it is not to be supposed that our Northern Brethren were Inattentive to their particular Interest. A navigation Act or the power to regulate Commerce in the Hands of the National Government . . . is

the "Tariff of Abominations"—to rue this day of reconciliation; Calhoun's *Disquisition on Government* was little more than an extension of the argument in the Convention against permitting a congressional majority to enact navigation acts.[63]

VI

Drawing on their vast collective political experience, utilizing every weapon in the politician's arsenal, looking constantly over their shoulders at their constituents, the delegates put together a Constitution. It was a makeshift affair; some sticky issues (for example, the qualification of voters) they ducked entirely; others they mastered with that ancient instrument of political sagacity, studied ambiguity (for example, citizenship), and some they just overlooked. In this last category, I suspect, fell the matter of the power of the federal courts to determine the constitutionality of acts of Congress. When the judicial article was formulated (Article III of the Constitution), deliberations were still in the stage where the legislature was endowed with broad power under the Randolph formulation, authority which by its own terms was scarcely amenable to judicial review. In essence, courts could hardly determine when ". . . the separate States are incompetent or . . . the harmony of the United States may be interrupted"; the National Legislature, as critics pointed out, was free to define its own jurisdiction. Later the definition of legislative authority was changed into the form we know, a series of stipulated powers, *but the delegates never seriously reexamined the jurisdiction of the judiciary under this new limited formulation.*[64] All arguments

what the Southern States have given in Exchange for the advantages we Mentioned." They concluded by explaining that while the Constitution did deal with other matters besides taxes—"there are other Considerations of great Magnitude involved in the system"—they would not take up valuable time with boring details! *Farrand*, III, 83–84.

[63]See John C. Calhoun, *A Disquisition on Government* (New York, 1943), pp. 21–25, 38. Calhoun differed from Mason, and others in the Convention who urged the two-thirds requirement, by advocating a functional or interest veto rather than some sort of special majority, *i.e.*, he abandoned the search for quantitative checks in favor of a qualitative solution.

[64]The Committee on Detail altered the general grant of legislative power envisioned by the Virginia Plan into a series of specific grants; these were examined closely between August 16 and August 23. One day only was devoted to the Judicial Article, August 27, and since no one raised the question of judicial review of Federal statutes, no light was cast on the matter. A number of random comments on the power of the judiciary were scattered throughout the discussions, but there was another variable which deprives them of much probative value: the proposed Council of Revision which

on the intention of the Framers in this matter are thus deductive and *a posteriori*, though some obviously make more sense than others.[65]

The Framers were busy and distinguished men, anxious to get back to their families, their positions, and their constituents, not members of the French Academy devoting a lifetime to a dictionary. They were trying to do an important job, and do it in such a fashion that their handwork would be acceptable to very diverse constituencies. No one was rhapsodic about the final document, but it was a beginning, a move in the right direction, and one they had reason to believe the people would endorse. In addition, since they had modified the impossible amendment provisions of the Articles (the requirement of unanimity which could always be frustrated by "Rogues Island") to one demanding approval by only three-quarters of the states, they seemed confident that gaps in the fabric which experience would reveal could be rewoven without undue difficulty.

So with a neat phrase introduced by Benjamin Franklin (but devised by Gouverneur Morris)[66] which made their decision sound unanimous, and an inspired benediction by the Old Doctor urging doubters to doubt their own infallibility, the Constitution was accepted and signed. Curiously, Edmund Randolph, who had played so vital a role throughout, refused to sign, as did his fellow Virginian George Mason and Elbridge Gerry of Massachusetts. Randolph's behavior was eccentric, to say the least—his excuses for refusing his signature have a factitious ring even at this late date; the best explanation seems to be that he was afraid that the Constitution would prove to be a liability in Virginia politics, where Patrick Henry was burning up the countryside with impassioned denunciations. Presumably, Randolph wanted to check the temper of the populace before he risked his reputation, and

---

would have joined the Executive with the judges in *legislative* review. Madison and Wilson, for example, favored this technique—which had nothing in common with what we think of as judicial review except that judges were involved in the task.

[65]For what it may be worth, I think that judicial review of congressional acts was logically on all fours with review of state enactments and that it was certainly consistent with the view that the Constitution could not be amended by the Congress and President, or by a two-thirds vote of Congress (overriding a veto), without the agreement of three-quarters of the states. *External* evidence from that time supports this view, see Charles Warren, *Congress, the Constitution, and the Supreme Court* (Boston, 1925), pp. 41–128, but the debates in the Convention prove nothing.

[66]Or so Madison stated, *Farrand*, II, 643. Wilson too may have contributed; he was close to Franklin and delivered the frail old gentleman's speeches for him.

perhaps his job, in a fight with both Henry and Richard Henry Lee.[67] Events lend some justification to this speculation: after much temporizing and use of the conditional subjunctive tense, Randolph endorsed ratification in Virginia and ended up getting the best of both worlds.

Madison, despite his reservations about the Constitution, was the campaign manager in ratification. His first task was to get the Congress in New York to light its own funeral pyre by approving the "amendments" to the Articles and sending them on to the state legislatures. Above all, momentum had to be maintained. The anti-Constitutionalists, now thoroughly alarmed and no novices in politics, realized that their best tactic was attrition rather than direct opposition. Thus they settled on a position expressing qualified approval but calling for a second Convention to remedy various defects (the one with the most demagogic appeal was the lack of a Bill of Rights). Madison knew that to accede to this demand would be equivalent to losing the battle, nor would he agree to conditional approval (despite wavering even by Hamilton). This was an all-or-nothing proposition: national salvation or national impotence with no intermediate positions possible. Unable to get congressional approval, he settled for second best: a unanimous resolution of Congress transmitting the Constitution to the states for whatever action they saw fit to take. The opponents then moved from New York and the Congress, where they had attempted to attach amendments and conditions, to the states for the final battle.[68]

At first the campaign for ratification went beautifully: within eight months after the delegates set their names on the document, eight states had ratified. Only in Massachusetts had the result been close (187–168). Theoretically, a ratification by one more state convention would set the new government in motion, but in fact until Virginia and New York acceded to the new Union, the latter was fiction. New Hampshire was the next to ratify;

---

[67]See a very interesting letter, from an unknown source in Philadelphia, to Jefferson, October 11, 1787: "Randolph wishes it well, & it is thought would have signed it, but he wanted to be on a footing with a popular rival." *Farrand*, III, 104. Madison, writing Jefferson a full account on October 24, 1787, put the matter more delicately—he was working hard on Randolph to win him for ratification: "[Randolph] was not inveterate in his opposition, and grounded his refusal to subscribe pretty much on his unwillingness to commit himself, so as not to be at liberty to be governed by further lights on the subject." *Ibid.*, p. 135.

[68]See Edward P. Smith, "The Movement Towards a Second Constitutional Convention in 1788," in J. F. Jameson, ed., *Essays in the Constitutional History of the United States* (Boston, 1889), pp. 46–115.

Rhode Island was involved in its characteristic political convulsions (the Legislature there sent the Constitution out to the towns for decision by popular vote and it got lost among a series of local issues);[69] North Carolina's convention did not meet until July and then postponed a final decision. This is hardly the place for an extensive analysis of the conventions of New York and Virginia. Suffice it to say that the Constitutionalists clearly outmaneuvered their opponents, forced them into impossible political positions, and won both states narrowly. The Virginia Convention could serve as a classic study in effective floor management: Patrick Henry had to be contained, and a reading of the debates discloses a standard two-stage technique. Henry would give a four-or-five-hour speech denouncing some section of the Constitution on every conceivable ground (the federal district, he averred at one point, would become a haven for convicts escaping from state authority!);[70] when Henry subsided, "Mr. Lee of Westmoreland" would rise and literally poleaxe him with sardonic invective (when Henry complained about the militia power, "Lighthorse Harry" really punched below the belt: observing that while the former Governor had been sitting in Richmond during the Revolution, *he* had been out in the trenches with the troops and thus felt better qualified to discuss military affairs).[71] Then the gentlemanly Constitutionalists (Madison, Pendleton and Marshall) would pick up the matters at issue and examine them in the light of reason.

Indeed, modern Americans who tend to think of James Madison as a rather dessicated character should spend some time with this transcript. Probably Madison put on his most spectacular demonstration of nimble rhetoric in what might be called "The Battle of the Absent Authorities." Patrick Henry in the course of one of his harangues alleged that Jefferson was known to be opposed to Virginia's approving the Constitution. This was clever: Henry hated Jefferson, but was prepared to use any weapon that came to hand. Madison's riposte was superb: First, he said that with all due respect to the great reputation of Jefferson, he was not in the country and therefore could not formulate an adequate judgment; second, no one should utilize the reputation of an

---

[69]See Bishop, *op. cit.*, *passim*.

[70]See Elliot's *Debates on the Federal Constitution* (Washington, 1836), Vol. 3, pp. 436–438.

[71]This should be quoted to give the full flavor: "Without vanity, I may say I have had different experience of [militia] service from that of [Henry]. It was my fortune to be a soldier of my country. . . . I saw what the honorable gentlemen did not see—our men fighting. . . ." *Ibid.*, p. 178.

outsider—the Virginia Convention was there to think for itself; third, if there were to be recourse to outsiders, the opinions of George Washington should certainly be taken into consideration; and finally, he knew from privileged personal communication from Jefferson that in fact the latter *strongly favored* the Constitution.[72] To devise an assault route into this rhetorical fortress was literally impossible.

VII

The fight was over; all that remained now was to establish the new frame of government in the spirit of its framers. And who were better qualified for this task than the Framers themselves? Thus victory for the Constitution meant simultaneous victory for the Constitutionalists; the anti-Constitutionalists either capitulated or vanished into limbo—soon Patrick Henry would be offered a seat on the Supreme Court[73] and Luther Martin would be known as the Federalist "bull-dog."[74] And irony of ironies, Alexander Hamilton and James Madison would shortly accumulate a reputation as the formulators of what is often alleged to be our political theory, the concept of "federalism." Also, on the other side of the ledger, the arguments would soon appear over what the Framers "really meant"; while these disputes have assumed the proportions of a big scholarly business in the last century, they began almost before the ink on the Constitution was dry. One of the best early ones featured Hamilton versus Madison on the scope of presidential power, and other Framers characteristically assumed positions in this and other disputes on the basis of their political convictions.

Probably our greatest difficulty is that we know so much more about what the Framers *should have meant* than they themselves did. We are intimately acquainted with the problems that their Constitution should have been designed to master; in short, we have read the mystery story backwards. If we are to get the right "feel" for their time and their circumstances, we must in Mait-

---

[72] *Ibid.*, p. 329.

[73] Washington offered him the Chief Justiceship in 1796, but he declined; Charles Warren, *The Supreme Court in United States History* (Boston, 1947), Vol. 1, p. 139.

[74] He was a zealous prosecutor of sedition in the period 1798–1800; with Justice Samuel Chase, like himself an alleged "radical" at the time of the Constitutional Convention, Martin hunted down Jeffersonian heretics. See James M. Smith, *Freedom's Fetters* (Ithaca, 1956) pp. 342–343.

land's phrase, ". . . think ourselves back into the twilight." Obviously, no one can pretend completely to escape from the solipsistic web of his own environment, but if the effort is made, it is possible to appreciate the past roughly on its own terms. The first step in this process is to abandon the academic premise that because we can ask a question, there must be an answer.

Thus we can ask what the Framers meant when they gave Congress the power to regulate interstate and foreign commerce, and we emerge, reluctantly perhaps, with the reply that (Professor Crosskey to the contrary notwithstanding)[75] they may not have known what they meant, that there may not have been any semantic consensus. The Convention was not a seminar in analytic philosophy or linguistic analysis. Commerce was *commerce* and if different interpretations of the word arose, later generations could worry about the problem of definition. The delegates were in a hurry to get a new government established; when definitional arguments arose, they characteristically took refuge in ambiguity. If different men voted for the same proposition for varying reasons, that was politics (and still is); if later generations were unsettled by this lack of precision, that would be their problem.

There was a good deal of definitional pluralism with respect to the problems the delegates did discuss, but when we move to the question of extrapolated intentions, we enter the realm of spiritu-

---

[75]Crosskey in his sprawling *Politics and the Constitution* (Chicago, 1953), 2 vols., has developed with almost unbelievable zeal and intricacy the thesis that the Constitution *was* designed to establish a centralized unitary state, but that the political leadership of the Republic in its formative years betrayed this ideal and sold the pass to states'-rights. While he has unearthed some interesting newspaper articles and other material, it is impossible for me to accept his central proposition. Madison and the other delegates, with the exceptions discussed in the text *supra*, did *want* to diminish the power of the states and create a vigorous national government. But they were not fools, and were, I submit, under no illusions when they departed from Philadelphia that this end had been accomplished. The crux of my argument is that *political realities* forced them to water down their objectives and they settled, like the good politicans they were, for half a loaf. The basic difficulty with Crosskey's thesis is that he knows too much—he assumes that the Framers had a perfectly clear idea of the road they were taking; with a semantic machete he cuts blandly through all the confusion on the floor of the meeting to the *real* meanings. Thus, despite all of his ornate research apparatus, there is a fundamentally non-empirical quality about Crosskey's work: at crucial points in the argument he falls back on a type of divination which can only be described as Kabbalistic. He may be right, for example, in stating (without any proof) that Richard Henry Lee did *not* write the "Letters from a Federal Farmer," but in this country spectral evidence has not been admissable since the Seventeenth Century.

alism. When men in our time, for instance, launch into elaborate talmudic exegesis to demonstrate that federal aid to parochial schools is (or is not) in accord with the intentions of the men who established the Republic and endorsed the Bill of Rights, they are engaging in historical Extra-Sensory Perception. (If one were to join this E. S. P. contingent for a minute, he might suggest that the hard-boiled politicians who wrote the Constitution and Bill of Rights would chuckle scornfully at such an invocation of authority: obviously a politician would chart his course on the intentions of the living, not of the dead, and count the numbers of Catholics in his constituency.)

The Constitution, then, was not an apotheosis of "constitutionalism," a triumph of architectonic genius; it was a patch-work sewn together under the pressure of both time and events by a group of extremely talented democratic politicians. They refused to attempt the establishment of a strong, centralized sovereignty on the principle of legislative supremacy for the excellent reason that the people would not accept it. They risked their political fortunes by opposing the established doctrines of state sovereignty because they were convinced that the existing system was leading to national impotence and probably foreign domination. For two years, they worked to get a convention established. For over three months, in what must have seemed to the faithful participants an endless process of give-and-take, they reasoned, cajoled, threatened, and bargained amongst themselves. The result was a Constitution which the people, in fact, by democratic processes, did accept, and a new and far better national government was established.

Beginning with the inspired propaganda of Hamilton, Madison and Jay, the ideological build-up got under way. *The Federalist* had little impact on the ratification of the Constitution, except perhaps in New York, but this volume had enormous influence on the image of the Constitution in the minds of future generations, particularly on historians and political scientists who have an innate fondness for theoretical symmetry. Yet, while the shades of Locke and Montesquieu *may* have been hovering in the background, and the delegates *may* have been unconscious instruments of a transcendent *telos,* the careful observer of the day-to-day work of the Convention finds no over-arching principles. The "separation of powers" to him seems to be a by-product of suspicion, and "federalism" he views as a *pis aller,* as the farthest point the delegates felt they could go in the destruction of state power without themselves inviting repudiation.

To conclude, the Constitution was neither a victory for abstract theory nor a great practical success. Well over half a million men had to die on the battlefields of the Civil War before certain constitutional principles could be defined—a baleful consideration which is somehow overlooked in our customary tributes to the farsighted genius of the Framers and to the supposed American talent for "constitutionalism." The Constitution was, however, a vivid demonstration of effective democratic political action, and of the forging of a national elite which literally persuaded its countrymen to hoist themselves by their own boot straps. American pro-consuls would be wise not to translate the Constitution into Japanese, or Swahili, or treat it as a work of semi-Divine origin; but when students of comparative politics examine the process of nation-building in countries newly freed from colonial rule they may find the American experience instructive as a classic example of the potentialities of a democratic elite.

The Theory of Human Nature in the American Constitution and the Method of Counterpoise

ARTHUR O. LOVEJOY

... In the late seventeenth and much of the eighteenth century man (as Vauvenargues put it) "was in disgrace with all thinking men" in the Western world—or at least with most of those who wrote disquisitions in prose or verse concerning him. He was described as a being actuated always by nonrational motives—by "passions," or arbitrary and unexamined prejudices, or vanity, or the quest of private economic advantage—and yet as always inwardly and incorrigibly assured that his motives *were* rational. When human nature was so conceived, it might naturally have been inferred that men were hopeless material for the construction of a peaceful, smoothly working, stable, and just political system, in which these diverse, conflicting, purely personal moti-

Reprinted with permission from *Reflections on Human Nature* (Baltimore: Johns Hopkins Press, 1961), 37–65.

vations would constantly be voluntarily subordinated to, and even made contributory to, "the general good." And such a view of human nature might well have appeared most of all incompatible with a scheme of government in which ultimate political power would be, through a wide (though still far from universal) extension of the franchise, placed in the hands of a multitude of individuals or groups prompted by such irrational and irreconcilable passions and prejudices. How could you build a safe, solid, and enduring structure out of bricks in which there were forces impelling them perpetually to push in different directions and to collide with one another? Yet it was precisely in the later eighteenth century that the scheme of "republican" government won the advocacy of political philosophers of immense influence in their time and made its first decisive advances; and (this is the particular fact relevant to our general subject which I wish to point out here) it was just at this time that the American Constitution was framed under the leadership of a group of extraordinarily able men who had few illusions about the rationality of the generality of mankind—who, in short, held in the main the theory of human nature and human motivations which was set forth in the preceding lecture.

This fact (for which I shall presently give some of the evidence) has the look of a paradox; but it is in large part (I do not say wholly) explained by the wide currency in the late seventeenth and the eighteenth century of two other conceptions, not hitherto mentioned, which implied that it is entirely possible to construct an ideal political society out of bad human materials —to frame a rational scheme of government, in which the general good will be realized, without presupposing that the individuals who exercise ultimate political power will be severally actuated in their use by rational motives, or primarily solicitous about the general good. Of these two conceptions, I shall try to elucidate and illustrate the first, which is the simpler and less far-reaching, in the present lecture. . . .

Although philosophers of the seventeenth and eighteenth centuries, when discoursing on the divine government of the world, often declared it to be axiomatic that the Creator always accomplishes his ends by the simplest and most direct means, they also tended to assume that he is frequently under the necessity of employing what may be called the method of counterpoise— accomplishing desirable results by balancing harmful things against one another. This was illustrated in the admirable contrivance on which popular expositions of the Newtonian celestial mechanics liked to dwell, whereby the planets had within them a centrifugal force which alone would have made them fly off into space in straight lines, and a centripetal force, which alone would have caused them to fall into the sun; happily counterbalancing one another, these two otherwise mischievous forces cause these bodies to behave as they should, that is, to roll round in their proper orbits. And human nature was increasingly conceived after the analogy of such a mechanical system. Voltaire proposed to amend the famous dictum of Descartes: "God, whom he called the eternal geometer, and whom I call the eternal mechanician (*machiniste*); and the passions are the wheels which make all these machines go."[1] The place of the method of counterpoise in the dynamics of human nature had been tersely pointed out by Pascal before 1660: "We do not sustain ourselves in a state of virtue by our own force, but by the counterpoise of two opposite faults, just as we stand upright between two contrary winds; remove one of these faults, we fall into the other."[2] La Rochefoucauld used a different simile to express the same conception: "The vices enter into the composition of the virtues as poisons enter into the composition of remedies. Prudence assembles and tempers them and makes them serve usefully against the evils of life."[3]

And the creator of a state, like the Creator of the universe and of man—and, in fact, as a *consequence* of this favorite method of the Author of Nature—must accomplish his lesser but beneficent design by pitting against one another forces (that is, human motives) which, taken separately, are disruptive or otherwise bad, or at the least nonmoral—since no other forces, no rational and virtuous motives, can be relied upon. He must harness together and counterbalance contrary defects and competing egoisms. It had been laid down by the judicious Hooker, in the earliest classic of English political thought, that

Laws politic, ordained for external order, are never framed as they should be, unless, presuming the will of man to be inwardly obstinate, rebellious, and averse from all obedience unto the sacred laws of his

---

[1] *Dieu et les hommes;* cf. also *Traité de Métaphysique,* 1734, Ch. VIII. For an example of the parallel of celestial and political mechanics, *cf.* Montesquieu, *De l'Esprit des lois,* Bk. III, ch. vii: "Ambition," or the desire for "honor," which is the "principle" of the monarchical form of government, "moves all the parts of the body politic; it unites them by its own action, and the result is that each individual serves the public interest while he believes that he is serving his own. . . . You might say that it is like the system of the universe, in which there is a force which incessantly moves all bodies away from the centre and a force of gravity which brings them back to it."

[2] *Pensées,* ed. Giraud, No. 359.

[3] *Maximes,* 182.

nature; unless, in a word, presuming man to be in regard of his depraved mind little better than a wild beast, they do accordingly provide
notwithstanding so to frame his outward actions that they be no hin-
drance unto the common good for which societies are instituted: unless
they do this, they are not perfect.[4]

This at least stated the problem: *how*, by means of what political
device, could you bring creatures whose wills were always moved
by irrational and "depraved" passions to behave in ways which
would not be inconsistent with the "common good"? There were
several proposed solutions to the problem; the one which here
concerns us and which was to play an extremely influential part
in eighteenth-century political thinking was the method of counterpoise. It was set forth in 1714 in doggerel verse by the very
injudicious Mandeville. As was his custom, he put it in the most
violently paradoxical form, describing a well-ordered state in
which,

> Though every part was full of Vice,
> Yet the whole Mass a Paradise.
> Such were the Blessings of that State,
> Their Crimes conspired to make them great . . .
> The worst of all the Multitude
> Did something for the Common Good.
> This was the State's Craft that maintained
> The Whole of which each part complain'd:
> This, as in Musick Harmony,
> Made jarrings in the main agree.[5]

But the textbook—though it was a very confused textbook—on
the theory of human nature which was most widely read and
admired in the middle decades of the eighteenth century was
provided by Alexander Pope. Every well-educated Englishman of
the period, in Britain and America, was acquainted with the
Essay on Man, and many of them doubtless knew its most famous
lines by heart. And one thesis concerning the *modus operandi* of
volition and the motivation of all of men's actions which the
poem set forth, especially in the Second Epistle, was essentially
the same as that in the lines which I have quoted from *The Fable
of the Bees*, though more elegantly expressed.[6] For Pope, too,
"statecraft" consisted in the recognition and application of the

---

[4]*Laws of Ecclesiastical Polity*, I (Everyman's Library ed., p. 188).
[5]*The Fable of the Bees*, ed. Kaye, I, p. 24.
[6]On the question of Pope's acquaintance with *The Fable of the Bees*, see
the Introduction to A. Hamilton Thompson's edition of the *Essay on Man*,
1913, p. xi. Mr. Thompson concludes that "it is certain that Pope knew
Mandeville's book," and that it "furnished a prominent portion of the argument of the Second Epistle."

two premises underlying the political method of counterpoise: that men never act from disinterested and rational motives, but that it is possible, none the less, to fashion a good "whole," a happy and harmonious State, by skillfully mixing and counter-balancing these refractory and separately antagonistic parts.

Since the *Essay on Man* is, I fear, much less familiar in the twentieth than it was in the eighteenth century, it is perhaps advisable to bring together here the principal passages illustrating the summary which I have just given. Men's actions, Pope de-clares, are always prompted by their passions, not by their reason. The latter, it is true, has an important part as a factor in human behavior, but it is an ancillary part. It enables us to judge of the means by which the passions, which are all "Modes of Self-Love," can be gratified, but it has no driving power.

> On life's vast ocean diversely we sail,
> Reason's the card, but Passion is the gale.[7]

The card (i.e., compass) neither propels the ship nor determines the direction in which it is to sail; it merely enables the mariner to know in which direction it is moving, or in what direction to steer in order to reach the port he desires. And the passions, which thus provide the sole dynamic factor in human behavior, are not only diverse but antagonistic to one another. Every indi-vidual's will is dominated by some obsessing "Master Passion," which is the "mind's disease":

> Reason itself but gives it edge and pow'r,
> As Heaven's blest beam turns vinegar more sour.[8]

That is one half of Pope's picture of the working of human moti-vations; but there is another half. Though these conflicting pas-sions cannot be got rid of, they can be so combined and made to counteract one another that the total result will be social peace and order; and this was the purpose of the Creator in making man:

> Passions, like elements, tho' born to fight,
> Yet, mix'd and soften'd, in His work unite:
> These, 'tis enough to temper and employ;
> But what composes Man, can Man destroy? . . .
> Each individual seeks a sev'ral goal,
> But Heav'ns great view is one, and that the whole.
> That, counterworks each folly and caprice,
> That, disappoints th' effect of every vice.[9]

---

[7]Epistle II, 107–108.
[8]Epistle II, 147–148.
[9]*Ibid.*, 111 ff., 235 ff.

Thus the statesman's task is to carry out this divine purpose by so adjusting the parts of "the whole" that "jarring interests" will

> of themselves create
> Th' according music of the well-mixed State.

By this means it will be possible for him to

> build on wants, and on defects of mind,
> The joy, the peace, the glory of mankind.[10]

To achieve this great end, in short, it is not at all necessary to assume that man is controlled by his reason; it is, on the contrary, necessary to assume that he is not—since that is the fact about him.

Two decades later, probably borrowing some of these ideas from Pope, the poet laureate of the time, William Whitehead, included a syncopated version of them in his poem "The Enthusiast";

> [God] bids the tyrant passions rage,
> He bids them war eternal wage,
> And combat each his foe,
> Till from dissensions concords rise,
> And beauties from deformities,
> And happiness from woe.

Vauvenargues wrote in 1746: "If it is true that one cannot eliminate vice, the science of those who govern consists in making it contribute to the common good." And Helvétius, later in the century, more diffusely versifies a particular form of the same general conception: every man always pursues his private interest, but the art of government lies in contriving an artificial identification of private with public interest—or at least, in persuading men that the two are identical:

> Le grand art de régner, l'Art du Législateur,
> Veut que chaque mortel qui sous ses lois s'enchaîne,
> En suivant le penchant où son plaisir l'entraîne,

---

[10]The last two quotations are from Epistles III, 239–244 and II, 247–248. The group of passages brought together above constitute the one consistent and coherent argument, on the subject with which this lecture is concerned, that is to be found in the *Essay*. But it must be added, and emphasized, that there are other passages inconsistent with them and with one another in that highly confused poem; these are chiefly due to Pope's timidity about assigning to that traditionally venerated faculty, the Reason, the subordinate and all-but-impotent role which was essential for his principal argument and was, as shown above, frequently insisted upon by him in the most unequivocal terms. His waverings and contradictions on this matter have been well pointed out by Thompson, *op. cit.*, p. 63, n. 197.

Ne puisse faire un pas qu'il ne marche à la fois
Vers le bonheur public, le chef-d'oeuvre des lois.
Selon qu'un Potentat est plus ou moins habile
A former, combiner cet Art si difficile,
D'unir et d'attacher, par un lien commun
A l'interêt de tous l'interêt de chacun,
Selon que bien ou mal il fonde la justice,
L'on chérit les vertus ou l'on se livre au vice.[11]

Bearing in mind these earlier statements of the two presuppositions of the method of counterpoise, as applied to the problem
of government, we are now ready to turn back to what happened
in Philadelphia in 1787 and, I think, to understand somewhat
better what it was that then happened. To any reader of *The
Federalist* it should be evident—though apparently it sometimes
has not been—that the chief framers of the Constitution of the
United States, who had been reared in the climate of opinion of
the mid-eighteenth century, accepted the same two presuppositions
and sought to apply them, for the first time in modern history,
in the actual and detailed planning of a system of government
not yet in existence. The ablest members of the Constitutional
Convention were well aware that *their* task—unlike that of the
Continental Congress of 1776—was not to lay down abstract
principles of political philosophy, not to rest the system they were
constructing simply upon theorems about the "natural rights" of
men or of States, though they postulated such rights. Their
problem was not chiefly one of political ethics but of practical
psychology, a need not so much to preach to Americans about
what they *ought* to do, as to predict successfully what they *would*
do, supposing certain governmental mechanisms were (or were
not) established. Unless these predictions were in the main
correct, the Constitution would fail to accomplish the ends for
which it was designed. And the predictions could be expected to
prove correct only if they were based upon what—in the eyes of
the chief proponents and defenders of the Constitution—seemed
a sound and realistic theory of human nature.

That theory was unmistakably set forth in what has come
to be the most famous of the *Federalist* papers (No. X), written
by James Madison, the member of the Convention who is, I suppose, now generally admitted to deserve, if any one member can
be said to deserve, the title of "Father of the Constitution."[12]
Since, however, it would be unsafe to assume that the argument

[11]Helvétius, *Poésies*, 1781, p. 111: "Épitre sur le plaisir."
[12]See the notable volume of Irving Brant, *James Madison, Father of the
Constitution*, 1950, especially pp. 154–155.

even of this celebrated essay is now familiar to most Americans, let me briefly summarize it, mostly in Madison's words. "The great menace," he writes, "to governments on the popular model" is "the spirit of faction." By a "faction," he explains he means "a number of citizens, whether amounting to a majority or a minority of the whole, who are united and actuated by some common impulse of passion or of interest adverse to the rights of other citizens, or to the permanent and aggregate interests of the community." There are two conceivable "methods of curing the mischiefs of faction: the one, by removing its causes, the other, by controlling its effects." The first method, however, is wholly inconsistent with popular government; you could abolish factions only by totally abolishing the "liberty" of individual citizens, i.e., their exercise, through the franchise, of the right severally to express and to seek to realize their own opinions and wishes with respect to the policies and acts of the government. But to expect that their exercise of that right will be, in general, determined by anything but what we now call "special interests" —which is what Madison chiefly meant by "the spirit of faction"[13] —is to expect an impossible transformation of human nature. "As long as the reason of man continues fallible, and he is at liberty to exercise it, different opinions will be formed." And "as long as the connection subsists between his reason and his self-love, his opinions and his passions will have a reciprocal influence upon each other. . . . A division of society into different interests and parties" will therefore be inevitable. Since, then, "the latent causes of faction are sown in the nature of man," the "indirect and remote considerations" which are necessary to "adjust these clashing interests and render them all subservient to the public good will rarely prevail over the immediate interest which one party has in disregarding the rights of another or the good of the whole."

But though the "causes" cannot be eliminated, the "effects" of the spirit of faction *can* be "controlled." How? By making sure, Madison answers, that the number and relative strength of the groups representing conflicting special interests will be such that

---

[13]The "passion" which Madison regarded as the chief source of the "spirit of faction" is economic self-interest. He was a pioneer of the conception of political struggles as, often disguised, class conflicts, and of economic determinism. But (unlike Marx) he also (to borrow Mr. Brant's summary on this point) "recognized the influence of differing opinions in religion, contrary theories of government, attachment to rival leaders, and many other points which stir the human passions and drive men into 'mutual animosities.'" (*James Madison, Father of the Constitution,* p. 173).

they will effectually counterbalance one another. When they do so, no part will be able to dominate the whole, to use all the legislative and executive power of the government for its own purposes. Each faction will be unable to get a majority vote in favor of its special interest because all the other factions will be opposed to it, and thereby (Madison assumes) the "general good," or the nearest practicable approximation to it, will be realized.

In thus invoking the method of counterpoise as the solvent of the (for him) crucial problem of political theory, Madison was at the same time defending one of the chief practical contentions of the group in the Convention of which he was the leader. The question at issue, as he formulates it in *Federalist* No. X, was "whether small or extensive republics are most favorable to the public weal"; but this question did not imply that there was any conflict of opinion as to the number of states which it was desirable to include in the new Union. No one proposed the actual exclusion from membership of any of the former thirteen colonies which were willing to ratify the Constitution. The real issue concerned the apportionment of legislative authority between the national government and the States. And (at this time) Madison was an extreme advocate of "national supremacy";[14] the States should, of course, have power to make laws on strictly and obviously local concerns, but "in all cases to which the separate States are incompetent, or in which the harmony of the United States may be interrupted by individual legislation,"[15] that power (and adequate means to enforce its decisions) should be assigned to the Federal Congress. By an "extensive republic," then, Madison means one of this centralized sort.

As to the choice between "small" and "extensive" republics, Madison, in *Federalist* No. X, argues vigorously in favor of the latter, mainly on the ground that it alone would ensure an adequate counterbalancing of the political power of the groups representing regional (which, as he recognizes, were in America often also economic) special interests. "The smaller the society, the fewer probably will be the distinct parties and interests composing it; the fewer the distinct parties and interests, the more frequently will a majority be found of the same party, and . . . the more easily will they concert and execute their plans of

---

[14]This has been conclusively shown by Mr. Brant, *cf. op. cit.*, pp. 24–25, 30–36, 60–61, and *passim*.

[15]The phrasing here is that of the "Virginia Plan." See Brant, *op. cit.*, pp. 24–25. This (as Brant has pointed out), though presented by Randolph, was merely an "echo" of Madison's proposals.

oppression." But if all these clashing factions are pitted against one another in a *single* legislative body, it is unlikely that any one of them will be strong enough to carry through any such "oppressive" designs. "Extend the sphere, and you take in a greater variety of parties and interests; you make it less probable that a majority of the whole will have a common motive to invade the rights of other citizens." "Extending the sphere" meant for Madison, it is evident, increasing both the number of groups participating in the central legislative authority and the number of subjects (touching more than merely local interests) on which it may legislate. The more "extended" it is *de jure*, the more restricted will be its power *de facto*. The decisive "advantage," in short, "of a large over a small republic" will "consist in the greater obstacles opposed to the concert and accomplishment of the secret wishes of an unjust and interested majority."

All this should be sufficient to justify the conclusion which I earlier propounded in advance of the proof of it, i.e., that the fundamental political philosophy of Madison (at this time) included two crucial propositions: (1) that the political opinions and activities of individuals will, with perhaps the rarest exceptions, always be determined by personal motives at variance with the general or "public" interest—in short, by bad motives; but (2) that, in framing a political constitution, you can construct a good whole out of bad parts, can make these conflicting private interests subservient to the public interest, simply by bringing all of them together upon a common political battleground where they will neutralize one another.

It has seemed to me worth while to present evidence for the first point at considerable length because there appears to be a still widely prevalent belief among Americans that the Founding Fathers were animated by a "faith in the people," a confidence in the wisdom of "the common man." This belief, to use the terminology of the logic books, is a grandiose example of the fallacy of division. For Madison, as we have seen—and in this he probably did not differ from the majority of his colleagues in the Convention—had *no* "faith in the people" *as individuals* acting in their political capacity. It is true that he recognized certain political *rights* of individual citizens—primarily the right to vote (with the large exceptions, *inter alia*, of women and Negroes) and to seek public office. It is also true that he sincerely believed, as apparently did many of his colleagues, that they themselves were disinterestedly constructing a scheme of government which would make for the good of the people as a whole and in the long run.[16] But "the people" as voters, the total electorate, was made up wholly of "factions," i.e., of individuals combined into rival political groups or parties; and a faction always strives to accomplish ends "adverse to the rights of other citizens, or to the permanent and aggregate interests of the community." "Faith in the people" is plainly and vigorously repudiated in *Federalist* No. X. But what Madison did have faith in was the efficacy, and probable adequacy, of the method of counterpoise as a corrective of the evils otherwise inevitably resulting from "government on the popular model," a "republican remedy for the diseases most incident to republican government."

One fundamental thesis in this lecture, the learned reader will note, precisely contradicts a historical generalization set forth in a celebrated, learned and brilliantly written book by a recent American historian. Carl Becker's *The Heavenly City of the Eighteenth-Century Philosophers* offers an enumeration of "four essential articles of the religion of the Enlightenment"; two of these articles are: "(1) Man is not natively depraved; . . . (3) Man is capable, guided solely by the light of reason and experience, of perfecting the good life on earth. . . . The Philosophers . . . knew instinctively that 'man in general' is natively good, easily enlightened, disposed to follow reason and common sense, generous and humane and tolerant, easily led by persuasion more than compelled by force; above all, a good citizen and a man of virtue." That there were some writers in the eighteenth century who would have subscribed to these articles, and that a tendency to affirm them was increasing, especially in France in the later decades of the century, is true. That the conception of the character and dominant motives of "man in general" formulated by Becker in the sentences quoted was held by most, or even by the most typical and influential, "eighteenth-century philosophers" is not true; it is a radical historical error. To assume its truth is to fail to see the most striking feature of the most widely prevalent opinion about human nature current in the period and to misapprehend the nature of the peculiar problem with which the

---

[16]This assumption of the disinterestedness of the makers of a Constitution —their exemption from the motivations controlling the political behavior of the rest of mankind—was psychologically almost indispensable in the Convention; certainly, few were likely to admit frankly that their own arguments were simply expressions of the "spirit of faction." But that they usually were so in fact is, I take it, now recognized by all competent historians; there are, indeed, few better examples of Madison's thesis—the shaping of political opinions by private, class, or sectional interests—than are to be found in the debates of the Convention.

"enlightened" and innovating political and social theorists and statesmen of that age were dealing. The question here, of course, like all historical questions, is one to be settled chiefly by documentary evidence; and it is partly for that reason that I have cited the *ipsissima verba* of the designers of our own Constitution. To these let us now return.

It is not solely in his argument on the division of powers between the national and state government, in the tenth *Federalist* paper, that Madison rests his case upon the two propositions of which I have been speaking. In his defense of all the major provisions of the Constitution concerning the internal structure of the national government itself—its division into three departments (legislative, executive, and judicial), the division of the legislature into two houses, the whole scheme of "checks and balances"—the same two premises are fundamental and decisive. When Madison undertakes to justify the separation of the Federal government into three mutually independent departments, his distrust of human nature and his conception of the way to offset its defects in planning a system of government are even more sharply expressed than in No. X. I hope those who are familiar with the text of *The Federalist* will forgive me for quoting from it at some length, for the benefit of those to whom it is not familiar:

The great security against a gradual concentration of the several powers in the same department, consists in giving to those who administer each department *the necessary means, and personal motives, to resist the encroachments of the others.* The provision for defence must in this case, as in all others, be made commensurate to the danger of attack. *Ambition must be made to counteract ambition. The interests of the man must be connected with the constitutional rights of the place.* It may be a reflection on human nature, that such devices should be necessary to control the abuses of government. *But what is government itself but the greatest of all reflections on human nature?* . . . *The policy of supplying, by opposite and rival interests, the defects of better motives* might be traced through the whole system of human affairs, private as well as public. We see it particularly displayed in all the subordinate distribution of power; where the constant aim is . . . that the private interest of every individual may be sentinel over the public interest.[17]

---

[17]*The Federalist,* No. LI; italics mine. Long attributed to Hamilton, this paper is now known to have been written by Madison; cf. Brant, *op. cit.,* pp. 184 and 486, n. 12. It should be mentioned that in a single sentence in this essay Madison writes: "A dependence on the people is, no doubt, the primary control on the government; but experience has taught mankind the

And this policy, Madison declares, is completely exemplified in the Constitution, which was then awaiting ratification.

> In the Federal Republic of the United States, whilst all authority in it will be derived from, and dependent on the society, the society itself will be broken into so many parts, interests, and classes of citizens, that the rights of individuals, or of the minority, will be in little danger from interested combinations of the majority. In a free government, the security for civil rights must be the same as that for religious rights. It consists in the one case in the multiplicity of interests, and in the other in the multiplicity of sects. The degree of security in both cases will depend on the number of interests and sects; and this may be presumed to depend on the extent of country and the number of people comprehended under the same government.[18]

In short, the bigger the country ("provided it lies within a practicable sphere"), the greater the assurance that "a coalition of the majority of the whole society could seldom take place upon any other principles than those of justice and the general good." It must be remembered that, in Madison's opinion, no coalition based upon *these* principles is likely except, perhaps, in times of grave national danger. Under such circumstances, there may be virtually universal agreement as to the measures necessary to avert the danger. But under normal conditions, the people will always be divided into factions, and it is essential that no faction—in other words, no *fraction* of the people—shall ever obtain a majority in the legislature. This, however, can easily be prevented by means of the counterposition of the factions to one another.

Madison's thesis here, then, may be summed up thus: The whole people has the sole right to rule, but no mere majority, *however large*, has that right. This seems a political paradox; but as actually applied—primarily, in the situation confronting the Convention itself—it resulted in the adoption of a series of compromises with which no faction was wholly satisfied, but which all, after much wrangling, were willing to accept, *faute de mieux*. Being under the practical necessity of arriving at *some* agreement, they reached a reluctant unanimity (barring a few

---

necessity of auxiliary precautions." But this seems no more than a prudent recognition of the fact that the general mass of voters possesses ultimate political power; and what Madison thought of "the people," in this sense, we have already seen. His chief concern was to prove the indispensability of the "auxiliary precautions." For the full presentation of the evidence that No. I, II, and the two preceding and seven following *Federalist* papers were composed by Madison, see Edward G. Bourne's study, "The Authorship of the *Federalist*," in his *Essays in Historical Criticism*, 1901.

[18]*Ibid.*

irreconcilable individuals) made necessary by the approximate counterbalancing of the conflicting groups and interests represented. And when embodied in the Constitution, these compromises for a time—though with steadily increasing tensions—*worked;* they held the Union together for more than seventy years. In this sense, and to this extent, Madison's theoretical principles may be said to have been pragmatically vindicated.

Lest it be supposed that faith in the method of counterpoise was peculiar to Madison among the members of the Convention, let me cite one more example from a member very different in temperament and character and in many of his opinions on specific issues. In the discussion of the powers of the "second branch" of the Federal legislature—i.e., the Senate—Gouverneur Morris delivered a characteristic speech in which he declared that the essential function of such a second chamber is "to check the precipitation, changeableness and excesses of the first branch." But "what qualities are necessary to constitute a check in this case? . . . The checking branch must have a personal interest in checking the other branch. One interest must be opposed to another interest. Vices as they exist must be turned against each other." Morris regarded the Senate—whose members, he thought, should hold office for life—as representing the interest of the propertied class. Doubtless, "the rich will strive to establish their dominion and to enslave the rest. They always did; they always will. The proper security against them is to form them into a separate interest. The two forces will then control each other. By thus combining and setting apart the aristocratic interest, the popular interest will be combined against it. There will be a mutual security." As the body representative of those who have "great personal property," the Senate will "love to lord it through pride. Pride is indeed, the great principle that actuates the poor and the rich. It is this principle which in the former resists, in the latter abuses, authority."[19]

But though Morris here voiced the same opinion of human motives that we have seen expressed by Madison and also, in order to offset the absence of "better motives," relied upon the counterbalancing of bad ones, he was in fact employing partially identical premises to support a different conclusion. For Madison, when writing in *The Federalist,* assumed that there would always be a "multiplicity" of such special interests and that the numerical

---

[19]Elliot's *Debates on the Adoption of the Federal Constitution,* V (1870), pp. 270 f.

ratios of the groups severally supporting them, or of their representatives in Congress, would be such that no coalition of them could ever obtain a majority.[20] But Morris—at least when making this speech—recognized only two permanently opposed forces in politics, the rich and the poor. And he cannot, of course, have supposed that these two would usually, or, indeed, ever, numerically counterbalance one another. They must therefore be *made* equal in legislative power—or, more precisely, in legislative impotence—by a specific constitutional provision; one of the Houses of Congress must be reserved for men having great wealth and the "aristocratic spirit," an American analogue of the House of Lords. True, Morris grants—human nature being what it is— such a body will always be inimical to the interests of "the rest," the nonpropertied classes. It is therefore necessary to have another chamber representative of the latter, to hold in check the former. But it is not in this latter consideration that Morris seems chiefly interested. What he wished to ensure was the protection of the vested interests of large property-holders. And he saw that the method of counterpoise, especially in the form which he proposed, was perfectly adapted to the accomplishment of this end. For the effect of that method, when applied to a legislative body,

---

[20]Why Madison made this assumption may seem at first hard to understand; he writes as if he, like Pope, accepted as evident beyond the need of proof the assumption that "jarring interests" will "*of themselves* create th' according music of the well-mix'd State"—though Madison adds, in substance, that they will not be well-mixed unless the mixture comprises *all* of them, in an "extensive republic." As a generalization the assumption was certainly not self-evident, nor particularly probable. But in fact Madison had specific reasons for the assumption, which he set forth in his speech in the Convention on June 28, 1787. He was then arguing (unsuccessfully, as it turned out) in favor of giving to the larger states more Senators than to the small states. To the objection that this would enable the larger states to combine to dominate the smaller ones, he replied that this could happen only if the larger states had common "interests," which they did not have. The three largest were Massachusetts, Pennsylvania, and Virginia. These were remote from one another; they differed in "customs, manners, and religion"; and, still more important, their trade interests were entirely "diverse." "Where," then, "is the probability of a combination? What the inducements?" Thus, it will be seen, Madison was here asserting an *actual* existing counterpoise of political forces in the Federal Union: where there is no identity of economic and other interests, there can be no "coalition," and therefore no majority in Congress for any one group. But since the proposal of unequal state representation in the Senate failed to carry, he turned, in the *Federalist*, to another and less specific argument: be the states equally or unequally represented in the "second chamber," there would in any case be a natural counterbalancing of voting strength among such a "multiplicity" of sections and economic interests and religious sects. And though Madison now gave no definite or cogent reasons for believing this to be true, it *was* true, subject to the qualifications above noted.

would be—as Madison's arguments said—to prevent any one of the opposing factions from ever accomplishing its purpose. A Senate that was representative exclusively of one economic class would never concur in any measure affecting class interests passed by a House that was representative of other classes. And it followed that "the poor" could never get a law passed which would be unfavorable to the economic interests of "the rich."[21]

Thus the method of counterpoise could, without relinquishment of its two essential premises, be proposed as a means to the realization of quite different designs with respect to the distribution of legislative power. But, whatever the purpose for which it might be advocated, it obviously could have only negative effects. It was simply a way of *preventing* new proposals from being adopted. If it ever became completely effective (which, of course, it never quite did), it could result only in a deadlock, an equilibrium of forces in which no movement in any direction would be possible. It therefore tended to crystallize the *status quo* and was naturally favored by those who wished to keep the existing political and economic order unchanged—or as little changed as possible. It was a device of conservatives to block innovations. Yet it could hardly be openly argued for upon traditionally conservative grounds—e.g., upon the assumption that change is in itself a bad thing or that the "aristocratic" and propertied class is wiser than, and morally superior to, the "lower classes." For it rested, as we have seen, upon the generalization that (certainly in politics) the aims and motives of virtually all individuals, and therefore of all "factions," are equally irrational and "interested," equally indifferent to the "general good"; and it was *only* upon this assumption that the scheme of equipoise, of rendering all factions *equally* impotent, could be consistently defended.

But this generalization, though indispensable to the argument,

---

[21]Madison, in spite of his usual argument based upon the existing multiplicity of interests and factions, recognized, like Morris, that the most serious conflict within the Union was that between only two factions; but for him, this was not a conflict between "the rich" and "the poor," but between two major sections of the country. In a memorably prophetic speech on June 29th he warned the Convention that "the great danger to our general government is, the great southern and northern interests being opposed to each other. Look to the votes in Congress [i.e., of the Confederation], and most of them stand divided by the geography of the country, not according to the size of the States." This supreme danger he hoped and believed could be averted by means of a balance of power in Congress between the two sections. So long as, by various compromises, that balance seemed to remain approximately undisturbed, Madison's hope was realized. As soon as the balance was patently overthrown, the danger which he pointed out became a tragic reality.

had some awkward consequences. It implied that, in political discussion and agitation, appeals to purely ethical standards and rational and disinterested ideals would be inappropriate and useless, since, by hypothesis, no such appeal could really influence the opinions and actions of the voters or legislators. But in practice such moral, or ostensibly moral, appeals were *not entirely* ineffective; and, once organized political parties were actually operating, their orators seldom, if ever, admitted that the policies they advocated were adverse "to the rights of others and the good of the whole"; on the contrary, they usually represented these policies as consistent with, or even required by, the highest moral principles, and they doubtless often believed this to be true. And though this usually was—and still is—simply "rationalization," even a rationalization is an admission that rational considerations, valid by criteria which are more than biases arising from private interests or from unexamined and unverifiable preconceptions, are relevant to the issue under discussion. However small the part which such considerations really play in the determination of individual opinions and individual behavior, as soon as you admit their relevance, and profess to justify your own contentions by them, you have accepted a change of venue to another and admittedly a higher court, in which the controversy must be fought out under the rules of that court, that is, rules of logical consistency and verifiable empirical evidence. In so far as those who invoked the method of counterpoise implicitly denied even the possibility of such a change of venue, they ignored a real aspect of the working of human nature in politics. But in saying this I am far from intending to imply that their assumptions about men's usual motivations, in their political opinions and actions, were false, or even that they were not the *more* pertinent and useful assumptions to apply to the immediate practical problems which confronted the Constitution-makers in 1787.

In these comments on the latent implications, the degree of validity, and the practical effect of the theory of counterpoise which so powerfully influenced the framing of the American Constitution, I have deviated from the primarily historical purpose of the present lecture. That purpose was not to evaluate but to illustrate the wide prevalence, even in the later eighteenth century, of a highly unfavorable appraisal of the motives generally controlling men's political (and other) behavior, and to explain in part the seemingly paradoxical fact that, in the very same period, the American republic was founded, largely by men who accepted that appraisal. This purpose has, I hope, now been sufficiently accomplished.

But there was, as I have already said, another idea, or complex of interrelated ideas, about the springs of action in men, which throughout the seventeenth and eighteenth centuries was even more widely prevalent than the conceptions underlying the method of counterpoise; and it had a broader scope, and could lead in part to different conclusions. Both, it is true, were in agreement on one fundamental premise already familiar to us: the assumption that man's "reason" has, at most, a secondary and a very small influence upon his conduct and that irrational or non-rational feelings and desires are the real efficient causes of all, or nearly all, of men's actions. And there followed from this assumption the practical corollary that one who wishes to control men's "outward conduct"—i.e., by means of a system of government—must do so by *employing* these nonrational forces, must (as Pope had said) "build on wants, and on defects of mind" the social and political structure which he seeks to realize.

Inasmuch as this general assumption underlay both the theory already expounded—that embodying the principle of counterpoise—and what as yet I can only refer to (since it has not yet been expounded) as the second theory, they may be considered species of the same genus. And, having thus one fundamental presupposition in common, they have often been lumped together as identical—by Pope, among others. But they were actually, in other respects, extremely dissimilar. Whereas the scheme of counterpoise, in order to offset the irrational and mutually antagonistic motivations of individuals, relied upon an essentially external, political, and quasi-mechanical device, the second theory found in the individual—in all individuals—a certain peculiarly potent type of motivation which, though admittedly a mode of self-love and certainly not "rational," was not necessarily mutually antagonistic or "adverse to the common good," but, on the contrary (as many writers maintained, though others denied), consisted of subjective forces which give rise to socially desirable "outward conduct," apart from any external controls. . . .

That Politics May Be Reduced to a Science: David Hume, James Madison, and the Tenth Federalist

DOUGLASS G. ADAIR

In June 1783, the war for American independence being ended, General Washington addressed his once-famous circular letter to the state governors with the hopeful prophecy that if the Union of the States could be preserved, the future of the Republic would be both glorious and happy. "The foundation of our Empire was not laid in the gloomy age of Ignorance and Superstition," Washington pointed out, "but at an Epocha when the rights of mankind were better understood and more clearly defined, than at any former period; the researches of the human mind after social happiness, have been carried to a great extent, the treasures of knowledge, acquired by the labours of Philosophers, Sages, and Legislators, through a long succession of years, are laid open for our use, and their collected wisdom may be happily applied in the Establishment of our forms of Government . . . At this auspicious period, the United States came into existence as a Nation, and if their Citizens should not be completely free and happy, the fault will be intirely their own."

The optimism of General Washington's statement is manifest; the reasons he advances for this optimism, however, seem to modern Americans a century and a half later both odd and naive, if not slightly un-American. For Washington here argues in favor of "the Progress of the Human Mind." Knowledge gradually acquired through "researches of the human mind" about the nature of man and government—knowledge which "the gloomy age of Ignorance and Superstition" did not have—gives Americans in 1783 the power to new-model their forms of government according to the precepts of wisdom and reason. The "Philosopher" as Sage and Legislator, General Washington hopes, will preside over the creation and reform of American political institutions.

Reprinted with permission from the *Huntington Library Quarterly*, XX, 4 (August, 1957), 343–360.

Note: Delivered at the Conference of Early American History at the Henry E. Huntington Library, February 9, 1957.

"Philosopher" as written here by Washington was a word with hopeful and good connotations. But this was 1783. In 1789 the French Revolution began; by 1792 "philosophy" was being equated with the guillotine, atheism, the reign of terror. Thereafter "philosopher" would be a smear-word, connoting a fuzzy-minded and dangerous social theorist—one of those impractical Utopians whose foolish attempts to reform society according to a rational plan created the anarchy and social disaster of the Terror. Before his death in 1799 Washington himself came to distrust and fear the political activities of philosophers. And in time it would become fashionable among both French conservatives and among all patriotic Americans to stress the sinister new implications of the word "philosophy" added after 1789 and to credit the French philosophers with transforming the French Revolution into a "bad" revolution in contrast to the "good" non-philosophical American Revolution. But this ethical transformation of the word still lay in the future in 1783. Then "philosophy" and "philosopher" were still terms evoking optimism and hopes of the high tide of Enlightenment on both sides of the Atlantic.

Dr. Johnson in his *Dictionary* helps us understand why Washington had such high regard for philosophy as our war for independence ended. "Philosophy," according to the lexicographer, was "knowledge natural or moral"; it was "hypothesis or system upon which natural effects are explained." "To philosophize," or "play the philosopher," was "to search into nature; to enquire into the causes of effects." The synonym of "Philosophy" in 1783 then was "Science"; the synonym of "Philosopher" would be our modern word (not coined until 1840) "Scientist," "a man deep in knowledge, either moral or natural."

Bacon, Newton, and Locke were the famed trinity of representative great philosophers for Americans and all educated inhabitants of Western Europe in 1783. Francis Bacon, the earliest prophet of philosophy as a program for the advancement of learning, had preached that "Knowledge is Power" and that Truth discovered by Reason through observation and free inquiry is as certain and as readily adapted to promote the happiness of human life, as Truth communicated to mankind through God's direct revelation. Isaac Newton, "the first luminary in this bright constellation," had demonstrated that Reason indeed could discover the laws of physical Nature and of Nature's God, while John Locke's researches into psychology and human understanding had definitely channeled inquiry toward the discovery of the immutable and universal laws of Human Nature. By the middle of the eighteenth century a multitude of researchers in all the countries of Europe were seeking, in Newtonian style, to advance the bounds of knowledge in politics, economics, law, and sociology. By the middle of the century the French judge and *philosophe* Montesquieu had produced a compendium of the behavioral sciences, cutting across all these fields in his famous study of *The Spirit of the Laws.*

However, Washington's assurance that already scientific knowledge about government had accumulated to such an extent that it could be immediately applied to the uses of "Legislators," pointed less toward France than toward Scotland. There, especially in the Scottish universities, had been developed the chief centers of eighteenth-century social science research and publication in all the world. The names of Francis Hutcheson, David Hume, Adam Smith, Thomas Reid, Lord Kames, Adam Ferguson, the most prominent of the Scottish philosophers, were internationally famous. In America the treatises of these Scots, dealing with history, ethics, politics, economics, psychology, and jurisprudence in terms of "system upon which natural effects are explained," had become the standard textbooks of the colleges of the late colonial period. At Princeton, at William and Mary, at Pennsylvania, at Yale, at King's, and at Harvard, the young men who rode off to war in 1776 had been trained in the texts of Scottish social science.

The Scottish system, as it had been gradually elaborated in the works of a whole generation of researchers, rested on one basic assumption, had developed its own special method, and kept to a consistent aim. The assumption was "that there is a great uniformity among the actions of men, in all nations and ages, and that human nature remains still the same, in its principles and operations. The same motives always produce the same actions; the same events follow from the same causes. . . . Would you know the sentiments, inclinations, and course of life of the Greeks and Romans? Study well the temper and actions of the French and English . . ."—thus David Hume, presenting the basis of a science of human behavior. The method of eighteenth-century social science followed from this primary assumption—it was historical-comparative synthesis. Again Hume: "Mankind are so much the same, in all times and places, that history informs us of nothing new or strange in this particular. Its chief use is only to discover the constant and universal principles of human nature, by showing men in all varieties and situations, and furnishing us with materials from which we may form our observations and become acquainted with the regular springs of human action and behavior."[1] Finally, the aim of studying man's behavior in its comparative-historical manifestations was for the purpose of prediction—philosophy would aid the legislator in making correct policy decisions. Comparative-historical studies of man in society would allow the discovery of the constant and universal principle of human nature, which, in turn, would allow at least some safe predictions about the effects of legislation "almost as general and certain . . . as any which the mathematical sciences will afford us." "Politics" (and again the words are Hume's) to some degree "may be reduced to a science."

By thus translating the abstract generalizations about "philosophy" in Washington's letter of 1783 into the concrete and particular type of philosophy to which he referred, the issue is brought into new focus more congenial to our modern understanding. On reviewing the specific body of philosophical theory and writing with which Washington and his American contemporaries were familiar, we immediately remember that "the collected wisdom" of at least some of the Scottish academic philosophers was applied to American legislation during the nineteenth century. It is obvious, for example, that the "scientific predictions," based on historical analysis, contained in Professor Adam Smith's *An Inquiry into the Nature and Causes of the Wealth of Nations* (London, 1776), concerning the role of free enterprise and economic productivity, was of prime significance in shaping the relations of the state with the American business community, especially after 1828. Washington's expectations of 1783 were thus accurate in the long-run view.[2]

---

[1]David Hume, "Of Liberty and Necessity," in *An Enquiry Concerning Human Understanding* (London, 1748). An examination of the social theory of the Scottish school is to be found in Gladys Bryson, *Man and Society: The Scottish Inquiry of the Eighteenth Century* (Princeton, 1945). Miss Bryson seems unaware both of the position held by Scottish social science in the curriculum of the American colleges after 1750—Princeton, for example, where nine members of the Constitutional Convention of 1787 graduated, was a provincial carbon-copy, under President Witherspoon, of Edinburgh—and of its influence on the revolutionary generation. For a brilliant analysis of Francis Hutcheson's ideas and his part in setting the tone and direction of Scottish research, as well as the trans-Atlantic flow of ideas between Scotland and the American colonies in the eighteenth century, with a persuasive explanation of why the Scots specialized in social science formulations that were peculiarly congenial to the American revolutionary elite, see Caroline Robbins, "When It Is That Colonies May Turn Independent," *William and Mary Quarterly*, 3rd ser., Vol. XI (April, 1954), pp. 214–251.

[2]The theoretical and prophetic nature of Adam Smith's classic when it was published in 1776 is today largely ignored by both scholars and spokesmen

It is the purpose of this paper, however, to show that Washington's immediate expectations of the creative role of "philosophy" in American politics were also accurate in the period in which he wrote. It is thus the larger inference of the following essay that "philosophy," or "the science of politics" (as defined above), was integral to the whole discussion of the necessity for a *more* perfect Union that resulted in the creation of the American Constitution of 1787.

It can be shown, though not in this short paper, that the use of history in the debates both in the Philadelphia Convention and in the state ratifying conventions is not mere rhetorical-historical window-dressing, concealing substantially greedy motives of class and property. The speakers were making a genuinely "scientific" attempt to discover the "constant and universal principles" of any republican government in regard to liberty, justice, and stability.

In this perspective the three hundred pages of comparative-historical research in John Adam's *Defence of the Constitutions of the United States* (1787), and the five-hour closely argued historical analysis in Alexander Hamilton's Convention Speech of June 18, 1787, were both "scientific" efforts to relate the current difficulties of the thirteen American republics to the universal tendencies of republicanism in all nations and in all ages. History, scientifically considered, thus helped *define* both the nature of the crisis of 1787 for these leaders and their audience, and also determined in large part the "reforms" that, it could be predicted, would end the crisis. To both Adams and Hamilton history proved (so they believed) that sooner or later the American people would have to return to a system of mixed or limited monarchy—so great was the size of the country, so diverse were the interests to be reconciled that no other system could be adequate in securing both liberty and justice. In like manner Patrick Henry's prediction, June 9, 1788, in the Virginia Ratifying Convention, "that one government [i.e., the proposed constitution] cannot reign over so extensive a country as this is, without absolute despotism" was grounded upon a "political axiom" scientifically confirmed, so he believed, by history.

The most creative and philosophical disciple of the Scottish school of science and politics in the Philadelphia Convention was

---

for the modern American business community. In 1776, however, Smith could only theorize from scattered historical precedents as to how a projective free enterprise system might work, because nowhere in his mercantilist world was a free enterprise system of the sort he described on paper actually operating.

James Madison. His effectiveness as an advocate of a new constitution, and of the particular constitution that was drawn up in Philadelphia in 1787, was certainly based in large part on his personal experience in public life and his personal knowledge of the conditions of America in 1787. But Madison's greatness as a statesman rests in part on his ability quite deliberately to set his limited personal experience in the context of the experience of men in other ages and times, thus giving extra reaches of insight to his political formulations.

His most amazing political prophecy, formally published in the tenth *Federalist,* was that the size of the United States and its variety of interests could be made a guarantee of stability and justice under the new constitution. When Madison made this prophecy the accepted opinion among all sophisticated politicians was exactly the opposite. It is the purpose of the following detailed analysis to show Madison, the scholar-statesman, evolving his novel theory, and not only using the behavioral science techniques of the eighteenth century, but turning to the writings of David Hume himself for some of the suggestions concerning an extended republic.

It was David Hume's speculations on the "Ideal of a Perfect Commonwealth," first published in 1752, that most stimulated James Madison's thought on factions.[3] In this essay Hume disclaimed any attempt to substitute a political Utopia for "the common botched and inaccurate governments" which seemed to serve imperfect men so well. Nevertheless, he argued, the idea of a perfect commonwealth "is surely the most worthy curiosity of any the wit of man can possibly devise. And who knows, if this controversy were fixed by the universal consent of the wise and learned, but, in some future age, an opportunity might be afforded of reducing the theory to practice, either by a dissolution of some old government, or by the combination of men to form a new one, in some distant part of the world." At the very end of Hume's essay was a discussion that could not help being of interest to Madison. For here the Scot casually demolished the Montesquieu small-republic theory; and it was this part of his essay, contained in a single page, that was to serve Madison in

---

[3]David Hume, *Essays, Moral, Political, and Literary* (London, 1875). Madison apparently used the 1758 edition, which was the most complete printed during the Scot's lifetime, and which gathered up into two volumes what he conceived of as the final revised version of his thoughts on the topics treated. Earlier versions of certain of the essays had been printed in 1742, 1748, 1752; there are numerous modern editions of the 1758 printing. All page references to Hume in this article are to the 1875 edition.

new-modeling a "botched" Confederation "in a distant part of the world." (I, 480–481, 492.)

Hume concluded his "Idea of a Perfect Commonwealth" with some observations on "the falsehood of the common opinion, that no large state, such as France or Great Britain, could ever be modelled into a commonwealth, but that such a form of government can only take place in a city or small territory." The opposite seemed to be true, decided Hume. "Though it is more difficult to form a republican government in an extensive country than in a city; there is more facility, when once it is formed, of preserving it steady and uniform, without tumult and faction."

The formidable problem of first unifying the outlying and various segments of a big area had thrown Montesquieu and like-minded theorists off the track, Hume believed. "It is not easy, for the distant parts of a large state to combine in any plan of free government; but they easily conspire in the esteem and reverence for a single person, who, by means of this popular favour, may seize the power, and forcing the more obstinate to submit, may establish a monarchical government." (I, 492.) Historically, therefore, it is the great leader who has been the symbol and engine of unity in empire building. His characteristic ability to evoke loyalty has made him in the past a mechanism both of solidarity and of exploitation. His leadership enables diverse peoples to work for a common end, but because of the power temptations inherent in his strategic position he usually ends as an absolute monarch.

And yet, Hume argued, this last step is not a rigid social law as Montesquieu would have it. There was always the possibility that some modern leader with the wisdom and ancient virtue of a Solon or of a Lycurgus would suppress his personal ambition and found a free state in a large territory "to secure the peace, happiness, and liberty of future generations." ("Of Parties in General," I, 127.) In 1776—the year Hume died—a provincial notable named George Washington was starting on the career that was to justify Hume's penetrating analysis of the unifying role of the great man in a large and variegated empire. Hume would have exulted at the discovery that his deductive leap into the future with a scientific prediction was correct: all great men who consolidated empires did not necessarily desire crowns.

Having disposed of the reason why monarchies had usually been set up in big empires and why it still was a matter of free will rather than necessity, Hume then turned to the problem of the easily founded, and unstable, small republic. In contrast to the large state, "a city readily concurs in the same notions of government, the natural equality of property favours liberty,[4] and the nearness of habitation enables the citizens mutually to assist each other. Even under absolute princes, the subordinate government of cities is commonly republican. . . . But these same circumstances, which facilitate the erection of commonwealths in cities, render their constitution more frail and uncertain. Democracies are turbulent. For however the people may be separated or divided into small parties, either in their votes or elections; their near habitation in a city will always make the force of popular tides and currents very sensible. Aristocracies are better adapted for peace and order, and accordingly were most admired by ancient writers; but they are jealous and oppressive." (I, 492.) Here, of course, was the ancient dilemma that Madison knew so well, re-stated by Hume. In the city where wealth and poverty existed in close proximity, the poor, if given the vote, might very well try to use the power of the government to expropriate the opulent. While the rich, ever a self-conscious minority in a republican state, were constantly driven by fear of danger, even when no danger existed in fact, to take aggressive and oppressive measures to head off the slightest threat to their power, position, and property.

It was Hume's next two sentences that must have electrified Madison as he read them: "In a large government, which is modelled with masterly skill, there is compass and room enough to refine the democracy, from the lower people, who may be admitted into the first elections or first concoction of the commonwealth, to the higher magistrates, who direct all the movements. At the same time, the parts are so distant and remote, that it is very difficult, either by intrigue, prejudice, or passion, to hurry them into any measures against the public interest." (I, 492.) Hume's analysis here had turned the small-territory republic theory upside down: *if* a free state could once be established in a large area, it would be stable and safe from the effects of faction. Madison had found the answer to Montesquieu. He

---

[4]Hume seems to be referring to the development in cities of a specialized product, trade, or industrial skill, that gives the small area an equal interest in a specific type of economic activity. All the inhabitants of Sheffield from the lowly artisan to the wealthiest manufacturer had an interest in the iron industry; every dweller in Liverpool had a stake in the prosperity of the slave trade. It was this regional unity of occupation that Hume was speaking of, not equality of income from the occupation, as is shown by the latter part of his analysis.

had also found in embryonic form his own theory of the extended federal republic.

Madison could not but feel that the "political aphorisms" which David Hume scattered so lavishly in his essays were worthy of his careful study. He re-examined the sketch of Hume's perfect commonwealth: "a form of government, to which," Hume claimed, "I cannot in theory discover any considerable objection." Hume suggested that Great Britain and Ireland—"or any territory of equal extent"—be divided into a hundred counties, and that each county in turn be divided into one hundred parishes, making in all ten thousand minor districts in the state. The twenty-pound freeholders and five-hundred-pound householders in each parish were to elect annually a representative for the parish. The hundred parish representatives in each county would then elect out of themselves one "senator" and ten county "magistrates." There would thus be in "the whole commonwealth, 100 senators, 1100 [sic] county magistrates, and 10,000 . . . representatives." Hume would then have vested in the senators the executive power: "the power of peace and war, of giving orders to generals, admirals, and ambassadors, and, in short all the prerogatives of a British King, except his negative." (I, 482–483.) The county magistrates were to have the legislative power; but they were never to assemble as a single legislative body. They were to convene in their own counties, and each county was to have one vote; and although they could initiate legislation, Hume expected the senators normally to make policy. The ten thousand parish representatives were to have the right to a referendum when the other two orders in the state disagreed.

It was all very complicated and cumbersome, but Hume thought that it would allow a government to be based on the consent of the "people" and at the same time obviate the danger of factions. He stated the "political aphorism" which explained his complex system.

> The lower sort of people and small proprietors are good judges enough of one not very distant from them in rank or habitation; and therefore, in their parochial meetings, will probably chuse the best, or nearly the best representative: But they are wholly unfit for county-meetings, and for electing into the higher offices of the republic. Their ignorance gives the grandees an opportunity of deceiving them.[5]

---

[5]*Essays*, I, 487. Hume elaborated his system in great detail, working out a judiciary system, the methods of organizing and controlling the militia,

This carefully graded hierarchy of officials therefore carried the system of indirect elections to a logical conclusion.

Madison quite easily traced out the origin of Hume's scheme. He found it in the essay entitled "Of the First Principles of Government." Hume had been led to his idea of fragmentizing election districts by his reading of Roman history and his contemplation of the historically verified evils incident to the direct participation of every citizen in democratical governments. The Scotsman had little use for "a republic," that is to say, a direct democracy. "For though the people, collected in a body like the Roman tribes, be quite unfit for government, yet when dispersed in small bodies, they are more susceptible both of reason and order; the force of popular currents and tides is, in a great measure, broken; and the public interest may be pursued with some method and constancy." (I, 113.) Hence, Hume's careful attempts to keep the citizens with the suffrage operating in thousands of artifically created electoral districts. And as Madison thought over Hume's theoretic system, he must suddenly have seen that in this instance the troublesome corporate aggressiveness of the thirteen American states could be used to good purpose. There already existed in the United States local governing units to break the force of popular currents. There was no need to invent an artificial system of counties in America. The states themselves could serve as the chief pillars and supports of a new constitution in a large-area commonwealth.

Here in Hume's *Essays* lay the germ for Madison's theory of the extended republic. It is interesting to see how he took these scattered and incomplete fragments and built them into an intellectual and theoretical structure of his own. Madison's first full statement of this hypothesis appeared in his "Notes on the Confederacy" written in April 1787, eight months before the final version of it was published as the tenth *Federalist*.[6] Starting with

---

etc. The Scot incidentally acknowledged that his thought and theories on the subject owed much to James Harrington's *Oceana* (London, 1656), "the only valuable model of a [perfect] commonwealth that has yet been offered to the public." For Hume thought that Sir Thomas More's *Utopia* and Plato's *Republic* with all other utopian blue-prints were worthless. "All plans of government, which suppose great reformation in the manners of mankind," he noted, "are plainly imaginary." *Ibid.*, 481.

[6]*Federalist*, X, appeared in *The New York Packet*, Friday, Nov. 23, 1787. There are thus three versions of Madison's theoretic formulation of how a properly organized republic in a large area, incorporating within its jurisdiction a multiplicity of interests, will sterilize the class conflict of the rich versus the poor: (1) the "Notes" of Apr. 1787; (2) speeches in the convention during June 1787; and (3) the final polished and elaborated form, in the *Federalist*, Nov. 1787.

the proposition that "in republican Government, the majority, however composed, ultimately give the law," Madison then asks what
is to restrain an interested majority from unjust violations of the
minority's rights? Three motives might be claimed to meliorate
the selfishness of the majority: first, "prudent regard for their own
good, as involved in the general . . . good"; second, "respect for
character"; and finally, religious scruples.[7] After examining each
in its turn Madison concludes that they are but a frail bulwark
against a ruthless party.

In his discussion of the insufficiency of "respect for character"
as a curb on faction, Madison again leans heavily upon Hume.
The Scot had stated paradoxically that it is "a just *political* maxim
that every man must be supposed a knave: Though at the same
time, it appears somewhat strange, that a maxim should be true
in *politics*, which is false in *fact* . . . men are generally more honest
in their private than in their public capacity, and will go greater
lengths to serve a party, than when their own private interest is
alone concerned. Honour is a great check upon mankind: But
where a considerable body of men act together, this check is, in
a great measure, removed; since a man is sure to be approved of
by his own party . . . and he soon learns to despise the clamours
of adversaries."[8] This argument, confirmed by his own experience,
seemed to Madison too just and pointed not to use, so under "Respect for character" he set down: "However strong this motive
may be in individuals, it is considered as very insufficient to restrain them from injustice. In a multitude its efficacy is diminished
in proportion to the number which is to share the praise or the
blame. Besides, as it has reference to public opinion, which, within
a particular society, is the opinion of the majority, the standard is
fixed by those whose conduct is to be measured by it."[9] The young
Virginian readily found a concrete example in Rhode Island, where
honor had proved to be no check on factious behavior. In a letter
to Jefferson explaining the theory of the new constitution, Madison
was to repeat his category of inefficacious motives,[10] but in formally presenting his theory to the world in the letters of Publius
he deliberately excluded it.[11] There was a certain disadvantage in

[7]James Madison, *Letters and Other Writings*, 4 vols. (Philadelphia, 1867),
I, 325–326.
[8]"Of the Independency of Parliament," *Essays*, I, 118–119.
[9]*Letters*, I, 326.
[10]*Ibid.*, p. 352, To Thomas Jefferson, Oct. 24, 1787.
[11]In Madison's earliest presentation of his thesis certain other elements
indicating his debt to Hume appear that have vanished in the *Federalist*.
In the "Notes on the Confederacy" the phrase "notorious factions and op-

making derogatory remarks to a majority that must be persuaded to adopt your arguments.

In April 1787, however, when Madison was writing down his first thoughts on the advantage of an extended government, he had still not completely thought through and integrated Hume's system of indirect elections with his own ideas. The Virginian, nevertheless, had not dismissed the subject from his thoughts. He had taken a subsidiary element of Hume's "Perfect Commonwealth" argument and developed it as the primary factor in his own theorem; but he was also to include Hume's major technique of indirect election as a minor device in the constitution he proposed for the new American state. As the last paragraph of "Notes on the Confederacy" there appears a long sentence that on its surface has little organic relation to Madison's preceding two-page discussion of how "an extensive Republic meliorates the administration of a small Republic."

An auxiliary desideratum for the melioration of the Republican form is such a process of elections as will most certainly extract from the mass of the society the purest and noblest characters which it contains; such as will at once feel most strongly the proper motives to pursue the end of their appointment, and be most capable to devise the proper means of attaining it.[12]

This final sentence, with its abrupt departure in thought, would be hard to explain were it not for the juxtaposition in Hume of the material on large area and indirect election.

When Madison presented his thesis to the electorate in the tenth *Federalist* as justification for a more perfect union, Hume's *Essays* were to offer one final service. Hume had written a scientific analysis on "Parties in General" as well as on the "Parties of Great Britain." In the first of these essays he took the position independently arrived at by Madison concerning the great variety of factions likely to agitate a republican state. The Virginian, with his characteristic scholarly thoroughness, therefore turned to Hume again when it came time to parade his arguments in full dress. Hume had made his major contribution to Madison's political

---

pressions which take place in corporate towns" (*Letters*, I, 327) recalls the original starting point of Hume's analysis in the "Perfect Commonwealth." Also the phraseology of the sentence: "The society becomes broken into a greater variety of interests . . . which check each other . . ." (ibid.), varied in the letter to Jefferson to: "In a large society, the people are broken into so many interests" (*ibid.*, 352), is probably a parallel of Hume's "The force of popular currents and tides is, in a great measure, broken." ("First Principles of Governments," *Essays*, I, 113.)

[12]*Letters*, I, 328.

philosophy before the Philadelphia Convention. Now he was to help in the final polishing and elaboration of the theory for purposes of public persuasion in print.

Madison had no capacity for slavish imitation; but a borrowed word, a sentence lifted almost in its entirety from the other's essay, and above all, the exactly parallel march of ideas in Hume's "Parties" and Madison's *Federalist*, X, show how congenial he found the Scot's way of thinking, and how invaluable Hume was in the final crystallizing of Madison's own convictions. "Men have such a propensity to divide into personal factions," wrote Hume, "that the smallest appearance of real difference will produce them." (I, 128.) And the Virginian takes up the thread to spin his more elaborate web: "So strong is this propensity of mankind to fall into mutual animosities, that where no substantial occasion presents itself, the most frivolous and fanciful distinctions have been sufficient to kindle their unfriendly passions and excite their most violent conflicts."[13] Hume, in his parallel passage, presents copious examples. He cites the rivalry of the blues and the greens at Constantinople, and recalls the feud between two tribes in Rome, the Pollia and the Papiria, that lasted three hundred years after everyone had forgotten the original cause of the quarrel. "If mankind had not a strong propensity to such divisions, the indifference of the rest of the community must have suppressed this foolish animosity [of the two tribes], that had not any aliment of new benefits and injuries. . . ." (I, 128–129.) The fine Latinity of the word "aliment"[14] apparently caught in some crevice of Madison's mind, soon to reappear in his statement, "Liberty is to faction what air is to fire, an aliment, without which it instantly expires."[15] So far as his writings show, he never used the word

---

[13]*The Federalist*, Max Beloff, ed. (Oxford and New York, 1948), No. X, p. 43. Hereafter page references to the *Federalist* will be to this edition.

[14]L. *alimentum*, fr. *alere* to nourish. Food; nutriment; hence, sustenance, means of support.—SYN. see PABULUM. This word is not a common one in 18th century political literature. Outside of *The Federalist* and Hume's essay I have run across it only in Bacon's works. To the man of the 18th century even the cognate forms "alimentary" (canal), and "alimony," so familiar to us in common speech, were still highly technical terms of medicine and law.

[15]*Federalist*, p. 42. Compare Hume's remarks: "In despotic governments, indeed, factions often do not appear; but they are not the less real; or rather, they are more real and more pernicious, upon that very account. The distinct orders of men, nobles and people, soldiers and merchants, have all a distinct interest; but the more powerful oppresses the weaker with impunity and without resistance; which begets a seeming tranquility in such governments." (I, 130.) Also see Hume's comparison of faction to "weeds . . . which grow most plentifully in the richest soil; and though absolute governments be not wholly free from them, it must be confessed, that they

again; but in this year of 1787 his head was full of such words
and ideas culled from David Hume.

When one examines these two papers in which Hume and
Madison summed up the eighteenth century's most profound
thought on party, it becomes increasingly clear that the young
American used the earlier work in preparing a survey on faction
through the ages to introduce his own discussion of faction in
America. Hume's work was admirably adapted to this purpose. It
was philosophical and scientific in the best tradition of the Enlightenment. The facile damnation of faction had been a commonplace in English politics for a hundred years, as Whig and Tory
vociferously sought to fasten the label on each other. But the Scot,
very little interested as a partisan and very much so as a social
scientist, treated the subject therefore in psychological, intellectual,
and socio-economic terms. Throughout all history, he discovered,
mankind has been divided into factions based either on personal
loyalty to some leader or upon some "sentiment or interest" common to the group as a unit. This latter type he called a "Real" as
distinguished from the "Personal" faction. Finally he subdivided
the "real factions" into parties based on "interest," upon "principle,"
or upon "affection." Hume spent well over five pages dissecting
these three types; but Madison, while determined to be inclusive,
had not the space to go into such minute analysis. Besides, he
was more intent now on developing the cure than on describing
the malady. He therefore consolidated Hume's two-page treatment
of "personal" factions, and his long discussion of parties based on
"principle and affection" into a single sentence. The tenth *Federalist* reads: "A zeal for different opinions concerning religion,
concerning government, and many other points, as well of speculation as of practice;[16] an attachment to different leaders am-

---

rise more easily, and propagate themselves faster in free governments,
where they always infect the legislature itself, which alone could be able,
by the steady application of rewards and punishments, to eradicate them"
(I, 127–128); and notice Madison's "The regulation of these various and
interfering interests forms the principal task of modern legislation, and
involves the spirit of party and faction in the necessary and ordinary operations of the government." (*Federalist*, p. 43.)

[16] This clause of Madison's refers to Hume's "parties from *principle*,
especially abstract speculative principle," in the discussion of which he includes "different political principles" and "principles of priestly government
. . . which has . . . been the poison of human society, and the source of
the most inveterate factions." Hume, in keeping with his reputation as the
great sceptic, feels that while the congregations of persecuting sects must
be called "factions of principle," the priests, who are "the prime movers"

bitiously contending for pre-eminence and power;[17] or to persons of other descriptions whose fortunes have been interesting to the human passions,[18] have, in turn, divided mankind into parties, inflamed them with mutual animosity, and rendered them much more disposed to vex and oppress each other than to cooperate for their common good."[19] It is hard to conceive of a more perfect example of the concentration of idea and meaning than Madison achieved in this famous sentence.

It is noteworthy that while James Madison compressed the greater part of Hume's essay on factions into a single sentence, he greatly expanded the quick sketch of the faction from "interest" buried in the middle of the philosopher's analysis. This reference, in Madison's hands, became the climax of his treatment and is the basis of his reputation in some circles as the progenitor of the theory of economic determinism. Hume had written that factions

---

in religious parties, are factious out of "interest." The word "speculation" that appears in Madison is rendered twice as "speculative" in Hume. (I, 130–132.)

[17]Here is Hume's "Personal" faction, "founded on personal friendship or animosity among such as compose the contending parties." Hume instances the Colonesi and Orsini of modern Rome, the Neri and Bianchi of Florence, the rivalry between the Pollia and Papiria of ancient Rome, and the confused mass of shifting alliances that marked the struggle between Guelfs and Ghibellines. (I, 128–129.)

[18]This phrase, which is quite obscure in the context, making a separate category of a type of party apparently just covered under "contending leaders," refers to the loyal bitter-end Jacobites of 18th-century England. These sentimental irreconcilables of the Squire Western ilk made up Hume's "party from *affection*." Hume explains: "By parties from affection, I understand those which are founded on the different attachments of men towards particular families and persons, whom they desire to rule over them. These factions are often very violent. [Hume was writing only three years before Bonnie Prince Charlie and the clans had frightened all England in '45]; though, I must own, it may seem unaccountable, that men should attach themselves so strongly to persons, with whom they are no wise acquainted, whom perhaps they never saw, and from whom they never received, nor can ever hope for any favour." (I, 133.)

The fact that Madison includes this category in his paper satisfies me that, when he came to write the tenth *Federalist* for publication, he referred directly to Hume's volume as he reworked his introduction into its final polished form. One can account for the other similarities in the discussion of faction as a result of Madison's careful reading of Hume's works and his retentive memory. But the inclusion of this "party from affection" in the Virginian's final scheme where its ambiguity indeed detracts from the force of the argument, puts a strain on the belief that it resulted from memory alone. This odd fourth classification, which on its face is redundant, probably was included because Hume's book was open on the table beside him, and because James Madison would leave no historical stone unturned in his effort to make a definitive scientific summary.

[19]*Federalist*, X, pp. 42–43.

from interest "are the most reasonable, and the most excusable. When two orders of men, such as the nobles and people, have a distinct authority in a government, not very accurately balanced and modelled, they naturally follow a distinct interest; nor can we reasonably expect a different conduct, considering that degree of selfishness implanted in human nature. It requires great skill in a legislator to prevent such parties; and many philosophers are of opinion, that this secret, like the *grand elixir*, or *perpetual motion*, may amuse men in theory, but can never possibly be reduced to practice." (I, 130.) With his uncomfortable thought Hume dismissed the subject of economic factions as he fell into the congenial task of sticking sharp intellectual pins into priestly parties and bigots who fought over abstract political principles.

Madison, on the contrary, was not satisfied with this cursory treatment. He had his own ideas about the importance of economic forces. All that Hume had to say of personal parties, of parties of principle, and of parties of attachment, was but a prologue to the Virginian's discussion of "the various and unequal distribution of property," throughout recorded history. "Those who hold, and those who are without property, have ever formed distinct interests in society. Those who are creditors, and those who are debtors, fall under a like discrimination. A landed interest, a manufacturing interest, a mercantile interest, a moneyed interest, with many lesser interests, grow up of necessity in civilized nations, and divide them into different classes actuated by different sentiments and views."[20] Here was the pivot of Madison's analysis. Here in this multiplicity of economic factions was "the grand elixir" that transformed the ancient doctrine of the rich against the poor into a situation that a skillful American legislator might model into equilibrium. Compound various economic interests of a large territory with a federal system of thirteen semi-sovereign political units, establish a scheme of indirect elections which will functionally bind the extensive area into a unit while "refining" the voice of the people, and you will have a stable republican state.

This was the glad news that James Madison carried to Philadelphia. This was the theory which he claimed had made obsolete the necessity for the "mixed government" advocated by Hamilton and Adams. This was the message he gave to the world in the first *Federalist* paper he composed. His own scientific reading of history, ancient and modern, his experience with religious factions in Virginia, and above all his knowledge of the scientific axiom

---

[20]*Federalist*, X, p. 43.

regarding man and society in the works of David Hume, ablest British philosopher of his age, had served him and his country well. "Of all men, that distinguish themselves by memorable achievements, the first place of honour seems due to Legislators and founders of states, who transmit a system of laws and institutions to secure the peace, happiness, and liberty of future generations." (I, 127.)

THE NATURE OF THE DEBATE

The philosophical and psychological bases for the divisions over the Constitution and the ways in which they were manifested in the ratification debate are analyzed in the following two selections. The first uses *The Federalist* as an index to the ideas, aspirations, and intentions of the Federalists and stresses their commitment to popular government. The second discusses the explicit arguments, implicit assumptions, and deep-seated anxieties that lay behind the Anti-Federalist opposition and locates that opposition squarely in the Anti-Federalist fear of the malignant effects of power.

MARTIN DIAMOND (b. 1919) is a member of the Department of Political Science at Claremont Men's College.

Democracy and The Federalist: A Reconsideration of the Framers' Intents

MARTIN DIAMOND

It has been a common teaching among modern historians of the guiding ideas in the foundation of our government that the Constitution of the United States embodied a reaction against the democratic principles espoused in the Declaration of Independence. This view has largely been accepted by political scientists and has therefore had important consequences for the way Amer-

Reprinted with permission from *The American Political Science Review*, LIII, 1 (March, 1959), 52–68.

Note: An earlier version of this was written at the request of the Fund for the Republic; the Fund's generous assistance is here gratefully acknowledged.

ican political development has been studied. I shall present here a contrary view of the political theory of the Framers and examine some of its consequences.

What is the relevance of the political thought of the Founding Fathers to an understanding of contemporary problems of liberty and justice? Four possible ways of looking at the Founding Fathers immediately suggest themselves. First, it may be that they possessed wisdom, a set of political principles still inherently adequate, and needing only to be supplemented by skill in their proper contemporary application. Second, it may be that, while the Founding Fathers' principles are still sound, they are applicable only to a part of our problems, but not to that part which is peculiarly modern; and thus new principles are needed to be joined together with the old ones. Third, it may be that the Founding Fathers have simply become [obsolete]; they dealt with bygone problems and their principles were relevant only to those old problems. Fourth, they may have been wrong or radically inadequate even for their own time.

Each of these four possible conclusions requires the same foundation: an understanding of the political thought of the Founding Fathers. To decide whether to apply their wisdom, or to add to their wisdom, or to reject it as irrelevant or as unwise, it is absolutely necessary to understand what they said, why they said it, and what they meant by it. At the same time, however, to understand their claim to wisdom is to evaluate it: to know wherein they were wise and wherein they were not, or wherein (and why) their wisdom is unavailing for our problems. Moreover, even if it turns out that our modern problems require wholly new principles for their solution, an excellent way to discover those new principles would be to see what it is about modernity that has outmoded the principles of the Founding Fathers. For example, it is possible that modern developments are themselves partly the outcome of the particular attempt to solve the problem of freedom and justice upon which this country was founded. That is, our modern difficulties may testify to fundamental errors in the thought of the Founding Fathers; and, in the process of discerning those errors, we may discover what better principles would be.

The solution of our contemporary problems requires very great wisdom indeed. And in that fact lies the greatest justification for studying anew the political thought of the Founding Fathers. For that thought remains the finest American thought on political matters. In studying them we may raise ourselves to their level. In achieving their level we may free ourselves from limitations that, ironically, they tend to impose upon us, *i.e.*, insofar as we tend to be creatures of the society they founded. And in so freeing ourselves we may be enabled, if it is necessary, to go beyond their wisdom. The Founding Fathers still loom so large in our life that the contemporary political problem of liberty and justice for Americans could be stated as the need to choose whether to apply their wisdom, amend their wisdom, or reject it. Only an understanding of them will tell us how to choose.

For the reflections on the Fathers which follow, I employ chiefly *The Federalist* as the clue to the political theory upon which rested the founding of the American Republic. That this would be inadequate for a systematic study of the Founding Fathers goes without saying. But it is the one book, "to which," as Jefferson wrote in 1825, "appeal is habitually made by all, and rarely declined or denied by any as evidence of the general opinion of those who framed and of those who accepted the Constitution of the United States, on questions as to its genuine meaning." As such it is the indispensable starting point for systematic study.

I

Our major political problems today are problems of democracy; and, as much as anything else, the *Federalist* papers are a teaching about democracy. The conclusion of one of the most important of these papers states what is also the most important theme in the entire work: the necessity for "a republican remedy for the diseases most incident to republican government."[1] The theme is clearly repeated in a passage where Thomas Jefferson is praised for displaying equally "a fervent attachment to republican government and an enlightened view of the dangerous propensities against which it ought to be guarded."[2] *The Federalist*, thus, stresses its commitment to republican or popular government, but, of course, insists that this must be an enlightened commitment.

But *The Federalist* and the Founding Fathers generally have not been taken at their word. Predominantly, they are understood as being only quasi- or even anti-democrats. Modern American historical writing, at least until very recently, has generally seen the Constitution as some sort of apostasy from, or reaction to, the radically democratic implications of the Declaration of Independ-

---

[1]*Federalist,* No. 10, p. 62. All references are to the Modern Library edition, ed. E. M. Earle.

[2]*Federalist,* No. 49, p. 327.

ence—a reaction that was undone by the great "democratic break-throughs" of Jeffersonianism, Jacksonianism, etc. This view, I believe, involves a false understanding of the crucial political issues involved in the founding of the American Republic. Further, it is based implicitly upon a questionable modern approach to democracy and has tended to have the effect, moreover, of rele-gating the political teaching of the Founding Fathers to the pre-democratic past and thus of making it of no vital concern to moderns. The Founding Fathers themselves repeatedly stressed that their Constitution was wholly consistent with the true prin-ciples of republican or popular government. The prevailing mod-ern opinion, in varying degrees and in different ways, rejects that claim. It thus becomes important to understand what was the relation of the Founding Fathers to popular government or de-mocracy.

I have deliberately used interchangeably their terms, "popular government" and "democracy." The Founding Fathers, of course, did not use the terms entirely synonymously and the idea that they were less than "democrats" has been fortified by the fact that they sometimes defined "democracy" invidiously in comparison with "republic." But this fact does not really justify the opinion. For their basic view was that *popular government was the genus, and democracy and republic were two species* of that genus of govern-ment. What distinguished popular government from other genera of government was that in it, political authority is "derived from the great body of the society, not from . . . [any] favoured class of it."[3] With respect to this decisive question, of where political authority is lodged, democracy and republic—as *The Federalist* uses the terms—differ not in the least. Republics, equally with democracies, may claim to be wholly a form of popular govern-ment. This is neither to deny the difference between the two, nor to depreciate the importance *The Federalist* attached to the differ-

---

[3]*Federalist,* No. 39, p. 244. Here Madison speaks explicitly of the republi-can form of government. But see on the same page how Madison compares the republican form with "every *other popular* government." Regarding the crucial question of the lodgement of political authority, Madison speaks of republic, democracy and popular government interchangeably. Consider that, in the very paper where he distinguishes so precisely between democracies and republics regarding direct versus representative rule, Madison defines his general aim both as a search for "a republican remedy" for republican diseases *and* a remedy that will "preserve the spirit and the form of *popular* government." (p. 58.) Interestingly, on June 6 at the Federal Convention, Madison's phrasing for a similar problem was the search for "the only defense against the inconveniences of democracy consistent with the *democratic* form of government." Madison, *Writings,* ed. G. Hunt, Vol. 3 (G. P. Putnam's Sons, New York, 1902), p. 103. Italics supplied throughout.

ence; but in *The Federalist's* view, the difference does not relate to the essential principle of popular government. Democracy means in *The Federalist* that form of popular government where the citizens "assemble and administer the government in person."[4] Republics differ in that the people rule through representatives and, of course, in the consequences of that difference. The crucial point is that republics and democracies are equally forms of popular government, but that the one form is vastly preferable to the other because of the substantive consequences of the difference in form. Those historians who consider the Founding Fathers as less than "democrats," miss or reject the Founders' central contention that, while being perfectly faithful to the *principle* of popular government, they had solved the *problem* of popular government.

In what way is the Constitution ordinarily thought to be less democratic than the Declaration? The argument is usually that the former is characterized by fear of the people, by preoccupation with minority interests and rights, and by measures therefore taken against the power of majorities. The Declaration, it is true, does not display these features, but this is no proof of a fundamental difference of principles between the two. Is it not obviously possible that the difference is due only to a difference in the tasks to which the two documents were addressed? And is it not further possible that the democratic principles of the Declaration are not only compatible with the prophylactic measures of the Constitution, but actually imply them?

The Declaration of Independence formulates two criteria for judging whether any government is good, or indeed legitimate. Good government must rest, procedurally, upon the consent of the governed. Good government, substantively, must do only certain things, *e.g.*, secure certain rights. This may be stated another way by borrowing a phrase from Locke, appropriate enough when discussing the Declaration. That "the people shall be judge" is of the essence of democracy, is its peculiar form or method of proceeding. That the people shall judge rightly is the substantive problem of democracy. But whether the procedure will bring about the substance is problematic. Between the Declaration's two criteria, then, a tension exists: consent can be given or obtained for governmental actions which are not right—at least as the men of 1776 saw the right. (To give an obvious example from their point of view: the people may freely but wrongly vote away the pro-

---

[4] *Federalist*, No. 10, p. 58.

tection due to property.) Thus the Declaration clearly contained, although it did not resolve, a fundamental problem. Solving the problem was not its task; that was the task for the framers of the Constitution. But the man who wrote the Declaration of Independence and the leading men who supported it were perfectly aware of the difficulty, and of the necessity for a "republican remedy."

What the text of the Declaration, taken alone, tells of its meaning may easily be substantiated by the testimony of its author and supporters. Consider only that Jefferson, with no known change of heart at all, said of *The Federalist* that it was "the best commentary on the principles of government which was ever written."[5] Jefferson, it must be remembered, came firmly to recommend the adoption of the Constitution, his criticisms of it having come down only to a proposal for rotation in the Presidency and for the subsequent adoption of a bill of rights. I do not, of course, deny the peculiar character of "Jeffersonianism" nor the importance to many things of its proper understanding. I only state here that it is certain that Jefferson, unlike later historians, did not view the Constitution as a retrogression from democracy. Or further, consider that John Adams, now celebrated as America's great conservative, was so enthusiastic about Jefferson's draft of the Declaration as to wish on his own account that hardly a word be changed. And this same Adams, also without any change of heart and without complaint, accepted the Constitution as embodying many of his own views on government.

The idea that the Constitution was a falling back from the fuller democracy of the Declaration thus rests in part upon a false reading of the Declaration as free from the concerns regarding democracy that the framers of the Constitution felt. Perhaps only those would so read it who take for granted a perfect, self-subsisting harmony between consent (equality) and the proper aim of government (justice), or between consent and individual rights (liberty). This assumption was utterly foreign to the leading men of the Declaration.

II

The Declaration has wrongly been converted into, as it were, a super-democratic document; has the Constitution wrongly been

[5]*The Works of Thomas Jefferson,* Paul L. Ford, ed. (The Federal Edition), Vol. 5 (G. P. Putnam's Sons, New York, 1904), p. 434.

converted in the modern view into an insufficiently democratic document? The only basis for depreciating the democratic character of the Constitution lies in its framers' apprehensive diagnosis of the "diseases," "defects" or "evil propensities" of democracy, and in their remedies. But if what the Founders considered to be defects *are* genuine defects, and if the remedies, without violating the principles of popular government, *are* genuine remedies, then it would be unreasonable to call the Founders anti- or quasi-democrats. Rather, they would be the wise partisans of democracy; a man is not a better democrat but only a foolish democrat if he ignores real defects inherent in popular government. Thus, the question becomes: are there natural defects to democracy and, if there are, what are the best remedies?

In part, the Founding Fathers answered this question by employing a traditional mode of political analysis. They believed there were several basic possible regimes, each having several possible forms. Of these possible regimes they believed the best, or at least the best for America, to be popular government, but only if purged of its defects. At any rate, an unpurged popular government they believed to be indefensible. They believed there were several forms of popular government, crucial among these direct democracy and republican—or representative—government (the latter perhaps divisible into two distinct forms, large and small republics). Their constitution and their defense of it constitute an argument for that form of popular government (large republic) in which the "evil propensities" would be weakest or most susceptible of remedy.

The whole of the thought of the Founding Fathers is intelligible and, especially, the evaluation of their claim to be wise partisans of popular government is possible, only if the words *"disease,"* *"defect,"* and *"evil propensity"* are allowed their full force. Unlike modern "value-free" social scientists, the Founding Fathers believed that true knowledge of the good and bad in human conduct was possible, and that they themselves possessed sufficient knowledge to discern the really grave defects of popular government and their proper remedies. The modern relativistic or positivistic theories, implicitly employed by most commentators on the Founding Fathers, deny the possibility of such true knowledge and therefore deny that the Founding Fathers *could* have been actuated by knowledge of the good rather than by passion or interest. (I deliberately employ the language of *Federalist* No. 10. Madison defined faction, in part, as a group "united and actuated by . . . passion, or . . . interest." That is, factions are groups *not*—as presumably the authors of *The Federalist* were—actuated by reason.) How this modern view of the value problem supports the conception of the Constitution as less democratic than the Declaration is clear. The Founding Fathers did in fact seek to prejudice the outcome of democracy; they sought to alter, by certain restraints, the likelihood that the majority would decide certain political issues in bad ways. These restraints the Founders justified as mitigating the natural defects of democracy. But, say the moderns, there are no "bad" political decisions, wrong-in-themselves, from reaching which the majority ought to be restrained. Therefore, ultimately, nothing other than the specific interests of the Founders can explain their zeal in restraining democracy. And inasmuch as the restraints were typically placed on the many in the interest of the propertied, the departure of the Constitution is "anti-democratic" or "thermidorean." In short, according to this view, there cannot be what the Founders claimed to possess, "an *enlightened* view of the dangerous propensities against which [popular government] . . . ought to be guarded," the substantive goodness or badness of such propensities being a matter of opinion or taste on which reason can shed no light.

What are some of the arrangements which have been considered signs of "undemocratic" features of the Constitution? The process by which the Constitution may be amended is often cited in evidence. Everyone is familiar with the arithmetic which shows that a remarkably small minority could prevent passage of a constitutional amendment supported by an overwhelming majority of the people. That is, bare majorities in the thirteen least populous states could prevent passage of an amendment desired by overwhelming majorities in the thirty-six most populous states. But let us, for a reason to be made clear in a moment, turn that arithmetic around. Bare majorities in the thirty-seven least populous states can pass amendments against the opposition of overwhelming majorities in the twelve most populous states. And this would mean in actual votes today (and would have meant for the thirteen original states) constitutional amendment by a minority against the opposition of a majority of citizens. My point is simply that, while the amending procedure does involve qualified majorities, the qualification is not of the kind that requires an especially large numerical majority for action.

I suggest that the real aim and practical effect of the complicated amending procedure was not at all to give power to minorities, but to ensure that passage of an amendment would require a *nationally* distributed majority, though one that legally could consist of a bare numerical majority. It was only adventitious that the procedure has the theoretical possibility of a minority blocking (or passing) an amendment. The aim of requiring nationally distributed majorities was, I think, to ensure that no amendment could be passed simply with the support of the few states or sections sufficiently numerous to provide a bare majority. No doubt it was also believed that it would be difficult for such a national majority to form or become effective save for the decent purposes that could command national agreement, and this difficulty was surely deemed a great virtue of the amending process. This is what I think *The Federalist* really means when it praises the amending process and says that "it guards equally against that extreme facility, which would render the Constitution too mutable; and that extreme difficulty, which might perpetuate its discovered faults."[6] All I wish to emphasize here is that the actual method adopted, with respect to the numerical size of majorities, is meant to leave all legal power in the hands of ordinary majorities so long as they are national majorities. The departure from simple majoritarianism is, at least, not in an oligarchic or aristocratic direction. In this crucial respect, the amending procedure does conform strictly to the principles of republican (popular) government.

Consider next the suffrage question. It has long been assumed as proof of an anti-democratic element in the Constitution that the Founding Fathers depended for the working of their Constitution upon a substantially limited franchise. Just as the Constitution allegedly was ratified by a highly qualified electorate, so too, it is held, was the new government to be based upon a suffrage subject to substantial property qualifications. This view has only recently been seriously challenged, especially by Robert E. Brown, whose detailed researches convince him that the property qualifications in nearly all the original states were probably so small as to exclude never more than twenty-five per cent, and in most cases as little as only five to ten per cent, of the adult white male population.[7] That is, the property qualifications were not designed to exclude the mass of the poor but only the small proportion which lacked a concrete—however small—stake in society, *i.e.*, primarily the transients or "idlers."

The Constitution, of course, left the suffrage question to the decision of the individual states. What is the implication of that fact for deciding what sort of suffrage the Framers had in mind?

---

[6] *Federalist*, No. 43, p. 286.
[7] *Middle Class Democracy and the Revolution in Massachusetts, 1691–1780.* (Cornell University Press, Ithaca, 1955).

The immediately popular branch of the national legislature was to be elected by voters who "shall have the qualifications requisite for electors of the most numerous branch of the State Legislature." The mode of election to the electoral college for the Presidency and to the Senate is also left to "be prescribed in each State by the legislature thereof." At a minimum, it may be stated that the Framers did not themselves attempt to reduce, or prevent the expansion of, the suffrage; that question was left wholly to the states—and these were, ironically, the very hotbeds of post-revolutionary democracy from the rule of which it is familiarly alleged that the Founders sought to escape.[8]

In general, the conclusion seems inescapable that the states had a far broader suffrage than is ordinarily thought, and nothing in the actions of the Framers suggests any expectation or prospect of the reduction of the suffrage. Again, as in the question of the amending process, I suggest that the Constitution represented no departure whatsoever from the democratic standards of the Revolutionary period, or from any democratic standards then generally recognized.[9]

What of the Senate? The organization of the Senate, its term of office and its staggered mode of replacement, its election by state legislatures rather than directly by the people, among other things, have been used to demonstrate the undemocratic character of the Senate as intended by the Framers. Was this not a device to represent property and not people, and was it not intended therefore to be a non-popular element in the government? I suggest, on the contrary, that the really important thing is that the Framers

---

[8]Madison must have thought that he had established this point beyond misinterpretation in *The Federalist,* No. 57. "Who are to be the electors of the federal representatives? Not the rich, more than the poor; not the learned, more than the ignorant; not the haughty heirs of distinguished names, more than the humble sons of obscurity and unpropitious fortune. The electors are to be the great body of the people of the United States. They are to be the same who exercise the right in every State of electing the corresponding branch of the legislature of the State." (p. 371.)

[9]This is not to deny the importance of the existing property qualifications for the understanding of the Founders' political theory. The legal exclusion from the franchise of even a very small portion of the adult population may have enormous significance for the politics and life of a country. This is obvious in the case of a racial, ethnic or religious minority. And the exclusion of otherwise eligible adult males on the grounds of poverty may be equally important. The property qualification clearly praises and rewards certain virtues, implies that the voter must possess certain qualities to warrant his exercise of the franchise, and aims at excluding a "rabble" from the operations of political parties. But important, therefore, as the property qualification was, it does not demonstrate that the Founding Fathers departed radically from the most important aspects of the principle of majority rule.

thought they had found a way to protect property *without* representing it. That the Founders intended the Senate to be one of the crucial devices for remedying the defects of democracy is certainly true. But *The Federalist* argues that the Senate, as actually proposed in the Constitution, was calculated to be such a device as would operate only in a way that "will consist . . . with the genuine principles of republican government."[10] I believe that the claim is just.

Rather than viewing the Senate from the perspective of modern experience and opinions, consider how radically democratic the Senate appears when viewed from a pre-modern perspective. The model of a divided legislature that the Founders had most in mind was probably the English Parliament. There the House of Lords was thought to provide some of the beneficial checks upon the popular Commons which it was hoped the Senate would supply in the American Constitution. But the American Senate was to possess none of the qualities which permitted the House of Lords to fulfill its role; *i.e.*, its hereditary basis, or membership upon election by the Crown, or any of its other aristocratic characteristics.[11] Yet the Founding Fathers knew that the advantages of having both a Senate and a House would "be in proportion to the dissimilarity in the genius of the two bodies."[12] What is remarkable is that, in seeking to secure this dissimilarity, they did not in any respect go beyond the limits permitted by the "genuine principles of republican government."

Not only is this dramatically demonstrated in comparison with the English House of Lords, but also in comparison with all earlier theory regarding the division of the legislative power. The aim of such a division in earlier thought is to secure a balance between the aristocratic and democratic elements of a polity. This is connected with the pre-modern preference for a *mixed* republic, which was rejected by the Founders in favor of a *democratic* republic. And the traditional way to secure this balance or mixture was to give one house or office to the suffrages of the few and one to the suffrages of the many. Nothing of the kind is involved in the American Senate. Indeed, on this issue, so often cited as evidence of the Founders' undemocratic predilections, the very opposite is the case. The Senate is a constitutional device which *par excellence* reveals the strategy of the Founders. They wanted something like the advantages earlier thinkers had seen in a mixed legislative

---

[10]*Federalist*, No. 62, p. 403.
[11]*Federalist*, No. 63, p. 415.
[12]*Federalist*, No. 62, p. 403.

power, but they thought this was possible (and perhaps preferable) without any introduction whatsoever of aristocratic power into their system. What pre-modern thought had seen in an aristocratic senate—wisdom, nobility, manners, religion, etc.—the Founding Fathers converted into stability, enlightened self-interest, a "temperate and respectable body of citizens." The qualities of a senate having thus been altered (involving perhaps comparable changes in the notion of the ends of government), it became possible to secure these advantages through a Senate based wholly upon popular principles. Or so I would characterize a Senate whose membership required no property qualification and which was appointed (or elected in the manner prescribed) by State legislatures which, in their own turn, were elected annually or biennially by a nearly universal manhood suffrage.

The great claim of *The Federalist* is that the Constitution represents the fulfillment of a truly novel experiment, of "a revolution which has no parallel in the annals of society," and which is decisive for the happiness of "the whole human race."[13] And the novelty, I argue, consisted in solving the problems of popular government by means which yet maintain the government "wholly popular."[14] In defending that claim against the idea of the Constitution as a retreat from democracy I have dealt thus far only with the easier task: the demonstration that the constitutional devices and arrangements do not derogate from the legal power of majorities to rule. What remains is to examine the claim that the Constitution did in fact remedy the natural defects of democracy. Before any effort is made in this direction, it may be useful to summarize some of the implications and possible utility of the analysis thus far.

Above all, the merit of the suggestions I have made, if they are accurate in describing the intention and action of the Founders, is that it makes the Founders available to us for the study of modern problems. I have tried to restore to them their *bona fides* as partisans of democracy. This done, we may take seriously the question whether they were, as they claimed to be, wise partisans of democracy or popular government. If they were partisans of democracy and if the regime they created was decisively democratic, then they speak to us not merely about bygone problems, not from a viewpoint—in this regard—radically different from our own, but as men addressing themselves to problems identical in

---

[13]*Federalist*, No. 14, p. 85.
[14]*Ibid.*, p. 81.

principle with our own. They are a source from within our own heritage which teaches us the way to put the question to democracy, a way which is rejected by certain prevailing modern ideas. But we cannot avail ourselves of their assistance if we consider American history to be a succession of democratizations which overcame the Founding Fathers' intentions. On that view it is easy to regard them as simply outmoded. If I am right regarding the extent of democracy in their thought and regime, then they are not outmoded by modern events but rather are tested by them. American history, on this view, is not primarily the replacement of a pre-democratic regime by a democratic regime, but is rather a continuing testimony to how the Founding Fathers' democratic regime has worked out in modern circumstances. The whole of our national experience thus becomes a way of judging the Founders' principles, of judging democracy itself, or of pondering the flaws of democracy and the means to its improvement.

III

What was the Founding Fathers' view of the good life? Upon what fundamental theoretical premises did that view of the good life depend? How comprehensive was their understanding of the dangers against which popular government was to be guarded? How efficacious were their remedies and what may have been the unanticipated costs of those remedies? These questions are clearly too vast to answer here and now. What follows is only a series of notes which bear upon the problems raised, and which I think may serve as general guides to what it is important to seek in studying the Founding Fathers.

The Federalist does not discuss systematically, as would a theoretical treatise, the question of the ends or purposes of government. That is, it does not deal systematically with philosophical issues. This is not to say that its authors did not have a view in such matters. But what that view was, and what are its implications for the understanding of the Constitution, is a subject on which I find it difficult to speak with confidence. I must still regard as open the question whether the authors of The Federalist, or the other leading founders, had themselves fully reflected on these matters, or whether they treated them as settled by thinkers like Locke and Montesquieu, or whether crucial premises in their thought were unreflectively taken for granted. But men cannot act on a political scale so vast as they did without having and employing a view of the politically fundamental; and it is this view which provides the crucial perspective for the understanding of their particular actions and thoughts.

Perhaps the most explicit fundamental utterance of *The Federalist* is the statement regarding

the great principle of self-preservation . . . the transcendent law of nature and of nature's God, which declares that the safety and happiness of society are the objects at which all political institutions aim, and to which all such institutions must be sacrificed.[15]

But self-preservation, it is made clear, includes more than mere preservation. This passage, which interestingly echoes the Declaration of Independence on the "laws of nature and of nature's God," emphasizes that preservation includes "happiness" as well as "safety." That is, *The Federalist* is aware of and explicitly rejects the kind of regime that would follow from a narrower view of self-preservation. For example, *The Federalist* seems explicitly to be rejecting Hobbes when, in another context, it rejects the view that "nothing less than the chains of despotism can restrain [men] from destroying and devouring one another."[16] But while it rejects the "chains of despotism," *i.e.*, the Hobbesean solution to the problem of self-preservation, it nonetheless seems to accept the Hobbesean statement of the problem. As it were, the primary fears of *The Federalist* are Hobbesean, that is, fears of "foreign war and domestic convulsion." Rejecting a despotic solution, the great aim of *The Federalist* is to supply a liberal and republican solution to the same problem. But while there is a great difference, never to be underestimated, between a liberal and a repressive, a republican and a monarchical solution, it may be that in making the same dangers and their solution *the* desideratum for the structure and functions of government much of the Hobbesean view is preserved.

The main object of *The Federalist* was to urge the necessity of a firm and energetic Union. The utility of such a Union, and therefore the chief ends it will serve, is that it will strengthen the American people against the dangers of "foreign war" and secure them from the dangers of "domestic convulsion." These functions of government are the most frequently discussed and the most vehemently emphasized in the whole work. To a very great extent, then, *The Federalist* determines the role of government with reference only, or primarily, to the extremes of external and internal

---

[15]*Federalist*, No. 43, p. 287.
[16]*Federalist*, No. 55, p. 365.

danger. It is to avoid the pre-civil forms of these dangers that men form government and it is the civil solution of these dangers which, almost exclusively, determines the legitimate objects of government. But again, *The Federalist* repeatedly emphasizes that a "novel" solution is at hand. The means now exist—and America is uniquely in a position to employ them—for a republican solution which avoids the extremes of tyranny and anarchy. But notice that, on this view, liberalism and republicanism are not the means by which men may ascend to a nobler life; rather they are simply instrumentalities which solve Hobbesean problems in a more moderate manner. It is tempting to suggest that if America is a "Lockean" nation, as is so often asserted, it is true in the very precise sense that Locke's "comfortable preservation" displaces the harshness of the Hobbesean view, while not repudiating that view in general.

To be sure, *The Federalist* does make other explicit statements regarding the ends of government. For example: "Justice is the end of government. It is the end of civil society."[17] But this statement, to the best of my knowledge, is made only once in the entire work; and the context suggests that "justice" means simply "civil rights" which in turn seems to refer primarily to the protection of economic interests. That justice has here this relatively narrow meaning, as compared with traditional philosophical and theological usage, is made more probable when we take account of the crucial statement in *Federalist* No. 10. There the "first object of government" is the protection of the diverse human faculties from which arise the "rights of property" and the unequal distribution of property. The importance of this statement of the function of government is underscored when it is recalled how large a proportion of *The Federalist* deals with the improvements in "commerce" made possible by the new Constitution. For example, in a list of the four "principal objects of federal legislation,"[18] three (foreign trade, interstate trade, and taxes) deal explicitly with commerce. The fourth, the militia, also deals with commerce insofar as it largely has to do with the prevention of "domestic convulsion" brought on by economic matters.

The very great emphasis of *The Federalist* on commerce, and on the role of government in nurturing it, may not be at all incompatible with the theme of "happiness" which is the most frequently occurring definition of the "object of government." The most definite statement is the following:

---

[17]*Federalist*, No. 51, p. 340.
[18]*Federalist*, No. 53, pp. 350–351.

A good government implies two things: first, fidelity to the object of government, which is the happiness of the people, secondly, a knowledge of the means by which that object can be best obtained.[19]

The Federalist is not very explicit in defining happiness. But there are firm indications that what it had in mind has little in common with traditional philosophical or theological understandings of the term. At one place, The Federalist indicates that happiness requires that government "provide for the security, advance the prosperity, [and] support the reputation of the commonwealth."[20] In another, happiness seems to require "our safety, our tranquility, our dignity, our reputation."[21] Part of what these words mean is made clear by the fact that they summarize a lengthy indictment of the Articles of Confederation, the particulars of which deal in nearly every case with commercial shortcomings. Happiness, "a knowledge of the means" to which The Federalist openly claims to possess, seems to consist primarily in physical preservation from external and internal danger and in the comforts afforded by a commercial society; which comforts are at once the dividends of security and the means to a republican rather than repressive security.

What is striking is the apparent exclusion from the functions of government of a wide range of non-economic tasks traditionally considered the decisive business of government. It is tempting to speculate that this reduction in the tasks of government has something to do with The Federalist's defense of popular government. The traditional criticism of popular government was that it gave over the art of government into the hands of the many, which is to say the unwise. It would be a formidable reply to reduce the complexity of the governmental art to dimensions more commensurate with the capacity of the many. I use two statements by Madison, years apart, to illustrate the possibility that he may have had something like this in mind. "There can be no doubt that there are subjects to which the capacities of the bulk of mankind are unequal."[22] But on the other hand, "the confidence of the [Republican party] in the capacity of mankind for self-government"[23] is what distinguished it from the Federalist party which distrusted that capacity. The confidence in mankind's

[19]Federalist, No. 62, p. 404.
[20]Federalist, No. 30, p. 186.
[21]Federalist, No. 15, p. 88.
[22]Letter to Edmund Randolph, January 10, 1788.
[23]Letter to William Eustis, May 22, 1823. The letters to Randolph and Eustis were brought to my attention by Ralph Ketcham's article, "Notes on James Madison's Sources for the Tenth Federalist Paper," Midwest Journal of Political Science, Vol. 1 (May, 1957).

capacities would seem to require having removed from government the subjects to which those capacities are unequal.

IV

So far as concerns those ends of government on which *The Federalist* is almost wholly silent, it is reasonable to infer that what the Founders made no provision for they did not rank highly among the legitimate objects of government. Other political theories had ranked highly, as objects of government, the nurturing of a particular religion, education, military courage, civic-spiritedness, moderation, individual excellence in the virtues, etc. On all of these *The Federalist* is either silent, or has in mind only pallid versions of the originals, or even seems to speak with contempt. The Founders apparently did not consider it necessary to make special provision for excellence. Did they assume these virtues would flourish without governmental or other explicit provision? Did they consciously sacrifice some of them to other necessities of a stable popular regime—as it were, as the price of their solution to the problem of democracy? Or were these virtues less necessary to a country when it had been properly founded on the basis of the new "science of politics"? In what follows I suggest some possible answers to these questions.

The Founding Fathers are often criticized for an excessive attention to, and reliance upon, mechanical institutional arrangements and for an insufficient attention to "sociological" factors. While a moderate version of this criticism may finally be just, it is nonetheless clear that *The Federalist* pays considerable and shrewd attention to such factors. For example, in *Federalist* No. 51, equal attention is given to the institutional and non-institutional strengths of the new Constitution. One of these latter is the solution to the "problems of faction." It will be convenient to examine *Federalist* No. 10 where the argument about faction is more fully developed than in No. 51. A close examination of that solution reveals something about *The Federalist's* view of the virtues necessary to the good life.

The problem dealt with in the tenth essay is how "to break and control the violence of faction." "The friend of popular governments never finds himself so much alarmed for their character and fate, as when he contemplates their propensity to this dangerous vice." Faction is, thus, *the* problem of popular government. Now it must be made clear that Madison, the author of this essay, was not here really concerned with the problem of faction generally. He devotes only two sentences in the whole essay to the dangers of *minority* factions. The real problem in a popular government, then, is *majority* faction, or, more precisely, *the* majority faction, *i.e.*, the great mass of the little propertied and unpropertied. This is the only faction that can "execute and mask its violence under the forms of the Constitution." That is, in the American republic the many have the legal power to rule and thus from them can come the greatest harm. Madison interprets that harm fairly narrowly; at least, his overwhelming emphasis is on the classic economic struggle between the rich and the poor which made of ancient democracies "spectacles of turbulence and contention." *The* problem for the friend of popular government is how to avoid the "domestic convulsion" which results when the rich and the poor, the few and the many, as is their wont, are at each others' throats. Always before in popular governments the many, armed with political power, invariably precipitated such convulsions. But the friend of popular government must find only "a republican remedy" for this disease which is "most incident to republican government." "To secure the public good and private rights against the danger of . . . [majority] faction, and at the same time to preserve the spirit and the form of popular government, is then the great object to which our inquiries are directed."

Without wrenching Madison's meaning too greatly, the problem may be put crudely this way: Madison gave a beforehand answer to Marx. The whole of the Marxian scheme depends upon the many—having been proletarianized—causing precisely such domestic convulsion and usurpation of property as Madison wished to avoid. Madison believed that in America the many could be diverted from that probable course. How will the many, *the* majority, be prevented from using for the evil purpose of usurping property the legal power which is theirs in a popular regime? "Evidently by one of two [means] only. Either the existence of the same passion or interest in a majority at the time must be prevented, or the majority, having such co-existent passion or interest, must be rendered, by their number and local situation, unable to concert and carry into effect schemes of oppression." But "we well know that neither moral nor religious motives can be relied on" to do these things. The "circumstance principally" which will solve the problem is the "greater number of citizens and extent of territory which may be brought within the compass" of large republican governments rather than of small direct democracies.

Rather than mutilate Madison, let me complete his thought

by quoting the rest of his argument before commenting on it:

The smaller the society, the fewer probably will be the distinct parties and interests, the more frequently will a majority be found of the same party; and the smaller the number of individuals composing a majority, and the smaller the compass within which they are placed, the more easily will they concert and execute their plans of oppression. Extend the sphere and you take in a greater variety of parties and interests; you make it less probable that a majority of the whole will have a common motive to invade the rights of other citizens; or if such a common motive exists, it will be more difficult for all who feel it to discover their own strength, and to act in unison with each other.

I want to deal only with what is implied or required by the first of the two means, *i.e.*, preventing the majority from having the same "passion or interest" at the same time. I would argue that this is the more important of the two remedial means afforded by a large republic. If the majority comes to have the same passion or interest and holds to it intensely for a period of only four to six years, it seems certain that it would triumph over the "extent of territory," over the barriers of federalism, and separation of powers, and all the checks and balances of the Constitution. I do not wish to depreciate the importance of those barriers; I believe they have enormous efficacy in stemming the tide Madison feared. But I would argue that their efficacy depends upon a prior weakening of the force applied against them, upon the majority having been fragmented or deflected from its "schemes of oppression." An inflamed Marxian proletariat would not indefinitely be deterred by institutional checks or extent of territory. The crucial point then, as I see it, is the means by which a majority bent upon oppression is prevented from ever forming or becoming firm.

Madison's whole scheme essentially comes down to this. The struggle of classes is to be replaced by a struggle of interests. The class struggle is domestic convulsion; the struggle of interests is a safe, even energizing, struggle which is compatible with, or even promotes, the safety and stability of society. But how can this be accomplished? What will prevent the many from thinking of their interest as that of the Many opposed to the Few? Madison, as I see it, implies that nothing can prevent it in a small democratic society where the many are divided into only a few trades and callings: these divisions are insufficient to prevent them from conceiving their lot in common and uniting for oppression. But in a large republic, numerous and powerful divisions will arise among the many to prevent that happening. A host of interests grows up "of necessity in civilized nations, and divide[s] them into different classes, actuated by different sentiments and views." "Civilized nations" clearly means here large, commercial societies. In a large commercial society the interest of the many can be fragmented into many narrower, more limited interests. The mass will not unite as a mass to make extreme demands upon the few, the struggle over which will destroy society; the mass will fragment into relatively small groups, seeking small immediate advantages for their narrow and particular interests.

If the Madisonian solution is essentially as I have described it, it becomes clear that certain things are required for the solution to operate. I only mention several of them. First, the country in which this is to take place will have to be profoundly democratic. That is, all men must be free—and even encouraged—to seek their immediate profit and to associate with others in the process. There must be no rigid class barriers which bar men from the pursuit of immediate interest. Indeed, it is especially the lowly, from whom the most is to be feared, who must feel most sanguine about the prospects of achieving limited and immediate benefits. Second, the gains must be real; that is, the fragmented interests must from time to time achieve real gains, else the scheme would cease to beguile or mollify. But I do not want to develop these themes here. Rather, I want to emphasize only one crucial aspect of Madison's design: that is, the question of the apparently narrow ends of society envisaged by the Founding Fathers. Madison's plan, as I have described it, most assuredly does not rest on the "moral and religious motives" whose efficacy he deprecated. Indeed there is not even the suggestion that the pursuit of interest should be an especially enlightened pursuit. Rather, the problem posed by the dangerous passions and interests of the many is solved primarily by a reliance upon passion and interest themselves. As Tocqueville pointed out, Americans employ the principle of "self-interest rightly understood."

The principle of self-interest rightly understood is not a lofty one, but it is clear and sure. It does not aim at mighty objects, but it attains . . . all those at which it aims. By its admirable conformity to human weaknesses it easily obtains great dominion; nor is that dominion precarious, since the principle checks one personal interest by another, and uses, to direct the passions, the very same instrument that excites them.[24]

---

[24]*Democracy in America*, Phillips Bradley, ed. (Knopf, New York, 1951) Vol. 2, pp. 122–123.

Madison's solution to his problem worked astonishingly well. The danger he wished to avert has been averted and largely for the reasons he gave. But it is possible to question now whether he did not take too narrow a view of what the dangers were. Living today as beneficiaries of his system, we may yet wonder whether he failed to contemplate other equally grave problems of democracy, or whether his remedy for the one disease has not had some unfortunate collateral consequences. The Madisonian solution involved a fundamental reliance on ceaseless striving after immediate interest (perhaps now immediate gratification). Tocqueville appreciated that this "permanent agitation . . . is characteristic of a peaceful democracy,"[25] one might even say, the price of its peace. And Tocqueville was aware of how great might be the price. "In the midst of this universal tumult, this incessant conflict of jarring interests, this continual striving of men after fortune, where is that calm to be found which is necessary for the deeper combinations of the intellect?"[26]

V

There is, I think, in *The Federalist* a profound distinction made between the qualities necessary for Founders and the qualities necessary for the men who come after. It is a distinction that bears on the question of the Founding Fathers' view of what is required for the good life and on their defense of popular government. Founding requires "an exemption from the pestilential influence of party animosities";[27] but the subsequent governing of America will depend on precisely those party animosities, moderated in the way I have described. Or again, founding requires that "reason" and not the "passions," "sit in judgment."[28] But, as I have argued, the society once founded will subsequently depend precisely upon the passions, only moderated in their consequences by having been guided into proper channels. The reason of the Founders constructs the system within which the passions of the men who come after may be relied upon.

Founders need a knowledge of the newly improved "science of politics" and a knowledge of the great political alternatives in order to construct a durable regime; while the men who come

[25]*Ibid.*, p. 42.
[26]*Idem.*
[27]*Federalist*, No. 37, p. 232.
[28]*Federalist*, No. 49, p. 331.

after need be only legislators who are but interested "advocates and parties to the causes they determine."[29] *The Federalist* speaks, as has often been observed, with harsh realism about the short-comings of human nature, but, as has not so often been observed, none of its strictures can characterize the Founders; they must be free of these shortcomings in order to have had disinterested and true knowledge of political things. While "a nation of philosophers is as little to be expected as the philosophical race of kings wished for by Plato,"[30] it is tempting to speculate that *The Federalist* contemplates a kind of philosopher-founder the posthumous dura-tion of whose rule depends upon "that veneration which time bestows on everything,"[31] and in particular on a regime well-founded. But once founded, it is a system that has no necessary place and makes no provision for men of the founding kind.

It is clear that not all now regarded as Founding Fathers were thought by the authors of *The Federalist* to belong in that august company. Noting that "it is not a little remarkable" that all previ-ous foundings of regimes were "performed by some individual citizen of pre-eminent wisdom and approved integrity,"[32] *The Federalist* comments on the difficulty that must have been experi-enced when it was attempted to found a regime by the action of an assembly of men. I think it can be shown that *The Federalist* views that assembly, the Federal Convention, as having been subject to all the weaknesses of multitudes of men. The real founders, then, were very few in number, men learned in the new science of politics who seized upon a uniquely propitious moment when their plans were consented to first by a body of respectable men and subsequently, by equally great good fortune, by the body of citizens. As it were, America provided a rare moment when "the prejudices of the community"[33] were on the side of wisdom. Not unnaturally, then, *The Federalist* is extremely reluctant to countenance any re-opening of fundamental questions or delay in ratifying the Constitution.

This circumstance—wisdom meeting with consent—is so rare that "it is impossible for the man of pious reflection not to per-ceive in it a finger of that Almighty hand."[34] But once consent has been given to the new wisdom, when the government has

---

[29]*Federalist*, No. 10, p. 56.
[30]*Federalist*, No. 49, p. 329.
[31]*Ibid.*, p. 328.
[32]*Federalist*, No. 38, p. 233.
[33]*Federalist*, No. 49, p. 329.
[34]*Federalist*, No. 38, p. 231.

been properly founded, it will be a durable regime whose perpetuation requires nothing like the wisdom and virtue necessary for its creation. The Founding Fathers' belief that they had created a system of institutions and an arrangement of the passions and interests, that would be durable and self-perpetuating, helps explain their failure to make provision for men of their own kind to come after them. Apparently, it was thought that such men would not be needed.

But does not the intensity and kind of our modern problems seem to require of us a greater degree of reflection and public-spiritedness than the Founders thought sufficient for the men who came after them? One good way to begin that reflection would be to return to their level of thoughtfulness about fundamental political alternatives, so that we may judge for ourselves wisely regarding the profound issues that face us. I know of no better beginning for that thoughtfulness than a full and serious contemplation of the political theory that informed the origin of the Republic, of the thought and intention of those few men who fully grasped what the "assembly of demi-gods" was doing.

Men of Little Faith:
The Anti-Federalists on the
Nature of Representative Government

CECELIA M. KENYON

One of the gravest defects of the late Charles Beard's economic interpretation of the Constitution is the limited perspective it has encouraged in those who have accepted it, and the block to fruitful investigation of the ideas and institutions of the Revolutionary Age to which it has been conducive. Like many theories influential in both the determination and the interpretation of historical events, Beard's thesis and its implications were never carefully analyzed either by himself or his followers. As a result, its impact on the study of American history produced certain effects not

Reprinted with permission from *The William and Mary Quarterly*, 3rd ser., XII, No. 1 (January, 1955), 3-43.

anticipated, which Beard himself must surely have regretted. The economic interpretation employed by him somewhat tentatively as a tool for analysis and research quickly became a methodological stereotype and led to a stereotypical appreciation of the Constitution and of the historical context in which it was created.

Beard's failure—perhaps it was deliberate refusal—to subject his thesis to rigorous analysis or to define it with precision makes it impossible to label him a clear-cut, thorough-going economic determinist. His position was always ambiguous and ambivalent, and in his later years he explicitly repudiated any monistic theory of causation.[1] Nevertheless, the thrust of *An Economic Interpretation of the Constitution* and the effects of its thesis as applied have frequently been those of simple and uncritical commitment to a theory of economic determinism.

Of these effects, the most significant has been a disinclination to explore the theoretical foundations of the Constitution. In the chapter entitled "The Constitution as an Economic Document," Beard presented the structure of the government, particularly the system of separation of powers and checks and balances, as the institutional means chosen by the Founding Fathers to protect their property rights against invasion by democratic majorities.[2]

---

[1] A critical and definitive study of Beard as an historian has not yet been done. Interesting commentaries on the ambiguity to be found in Beard's thesis are Max Lerner's "Charles A. Beard," in his *Ideas Are Weapons* (New York, 1939), pp. 161–162, and Richard Hofstadter's "Charles Beard and the Constitution," in *Charles A. Beard: An Appraisal,* edited by Howard K. Beale (University of Kentucky Press, 1954). Hofstadter also cites the different attitudes toward the Constitution and its framers reflected in the Beards' *The Rise of American Civilization* (1927) and their *Basic History of the United States* (1944). Beale's essay in the same collection, "Charles Beard: Historian," recounts in broad terms the shifts in Beard's historiographical thought throughout his career. It is with the Beard of the earlier period that this essay is concerned, for this was the period of his most influential works.

[2] Charles A. Beard, *An Economic Interpretation of the Constitution* (New York, 1913), Ch. VI, especially pp. 154–164. See also the succinct statement in *The Economic Basis of Politics* (New York, 1922), pp. 66–67: "Under the circumstances the framers of the Constitution relied, not upon direct economic qualification, but upon checks and balances to secure the rights of property—particularly personal property—against the assaults of the farmers and the proletariat." In Charles and Mary Beard's *The Rise of American Civilization* (New York, 1927), the theme is continued: "Almost unanimous was the opinion that democracy was a dangerous thing, to be restrained, not encouraged, by the Constitution, to be given as little voice as possible in the new system, to be hampered by checks and balances." (p. 315; cf. p. 326.) It was this position which the Beards had apparently abandoned by the 1940's. The attitude of *The Republic* (1942), and of *The Basic History* (1944), is one of appreciatior. of the authors of the Constitution, not condemnation.

This interpretation, or variations of it, has been widely accepted, though it has been frequently challenged both directly and indirectly.[3] Its tendency is to dispose of the institutional thought of the men who framed the Constitution as ideological response to economic interest. The present essay offers yet another challenge to this position, not by further examination of the Constitution or its authors, but by analysis of the Anti-Federalist position of 1787–1788.

Perhaps because theirs was the losing side, the political thought of the Anti-Federalists has received much less attention than that of the Founding Fathers. Since they fought the adoption of a Constitution which they thought to be aristocratic in origin and intent, and which by Beardian criteria was inherently anti-democratic in structure, there has been some tendency to characterize them as spokesmen of eighteenth-century democracy. But their theory of republican government has never been closely analyzed, nor have the areas of agreement and disagreement between them and the Federalists been carefully defined. It is the purpose of this essay to explore these topics. A very large proportion of the people in 1787–1788 were Anti-Federalists, and a knowledge of their ideas and attitudes is essential to an understanding of American political thought in the formative years of the republic.

Implicit in this purpose is the thesis that the ideological context of the Constitution was as important in determining its form as were the economic interests and motivations of its framers, and that the failure of Beard and his followers to examine this context has rendered their interpretation of the Constitution and its origin necessary partial and unrealistic.

Beard's conclusions rested on two assumptions or arguments. One was that the framers of the Constitution were motivated by

---

[3]In 1936 Maurice Blinkoff published a study of the influence of Beard on American historiography and came to the conclusion that authors of college history textbooks had adopted Beard's views "with virtual unanimity." *The Influence of Charles A. Beard upon American Historiography*, University of Buffalo Studies, XII (May, 1936), p. 36. I have not conducted a comprehensive survey, but it seems to me that Blinkoff's conclusions would probably not be accurate for today.

For challenges to the Beard position, the reader may consult the survey of reviews of *An Economic Interpretation of the Constitution* cited in Blinkoff, as well as some of the selections in the *Amherst Problems in American Civilization* series; Earl Latham, editor, *The Declaration of Independence and the Constitution* (Boston, 1949), though this collection is, in the opinion of the author, biased in favor of the Beard interpretation. See also B. F. Wright, "The Origin of Separation of Powers in America," *Economica*, May, 1933; and "The Federalist on the Nature of Political Man," *Ethics*, Vol. LIX, No. 2, Part II (January, 1949); and Douglass Adair, "The Tenth Federalist Revisited," *William and Mary Quarterly*, 3rd ser., Vol. VIII (January, 1951).

their class and perhaps their personal economic interests; a great deal of evidence, drawn from more or less contemporary records, was presented to support this part of the thesis. A second assumption was that the system of separation of powers and checks and balances written into the Constitution was undemocratic. In making this second assumption Beard was more influenced by the ideas of the Populist and Progressive movements of his own time, I think, than by a study of the political beliefs current in 1787. He was preoccupied in 1913 with his period's interest in reforming the structure of the national government to make it more democratic, which by his standards meant more responsible to simple majority rule. Thus he judged an eighteenth-century frame of government by a twentieth-century political doctrine. The effect was to suggest by implication that the men who in 1787–1788 thought the Constitution aristocratic and antagonistic to popular government thought so for the same reasons as Beard.[4] The evidence shows clearly that their reasons were frequently and substantially different. These differences serve to illuminate the context of the Constitution and to illustrate the evolutionary character of American political thought.

II

At the center of the theoretical expression of Anti-Federalist opposition to increased centralization of power in the national government was the belief that republican government was possible only for a relatively small territory and a relatively small

---

[4]There is no doubt at all that many of the Anti-Federalists did regard the Constitution as dangerous and aristocratic, and its framers and supporters likewise. They were acutely suspicious of it because of its class origin and were on the lookout for every evidence of bias in favor of the "aristocrats" who framed it. Note, for example, the attitude of Amos Singletary expressed in the Massachusetts ratifying convention: "These lawyers, and men of learning and moneyed men, that talk so finely, and gloss over matters so smoothly, to make us poor illiterate people swallow down the pill, expect to get into Congress themselves; they expect to be managers of this Constitution, and get all the power and all the money into their own hands, and then they will swallow up all us little folks like the great *Leviathan*; yes, just as the whale swallowed up Jonah!" Jonathan Elliot, *The Debates in Several State Conventions on the Adoption of the Federal Constitution as Recommended by the General Convention at Philadelphia, in 1787*, Second Edition, 5 vols. (Philadelphia, 1896), II, p. 102. See also reference to this attitude in a letter from Rufus King to James Madison, January 27, 1788. This letter is to be found in the *Documentary History of the Constitution of the United States of America, 1786–1870* (Washington, 1894–1905), 5 vols.; IV, p. 459. A similar feeling was reported to exist in the New Hampshire convention. See John Langdon to George Washington, February 28, 1788, *ibid.*, p. 524.

and homogeneous population. James Winthrop of Massachusetts expressed a common belief when he said, "The idea of an un-compounded republick, on an average one thousand miles in length, and eight hundred in breadth, and containing six millions of white inhabitants all reduced to the same standard of morals, of habits, and of laws, is in itself an absurdity, and contrary to the whole experience of mankind."[5] The last part of this statement, at least, was true; history was on the side of the Anti-Federalists. So was the authority of contemporary political thought. The name of Montesquieu carried great weight, and he had taught that republican governments were appropriate for small territories only. He was cited frequently, but his opinion would probably not have been accepted had it not reflected their own experience and inclinations. As colonials they had enjoyed self-government in colony-size packages only and had not sought to extend its operation empire-wise. It is significant that the various proposals for colonial representation in Parliament never grew deep roots during the debate preceding the Revolution. This association of self-government with relatively small geographical units rein-forced Montesquieu's doctrine and led to further generalizations. A large republic was impossible, it was argued, because the center of government must necessarily be distant from the people. Their interest would then naturally decrease; and when this happened, "it would not suit the genius of the people to assist in the govern-ment," and "Nothing would support the government, in such a case as that, but military coercion."[6] Patrick Henry argued that republican government for a continent was impossible because it was "a work too great for human wisdom."[7]

Associated with the argument regarding size was the assump-tion that any people who were to govern themselves must be relatively homogeneous in interest, opinion, habits, and mores. The theme was not systematically explored, but it apparently stemmed from the political relativism prevalent at the time,[8] and

---

[5]The *Agrippa* Letters in Paul Leicester Ford, *Essays on the Constitution of the United States* (Brooklyn, 1892), p. 65. See also pp. 91–92.

[6]Elliot, IV, p. 52.

[7]Elliot, III, p. 164; cf. III, pp. 607 ff.; II, pp. 69, 335; the *Centinel* Letters in John Bach McMaster and Frederick D. Stone, editors, *Pennsylvania and the Federal Constitution, 1787–1788* (Historical Society of Pennsylvania, 1888), p. 572; R. H. Lee, "Letters of a Federal Farmer," in Paul Leicester Ford, *Pamphlets on the Constitution of the United States* (Brooklyn, 1888), p. 288; George Clinton, *Cato*, in Ford, *Essays*, pp. 256 ff.

[8]Political relativism had long been a part of the colonial heritage. Seven-teenth-century Puritans, who were sure that God had regulated many aspects of life with remarkable precision, believed that He had left each people

from the recent experience of conflicts of interest between the colonies and Great Britain, and later between various states and sections of the new confederation.

It is not easy to measure the relative strength of national and state sentiment in either individuals or groups,[9] but it is clear that the Anti-Federalists were conscious of, and emphasized, the cultural diversity of the peoples in the thirteen states. They argued that no one set of laws could operate over such diversity. Said a Southerner, "We see plainly that men who come from New England are different from us."[10] He did not wish to be governed either with or by such men. Neither did the New Englanders wish to share a political roof with Southerners. "The inhabitants of warmer climates are more dissolute in their manners, and less industrious, than in colder countries. A degree of severity is, therefore, necessary with one which would cramp the spirit of the other. . . . It is impossible for one code of laws to suit Georgia and Massachusetts."[11] To place both types of men under the same government would be abhorrent and quite incompatible with the retention of liberty. Either the new government would collapse, or it would endeavor to stamp out diversity and level all citizens to a new uniformity in order to survive. Such was the reasoning of the leading New England publicist, James Winthrop. His indebtedness to Montesquieu is obvious. His failure to grasp the principles of the new federalism is also clear; for the purposes of this argument, and indeed for almost all of their arguments, he and his colleagues refused to consider the proposed government as one of limited, enumerated powers. They constantly spoke and wrote as if the scope and extent of its powers would be the same as those of the respective state governments, or of a unified national government.[12]

In addition to the absence of cultural homogeneity, the Anti-Federalists emphasized the clash of specific economic and political

---

considerable freedom in the choice of their form of government. The secularized legacy of this belief prevailed throughout the era of framing state and national constitutions. Fundamental principles derived from natural law were of course universally valid, and certain "political maxims" regarding the structure of the government very nearly so, but the embodiment of these general truths in concrete political forms was necessarily determined by the nature and circumstances of the people involved.

[9]On this subject see John C. Ranney, "The Bases of American Federalism," *William and Mary Quarterly*, 3rd ser., Vol. III, No. 1 (January, 1946).

[10]Elliot, IV, p. 24.

[11]From the *Agrippa* Letters, Ford, *Essays*, p. 64.

[12]It was this misunderstanding of the proposed new system which Madison attempted to remove in *Federalist* 39.

interests. These were primarily sectional,[13] and were of more acute concern in the South than in the North. In Virginia, for example, George Mason expressed the fear that the power of Congress to regulate commerce might be the South's downfall. In Philadelphia he had argued that this power be exercised by a two-thirds majority, and he now feared that by requiring only a simple majority "to make all commercial and navigation laws, the five southern states (whose produce and circumstances are totally different from those of the eight northern and eastern states) will be ruined. . . ."[14] It was also argued in several of the Southern conventions that a majority of the Eastern states might conspire to close the Mississippi,[15] and that they might eventually interfere with the institution of slavery.[16] In New England and the Middle states, there was less feeling that the interests of the entire section were in jeopardy, and therefore less discussion of these concrete issues and their divisive effect. One writer did strike out at the Federalist plea for a transcendent nationalism and repudiated the notion of sacrificing local interests to a presumed general interest as unrealistic and prejudicial to freedom. "It is vain to tell us that we ought to overlook local interests. It is only by protecting local concerns that the interest of the whole is preserved." He went on to say that men entered into society for egoistic rather than altruistic motives, that having once done so, all were bound to contribute equally to the common welfare, and that to call for sacrifices of local interest was to violate this principle of equality and to subvert "the foundation of free government."[17]

There was much to be said for Winthrop's argument. It was an unequivocal statement of the principle that self-interest is the primary bond of political union. It was also an expression of an attitude which has always played a large part in our national politics: a refusal to sacrifice—sometimes even to subordinate— the welfare of a part to that of the whole. Pursuit of an abstract national interest has sometimes proved dangerous, and there was a healthy toughness in the Anti-Federalist insistence on the im-

---

[13]Curiously enough, the Big-Little State fight, which almost broke up the Convention, played very little part in the ratification debates. And ironically one of the evidences of ideological unity which made the "more perfect union" possible was the similarity of arguments put forth by the Anti-Federalists in their respective states.

[14]"Objections," Ford, *Pamphlets*, p. 331.

[15]Elliot, III, p. 326.

[16]Elliot, IV, pp. 272–273.

[17]*Agrippa* Letters, Ford, *Essays*, p. 73.

portance of local interests. But Winthrop skirted around the really difficult questions raised by his argument, which were also inherent in the Anti-Federalist position that the size of the United States and the diversity which existed among them were too great to be consistent with one republican government operating over the whole. No one would deny that a certain amount of unity or consensus is required for the foundation of popular, constitutional government; not very many people—now or in 1787—would go as far as Rousseau and insist on virtually absolute identity of interest and opinion. The Anti-Federalists were surprisingly close to Rousseau and to the notions of republicanism which influenced him, but they were sensible, practical men and did not attempt to define their position precisely. Consequently they left untouched two difficult questions: how much, and what kind of unity is required for the foundation of any republican government, large or small; and how, in the absence of perfect uniformity, are differences of opinion and interest to be resolved?

III

The Anti-Federalist theory of representation was closely allied to the belief that republican government could operate only over a small area. The proposed Constitution provided that the first House of Representatives should consist of sixty-five members, and that afterwards the ratio of representation should not exceed one representative for thirty thousand people. This provision was vigorously criticized and was the chief component of the charge that the Constitution was not sufficiently democratic. The argument was two-fold: first, that sixty-five men could not possibly represent the multiplicity of interests spread throughout so great a country; second, that those most likely to be left out would be of the more democratic or "middling" elements in society. The minority who voted against ratification in the Pennsylvania Convention calculated that the combined quorums of the House and Senate was only twenty-five, and concluded that this number plus the President could not possibly represent "the sense and views of three or four millions of people, diffused over so extensive a territory, comprising such various climates, products, habits, interests, and opinions. . . ."[18] This argument, accompanied with

---

[18]"Address and Reasons of Dissent of the Minority of the Convention of Pennsylvania to their Constituents," reprinted in McMaster and Stone, *Pennsylvania and the Constitution*, p. 472.

the same calculus, was repeated many times during the ratification debate.

Almost all of the leaders of the opposition laid down what they believed to be the requisites of adequate representation, and there is a remarkable similarity in their definitions. George Mason, speaking in the Virginia Convention against giving the central government the power of taxation, based his argument on the inadequacy of representation as measured by his criteria: "To make representation real and actual, the number of representatives ought to be adequate; they ought to mix with the people, think as they think, feel as they feel,—ought to be perfectly amenable to them, and thoroughly acquainted with their interest and condition."[19] In his *Letters of a Federal Farmer*, Richard Henry Lee developed the same idea further:

. . . a full and equal representation is that which possesses the same interests, feelings, opinions, and views the people themselves would were they all assembled—a fair representation, therefore, should be so regulated, that every order of men in the community, according to the common course of elections, can have a share in it—in order to allow professional men, merchants, traders, farmers, mechanics, etc. to bring a just proportion of their best informed men respectively into the legislature, the representation must be considerably numerous.[20]

It was the contention of the Anti-Federalists that because of the small size of the House of Representatives, the middle and lower orders in society would not be elected to that body, and that consequently this, the only popular organ of the government, would not be democratic at all. It would, instead, be filled by aristocrats, possibly by military heroes and demagogues.[21] Why should this be? Lee asserted simply that it would be "in the nature of things." Mason seems to have assumed it without any comment or argument. Patrick Henry reasoned that since the candidates would be chosen from large electoral districts rather than from counties, they would not all be known by the electors, and "A common man must ask a man of influence how he is to proceed, and for whom he must vote. The elected, therefore, will be careless of the interest of the electors. It will be a common job to

---

[19]Elliot, III, p. 32.

[20]Ford, *Pamphlets*, pp. 288–289.

[21]This idea appeared frequently in Anti-Federalist arguments. See, for example, the "Address and Dissent of the Minority. . . ," McMaster and Stone, *Pennsylvania and the Constitution*, pp. 472, 479; Lee, "Letters of a Federal Farmer," Ford, *Pamphlets*, p. 295; Elliot, III, pp. 266–267, 426 (George Mason).

extort the suffrages of the common people for the most influential characters."[22] This argument reflects one of the basic fears of the Anti-Federalists: loss of personal, direct contact with and knowledge of their representatives. They sensed quite accurately that an enlargement of the area of republican government would lead to a more impersonal system, and that the immediate, individual influence of each voter over his representative would be lessened.

The most elaborate explanation of the anticipated results of the electoral process was given by the moderate Anti-Federalist in New York, Melancton Smith. He argued that very few men of the "middling" class would choose to run for Congress, because the office would be "highly elevated and distinguished," the style of living probably "high." Such circumstances would "render the place of a representative not a desirable one to sensible, substantial men, who have been used to walking in the plain and frugal paths of life." Even if such should choose to run for election, they would almost certainly be defeated. In a large electoral district it would be difficult for any but a person of "conspicuous military, popular, civil, or legal talents" to win. The common people were more likely to be divided among themselves than the great, and "There will be scarcely a chance to their uniting in any other but some great man, unless in some popular demagogue, who will probably be destitute of principle. A substantial yeoman, of sense and discernment, will hardly ever be chosen."[23] Consequently, the government would be controlled by the great, would not truly reflect the interests of all groups in the community, and would almost certainly become oppressive.

Anti-Federalists in Massachusetts were also uneasy about the capacity of the people to elect a legislature which would reflect their opinions and interests. The arguments emphasized geographical as well as class divisions, and expressed the fear and suspicion felt by the western part of the state toward Boston and the other coastal towns. It was predicted that the latter would enjoy a great advantage under the new system, and this prediction was supported by a shrewd analysis in the *Cornelius* Letter:

The citizens in the seaport towns are numerous; they live compact; their interests are one; there is a constant connection and intercourse between them; they can, on any occasion, centre their votes where they please. This is not the case with those who are in the landed

---

[22]Elliot, III, p. 322.
[23]Elliot, II, p. 246.

interest; they are scattered far and wide; they have but little inter-course and connection with each other. To concert uniform plans for carrying elections of this kind is entirely out of their way. Hence, their votes if given at all, will be no less scattered than are the local situations of the voters themselves. Wherever the seaport towns agree to centre their votes, there will, of course, be the greatest number. A gentleman in the country therefore, who may aspire after a seat in Congress, or who may wish for a post of profit under the federal government, must form his connections, and unite his interest with those towns. Thus, I conceive, a foundation is laid for throwing the whole power of the federal government into the hands of those who are in the mercantile interest; and for the landed, which is the great interest of this country to lie unrepresented, forlorn and without hope.[24]

What the Anti-Federalists feared, in other words, was the superior opportunities for organized voting which they felt to be inherent in the more thickly populated areas. They shared with the authors of *The Federalist* the fear of party and faction in the eighteenth-century American sense of those words. But they also feared, as the preceding analyses show, the essence of party in its modern meaning, i.e., organizing the vote, and they wanted constituencies sufficiently small to render such organization un-necessary.

This belief that larger electoral districts would inevitably be to the advantage of the well-to-do partially explains the almost complete lack of criticism of the indirect election of the Senate and the President. If the "middling" class could not be expected to compete successfully with the upper class in Congressional elections, still less could they do so in statewide or nation-wide elections. It was a matter where size was of the essence. True representation—undistorted by party organization—could be achieved only where electoral districts were small.

IV

The conception of the representative body as a true and faithful miniature of the people themselves was the projection of an ideal —almost a poetic one. Very few of its proponents thought it could actually be realized. In the Anti-Federalist attack on the Consti-tution, it served as a foil for an extraordinary picture of antici-

---

[24]The *Cornelius* Letter is reprinted in Samuel Bannister Harding, *The Contest over the Ratification of the Federal Constitution in the State of Massachusetts* (New York, 1896). See pp. 123–124.

pated treachery on the part of the representatives to be elected under the proposed government. No distinction was made on the basis of their method of election, whether directly or indirectly by the people. All were regarded as potential tyrants.

This attack stemmed directly from the Anti-Federalist conception of human nature. They shared with their opponents many of the assumptions regarding the nature of man characteristic of American thought in the late eighteenth century. They took for granted that the dominant motive of human behavior was self-interest, and that this drive found its most extreme political expression in an insatiable lust for power. These were precisely the characteristics with which the authors of *The Federalist Papers* were preoccupied.[25] Yet the Anti-Federalists chided the Federalists for their excessive confidence in the future virtue of elected officials, and criticized the Constitution for its failure to provide adequate protection against the operation of these tyrannical drives. There is surely an amusing irony to find the Founding Fathers, who prided themselves on their realism, and who enjoy an enviable reputation for that quality today, taken to task for excessive optimism. But they had to meet this charge again and again. Thus Caldwell in the North Carolina Convention found it "remarkable,—that gentlemen, as an answer to every improper part of it [the Constitution], tell us that every thing is to be done by our own representatives, who are to be good men. There is no security that they will be so, or continue to be so."[26] In New York Robert Lansing expressed the same feeling in a passage strikingly reminiscent of the famous paragraph in Madison's *Federalist* 51:

Scruples would be impertinent, arguments would be in vain, checks would be useless, if we were certain our rulers would be good men; but for the virtuous government is not instituted: its object is to restrain and punish vice; and all free constitutions are formed with two views—to deter the governed from crime, and the governors from tyranny.[27]

---

[25]See B. F. Wright, *"The Federalist* on the Nature of Political Man," *Ethics* (January, 1949).

[26]Elliot, IV, p. 187; cf. pp. 203–204, and III, p. 494. Caldwell's statement is very similar to Madison's comment in *Federalist* 10: "It is in vain to say that enlightened statesmen will be able to adjust these clashing interests and render them all subservient to the public good. Enlightened statesmen will not always be at the helm."

[27]Elliot, II, pp. 295–296. Madison's declaration was this: "But what is government itself, but the greatest of all reflections on human nature? If men were angels, no government would be necessary. If angels were to govern men, neither external nor internal controls on government would be

This and many other similar statements might have been used interchangeably by either side in the debate, for they symbolized an attitude deeply embedded and widely dispersed in the political consciousness of the age. There were frequent references to "the natural lust of power so inherent in man";[28] to "the predominant thirst of dominion which has invariably and uniformly prompted rulers to abuse their power";[29] to "the ambition of man, and his lust for domination";[30] to rulers who would be "men of like passions," having "the same spontaneous inherent thirst for power with ourselves."[31] In Massachusetts, another delegate said, "we ought to be jealous of rulers. All the godly men we read of have failed; nay, he would not trust a 'flock of Moseses.' "[32]

It is to be noted that this dreadful lust for power was regarded as a universal characteristic of the nature of man, which could be controlled but not eradicated. The Anti-Federalists charged that the authors of the Constitution had failed to put up strong enough barriers to block this inevitably corrupting and tyrannical force. They painted a very black picture indeed of what the national representatives might and probably would do with the unchecked power conferred upon them under the provisions of the new Constitution. The "parade of imaginary horribles" has become an honorable and dependable technique of political debate, but the marvelous inventiveness of the Anti-Federalists has rarely been matched. Certainly the best achievements of their contemporary opponents were conspicuously inferior in dramatic quality, as well as incredibly unimaginative in dull adherence to at least a semblance of reality. The anticipated abuses of power, some real, some undoubtedly conjured as ammunition for debate, composed a substantial part of the case against the Constitution, and they must be examined in order to get at the temper and quality of Anti-Federalist thought as well as at its content. Their source was ordinarily a distorted interpretation of some particular clause.

One clause which was believed to lay down a constitutional road to legislative tyranny was Article I, Section 4: "The times,

---

necessary. In framing a government which is to be administered by men over men, the great difficulty lies in this: you must first enable the government to control the governed; and in the next place oblige it to control itself."

[28]Mason in Virginia, Elliot, III, p. 32.
[29]Henry in Virginia, *ibid.*, p. 436.
[30]"Letters of Luther Martin," Ford, *Essays*, p. 379.
[31]Barrell in Massachusetts, Elliot, II, p. 159.
[32]White in Massachusetts, Elliot, II, p. 28.

places, and manner of holding elections for senators and representatives, shall be prescribed in each state by the legislature thereof; but the Congress may, at any time, by law, make or alter such regulations, except as to the places of choosing senators." Here was the death clause of republican government. "This clause may destroy representation entirely," said Timothy Bloodworth of North Carolina.[33] If Congress had power to alter the times of elections, Congress might extend its tenure of office from two years to four, six, eight, ten, twenty, "or even for their natural lives."[34] Bloodworth and his colleagues feared the worst. In Massachusetts, where debate over this clause occupied a day and a half, the primary fear was that Congress, by altering the places of election, might rig them so as to interfere with a full and free expression of the people's choice. Pierce suggested that Congress could "direct that the election for Massachusetts shall be held in Boston," and then by pre-election caucus, Boston and the surrounding towns could agree on a ticket "and carry their list by a major vote."[35] In the same state the delegate who would not trust "a flock of Moseses" argued thus: "Suppose the Congress should say that none should be electors but those worth 50 or a £100 sterling; cannot they do it? Yes, said he, they can; and if any lawyer . . . can beat me out of it, I will give him ten guineas."[36] In Virginia, George Mason suggested that Congress might provide that the election in Virginia should be held only in Norfolk County, or even "go farther, and say that the election for all the states might be had in New York. . . ."[37] Patrick Henry warned, "According to the mode prescribed, Congress may tell you that they have a right to make the vote of one gentleman go as far as the votes of a hundred poor men."[38]

Any of these acts would have been a flagrant abuse of power, but no more so than that which Mason and others predicted under Article II, Section 2, which gave to the President the power to make treaties with the advice and consent of two-thirds of the senators present. This power was believed to be fraught with danger, particularly among Southerners, who feared that the majority of Northern states might use it to give up American

[33]Elliot, IV, p. 55.
[34]Elliot, IV, pp. 51–52, 55–56, 62–63, 87–88.
[35]Elliot, II, p. 22.
[36]Elliot, II, p. 28.
[37]Elliot, III, pp. 403–404.
[38]Elliot, III, p. 175. Cf. *Centinel*, McMaster and Stone, *Pennsylvania and the Constitution*, p. 598, and James Winthrop in the *Agrippa* Letters, Ford, *Essays*, p. 105.

rights of navigation on the Mississippi. The North would not have a two-thirds majority of the entire Senate, of course, but Mason suggested that when a "partial" treaty was involved, the President would not call into session senators from distant states, or those whose interests would be affected adversely, but only those he knew to be in favor of it.[39] His colleague, William Grayson, suggested the similarly treacherous prospect of such a treaty's being rushed through while members from the Southern states were momentarily absent from the floor of the Senate: "If the senators of the Southern States be gone but one hour, a treaty may be made by the rest. . . ."[40]

This fear at least had some foundation in fact—there *was* a conflict of interest between North and South over the Mississippi. It would seem that the fear expressed in North Carolina by Abbott on behalf of "the religious part of the society" was pure fantasy: "It is feared by some people, that, by the power of making treaties, they might make a treaty engaging with foreign powers to adopt the Roman Catholic religion in the United States. . . ."[41]

This was not the only provision objected to by "the religious part of the society." They were greatly displeased with the last clause of Article VI, Section 3: "but no religious test shall ever be required as a qualification to any office or public trust under the United States." In the same speech quoted above, Abbott reported, presumably on behalf of his constituents, "The exclusion of religious tests is by many thought dangerous and impolitic." For without such, "They suppose . . . pagans, deists, and Mahometans might obtain offices among us, and that the senators and representatives might all be pagans."[42] David Caldwell thought that the lack of a religious qualification constituted "an invitation for Jews and pagans of every kind to come among us," and that since the Christian religion was acknowledged to be the best for making "good members of society . . . those gentlemen who formed this Constitution should not have given this invitation to Jews and heathens."[43] Federalist James Iredell reported a pamphlet in circulation "in which the author states, as a very serious danger,

---

[39]Elliot, III, p. 499.

[40]Elliot, III, p. 502.

[41]Elliot, IV, pp. 191–192. Abbot was not an Anti-Federalist, but was, according to L. I. Trenholme, in *The Ratification of the Federal Constitution in North Carolina* (New York, 1932), something of an independent. See p. 178. He voted for ratification.

[42]Elliot, IV, p. 192.

[43]*Ibid.*, p. 199.

that the pope of Rome might be elected President."[44] This unwittingly placed fresh ammunition at the disposal of the opposition. An Anti-Federalist admitted that he had not at first perceived this danger and conceded that it was not an immediate one. "But," said he, "let us remember that we form a government for millions not yet in existence. I have not the art of divination. In the course of four or five hundred years, I do not know how it will work. This is most certain, that Papists may occupy that chair, and Mahometans may take it. I see nothing against it. There is a disqualification, I believe, in every state in the Union—it ought to be so in this system."[45]

It is to be noted that these fears were fears of the majority of electors as well as of their elected representatives, and that these statements can hardly be said to glow with the spirit of liberty and tolerance. These beliefs were undoubtedly not shared by all Anti-Federalists, but they would not have been expressed so vigorously in the convention debates had they not represented a sizeable segment of constituent opinion.

Another provision severely and dramatically criticized was that which gave to Congress exclusive jurisdiction over the future site of the national capital and other property to be purchased for forts, arsenals, dockyards, and the like.[46] It was predicted that the ten-mile square area would become an enormous den of tyranny and iniquity. In New York George Clinton warned "that the ten miles square . . . would be the asylum of the base, idle, avaricious and ambitious. . . ."[47] In Virginia Patrick Henry pointed out that this provision, combined with the necessary and proper clause, gave Congress a right to pass "any law that may facilitate the execution of their acts," and within the specified area to hang "any man who shall act contrary to their commands . . . without benefit of clergy."[48] George Mason argued that the place would

---

[44]*Ibid.*, p. 195.

[45]*Ibid.*, p. 215. This quotation transmits a sense of the method of Anti-Federalist debate admirably. A similar statement by Amos Singletary of Massachusetts gives something of the flavor of the thinking done by the honest and pious patriots of the back country, in which opposition to the Constitution was strong: "The Hon. Mr. Singletary thought we were giving up all our privileges, as there was no provision that men in power should have any *religion*, and though he hoped to see Christians, yet by the Constitution, a Papist, or an Infidel, was as eligible as they. It had been said that men had not degenerated; he did not think that men were better now than when men after God's own heart did wickedly. He thought, in this instance, we were giving great power to we know not whom." Elliot, II, p. 44.

[46]Article I, Section 8.

[47]The *Cato* Letters; reprinted in Ford, *Essays*, p. 265.

[48]Elliot, III, p. 436.

make a perfect lair for hit-and-run tyrants. For if any of the government's "officers, or creatures, should attempt to oppress the people, or should actually perpetuate the blackest deed, he has nothing to do but get into the ten miles square. Why was this dangerous power given?"[49] One man observed that the Constitution did not specify the location of this site, and that therefore Congress was perfectly free to seat itself and the other offices of government in Peking. All in all, a terrible prospect: the Pope as President, operating from a base in Peking, superintending a series of hangings without benefit of clergy! Or worse.

There was no bill of rights in the Constitution. This caused genuine fear for the security of some of the liberties thus left unprotected. The fear itself, though real and well founded, frequently found expression in melodramatically picturesque terms. The Anti-Federalists sometimes mentioned freedom of the press and freedom of conscience,[50] but they were primarily preoccupied with the failure of the Constitution to lay down the precious and venerable common-law rules of criminal procedure. The Constitution guaranteed the right of trial by jury in all criminal cases[51] except impeachment, but it did not list the procedural safeguards associated with that right. There was no specification that the trial should be not merely in the state but in the vicinity where the crime was committed (which was habitually identified with the neighborhood of the accused); there were no provisions made for the selection of the jury or of the procedure to be followed; there were no guarantees of the right to counsel, of the right not to incriminate oneself; there was no prohibition against cruel and unusual punishments. In short, there were few safeguards upon which the citizen accused of crime could rely.[52] Apprehen-

---

[49]*Ibid.*, p. 431.

[50]The expressed fear that Roman Catholicism might be established by treaty did not reflect any strong belief in religious freedom. It was nothing more than simple anti-Catholicism, as the remarks about the lack of a religious qualification for office-holding clearly indicate. On the other hand, there was some concern expressed in Pennsylvania over the rights of conscientious objectors to military service. See McMaster and Stone, *Pennsylvania and the Constitution*, pp. 480–481.

[51]Article III, Section 2. The Constitution made no provision for jury trial in civil cases, because different procedures in the several states had made the formulation of a general method difficult. The Anti-Federalists leaped to the conclusion that the lack of a written guarantee of this right meant certain deprivation of it, and they professed to be thoroughly alarmed. But their primary fear centered around what they regarded as the inadequate guarantees of the right of trial by jury in criminal cases.

[52]If George Washington's word is to be trusted, the actions of the Founding Fathers with respect to trial by jury and a bill of rights did not stem from any sinister motives. In a letter to Lafayette on April 28, 1788, he

sion concerning the latitude left to Congress in this matter was expressed in several conventions;[53] it was Holmes of Massachusetts who painted the most vivid and fearful picture of the possible fate of the unfortunate citizen who ran afoul of federal law. Such an individual might be taken away and tried by strangers far from home; his jury might be handpicked by the sheriff, or hold office for life; there was no guarantee that indictment should be by grand jury only, hence it might be by information of the attorney-general, "in consequence of which the most innocent person in the commonwealth may be . . . dragged from his home, his friends, his acquaintance, and confined in prison. . . ." "On the whole," said Holmes, ". . . we shall find Congress possessed of powers enabling them to institute judicatories little less inauspicious than a certain tribunal in Spain, which has long been the disgrace of Christendom: I mean that diabolical institution, the *Inquisition*. . . . They are nowhere restrained from inventing the most cruel and unheard-of punishments and annexing them to crimes; and there is no constitutional check on them, but that *racks* and *gibbets* may be amongst the most mild instruments of their discipline."[54]

Should Congress have attempted any of these actions, it would have amounted to a virtual *coup d'état* and a repudiation of republicanism.[55] The advocates of the Constitution argued that such abuse of power could not reasonably be expected on the part of representatives elected by the people themselves. This argument

gave this explanation: ". . . There was not a member of the convention, I believe, who had the least objection to what is contended for by the Advocates for a *Bill of Rights* and *Tryal by Jury*. The first, where the people evidently retained everything which they did not in express terms give up, was considered nugatory. . . . And as to the second, it was only the difficulty of establishing a mode which should not interfere with the fixed modes of any of the States, that induced the Convention to leave it, as a matter of future adjustment." *Documentary History of the Constitution*, Vol. IV, pp. 601–602.

[53]In New York, see Elliot, II, p. 400; Virginia, III, pp. 523 ff., North Carolina, IV, pp. 143, 150, 154–155.

[54]Elliot, II, pp. 109–111.

[55]This method of arguing drove the Federalists to exasperation more than once, as when one delegate in the Virginia Convention, an infrequent speaker, lost patience with Patrick Henry's "bugbears of hobgoblins" and suggested that "If the gentleman does not like this government, let him go and live among the Indians." Elliot, III, p. 580; cf. pp. 632, 644. Also note the reporter's tongue-in-cheek note on Henry's opposition to the President's power of Commander-in-Chief: "Here Mr. Henry strongly and pathetically expatiated on the probability of the President's enslaving America, and the horrid consequences that must result." *Ibid.*, p. 60. But Henry, who was so good at this technique himself, attacked it in his opponents. See *ibid.*, p. 140.

was not satisfactory to the Anti-Federalists. They reiterated again and again the universal perfidy of man, especially men entrusted with political power, and emphasized the necessity of providing adequate protection against manifestations of human depravity. They charged that the authors and advocates of the Constitution were about to risk their liberties and those of all of the people on the slim possibility that the men to be elected to office in the new government would be, and would always be, good men.[56]

The Federalists also argued that election would serve as a check, since the people could remove unfaithful or unsatisfactory representatives, and since knowledge of this would make the latter refrain from incurring the displeasure of their constituents. This argument was flatly rejected. Patrick Henry stated his position emphatically during the course of his objection to Congressional power of taxation:

I shall be told in this place, that those who are to tax us are our representatives. To this I answer, that there is no real check to prevent their ruining us. There is no actual responsibility. The only semblance of a check is the negative power of not re-electing them. This, sir, is but a feeble barrier, when their personal interest, their ambition and avarice, come to be put in contrast with the happiness of the people. All checks founded on anything but self-love, will not avail.[57]

In North Carolina the same opinion was expressed in a rather remarkable interchange. Taylor objected to the method of impeachment on the ground that since the House of Representatives drew up the bill of indictment, and the Senate acted upon it, the members of Congress themselves would be virtually immune to this procedure. Governor Johnston answered that impeachment was not an appropriate remedy for legislative misrule, and that "A representative is answerable to no power but his constituents. He is accountable to no being under heaven but the people who appointed him." To this, Taylor responded simply, "that it now appeared to him in a still worse light than before."[58] Johnston stated one of the great principles of representative government; it merely deepened Taylor's fear of Congress. He and his fellow Anti-Federalists strongly wished for what Madison had referred to as "auxiliary precautions" against possible acts of legislative tyranny.

[56]See above, pp. 13–15.
[57]Elliot, III, p. 167; cf. p. 327.
[58]Elliot, IV, pp. 32–34.

V

These additional safeguards were of two kinds: more explicit limitations written into the Constitution, and more institutional checks to enforce these limitations.

In recent years the Constitution has been much admired for its brevity, its generality, its freedom from the minutiae which characterized nineteenth-century constitutions. These qualities were feared and not admired by the Anti-Federalists. They wanted detailed explicitness which would confine the discretion of Congressional majorities within narrow boundaries. One critic complained of "a certain darkness, duplicity and studied ambiguity of expression running through the whole Constitution. . . ."[59] Another said that "he did not believe there existed a social compact on the face of the earth so vague and so indefinite as the one now on the table."[60] A North Carolinian demanded to know, "Why not use expressions that were clear and unequivocal?"[61] Later, he warned, "Without the most express restrictions, Congress may trample on your rights."[62] Williams of New York expressed the general feeling when he said in that state's convention, "I am, sir, for certainty in the establishment of a constitution which is not only to operate upon us, but upon millions yet unborn."[63] These men wanted everything down in black and white, with no latitude of discretion or interpretation left to their representatives in Congress. It was an attitude which anticipated the later trend toward lengthy constitutions filled with innumerable and minute restrictions on the legislatures.

To no avail did the Federalists argue that if future representatives should indeed prove to be so treacherous and tyrannical as to commit the horrible deeds suggested, then mere guarantees on paper would not stop them for a minute. It is easy to call the Anti-Federalist attitude unrealistic, but to do so is to miss a large part of its significance. Like the Founding Fathers, like all men

---

[59]Thomas B. Wait to George Thatcher, January 8, 1788, in "The Thatcher Papers," selected from the papers of Hon. George Thatcher, and communicated by Captain Goodwin, U.S.A., *The Historical Magazine*, November and December, 1869 (Second Series, Vols. 15–16), No. V, p. 262.
[60]Elliot, III, p. 583.
[61]Elliot, IV, p. 68; cf. pp. 70, 153, 154–155, 168.
[62]*Ibid.*, p. 167.
[63]Elliot, II, p. 339.

of their age, they were great constitutionalists. They were also first-generation republicans, still self-consciously so, and aware that their precious form of government was as yet an experiment and had not proved its capacity for endurance. Its greatest enemy was man's lust for power, and the only thing which could hold this in check, they were convinced, was a carefully written and properly constructed constitution. They placed even greater emphasis on the structure of government than did the Founding Fathers, and refused to take for granted, as the latter did, that the "genius" of the country was republican, and that the behavior of the men to be placed in office would in general be republican also.

The Anti-Federalists wanted a more rigid system of separation of powers, more numerous and more effective checks and balances, than the Founding Fathers had provided.[64] They thought this elementary principle of good government, this "political maxim," had been violated, and that corruption leading to tyranny would be the inevitable result. That the doctrine celebrated by Montesquieu did enjoy the status of "maxim" seems unquestionable. Violation of separation of powers was one of George Mason's major objections to the Constitution.[65] Richard Henry Lee made the same protest,[66] and further lamented that there were no "checks in the formation of the government, to secure the rights of the people against the usurpations of those they appoint to govern. . . ."[67] James Monroe said that he could "see no real checks in it."[68] It is no wonder that an obscure member of the Virginia Convention, when he rose with great diffidence to make his only speech, chose safe and familiar ground to cover:

That the legislative, executive, and judicial powers should be separate and distinct, in all free governments, is a political fact so well established, that I presume I shall not be thought arrogant, when I affirm that no country ever did, or ever can, long remain free, where they are blended. All the states have been in this sentiment when they

---

[64]Thus in *The Federalist* 47, Madison felt obliged to defend the Constitution against this charge. This was first pointed out to me by B. F. Wright and was the origin of the present essay. See the discussion in his article "*The Federalist* on the Nature of Political Man," *Ethics* (January, 1949), especially pp. 7 ff.

[65]"Objections of the Hon. George Mason, to the proposed Federal Constitution. Addressed to the Citizens of Virginia." Ford, *Pamphlets*, p. 330.

[66]"Letters of a Federal Farmer," Ford, *Pamphlets*, p. 299.

[67]*Ibid.*, p. 318.

[68]Elliot, III, p. 219.

formed their state constitutions, and therefore have guarded against the danger; and every schoolboy in politics must be convinced of the propriety of the observation; and yet, by the proposed plan, the legislative and executive powers are closely united. . . .[69]

In Pennsylvania, whose Revolutionary state constitution had embodied very little of separation of powers, an apparent return to Montesquieu's doctrine led to criticism of the Constitution. In the ratifying convention, one of the amendments submitted had for its purpose "That the legislative, executive, and judicial powers be kept separate. . . ."[70] In that same state, the leading Anti-Federalist pamphleteer "Centinel," who is believed to have been either George Bryan, a probable co-author of the 1776 Constitution and formerly in sympathy with the ideas of Tom Paine on this subject, or his son Samuel, now expressed himself in the usual manner:

This mixture of the legislative and executive moreover highly tends to corruption. The chief improvement in government, in modern times, has been the complete separation of the great distinctions of power; placing the *legislative* in different hands from those which hold the *executive;* and again severing the *judicial* part from the ordinary *administrative.* "When the legislative and executive powers (says Montesquieu) are united in the same person, or in the same body of magistrates, there can be no liberty."[71]

The Anti-Federalists were just as unequivocal about the inadequacy of the Constitution's system of checks and balances. Patrick Henry hit his top form when he took up the matter in Virginia: "There will be no checks, no real balances, in this government. What can avail your specious, imaginary balances, your rope-dancing, chain-rattling, ridiculous ideal checks and contrivances?"[72] Later in the Convention he argued that what checks there were had no practical value at all—for reasons which must cloud his reputation as a spokesman for the masses imbued with the radical spirit of Revolutionary democracy: "To me it appears that there is no check in that government. The President, senators, and representatives, all, immediately or mediately, are the

---

[69] *Ibid.,* p. 608.
[70] McMaster and Stone, *Pennsylvania and the Constitution,* p. 423. See also pp. 475–477 for discussion back of this.
[71] McMaster and Stone, *Pennsylvania and the Constitution,* p. 587.
[72] Elliot, III, p. 54.

choice of the people."[73] His views were echoed by his colleague, William Grayson.[74]

In New York, Melancton Smith returned to the subject several times, arguing, because there would eventually be corruption in Congress, "It is wise to multiply checks to a greater degree than the present state of things requires."[75] In Massachusetts James Winthrop tied up the concept of separation of powers with checks and balances very neatly. "It is now generally understood that it is for the security of the people that the powers of the government should be lodged in different branches. By this means publick business will go on when they all agree, and stop when they disagree. The advantage of checks in government is thus manifested where the concurrence of different branches is necessary to the same act. . . ."[76]

There can be little doubt that the Anti-Federalists were united in their desire to put more checks on the new government. This was natural, since they greatly feared it. Expressions of the opposite opinion were extremely rare. Rawlins Lowndes in South Carolina remarked casually and without elaboration that it was possible to have too many checks on a government.[77] George Clinton and the Pennsylvanian "Centinel" both warned that a government might become so complex that the people could not understand it,[78] but both men expressed the usual fear of abuse

---

[73]*Ibid.*, p. 164. He then went on to point out that the British House of Lords constituted a check against both the King and the Commons, and that this check was founded on "self-love," i.e., the desire of the Lords to protect their interests against attack from either of the other two branches of the government. This consideration, he said, prevailed upon him "to pronounce the British government superior, in this respect, to any government that ever was in any country. Compare this with your Congressional checks. . . . Have you a resting-place like the British government? Where is the rock of your salvation? . . . Where are your checks? You have no hereditary nobility—an order of men to whom human eyes can be cast up for relief; for, says the Constitution, there is no title of nobility to be granted. . . . In the British government there are real balances and checks: in this system there are only ideal balances." *Ibid.*, pp. 164–165.

[74]*Ibid.*, pp. 421, 563. Grayson also expressed his preference for a form of government—if there was to be a national government at all—far less popular than the one proposed. He favored one strikingly similar to the plan Hamilton had suggested in Philadelphia, a president and senate elected for life, and a lower house elected for a three-year term. See *Elliot*, III, p. 279.

[75]Elliot, II, pp. 259, 315.

[76]*Agrippa* Letters in Ford, *Essays*, p. 116.

[77]Elliot, IV, pp. 308–309.

[78]Clinton's *Cato* Letters in Ford, *Essays*, p. 257; *Centinel* in McMaster and Stone, *Pennsylvania and the Constitution*, p. 569. "Centinel" expressed a desire for a unicameral legislature.

of power,[79] and "Centinel" paid his respects to Montesquieu and explicitly criticized the inadequacy of checks by the President or the House of Representatives on the Senate.[80]

Thus no one, so far as I have been able to discover, attacked the general validity of the system of separation of powers and checks and balances. The Anti-Federalists were staunch disciples of Montesquieu on this subject, and they would have found quite unacceptable J. Allen Smith's dictum that "The system of checks and balances must not be confused with democracy; it is opposed to and cannot be reconciled with the theory of popular government."[81]

Although there was much oratory about the Founding Fathers' deviation from Montesquieu's doctrine, there were surprisingly few proposals for specific alterations in the structure of the new government. Of these, the most important was a change in the relationship between President and Senate. The latter's share in the treaty-making and appointing powers was believed to be a dangerous blending of executive and legislative power which ought to have been avoided. Possibly because of their recent memory of the role of the colonial governor's council, possibly because there was no clear provision in the Constitution for an executive cabinet or council, the Anti-Federalists saw the Senate very much in the latter's role and expected it to play a very active and continuous part in giving advice to the President. This was clearly contrary to the doctrine of the celebrated Montesquieu—at least it seemed so to them.

The result would certainly be some form of joint Presidential-Senatorial tyranny, it was argued, but as to which of the two departments would be the stronger of the "partners in crime," the Anti-Federalists were not agreed. Patrick Henry said that the President, with respect to the treaty-making power, "as distinguished from the Senate, is nothing."[82] Grayson, with the North-South division in mind, predicted a *quid pro quo* alliance between the President and "the seven Eastern states." "He will accommodate himself to their interests in forming treaties, and they will continue him perpetually in office."[83] Mason predicted a "marriage" between the President and Senate: "They will be continu-

---

[79]Clinton in Ford, *Essays,* pp. 261, 266; *Centinel* in McMaster and Stone, *Pennsylvania and the Constitution,* p. 617.

[80]McMaster and Stone, *Pennsylvania and the Constitution,* pp. 586–587, 475–477.

[81]*The Spirit of American Government* (New York, 1907), p. 9.

[82]Elliot, III, p. 353.

[83]*Ibid.,* p. 492.

ally supporting and aiding each other: they will always consider their interest as united. . . . The executive and legislative powers, thus connected, will destroy all balances. . . ."[84] "Centinel" of Pennsylvania also feared that the President would not be strong enough to resist pressure from the Senate, and that he would join with them as "the head of the aristocratic junto."[85] Spencer of North Carolina, in support of a remedy in which all of the above men concurred, argued that with an advisory council entirely separate from the legislature, and chosen from the separate states, the President "would have that independence which is necessary to form the intended check upon the acts passed by the legislature before they obtain the sanction of laws."[86]

Although the prevailing opinion thus seemed to be that the President was not strong enough, there were some who believed that he was too strong. George Clinton argued that the extensive powers given to him, combined with his long tenure of office, gave him both "power and time sufficient to ruin his country." Furthermore, since he had no proper council to assist him while the Senate was recessed, he would be without advice, or get it from "minions and favorites"—or "a great council of state will grow out of the principal officers of the great departments, the most dangerous council in a free country."[87]

One man in North Carolina, the only one to the best of my knowledge, departed from the ordinary Anti-Federalist line of attack and criticized the executive veto from a clear majoritarian position. It was Lancaster, who projected the hypothetical case of a bill which passed the House of Representatives unanimously, the Senate by a large majority, was vetoed by the President and returned to the Senate, where it failed to get a two-thirds vote. The House would never see it again, said Mr. Lancaster, and thus, "This is giving a power to the President to overrule fifteen members of the Senate and every member of the House of Representatives."[88]

Except for Lancaster, most Anti-Federalists feared the Senate more than the President, but all feared the two in combination and wanted some checks against them. The separate advisory council for the President was one, and shorter terms and/or compulsory rotation for Senators and President, plus the power

---

[84]*Ibid.*, pp. 493–494.
[85]McMaster and Stone, *Pennsylvania and the Constitution*, p. 586.
[86]Elliot, IV, pp. 117–118.
[87]*Cato Letters*, Ford, *Essays*, pp. 261–262.
[88]Elliot, IV, p. 214.

of state recall of the former, were others. Direct, popular election of either was *not* proposed.

Since most of the state executives and legislators held office for annual or biennial terms, one would naturally expect the substantially longer tenure of the President and Senate to be severely criticized. There were numerous objections to the six-year term of Senators, some to the four-year term of the President, and a few to the two-year term of members of the House of Representatives. It is to be noted, however, that there was no serious attempt to shorten the length of term of any of these officers, nor was there any attempt to make the tenure of either the President or the Senate correspond with that of the House. It was agreed that the two houses should "afford a mutual check" on each other,[89] and that the "stability" provided by the Senate "was essential to good government."[90]

The most insistent and repeated criticism was the failure of the Constitution to provide for the compulsory rotation of office for Senators and the President. "Nothing is so essential to the preservation of a republican government as a periodical rotation," said George Mason,[91] and Melancton Smith pronounced it "a very important and truly republican institution."[92] They greatly feared that President and Senators would be perpetually re-elected, and in effect hold office for life. Mason, for example, was quite content for the Senate to serve six years, and the President even eight, but he believed that without rotation, the new government would become "an elective monarchy."[93] The President would be able to perpetuate himself forever, it was assumed, because his election would always be thrown into the House of Representatives. In that body, corruption, intrigue, foreign influence, and above all else, the incumbent's use of his patronage, would make it possible for every man, once elected, to hold office for life. Senators would "hold their office perpetually,"[94] by corrupting their electors, the state legislatures. In New York, where the subject was debated very thoroughly, the Anti-Federalists were challenged to show how such corruption could take place, and continue for life, among a group which was continuously subject to popular election, and which would presumably not be perma-

---

[89]Elliot, II, p. 308 (Lansing).
[90]*Ibid.*, p. 309 (Smith).
[91]Elliot, III, p. 485.
[92]Elliot, II, p. 310.
[93]Elliot, III, p. 485.
[94]Elliot, II, p. 309 (Smith).

nent. To this challenge Lansing replied, "It is unnecessary to particularize the numerous ways in which public bodies are accessible to corruption. The poison always finds a channel, and never wants an object."[95] No distinction as to comparative corruptibility was made between national and state representatives.

To Federalist objections that compulsory rotation constituted an abridgment of the people's right to elect whomsoever they wished, Melancton Smith replied impatiently, "What is government itself but a restraint upon the natural rights of the people? What constitution was ever devised that did not operate as a restraint on their natural liberties?"[96] Lansing conceded that rotation placed a restriction on the people's free choice of rulers, but he thought this beneficial: "The rights of the people will be best supported by checking, at a certain point, the current of popular favor, and preventing the establishment of an influence which may leave to elections little more than the form of freedom."[97]

The power of recall by state legislatures was associated with compulsory rotation as a means of preventing senatorial abuse of power. Not only would it enforce strict responsibility of senators to their electors, but in so doing it would protect the interests and preserve the sovereignty of the separate states. For these reasons, its adoption was strongly pressed in several of the ratifying conventions. Beyond these reasons, which were primary, recall combined with rotation would have a secondary beneficent result. It would serve to prevent the perpetuation of intra-legislative parties and factions—something which the Anti-Federalists feared quite as much as their opponents. Even if the power of recall should not actually be used, said Lansing, it would "destroy party spirit."[98] When his opponents turned this argument against him, and suggested that factions within the state legislatures might use the power to remove good, honorable, and faithful men from the Senate, the answer was that the legislatures had not abused the power under the Articles of Confederation and would almost certainly not do so in the future, and that even if they did, ample opportunity would be provided for the displaced senator to defend himself. The influence of "ambitious and designing men" would be detected and exposed, and the error easily corrected.[99] A curious "Trust them, trust them not" attitude toward

---

[95] Elliot, II, p. 295.
[96] *Ibid.*, p. 311.
[97] *Ibid.*, p. 295. It was in this debate that Lansing made the Madisonian statement quoted above.
[98] Elliot, II, p. 290.
[99] *Ibid.*, p. 299.

the state legislatures is thus revealed. They could not be trusted to refuse re-election to unfaithful or ambitious senators, though they could be trusted to remove the same and to leave in office all those who deserved well of them and of their constituents.

From this it is clear that the Anti-Federalists were not willing to trust either upper or lower house of the proposed national Congress; neither were they willing to trust their own state legislatures completely, though they had less fear of the latter because these could be kept under closer observation.

The same attitude is indicated by Anti-Federalist reaction to the restrictions placed on state legislatures by Article I, Section 10 of the Constitution, and to the then potential review of both state and national legislation by the Supreme Court.

Of the latter prospect, frequently said to have been one of the great bulwarks erected against the democratic majority, very little was said during the ratification debate. There was no explicit provision for judicial review in the Constitution, and it is probably not possible to prove conclusively whether or not its authors intended the Supreme Court to exercise this power. The evidence suggests that they probably assumed it would. Hamilton's *Federalist* 78 supports this view. The issue was never debated in the state conventions, and there are almost no references to it in any of the Anti-Federalist arguments. Since *Federalist* 78 was published before the Virginia, New York, and North Carolina Conventions met, this lack of discussion is significant and would seem to reflect lack of concern. There was severe criticism of Article III, particularly in Virginia, but it centered around the jurisdiction of the lower federal courts to be established by Congress, not around the Supreme Court. The issue was entirely one of state courts versus federal courts, not of courts versus legislatures.

The single direct reference to judicial review made in the Virginia Convention—at least the only one I have found—suggests that this institution was, or would have been, thoroughly congenial to the Anti-Federalists. The statement was made by Patrick Henry:

Yes, sir, our judges opposed the acts of the legislature. We have this landmark to guide us. They had fortitude to declare that they were the judiciary, and would oppose unconstitutional acts. Are you sure that your federal judiciary will act thus? Is that judiciary as well constructed, and as independent of the other branches, as our state judiciary? Where are your landmarks in this government? I will be bold to say you cannot find any in it. I take it as the highest encomium on this country, that the acts of the legislature, if unconstitutional, are liable to be opposed by the judiciary.[100]

There was nothing equivocal about Henry's attitude. It elicited no comment. Possibly neither side wished to commit itself; more likely the statement was lost and forgotten after brighter flames had issued from the great orator's fire. What is really significant, however, is the complete absence of debate over judicial review. The Anti-Federalists probed the Constitution for every conceivable threat, explicit or implicit, to their conception of free and popular government. If they had considered judicial review such a threat, they would surely have made the most of it, and particularly after *Federalist* 78 was published.

There was also comparatively little attention given to the restrictions which Article I, Section 10 of the Constitution placed on the state legislatures. Among other things, the states were forbidden to coin money, emit bills of credit, make anything but gold or silver legal tender for the payment of debts, or pass any law impairing the obligations of contracts. These are the provisions which recent historians have emphasized as designed to protect the property of the conservative class against the onslaughts of the radical democratic majority. The Anti-Federalists had very little to say about these provisions. The notation of the New York Convention's action is significant: "The committee then proceded through sections 8, 9, and 10, of this article [I], and the whole of the next, with little or no debate."[101] In Virginia and the Carolinas there was more discussion, but nothing like a full-dress debate, and very little indication of any strong or widespread opposition. In fact, Patrick Henry said that the restrictions were "founded in good principles,"[102] and William Grayson said of the prohibition against paper money, "it is unanimously wished by every one that it should not be objected to."[103] Richard Henry Lee expressed his preference for paper money to be issued by Congress only.[104] Of the few objections or doubts expressed, these were typical. Henry in Virginia and Galloway in North Carolina both expressed a fear that the contract clause might be interpreted to force the states to redeem their respective shares of the depreciated Continental currency and of state securities at face value.[105]

---

[100]*Elliot*, III, p. 325.

[101]Elliot, II, p. 406.

[102]Elliot, III, p. 471.

[103]*Ibid.*, p. 566.

[104]J. C. Ballagh, editor, *The Letters of Richard Henry Lee*, 2 vols. (New York, 1911–1914), pp. 421–422.

[105]Elliot, III, pp. 318–319; IV, p. 190.

Henry was also angry because of the necessary implication that the states were too "depraved" to be trusted with the contracts of their own citizens.[106] With regard to the prohibition of paper money, two men in North Carolina defended the previous state issue as having been a necessary expedient in troublesome times, but did not seem to object to the prohibition of future issues.[107] One man argued against this clause and the supreme law clause on the ground that the effect might be to destroy the paper money already in circulation and thereby create great confusion.[108] His contention was denied.[109] These remarks, none of which expressed direct opposition, were typical. In South Carolina, however, Rawlins Lowndes came out flatly against this restriction, defended the previous issue of paper money and the right of the state to make further issues in the future.[110] His position appears to have been the exception, at least of those which were expressed openly and publicly on the various convention floors.[111]

The response of the Anti-Federalists to these important limitations on the power of the states can accurately be described, I think, as one of over-all approbation tempered by some doubts caused by fear that they would be applied retroactively. This attitude is in rather curious contrast with the extremely jealous reaction to other changes in federal-state relations for which the Constitution provided. There were violent objections to federal control over state militia, to Congressional power to tax and to regulate commerce, to the creation of an inferior system of federal courts. All these things brought forth loud cries that the

---

[106]Elliot, III, p. 156.

[107]*Ibid.*, IV, pp. 88, 169–170.

[108]*Ibid.*, pp. 180, 184–185.

[109]*Ibid.*, pp. 181–185.

[110]*Ibid.*, pp. 289–290.

[111]There appears to have been more opposition to the provisions of Article I, Section 10 expressed outside of the Convention than inside. See Trenholme, *Ratification in North Carolina*, p. 42, and Clarence E. Miner, *The Ratification of the Federal Constitution in New York*, Studies in History, Economics and Public Law, Vol. XCIV, No. 3, Whole No. 214, Columbia University (New York, 1921), for the extra-Convention debate in New York. It may be that this was one of the subjects the Anti-Federalists preferred not to debate for the official record. See Trenholme, pp. 166–167, for a discussion of the refusal of North Carolina Anti-Federalists to state in the Convention objections to the Constitution being made outside. There was also apparently a similar situation during the Virginia Convention, where the Federalists objected to what was happening "outdoors." See Elliot, III, p. 237. See also the remarks of Alexander C. Hanson, a member of the Maryland Convention. In discussing these provisions, of which he strongly approved, he wrote, "I have here perhaps touched a string, which secretly draws together many of the foes to the plan." In *Aristides*, "Remarks on the Proposed Plan of a Federal Government," Ford, *Pamphlets*, p. 243.

states would be swallowed up by the national government. These important restrictions on the economic powers of the states were received with relative silence. There was apparently very little objection to these limitations on the power of state legislative majorities.

It remains to consider the extent to which the general Anti-Federalist distrust of their representatives, particularly those who were to serve in the national government but also those who served in their state legislatures, reflected also a distrust of the majorities who elected them, that is to say, of the people themselves. The answer is partly wrapped up in the whole complex of ideas constituting the Anti-Federalist conception of republican government, which I shall attempt to draw together in the concluding section of this essay. Some parts of the answer can be put into the record here.

The attitude of the Anti-Federalists toward the people as distinguished from their representatives, and toward the general problem of majority rule, was not radically different from that of their opponents. It is a curious and remarkable fact that during the course of this great debate in which the most popular national constitution ever framed was submitted to the public for the most popular mode of ratification yet attempted, there was very little tendency on either side to enthrone "the people" or to defer automatically to their judgment. Neither side showed the slightest inclination to use as its slogan, "Vox populi vox Dei." Rather was the contrary true, and some of the Anti-Federalist expressions of this attitude could easily have fitted into the dark picture of human nature presented in *The Federalist*. Indeed, the speeches and essays of the Anti-Federalists were peculiarly lacking in the great expressions of faith in the people which are to be found in the writings of Jefferson, and even occasionally in *The Federalist* itself. This is partly to be accounted for because their position was a negative one; they attacked the proposed system on the ground that it would be destructive of liberty.

It was therefore perhaps natural that they sometimes expressed fear about what may be called the constituent capacity of the people—the capacity of the people to act wisely in the actual choice of a constitution. They were afraid that the people might not see in the proposed new government all of the dangers and defects which they themselves saw. And there were gloomy comments about lack of stability. Said George Clinton in the New York Convention, "The people, when wearied with their distresses, will in the moment of frenzy, be guilty of the most imprudent and desperate measures. . . . I know the people are too apt to vibrate from one extreme to another. The effects of this disposition are what I wish to guard against."[112] His colleague, Melancton Smith, spoke in a similar vein:

Fickleness and inconstancy, he said, were characteristics of a free people; and, in framing a constitution for them, it was, perhaps, the most difficult thing to correct this spirit, and guard against the evil effects of it. He was persuaded it could not be altogether prevented without destroying their freedom. . . . This fickle and inconstant spirit was the more dangerous in bringing about changes in the government.[113]

It was "Centinel," author or son of the author of Pennsylvania's revolutionary Constitution, who expressed the gravest doubts about the capacity of the people to make a wise choice in the form of government, and who expounded a kind of Burkeian conservatism as the best guarantor of the people's liberties. In a passage apparently aimed at the prestige given to the proposed Constitution by the support of men like Washington and Franklin, "Centinel" wrote that "the science of government is so abstruse, that few are able to judge for themselves." Without the assistance of those "who are competent to the task of developing the principles of government," the people were "too apt to yield an implicit assent to the opinions of those characters whose abilities are held in the highest esteem, and to those in whose integrity and patriotism they can confide. . . ." This was dangerous, because such men might easily be dupes, "the instruments of despotism in the hands of the *artful and designing.*" "Centinel" then continued:

If it were not for the stability and attachment which time and habit gives to forms of government, it would be in the power of the enlightened and aspiring few, if they should combine, at any time to destroy the best establishments, and even make the people the instruments of their own subjugation.

The late revolution having effaced in a great measure all former habits, and the present institutions are so recent, that there exists not that great reluctance to innovation, so remarkable in old communities, and which accords with reason, for the most comprehensive mind cannot foresee the full operation of material changes on civil polity; it is the genius of the common law to resist innovation.[114]

Later in the same series of articles, "Centinel" pronounced "this reluctance to change" as "the greatest security of free govern-

---

[112]Elliot, II, p. 359.
[113]Elliot, II, p. 225.
[114]McMaster and Stone, *Pennsylvania and the Constitution*, pp. 566–567.

ments, and the principal bulwark of liberty."[115] This attitude provides an interesting comparison with the unquestioning assumption in the Federal Convention that the proposed Constitution would be submitted to the people for their verdict, and with the level of popular understanding of political affairs to which the essays of the *Federalist Papers* were addressed.

Serious reservations about the capacity of the people as electors were implicit in several of the arguments noted above. The advocacy of religious qualifications for office-holding indicated a desire to restrict the choice of the electorate to certified Protestants, and the demand for compulsory rotation of senators and President rested on the fear that corruption of both state and national legislatures by the incumbents of those offices could not be prevented by the feeble check of popular election. Perhaps most important was the belief that the people, voting in the large constituencies provided for by the Constitution, would either lose elections to their presumed aristocratic opponents because of the latter's superior capacity for organization, or would themselves let their choice fall on such aristocrats, or be deceived by ambitious and unscrupulous demagogues.

There was no more confidence in the inherent justice of the will of the majority than there was in its electoral capacity. Since the Anti-Federalists were skeptical that constituent opinion would be adequately reflected in the national legislature, they were less inclined than the Federalists to regard the government as the instrument of the people or of the majority. When they did so, there was not the slightest tendency to consider its decisions "right" *because* they were majority decisions. Rather was there always some standard of right and justice, independent of the majority's will, to which that will ought to conform. The Anti-Federalists were perfectly consistent in their conception of political behavior and did not regard a majority as superior to the sum of its parts, that is to say, of individual men motivated by self-interest and subject to a natural lust for power. There was very little discussion of majority rule and minority rights as fundamental principles of representative government, but the general attitude of the Anti-Federalists is, I think, reasonably clear.

They assumed, of course, that in a republican form of govern-

---

[115]*Ibid.*, p. 655. It may be noted that this Burkeian friend of Tom Paine had not undertaken to submit the radical revolutionary Constitution of Pennsylvania to the people of that state for full, free, and deliberate debate, but had rushed its ratification through the legislature with most unseemly haste.

ment, the majority must rule. But they also assumed that the will of the majority ought to be limited, especially when the "majority" was a legislative one. They demanded a bill of rights, with special emphasis on procedural protections in criminal cases, and vehemently repudiated the somewhat spurious Federalist argument that a bill of rights was not necessary in a government ruled by the people themselves. To this, James Winthrop replied:

> . . . that the sober and industrious part of the community should be defended from the rapacity and violence of the vicious and idle. A bill of rights, therefore, ought to set forth the purposes for which the compact is made, and serves to secure the minority against the usurpation of the majority. . . . The experience of all mankind has proved the prevalence of a disposition to use power wantonly. It is therefore as necessary to defend an individual against the majority in a republick as against the king in a monarchy.[116]

The reaction of the Anti-Federalists to the restrictions imposed on state legislative majorities by Article I, Section 10 of the Constitution is also relevant at this point. These provisions were certainly intended to protect the rights of property against legislative invasion by majorities. If there had been any spirit of doctrinaire majoritarianism among the opponents of the Constitution, this would surely have been the occasion to express it, and in quite unequivocal terms. There was very little open criticism of these provisions, none on the grounds that they violated the principle of majority rule or that they were designed to protect the interests of the upper classes.[117] What criticism there was, was expressed largely in terms of practical considerations.

Distrust of majority factions in much the same sense as Madison's was emphatically expressed by the one sector of Anti-Federalism which constituted the most self-conscious minority. Southerners felt keenly the conflict of interest between North and South and were vehemently opposed to surrendering themselves to the majority of the seven Eastern states. One of the reasons for George Mason's refusal to sign the Constitution had been his failure to get adopted a two-thirds majority vote for all laws affecting commerce and navigation. His fears for the South's interests were shared by his fellow Southerners and were frequently expressed in the Convention debates. "It will be a government of a faction," said

---

[116]*Agrippa* Letters, Ford, *Essays*, p. 117. See also Elliot, III, p. 499, for a similar statement from William Grayson.

[117]See above, footnote 111, for discussion of the possibility of more criticism expressed outside of the conventions.

William Grayson, "and this observation will apply to every part of it; for, having a majority, they may do what they please."[118] Other colleagues in Virginia joined in this distrust of the anticipated Northern majority uniting to oppress the South.[119] In North and South Carolina it was much the same. Bloodworth lamented, "To the north of the Susquehanna there are thirty-six representatives, and to the south of it only twenty-nine. They will always outvote us."[120] In South Carolina, Rawlins Lowndes predicted that "when this new Constitution should be adopted, the sun of the Southern States would set, never to rise again." Why? Because the Eastern states would have a majority in the legislature and would not hesitate to use it—probably to interfere with the slave trade, "because they have none themselves, and therefore want to exclude us from this great advantage."[121]

There was, then, no doctrinaire devotion to majoritarianism. It was assumed that oppression of individuals or of groups might come from majorities of the people themselves as well as from kings or aristocrats.

VI

For a generation the *Economic Interpretation of the Constitution* has exerted a deep and extensive influence over students of American history and government. The conception of the Constitution as the product of a conservative reaction against the ideals of the Revolution has been widely accepted, and Beard's analysis of the document itself commonly followed. According to this interpretation, the Founding Fathers secured their property rights by placing certain restrictions on state legislatures and by setting up a government in which the system of separation of powers, with checks and balances, indirect elections, staggered terms of office, and a national judiciary with the potential power of judicial review, would restrain the force of turbulent, democratic majorities. Surprisingly little attention has been devoted to the Anti-Federalists, but it is implied that they were the true heirs of the Revolutionary tradition—equally devoted to individual liberty and majority rule. The Federalists' desire for strong central government and the Anti-Federalists' fear of such are also considered, but the allegedly undemocratic structure of the national government itself is

---

[118]Elliot, III, p. 492.
[119]*Ibid.*, pp. 152, 221–222.
[120]Elliot, IV, p. 185.
[121]*Ibid.*, p. 272.

strongly emphasized. This aspect of the Beard thesis is open to question.

For the objections of the Anti-Federalists were not directed toward the barriers imposed on simple majority rule by the Constitution. Advocates and opponents of ratification may have belonged to different economic classes and been motivated by different economic interests. But they shared a large body of political ideas and attitudes, together with a common heritage of political institutions. For one thing, they shared a profound distrust of man's capacity to use power wisely and well. They believed self-interest to be the dominant motive of political behavior, no matter whether the form of government be republican or monarchical, and they believed in the necessity of constructing political machinery that would restrict the operation of self-interest and prevent men entrusted with political power from abusing it. This was the fundamental assumption of the men who wrote the Constitution, and of those who opposed its adoption, as well.

The fundamental issue over which Federalists and Anti-Federalists split was the question whether republican government could be extended to embrace a nation, or whether it must be limited to the comparatively small political and geographical units which the separate American states then constituted. The Anti-Federalists took the latter view; and in a sense they were the conservatives of 1787, and their opponents the radicals.

The Anti-Federalists were clinging to a theory of representative government that was already becoming obsolete, and would have soon become so even had they been successful in preventing the establishment of a national government. Certainly it was a theory which could never have provided the working principles for such a government. For the Anti-Federalists were not only localists, but localists in a way strongly reminiscent of the city-state theory of Rousseau's *Social Contract*. According to that theory, a society capable of being governed in accordance with the General Will had to be limited in size, population, and diversity. The Anti-Federalists had no concept of a General Will comparable to Rousseau's, and they accepted the institution of representation, where he had rejected it. But many of their basic attitudes were similar to his. Like him, they thought republican government subject to limitations of size, population, and diversity; and like him also, they thought the will of the people would very likely be distorted by the process of representation. In fact, their theory of representation and their belief that republican government could not be extended nation-wide were integrally related.

They regarded representation primarily as an institutional substitute for direct democracy and endeavored to restrict its operation to the performance of that function; hence their plea that the legislature should be an exact miniature of the people, containing spokesmen for all classes, all groups, all interests, all opinions, in the community; hence, too, their preference for short legislative terms of office and their inclination, especially in the sphere of state government, to regard representatives as delegates bound by the instructions of constituents rather than as men expected and trusted to exercise independent judgment. This was a natural stage in the development of representative government, but it contained several weaknesses and was, I think, already obsolete in late eighteenth-century America.

Its major weaknesses were closely akin to those of direct democracy itself, for representation of this kind makes difficult the process of genuine deliberation, as well as the reconciliation of diverse interests and opinions. Indeed, it is notable, and I think not accidental, that the body of Anti-Federalist thought as a whole showed little consideration of the necessity for compromise. The Founding Fathers were not democrats, but in their recognition of the role which compromise must play in the process of popular government, they were far more advanced than their opponents.

It is clear, too, that the same factors limiting the size and extent of direct democracies would also be operative in republics where representation is regarded only as a substitute for political participation by the whole people. Within their own frame of reference, the Anti-Federalists were quite right in insisting that republican government would work only in relatively small states, where the population was also small and relatively homogeneous. If there is great diversity among the people, with many interests and many opinions, then all cannot be represented without making the legislature as large and unwieldy as the citizen assemblies of ancient Athens. And if the system does not lend itself readily to compromise and conciliation, then the basis for a working consensus must be considerable homogeneity in the people themselves. In the opinion of the Anti-Federalists, the American people lacked that homogeneity.[122] This Rousseauistic vision of a small,

---

[122] I do not mean to suggest that the Anti-Federalist attitude concerning homogeneity and what modern social scientists refer to as *consensus* was hopelessly wrong. A degree of both is necessary for the successful operation of democracy, and the concept itself is an extremely valuable one. I would merely contend that the Federalist estimate of the degree required was both more liberal and more realistic. On the subject of the extent to which the American people were united in tradition, institutions, and ideas in 1787–1788, see Ranney, "Bases of American Federalism."

simple, and homogeneous democracy may have been a fine ideal, but it *was* an ideal even then. It was not to be found even in the small states, and none of the Anti-Federalists produced a satisfactory answer to Madison's analysis of the weaknesses inherent in republicanism operating on the small scale preferred by his opponents.

Associated with this theory of representation and its necessary limitation to small-scale republics was the Anti-Federalists' profound distrust of the electoral and representative processes provided for and implied in the proposed Constitution. Their ideal of the legislature as an "exact miniature" of the people envisaged something not unlike the result hoped for by modern proponents of proportional representation. This was impossible to achieve in the national Congress.[123] There would not and could not be enough seats to go around. The constituencies were to be large—the ratio of representatives to population was not to exceed one per thirty thousand—and each representative must therefore represent not one, but many groups among his electors. And whereas Madison saw in this process of "filtering" or consolidating public opinion a virtue, the Anti-Federalists saw in it only danger. They did not think that a Congress thus elected could truly represent the will of the people, and they particularly feared that they themselves, the "middling class," to use Melancton Smith's term, would be left out.

They feared this because they saw clearly that enlarged constituencies would require more pre-election political organization than they believed to be either wise or safe. Much has been written recently about the Founding Fathers' hostility to political parties. It is said that they designed the Constitution, especially separation of powers, in order to counteract the effectiveness of parties.[124] This is partly true, but I think it worth noting that the contemporary opponents of the Constitution feared parties or factions in the Madisonian sense just as much as, and that they feared parties in the modern sense even more than, did Madison himself. They feared and distrusted concerted group action for the purpose of "centering votes" in order to obtain a plurality, because they believed this would distort the automatic or natural expression of the people's will. The necessity of such action in large electoral districts would work to the advantage of the upper classes, who, because of their superior capacity and opportunity for organiza-

---

[123]Nor for that matter, has it been the pattern of representation in state legislatures.

[124]See, e.g., E. E. Schattschneider, *Party Government* (New York, 1942), pp. 4 ff.

tion of this kind, would elect a disproportionate share of repre-sentatives to the Congress. In other words, the Anti-Federalists were acutely aware of the role that organization played in the winning of elections, and they were not willing to accept the "organized" for the "real" majority. Instead they wanted to retain the existing system, where the electoral constituencies were small, and where organization of this kind was relatively unnecessary. Only then could a man vote as he saw fit, confident that the result of the election would reflect the real will of the people as exactly as possible.

Distrust of the electoral process thus combined with the localist feelings of the Anti-Federalists to produce an attitude of profound fear and suspicion toward Congress. That body, it was felt, would be composed of aristocrats and of men elected from far-away places by the unknown peoples of distant states. It would meet at a yet undesignated site hundreds of miles from the homes of most of its constituents, outside the jurisdiction of any particular state, and protected by an army of its own making. When one sees Congress in this light, it is not surprising that the Anti-Federalists were afraid, or that they had little faith in elections as a means of securing responsibility and preventing Congressional tyranny.[125]

Their demand for more limitations on Congressional power was perfectly natural. These were believed to be necessary in any gov-ernment because of the lust for power and the selfishness in its use which were inherent in the nature of man. They were doubly necessary in a government on a national scale. And so the Anti-Federalists criticized the latitude of power given to Congress under Article I and called for more detailed provisions to limit the scope of Congressional discretion. We are certainly indebted to them for the movement that led to the adoption of the Bill of Rights, though they were more concerned with the traditional common-law rights of procedure in criminal cases than with the provisions of the First Amendment. They were at the same time forerunners of the unfortunate trend in the nineteenth century toward lengthy and cumbersome constitutions filled with minute restrictions upon the various agencies of government, especially the legislative branch. The generality and brevity which made the national Constitution

---

[125] It is worth noting again that the abuses of power dwelt upon by the Anti-Federalists were usually extreme ones, almost amounting to a complete subversion of republican government. They did not regard as of any value the Federalists' argument that a desire to be re-elected would serve to keep the representatives in line. The Federalists had no clear idea of politics as a profession, but they were close to such a notion.

a model of draftsmanship and a viable fundamental law inspired in the Anti-Federalists only fear.

They repeatedly attacked the Constitution for its alleged departure from Montesquieu's doctrine of separation of powers, emphasized the inadequacy of the checks and balances provided within the governmental structure, and lamented the excessive optimism regarding the character and behavior of elective representatives thus revealed in the work of the Founding Fathers. It is significant, in view of the interpretation long and generally accepted by historians, that *no one* expressed the belief that the system of separation of powers and checks and balances had been designed to protect the property rights of the well-to-do. Their positive proposals for remedying the defects in the system were not numerous. They objected to the Senate's share in the appointive and treaty-making powers and called for a separate executive council to advise the President in the performance of these functions. Shorter terms were advocated for President and Congress, though not as frequently or as strongly as required rotation for senators and President. No one suggested judicial review of Congressional legislation, though Patrick Henry attacked the Constitution because it did not explicitly provide for this safeguard to popular government.

Had the Constitution been altered to satisfy the major structural changes desired by the Anti-Federalists, the House of Representatives would have been considerably larger; there would have been four rather than three branches of the government; the President would have been limited, as he is now, to two terms in office; the senators would have been similarly limited and also subject to recall by their state governments. These changes might have been beneficial. It is doubtful that they would have pleased the late Charles Beard and his followers; it is even more doubtful that they would have facilitated the operation of unrestrained majority rule. Certainly that was not the intention of their proponents.

The Anti-Federalists were not latter-day democrats. Least of all were they majoritarians with respect to the national government. They were not confident that the people would always make wise and correct choices in either their constituent or electoral capacity, and many of them feared the oppression of one section in the community by a majority reflecting the interests of another. Above all, they consistently refused to accept legislative majorities as expressive either of justice or of the people's will. In short, they distrusted majority rule, at its source and through the only possible means of expression in governmental action over a large and populous nation, that is to say, through representation. The last thing in the world they wanted was a national democracy which would permit Congressional majorities to operate freely and without restraint. Proponents of this kind of majority rule have almost without exception been advocates of strong, positive action by the national government. The Anti-Federalists were not. Their philosophy was primarily one of limitations on power, and if they had had their way, the Constitution would have contained more checks and balances, not fewer. Indeed it seems safe to say that the Constitution could not have been ratified at all had it conformed to the standards of democracy which are implicit in the interpretation of Beard and his followers. A national government without separation of powers and checks and balances was not politically feasible. In this respect, then, I would suggest that his interpretation of the Constitution was unrealistic and unhistorical.

The Anti-Federalists may have followed democratic principles within the sphere of state government and possibly provided the impetus for the extension of power and privilege among the mass of the people, though it is significant that they did not advocate a broadening of the suffrage in 1787–1788 or the direct election of the Senate or the President. But they lacked both the faith and the vision to extend their principles nation-wide. It was the Federalists of 1787–1788 who created a national framework which would accommodate the later rise of democracy.

{ *VII* }

ACHIEVEMENTS
AND
PERSPECTIVES

The philosophical thrust of the Revolution, its meaning to the men who led it and to the modern world, the nature of its objectives, and some of the ways in which it may be regarded as a success are discussed in the following selections. The first selection shows how the Revolution presented American leaders with a formidable intellectual challenge and describes three notable principles —in the view of the author, the three most important intellectual achievements of the Revolution—that the men of the Revolution developed to meet that challenge. The second analyzes the impulses and assumptions behind the Revolution and the fetish of constitution-making which accompanied it. By comparisons with similar phenomena in the French Revolution and the later revolutionary tradition, the author suggests how these and other factors unique to the American experience helped to make the American Revolution a success.

HANNAH ARENDT (b. 1906), a political philosopher and social critic, is a member of the Institute for Advanced Study at Princeton.

The American Revolution Considered As an Intellectual Movement

EDMUND S. MORGAN

In 1740 America's leading intellectuals were clergymen and thought about theology; in 1790 they were statesmen and thought about politics. A variety of forces, some of them reaching deep

Reprinted with permission from Morton White and Arthur M. Schlesinger, Jr., eds., *Paths of American Thought* (Boston: Houghton Mifflin, 1963), 11, 22–33.

into the colonial past, helped to bring about the transformation,
but it was so closely associated with the revolt from England that
one may properly consider the American Revolution, as an intellectual movement, to mean the substitution of political for clerical
leadership and of politics for religion as the most challenging area
of human thought and endeavor.

• • •

Although the clergy were a powerful influence in molding
American political opinion during the Revolutionary period, they
did not recover through politics the intellectual leadership they
had already begun to lose. Their own principles barred them from
an active role in politics. While they had always given political
advice freely and exercised their influence in elections, most of
them would have considered it wrong to sit in a representative
assembly, on a governor's council, or on the bench. To them as to
their Puritan ancestors the clerical exercise of temporal powers
spelled Rome. A minister's business was, after all, the saving of
souls. By the same token, however outraged he might be by the
actions of the English government, however excited by the
achievement of American independence, a minister could not devote his principal intellectual effort to the expounding of political
ideas and political principles. As the quarrel with England developed and turned into a struggle for independence and nationhood, though the ministers continued to speak up on the American
side, other voices commanding greater attention were raised by
men who were free to make a career of politics and prepared to
act as well as talk.

There had always, of course, been political leaders in the colonies, but hitherto politics had been a local affair, requiring at
most the kind of talents needed for collecting votes or pulling
wires. A colonial legislative assembly might occasionally engage
in debates about paper money, defense, or modes of taxation; but
the issues did not reach beyond the borders of the colony involved
and were seldom of a kind to challenge a superior mind. No American debated imperial policy in the British Parliament, the Privy
Council, or the Board of Trade. The highest political post to which
a man could aspire in the colonies was that of governor, and
everywhere except in Connecticut and Rhode Island, this was obtained not through political success but through having friends in
England. Few native Americans ever achieved it or even tried to.

But the advent of Parliamentary taxation inaugurated a quarter-
century of political discussion in America that has never since
been matched in intensity. With the passage of the Stamp Act in

1765, every colonial legislature took up the task of defining the structure of the British empire; and as colonial definitions met with resistance from England, as the colonies banded together for defense and declared their independence, politics posed continental, even global, problems that called forth the best efforts of the best American minds. In no other period of our history would it be possible to find in politics five men of such intellectual stature as Benjamin Franklin, John Adams, Alexander Hamilton, James Madison, and Thomas Jefferson; and there were others only slightly less distinguished.

Whether they hailed from Pennsylvania or Virginia, New England or New York, the men who steered Americans through the Revolution, the establishment of a new nation, and the framing of the Constitution did not for the most part repudiate the political ideas inherited from the period of clerical dominance. Like the clergy, they started from a conviction of human depravity; like the clergy, they saw government originating in compact, and measured governmental performance against an absolute standard ordained by God. Like the clergy too, they found inspiration in the example of seventeenth-century Englishmen. Sometimes they signed their own attacks on George III or his ministers with the names of John Hampden, William Pym, or other Parliamentary heroes in the struggle against Charles I. They read the works of Harrington and of Harrington's later admirers; and after the Declaration of Independence, when they found themselves in a position similar to that of England in the 1650's, they drew heavily on the arsenal of political ideas furnished by these latter-day republicans.

Indeed, most of the ideas about government which American intellectuals employed first in their resistance to Parliament, and then in constructing their own governments, had been articulated earlier in England and were still in limited circulation there. The social compact, fundamental law, the separation of powers, human equality, religious freedom, and the superiority of republican government were continuing ideals for a small but ardent group of Englishmen who, like the Americans, believed that the British constitution was basically republican and drew inspiration from it while attacking the ministers and monarch who seemed to be betraying it.[1] It is perhaps no accident that the work in which Americans first repudiated monarchy, *Common Sense*, was

[1]See Caroline Robbins, *The Eighteenth-Century Commonwealthman* (Cambridge, Mass., 1959).

written by an Englishman, Thomas Paine, who had come to America only two years before.

But if Englishmen supplied the intellectual foundations both for the overthrow of English rule and for the construction of republican government, Americans put the ideas into practice and drew on American experience and tradition to devise refinements and applications of the greatest importance. That republican ideas, which existed in a state of obscurity in England, should be congenial in the colonies, was due in the first place to the strong continuing Calvinist tradition which had been nourished over the years by the American clergy. But fully as important was the fact that during a hundred and fifty years of living in the freedom of a relatively isolated and empty continent, the colonists had developed a way of life in which republican ideas played a visible part. When Parliamentary taxation set Americans to analyzing their relationship to the mother country, they could not escape seeing that the social, economic, and political configuration of America had diverged from that of England in ways that made Americans better off than Englishmen. And the things that made them better off could be labeled republican.

England's practical experience with republicanism had lasted only eleven years. With the return of Charles II in 1660, Englishmen repudiated their republic and the Puritans who had sponsored it. Though a small minority continued to write and talk about republicanism and responsible government, they wielded no authority. The House of Commons grew more powerful but less common, and the main current of English national life flowed in the channels of monarchy, aristocracy, and special privilege. Americans, by contrast, though formally subjects of the king, had lived long under conditions that approximated the ideals of the English republican theorists. Harrington thought he had found in the England of his day the widespread ownership that seemed to him a necessary condition for republican government; but throughout the colonies ownership of property had always been more widespread than in England. Furthermore no member of the nobility had settled in America, so that people were accustomed to a greater degree of social as well as economic equality than existed anywhere in England.

During the 1640's and 1650's England had seen a rapid multiplication of religious sects, which produced a wide belief in religious freedom, but after the Anglican Church had reimposed its controls in the 1660's, the most that other denominations could hope for was toleration. In America, religious diversity had steadily increased, and with it came a religious freedom which, if still imperfect, surpassed anything England had ever known.

Though the English people had twice removed an unsatisfactory king, in 1649 and in 1688, the English government remained far less responsible and far less responsive to the people than any colonial government. While the members of Parliament disclaimed any obligation to their immediate constituents, the members of American representative assemblies knew that they were expected to look after the interests of the people who elected them. Nor were the voters in America only a small minority of the population as in England. In most colonies probably the great majority of adult males owned enough property to meet the qualification (which varied from colony to colony) for voting. In England, the government paid hundreds of office-holders whose offices, carrying no duties, existed solely for the enrichment of those who held them. In the colonies such sinecures were few. Americans thought that government existed to do a job, and they created no offices except for useful purposes.

Thus when the quarrel with Parliament began, the colonists already had what English reformers wanted. And the colonists were inclined to credit their good fortune not to the accident of geography but to their own superior virtue and political sophistication. The interpretation was not without foundation: since Calvinist traditions were still strong among them and since they had often learned of British republican ideas through the sermons of Calvinist clergymen, Americans retained what the Enlightenment had dimmed in England and Europe, a keen sense of human depravity and of the dangers it posed for government. Although their own governments had hitherto given little evidence of depravity, by comparison with those of Europe, they were expert at detecting it in any degree. They had always been horrified by the open corruption of British politics and feared it would lead to tyranny. When Parliament attempted to tax them and sent swarms of customs collectors, sailors, and soldiers to support the attempt, their fears were confirmed. In resisting the British and in forming their own governments, they saw the central problem as one of devising means to check the inevitable operation of depravity in men who wielded power. English statesmen had succumbed to it. How could Americans avoid their mistakes?

In the era of the American Revolution, from 1764 to 1789, this was the great intellectual challenge. Although human depravity continued to pose as difficult theological problems as ever, the best minds of the period addressed themselves to the rescue, not of souls, but of governments, from the perils of corruption. Of course the problem was not new, nor any more susceptible of final solution than it had been in an earlier time, but Americans in the Revolutionary period contributed three notable principles to men's efforts to deal with it.

The first principle, which evolved from the struggle with Parliament, was that the people of one region ought not to exercise dominion over those of another, even though the two may be joined together. It was an idea that overlapped and greatly facilitated the slower but parallel development of the more general belief in human equality. In objecting to British taxation in 1764 the colonists had begun by asserting their right to equal treatment with the king's subjects in Great Britain: Englishmen could not be taxed except by their representatives; neither therefore could Americans. Within a year or two the idea was extended to a denial that Parliament, representing the electors of Great Britain, could exercise any authority over the colonies. The empire, according to one American writer, was "a confederacy of states, independent of each other, yet united under one head," namely the king. "I cannot find," said another, "that the inhabitants of the colonies are dependent on the people of Britain, or the people of Britain on them, any more than Kent is on Sussex, or Sussex on Kent."[2]

It took varying lengths of time for other Americans to reach the position thus anonymously expressed in the press in 1765 and 1766. Franklin stated it later in 1766;[3] Jefferson, James Wilson, and John Adams had all expressed it by the beginning of 1775.[4] It was frequently buttressed by the citation of precedents from English constitutional history, but it rested on a principle capable of universal application, the principle stated in the preamble of the Declaration of Independence, that every people is entitled, by the laws of nature and of nature's God, to a separate and equal station.

Before Independence this principle offered a means of reorganizing the British empire so as to defeat the tyranny which Americans thought English statesmen were developing in the

---

[2]E. S. Morgan, *Prologue to Revolution: Sources and Documents on the Stamp Act Crisis* (Chapel Hill, N.C., 1959), pp. 73, 91.

[3]Verner Crane, *Benjamin Franklin's Letters to the Press, 1758–1775* (Chapel Hill, N.C., 1950), p. xlii.

[4]Thomas Jefferson, *A Summary View of the Rights of British America* (Williamsburg, 1774); James Wilson, *Considerations on the Nature and the Extent of the Legislative Authority of the British Parliament* (Philadelphia, 1774); John Adams, *Works*, C. F. Adams, ed. (Boston, 1850–1856) IV, 3–177.

extension of taxation. If a British legislature, in which the colonists were not represented, could govern them, then neither British nor colonial freedom could be safe. Americans without a voice in the government could not defend their rights against corrupt rulers. Englishmen, relieved of expenses by American taxation, might rejoice for the moment, but their rulers, no longer dependent on them financially, would be able to govern as they pleased and would eventually escape popular control altogether. The only solution was to give each legislature power only over the people who chose it.

In the 1770's England was unwilling to listen to the colonial arguments, but ultimately adopted the American principle in forming the Commonwealth of Nations. The independent United States applied the principle not only in the confederation of states but in the annexation of other areas. When Virginia in 1781 offered the United States Congress her superior claim to the old Northwest, it was with the stipulation that the region be divided into separate republican states, each of which was to be admitted to the Union on equal terms with the old ones. The stipulation, though not accepted by Congress at the time, was carried out in Jefferson's land ordinance of 1784 and in the Northwest Ordinance of 1787 which superseded it. The United States never wavered from the principle until after the Spanish-American War, when it temporarily accepted government of areas which it had no intention of admitting to the union on equal terms.

The second contribution of the American Revolutionists was an application of the assumption, implicit in the whole idea of a compact between rulers and people, that a people can exist as a people before they have a government and that they can act as a people independently of government. The Puritans had distinguished between the compact of a group of individuals with God, by which they became a people, and the subsequent compact between this people and their rulers, by which government was created. John Locke had similarly distinguished between the dissolution of society and of government, and so, at least tacitly, had the Revolutionists. They would have been more daring, not to say foolhardy, if they had undertaken to destroy the bonds of society as well as of government. But in their haste to form new governments after the royal government in each colony dissolved, the Revolutionists followed a procedure that did not clearly distinguish the people from the government. Provincial congresses, exercising a *de facto* power, drafted and adopted permanent constitutions, which in most cases then went into effect without submission to a popular vote.

When the Massachusetts provincial congress proposed to follow this procedure in 1776, the citizens of the town of Concord pointed out the dangerous opening which it offered to human depravity. A *de facto* government that legitimized itself could also alter itself. Whatever safeguards it adopted against corruption could easily be discarded by later legislators: "a Constitution alterable by the Supreme Legislative is no Security at all to the Subject against any Encroachment of the Governing part on any or on all of their Rights and priviliges." The town therefore suggested that a special popularly elected convention be called for the sole purpose of drafting a constitution, which should then be submitted to the people for approval.[5]

It is impossible to determine who was responsible for Concord's action, but the protest displays a refinement in the application of republican ideas that does not appear to have been expressed before. Concord's suggestion was eventually followed in the drafting and adoption of the Massachusetts constitution of 1780 and of every subsequent constitution established in the United States. By it the subservience of government to the people was secured through a constitution clearly superior to the government it created, a constitution against which the people could measure governmental performance and against which each branch of government could measure the actions of the other branches. The separation of governmental powers into a bicameral legislature, an executive, and a judiciary, which was an older and more familiar way of checking depravity, was rendered far more effective by the existence of a written constitution resting directly on popular approval. The written constitution also proved its effectiveness in later years by perpetuating in America the operation of judicial review, of executive veto, and of a powerful upper house of the legislature, all of which had been or would be lost in England, where the constitution was unwritten and consisted of customary procedures that could be altered at will by Parliament.

Thus by the time the Revolution ended, Americans had devised a way to establish the superiority of the people to their government and so to control man's tyranny over man. For the same purpose Americans had formulated the principle that no people

---

[5]Robert J. Taylor, ed., *Massachusetts, Colony to Commonwealth: Documents on the Formation of its Constitution, 1775–1780* (Chapel Hill, N.C. 1961), p. 45.

should exercise dominion over another people. But the way in which they first employed the latter principle in running the new nation did not prove satisfactory. As thirteen colonies the people of America had joined to combat Parliamentary taxation, and the result had been thirteen independent republics. It had been an exhilarating experience, and it had led them almost from the beginning to think of themselves in some degree as one people. But the thought was not completed: they did not coalesce into one republic with one government. Instead, as thirteen separate and equal peoples, they set up a "perpetual union" in which they were joined only through a Congress in which each state had one vote. They gave the Congress responsibility for their common concerns. But they did not give it the ordinary powers of a government to tax or legislate.

Because of the straightforward equality of the member states and because the Congress did not possess the means by which governments generally ran to tyranny, the confederation seemed a safe shape in which to cast the new nation. Actually danger lurked in the fact that the Congress had insufficient power to carry out the responsibilities which the states assigned to it. After the British troops were defeated and the need for united action became less obvious, state support of the Congress steadily declined. Without coercive powers, the Congress could not act effectively either at home or abroad, and the nation was increasingly exposed to the danger of foreign depredations. At the same time, the state governments were proving vulnerable to manipulation by corrupt or ambitious politicians and were growing powerful at the expense not only of the Congress but of the people. Some undertook irresponsible inflationary measures that threatened property rights. Unless the state governments were brought under more effective control, local demagogues might destroy the union and replace the tyranny of Parliament with a new domestic brand.

Although a few men foresaw the drawbacks of a weak Congress from the beginning, most people needed time to show them. The Massachusetts legislature, perceiving that the experience of the state could be applied to the whole United States, in 1785 suggested a national constitutional convention to create a central authority capable of acting effectively in the interests of the whole American people. But in 1785, Americans were not yet convinced that what they had was inadequate. The Massachusetts delegates to the Congress replied to their state's suggestion with the same arguments that had in the first place prompted Americans to base their union on a weak coordinative Congress rather than a real national government: it would be impossible, they said, to prevent such a government from escaping popular control. With headquarters remote from most of its constituents, with only a select few from each state engaged in it, a national government would offer too many opportunities for corruption.[6] The fear was supported by the views of respected European political thinkers. Montesquieu, who had been widely read in America, maintained that republican government was suited only to small areas. A confederation of republics might extend far, but a single republican government of large extent would either fall a prey to the ambitions of a few corrupt individuals, or else it would break up into a number of smaller states.[7]

These sentiments were so widely held that they prevented any effort to establish a national government until 1787. And when a convention was finally called in that year it was charged, not to create a new government, but simply to revise the Articles of Confederation. The members of the convention, without authorization, assumed the larger task and turned themselves into a national Constitutional Convention. They did so because they became convinced that, contrary to popular belief, a large republic would not necessarily succumb to corruption. The man who persuaded the Convention, insofar as any one man did it, was James Madison, one of the delegates from Virginia.

In the month before the Convention assembled, Madison had drawn up some observations on the "Vices of the Political System of the United States." Following a hint thrown out by David Hume, he reached the conclusion that "the inconveniencies of popular States contrary to the prevailing Theory, are in proportion not to the extent, but to the narrowness of their limits." In the state governments that had operated since 1776, the great defect was a tendency of the majority to tyrannize over the minority. Madison took it as axiomatic that "in republican Government the majority however composed, ultimately give the law." Unless a way could be found to control them, the majority would inevitably oppress the minority, because the individuals who made up the majority were as susceptible as any king or lord to the operation of human depravity. The most effective curb, Madison suggested, was to make the territory of the republic so large that a majority

[6]Edmund C. Burnett, ed., *Letters of Members of the Continental Congress* (Washington, 1921–1936), VIII, 206–210.

[7]Montesquieu, *Spirit of the Laws* (New York, 1949), p. 120 (Book VIII, c. 16).

would have difficulty forming. Men being hopelessly selfish would inevitably seek to capture the government for selfish purposes, and in a small republic they might easily form combinations to secure the necessary majority. But in a large republic, "the Society becomes broken into a greater variety of interests, of pursuits of passions, which check each other, whilst those who may feel a common sentiment have less opportunity of communication and concert."[8]

This insight, later given classic expression in the tenth *Federalist* paper, was the most fruitful intellectual achievement of the Revolutionary period, the third of the three principles mentioned earlier. It gave Madison and his colleagues at Philadelphia the courage to attempt a republican government for the whole nation. The constitution which they drew up would provide the American peoples with a government that would effectively make them one people. The government would incorporate all the protections to liberty that they still cherished from their British heritage; it would preserve both imported and home-grown republican traditions; and it would employ the political principles developed during the Revolution. It would be a government inferior to the people and one in which no people should have dominion over another, a government in which almost every detail was prompted by the framers' determination to control the operation of human depravity. Many Americans, doubting that the safeguards would work, opposed the adoption of the Constitution. But the character of American politics from 1789 to the present day has borne out Madison's observation: majorities in the United States have been composed of such a variety of interests that they have seldom proved oppressive, and the national government has been a stronger bulwark of freedom than the state governments.

The establishment of a national republic renewed the challenge which the contest with Great Britain had presented to the best minds of America. In the Constitutional Convention and in the conduct of the new national government, Americans found scope for talents that the Revolution had uncovered. Jefferson, Hamilton, Madison, and John Adams received from national politics the stimulus that made them great. The writings in which they embodied their best thoughts were state papers.

In the course of the nineteenth century the stimulus was somehow lost, in hard cider, log cabins, and civil war. Intellect moved

---

[8]James Madison, *Writings*, Gaillard Hunt, ed. (New York, 1900–1910), II, 361–369.

away from politics; and intellectual leadership, having passed from clergy to statesmen, moved on to philosophers, scientists, and novelists. But during the brief period when America's intellectual leaders were her political leaders, they created for their country the most stable popular government ever invented and presented to the world three political principles which men have since used repeatedly and successfully to advance human freedom and responsible government.

Constitutio Libertatis

HANNAH ARENDT

I

That there existed men in the Old World to dream of public freedom, that there were men in the New World who had tasted public happiness—these were ultimately the facts which caused the movement for restoration, for recovery of the old rights and liberties, to develop into a revolution on either side of the Atlantic. And no matter how far, in success and failure, events and circumstances were to drive them apart, the Americans would still have agreed with Robespierre on the ultimate aim of revolution, the constitution of freedom, and on the actual business of revolutionary government, the foundation of a republic. Or perhaps it was the other way round and Robespierre had been influenced by the course of the American Revolution when he formulated his famous "Principles of Revolutionary Government." For in America the armed uprising of the colonies and the Declaration of Independence had been followed by a spontaneous outbreak of constitution-making in all thirteen colonies—as though, in John Adams' words, "thirteen clocks had struck as one"—so that there existed no gap, no hiatus, hardly a breathing spell between the war of liberation, the fight for independence which was the condition for freedom, and the constitution of the new states. Although it is true that "the first act of the great drama," the

From On Revolution by Hannah Arendt, 139–153, 164–178, 300–304, 306–310. Copyright © 1963 by Hannah Arendt. All rights reserved. Reprinted by permission of The Viking Press, Inc.

"late American war," was closed before the American Revolution had come to an end,[1] it is equally true that these two altogether different stages of the revolutionary process began at almost the same moment and continued to run parallel to each other all through the years of war.

The importance of this development can hardly be overestimated. The miracle, if such it was, that saved the American Revolution was not that the colonists should have been strong and powerful enough to win a war against England but that this victory did not end "with a multitude of Commonwealths, Crimes and Calamities . . . ; till at last the exhausted Provinces [would] sink into Slavery under the yoke of some fortunate Conqueror,"[2] as John Dickinson had rightly feared. Such is indeed the common fate of a rebellion which is not followed by revolution, and hence the common fate of most so-called revolutions. If, however, one keeps in mind that the end of rebellion is liberation, while the end of revolution is the foundation of freedom, the political scientist at least will know how to avoid the pitfall of the historian who tends to place his emphasis upon the first and violent stage of rebellion and liberation, on the uprising against tyranny, to the detriment of the quieter second stage of revolution and constitution, because all the dramatic aspects of his story seem to be contained in the first stage and, perhaps, also because the turmoil of liberation has so frequently defeated the revolution. This temptation, which befalls the historian because he is a storyteller, is closely connected with the much more harmful theory that the constitutions and the fever of constitution-making, far from expressing truly the revolutionary spirit of the country, were

---

[1]There is perhaps nothing more detrimental to an understanding of revolution than the common assumption that the revolutionary process has come to an end when liberation is achieved and the turmoil and the violence, inherent in all wars of independence, has come to an end. This view is not new. In 1787, Benjamin Rush complained that "there is nothing more common, than to confound the term of American revolution with those of the late American war. The American war is over: but this is far from being the case with the American revolution. On the contrary, nothing but the first act of the great drama is closed. It remains yet to establish and perfect our new forms of government." (In Hezekiah Niles, Principles and Acts of the Revolution [Baltimore, 1822] p. 402.) We may add that there still is nothing more common than to confound the travail of liberation with the foundation of freedom.

[2]These fears were expressed in 1765, in a letter to William Pitt in which Dickinson had voiced his assurance that the colonies would win a war against England. See Edmund S. Morgan, The Birth of the Republic, 1763–89, Chicago, 1956, p. 136.

in fact due to forces of reaction and either defeated the revolution or prevented its full development, so that—logically enough—the Constitution of the United States, the true culmination of this revolutionary process, is understood as the actual result of counter-revolution. The basic misunderstanding lies in the failure to distinguish between liberation and freedom; there is nothing more futile than rebellion and liberation unless they are followed by the constitution of the newly won freedom. For "neither morals, nor riches, nor discipline of armies, nor all these together will do without a constitution" (John Adams).

Yet even if one resists this temptation to equate revolution with the struggle for liberation, instead of identifying revolution with the foundation of freedom, there remains the additional, and in our context more serious, difficulty that there is very little in form or content of the new revolutionary constitutions which was even new, let alone revolutionary. The notion of constitutional government is of course by no means revolutionary in content or origin; it means nothing more or less than government limited by law, and the safeguard of civil liberties through constitutional guarantees, as spelled out by the various bills of rights which were incorporated into the new constitutions and which are frequently regarded as their most important part, never intended to spell out the new revolutionary powers of the people but, on the contrary, were felt to be necessary in order to limit the power of government even in the newly founded body politic. A bill of rights, as Jefferson remarked, was "what the people are entitled to against every government on earth, general or particular, and what no just government should refuse, or rest on inference."[3]

In other words, constitutional government was even then, as it still is today, limited government in the sense in which the eighteenth century spoke of a "limited monarchy," namely, a monarchy limited in its power by virtue of laws. Civil liberties as well as private welfare lie within the range of limited government, and their safeguard does not depend upon the form of government. Only tyranny, according to political theory a bastard form of government, does away with constitutional, namely, lawful government. However, the liberties which the laws of constitutional government guarantee are all of a negative character, and this includes the right of representation for the purposes of taxation which later became the right to vote; they are indeed "not

---

[3] In a letter to James Madison of December 20, 1787.

powers of themselves, but merely an exemption from the abuses of power";[4] they claim not a share in government but a safeguard against government. Whether we trace the notion of this constitutionalism back to Magna Charta and hence to feudal rights, privileges, and pacts concluded between the royal power and the estates of the kingdom, or whether, on the contrary, we assume that "nowhere do we find modern constitutionalism until an effective central government has been brought into existence,"[5] is relatively unimportant in our context. If no more had ever been at stake in the revolutions than this kind of constitutionalism, it would be as though the revolutions had remained true to their modest beginnings when they still could be understood as attempts at restoration of "ancient" liberties; the truth of the matter, however, is that this was not the case.

There is another and perhaps even more potent reason why we find it difficult to recognize the truly revolutionary element in constitution-making. If we take our bearings not by the revolutions of the eighteenth century but by the series of upheavals that followed upon them throughout the nineteenth and twentieth centuries, it seems as though we are left with the alternative between revolutions which become permanent, which do not come to an end and do not produce their end, the foundation of freedom, and those where in the aftermath of revolutionary upheaval some new "constitutional" government eventually comes into existence that guarantees a fair amount of civil liberties and deserves, whether in the form of a monarchy or a republic, no more than the name of limited government. The first of these alternatives clearly applies to the revolutions in Russia and China, where those in power not only admit that fact but boast of having maintained indefinitely a revolutionary government; the second alterna-

---

[4] It is seldom recognized and of some importance that, to put it in Woodrow Wilson's words, "power is a positive thing, control a negative thing," and that "to call these two things by the same name is simply to impoverish language by making one word serve for a variety of meanings" (An Old Master and Other Political Essays, 1893, p. 91). This confusion of the power to act with the right to control the "organs of initiative" is of a somewhat similar nature as the previously mentioned confusion of liberation with freedom. The quotation in the text is from James Fenimore Cooper, The American Democrat (1838).

[5] The latter is the view of Carl Joachim Friedrich, Constitutional Government and Democracy, revised edition, 1950. For the former—that "the clauses in our American constitutions are . . . mere copies of the thirty-ninth article of Magna Charta"—see Charles E. Shattuck, "The True Meaning of the Term 'Liberty' in the Federal and State Constitutions," Harvard Law Review, 1891.

tive applies to the revolutionary upheavals which swept nearly all European countries after the First World War, as well as to many colonial countries that won their independence from European rule after the Second World War. In these cases, constitutions were by no means the result of revolution; they were imposed, on the contrary, after a revolution had failed, and they were, at least in the eyes of the people living under them, the sign of its defeat, not of its victory. They were usually the work of experts, though not in the sense in which Gladstone had called the American Constitution "the most wonderful work ever struck off at a given time by the brain and purpose of man," but rather in the sense in which Arthur Young even in 1792 felt that the French had adopted the "new word," which "they use as if a constitution was a pudding to be made by a recipe."[6] Their purpose was to stem the tide of revolution, and if they too served to limit power, it was the power of the government as well as the revolutionary power of the people whose manifestation had preceded their establishment.

One, and perhaps not the least, of the troubles besetting a discussion of these matters is merely verbal. The word "constitution" obviously is equivocal in that it means the act of constituting as well as the law or rules of government that are "constituted," be these embodied in written documents or, as in the case of the British constitution, implied in institutions, customs, and precedents. It is clearly impossible to call by the same name and to expect the same results from those "constitutions" which a non-revolutionary government adopts because the people and their revolution had been unable to constitute their own government, and those other "constitutions" which either, in Gladstone's phrase, "had proceeded from progressive history" of a nation or were the result of the deliberate attempt by a whole people at founding a new body politic. The distinction as well as the confusion are perfectly apparent in the famous definition of the word by Thomas Paine, a definition in which he only summed up and reasoned out what the fever of American constitution-making

---

[6]Quoted from Charles Howard McIlwain, *Constitutionalism, Ancient and Modern*, Ithaca, 1940. Those who wish to see this matter in historical perspective may recall the fate of Locke's constitution for Carolina, which was perhaps the first constitution framed by an expert and then offered to a people. William C. Morey's verdict, "It was created out of nothing, and it soon relapsed into nothing," has been true for almost all of them ("The Genesis of a Written Constitution," in *American Academy of Politics and Social Science*, Annals I, April, 1891).

must have taught him: "A constitution is not the act of a government, but of a people constituting a government."[7] Hence the need in France as in America for constituent assemblies and special conventions whose sole task it was to draft a constitution; hence also the need to bring the draft home and back to the people and have the Articles of Confederacy debated, clause by clause, in the town-hall meetings and, later, the articles of the Constitution in the state congresses. For the point of the matter was not at all that the provincial congresses of the thirteen colonies could not be trusted to establish state governments whose powers were properly and sufficiently limited, but that it had become a principle with the constituents "that the people should endow the government with a constitution and not vice versa."[8]

A brief glance at the various destinies of constitutional government outside the Anglo-American countries and spheres of influence should be enough to enable us to grasp the enormous difference in power and authority between a constitution imposed by a government upon a people and the constitution by which a people constitutes its own government. The constitutions of experts under which Europe came to live after the First World War were all based, to a large extent, upon the model of the American Constitution, and taken by themselves they should have worked well enough. Yet the mistrust they have always inspired in the people living under them is a matter of historical record as is the fact that fifteen years after the downfall of monarchical government on the European continent more than half of Europe lived under some sort of dictatorship, while the remaining constitutional governments, with the conspicuous exception of the Scandinavian countries and of Switzerland, shared the sad lack of power, au-

---

[7] Or, phrased somewhat differently: "A constitution is a thing *antecedent* to a government, and a government is only the creature of a constitution." Both phrases occur in the second part of *The Rights of Man*.

[8] According to Morgan, *op. cit.*, "Most states allowed their provincial congresses to assume the task of drafting a constitution and putting it into effect. The people of Massachusetts seem to have been the first to see the danger of this procedure. . . . Accordingly a special convention was held in 1780 and a constitution established by the people acting independently of government. . . . Though by this time it was too late for the states to use it, the new method was shortly followed in creating a government for the United States" (p. 91). Even Forrest McDonald, who holds that the state legislatures were "circumvented" and ratifying conventions elected because "ratification would [have been] much more difficult . . . if the Constitution had to overcome the machinations . . . of the legislatures," concedes in a footnote: "In point of legal theory, ratification by state legislatures would be no more binding than any other laws and could be repealed by subsequent legislatures." See *We the People: The Economic Origins of the Constitution*, Chicago, 1958, p. 114.

thority, and stability which even then was already the outstanding characteristic of the Third Republic in France. For lack of power and the concomitant want of authority have been the curse of constitutional government in nearly all European countries since the abolition of absolute monarchies, and the fourteen constitutions of France between 1789 and 1875 have caused, even before the rainfall of postwar constitutions in the twentieth century, the very word to become a mockery. Finally, we may remember, the periods of constitutional government were nicknamed times of the "system" (in Germany after the First World War and in France after the Second), a word by which the people indicated a state of affairs where legality itself was submerged in a system of half-corrupt connivances from which every right-minded person should be permitted to excuse himself since it hardly seemed worth while even to rise in revolt against it. In short, and in the words of John Adams, "a constitution is a standard, a pillar, and a bond when it is understood, approved and beloved. But without this intelligence and attachment, it might as well be a kite or balloon, flying in the air."[9]

The difference between a constitution that is the act of government and the constitution by which people constitute a government is obvious enough. To it must be added another difference which, though closely connected with it, is much more difficult to perceive. If there was anything which the constitution-makers of the nineteenth and twentieth centuries had in common with their American ancestors in the eighteenth century, it was a mistrust in power as such, and this mistrust was perhaps even more pronounced in the New World than it ever had been in the old countries. That man by his very nature is "unfit to be trusted with unlimited power," that those who wield power are likely to turn into "ravenous beasts of prey," that government is necessary in order to restrain man and his drive for power and, therefore, is (as Madison put it) a "reflection upon human nature"—these were commonplaces in the eighteenth century no less than in the nineteenth, and they were deeply ingrained in the minds of the Founding Fathers. All this stands behind the bills of rights, and it formed the general agreement on the absolute necessity of constitutional government in the sense of limited government; and yet, for the American development it was not decisive. The founders' fear of too much power in government was checked by

---

[9]Quoted from Zoltan Haraszti, *John Adams and the Prophets of Progress,* Cambridge, Mass., 1952, p. 221.

their great awareness of the enormous dangers to the rights and liberties of the citizen that would arise from within society. Hence, according to Madison, "it is of great importance in a republic, not only to guard the society against the oppression of its rulers; but to guard one part of the society against the injustice of the other part," to save "the rights of individuals, or of the minority . . . from interested combinations of the majority."[10] This, if nothing else, required the constitution of public, governmental power whose very essence could never be derived from something which is a mere negative, i.e., constitutional limited government, although European constitution-makers and constitutionalists saw in it the quintessence of the blessings of the American Constitution. What they admired, and from the viewpoint of Continental history rightly, was in fact the blessings of "mild government" as it had developed organically out of British history, and since these blessings were not only incorporated into all constitutions of the New World but most emphatically spelled out as the inalienable rights of all men, they failed to understand, on one hand, the enormous, overriding importance of the foundation of a republic and, on the other, the fact that the actual content of the Constitution was by no means the safeguard of civil liberties but the establishment of an entirely new system of power.

In this respect, the record of the American Revolution speaks an entirely clear, unambiguous language. It was not constitutionalism in the sense of "limited," lawful government that preoccupied the minds of the founders. On this they were agreed beyond the need for discussion or even clarification, and even in the days when feeling against England's king and Parliament ran highest in the country, they remained somehow conscious of the fact that they still dealt with a "limited monarchy" and not with an absolute prince. When they declared their independence from this government, and after they had forsworn their allegiance to the crown, the main question for them certainly was not how to limit power but how to establish it, not how to limit government but how to found a new one. The fever of constitution-making which gripped the country immediately after the Declaration of Independence prevented the development of a power vacuum, and the establishment of new power could not be based upon what had always been essentially a negative on power, that is, the bills of rights.

This whole matter is so easily and frequently confused because

---

[10]See *The Federalist,* no. 51.

of the important part the "Declaration of the Rights of Man and the Citizen" came to play in the course of the French Revolution, where these rights indeed were assumed not to indicate the limitations of all lawful government, but on the contrary to be its very foundation. Quite apart from the fact that the declaration "All men are born equal," fraught with truly revolutionary implications in a country which still was feudal in social and poltical organization, had no such implications in the New World, there is the even more important difference in emphasis with regard to the only absolutely new aspect in the enumeration of civil rights, and that is that these rights were now declared solemnly to be rights of all men, no matter who they were or where they lived. This difference in emphasis came about when the Americans, though quite sure that what they claimed from England were "the rights of Englishmen," could no longer think of themselves in terms of "a nation in whose veins the blood of freedom circulates" (Burke); even the trickle of immigrants of non-English and non-British stock in their midst was enough to remind them: "Whether you be English, Irish, Germans, or Swedes, . . . you are entitled to all the liberties of Englishmen and the freedom of this constituition."[11] What they were saying and proclaiming was in fact that those rights which up to now had been enjoyed only by Englishmen should be enjoyed in the future by all men[12]—in other words, all men should live under constitutional, "limited" government. The proclamation of human rights through the French Revolution, on the contrary, meant quite literally that every man by virtue of being born had become the owner of certain rights. The consequences of this shifted emphasis are enormous, in practice no less than in theory. The American version actually proclaims no more than the necessity of civilized government for all mankind; the French version, however, proclaims the existence of rights independent of and outside the body politic, and then goes on to equate these so-called rights, namely the rights of man *qua* man, with the rights of citizens. In our context, we do not need to insist on the perplexities inherent in the very

---

[11]These are the words of a Pennsylvanian, and "Pennsylvania, the most thoroughly cosmopolitan colony, had almost as many people of English descent as of all other nationalities put together." See Clinton Rossiter, *The First American Revolution*, New York, 1956, pp. 20 and 228.

[12]Even in the early sixties, "James Otis envisaged the transformation within the British constitution of the common-law rights of Englishmen into the natural rights of man, but he also saw these natural rights as limitations upon the authority of government." William S. Carpenter, *The Development of American Political Thought*, Princeton, 1930, p. 29.

concept of human rights nor on the sad inefficacy of all declarations, proclamations, or enumerations of human rights that were not immediately incorporated into positive law, the law of the land, and applied to those who happened to live there. The trouble with these rights has always been that they could not but be less than the rights of nationals, and that they were invoked only as a last resort by those who had lost their normal rights as citizens.[13] We need only to ward off from our considerations the fateful misunderstanding, suggested by the course of the French Revolution, that the proclamation of human rights or the guarantee of civil rights could possibly become the aim or content of revolution.

The aim of the state constitutions which preceded the Constitution of the Union, whether drafted by provincial congresses or by constitutional assemblies (as in the case of Massachusetts), was to create new centers of power after the Declaration of Independence had abolished the authority and power of crown and Parliament. On this task, the creation of new power, the founders and men of the Revolution brought to bear the whole arsenal of what they themselves called their "political science," for political science, in their own words, consisted in trying to discover "the forms and combinations of power in republics."[14] Highly aware of their own ignorance on the subject, they turned to history, collecting with a care amounting to pedantry all examples, ancient and modern, real and fictitious, of republican constitutions; what they tried to learn in order to dispel their ignorance was by no means the safeguards of civil liberties—a subject on which they certainly knew much more than any previous republic— but the constitution of power. This was also the reason for the enormous fascination exerted by Montesquieu, whose role in the American Revolution almost equals Rousseau's influence on the course of the French Revolution; for the main subject of Montesquieu's great work, studied and quoted as an authority on government at least a decade before the outbreak of the Revolution, was indeed "the constitution of political freedom,"[15] but the word

---

[13]On the perplexities, historical and conceptual, of the Rights of Man, see the extensive discussion in the author's *Origins of Totalitarianism*, revised edition, New York, 1958, pp. 290–302.

[14]The words are Benjamin Rush's in Niles, *op. cit.*, p. 402.

[15]No other passage from the "divine writings" of the "great Montesquieu" is more frequently quoted in the debates than the famous sentence about England: "Il y a aussi une nation dans le monde qui a pour objet direct de sa constitution la liberté politique" (*Esprit des Lois*, XI, 5). For the enormous influence of Montesquieu on the course of the American Revolution, see especially Paul Merrill Spurlin, *Montesquieu in America, 1760–1801*, Baton Rouge, Louisiana, 1940, and Gilbert Chinard, *The Commonplace Book of Thomas Jefferson*, Baltimore and Paris, 1926.

"constitution" in this context has lost all connotations of being a negative, a limitation and negation of power; the word means, on the contrary, that the "grand temple of federal liberty" must be based on the foundation and correct distribution of power. It was precisely because Montesquieu—unique in this respect among the sources from which the founders drew their political wisdom —had maintained that power and freedom belonged together, that, conceptually speaking, political freedom did not reside in the I-will but in the I-can, and that therefore the political realm must be construed and constituted in a way in which power and freedom would be combined, that we find his name invoked in practically all debates on constitution.[16] Montesquieu confirmed what the founders, from the experience of the colonies, knew to be right, namely, that liberty was "a natural Power of doing or not doing whatever we have a Mind," and when we read in the earliest documents of colonial times that "deputyes thus chosen shall have *power and liberty* to appoynt" we can still hear how natural it was for these people to use the two words almost as synonyms.[17]

It is well known that no question played a greater role in these debates than did the problem of the separation or the balance of powers, and it is perfectly true that the notion of such a separation was by no means Montesquieu's exclusive discovery. As a matter of fact, the idea itself—far from being the outgrowth of a mechanical, Newtonian world view, as has recently been suggested—is very old; it occurs, at least implicitly, in the traditional discussion of mixed forms of government and thus can be traced back to Aristotle, or at least to Polybius, who was perhaps the first to be aware of some of the advantages inherent in mutual checks and balances. Montesquieu seems to have been unaware of this historical background; he had taken his bearings by what he believed to be the unique structure of the English constitution, and whether or not he interpreted this constitution correctly is of no relevance today and was of no great importance even in the eighteenth century. For Montesquieu's discovery actually concerned the nature of power, and this discovery stands in so flagrant a contradiction to all conventional notions on this matter

---

[16]Montesquieu distinguishes between philosophic freedom, which consists "in the exercise of will" (*Esprit des Lois* XII, 2), and political freedom, which consists in *pouvoir faire ce que l'on doit vouloir* (*ibid.*, XI, 3), whereby the emphasis is on the word *pouvoir*. The element of power in political freedom is strongly suggested by the French language, in which the same word, *pouvoir*, signifies power and "to be able."

[17]See Rossiter, *op. cit.*, p. 231, and "The Fundamental Orders of Connecticut" of 1639 in *Documents of American History*, Henry Steele Commager, ed., New York, 1949, 5th edition.

that it has almost been forgotten, despite the fact that the foundation of the republic in America was largely inspired by it. The discovery, contained in one sentence, spells out the forgotten principle underlying the whole structure of separated powers: that only "power arrests power," that is, we must add, without destroying it, without putting impotence in the place of power.[18] For power can of course be destroyed by violence; this is what happens in tyrannies, where the violence of one destroys the power of the many, and which therefore, according to Montesquieu, are destroyed from within: they perish because they engender impotence instead of power. But power, contrary to what we are inclined to think, cannot be checked, at least not reliably, by laws, for the so-called power of the ruler which is checked in constitutional,

---

[18]The sentence occurs in XI, 4 and reads as follows: "Pour qu'on ne puisse abuser du pouvoir, il faut que, par la disposition des choses, le pouvoir arrête le pouvoir." At first glance, even in Montesquieu this seems to mean no more than that the power of the laws must check the power of men. But this first impression is misleading, for Montesquieu does not speak of laws in the sense of imposed standards and commands but, in full agreement with the Roman tradition, understands by laws *les rapports qui se trouvent entre [une raison primitive] et les différents êtres, et les rapports de ces divers êtres entre eux* (I, 1). Law, in other words, is what relates, so that religious law is what relates man to God and human law what relates men to their fellow men. (See also Book XXVI, where the first paragraphs of the whole work are treated in detail.) Without divine law there would be no relation between man and God, without human law the space between men would be a desert, or rather there would be no in-between space at all. It is within this domain of *rapports,* or lawfulness, that power is being exerted; non-separation of power is not the negation of lawfulness, it is the negation of freedom. According to Montesquieu, one could very well abuse power and stay within the limits of the law; the need for limitation—*la vertu même a besoin de limites* (XI, 4)—arises out of the nature of human power, and not out of an antagonism between law and power.

Montesquieu's separation of power, because it is so intimately connected with the theory of checks and balances, has often been blamed on the scientific, Newtonian spirit of the time. Yet nothing could be more alien to Montesquieu than the spirit of modern science. This spirit, it is true, is present in James Harrington and his "balance of property," as it is present in Hobbes; no doubt this terminology drawn from the sciences carried even then a great deal of plausibility—as when John Adams praises Harrington's doctrine for being "as infallible a maxim in politics as that action and reaction are equal in mechanics." Still, one may suspect that it was precisely Montesquieu's political, non-scientific language which contributed much to his influence; at any rate, it was in a non-scientific and non-mechanical spirit and quite obviously under the influence of Montesquieu that Jefferson asserted that "the government we fought for . . . should not only be founded on free principles" (by which he meant the principles of limited government), "but in which the powers of government should be so divided and balanced among several bodies of magistracy, as that no one could transcend their legal limits, without being effectually checked and restrained by the others." *Notes on the State of Virginia,* query XIII.

limited, lawful government is in fact not power but violence, it is the multiplied strength of the one who has monopolized the power of the many. Laws, on the other hand, are always in danger of being abolished by the power of the many, and in a conflict between law and power it is seldom the law which will emerge as victor. Yet even if we assure that law is capable of checking power —and on this assumption all truly democratic forms of government must rest if they are not to degenerate into the worst and most arbitrary tyranny—the limitation which laws set upon power can only result in a decrease of its potency. Power can be stopped *and* still be kept intact only by power, so that the principle of the separation of power not only provides a guarantee against the monopolization of power by one part of the government, but actually provides a kind of mechanism, built into the very heart of government, through which new power is constantly generated, without, however, being able to overgrow and expand to the detriment of other centers or sources of power. Montesquieu's famous insight that even virtue stands in need of limitation and that even an excess of reason is undesirable occurs in his discussion of the nature of power;[19] to him, virtue and reason were powers rather than mere faculties, so that their preservation and increase had to be subject to the same conditions which rule over the preservation and increase of power. Certainly it was not because he wanted less virtue and less reason that Montesquieu demanded their limitation.

This side of the matter is usually overlooked because we think of the division of power only in terms of its separation in the three branches of government. The chief problem of the founders, however, was how to establish union out of thirteen "sovereign," duly constituted republics; their task was the foundation of a "confederate republic" which—in the language of the time, borrowed from Montesquieu—would reconcile the advantages of monarchy in foreign affairs with those of republicanism in domestic policy.[20]

---

[19]*Esprit des Lois* XI, 4 and 6.

[20]Thus, James Wilson held that "a Federal Republic . . . as a species of government . . . secures all the internal advantages of a republic; at the same time that it maintains the external dignity and force of a monarchy" (quoted from Spurlin, *op. cit.*, p. 206). Hamilton, *The Federalist*, no. 9, arguing against the opponents of the new Constitution who, "with great assiduity, cited and circulated the observations of Montesquieu on the necessity of a contracted territory for a republican government," quoted at length from *L'Esprit des Lois* to show that Montesquieu "explicitly treats of a Confederate Republic as the expedient for extending the sphere of popular government, and reconciling the advantages of monarchy with those of republicanism."

And in this task of the Constitution there was no longer any question of constitutionalism in the sense of civil rights—even though a Bill of Rights was then incorporated into the Constitution as amendments, as a necessary supplement to it—but of erecting a system of powers that would check and balance in such a way that the power neither of the union nor of its parts, the duly constituted states, would decrease or destroy one another.

How well this part of Montesquieu's teaching was understood in the days of the foundation of the republic! On the level of theory, its greatest defender was John Adams, whose entire political thought turned about the balance of powers. And when he wrote: "Power must be opposed to power, force to force, strength to strength, interest to interest, as well as reason to reason, eloquence to eloquence, and passion to passion," he obviously believed he had found in this very opposition an instrument to generate more power, more strength, more reason, and not to abolish them.[21] On the level of practice and the erection of institutions, we may best turn to Madison's argument on the proportion and balancing of power between the federal and the state governments. Had he believed in the current notions of the indivisibility of power—that divided power is less power[22]—he would have concluded that the new power of the union must be founded on powers surrendered by the states, so that the stronger the union was to be, the weaker its constituent parts were to become. His point, however, was that the very establishment of the Union had founded a new source of power which in no way drew its strength from the powers of the states, as it had not been established at their expense. Thus he insisted: "Not the states ought to surrender their powers to the national government, rather the powers of the central government should be greatly enlarged. . . . It should be set as a check upon the exercise by the state governments of the

---

[21]From Haraszti, *op. cit.*, p. 219.

[22]Such notions, of course, were also quite current in America. Thus John Taylor of Virginia argued against John Adams as follows: "Mr. Adams considers our division of power as the same principle with his balance of power. We consider these principles as opposite and inimical. . . . Our principle of division is used to reduce power to that degree of temperature which may make it a blessing and not a curse. . . . Mr. Adams contends for a government of orders, as if power would be a safe sentinel over power, or the devil over Lucifer. . . ." (See William C. Carpenter, *op. cit.*) Taylor, because of his mistrust in power, has been called the philosopher of Jeffersonian democracy; however, the truth of the matter is that Jefferson, no less than Adams or Madison, emphatically held that it was the balancing of powers and not the division of power which was the proper remedy for despotism.

considerable powers which must still remain with them."[23] Hence, "if [the governments of the particular states] were abolished, the general government would be compelled by the principle of self-preservation to reinstate them in their proper jurisdiction."[24] In this respect, the great and, in the long run, perhaps the greatest American innovation in politics as such was the consistent abolition of sovereignty within the body politic of the republic, the insight that in the realm of human affairs sovereignty and tyranny are the same. The defect of the Confederacy was that there had been no "partition of power between the General and the Local Governments"; and that it had acted as the central agency of an alliance rather than as a government; experience had shown that in this alliance of powers there was a dangerous tendency for the allied powers not to act as checks upon one another but to cancel one another out, that is, to breed impotence.[25] What the founders were afraid of in practice was not power but impotence, and their fears were intensified by the view of Montesquieu, quoted throughout these discussions, that republican government was effective only in relatively small territories. Hence, the discussion turned about the very viability of the republican form of government, and both Hamilton and Madison called attention to another view of Montesquieu, according to which a confederacy of republics could solve the problems of larger countries under the condition that the constituted bodies—small republics—were capable of constituting a new body politic, the confederate republic, instead of resigning themselves to a mere alliance.[26]

Clearly, the true objective of the American Constitution was not to limit power but to create more power, actually to establish and duly constitute an entirely new power center, destined to compensate the confederate republic, whose authority was to be exerted over a large, expanding territory, for the power lost through the separation of the colonies from the English crown. This complicated and delicate system, deliberately designed to keep the power potential of the republic intact and prevent any of the multiple power sources from drying up in the event of further expansion, "of being increased by the addition of other members," was entirely

---

[23]See Edward S. Corwin, "The Progress of Constitutional Theory between the Declaration of Independence and the Meeting of the Philadelphia Convention," *American Historical Review*, Vol. 30, 1925.

[24]*The Federalist*, no. 14.

[25]Madison in a letter to Jefferson, October 24, 1787, in Max Farrand, *Records of the Federal Convention of 1787*, New Haven, 1937, vol. 3, p. 137.

[26]For Hamilton, see note 20; for Madison, *The Federalist*, no. 43.

the child of revolution.[27] The American Constitution finally consolidated the power of the Revolution, and since the aim of revolution was freedom, it indeed came to be what Bracton had called *Constitutio Libertatis,* the foundation of freedom.

To believe that the short-lived European postwar constitutions or even their predecessors in the nineteenth century, whose inspiring principle had been distrust of power in general and fear of the revolutionary power of the people in particular, could constitute the same form of government as the American Constitution, which had sprung from confidence in having discovered a power principle strong enough to found a perpetual union, is to be fooled by words.

• • •

II

The great and fateful misfortune of the French Revolution was that none of the constituent assemblies could command enough authority to lay down the law of the land; the reproach rightly leveled against them was always the same: they lacked the power to constitute by definition; they themselves were unconstitutional. Theoretically, the fateful blunder of the men of the French Revolution consisted in their almost automatic, uncritical belief that power and law spring from the selfsame source. Conversely, the great good fortune of the American Revolution was that the people of the colonies, prior to their conflict with England, were organized in self-governing bodies, that the revolution—to speak the language of the eighteenth century—did not throw them into a state of nature,[28] that there never was any serious questioning of the *pouvoir constituant* of those who framed the state constitutions and, eventually, the Constitution of the United States. What Madi-

---

[27]James Wilson, commenting on Montesquieu's Federal Republic, explicitly mentions that "it consists in assembling distinct societies which are consolidated into a new body, capable of being increased by the addition of other members—an expanding quality peculiarly fitted to the circumstances of America" (Spurlin, op. cit., p. 206).

[28]That there existed a few isolated instances in which resolutions were passed to the effect that "the whole procedure of the Congress was unconstitutional," and that "when the Declaration of Independence took place, the Colonies were absolutely in a state of nature," is of course no argument against this. For the resolutions of some New Hampshire towns, see Merrill Jensen, "Democracy and the American Revolution," *Huntington Library Quarterly,* XX, no. 4, 1957.

son proposed with respect to the American Constitution, namely, to derive its "general authority . . . entirely from the subordinate authorities,"[29] repeated only on a national scale what had been done by the colonies themselves when they constituted their state governments. The delegates to the provincial congresses or popular conventions which drafted the constitutions for state governments had derived their authority from a number of subordinate, duly authorized bodies—districts, counties, townships; to preserve these bodies unimpaired in their power was to preserve the source of their own authority intact. Had the Federal Convention, instead of creating and constituting the new federal power, chosen to curtail and abolish state powers, the founders would have met immediately the perplexities of their French colleagues; they would have lost their *pouvior constituant*—and this, probably, was one of the reasons why even the most convinced supporters of a strong central government did not want to abolish the powers of state governments altogether.[30] Not only was the federal system the sole alternative to the nation-state principle; it was also the only way not to be trapped in the vicious circle of *pouvoir constituant* and *pouvoir constitué.*

The astounding fact that the Declaration of Independence was preceded, accompanied, and followed by constitution-making in all thirteen colonies revealed all of a sudden to what an extent an entirely new concept of power and authority, an entirely novel idea of what was of prime importance in the political realm had already developed in the New World, even though the inhabitants of this world spoke and thought in the terms of the Old World and referred to the same sources for inspiration and confirmation of their theories. What was lacking in the Old World were the townships of the colonies, and, seen with the eye of a European observer, "the American Revolution broke out, and the doctrine of the sovereignty of the people came out of the townships and took possession of the state."[31] Those who received the power to

---

[29]In a letter to Jefferson, October 24, 1787, in Farrand, *Records of the Federal Convention*, III, p. 137.

[30]Winton U. Solberg, in his introduction to *The Federal Convention and the Formation of the Union of the American States*, New York, 1958, rightly stresses that the Federalists "wished definitely to subordinate the states, but they did not, with two exceptions, desire to destroy the states" (p. cii). Madison himself once said "he would preserve the State rights as carefully as the trials by jury" (*ibid.*, p. 196).

[31]Tocqueville, *Democracy in America*, New York, 1945, vol. I, p. 56. The extraordinary degree of political articulation of the country may be realized by the fact that there were more than 550 such towns in New England alone in 1776.

constitute, to frame constitutions, were duly elected delegates of constituted bodies; they received their authority from below, and when they held fast to the Roman principle that the seat of power lay in the people, they did not think in terms of a fiction and an absolute, the nation above all authority and absolved from all laws, but in terms of a working reality, the organized multitude whose power was exerted in accordance with laws and limited by them. The American revolutionary insistence on the distinction between a republic and a democracy or majority rule hinges on the radical separation of law and power, with clearly recognized different origins, different legitimations, and different spheres of application.

What the American Revolution actually did was to bring the new American experience and the new American concept of power out into the open. Like prosperity and equality of condition, this new power concept was older than the Revolution, but unlike the social and economic happiness of the New World—which would have resulted in abundance and affluence under almost any form of government—it would hardly have survived without the foundation of a new body politic, designed explicitly to preserve it; without revolution, in other words, the new power principle would have remained hidden, it might have fallen into oblivion or be remembered as a curiosity, of interest to anthropologists and local historians, but of no interest to statecraft and political thought.

Power—as the men of the American Revolution understood it as a matter of course because it was embodied in all institutions of self-government throughout the country—was not only prior to the Revolution, it was in a sense prior to the colonization of the continent. The Mayflower Compact was drawn up on the ship and signed upon landing. For our argument, it is perhaps of no great relevance, though it would be interesting to know, whether the Pilgrims had been prompted to "covenant" because of the bad weather which prevented their landing farther south within the jurisdiction of the Virginia Company that had granted them their patent, or whether they felt the need to "combine themselves together" because the London recruits were an "undesirable lot" challenging the jurisdiction of the Virginia Company and threatening to "use their owne libertie."[32] In either case, they obviously feared the so-called state of nature, the untrod wilderness, unlimited by any boundary, as well as the unlimited initiative of

[32]The bad-weather theory, which I find rather suggestive, is contained in the "Massachusetts" article in the *Encyclopædia Britannica*, 11th edition, vol. XVII. For the perhaps more probable alternative, see the introduction to the "Mayflower Compact" in Commager, *op. cit.*

men bound by no law. This fear is not surprising; it is the justified fear of civilized men who, for whatever reasons, have decided to leave civilization behind them and strike out on their own. The really astounding fact in the whole story is that their obvious fear of one another was accompanied by the no less obvious confidence they had in their own power, granted and confirmed by no one and as yet unsupported by any means of violence, to combine themselves together into a "civil Body Politick" which, held together solely by the strength of mutual promise "in the Presence of God and one another," supposedly was powerful enough to "enact, constitute, and frame" all necessary laws and instruments of government. This deed quickly became a precedent, and when, less than twenty years later, colonists from Massachusetts emigrated to Connecticut, they framed their own "Fundamental Orders" and "plantation covenant" in a still uncharted wilderness, so that when the royal charter finally arrived to unite the new settlement into the colony of Connecticut it sanctioned and confirmed an already existing system of government. And precisely because the royal charter of 1662 had only sanctioned the Fundamental Orders of 1639, the selfsame charter could be adopted in 1776, virtually unchanged, as "the Civil Constitution of this State under the sole authority of the people thereof, independent of any King and Prince whatever."

Since the colonial covenants had originally been made without any reference to king or prince, it was as though the Revolution liberated the power of covenant and constitution-making as it had shown itself in the earliest days of colonization. The unique and all-decisive distinction between the settlements of North America and all other colonial enterprises was that only the British emigrants had insisted, from the very beginning, that they constitute themselves into "civil bodies politic." These bodies, moreover, were not conceived as governments, strictly speaking; they did not imply rule and the division of the people into rulers and ruled. The best proof of this is the simple fact that the people thus constituted could remain, for more than a hundred and fifty years, the royal subjects of the government of England. These new bodies politic really were "political societies," and their great importance for the future lay in the formation of a political realm that enjoyed power and was entitled to claim rights without possessing or claiming sovereignty.[33] The greatest revolutionary innovation, Madison's discovery of the federal principle for the foundation of

---

[33] The important distinction between states that are sovereign and those that are "only political societies" was made by Madison in a speech in the Federal Convention. See Solberg, *op. cit.*, p. 189, note 8.

large republics, was partly based upon an experience, upon the intimate knowledge of political bodies whose internal structure predetermined them, as it were, and conditioned its members for a constant enlargement whose principle was neither expansion nor conquest but the further combination of powers. For not only the basic federal principle of uniting separate and independently constituted bodies, but also the name "confederation" in the sense of "combination" or "cosociation" was actually discovered in the earliest times of colonial history, and even the new name of the union to be called United States of America was suggested by the short-lived New England Confederation to be "called by the name of United Colonies of New England."[34] And it was this experience, rather than any theory, which emboldened Madison to elaborate and affirm a casual remark of Montesquieu, namely that the republican form of government, if based upon the federal principle, was appropriate for large and growing territories.[35]

---

[34]See the "Fundamental Orders of Connecticut" of 1639 and "The New England Confederation" of 1643 in Commager, *op. cit.*

[35]Benjamin F. Wright—especially in the important article "The Origins of the Separation of Powers in America" in *Economica*, May, 1933—has argued in a similar vein that "the framers of the first American constitutions were impressed by the separation of powers theory only because their own experience . . . confirmed its wisdom"; and others have followed him. Sixty or seventy years ago, it was almost a matter of course for American scholarship to insist on an unbroken, autonomous continuity of American history culminating in the Revolution and the establishment of the United States. Since Bryce had related the American constitution-making to the royal colonial charters by which the earliest English settlements were established, it had been current to explain the origin of a written constitution as well as the unique emphasis on statutory legislation by the fact that the colonies were subordinate political bodies, which derived from trading companies and were capable of assuming powers only so far as delegated by special grants, patents, and charters. (See William C. Morey's "The First State Constitutions" in *Annals of the American Academy of Political and Social Science*, September, 1893, vol. IV, and his essays on the Written Constitution, quoted in Note 6.) Today this approach is much less common, and the emphasis on European influences, British or French, is more widely accepted. There are various reasons for this shift in emphasis in American historical scholarship, among them the strong recent influence of the history of ideas, which obviously directs its attention to intellectual precedent rather than to political event, as well as the slightly older abandonment of isolationist attitudes. All this is quite interesting but of no great relevance in our context. What I should like to underline here is that the importance of royal or company charters seems to have been stressed at the expense of the far more original and more interesting covenants and compacts which the colonists made amongst themselves. For it seems to me that Merrill Jensen—in his more recent article, *op. cit.*—is entirely right when he states: "The central issue in seventeenth-century New England . . . was the source of authority for the establishment of government. The English view was that no government could exist in a colony without a grant of power from the Crown. The opposite view, held by certain English dissenters in New England, was that a group of people could create a valid government for

John Dickinson, who once almost casually remarked, "Experience must be our only guide. Reason may mislead us,"[36] may have been dimly aware of this unique but theoretically inarticulate background of the American experiment. It has been said that "America's debt to the idea of the social contract is so huge as to defy measurement,"[37] but the point of the matter is that the early colonists, not the men of the Revolution, "put the idea into practice," and they certainly had no notion of any theory. On the contrary, if Locke in a famous passage states, "That which begins and actually constitutes any political society is nothing but the consent of any number of freemen capable of majority, to unite and incorporate into such society," and then calls this act the "beginning to any lawful government in the world," it rather looks as though he was more influenced by the facts and events in America, and perhaps in a more decisive manner, than the founders were influenced by his *Treatises of Civil Government*.[38] The proof of the matter—if proof in such matters can exist at all—lies in the curious and, as it were, innocent way in which Locke construed this "original compact," in line with the current social-contract theory, as a surrender of rights and powers to either the government or the community, that is, not at all as a "mutual" contract but as an agreement in which an individual person resigns his power to some higher authority and consents to be ruled in exchange for a reasonable protection of his life and property.[39]

Before we proceed, we must recall that in theory the seventeenth century clearly distinguished between two kinds of "social contract." One was concluded between individual persons and supposedly gave birth to society; the other was concluded between a people and its ruler and supposedly resulted in legitimate govern-

themselves by means of a covenant, compact, or constitution. The authors of the Mayflower Compact and the Fundamental Orders of Connecticut operated on this assumption. . . . It is the basic assumption of the Declaration of Independence, a portion of which reads much like the words of Roger Williams written 132 years earlier."

[36]Quoted from Solberg, *op. cit.*, p. xcii.

[37]Thus Rossiter, *op. cit.*, p. 132.

[38]The uniqueness of the Mayflower Compact was stressed time and again in this period of American history. Thus, James Wilson, referring to it in a lecture in 1790, reminds his audience that he is presenting "what, as to the nations in the Transatlantic world, must be searched for in vain—an original compact of a society, on its first arrival in this section of the globe." And the early histories of America are still quite explicitly insisting on "a spectacle . . . which rarely occurs, of contemplating a society in the first moment of its political existence," as the Scottish historian William Robertson put it. See W. F. Craven, *The Legend of the Founding Fathers*, New York, 1956, pp. 57 and 64.

[39]See especially *op. cit.*, Section 131.

ment. However, the decisive differences between these two kinds (which have hardly more in common than a commonly shared and misleading name) were early neglected because the theorists themselves were primarily interested in finding a universal theory covering all forms of public relationships, social as well as political, and all kinds of obligations; hence, the two possible alternatives of "social contract," which, as we shall see, actually are mutually exclusive, were seen, with more or less conceptual clarity, as aspects of a single twofold contract. In theory, moreover, both contracts were fictions, the fictitious explanation of existing relationships between the members of a community, called society, or between this society and its government; and while the history of the theoretical fictions can be traced back deep into the past, there had been no instance, prior to the colonial enterprise of the British people, when even a remote possibility of testing their validity in actual fact had presented itself.

Schematically, the chief differences between these two kinds of social contract may be enumerated as follows: The mutual contract by which people bind themselves together in order to form a community is based on reciprocity and presupposes equality; its actual content is a promise, and its result is indeed a "society" or "cosociation" in the old Roman sense of *societas*, which means alliance. Such an alliance gathers together the isolated strength of the allied partners and binds them into a new power structure by virtue of "free and sincere promises."[40] In the so-called social contract between a given society and its ruler, on the other hand, we deal with a fictitious, aboriginal act on the side of each member, by virtue of which he gives up his isolated strength and power to constitute a government; far from gaining a new power, and possibly more than he had before, he resigns his power such as it is, and far from binding himself through promises, he merely expresses his "consent" to be ruled by the government, whose power consists of the sum total of forces which all individual persons have channeled into it and which are monopolized by the government for the alleged benefit of all subjects. As far as the individual person is concerned, it is obvious that he gains as much power by the system of mutual promises as he loses by his consent to a monopoly of power in the ruler. Conversely, those who "covenant and combine themselves together" lose, by virtue of reciprocation, their isolation, while in the other instance it is precisely their isolation which is safeguarded and protected.

---

[40]See the Cambridge Agreement of 1629 in Commager, *op. cit.*

Whereas the act of consent, accomplished by each individual person in his isolation, stands indeed only "in the Presence of God," the act of mutual promise is by definition enacted "in the presence of one another"; it is in principle independent of religious sanction. Moreover, a body politic which is the result of covenant and "combination" becomes the very source of power for each individual person who outside the constituted political realm remains impotent; the government which, on the contrary, is the result of consent acquires a monopoly of power so that the governed are politically impotent so long as they do not decide to recover their original power in order to change the government and entrust another ruler with their power.

In other words, the mutual contract where power is constituted by means of promise contains *in nuce* both the republican principle, according to which power resides in the people, and where a "mutual subjection" makes of rulership an absurdity—"if the people be governors, who shall be governed?"[41]—and the federal principle, the principle of "a Commonwealth for increase" (as Harrington called his utopian *Oceana*), according to which constituted political bodies can combine and enter into lasting alliances without losing their identity. It is equally obvious that the social contract which demands the resignation of power to the government and the consent to its rule contains *in nuce* both the principle of absolute rulership, of an absolute monopoly of power "to overawe them all" (Hobbes) (which, incidentally, is liable to be construed in the image of divine power, since only God is omnipotent), and the national principle according to which there must be one representative of the nation as a whole, and where the government is understood to incorporate the will of all nationals.

---

[41]In these words, John Cotton, Puritan minister and "The Patriarch of New England" in the first half of the seventeenth century, raised his argument against democracy, a government not fit "either for church or commonwealth." Here and in the following, I try to avoid as much as possible a discussion of the relationship between Puritanism and American political institutions. I believe in the validity of Clinton Rossiter's distinction "between Puritans and Puritanism, between the magnificent autocrats of Boston and Salem and their inherently revolutionary way of life and thought" (*op. cit.*, p. 91), the latter consisting in their conviction that even in monarchies God "referreth the sovereigntie to himselfe" and their being "obsessed with the covenant or contract." But the difficulty is that these two tenets are somehow incompatible, the notion of covenant presupposes no-sovereignty and no-rulership, whereas the belief that God retains his sovereignty and refuses to delegate it to any earthly power "setteth up Theocracy . . . as the best form of government," as John Cotton rightly concluded. And the point of the matter is that these strictly religious influences and movements, including the Great Awakening, had no influence whatsoever on what the men of the Revolution did or thought.

"In the beginning," Locke once remarked, "all the world was America." For all practical purposes, America should have presented to the social-contract theories that beginning of society and government which they had assumed to be the fictitious condition without which the existing political realities could be neither explained nor justified. And the very fact that the sudden rise and great variety of social-contract theories during the early centuries of the modern age were preceded and accompanied by these earliest compacts, combinations, cosociations, and confederations in colonial America would indeed be very suggestive, if it were not for the undeniable other fact that these theories in the Old World proceeded without ever mentioning the actual realities in the New World. Nor are we entitled to assert that the colonists, departing from the Old World, took with them the wisdom of new theories, eager, as it were, for a new land in which to test them out and to apply them to a novel form of community. This eagerness for experimentation, and the concomitant conviction of absolute novelty, of a *novus ordo saeclorum*, was conspicuously absent from the minds of the colonists, as it was conspicuously present in the minds of those men who one hundred and fifty years later were to make the Revolution. If there was any theoretical influence that contributed to the compacts and agreements in early American history, it was, of course, the Puritans' reliance on the Old Testament, and especially their rediscovery of the concept of the covenant of Israel, which indeed became for them an "instrument to explain almost every relation of man to man and man to God." But while it may be true that "the Puritan theory of the origin of the church in the consent of the believers led directly to the popular theory of the origin of government in the consent of the governed,"[42] this could not have led to the other much less current theory of the origin of a "civil body politic" in the mutual promise and binding of its constituents. For the Biblical covenant as the Puritans understood it was a compact between God and Israel by virtue of which God gave the law and Israel consented to keep it, and while this covenant implied government by consent, it implied by no means a political body in which rulers and ruled would be equal, that is, where actually the whole principle of rulership no longer applied.[43]

---

[42]Rossiter, *op. cit., loc. cit.*
[43]A magnificent example of the Puritan notion of covenant is contained in a sermon by John Winthrop, written aboard the *Arbella* on the way to America: "Thus stands the cause between God and us, we are entered into Covenant with him for this work, we have taken out a Commission, the

Once we turn from these theories and speculations about influences to the documents themselves and their simple, uncluttered, and often awkward language, we see immediately that it is an event rather than a theory or a tradition we are confronted with, an event of the greatest magnitude and the greatest import for the future, enacted on the spur of time and circumstances, and yet thought out and considered with the greatest care and circumspection. What prompted the colonists "solemnly and mutually in the Presence of God and one another, [to] covenant and combine ourselves together into a civil Body Politick . . . ; and by virtue hereof [to] enact, constitute, and frame, such just and equal Laws, Ordinances, Acts, Constitutions, and Offices, from time to time, as shall be thought most meet and convenient for the general Good of the Colony; unto which we promise all due Submission and Obedience" (as the Mayflower Compact has it), were the "difficulties and discouragements which in all probabilities must be forecast upon the execution of this business." Clearly the colonists, even before embarking, had rightly and thoroughly considered "that this whole adventure growes upon the joint confidence we have in each others fidelity and resolution herein, so as no man of us would have adventured it without assurance of the rest." Nothing but the simple and obvious insight into the elementary structure of joint enterprise as such, the need "for the better encouragement of ourselves and others that shall joyne with us in this action," caused these men to become obsessed with the notion of compact and prompted them again and again "to promise and bind" themselves to one another.[44] No theory, theological or political or philosophical, but their own decision to leave the Old World behind and to venture forth into an enterprise entirely of their own led into a sequence of acts and occurrences in which they would have perished, had they not turned their minds to the matter long and intensely enough to discover, almost by inadvertence, the elementary grammar of political action and its more complicated syntax, whose rules determine the rise and fall of human power. Neither grammar nor syntax was something altogether new in the

Lord hath given us leave to draw our own Articles, we have professed to enterprise these actions upon these and these ends, we have hereupon besought him of favor and blessing: Now if the Lord shall please to hear us, and bring us in peace to the place we desire, then hath he ratified this Covenant and sealed our Commission" (quoted from Perry Miller, *The New England Mind: The Seventeenth Century*, Cambridge, Mass., 1954, p. 477).

[44]Thus in the Cambridge Agreement of 1629, drafted by some of the leading members of the Massachusetts Bay Company before they embarked for America. Commager, *op. cit.*

history of Western civilization; but to find experiences of equal import in the political realm and to read a language of equal authenticity and originality—namely, so incredibly free of conventional idioms and set formulas—in the huge arsenal of historical documents, one might have to go back into a very distant past indeed, a past, at any rate, of which the settlers were totally ignorant. What they discovered, to be sure, was no theory of social contract in either of its two forms, but rather the few elementary truths on which this theory rests.

For our purpose in general, and our attempt to determine with some measure of certainty the essential character of the revolutionary spirit in particular, it may be worth while to pause here long enough to translate, however tentatively, the gist of these pre-revolutionary and even pre-colonial experiences into the less direct but more articulate language of political thought. We then may say that the specifically American experience had taught the men of the Revolution that action, though it may be started in isolation and decided upon by single individuals for very different motives, can be accomplished only by some joint effort in which the motivation of single individuals—for instance, whether or not they are an "undesirable lot"—no longer counts, so that homogeneity of past and origin, the decisive principle of the nation-state, is not required. The joint effort equalizes very effectively the differences in origin as well as in quality. Here, moreover, we may find the root of the surprising so-called realism of the Founding Fathers with respect to human nature. They could afford to ignore the French revolutionary proposition that man is good outside society, in some fictitious original state, which, after all, was the proposition of the Age of Enlightenment. They could afford to be realistic and even pessimistic in this matter because they knew that whatever men might be in their singularity, they could bind themselves into a community which, even though it was composed of "sinners," need not necessarily reflect this "sinful" side of human nature. Hence, the same social state which to their French colleagues had become the root of all human evil was to them the only reasonable hope for a salvation from evil and wickedness at which men might arrive even in this world and even by themselves, without any divine assistance. Here, incidentally, we may also see the authentic source of the much misunderstood American version of the then current belief in the perfectibility of man. Before American common philosophy fell prey to Rousseauan notions in these matters—and this did not happen prior to the nineteenth century—American faith was not at all based on a semi-religious trust in human nature but, on the contrary, on the possibility of checking human nature in its singularity by virtue of common bonds and mutual promises. The hope for man in his singularity lay in the fact that not man but men inhabit the earth and form a world between them. It is human worldliness that will save men from the pitfalls of human nature. And the strongest argument, therefore, John Adams could muster against a body politic dominated by a single assembly was that it was "liable to all the vices, follies and frailties of an individual."[45]

Closely connected with this is an insight into the nature of human power. In distinction to strength, which is the gift and the possession of every man in his isolation against all other men, power comes into being only if and when men join themselves together for the purpose of action, and it will disappear when, for whatever reason, they disperse and desert one another. Hence, binding and promising, combining and covenanting are the means by which power is kept in existence; where and when men succeed in keeping intact the power which sprang up between them during the source of any particular act or deed, they are already in the process of foundation, of constituting a stable worldly structure to house, as it were, their combined power of action. There is an element of the world-building capacity of man in the human faculty of making and keeping promises. Just as promises and agreements deal with the future and provide stability in the ocean of future uncertainty where the unpredictable may break in from all sides, so the constituting, founding, and world-building capacities of man concern always not so much ourselves and our own time on earth as our "successor," and "posterities." The grammar of action: that action is the only human faculty that demands a plurality of men; and the syntax of power: that power is the only human attribute which applies solely to the worldly in-between space by which men are mutually related, combine in the act of foundation by virtue of the making and the keeping of promises, which, in the realm of politics, may well be the highest human faculty.

In other words, what had happened in colonial America prior to the Revolution (and what had happened in no other part of the world, neither in the old countries nor in the new colonies) was, theoretically speaking, that action had led to the formation of power and that power was kept in existence by the then newly discovered means of promise and covenant. The force of this

---

[45] See *Thoughts on Government* (1776), *Works*, Boston, 1851, IV, 195.

power, engendered by action and kept by promises, came to the fore when, to the great surprise of all the great powers, the colonies, namely, the townships and provinces, the counties and cities, their numerous differences amongst themselves notwithstanding, won the war against England. But this victory was a surprise only for the Old World; the colonists themselves, with a hundred and fifty years of covenant-making behind them, rising out of a country which was articulated from top to bottom—from provinces or states down to cities and districts, townships, villages, and counties—into duly constituted bodies, each a commonwealth of its own, with representatives "freely chosen by the consent of loving friends and neighbors,"[46] each, moreover, designed "for increase" as it rested on the mutual promises of those who were "cohabiting" and who, when they "conioyned [them] selves to be as one Publike State or Commonwealth," had planned not only for their "successors" but even for "such as shall be adioyned to [them] att any tyme hereafter,"[47]—the men who out of the uninterrupted strength of this tradition "bid a final adieu to Britain" knew their chances from the beginning; they knew of the enormous power potential that arises when men "mutually pledge to each other [their] lives, [their] Fortunes and [their] sacred Honor."[48]

---

[46]This is from the Plantation agreement at Providence, which founded the town of Providence in 1640 (Commager, *op. cit.*). It is of special interest as the principle of representation is found here for the first time, and also because those who were "so betrusted" agreed "after many Considerations and Consultations of our owne State and also of States abroad in way of government" that no form of government would be so "suitable to their Condition as government by way of Arbitration."

[47]Thus in the Fundamental Orders of Connecticut of 1639 (Commager, *op. cit.*), which Bryce (*American Commonwealth*, vol. I, p. 414, note) has called "the oldest truly political constitution in America."

[48]The "final adieu to Britain" occurs in the Instructions from the Town of Malden, Massachusetts, for a Declaration of Independence, May 27, 1776 (Commager, *op. cit.*). The fierce language of these instructions, the town renouncing "with disdain our connexion with a kingdom of slaves," shows how right Tocqueville was when he traced the origin of the American Revolution to the spirit of the townships. Interesting for the popular strength of republican sentiment throughout the states is also Jefferson's testimony in *The Anas*, February 4, 1818 (*The Complete Jefferson*, Saul Padover, ed. New York, 1943, p. 1206 ff.); it shows very convincingly that if "the contests of that day were contests of principle between the advocates of republican and those of kingly government," it was the republican opinions of the people that eventually settled the difference of opinion among the statesmen. How strong republican sentiments were even before the Revolution because of this unique American experience is evident in John Adams' early writings. In a series of papers written in 1774 for the *Boston Gazette*, he wrote: "The first planters of Plymouth were 'our ancestors' in the strictest sense. They had no charter or patent for the land they took possession of; and derived no authority from the English parliament or crown to set up their government. They purchased land of the Indians, and

This was the experience that guided the men of the Revolution; it had taught not only them but the people who had delegated and "so betrusted" them, how to establish and found public bodies, and as such it was without parallel in any other part of the world. The same, however, is by no means true of their reason, or rather reasoning, of which Dickinson rightly feared that it might mislead them. Their reason, indeed, both in style and content was formed by the Age of Enlightenment as it had spread to both sides of the Atlantic; they argued in the same terms as their French or English colleagues, and even their disagreements were by and large still discussed within the framework of commonly shared references and concepts. Thus, Jefferson could speak of the consent by the people from which governments "derive their just powers" in the same Declaration which he closes on the principle of mutual pledges, and neither he nor anybody else became aware of the simple and elementary difference between the two types of social-contract theory. This lack of conceptual clarity and precision with respect to existing realities and experiences has been the curse of Western history ever since, in the aftermath of the Periclean Age, the men of action and the men of thought parted company and thinking began to emancipate itself altogether from reality, and especially from political factuality and experience. The great hope of the modern age and the modern age's revolutions has been, from the beginning, that this rift might be healed; one of the reasons why this hope thus far has not been fulfilled, why, in the words of Tocqueville, not even the New World could bring forth a new political science, lies in the enormous strength and resiliency of our tradition of thought, which has withstood all the reversals and transformation of values through which the thinkers of the nineteenth century tried to undermine and to destroy it.

However that may be, the fact of the matter, as it relates to the American Revolution, was that experience had taught the colonists that royal and company charters confirmed and legalized rather than established and founded their "commonwealth," that they were "subject to the laws which they adopted at their first settlement, and to such others as have been since made by their respective Legislatures," and that such liberties were "confirmed by the political constitutions they have respectively assumed, and

---

set up a government of their own, on the simple principle of nature; . . . and [they] continued to exercise all the powers of government, legislative, executive, and judicial, upon the plain ground of an *original contract among independent individuals*." (My italics.) See *Novanglus, Works*, vol. IV, p. 110.

also by several charters of compact from the Crown."[49] It is true, "the colonial theorists wrote much about the Birtish constitution, the rights of Englishmen, and even of the laws of nature, but they accepted the British assumption that colonial governments derived from British charters and commissions."[50] Yet the essential point even in these theories was the curious interpretation, or rather misinterpretation, of the British constitution as a fundamental law which could limit the legislative powers of Parliament. This, clearly, meant understanding the British constitution in the light of American compacts and agreements, which indeed were such "fundamental Law," such "fixed" authority, the "bounds" of which even the supreme legislature might not "overlap . . . without destroying its own foundation." It was precisely because the Americans so firmly believed in their own compacts and agreements that they would appeal to a British constitution and their "constitutional Right," "exclusive of any Consideration of Charter Rights"; whereby it is even relatively unimportant that they, following the fashion of the time, asserted this to be an "unalterable Right, in nature," since, to them at least, this right had become law only because they thought it to be "ungrafted into the British Constitution, as a fundamental Law."[51]

And again, experience had taught the colonists enough about the nature of human power to conclude from the by no means intolerable abuses of power by a particular king that kingship as such is a form of government fit for slaves, and that "an American republic . . . is the only government which we wish to see established; for we can never be willingly subject to any other King than he who, being possessed of infinite wisdom, goodness and rectitude, is alone fit to possess unlimited power";[52] but the colo-

---

[49]This is from a Resolution of Freeholders of Albemarle County, Virginia, July 26, 1774, which was drafted by Jefferson. The royal charters are mentioned almost as an afterthought, and the curious term "charter of compact," which reads like a contradiction in terms, shows clearly that it was compact, and not charter, that Jefferson had in mind (Commager, *op. cit.*). And this insistence on compact at the expense of royal or company charters is by no means a consequence of revolution. Almost ten years before the Declaration of Independence, Benjamin Franklin argued "that parliament was so far from having a hand in the work of original settlement that it actually took no kind of notice of them, till many years after they were established" (Craven, *op. cit.*, p. 44).

[50]Merrill Jensen, *op. cit.*

[51]This is from the Massachusetts Circular Letter, protesting the Townshend Acts of February 11, 1768, drafted by Samuel Adams. According to Commager, these addresses to the British Ministry present "one of the earliest formulations of the doctrine of fundamental law in the British constitution."

[52]From the Instructions of the Town of Malden, as quoted in note 48.

nial theorists were still debating at length the advantages and disadvantages of the various forms of government—as though there were any choice in this matter. Finally, it was experience—"the unified wisdom of North America . . . collected in a general congress"[53]—rather than theory or learning, that taught the men of the Revolution the real meaning of the Roman *potestas in populo*, that power resides in the people. They knew that the principle of *potestas in populo* is capable of inspiring a form of government only if one adds, as the Romans did, *auctoritas in senatu*, authority resides in the senate, so that government itself consists of both power and authority, or, as the Romans had it, *senatus populusque Romanus*. What the royal charters and the loyal attachment of the colonies to king and Parliament in England had done for the people in America was to provide their power with the additional weight of authority; so that the chief problem of the American Revolution, once this source of authority had been severed from the colonial body politic in the New World, turned out to be the establishment and foundation not of power but of authority.

---

[53]As the Virginia Instructions to the Continental Congress of August 1, 1774, put it (Commager, *op. cit.*).

SELECTIVE BIBLIOGRAPHY

Most of the important writings on the American Revolution have been discussed at some length in the introductory essay. No consideration was given in that essay, however, to biographies or works on either the military or diplomatic aspects of the Revolution. Wesley Frank Craven, "The Revolutionary Era," in John Higham, ed., *The Reinterpretation of American History* (London, 1962), comments on some of the more important of the recent biographical studies; Don Higginbotham, "American Historians and the Military History of the American Revolution," *American Historical Review*, LXXX (1964), 18–34 is an excellent analysis of recent literature on the war itself; and Samuel Flagg Bemis, *The Diplomacy of the American Revolution* (New York, 1935) and Richard B. Morris, *The Peacemakers* (New York, 1965) are the standard works on Revolutionary diplomacy. Other treatments of the historiography of the Revolution not mentioned in the introductory essay are Page Smith, "David Ramsay and the Causes of the American Revolution," *William and Mary Quarterly*, 3rd ser., XVII (1960), 51–77, and Peter Marshall, "Radicals, Conservatives and the American Revolution," *Past and Present*, XXIII (1962), 44–56.

General collections of primary sources, all of which are available in paper editions, are Samuel Eliot Morison, ed., *Sources and Documents Illustrating the American Revolution 1764–1788 and the Formation of the American Constitution* (Oxford, 1923); Max Beloff, ed., *The Debate over the American Revolution, 1761–1783* (London, 1949); Jack P. Greene, ed., *Colonies to Nation, 1763–1789* (New York, 1967); and John Braeman, ed., *The Road to Independence: A Documentary History of the Causes of the American Revolution: 1763–1776* (New York, 1963).

For a continuous and reasonably detailed narrative of the entire Revolutionary era, the reader will do best to read the following three volumes in sequence: John C. Miller, *Origins of the American Revolution* (Boston, 1943); John Richard Alden, *The American Revolution 1775–1783* (New York, 1954); and Andrew Cunningham McLaughlin, *The Confederation and the Constitution 1783–1789* (New York, 1905). The best brief history is by Edmund S. Morgan, *The Birth of the Republic 1763–89* (Chicago, 1956).

INDEX